Pyrrhic Victory

Pyrrhic Victory

FRENCH STRATEGY AND

OPERATIONS IN THE GREAT WAR

Robert A. Doughty

The Belknap Press of Harvard University Press

Cambridge, Massachusetts · London, England

2005

Library of Congress Cataloging-in-Publication Data

Doughty, Robert A.
Pyrrhic victory : French strategy and operations in the Great War / Robert A. Doughty.
p. cm.
Includes bibliographical references and index.
ISBN 0-674-01880-X (alk. paper)
1. World War, 1914–1918—France. 2. Strategy—History—20th century.
3. France—Military policy. 4. France—History, Military—20th century. I. Title.

D548.D68 2005
940.4'012—dc22   2005041172

To the soldiers of the Great War

∾

May their sacrifices and devotion to duty never be forgotten

Contents

Maps

Preface

WHILE WORKING on this book, I have visited France often and have gained a deep appreciation of its people and their customs. I learned that one cannot write a book about France and the Great War without walking battlefields, visiting memorials and historic sites, working many hours in archives and libraries, exploring cemeteries, spending nights in delightful hotels, and enjoying superb food and drink. I also learned that one cannot do all these things without coming into frequent contact with the people of France. While some of my understanding of the Great War has come from such things as my skill at deciphering illegible handwriting, much has come from the assistance and ideas many of them provided me.

Foremost among those in France who have assisted me are the courteous and competent professionals at the Service historique de l'armée de terre, the Bibliothèque nationale de France, the Centre historique des archives nationales, and the Bibliothèque de l'Institut de France. I am especially indebted to Colonel Frédéric Guelton, Directeur des recherches du Service historique de l'armée de terre. I have benefited enormously from his assistance, as well as from his advice and insights. I also am indebted to Professor Maurice Vaïsse, Directeur du Centre d'études d'histoire de la défense, who helped me gain access to key libraries and archives. I am grateful to the de Laguiche family, who tolerated my frequent e-mail messages and allowed me to view their family's diaries and papers. I am also appreciative of the assistance furnished by the kind people who run the Hotel Océanic in Paris. Over the years they have provided me with a clean, secure, quiet place to sleep, with directions and advice about restaurants and places to shop, and with unfailingly warm greetings when I stepped through the front door.

On this side of the Atlantic, I have benefited from grants from the Faculty Development Research Fund at the United States Military Academy. Here I wish to thank not only those who have donated to this fund but also those who oversee the fund and have seen my research as fitting within its goals. I also greatly appreciate the support of those who work in interlibrary loan in the cadet library at West Point. Over the years they have routinely done the impossible by locating obscure books and journals and providing them in a reasonable time. I owe thanks also to Frank Martini for his great skill and creativity in producing the maps for this book. In addition to the anonymous readers who formally critiqued my manuscript, other scholars interested in the Great War have considered my ideas over the years and offered constructive criticism. Foremost among these are Dennis Showalter, Doug Porch, Bill Dean, Jack Tunstall, John Morrow, Robert Bruce, and Father Don Smythe. I am also indebted to Kathleen McDermott and other members of the editorial staff at Harvard University Press. Their friendly and flexible support helped me finish this work despite the heavy demands of my other duties. Finally, I have benefited frequently from discussions about my research with faculty members of the Department of History at West Point. I remain in awe not only of their professionalism but also of their intellect and creativity.

As I did the research for this book, I thought a lot about the soldiers who fought and died in this war. One cannot look at the still-scarred earth at Souchez, Vauquois, Perthes, Verdun, or a hundred other places without reflecting on the motivations and aspirations of the men who fought there, men who had only a partial understanding of the strategic and operational concepts that placed them there. Decades after they crawled out of their holes and did their duty, I admire their mustering the courage to do so. With great respect, I dedicate this book to the soldiers of the Great War.

In a book with a subject as broad as this, there are bound to be errors. Whatever the contributions of the many people who helped me avoid the errors of fact or interpretation that are no longer part of this work, I alone am responsible for any inaccuracies or omissions that remain.

Introduction

I N AUGUST 1914 the French went to war confident of victory. Despite huge casualties and enormous costs, political and military leaders continued pressing for victory for the next four years. To defeat the Germans they devised new strategies, developed new weapons, formulated new doctrines, launched different kinds of operations, and achieved an unparalleled level of industrial mobilization. Although they emerged victorious, they sacrificed the lives and bodies of their young men, exhausted the resources of their nation, and mortgaged their country's future.

In 1994 Jean-Baptiste Duroselle noted that on average 890 French soldiers died on each of the 1,560 days of the war.[1] In September 1922 André Tardieu offered a broader description of the burden of France's victory:

> The war bled us terribly. Out of our population of less than 38,000,000 there were mobilized 8,500,000; 5,300,000 of them were killed or wounded (1,500,000 killed, 800,000 *mutilés*, 3,000,000 wounded), not counting 500,000 men who have come back to us from German prisons in very bad physical condition.
>
> Almost 4,000,000 hectares of land were devastated,[2] together with 4,000 towns and villages, 600,000 buildings were destroyed,

1

among them 20,000 factories and workshops, besides 5,000 kilometers of railroads and 53,000 kilometers of roads. About 1,400,000 head of cattle were carried off. Altogether a quarter of our productive capital was annihilated.

The financial consequences of the annihilation of all these resources bear down on us heavily today. The war cost us 150 billions of francs. The damage to property and persons comes to 200 billions. Our ordinary budget has increased from $4\frac{1}{2}$ billions to 25 billions; our debt from 36 billions to 330 billions. . . .

To measure what we have undergone, suppose that the war had taken place in America, and that you had suffered proportionately. You would have had 4,000,000 of your men killed and 10,000,000 wounded [out of a population of 110,000,000 in 1922]. All your industries from Washington to Pittsburgh would have ceased to exist. All your coal mines would have been ruined. That is what the war would have meant to you. That is what it has meant to us.[3]

In the decades following the Great War the enormity of these consequences raised questions about whether the war's outcome was worth the price paid. Aware of the high losses and small gains common to many operations, historians and military professionals sometimes dismissed the French effort as irrational and impulsive. Instead of carefully considered actions, critics found only mindless assaults and senseless blunders. Over time the notion of France's war effort as a series of ill-conceived but energetically executed operations with no connection to a coherent national strategy became a cliché.

The real story is significantly different. From the first day of the war to the last, French grand strategy rested upon the idea of waging a multifront war against the Central Powers. By maintaining pressure on several fronts, French leaders believed France and its allies could force Germany and Austria-Hungary to spread their forces and prevent them from concentrating overwhelming force against one of the Entente powers. Within the framework of this grand strategy, military leaders attempted to coordinate their operations with their allies and usually launched operations only after thorough analysis and careful consideration of alternatives. Commanders routinely directed their operations toward objectives linked to broader goals of strategy or policy. As the French developed their strategy and prepared their operations, they proceeded pragmatically, by trial and error, rather than by intuition or impulse. They also relied on reason and science in seeking numerous innovations in technology and doctrine. Although they failed to drive the Germans out of France until the final days of the war, their losses came more from a refusal to quit fighting—and from German combat power—than from a vain search for glory or an unwillingness to innovate and adapt.

Clearly, the political and military leaders who devised strategy and launched operations from 1914 to 1918 did not know the outcome of their actions and could only hope for the best. They made many mistakes, and had they known beforehand that so many operations would fail and the price would be so high, they undoubtedly would have fought the war very differently. War, as Clausewitz taught us, is an extension of politics, but it is waged against an opponent who acts and reacts on his own. War also is shaped by the friction and fog of battle and by the primitive emotions of pride, passion, vengeance, and irrationality. Those who believe that wars can be surgical, that they can be won with "shock and awe," or that they can be directed toward a precise endgame or end state know little about the Great War. In the final analysis, war is far more than an extension of politics or the image one sees on a computer or television screen. It is the most complex, demanding, and unpredictable of all human endeavors—as the French learned from 1914 to 1918.

CHAPTER 1

The Transformation of the French Army

A FTER THE DÉBACLE OF 1870–1871 and the unification of Germany, the leaders of the new Third Republic moved quickly to reorganize and reform the French army. In 1874 a committee in the National Assembly charged with proposing a new law on the administration of the army began its report by stating: "The misfortunes of the 1870 campaign demonstrated the inferiority of our military. This unhappy experience convinced us that we cannot stamp our foot upon the ground and expect invincible armies to emerge, that on the contrary we must prepare and organize in advance the armed forces of the nation if we want them, at the time of danger, to be ready for prompt and energetic action."[1] An earlier report had stated: "We were beaten by the absence of preparation, organization, and direction, and by the small number of our soldiers more than by the arms of our enemies."[2] As France's political and military leaders shaped the armed forces for future challenges, their reforms reflected these harsh lessons. Instead of improvisation, success required solid organizations, well-trained and motivated leaders and soldiers, and thorough preparation. Success also required up-to-date weapons, equipment, and doctrine.

The path to success, however, was neither obvious nor simple. France's political and military leaders could not copy the institutions and methods of the Germans, for France's strategic situation, political and economic systems, and historical traditions required something different. These leaders also had to blaze a path through uncharted territory amidst a true "revolution in military affairs," when technological and scientific advances and broad political, economic, and social changes were altering the nature of war. Additionally, the transition from the Second Empire to the Third Republic created legitimate concerns about the military's acceptance of republican institutions. Several crises, especially the Dreyfus Affair of the 1890s and the *Affaire des Fiches* of 1904–1905, deepened distrust between political and military authorities and disrupted efforts to reform the French army. As the international environment became more threatening, especially after the German gunboat *Panther* visited Agadir, Morocco, in July 1911, the desire to improve the army and accelerate the pace of reform overshadowed concerns about the political reliability of the military.

As a consequence of numerous changes, the French army that went into battle in August 1914 differed dramatically from that of 1870. Important modifications to French strategy, doctrine, organizations, and equipment had occurred. While some changes came from identifying shortcomings in the Franco-Prussian War, others came from adapting the military to the ideals and institutions of the Third Republic. Especially noteworthy—despite passionate disagreement about the role and organization of the reserves and the length of service for conscripts—was the dismantling of the professional, long-service army of Napoleon III and the building of a national army based upon conscription. Further changes came from the adoption of wireless telegraphs, machine guns, repeating rifles, and rapid-fire artillery, as well as other weapons and equipment. Though the uniforms were essentially those of the Second Empire, the weapons, transport systems (railways, trucks, airplanes), and communications systems (telephones and wireless telegraph) were not. The strategic situation also changed: whereas France had faced Prussia and its allies alone in 1870, it had strong diplomatic and military ties with Russia and Great Britain in 1914. The prewar years thus saw marked improvement in France's military forces and strategic situation and a gradual increase in the military's self-confidence. Although severe deficiencies became apparent in the first months of the Great War, prewar improvements enabled the French to perform much better in August–September 1914 than in 1870 and to win the "miracle of the Marne."

Of the numerous changes occurring after 1871, none had a greater effect on French strategy and operations in the Great War than those affecting the High Command. Despite widespread recognition of the need for long-term preparation, French political leaders had adamantly refused for years to create a powerful military hierarchy, dominated by uniformed officers who controlled strategic planning and preparation for war. Not until the very eve of the war did the French have something comparable to the German High Command and its General Staff. In the newly established Third Republic, the president served as the titular head of the armed forces, but the minister of war functioned as the army's chief and directed not only its day-to-day administration but also its long-term preparation for war. An 1874 report on the administration of the army emphasized the power of the minister of war:

> The minister alone has responsibility for the direction of programs and the use of funds that are allocated to him by the budget. This responsibility is indivisible; it cannot be delegated. . . . To work in harmony, everything must be connected to a center from which emanates a common policy. The minister is this center. He is the head of the administration [of the army]; he alone works with the National Assembly.[3]

Still remembering the army's role in Louis Napoleon's coup of December 1851, the Republic's leaders expected the minister of war to maintain a tight rein on the army and to keep politics out of the barracks. The fact that ministers often served for only one year or less, however, severely limited their ability to achieve significant reforms. Moreover, the fact that ministers usually were general officers made them sometimes reluctant to offend the army's senior generals and thereby jeopardize their own future careers when they left their political position. One of them, General Jean Thibaudin, so offended the army's senior generals that he remained unassigned for nearly two years before being given fewer responsibilities than those he had had before becoming minister of war. The result was a cumbersome High Command, one in which change occurred only with great difficulty and in which solidly entrenched bureau-crats easily stalled initiatives from "ephemeral" ministers of war and de-layed unwanted programs or actions.

Inefficiencies also came from the organization of the staff supporting the minister of war. Initially the General Staff was little more than the mil-itary cabinet of the minister, but in 1874 the French enlarged and re-named it the General Staff of the Minister of War, thereby indicating not only its expanded role but also its subordination to the minister. Wary political leaders at first refused to follow the Germans and designate a chief of staff, but they finally created the position of Chief of Staff of the Minister of War. This title made it clear that he had no authority over the army and was subordinate to the minister. In 1890 Charles de Freycinet, the first civilian minister of war, managed to get the names changed to General Staff of the Army and Chief of Staff of the Army, but republican leaders remained reluctant to appoint a single general officer head of the army during peacetime or to create a strong military hierarchy or com-mand structure.

The French partially compensated for the lack of a formal military hi-erarchy with real authority by establishing the Superior Council of War and the Superior Council of National Defense. The former was created in 1872, had the president of the Republic as its chair, and included the president of the Council of Ministers (premier) and its senior generals. The council was supposed to be consulted "in a general manner, on all measures able to affect the constitution of the army and the manner in which it would be employed."[4] The Superior Council of National De-fense, created by a decree on April 3, 1906, had a much broader mandate. With the president of the Third Republic presiding, the council in-cluded the premier and the ministers of war, navy, foreign affairs, finances, and colonies. The ranking officers in the army and navy also at-tended but not as voting members. Not a decisionmaking body, the coun-cil provided a forum for the discussion of "all questions relating to na-tional defense"[5] and often assembled prior to a meeting of the Council of Ministers. Though both councils only provided advice, they played large roles in shaping national security policy and influencing military strategy.

Of the two councils, the Superior Council of War played a particularly important role in giving voice to the army's concerns and providing a forum in which senior officers could give technical military advice to the government. Before 1870 France did not have corps headquarters in peacetime, much less functioning field armies, and the army's performance in combat in 1870–1871 suffered because of the inexperience of commanders and staffs of newly formed units. After 1871 political leaders permitted the organization of corps in peacetime, but many republicans, fearing another Louis Napoleon, opposed the creation of field army headquarters. Between 1888 and 1891, while Freycinet was minister of war, France took several important steps toward establishing field army headquarters as temporary, skeleton units during peacetime. Although field army commanders had "no actual right of command," they had much greater influence than in the past over the preparation and mobilization of their commands in the event of war.[6] Many of these general officers also served on the Superior Council of War and thus were able to communicate their concerns to the Republic's political leaders.

By the late 1880s, thanks especially to the efforts of Freycinet, the French had improved the effectiveness of their High Command, but political leaders still refused to appoint a general officer to command the army during peacetime. Instead, they appointed one general officer as chief of staff of the army and another as the vice president of the Superior Council of War. The former worked closely with the minister of war (who could be an army officer) in administering the day-to-day activities of the army; the latter had no command authority but nonetheless had responsibilities associated with preparing the army for war. Known as the "generalissimo," the vice president of the Superior Council was the designated commander of French forces in the event of war. The Superior Council included generals who would command France's forces in war, but neither the council nor the vice president could make decisions; they could only tender advice to the minister of war. Though this arrangement gave the minister of war great power over the army, it resulted in numerous inefficiencies, particularly since the chief of staff worked independently from the vice president of the Superior Council.[7]

As the international situation became more tense in 1911, representatives in the Senate and Chamber of Deputies became concerned about the effectiveness of the High Command. When a senator questioned the minister of war, General François Goiran, in June 1911 about the relationship between the government and its senior generals, Goiran responded that the government controlled wartime strategy and operations and the minister of war executed the directives of the government. He also explained that there was no peacetime commander; there was only a vice president of the Superior Council of War, who would assume command of the armies of the northeast in wartime. Though Goiran's response was technically correct and agreed with existing legislation, his comments caused great dismay among the parliamentary representatives and resulted in a heated discussion, particularly in the Chamber of Deputies, about the relationship between political and military authorities. During this discussion one conservative representative said: "Unity of command, gentlemen, that is the main issue. . . . When the guns begin to speak, diplomacy should be silent, and at the same time all the deliberative bodies—Council of Ministers, Council of Defense, Superior Council of War—who have studied, weighed, tried to foresee all the eventualities during peacetime should yield to the sole and single leader of all the national forces, the generalissimo."[8] Despite Goiran's best efforts, the legislators rejected his explanation and overthrew the government. This action clearly indicated that the legislators understood the importance of unity of command and wanted to give more authority to the officer who would command French forces in time of war.

The new minister of war, Adolphe Messimy, assumed his duties a few days before the appearance of the German gunboat *Panther* off the port of Agadir. In the ensuing crisis a wave of nationalism and anti-German sentiment swept through France, and a renewed interest in improving chances of victory over Germany swept through Paris. Messimy later said, "I arrived at the Ministry [of War] on June 30, 1911, with the mandate given to me by the Chamber [of Deputies] to concentrate all my efforts on a reorganization of the High Command."[9] The Moroccan crisis had created an environment in which the new minister of war could make significant adjustments, and Messimy—a former infantry officer who had left active duty in 1899 but remained in the reserves and who professed great admiration for Napoleon[10]—had strong ideas about what needed to be done. Though he remained in office only from June 30, 1911, to January 12, 1912, he made several changes that strengthened the High Command and shaped France's strategy and operations during the Great War.

The most important of these changes involved raising General Joseph Joffre to the highest position in the French army and giving him new powers.

The appointment of Joffre came after Messimy lost confidence in General Victor Michel, the vice president of the Superior Council of War. In his memoirs, Messimy explained why he relieved Michel: "His authority—that imponderable but necessary element which makes a leader—was nil." Three of France's most respected generals (Yvon Dubail, Pol Durand, and Joseph Gallieni) told Messimy that Michel was "incapable of commanding," and one added, "Michel is a national danger."[11] The army's senior generals also lacked confidence in Michel because he criticized the notion of the *offensive à outrance* as articulated by Lieutenant Colonel Louis Loyseau de Grandmaison and he supported a new strategy relying heavily on reserves. Messimy shared the army's faith in the offensive, a factor that undoubtedly further eroded his confidence in Michel. When he met with Michel and informed him that his colleagues on the Superior Council of War lacked confidence in him, Michel countered that the new minister of war had not attended a meeting of the council and thus had had no occasion to judge the attitudes of its members. During his short tenure as vice president of the council, Michel had formed new ideas about France's strategy and the organization of the army, and he asked permission to present to the council his plan for reorganizing the army. Messimy agreed, but it was clear that Michel had to sell his ideas to the Superior Council if he were to maintain his position.

Between 1871 and 1911 French strategy and war plans had changed considerably. Following the Franco-Prussian War, the Germans had taken the provinces of Alsace and Lorraine and deprived France of the natural barriers of the Rhine River and Vosges Mountains, which had protected the old northeastern frontier. Though the border after 1871 meandered considerably, it extended in a straight-line distance across 290 kilometers from the English Channel to the southwest corner of Luxembourg and 250 kilometers from the latter point to Switzerland. Along the Belgian frontier, Sedan lay 70, Mézières 85, and Maubeuge 150 kilometers from the southwest corner of Luxembourg.

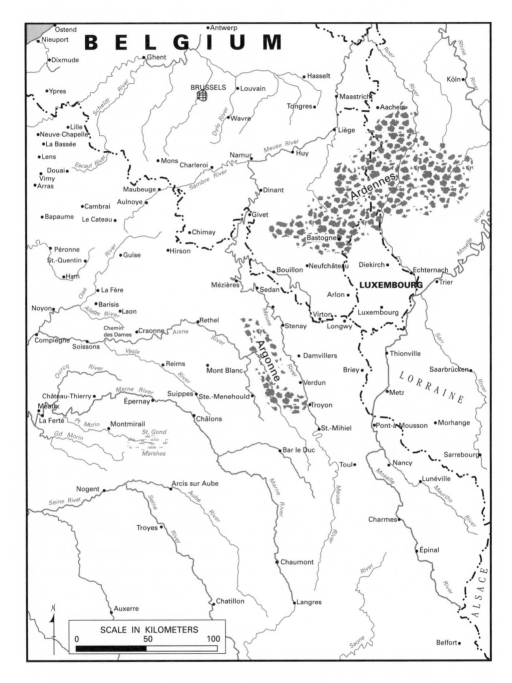

North and northeastern France

Under the guiding hand of General Raymond Séré de Rivières, the French built a defensive line between 1874 and 1880 in the northeast between Verdun and Toul and another between Épinal and Belfort, with the main fortifications surrounding those four cities. Except for Belfort, which was about twenty kilometers from the junction of the German and Swiss borders, the fortified line lay forty kilometers west of the German frontier and extended sixty-five kilometers between Verdun and Toul and between Épinal and Belfort. The Meuse River flowed between Givet, Mézières, Verdun, and Toul, and a small branch of the Moselle flowed between Épinal and Belfort. A seventy-kilometer gap—known as the Charmes Gap—lay between Toul and Épinal, and forward of this gap sat the city of Nancy, only a dozen kilometers from the German border. Recognizing the need for depth and for fortifications to block an enemy's moves around the flanks of the Verdun-Toul and Épinal-Belfort lines, the French began building fortifications on the right between Langres and Dijon and on the left between La Fère and Reims and between Valenciennes and Maubeuge but did not finish them.[12]

Early plans, which were essentially concentration plans and not war plans, emphasized the defense and took advantage of the Meuse and the branches of the Moselle, which ran almost parallel to the northeastern border. By the late 1880s, completion of the fortresses between Verdun and Belfort and improvement of the railways from central to northeastern France enabled the French to consider attacking after initially defending. Not until relations with Russia improved in 1891 and Plan XI was completed in August of that year, however, did the French anticipate having a choice between attacking or defending at the beginning of a war with Germany, and not until the completion of Plan XII in February 1892 did the French consider launching an immediate offensive into Germany. Nevertheless Plans XI through XVI rested primarily on a defensive-offensive strategy in which French forces initially defended and then counterattacked.[13]

Beginning in 1888 the French paid more attention to the possibility of the Germans' moving north of Verdun or advancing through Belgium. As early as February 1892 Plan XII included a contingency for a German violation of Belgian neutrality. In early 1904 planners became particularly interested in this contingency after a German, apparently a general officer attached to the General Staff in Berlin, sold a copy of the German concentration plan to French intelligence. Calling himself "The Avenger," the mysterious individual concealed his identify by covering his face with bandages and met with French officials three times. In these meetings he outlined German mobilization procedures and war plans.[14] As a consequence of the Avenger's revelations, as well as other intelligence, the French modified Plan XV in March 1906 to take into account the possibility of the Germans' passing through Belgium to the north of Verdun. Some high-ranking officers refused to believe the Germans would violate Belgian neutrality. Nevertheless, military leaders, who had nothing more than covering forces north of Verdun or along the Belgian frontier in the late 1880s, increased the number of forces north and northwest of Verdun with each new plan.

Completed in March 1909, Plan XVI placed more emphasis than previous plans on the possibility of the Germans' moving through Luxembourg or Belgium. In February 1908 General Henri de Lacroix, then the vice president of the Superior Council of War, presented to the council an analysis that emphasized the German tradition of enveloping its opponent's flanks. He foresaw the Germans' sending two armies around the flank of French fortifications and passing through Luxembourg and eastern Belgium, one army emerging from the Ardennes at Verdun and the other at Sedan.[15] Despite concern about the Germans' moving through Belgium, de Lacroix did not propose placing large French forces along the frontier of eastern Belgium. Instead, he proposed adjusting the organization and location of French units to give additional power to a defensive-offensive strategy. To provide additional forces for a counterattack, he suggested organizing a new army, Sixth Army, and placing it near Châlons, eighty kilometers west of Verdun, so it could move easily toward Toul in the center, Verdun on the left, or Sedan-Mézières in the left rear. Though he anticipated an envelopment from the Germans, he envisaged only a shallow advance through eastern Belgium and did not anticipate a deep envelopment through central Belgium.

When Michel became vice president of the Superior Council of War in 1910, he had reservations about Plan XVI and much greater concerns than de Lacroix about the Germans' moving through Belgium. Before Messimy became minister of war, Michel had submitted a report in which he foresaw the Germans' seeking a victory in central Belgium, not in Lorraine or eastern Belgium. Given the strength of French defenses in Lorraine, the difficulty of passing through the numerous natural obstacles in eastern Belgium, and the presence of modern railways between Bonn, Köln, and Düsseldorf, Michel expected the Germans to concentrate their forces in the north and to seek a "definitive solution in the very heart of Belgium." To respond to this threat, he suggested a new strategy: defend on the right from Belfort to Mézières and launch a "vigorous offensive" on the left toward Antwerp, Brussels, and Namur.[16] Since French forces could not occupy such a vast front without complete integration of the reserves, Michel also proposed a reorganization of the army, primarily through the adoption of what he called the "demi-brigade," a formation used during the wars of the French Revolution to integrate active and reserve forces. In essence, an active regiment and a reserve regiment would form a demi-brigade, thereby doubling the size of each brigade, division, and corps.[17] Michel presented his ideas on reorganizing the army to the Superior Council on July 19, 1911,[18] and the response to his proposal is apparent in a reference to him by an undersecretary in the Ministry of War as a "looney."[19] When the council rejected his proposal to form demi-brigades and reorganize the army, it rendered impossible his proposal to change French strategy, spread French forces from Belfort to Mézières, and then drive toward Antwerp, Brussels, and Namur.

The resignation of Michel two days later gave Messimy the opportunity to choose a new leader for the French army. He identified three candidates. His first choice was General Joseph Gallieni, a distinguished soldier who had made his reputation policing France's colonies; but Gallieni refused the position because he had only two and a half years before mandatory retirement and because he thought it inappropriate to accept the position after playing a key role in Michel's ouster. Messimy's next choice was General Paul Pau, who had been the army's choice for vice president of the Superior Council when Michel had been chosen. After Pau said he would take the position only if he could choose all general officers, Messimy went to his third choice, General Joseph Joffre. Joseph Caillaux, the premier, preferred Gallieni but accepted Joffre after

Messimy emphasized Gallieni's age and his having only a few years until retirement.[20]

A graduate of the École Polytechnique and an engineer, the fifty-nine-year-old Joffre came from a middle-class family and considered himself a moderate republican. In a variety of assignments in the army, he had demonstrated strong organizational skills and an unusual capacity to handle positions of great responsibility. He had performed well as an engineer in the construction of fortifications on the northeastern frontier of France and distinguished himself when he served in the colonies. After serving in Formosa and Indochina, he had led a small force 500 miles across the Sudan desert to Timbuktu in December 1893 and restored control over an area in which rebellious natives had recently massacred a French column. His outstanding performance in organizing the port of Diégo Suarez, on the northern tip of Madagascar, and building fortifications around the port earned Gallieni's strongest praise and his affirmation that Joffre should rise to the highest levels in the French army.[21] After leaving Madagascar and returning to France, Joffre commanded 6th Division (which had its headquarters in Paris) and II Corps (which had its headquarters in Amiens, 100 kilometers north of Paris) and served as director of engineers. When he was appointed director of support services in January 1910, he gained a seat on the Superior Council of War and became the youngest member of that body. His position as director of support services enabled him to gain a better understanding of logistics and railway transportation, an understanding that served him well in subsequent years. In the eyes of some French officers, such as General Hubert Lyautey, Joffre was a far better logistician than an operational commander or strategic thinker.

Yet, unlike most French officers, Joffre had dealt often with civilian authorities as he climbed the ladder of success, and he had developed a shrewd understanding of how to deal with them. Unlike officers such as Pau, Ferdinand Foch, or Édouard de Curières de Castelnau, who were known for their conservative or Catholic views, Joffre was known for his republican views. Some officers referred to him as "the crab" not only because of his thick girth but also because he never moved to the right politically. As he dealt with his civilian superiors, he sometimes made unreasonable demands on them or ignored them, but he cagily avoided placing them in embarrassing circumstances or giving them impossible choices such as Pau had done with Messimy. Joffre's political skills also extended into the diplomatic arena. In October 1913 the Russian minister of foreign affairs, Sergei Sazonov, praised Joffre for the diplomatic skills he demonstrated while attending autumn maneuvers in Russia and compared him very favorably with senior Russian officers, who, he said, showed no interest in diplomats.[22]

Though neither brilliant nor a conversationalist, Joffre was far from being as dull as some historians have portrayed him. Those who attended meetings or conferences with him discovered him to be an intelligent, articulate proponent of his ideas. In July 1913 Joffre spoke to the Chamber of Deputies in support of the law on three years of military service and earned praise for his performance. One politician in the audience observed that "even the socialists listened with deference."[23] After World War I David Lloyd George wrote: "As to his gifts as an orator, I feel that as an old Parliamentarian I am quite equal to forming a judgment, and quite entitled to state it. He was one of the most forceful and dramatic speakers I heard at any conference which I ever attended."[24] A man of extraordinary will and obstinate determination, Joffre remained calm and composed under the most demanding circumstances. He preferred receiving proposals in writing from his staff and, after receiving a proposal, would withdraw to a corner, close his eyes, and remain absorbed for a lengthy period as he pondered strategic or operational choices. As events swirled around him and as his staff awaited momentous decisions, he went to bed early each night and left strict orders not to be awakened. Though not inclined to philosophical discussions, he appreciated intelligent people and surrounded himself with bright, energetic officers, a preference that led some critics to accuse him of being dominated by his staff. Those who worked directly for him and knew him well, however, rejected such criticisms. One of them wrote, "I know of nothing which could be more false. He was incontestably the boss, and those who did not tremble before him were rare."[25] Joffre showed no patience for those who failed or who proved incompetent and sometimes exploded in a short but violent fit of temper when a subordinate objected to an order or indirectly criticized him. From 1911 until December 1916 he dominated his staff and the French army.

With Joffre chosen as Michel's successor, Messimy ended the duality of the High Command by uniting the functions of the vice president of the Superior Council and the chief of staff of the army. A decree on July 28 named Joffre chief of the General Staff and reorganized the High Command, placing it—in the words of Messimy—"completely and without reserve under Joffre's direction."[26] Messimy appointed General Yvon Dubail chief of staff of the army and, except for issues dealing with personnel and logistical support, made him subordinate to Joffre. Though Joffre wanted Foch to be his first deputy, Messimy refused to appoint him, so Joffre chose General de Castelnau, who had worked on Plan XVI and was thoroughly familiar with the administrative procedures of the War Ministry. Foch, Dubail, and Castelnau would later serve Joffre as army-group commanders.

Shortly after Joffre's appointment, the High Command began an assessment not only of France's strategy in a campaign against Germany but also of its grand strategy. Part of this assessment included meetings on October 16, 1911, between representatives of the ministries of War and Foreign Affairs. In preparation for this meeting, the Operations Bureau of the General Staff completed a strategic assessment that reviewed the major powers of Europe and their probable actions in the event of a war between France and Germany. The purpose of the study and the meeting was to determine whether the Ministry of Foreign Affairs agreed with the General Staff's assessment of the "grouping of powers that could be produced in the event of a war between France and Germany." The authors of the October 1911 assessment believed Russia and Great Britain would join France, and Austria—and perhaps Spain—would join Germany. They expected Italy, Switzerland, Holland, and Luxembourg to be neutral. They also believed military operations would cover a "considerable" part of Belgium.[27] While the strategic assessment drew no surprising conclusions, its existence demonstrates the breadth of the review conducted in 1911 and 1912. In preparation for a meeting of the Superior

Council of National Defense on January 9, 1912, its staff completed a twenty-five-page assessment that demonstrated the confidence and goals of the High Command:

> France and its allies should focus on a common objective, conform-
> ing to the well-understood interests of each of the states in the co-
> alition. This simple and precise objective CONSISTS OF CRUSHING
> GERMANY [*sic*]. With it vanquished, Austria can no longer oppose
> the progress of Russia in the east; England will retain its mastery of
> the seas; France will regain its lost provinces—the framework of the
> Triple Alliance will collapse with a single blow.[28]

As part of this broad review, Joffre revised French strategy and war plans. Dismissing Michel's concept of defending along the entire Belgian frontier, Joffre modified Plan XVI so that French forces could cover more but not all of the frontier. To increase the number of divisions immedi-ately available, a prerequisite for covering a longer front, he shifted forces from the Italian border and moved units from the second line (including reserve units) into the front line. In his memoirs, Joffre claimed to have increased the number of divisions available immediately from thirty-eight to fifty-eight. He then arranged to shift Fifth Army farther to the left, as far west as Mézières, and to push Sixth Army closer to Verdun and the Belgian frontier west of Luxembourg.[29] These changes placed two French armies (seven corps) near the Belgian border and provided some protection against a German attempt to envelop the French flank by driv-ing around Verdun or as deep as Sedan or Mézières. Joffre also shifted French strategy from defensive-offensive and placed greater emphasis on an immediate offensive. He published the new variation of Plan XVI on September 6, only six weeks after becoming chief of the General Staff.[30]

During the next several months Joffre continued to consider French strategy and to contemplate the possibility of a German advance into Bel-gium. The French staff focused on three alternatives for the Germans: first, respect neutral Belgium and Luxembourg and make an attack into strong French defenses along the Verdun-Toul-Épinal-Belfort line; sec-ond, attack through Luxembourg toward or around Verdun and follow this with a limited and perhaps delayed advance into Belgium; and third, defend in Lorraine and attack through Belgium. Of these alternatives, the third appeared most likely, since it corresponded to a recent German war game, used German fortifications between Metz and Thionville to great advantage, and threatened the flank of any French offensive advancing between Metz and Strasbourg. In particular, German efforts to strengthen fortifications between Metz and Thionville (opposite French defenses from Verdun to Toul) convinced Joffre that the Germans intended to drive through Belgium. During this period of analysis, his views toward Belgium changed from a belief that violating Belgian territory first could cause Britain and Italy to side against France to a belief that the only territory suitable for a decisive battle with Germany lay in Belgium.[31]

At a meeting of the Superior Council of National Defense on January 9, 1912 (the one for which the council's staff had prepared a strategic assessment advocating "crushing Germany"), political and military leaders addressed France's grand strategy. Quickly agreeing that Germany was the principal adversary against which France and its allies should concentrate all their resources, they welcomed the possibility of Russia's having 500,000 men ready for an offensive by the fifteenth day of mobilization. Though the prospect of a war with Germany immediately raised the question of Belgium, the council noted Great Britain's concerns about Belgium's neutrality. With Joffre's concurrence, the council finally agreed that French forces could "penetrate the territory of Belgium at the first news of the violation of that territory by the German army."[32] Premier Caillaux emphasized, however, "Not one French soldier will put a foot on the soil of Belgium if the Germans respect the treaties [of neutrality]."[33] In sharp contrast, the minister of foreign affairs expressed no reservations about France's troops violating Luxembourg's borders, since that small country was "enfeoffed to Germany." For France's "secondary frontiers," the Alps and Pyrenees, the council agreed that reserve or territorial forces could provide sufficient protection. Focusing primarily on landpower and the prospects of a war with Germany, the council had few comments about seapower except its importance in transporting troops from North Africa.

The meeting covered other important aspects of France's military preparation. In one of the few instances in which the subject was even addressed, the council discussed industrial mobilization, noting that "most of our industrial establishments are not prepared [to increase production greatly] and to fulfill the orders that will be sent to them." Also in the category of issues about which little was done, council members expressed regrets about the slowness of the technical services in developing heavy artillery. Additionally, the council considered the number of artillery rounds stockpiled for each artillery piece and agreed to increase the number from 1,280 to 1,500.

The meeting of the Superior Council of National Defense in January 1912 thus covered the broadest aspects of military preparation and provided ample reason for everyone to feel that France was on the right track. The president of the Third Republic, Armand Fallières, complimented Joffre on the army's resolve "to march straight for the enemy without any second thoughts."[34] With the council's blessings, Joffre had the license to make significant changes in French strategy and war plans, but France's political leaders had refused to give him permission to violate Belgium's neutrality before the Germans did.

Shortly after this important meeting of the Superior Council of National Defense, the Caillaux government fell, the Poincaré government assumed power, and Alexandre Millerand replaced Messimy as the minister of war. On the day Millerand entered office, he met with Joffre and expressed reservations, according to Joffre, about the chief of staff of the army's dealing directly with the minister of war rather than with the chief of the General Staff on issues pertaining to personnel and logistical support. Shortly thereafter Millerand used a presidential decree to abolish the functions of chief of staff of the army and make Castelnau the deputy chief of the General Staff, working for Joffre. Dubail departed Paris for command of a corps. As Joffre noted in his memoirs, this action completely ended the duality of the High Command and gave him enormous powers over the army by shifting powers from the minister of war and chief of staff of the army to the chief of the General Staff. Joffre noted: "It was the first time that such powers were confided to a single man; I had authority over the training of the army, its doctrine, its regulations, its mobilization, its concentration. For questions of promotion, the new

minister told me it was his intention to consult me. For the first time . . .
the leader [who would be] responsible [for the army] in wartime would
have the authority in peacetime to prepare for war."[35]

The limitations on Joffre's powers, however, became apparent when
he sought permission from political authorities to advance into Belgium
prior to a German violation of Belgian neutrality. The opportunity to
raise the issue came when the new premier, Raymond Poincaré, held a
meeting of political and military leaders on February 21, 1912, to review
military agreements with Britain and Russia. As part of this review, Joffre
focused on operational alternatives on the northeastern frontier and explained that enemy fortifications and natural obstacles severely limited
the opportunity to attack into Alsace and Lorraine. In Lorraine the German fortified system extended from Metz twenty-five kilometers north to
Thionville and blocked any hopes of attacking north of Metz. South of
Metz, an eighty-kilometer gap existed between the Metz-Thionville
fortifications and the Vosges Mountains, but several lakes blocked part of
this gap, leaving two corridors, one thirty kilometers wide and the other
twenty. In Alsace an offensive against Strasbourg would accomplish little
because of the natural barrier of the Rhine. Joffre concluded that favorable terrain for an advance did not exist in Alsace or Lorraine and that an
"infinitely more advantageous" opportunity for offensive action existed
in Belgium. By striking in Belgium, the French could avoid the enemy's
fortifications at Metz-Thionville, threaten German lines of communication, and use the British more effectively.[36]

Despite the attractiveness of Joffre's appeal, Poincaré—like Caillaux
before him—refused to let French forces enter Belgium before a German
violation of neutrality. The premier insisted that Belgium would never
agree to France's violating its neutrality and that a violation would probably result in its joining Germany. More important, a violation of Belgium's neutrality could cause Britain not to support France. Poincaré's
only concession was his willingness to accept a violation of Belgium's
neutrality if a "positive menace of German invasion" existed. The difficulty, however, as Joffre pointed out in his memoirs, was determining
what constituted a "positive menace."[37] After the meeting, diplomatic
and military officials probed the willingness of the British to countenance
a violation of Belgium's neutrality, but blunt advice in late November

from General Sir Henry Wilson, the British director of military operations, about not violating Belgium's neutrality ended Joffre's efforts. Two premiers, Caillaux and Poincaré, had adamantly opposed violating Belgium's neutrality, and he had no choice but to accept their decision.,

Despite restrictions on violating Belgium's neutrality, Joffre preferred an offensive strategy rather than a defensive-offensive one. He also saw significant advantages in forcing Germany to fight on two or more fronts. These advantages had long been obvious and had encouraged France to complete a military convention with the Russians. The final draft of the convention, though emphasizing the defensive nature of the Franco-Russian Alliance, pledged both powers to concentrate their forces against Germany. Completed in late 1892 and formally acknowledged with an exchange of notes in December 1893 and January 1894, the convention stipulated: "These forces shall be engaged to the utmost, as quickly as possible, in such a manner that Germany has to fight at the same time in the east and the west."[38] The military convention established the foundation for French strategy for the next twenty-five years by creating the real possibility of a two-front war against Germany and raising to new heights the importance of mobilizing first. The goal of a two-front war also made Russia, not Britain, France's principal ally in a war against Germany.

Staff talks between the French and Russians ensured that both countries understood and implemented the provisions of the 1894 military convention. Although the poor performance of the Russians in the Russo-Japanese War created doubts in France about the wisdom of relying on them, staff talks, as required by the convention, occurred in 1900, 1901, 1906, 1907, and 1908. In 1910 the two powers affirmed the discussions of previous meetings and emphasized that "defeat of the German armies remains, no matter what the circumstances, the first and principle objective of the allied armies." The generals representing the two countries agreed that Germany would probably direct its principal effort against France at the beginning of a war and send only three to five corps, plus a few reserve divisions, against Russia. The French representative also indicated France's intention to launch an "all-out and immediate" offensive against Germany at the beginning of a war.[39] With the permission of Paris, the French military attaché in Berlin held detailed talks with the Russian military attaché about the strategic implications of the

Franco-Russian military convention and the need for a Russian attack very early in the war. The French officer insisted that a war with France and Russia against Germany could be over in a month and emphasized the importance of both powers' attacking immediately. He concluded, "Even if beaten the French army will have opened the way for the Russian offensive and assured the final success [of the two allies]."[40]

Subsequent talks in 1911, 1912, and 1913 confirmed Germany's defeat as the "first and principal objective" of France and Russia and the defeat of Germany's allies as subordinate objectives. In each of the staff talks from 1910 to 1913 military representatives of the two countries explicitly addressed the meaning of the word "defensive" in the convention's preamble. In each meeting the generals agreed to keep the word, since the alliance was defensive, but they also agreed that the presence of the word did not rule out the possibility of offensive operations—even at the beginning of a war. Additionally, the meetings reinforced the requirement for rapid mobilization and offensives by France and Russia. In August 1913 the Russians agreed to begin an offensive on the fourteenth day after mobilization, and both allies promised to send their offensives into the "heart" of Germany.[41] The staff talks in 1911, 1912, and 1913 also provided information to the French about the readiness of the Russians for war, and they grew increasingly confident that the Russians could mount a strong offensive against Germany. The several staff talks and the constant pressure on Russia to launch an offensive against Germany, if war came, encouraged France's political and military leaders to abide by the military convention and to launch an offensive as soon as possible. Had the Russians, Joffre recognized, sensed any reservations among the French about launching an immediate offensive, they might not have attacked at the beginning of a war with Germany.

When Joffre participated in the staff talks in 1912 and 1913, he provided substantial information about his strategy in the event of a war with Germany. He later insisted that he kept his options open and did not commit himself to a course of action until after the situation at the beginning of a war became apparent, but even if he did not specify the exact location of the attack, he clearly communicated during the staff talks with Russia his intention to attack from northeastern France and his desire for simultaneous offensives. As in previous staff talks, Joffre and the Russian representative agreed in July 1912 that in the event of war Germany probably would deploy the principal part of its forces first against France and would leave only minimal forces against Russia. Recent improvements of German railroads in the Eifel, a German region northeast of Luxembourg, confirmed in Joffre's mind the Germans' intention to attack first. He assured the Russian representative that France would abide by article 3 of the military convention, which required France to have 1,300,000 soldiers participate in a "vigorous and determined" offensive against Germany.[42] The following year, Joffre was even more explicit. He promised that France would engage "nearly all its forces" on the northeastern frontier and would commence offensive operations on the eleventh day after mobilization. He also noted that the number of forces he would send into battle exceeded by more than 210,000 the number required by the convention. He and the Russian representative agreed:

> With regard to the conduct of operations, it is especially necessary that the allied armies obtain a decisive success as rapidly as possible. A check of the French armies at the beginning of a war will permit Germany to transfer to the Eastern Front part of its forces which have already fought against France. If, on the contrary, French armies obtain a success rapidly against the forces concentrated by Germany before them, this success will equally facilitate operations by the Russian armies, since the forces concentrated by Germany on the Western Front cannot possibly be transferred to the east. Thus, it is essential that French armies have numerical superiority over Germany forces in the west. This condition will be realized easily if Germany has to guard its eastern frontier with large forces.[43]

Joffre's strategic and operational concepts thus looked beyond the simple effect of France's acting against Germany and were linked inextricably to a simultaneous offensive by Russia. The location of his attack, however, remained uncertain. The French could attack into Alsace-Lorraine or Belgium or both.

As part of the effort to coordinate simultaneous attacks, France and Russia worked diligently to establish reliable wireless contact. As early as 1909, the two allies had two wireless telegraph routes, one connecting

Bobruisk (140 kilometers southeast of Minsk) to Paris directly and the other connecting Bobruisk to Sebastopol and then to Bizerte.[44] Another link evidently connected Bizerte with Paris. By July 1913 wireless communications between Paris and Bobruisk were open each day between 0600 and 0800 and 2000 and 2400 hours. As a backup, the links between Sebastopol and Bizerte were open each night between midnight and 0200.[45] By August 1914 the framework of French strategy—in the sense of its being part of an alliance strategy—was firmly in place, as were the communications to ensure continued coordination.

Outside the strategic arena, the second factor influencing Joffre to plan for an attack at the beginning of a war with Germany came from his own faith in the offense. Beginning in the early 1890s, the thinking of the French army had moved gradually from an emphasis on the defense to an emphasis on the offense. Some of this change stemmed from the desire to launch an offensive against Germany and compel it to fight a two-front war. Other pressure for change came from a misreading of the effect of new technological advances, such as smokeless gunpowder, rapid-firing artillery, magazine-fed rifles, and machine guns. From 1900 to 1905 the French placed more emphasis on the defense, but as the army's capabilities improved, its interest in the offense increased. Important support for the offensive came from military intellectuals such as Charles Ardant du Picq, Ferdinand Foch, and Henri Bonnal. More than any other theories, du Picq's ideas about "moral ascendancy" permeated the entire French army and provided the inspiration for the *offensive à outrance*. According to du Picq, the side with the superior "resolution to advance" would prevail, even if its weapons and equipment were equal or inferior to those of its opponent.[46] Foch argued in 1903 that improvements in firearms favored the offensive. He calculated how an attack with two battalions against one battalion would result in the attacking troops' firing some 10,000 more bullets than the defenders. By comparing this with the smaller advantage provided by earlier rifles, Foch confidently predicted that increases in firepower favored the attacker and would enable him to gain "moral superiority."[47] Bonnal added a special spin to these ideas by arguing that the first great battle between mass armies would be decisive.

Since huge conscript armies, he said, did not have the discipline and experience of professional armies, panic would spread quickly and magnify the effect of any defeat.[48] A future war would thus be short, and both sides would rely on the offensive in order to win the first battle and gain a decisive victory. Such ideas captured the imagination of many officers who thought that the offensive, more than the defensive, accorded with the national temperament of the French.

After becoming chief of the General Staff and gaining greater powers than his predecessors, Joffre began what he later called the "transformation" of the French army.[49] As part of this effort he firmly integrated the *offensive à outrance* into the thinking of the French army and thereby had greater influence than du Picq, Foch, Bonnal, or any other leader. Joffre became the chief of the General Staff only five months after Loyseau de Grandmaison, the head of the Operations Bureau of the General Staff, gave his famous lectures on tactics in February 1911. In those lectures Grandmaison criticized the "nearly complete atrophy" of the offensive spirit in the French army.[50] Had Michel remained chief of staff of the army, his reservations about Grandmaison and the *offensive à outrance* might have limited some of its pernicious effects, but Joffre welcomed the new ideas and resolved to develop a new doctrine through numerous maneuvers and map exercises and to transform the army.

After months of hard work, a "logical and sensible doctrine of the offensive," to use Joffre's words, emerged. In October 1913 the French codified their new doctrine in a new regulation on the operations of large units (corps, army, and army group), and in December 1913 in one on smaller units (regiment, brigade, and division). In reality, the October regulations focused on the operational level of war and the December regulations on the tactical level. As for the significance of the two regulations, the commission that wrote the October 1913 version explained, "The French army, returning to its traditions, accepts no law in the conduct of operations other than the offensive." The October 1913 regulations emphasized: "Only the offensive yields positive results." The will to fight became all-important: "Battles are above all moral contests. Defeat is inevitable when hope for victory ceases. Success will come, not to the one who has suffered the least losses, but to the one whose will is the steadiest and whose morale is the most highly tempered." The regulations also stated:

An energetic commander-in-chief, having confidence in himself, in his subordinates, in his troops, will never yield the initiative to his adversary under the pretext of awaiting better intelligence. At the beginning of the war, he will launch operations of such violence and fury that the enemy, weakened in its morale and paralyzed in its action, will be reduced, perhaps, to remaining on the defensive.[51]

The new regulations saw little value in the defense. For example, the commission that wrote the December 1913 regulations criticized the 1895 regulations for considering the defense as a way of "drawing the enemy onto terrain where one can fight him under the best conditions." Rejecting this concept, the December regulations asserted: "Only the offensive can break the will of the adversary. The necessity to economize forces in order to give greater power to attack can result in the assumption of the defensive in certain zones. But, by itself, the defense can contain the enemy only during a limited time; it can never gain success." The regulations added: "Once begun, combat is pushed to the end; success depends more on the vigor and the tenacity of execution than on the skill of combined actions. All units thus are employed with the most extreme energy."[52]

The December 1913 regulations also emphasized a new relationship between artillery and infantry. The commission writing the regulations explained that the principal changes from the 1895 regulations pertained to the employment of artillery. The 1895 regulations had said, "The artillery begins the combat, prepares partial attacks as well as the decisive attack, and finishes the battle."[53] The report with the December 1913 edition said, however, "The artillery does not prepare attacks; it supports them."[54] In other words, instead of blasting enemy positions for long periods before an infantry assault, artillery fired primarily during an attack. Additionally, the regulations for the employment of field artillery emphasized the economical use of ammunition and went so far as to warn against the massive use of artillery. Whereas previous regulations had envisaged the artillery firing many rounds and blasting enemy positions for long periods prior to an assault, the new regulations on artillery published on the eve of the Great War warned against the massive use of artillery and called for support only during the infantry's advance. The field service regulations asserted that artillery had only a limited effect against an entrenched enemy and added, "To force an adversary out of his cover, it is necessary to attack with the infantry."[55] The infantry regulations of April 1914 asserted that the "supreme weapon" of the infantry was the bayonet. After the infantrymen fixed bayonets, they would advance— wearing a blue coat, red trousers, and a blue cap with red top—with their officers leading in the front and with drums and bugles sounding the charge.[56] The attacking troops would supposedly gain a superiority of fire with the rapid and intense fire of the 75-mm cannon and with a hail of bullets from the advancing soldiers. When they closed with the enemy soldiers, they would throw themselves into their ranks and finish the fight with the bayonet and superior courage. Such ideas would cost the French thousands of casualties in the opening battles of 1914. In numerous cases officers refused to lie on the ground or seek cover when under fire, and infantry units charged forward with little or no artillery support. These "glorious" actions bled many of the best soldiers from French units.

Although Joffre's exact role in infusing such ideas throughout the army is not completely clear, and although numerous senior officers and commissions willingly contributed, there is no doubt that he bears the ultimate responsibility for those ideas and their effects. The French army may have become captivated by what Joffre called the "mystique of the offensive" and the "cult of the offensive,"[57] but he purposely used the abundant powers given him by Messimy and Millerand to modify the army's doctrine and regulations and to raise emphasis on the offensive to new heights. And he did nothing before August 1914 to curb the excessive emphasis on the offensive and to establish a better balance between the offense and the defense in the French army. In the end, the significance of Joffre's role is best weighed by recalling that Michel publicly criticized Grandmaison's ideas.

In his memoirs Joffre acknowledged his role in formulating the new offensive doctrine, but he denied responsibility for the murderous results. He explained, "It takes a long time for a doctrine to penetrate into every echelon, especially after a period of moral anarchy similar to that through which the army had passed." He also criticized French soldiers for "not taking into account the nature of modern war, which no longer permits attacks like those made during the time of muzzle-loading rifles and cannon."[58] In other words, Joffre defended his reliance on the offensive at the strategic and operational levels, but he criticized tactical commanders who launched infantry assaults without providing adequate support and preparation and who wasted the lives of their soldiers. Long separated by time and geography from the disastrous assaults, the retired Marshal of France offered no explanation in his memoirs of what he had done to limit the excesses of the *offensive à outrance* or to ensure that tactical commanders knew how to conduct well-prepared and supported attacks.

Joffre also contributed directly and indirectly to France's weakness in heavy artillery, but he had less influence over the development of artillery materiel in the French army than on the development of its doctrine. Among the most controversial issues pertaining to the Great War was the small amount of heavy artillery possessed by the French in August 1914. When the French mobilized, they had 4,076 75-mm cannon (plus 666 in reserve) but only 308 heavy field artillery pieces: 104 155-mm Rimailho, 84 120-mm short-range Baquet, and 120 120-mm long-range de Bange models. In addition they had some 7,300 guns (ranging in caliber from 80-mm to 155-mm) in various arsenals and fortified positions.[59] Many of these were obsolete; most were suitable for use only in fortifications or sieges because of their great weight and lack of mobility. The key shortage was in heavy field artillery that could be moved from one point on the battlefield to another. While the French had 308 of these pieces, the Germans had 848, most of which had greater range and higher rates of fire than those of the French.

As early as 1909 the French recognized the requirement for additional heavy artillery. Despite the apparent strengths of their own 75-mm cannon, the French followed German military activities and monitored their potential adversary's adoption of 105-mm and 150-mm guns and the improvement of their 77-mm guns between 1907 and 1909. Though some French artillerists preferred to hit a target with numerous smaller shells rather than a few heavy shells and denied the need for longer-range pieces,[60] many recognized the advantages of longer-range pieces and heavier shells. Most also recognized that the flat trajectory of the 75-mm gun kept it from occupying and firing from defilade positions and prevented its rounds from hitting targets on the reverse slope of hills. The inability to hit targets on reverse slopes caused the French more concern than did German advantages in range, since the useful range of the artillery, the French believed, was restricted to the five or six kilometers a commander of a battery could see and since the French expected the movement of their mobile batteries to protect them against the longer-range counterbattery fire of the German pieces.[61]

Because of the army's concerns about defilade firing, the Superior Council of War recommended in 1909 the development of a "light Howitzer" that would have a higher trajectory than that of the 75-mm gun.[62] Although the French had developed a 155-mm short-range Rimailho cannon, the generals wanted a more mobile 120-mm Howitzer, capable of following the infantry more closely. In essence, they foresaw a war of movement and wanted mobile heavy artillery that could keep up with the infantry in the field. In the winter of 1910–11 the French legislature expressed concern about the army's failure to develop heavy field artillery. The legislators noted that whereas the Germans had developed heavy artillery capable of being used in an offensive maneuver, the French had developed pieces suitable for use only in a static siege. They then urged the development of new guns. In July 1911 the Superior Council of War again addressed the issue of artillery. On the same day that General Michel presented his proposal for reorganizing the army, Joffre led the discussion of artillery, and at its conclusion the council supported adoption of a "light Howitzer." During this meeting, Messimy expressed surprise when he realized French artillery had not changed significantly since the Fashoda crisis of 1898. Offering an objection that others would repeat on numerous occasions in the future, Michel opposed the proposal because it would multiply the number of calibers (and hence difficulties of supply) in the artillery.[63]

To bypass the resistance of the artillery's technical services to heavy artillery and additional calibers, Messimy formed a special commission under General Léon de Lamothe and ordered it to consider alternatives. In October 1911 Lamothe gave the committee's first proposal to the minister of war and called for a light Howitzer that was as mobile as the 75-mm cannon but capable of producing greater destruction and demoralization among the enemy. He also called for a "long cannon" with a range of twelve to thirteen kilometers and light enough to be drawn by six to eight horses.[64] In February 1912 the Puteaux arsenal presented two pieces for testing, one of which was a 120-mm gun and the other a hybrid model that could be switched from 75-mm to 120-mm by changing tubes. Neither model was acceptable. A few months later Schneider manufacturing presented two pieces for testing, one of which was a 105-mm gun built for the Bulgarians and the other a 106.7-mm gun built for the Russians. The latter gun proved partially satisfactory, but the commission refused to approve it without additional testing. In January 1913 the commission approved the improved Schneider gun but ordered its caliber reduced to 105-mm. In April France ordered 220 of the improved Schneider 105-mm Howitzers, which had a range of 12.3 kilometers.

The artillery's technical services, however, strongly objected to the order. In their minds there was little difference between the 75-mm and the 105-mm, and they, like Michel, disliked increasing the number of calibers. Recognizing that those advocating the 105-mm were concerned primarily with providing defilade fire, the technicians came up with a modification to the 75-mm. By adding fins to the round *(plaquette Maladrin),* the technicians gave the round a much more curved trajectory and enabled it to strike defilade targets at short ranges. Arguing that this modification decreased the need for the 105-mm, the technicians convinced the minister of war to reduce the order for the 105-mm from 220 to 36, all of which appeared just as the war started.

Recognizing that some German artillery pieces had a greater range and larger projectile than the 105-mm, the minister of war ordered development of a 135-mm gun that could keep up with the infantry and fire a forty-kilogram projectile sixteen to eighteen kilometers. Since developing a completely new gun could take as long as five years, the French initiated a program to modify existing 120-mm and 155-mm long-range guns and provide them with greater mobility and range. Placing the tube of the 120-mm long-range gun on the carriage of the 155-mm short-range gun in July 1913 yielded significant improvements. Another important enhancement occurred after the French, still concerned about mobility, tested a Schneider carriage for the 155-mm long-range gun in October 1913. The carriage was a modification of one built for the Russians, and its adoption added two to three kilometers to the range of the 155-mm long-range gun. Although these efforts helped a little, they had occurred too late to affect the war's first battles. Over the longer term, much of the delay obviously came, as the Superior Council of War noted in January 1912, from the technical services' greater interest in technological innovation than in producing an acceptable, but not highly advanced, weapon that met the basic needs of the army.[65]

In his memoirs Joffre asserted that when he became the chief of the General Staff, he worked diligently to increase France's heavy artillery. He nevertheless admitted that he had submitted an unnecessarily optimistic comparison in January 1914 of French and German capabilities in heavy artillery. His study had concluded that France's 155-mm, 120-mm, and 105-mm artillery could respond adequately to Germany's artillery in those rare instances in which the 75-mm was inadequate. His study also argued the 75-mm was adequate in most cases: "A mobile artillery, knowing how to utilize the terrain, will rarely have need of a long-range cannon to place itself a good distance from the enemy."[66] Joffre attempted to justify the unfortunate study by saying that France's inferiority was obvious to everyone and that he had submitted it for "reasons of morale." He also claimed that the study did nothing more than say that short-range heavy artillery was "sometimes necessary and not always indispensable."[67] In reality Joffre and most French officers could foresee situations in which heavy artillery would be useful, but since they expected a series of highly mobile battles, few desired to burden the corps or divisions with relatively immobile heavy artillery. All had complete confidence in their quick-firing 75-mm cannon, the best in the world, and almost none questioned having 120 75-mm cannon in a corps while the Germans had 108 77-mm, 36 105-mm, and 16 150-mm.

On October 15, 1913, when the Superior Council of War discussed the distribution and use of the limited number of heavy artillery pieces, Joffre opposed placing France's few heavy pieces in the army's corps and instead supported placing them in separate regiments and then assigning these regiments to support the five field armies established in Plan XVII. Such a distribution made heavy artillery available throughout the five armies and did not hamper the mobility of divisions and corps. In essence, Joffre expected the heavy artillery to function as siege artillery, not field artillery. The council agreed with him and recommended combining the heavy artillery batteries into five regiments.[68] The government approved this recommendation in April 1914, but since the regiments were not completely ready, the French army had only sixteen battalions (or sixty-one batteries) of heavy artillery in August 1914. Such a distribution of heavy artillery nonetheless coincided perfectly with Joffre's view that such pieces were "sometimes necessary and not always indispensable." Placing heavy artillery at field army level, and not at division or corps level, also guaranteed that the ponderous weapons would remain far in the rear and be used only on fortified targets.

Given the reluctance of the artillery community to demand heavier, longer-range pieces and given their success in stymieing reform, Joffre escapes some of the blame for the artillery's weakness, but he never used his energy and his authority to improve artillery in the way he used them to change French doctrine. Even if he had been sympathetic to the need for more heavy pieces, his interest in the 105-mm was driven more by his concern with defilade fire than with a desire for heavy artillery or a concern about counterbattery fire. More significantly, his explanation of his unnecessarily optimistic comparison in January 1914 of French and German artillery is undoubtedly as disingenuous as his defense of his offensive doctrine and his criticism of French commanders for not conducting tactical attacks correctly. After the war Messimy acknowledged that "responsibility for the French army's not having heavy artillery at the declaration of war falls principally on the artillery's technical services. . . . There is no doubt that Joffre and the General Staff of the army were wrong not to overcome this obstacle."[69] In July 14, 1914, however, when Poincaré presided over a special ceremony in which three new heavy artillery and three engineer regiments received their colors, those attending the ceremony had few doubts about France's artillery or its readiness for war.

Joffre's transformation of the French army prepared it for a short war. He did this even though he had acknowledged in a meeting of the Superior Council of National Defense on 21 February 1912 that a war with Germany could last for an "indefinite period." If France were victorious in the initial battles, it still would take six months to march to the Rhine, he argued, where the strongest national resistance of Germany would begin. Or, if France were beaten in the initial battles, it would take the Germans

four months to march deep enough into France to face the strongest national resistance.[70] Despite the possibility of a war lasting an "indefinite
period," military leaders made almost no preparations for a long war. In
his memoirs Joffre defended this focus on a short war by citing a 1909 assertion by General Alfred von Schlieffen that a future war would last no
longer than the first battles because of "pacifist tendencies in the majority
of the European people." Accordingly, Joffre reasoned, the French had to
enter battle with all their forces and had to prepare for a short war.[71] In
truth, however, the French on their own had concluded that a war with
Germany would be short. The October 1913 field service regulations explained: "The nature of war, the size of forces involved, the difficulties of
resupplying them, the interruption of the social and economic life of the
country, all encourage the search for a decision in the shortest possible
time in order to terminate the fighting quickly."[72] Even those officers who
rejected the notion of a short war did not anticipate a war lasting longer
than a year.

Several preparatory measures taken by the French suggest some
awareness of the possibility of something other than a short war. As the
most notable exception to the army's preparing to live off its stocks,
French planners anticipated the daily manufacture of 13,600 rounds of
75-mm ammunition within eighty-one days after mobilization. Yet such a
rate proved far below what was required. Also, arrangements with the
British allowed French naval forces to concentrate on the western Mediterranean and transport troops and supplies to France. While much of
the public discussion of colonial troops concerned Charles Mangin's
force noire from Africa and its long-term contribution,[73] the Superior
Council of National Defense focused primarily on transporting XIX
Corps quickly from Algeria and achieving numerical equality with German forces in the first battles.[74] Finally, another preparatory step ensured
the stockpiling of food for Paris, as well as for other fortified areas. When
the war began, Paris accumulated food supplies (including potatoes, con-
densed milk, starchy foods, and salt).[75] Yet the rationale for this stockpiling was based less on the prospect of a long war than on fears of another
siege such as the one of 1870–1871.

Although preparation for a short war ultimately enabled France to
avoid defeat in the opening campaign of World War I, it also contributed

to France's disastrously inadequate preparation for the enormous economic and industrial demands of the war. One officer who studied industrial mobilization acknowledged, "Before the war began in 1914, we never thought in France about the mobilization of our industry."[76] Since everyone expected a short war, logisticians assumed that munitions and equipment already manufactured in peacetime would meet the army's immediate needs and that a simple acceleration of manufacturing would replace those items consumed in wartime. As a postwar parliamentary commission concluded, the failure to comprehend the relationship between industrial production and military operations, and the unwillingness to think of anything but a short war, contributed to Joffre's paying no attention to defending or retaining the Briey basin, the loss of which deprived France of 83 percent of its production of iron ore, 62 percent of its cast iron, and 60 percent of its steel.[77] The failure to prepare, or even think through, industrial mobilization eventually cost the French thousands of lives when their soldiers had to fight without adequate weapons and supplies.

In contrast to the failure to think through industrial mobilization, military leaders paid close attention to the mobilization of personnel. They knew that France had gone to war in 1870 with little or no preparation to mobilize conscripts and organize units effectively, and that the chaotic results had contributed substantially to its defeat. Beyond this historical experience, the focus on a short war created great interest in putting all available men into uniform and integrating them into the army quickly and efficiently. Additionally, after the Germans increased the number of active forces in their army in 1911, 1912, and 1913, political and military leaders feared they could mobilize quickly, attack without warning, and disrupt France's mobilization. In July–August 1913, the adoption of three years' military service enabled the French to have three "classes" on active duty and increased the size of the active force to about 700,000 soldiers. According to Joffre, it also "reinforced the covering force, facilitated mobilization, and considerably improved the quality of the troops."[78] As a result of these and other improvements, the army became more capable of an immediate offensive upon mobilization, and plans for concentrating on the northeastern frontier incorporated some reserve divisions in the front line.[79] In June 1914, shortly before becoming minister of war again, Messimy stated: "Today . . . the mobilization order places the entire country under arms and transforms it into a formidable army capable of maneuvering and winning, not in several months, not in several weeks, but in just a few days."[80]

The army's preparation for a short war accorded with the expectations of most political leaders and found few naysayers. In contrast, the adoption of three years of military service in July–August 1913 occurred only after intense parliamentary debate and public protests in several garrisons. While Joffre considered three years' service essential for providing trained soldiers who could deliver a vigorous offensive early in a war, most critics of the new law ignored the question of a long or short war and instead focused on the capabilities and role of the reserves and the burden of military service. In such an environment no military leader could insist on preparing for a long war, even though some anticipated France's being joined by Russia and Great Britain and foresaw a war being waged over stakes far grander—the redrawing of the map of Europe "from top to bottom"[81]—than those associated with a brief military campaign.

With the broad outlines of France's strategy sketched by the requirement to launch an offensive simultaneously with Russia, by Joffre's preference for an offensive, and by Caillaux's and Poincaré's having ruled out violating Belgium's neutrality, the army's staff carefully considered the Germans' capability to advance through Belgium. The key question pertained to the number of German corps and the role of their reserve formations. After adding two corps in 1912, the German army—according to French calculations—had twenty-five corps. If the Germans defended East Prussia against the Russians and Lorraine against the French, they did not have enough corps, the French reasoned, to concentrate a force large enough for a deep drive across central Belgium, west of the Meuse-Sambre rivers through Liège, Namur, Charleroi, and Maubeuge. Castelnau, the deputy chief of the General Staff, assured Joffre that if the Germans tried to go beyond the Liège-Namur line, they would "dangerously overextend their front and have an insufficient density for a vigorous action." The Germans could extend their forces and amass a large force for an advance west of the Meuse-Sambre rivers only by integrating reserve units into the front line and using them the same way they would use active units. The French did not expect the Germans to use their reserves as "shock" troops, an impression reinforced by the fact that the Germans provided their reserves with less artillery than they did active units.[82] Thus Joffre accepted the likelihood of Germany's violating Belgian neutrality and advancing around the flank of the Verdun-Toul-Épinal-Belfort fortifications, but he did not think the Germans had sufficient active forces to make a deep envelopment beyond the Liège-Namur-Charleroi-Maubeuge line. Additionally, he thought such a deep maneuver would leave the Germans few forces for eastern Belgium and Luxembourg.

After publishing modifications to Plan XVI in September 1911, Joffre and his staff spent more than a year and a half revising French plans for concentrating forces on the frontier in the event of war. On April 18, 1913, Joffre presented his new concept to the Superior Council of War, which supported it unanimously.[83] After the minister of war approved the proposed concept, Joffre completed and published the plan. On February 7, 1914, his staff finished the main parts of Plan XVII and issued copies to each designated army commander. The staff finally completed all documents in the plan on May 1. Though Plan XVII was a concentration plan and not a war plan, the main body of the document stated, "The intention of the commander-in-chief is to deliver, with all forces assembled, an attack against the German armies."[84] Later events would determine Joffre's strategy and the operations to accomplish the goals of that strategy, but he refused to remain behind the northeastern fortifications and intended to concentrate French forces so they could attack north or south of Metz-Thionville or north into Belgium toward Arlon and Neufchâteau.

Plan XVII envisaged France's having five armies in the northeast. From right to left, Joffre placed First, Second, Third, and Fifth armies along the German, Luxembourg, and Belgian frontier. Fourth Army remained in reserve behind Second and Third armies, where it could move to the right if the Germans came through Switzerland or to the left if they came through Belgium. Fifth Army, which had five infantry corps and a cavalry corps, occupied a broad front beginning east of the point where the eastern border of Luxembourg touched France and extending west beyond Mézières to Hirson. Joffre also had four "Reserve Division groups," each of which had three divisions. After positioning First Group on the right of First Army and Fourth Group on the left of Fifth Army, he placed Second and Third groups behind Second and Third armies. Thus, Plan XVII had about the same forces along the Luxembourg and Belgian frontier that Joffre's modified version of Plan XVI had had.

By virtue of Plan XVII, French forces occupied a central strategic position and could respond to whatever move the Germans made. Each army commander received specific instructions, as well as the mission of the armies on his flank. In the broadest sense, these specific instructions provided Joffre with options for attacking north into Belgium toward Arlon and Neufchâteau or north or south of Metz-Thionville. In Plan XVII's specific instructions, First and Second armies were ordered to prepare to attack south of Metz-Thionville. Third Army focused on Metz-Thionville; it would either invest Metz or throw back any enemy forces coming from the Metz-Thionville fortifications. Focusing north, Fifth Army prepared to attack north of Metz-Thionville or into Belgium. Since it had the mission of preparing to attack the right wing of the main enemy force, the direction of its attack depended on whether the Germans entered neutral Luxembourg and Belgium. If the Germans did not violate the territory of Luxembourg or Belgium, Fifth Army would attack north of Thionville into Lorraine but would retain sufficient forces along the Belgian frontier to protect against a subsequent German move deep into Belgium. If the Germans entered Belgium, Fifth Army would advance north into Belgium toward Neufchâteau. In this latter case, Fourth Army would advance toward Arlon on the right of Fifth Army and left of Third Army. If the Germans did not violate the territory of Luxembourg or Belgium, Fourth Army would enter the line between Second and Third armies and participate in the Lorraine attack.

As for allies, the "crushing" of Germany could be accomplished only with the cooperation of Great Britain and Russia, but France and Britain had a long history of disputes and conflicts. As late as 1902, the French had had a highly classified plan for a surprise invasion of the British Isles with 65,000 men.[85] The British had their own reservations; in 1908, four years after signing the agreement with Paris, some high-ranking political leaders had expressed a belief that the French would side with the Russians in the event of a conflict between Britain and Russia.[86] Despite these mutual doubts, France had courted Britain and in April 1904 signed the Anglo-French Entente, an agreement that did little more than liquidate outstanding colonial differences. Not until later did discussions between army and naval staffs increase the significance of what became known as the Entente Cordiale. In essence, the evolving strategic situation and the dividing of Europe into armed camps brought London and Paris together. In a meeting of the Superior Council of War in 1906, Georges Clemenceau noted: "In the actual political situation, it is impossible to imagine France entering a conflict with Germany without having the support of England."[87] Despite this strategic reality, British authorities made two points very clear from the earliest moment in the negotiations between the two military staffs. First, France should violate Belgian neutrality only after Germany had done so. Second, the military discussions and arrangements were, as one memorandum stated, "not binding on the [British] Government."[88]

From the earliest years of the Entente, the British appeared to be more willing to provide naval forces than land forces. At a meeting of the Superior Council of National Defense on February 21, 1912, the minister of the navy summarized arrangements with the British Admiralty: "The English fleet is charged with operations in the North Sea, the English Channel, and the Atlantic Ocean; the French fleet is charged with operations in the Mediterranean."[89] The French welcomed this division of responsibilities, for concentrating its fleet in the Mediterranean gave France, as Joffre explained in May 1913, "absolute mastery of the western Mediterranean." As a result, troops could be transported easily from North Africa to French ports.[90]

British commitment of land forces remained much less certain. By early 1906 the French nonetheless anticipated the British landing six infantry divisions, one "mounted" division, and four brigades of cavalry.[91] By July 1911 they expected the same number of divisions but only two cavalry brigades, totaling some 150,000 men and 67,000 horses.[92] The value of this relatively small force was explained in an intelligence assessment in 1912: "In the event that English troops participate in operations with ours, the active forces placed in the line by France and England clearly will be superior to the German forces."[93] No one expected the

British forces to add considerably to the fighting power of the French, and everyone knew that the British could be delayed for "political or naval reasons."[94] In 1919 Joffre acknowledged, "Personally, I was convinced that they would come, but in the end there was no formal commitment on their part. There were only studies on embarking and debarking and on the positions that would be reserved for their troops."[95] Until Britain declared war on Germany and began moving troops, the French had no guarantee of British support.

Despite continuing doubts, a secret annex to Plan XVII dealt with British land forces, known as "Army W." On the basis of a transportation plan completed in March 1913, the French expected the British to have one cavalry and six infantry divisions in France sixteen days after mobilization.[96] If the British arrived on time, Joffre expected them to move into position on the left of Fifth Army in the vicinity of Hirson (fifty kilometers west of Mézières) and, according to Sir John French, "act on the left of the French army against the right German flank."[97] Since the time required to transport the British to the continent corresponded to the time required to mobilize the entire French army, Joffre could expect prompt assistance, but given the possibility of a delay in the British decision to mobilize or a problem in transportation, he could not let the success of the entire campaign depend on British participation. Additionally, the secrecy and sensitivity of conversations between Paris and London prevented any open mention of British assistance. The British thus added to the number of allied soldiers who could participate in a campaign against Germany and enabled the French to concentrate their fleet in the Mediterranean and move troops more readily from Africa, but the French relied much more heavily on and expected much more of the Russians.

In the end, French strategic thinking suffered from several flaws, the most serious of which stemmed from the assumption that the Germans had insufficient forces to drive across Belgium deep into the French rear. Joffre and his planners expected the enemy to advance through Luxembourg and Belgium, but virtually no one in France anticipated the Germans' sending two armies north of the Meuse-Sambre rivers through Liège, Namur, Charleroi, and Maubeuge. To make matters worse, Plan XVII placed three-quarters of the French army south of Verdun and set the framework for an advance into Alsace and Lorraine. Ironically, if not foolishly, Joffre accepted this distribution of his forces even though he had emphasized the difficulties of an advance into the two former provinces when he attempted to convince Caillaux and Poincaré to let French forces violate Belgium's neutrality. Finally, the revision of French strategy produced no new thoughts about increasing industrial production for a long war or adding significantly more heavy artillery.[98]

Two different commanders of Fifth Army, which under Plan XVII occupied a position on Joffre's extreme left, complained before the outbreak of war about the maldistribution of forces. General Gallieni, who commanded Fifth Army until his retirement on April 24, 1914, expressed strong doubts about the strength and mission of his army shortly after publication of Plan XVII. Using several map exercises to assess possible operations, Gallieni concluded that Fifth Army did not have sufficient forces to move into Belgium. He demanded more troops and insisted that fortifications at Maubeuge be improved.[99] His successor, General Charles Lanrezac, also submitted a report in late July 1914 expressing doubts about Fifth Army's ability to march into Belgium. According to Lanrezac, Fifth Army could not reach key positions in Belgium before the Germans; its front had to be shortened by moving his right boundary farther to the west; and it could march into Belgium only if Fourth Army advanced on its right. More important, an offensive toward Neufchâteau would succeed only if the Germans were advancing no deeper than Sedan. The Fifth Army commander believed, however, that the enemy would drive deeper into Belgium than Sedan, and as evidence mounted that the enemy might advance deeper, he cited a German war game of 1911 in which three armies had marched across Belgium, the southernmost of which had crossed the Meuse south of Namur. Lanrezac explained, "It is clear that Fifth Army, once engaged in the direction of Neufchâteau, cannot parry this last eventuality."[100] Lanrezac later insisted that Joffre paid no attention to his comments, but Lanrezac's report did not arrive until August 1, the date French political leaders authorized mobilization. According to Joffre he did not respond to Lanrezac's study because it was "premature" to discuss the strategic situation with an army commander when the situation was still unfolding.[101]

In the years immediately preceding the war, the French High Command received intelligence that provided valuable insights into German capabilities. Among the items acquired by intelligence were copies of war games conducted by German units in 1912 and 1913. Although most of these war games did not yield explicit information about German capabilities and intentions,[102] one in 1912 did address directly the question of concentrating against Russia or France and concluded that German forces should concentrate on "wiping out the French army."[103] French intelligence also acquired a copy of the 1911 handbook for German General Staff officers. This handbook described the role of reserve units and clearly anticipated their being integrated into active units. Unlike the 1902 edition, it also had information about the military forces of Great Britain, Belgium, and Holland.[104]

According to Joffre, he received assessments of German efforts to improve the quality of the reserves and thereby enable them to advance with active units. He also received an analysis of Germany's mobilization plan, a copy of which was obtained by French agents. The mobilization plan stated that "reserve troops will be employed the same as active troops."[105] French analysis of the document noted this important sentence but concluded that "the reserve corps, destined to be employed in operations [the same] as the active corps, has become, according to the new mobilization plan, more homogeneous and better led but has remained lighter than the active corps."[106] In his memoirs Joffre noted his awareness that German reserve units needed additional "capable" officers and had only two battalions of artillery in a division. He also asserted that the role assigned to reserve units appeared to be different from that of active units.[107] In other words, the Germans had not given their reserve units enough combat power for them to deliver the "shock" of frontline troops. Consequently, before the beginning of the war he remained confident that the Germans did not have sufficient units to drive west of the Meuse-Sambre rivers and simultaneously have a strong force in central Belgium.

While Plan XVII provided for the mobilization and concentration of the French army in the northeast and included alternatives for possible maneuver, it was not a blueprint for strategy and operations in August 1914. In his memoirs Joffre explained that even though the plan established the broad outlines of possible maneuvers, it was "impossible to fix a definitive maneuver for execution a long time in advance."[108] According to Joffre a wide variety of information, "as much diplomatic and political

as military," would arrive incrementally after mobilization and would require modification of any plan completed in peacetime;[109] hence he
chose to delay final decisions about strategy and operations until the military and political situation became clear in the opening days of the war.
Moreover, establishing a plan of operations in peacetime would permit
"meddling of the government in military operations." Though convinced
that French forces would have to advance into Belgium, Joffre knew
better than to disobey his political superiors flagrantly and to initiate
preparations for an advance. Consequently, as he acknowledged in his
memoirs, he concealed his intentions. The alternatives in Plan XVII, he
insisted, provided sufficient guidelines for French forces to plan and prepare. However, he "always" considered maneuver into Belgium France's
"most desirable" course of action.[110]

Joffre's reluctance to share his concept of operations with his political
superiors and his subordinate commanders or to commit himself to a
course of action prior to the war became apparent in a meeting with his
army commanders in early August 1914. When General Dubail, commander of First Army and a participant in the staff talks with Russia,
asked for additional troops for his attack into Alsace, Joffre coyly responded, "That's your plan, not mine."[111]

In fact Plan XVII did nothing more than concentrate French forces in
the northeast and provide alternatives for several possible maneuvers. If
the Germans avoided Belgium, French forces could advance on both
sides of the Metz-Thionville fortifications. If the Germans entered Belgium, the French could send three armies toward Neufchâteau and Arlon
which lay on the two best east-west routes through eastern Belgium.
While Plan XVII placed French forces along the Franco-Belgian and
Franco-German border, Joffre would determine his wartime strategy and
design the operations to support that strategy after his forces were located along the border and hostilities began.

Messimy's choice of Joffre in July 1911 thus had a profound effect upon
the war plans, doctrine, and weapons of the French army. Joffre dominated war planning, increased emphasis on the offensive, permitted fundamental changes in the doctrinal relationship between artillery and infantry, and failed to act energetically to improve heavy field artillery. After
the war, Messimy admitted, "I have often vehemently reproached myself

for not having chosen Gallieni."[112] Additionally, Messimy set the framework for the relationship between political and military authorities in the Great War when he ended the duality of the High Command in July 1911 and appointed Joffre chief of the General Staff. As David B. Ralston noted, the Chamber of Deputies and Senate voiced few objections to Messimy's or Millerand's changes. After one legislator questioned the legality of the reform, the government received an overwhelming vote of confidence, 338 to 7, in the Chamber of Deputies. As a consequence of the decrees of July 1911 and January 1912, Ralston asserted, "Joffre now had a greater degree of control over the functioning of the French army than any general since Bonaparte."[113] In fact Joffre's powers were limited by the government and were far less than those of Bonaparte. As Douglas Porch observed, "the war minister remained the constitutional head of the forces and the acknowledged army chief."[114] Moreover, even Joffre could not ignore the obstacles placed in his path by parochial bureaucrats in the High Command.

The relationship between political and military authorities during wartime had been spelled out in the October 1913 regulations on the operations of large units. Approved by a presidential decree and based on a report submitted by the minister of war, the first paragraph of the regulations said:

> The government, which has responsibility for the vital interests of the country, alone has the authority to fix the political objective of a war. If the struggle extends to several frontiers, it designates the principal adversary against which the greater part of the national forces should be directed. It consequently distributes the means of action and all types of resources and places them entirely at the disposition of the generals charged with being commanders-in-chief of the various theaters of operation.[115]

Neither the 1883 nor the 1895 field service regulations had included such an assertion.

The paragraph in the October 1913 regulations on the government's fixing the political objectives of a war also provided senior military commanders with substantial authority. Since the regulations had the authority of a presidential decree and thus the force of law, they carried substantial weight in political and military circles. They also reflected the agreement carved out between political and military leaders. Although this agreement gave the government responsibility for fixing political objectives and choosing commanders-in-chief for the various theaters, it left little room for the government to do anything with regard to the various theaters other than identifying the objective to be attained and distributing personnel, units, and resources for the accomplishment of that objective. Questions of strategy and operations remained the preserve of the commanders-in-chief; the government was left to choose among different strategies and different theaters through its distribution of resources.

Key political leaders supported the division of responsibility envisaged by the October 1913 regulations. Not surprisingly, one of these was Messimy, who again served as minister of war during the first government of René Viviani, which lasted from June 13 until August 26, 1914. As France began mobilizing, Messimy met with Joffre and discussed their relationship. They agreed that "the political direction of the war belongs properly to the government. The conduct of operations belongs exclusively to the commander-in-chief."[116] Thus, France entered the war with an offensive strategy placing special emphasis on attacks and mobile operations and with Joffre in almost complete control of French strategy and operations.

The army that entered the Great War differed dramatically from the poorly organized and led forces of 1870 or the undisciplined mob of 1871. Joffre and other French leaders had transformed the French army, but that transformation had produced an army that would suffer high casualties while winning the "miracle" of the Marne, not one that was prepared for the long, destructive, costly war that followed. Unaware of the mismatch between his army's capability and the challenges it would soon face but optimistic about the "wholehearted support of Russia," Joffre welcomed the prospect of war with Germany. After visiting "the leading military men" of France in February 1913, General Sir Henry Wilson reported that "the soldiers are of the opinion that it would be far better for France if a conflict were not too long postponed."[117]

CHAPTER 2

The War of Movement

1914

IN THE WEEKS following the assassination of Archduke Franz Ferdinand on June 28, 1914, very few people in France believed they faced a
grave crisis or thought a massively destructive and costly war was imminent. Most paid closer attention to the sensational events surrounding
the trial of Henriette Caillaux, the wife of Joseph Caillaux, former premier of France, than to the flurry of diplomatic messages coming from
Europe's capitals. They were fascinated by the story of Madame
Caillaux's having killed the editor of *Le Figaro* to keep him from publishing love letters that her husband had written her before leaving his first
wife. More aware of the danger, France's political leaders monitored the
unfolding international crisis carefully, and, to avoid inflaming domestic
opposition and damaging the Entente with Great Britain, they refrained
from taking any steps publicly that would appear provocative. If war
came, they wanted France's actions to be seen at home and abroad as defensive, and they wanted Germany, not France, to incur blame for any escalation of the crisis. Above all, they did not want to risk losing the support of France's allies, Russia and Great Britain, or entering a future
conflict with the French people divided. Amidst the escalating crisis,
however, they did not remain passive. While urging restraint by the
Austrians, they took several less cautious steps to ensure that, if war

came, France and Russia would launch simultaneous offensives against Germany.

On July 16 the president of the Third Republic, Raymond Poincaré, and the premier, René Viviani, traveled to Russia. In recent years historians have considered Poincaré and Viviani's trip to Russia as evidence of France's peaceful intentions. As Jean-Jacques Becker suggested, "It is hard to imagine the leaders of the country indulging in the joys of tourism . . . having plotted the outbreak of a European war."[1] Yet an assessment of the importance of this visit, which was scheduled months before the assassination of Archduke Ferdinand, is different if one views the visit not as a goodwill trip but as an opportunity for France's leaders to consult with its most important military ally. With greater confidence in the readiness of France's and Russia's military forces, neither Poincaré nor Viviani saw any reason to yield in the increasingly tense Balkans. They may not have wanted war, but their firm stance toward Vienna and Berlin and their personal assurances of France's full support at this crucial moment bolstered the Russians' resolve and increased the chances of war.

Amidst rumors of impending Austrian action against Serbia, Poincaré and Viviani participated in several discussions with Tsar Nicholas II and Sergei Sazonov, the Russian minister of foreign affairs. In contrast to what had happened during Poincaré's visit to Russia in August 1912, the two French leaders spent little time explaining the conditions under which France was not obligated to come to Russia's aid. Though not promising unqualified support for whatever the Russians decided to do, they reviewed the dangers that could result from any démarche from Austria-Hungary and agreed that France would cooperate with Russia to prevent any intervention in the internal affairs of Serbia. To highlight France's support the two leaders reaffirmed the alliance's obligations, and at a dinner with the tsar Poincaré offered a formal toast to the "indissoluble alliance that unites the two nations." At a reception in the Winter Palace he also warned the Austrian ambassador that Serbia had friends and that any attempt to bully Serbia into submission could endanger the peace.[2] After the discussions, Viviani and Sazonov sent similar messages to Vienna directing their respective ambassadors to advise the Austrians to be cautious. To avoid any appearance of "brinksmanship" or purposeful escalation of the crisis, both warned their ambassadors not to let their diplomatic efforts appear carefully coordinated with other members of the Entente.[3]

As the two French leaders left St. Petersburg on July 23, neither anticipated a dramatic worsening of the crisis. In his parting comments Viviani urged the Russians to be prudent but repeated that France would fulfill the obligations of the alliance. About five hours earlier, however, Vienna had delivered its ultimatum to Belgrade, and the rush to war began not long after the ship carrying the two Frenchmen sailed for Stockholm. When the Austrian ambassador met with Sazonov the following morning and gave him a copy of the ultimatum, the foreign minister immediately met with the Russian chief of staff and raised the question of a partial mobilization against Austria. According to Luigi Albertini, Sazonov acted "with characteristic haste and with effects that were fatal."[4] The next day, July 25, the tsar met with the Russian Council of Ministers and decided to initiate preparations for mobilizing thirteen corps against Austria. Though the Russian leaders hoped the partial mobilization would limit the crisis, some military leaders recognized its broader implications. That day a Russian general officer told the French military attaché, "Finally we will march together. Fighting at the same time the Germans and Austrians!"[5] Despite the worsening situation, Poincaré and Viviani continued their scheduled visit to Stockholm. They departed immediately, however, on July 27, when the Austrians began mobilizing against the Serbs.

As the two French leaders hurried back to Paris, Adolphe Messimy, the minister of war, welcomed the prospect of war. In a letter in April 1915 to his former mistress, Messimy bragged about having been "the right man in the right place" who had had the "courage" to "take the steps that were exactly the right ones."[6] That "courage" initially manifested itself on the evening of July 24, when he met in Paris with other high-ranking officials to discuss the Austrian ultimatum. Commenting on Messimy's enthusiasm, one political leader said, "He wanted to contact Italy, to telephone here, to telephone there." Another described him as "too active."[7] That evening Messimy met with Joffre and told him that France might go to war. When Joffre responded calmly, "Very well, sir, we will fight if it is necessary," Messimy energetically shook his hand and said, "Bravo!" The two then reviewed the steps that needed to be taken if war came.[8] They had presided over the transformation of the French army, and both had great confidence in its ability to perform well in a war against Germany, especially if French operations were coordinated with those of the Russians.

At the height of the Moroccan crisis in August 1911, the premier of France, Caillaux, had chosen to compromise rather than fight when Joffre acknowledged that the French had less than a 70 percent chance of victory. Over the next three years the French became increasingly confident of their ability to prevail in a conflict with the Germans. In late 1912, amidst the tension preceding the first Balkan war, the General Staff concluded that if the Austrians intervened in the Balkans and the Germans assisted them, the strategic situation favored the Entente powers. Joffre's assessment of the limitations imposed on a Russian offensive by their railways, however, led Paris to urge restraint on St. Petersburg. As the Russians continued to make improvements, Joffre compared their progress favorably in August 1913 with that made in France after the Franco-Prussian War. By July–August 1914 his confidence and Messimy's eagerness overshadowed any doubts about France's chances of victory.

On July 25, after Serbia responded conditionally to the ultimatum and Vienna severed diplomatic relations, Messimy—with the approval of the Council of Ministers—ordered the recall of all general officers who were absent from their posts. He also asked the African Section of the army's General Staff about the readiness of French regiments in North Africa.[9] These regiments would be needed in a campaign against Germany and would have to be transported to France very quickly in the event of a crisis. That same day, Paris reminded local officials of their responsibility to arrest people listed on the "Carnet B" if mobilization occurred; French bureaucrats had compiled a list of about 2,500 people who might disrupt mobilization and arranged for local officials to arrest them when ordered. The next day Messimy—again with the approval of the Council of Ministers—recalled all officers from leave and canceled all scheduled movements of troops. The minister of the navy also alerted naval forces at Toulon and Cherbourg to remain in port and to fill their ammunition stocks. Agents in Alsace and Lorraine had reported the Germans occupying fortifications at Metz, installing telephone lines, and reconnoitering the frontier, and the French took steps to permit rapid mobilization if such a measure became necessary.

Beginning on July 27, Messimy went beyond simple precautionary steps. He warned General Hubert Lyautey to begin preparations for abandoning most of Morocco and Algeria and sending the bulk of his troops—except for those guarding the cities—to France.[10] He later said that his message was not simply a warning but a "formal" order to send most of the forces in North Africa to France.[11] Amidst the escalating crisis, Joffre convinced Messimy to encourage St. Petersburg to abide by the Franco-Russian agreements and, if hostilities occurred, to launch an offensive without delay into East Prussia. After the war, Messimy acknowledged having done so: "Through our military attaché, by the channel of the Foreign Ministry and our St. Petersburg ambassador, I urged with all my might that, in spite of the slowness of Russian mobilization, the tsar's armies should take the offensive in East Prussia as soon as possible."[12] In St. Petersburg the wife of the French military attaché wrote in her diary, "they were communicating with Paris all night [of July 27–28]; the two general staffs are in permanent contact."[13] Though Germany's declaration of war was still a week away, neither Messimy nor Joffre wanted to risk Germany's gaining an edge by mobilizing first and striking before France was ready. And both wanted simultaneous offensives by France and Russia against Germany.

After Austria declared war on Serbia on July 28, the rush to war accelerated. That day the French ordered all troops on pass or leave to report to their units. Joffre asked Messimy for permission to order covering forces to the border, but the minister refused because he wanted to avoid any openly provocative steps that could "poison" diplomatic efforts. Such a "grave" decision, Messimy believed, had to wait until the return of Poincaré and Viviani from Russia.[14] The following day, after Poincaré and Viviani arrived in Paris, the Council of Ministers met at 1700 hours and decided not to send covering forces to the border. Meanwhile the Germans had reinforced their border troops, pushed patrols up to the frontier, strengthened communications, placed guards at key railway stations, and barred roads coming from France. Later that night, July 29–30, the Russian ambassador in Paris received a telegram from St. Petersburg directing him to inform the French that Russia was about to accelerate its preparations for war and to thank them for their assurances of support.[15] Disturbed by the quickening pace of events and by this telegram's suggestion of unqualified French support for Russia, Viviani, accompanied by Messimy, awakened Poincaré at 0200 hours and discussed sending a telegram to the Russians urging them not to do anything that the Germans could use as a "pretext" for total or partial mobilization. Dispatched at 0700, the telegram also reaffirmed France's resolve to "fulfill all the obligations of the [Franco-Russian] Alliance."[16]

That same morning, July 30, Joffre met with Messimy and insisted that the government approve placing the entire covering force on the frontier. War was inevitable, he believed, and France could delay no longer. In one of its several meetings that day, the Council of Ministers discussed the crisis. Though no formal minutes exist, Abel Ferry, the undersecretary of state for foreign affairs, recorded the main points: "For the sake of public opinion, let the Germans put themselves in the wrong." He also noted, "Mobilize but do not concentrate."[17] Acceding to Joffre's request, the council approved placing part of France's covering forces along the border but insisted that they be kept ten kilometers from the frontier. Keeping troops away from the border not only reduced chances of an accidental clash with German troops but also demonstrated to London, as well as to the public, that French political leaders were doing everything possible to avoid provoking a war. Additionally, the council ruled out summoning any reservists and allowed movement only of those troops close enough to march, rather than ride the railway, to the frontier. Though Joffre considered the actions far too timid, the careful steps reinforced the appearance that France was the victim and was trying to keep the crisis from escalating.

The veneer of caution, however, concealed much riskier actions. After Viviani dispatched his telegram at 0700 hours urging the Russians not do anything to give the Germans an excuse for mobilization, the Council of Ministers discussed, according to Ferry's notes, a very different policy: "Do not stop Russian mobilization." The head of the political division of the Ministry of Foreign Affairs, Pierre de Margerie, then met with the Russian ambassador and suggested not that military preparations be curtailed but that they be "less open and less provocative." Emphasizing the same idea, Messimy met with the Russian military attaché and suggested the Russians "in the interests of peace" announce they were slowing their mobilization "temporarily." The Russians, after making such an announcement, could "continue or even accelerate" their mobilization but would have to refrain "as much as possible" from the "mass transport of troops."[18] As Albertini noted, the message from the Russian ambassador summarizing Margerie's and Messimy's advice probably did not reach St. Petersburg until after the Russian order for general mobilization had been issued. Yet, as Sidney B. Fay observed, Paris sent St. Petersburg no unequivocally clear message at this crucial moment about delaying general mobilization until all diplomatic efforts had failed.[19] None of the political leaders, including Poincaré, was as eager for war as Messimy, but none of them wanted to do anything that would disrupt the chances of simultaneous French and Russian offensives against Germany.

As Austria and Russia began complete mobilization on July 30–31, Joffre demanded permission on Friday, July 31, to place the entire covering force along the border. After citing German steps toward mobilization, he argued that further delays could result in France's having to abandon part of its territory and, threatening to resign, insisted he could not accept responsibility for such an outcome. Late that afternoon, after the Council of Ministers met, Viviani reluctantly approved sending the entire covering force to the border but again ordered it to remain ten kilometers from the frontier. At around 1900 hours the German ambassador met with Viviani and informed him that Germany had demanded formally that Russia cease mobilizing. He then asked whether France would remain neutral in the event of war between Germany and Russia and said he would return at 1300 hours the following day to receive France's response. Upon hearing this news Joffre demanded authority for complete mobilization of the French army, but the government refused. Messimy gave Joffre permission, however, to send a warning order to major commanders informing them that the mobilization order would probably be dispatched the following day. Shortly after midnight the Russian military attaché wired St. Petersburg that Messimy had told him "enthusiastically" about the "firm decision" of the government to go to war and asked him to remind Russian authorities that the French High Command wanted the Russians to direct "all" their efforts against Germany.[20]

On Saturday, August 1, Viviani met with the German ambassador and, avoiding any hint of provocation, informed him that should war break out between Germany and Russia, France would defend its interests. Before this meeting Viviani had conferred with Poincaré, who again had emphasized, "It is better to have war declared on us."[21] Early that Saturday morning Joffre had presented Messimy a note in which he again argued that further delays in ordering general mobilization would give the Germans a head start of several days and possibly a decisive advantage. At a hastily called meeting, the Council of Ministers decided that it could not delay mobilization any longer and authorized the minister of war to issue the order that afternoon. At 1530 hours Messimy signed the mobilization order that by August would expand the metropolitan army from 884,000 soldiers to 2,689,000, plus another 408,000 in administrative and public services. Twenty-five minutes later the news flashed via telegram across France that the first day of mobilization would be the next day, Sunday, August 2. At 1700 hours the government sent another telegram reminding unit commanders not to get closer to the border than ten kilometers. A message to the French people said: "Mobilization is not war. In the present circumstances it appears, to the contrary, as the best means of assuring peace with honor."[22]

Mobilization may not have been war, but war nonetheless came. That same day, August 1, Germany declared war on Russia, and the next day small groups of German troops crossed the French border at several points. On August 3 Germany declared war on France. On August 4 the French Senate and Chamber of Deputies met in a joint session, and a succession of political leaders gave passionate, emotional speeches. In his address Premier Viviani read a message from President Poincaré asserting that France was the victim of a "premeditated and brutal aggression."[23] Other speakers reviewed the sequence of events and accused Germany of having started the war. Later that day a proclamation signed by the president of the Republic and the Council of Ministers said: "At this time, there are no more parties. There is only eternal France."[24] In an unprecedented show of unity, legislators in the Senate and Chamber of Deputies approved all the government's proposals pertaining to financing and waging the war. Shortly after approving laws enabling the government to wage war in their absence, they closed for an indefinite period.

Clearly, the effort to "let the Germans put themselves in the wrong" had succeeded, for public opinion strongly supported the idea that France had done everything possible to avoid war. Concrete evidence of a united France came from the thousands of young men affected by the mobilization order. While the General Staff had expected 10 percent not to report, only a small number (1.22 percent for the conscription class of 1914, for example) refused to report for duty.[25] Even the assassination of the Socialist leader Jean Jaurès failed to inflame opposition to the war. As Jean-Jacques Becker said, "Convinced that they were victims of aggression, the French, who for the most part had neither wanted nor really expected the conflict, firmly decided to pick up the gauntlet."[26] The Council of Ministers recognized broad support for the war and, over Messimy's objections, decided not to arrest those listed on the Carnet B.

The effort to "let the Germans put themselves in the wrong" also succeeded internationally. Early on the morning of August 4, Germany informed Belgium that it would use "force of arms" to enter Belgian territory; two hours later German soldiers crossed the frontier. Brussels immediately appealed to France, Britain, and Russia for assistance, and at midnight Britain declared itself in a state of war with Germany. Europe quickly split into two warring camps, with France, Britain, and Russia on one side and Germany and Austria on the other. Italy, Romania, Bulgaria, and Greece remained neutral, as did the Ottoman Empire (but not for long). Unlike in 1870, France went to war with powerful allies at its side.

Notwithstanding the commonly accepted notion that the French entered the war amidst an outpouring of enthusiasm, they entered the war less with enthusiasm than with determination to defend their national territory. Except for slogans about fighting for "liberty and justice," a united France avoided defining its war aims in the first days of the war and did not define any precisely until July 1916. Over time the regaining of Alsace-Lorraine became a commonly accepted goal, as did the refusal to accept a negotiated end to the war.[27] Despite the politicians' reluctance to compile a formal list, military officials did discuss war aims. One undated "think piece" in the files of the minister of war called for reducing Germany's territory and thereby its population from 67,000,000 to 25,000,000 or 30,000,000, taking away all its colonies, separating the west bank of the Rhine from it, turning over Alsace-Lorraine and the Saar to France, and forcing it to pay huge damages.[28] As the war proceeded, passion and hatred soon replaced bureaucratic calculations. General Philippe Pétain later told his soldiers, "It is necessary to fight to the end.

It is necessary that the world be delivered from the fear of being dominated by the new barbarians." He also said, "It is necessary that the crimes they have committed against our villages and our historical monuments [be punished]; [that] the outrages they have perpetrated against our women, our elderly, and our children be punished; that the blood of our young men that they have spilled be avenged."[29]

Prior to any formal declaration of war against France, Joffre and Messimy met on August 1 and agreed that although the government determined the political objectives of the war, the conduct of the war belonged "exclusively" to the general-in-chief. After small groups of German soldiers crossed the French frontier on August 2, the day before the Germans declared war, the minister of war informed Joffre that he had "absolute liberty of movement for executing his plans even if this results in the crossing of the German [but not Belgian] frontier."[30] At 1730 hours, Joffre sent a warning order to the commanders of the six corps in the covering force and said, "The intention of the commander-in-chief is not to launch a general offensive until his forces are assembled."[31] The warning order gave specific missions to each of the corps in the covering force. Of these units, VII Corps prepared to advance toward Mulhouse (in Alsace, thirty-five kilometers northeast of Belfort), while XX Corps prepared to advance toward Nancy. After receiving conclusive evidence that Germany had violated Luxembourg's neutrality, Joffre ordered Fourth Army, which was assembling to the rear of Second and Third armies, to enter the line between Third and Fifth armies and prepare to attack north of Verdun. He also informed Fifth Army of the change. Yet, as he stated in his memoirs, "It was still too early to announce formally my intention to operate in Belgium."[32]

On the morning of August 4 Messimy wired Joffre that Germany had declared war on France and that Italy had declared its neutrality. Believing that Germany wanted France to violate Belgium's neutrality first, the minister formally forbade any move into Belgium even by cavalrymen and aviators. By the time his message had arrived, however, German soldiers had entered Belgium. Specially trained units had advanced quickly toward Liège to capture the city and the fortresses around it so that two

German armies could advance through the narrow gap between the Netherlands and Liège. The Belgians immediately appealed for help and informed Paris and London that French and British troops could enter Belgium. Late that night the French received additional information about the German advance toward Liège. The telegram from Brussels said that the main German forces had not crossed the Meuse. The next day, August 5, Joffre sent aircraft and dirigibles over Belgium and authorized cavalry to enter Belgium. He also left Paris for Vitry-le-François, where his headquarters, the Grand quartier général, or GQG, was located.

Joffre's control over French strategy was now complete. Keeping his thoughts to himself, he had carefully analyzed the challenges France might face in a campaign against Germany, and he now began shaping his strategy. First and foremost, he had to know what the Germans would do; hence he did not complete the design of his strategy until after the enemy began advancing and did not inform his subordinates fully until a week after mobilization. Second, his strategy depended on simultaneous attacks from France and Russia. Grand Duke Nicholas, who was named commander of Russian forces on August 2, dispelled fears of Russian timidity when he said, "I am resolved to launch an offensive as soon as possible, and I will make an all-out attack."[33] After subsequent messages from the French ambassador to Russia indicated that the grand duke would begin his offensive on August 14, Joffre resolved to launch an attack into Alsace-Lorraine on the same day and thereby comply with the provisions of the Franco-Russian Alliance. Meanwhile he bided his time and, even though he expected the main German advance to come through Belgium, awaited additional information before shaping his main attack.

Keenly aware of the French desire to recover the two "lost" provinces, he also began preparations for sending a small force into Alsace. This operation would begin before his main attack and would demonstrate to the Russians, as well as to the French, the readiness and willingness of the army to fight. Having already alerted the First Army commander to the possibility of a small offensive toward Mulhouse in German-held Alsace, on August 5 he ordered the attack to commence on August 7. Although the commander of VII Corps, which had responsibility for the drive into

Alsace, reported a large concentration of enemy troops in the area and expressed some reluctance to advance, Joffre refused to delay the attack and ordered VII Corps forward. The offensive, which was little more than a large-scale raid, involved two infantry divisions and one infantry brigade. One of the first actions occurred at Altkirch (fifteen kilometers south of Mulhouse). With little or no reconnaissance or preparation, one of the regiments fixed bayonets and launched an energetic assault against the small German elements in the town. The regimental commander led the assault, sitting astride a handsome white horse. Although he was wounded in the battle, his regiment finally managed to secure the small town. Except for the fight at Altkirch, the French encountered no strong resistance during their twenty-five-kilometer advance toward Mulhouse, and French units entered the city without opposition at 1500 hours on August 8. They were welcomed by thousands of Alsatians who lined the roads and cheered "Vive la France!" Despite the initial explosion of enthusiasm throughout France at the news of the victory, indications of future difficulties appeared when the small force failed to make further advances and the Germans drove them back on August 10.

As the nation welcomed the news of French soldiers having entered Alsace, Joffre issued his General Instructions No. 1 on August 8 and finally revealed his strategic concept, the goal of which was destruction of enemy forces, not occupation of territory. In essence, he would jab with his right and attempt a knockout blow with his left, for the offensive on the right was a supporting attack and the offensive on the left his main attack. While the offensive on the right and the raid into Alsace fixed the German left and drew enemy forces to the south, the subsequent main attack on his left would strike the German center and unhinge the enemy forces advancing into central Belgium. Joffre expected his main attack to avoid the powerful enemy force driving toward his left through central Belgium and to strike the enemy's less dense, more vulnerable center in eastern Belgium. Thus, he intended to send the First and Second armies on his right into Lorraine, south of the German fortifications of Metz-Thionville, and the Third and Fourth armies on his left into Belgium and Luxembourg, north of the German fortifications of Metz-Thionville. Aware of the possibility of a deep envelopment by the Germans, Joffre also ordered Fourth Reserve Division Group to occupy a "fortified position" near Hirson on his extreme left to guard against an attack from the north or east. This order enabled the French to watch the Chimay Gap and provided insurance against the Germans' sweeping as deep as the eastern bank of the Meuse-Sambre rivers.[34]

Joffre's concept of operations—a two-pronged attack with an advance on each side of the Metz-Thionville fortifications—rested on the assumption that the major part of the German army was in Luxembourg and around Metz-Thionville and that smaller forces had entered Belgium to the north of Luxembourg. An intelligence assessment on August 9 identified (from north to south) as many as six active corps between Liège and the northern tip of Luxembourg, four in Luxembourg north of Thionville, four near Metz, three near Strasbourg, and one near Freiburg (forty kilometers northeast of Mulhouse). Counting the four corps arrayed against Russia, the report identified the location of all but five of the twenty-six active German corps and paid little or no attention to the enemy's reserve corps. The French suspected that the remaining corps were in the vicinity of Luxembourg and Metz-Thionville.[35] Joffre expected the Germans to attempt an envelopment through Belgium but not to make their main attack any deeper than Sedan or Mézières.

When Joffre learned that British forces arriving on the continent would not be ready for action until August 26 and that they would consist of four rather than six infantry divisions, he decided to attack without them. First and Second armies appeared strong enough to handle any enemy forces they encountered on the French right, and Third, Fourth, and Fifth armies could advance into Belgium when the enemy's intentions became more apparent. After the Second Army commander expressed concerns about not being ready to march until August 17, Joffre, anxious to attack at the same time as the Russians, insisted that the time of the offensive be sooner. The Second Army commander quickly agreed to attack on August 14.

With the date of the attack on his right set, Joffre issued final orders to his subordinate commanders. On his right he sent First and Second armies into Lorraine, south of the German fortifications of Metz-Thionville; the two armies moved forward between Toul and Épinal in the gap separating the French fortifications of Verdun-Toul and Épinal-Belfort. On the right First Army would make the main attack with its four corps. The army's objectives were Sarrebourg (sixty kilometers east of Nancy) and Donon (twenty-five kilometers south of Sarrebourg); Donon was a German strong point deep in the Vosges that commanded a key valley running through the mountains.[36] First Army also had the mission of seizing several key passes in the Vosges Mountains thirty kilometers south of Donon, but Joffre ordered it to seize these before launching its main attack on August 14. To support First Army, he ordered Second Army to advance toward Morhange (forty-five kilometers northeast of Nancy) with two corps on First Army's left and, with its other units arrayed in echelon farther on the left, to guard against the possibility of a German thrust from Metz.

Though simple in conception, Joffre's drive into Alsace-Lorraine was extremely difficult to execute, for as the two armies advanced their fronts became progressively larger. First Army's task was particularly difficult, for it had to attack in divergent directions (northeast toward Sarrebourg and east toward Donon) across a front that stretched more than eighty kilometers over rugged terrain. Though in less difficult terrain, Second Army advanced toward Morhange on a front that eventually extended across seventy kilometers. That Joffre would even consider such a complex operation is an indication of his inexperience; he would never have attempted such an operation later in the war. At this point, however, peacetime maneuvers shaped his thinking more than wartime experience.

As the French prepared their offensive, Joffre began replacing weak commanders. Concerned about the performance of VII Corps, which had advanced slowly toward Mulhouse and then been driven back by an enemy counterattack, Joffre relieved its commander and others who failed to perform to his expectations. Messimy strongly supported his weeding the officer corps of men who performed poorly and proposed holding courts-martial and shooting those officers who showed "weakness or pusillanimity."[37] Between August 2 and September 6 Joffre relieved two army, ten corps, and thirty-eight division commanders.[38] He placed these officers at the disposal of the minister of war, who did not want to bring the dissatisfied generals to Paris and elected instead to send them to Limoges. From this city came the term to describe those relieved of their duties, the "*limogés.*" Though Joffre sometimes relieved officers unjustly, the example of the *limogés* did much to strengthen his control of the army, and the promotion of hard-nosed, self-confident fighters into important leadership positions did much to improve the army's performance.

Also in preparation for the attack, Joffre reorganized the units on his extreme right. After relieving the VII Corps commander, Joffre placed VII Corps, two additional infantry divisions, a cavalry division, and First Reserve Division Group in the newly formed Army of Alsace and made General Pau its commander. He gave Pau the mission of securing the French right flank and thereby freed First Army to concentrate on its attack into Lorraine. With the formation of the Army of Alsace, the French had (from south to north) the Army of Alsace, First Army, and Second Army. In an indication of his priorities, Joffre pulled two corps out of Castelnau's Second Army, which originally had five plus a reserve division group, and kept them under his own control for possible use on the Belgian frontier. One of these, IX Corps, would participate in the first phase of the upcoming offensive into Lorraine and then be transferred north.

On the morning of the August 14 Joffre's offensive on his right began. The previous day the French ambassador in St. Petersburg, Maurice Paléologue, had verified that the Russians would begin their offensive at dawn on the fourteenth. First Army sent two corps east into the Vosges and two corps northeast toward Sarrebourg while Second Army had two corps advance on First Army's left. The remainder of Second Army (one corps and a reserve division group) advanced toward Morhange more slowly, moving in echelon and guarding against a German thrust from Metz into the left flank of the advancing French forces. Since the newly formed Army of Alsace on Joffre's extreme right was not yet ready to move, the First Army commander used a corps to cover his right as he advanced. In compliance with Joffre's orders First Army, beginning on August 8, had seized several passes in the Vosges, but in a portent of the future the Germans had killed and wounded as many as 600 French soldiers near one of the passes and strongly resisted several of these advances. The seizure of the passes nevertheless provided some protection to the army's right flank as it marched toward Sarrebourg and Donon. After First Army began moving, Joffre cautioned the army commander,

Dubail, not to let his forces advance in "diverging" directions, but he nonetheless emphasized the importance of advancing simultaneously northeast toward Sarrebourg, east toward Donon, and southeast toward the Vosges passes.[39]

The first day of the attack proceeded smoothly as the enemy withdrew in the face of French troops. By that evening First Army had seized Donon as well as several key positions in the Vosges, while its two left corps had advanced ten to twelve kilometers toward Sarrebourg. As night fell, 26th Division, which was part of XIII Corps's move toward Sarrebourg, launched an unfortunate attack against the village of Cirey. The after-action report of the division explained what happened:

> The attack seemed close to success when a bugle unwisely sounded the charge around 1845 hours. . . . On this signal, the infantry leaders launched their assault. . . . They crossed an area covered by enemy artillery and machine guns. Officer losses were such that the attack failed . . . and the reconstitution of units became extremely difficult. All the energy of the officers and men was devoted to [reconstituting the unit]. . . . The exhaustion of the men is extreme. The division is incapable of undertaking an offensive tomorrow.[40]

As First and Second armies marched forward on the second day, an early report from Second Army suggested the extent of the difficulties confronting the French: "The troops, infantry and artillery, have been sorely tested. Our artillery is held at a distance by the long-range artillery of our enemy; it cannot get close enough for counterbattery fire. Our infantry has attacked with élan, but they have been halted primarily by enemy artillery fire and by unseen enemy infantry hidden in trenches." By 0900 hours on the second day of the offensive Second Army had suffered more than 1,000 wounded and an unknown number killed.[41] A message from Castelnau, the Second Army commander, to Joffre explained that a deadly battle was occurring on the front of his army and added, "It is necessary . . . to conquer approach positions successively and to occupy them solidly with field fortifications (extensive trenches, shelter against shrapnel, helmets for riflemen, etc.)." Castelnau also recommended extensive preparation for an attack and heavy firing by artillery prior to a coordinated infantry and artillery attack against an objective.[42] In short, the bankruptcy of French tactical doctrine and the inadequacy of their artillery should have been apparent by the end of the second day. The enemy's retreat, however, dispelled any doubts in Joffre's headquarters about the effectiveness of French methods. A note from Joffre to his army commanders said, "The fighting thus far has demonstrated the admirable offensive qualities of our infantry." The only admission of doctrinal shortcomings came in his assertion that "attacks will be more crushing, less costly when they are prepared more carefully."[43]

As First and Second armies moved forward slowly, intelligence reports suggested that they were approaching the enemy's main line of resistance and that the enemy was prepared to launch a strong attack. Despite these reports, the two army commanders remained confident of their ability to defeat the Germans and continued advancing. On August 16 enemy resistance consisted primarily of long-range artillery fire, and on the following day the First Army commander shifted more of his forces into the advance toward Sarrebourg. When Joffre learned that the Germans had evacuated Sarrebourg, he ordered Second Army to maintain contact on its right with First Army but to shift the direction of its advance toward the north. This order played directly into the enemy's hands, focusing the attention of First and Second armies in different directions.

When the Germans counterattacked on August 20, little liaison or coordination existed between First and Second armies, and the French fought two separate and distinct battles, both of which they lost. As shaken elements of First and Second armies fell back in disorder to new positions, Dubail and Castelnau worked energetically to reorganize their armies. Fortunately for the French the Germans advanced slowly. Castelnau anchored Second Army's left wing on the previously prepared fortifications east of Nancy and extended his forces south to reestablish contact with First Army. At midmorning on August 22, however, the enemy struck Second Army's right and drove it back. By the following evening Second Army's right was twenty-five kilometers behind where it had started on August 14. As the Germans pounded Second Army's right, First Army, though not pressed as hard by the enemy, withdrew but maintained contact with the battered Second Army. Beginning on August 24, in what became known as the battle of Charmes Gap, the two armies counterattacked and slowly pushed the Germans back. By early September they once again occupied the approximate position from which they had begun their offensive on August 14.

As the battle unfolded on the right, Joffre's intention—as he explained to Dubail and Castelnau on August 21—was for First and Second armies to "retain and draw toward them an important part of the opposing forces,"[44] since the main French effort consisted of a "maneuver" farther north into Belgium and Luxembourg. The purpose of this maneuver was to strike what Joffre identified as the "most sensitive point" in the German disposition and destroy the main enemy force. Just before First and Second armies attacked into Alsace-Lorraine on August 14, however, several factors, including German cavalry attempting to seize bridges across the Meuse River south of Namur, led to a fresh assessment by the High Command and the realization that the Germans intended to strike deeper into Belgium than previously thought. Joffre informed his subordinate commanders on August 15 and the British commander the following day that the enemy would make his main effort with his right wing and strike north of Givet, which lay along the Meuse River forty kilometers north of Mézières. Such an attack would take advantage of the road network, which generally ran from northeast to southwest, and would place the Germans deep in the French rear; but Joffre still did not expect significant enemy forces to cross the Meuse. With increased evidence of the Germans' having strengthened their right, he assumed that the enemy commander had weakened his center in order to strengthen his right. He also expected another group of enemy forces to strike along the Belgian frontier at Sedan and Montmédy (thirty-five kilometers southeast of Sedan).

On the morning of August 18, two days before the German counterattack in Lorraine, Joffre issued additional instructions to the three armies on his left and adjusted their mission and composition to correspond with his latest understanding of the enemy's location. He said, "Third, Fourth, and Fifth French armies, acting in concert with the British and Belgian armies, have the objective of the German forces assembled around Thionville in Luxembourg and in Belgium." The Germans appeared, according to Joffre, to have thirteen to fifteen corps assembled between Liège and Thionville. They had divided these corps into two principal groups: in the north, between Liège and Bastogne, seven or eight corps and four cavalry divisions; in the south, between Bastogne and Thionville, six or seven corps and two or three cavalry divisions.[45] An intelligence report on that same day identified two cavalry divisions on the west bank of the Meuse.

Joffre aimed Third and Fourth armies at the enemy forces between Bastogne and Thionville, which were expected to head toward Sedan and Montmédy. By attacking and defeating this group, which he thought was smaller than the force heading toward Givet, he hoped to halt the advance of the German main attack. As will be explained below, he also modified the composition and mission of Fifth Army and aimed it toward the main German force, which he expected to move north of Givet. After Third and Fourth armies defeated the enemy forces between Liège and Bastogne, he expected Fourth Army to turn west and strike the enemy's main force in the left flank. Defeat or victory thus rested in the hands of Third and Fourth armies, and to ensure their success, Joffre transferred XI Corps from Fifth Army to Fourth Army and IX Corps from Third Army to Fourth Army, thereby giving Fourth Army six corps.

After issuing the attack order on August 18 Joffre held Third and Fourth armies in place for the next two days. On August 19 aerial observers and cavalry reconnaissance reported few enemy forces to the immediate front of the two armies but found more enemy advancing toward the northwest, forty to fifty kilometers forward of French outposts. An intelligence report from Joffre's headquarters that day included a Belgian report of "important" enemy forces, probably General Karl von Bülow's Second Army, crossing the Meuse just south of Liège. In midmorning Joffre gave Fourth Army permission to secure passages across the Semois River, which meandered through the difficult terrain of the Ardennes just over the frontier north of Sedan. As the day progressed and reports of enemy forces moving across the front of Third and Fourth armies increased, the Fourth Army commander requested permission to advance into Belgium, but Joffre said no, since the Germans had not yet launched their offensive. Intelligence reports indicated, he explained, that the Germans had not yet made important movements across the Meuse between Huy (twenty-five kilometers southwest of Liège) and Givet, and that enemy forces in the Huy-Givet region seemed to be marching toward the

Belgian army. Joffre warned the Fourth Army commander, "I draw your attention to the necessity of not revealing our maneuver prior to the moment when it is unleashed." He explained that the Germans wanted to "bait" the French into attacking prematurely and that he wanted to avoid this "trap."[46]

The Fourth Army commander explained Joffre's reasoning to his corps commanders. By letting the enemy advance across the front of Third and Fourth armies, the French permitted the Germans to strip the Luxembourg region of troops, thereby increasing the chances of Third and Fourth armies' success. If the French attacked too early, they would advance into a "trap" set for them by the Germans.[47] If they attacked at the appropriate time, they would strike the less "dense" center of the German formation and disrupt the entire attack.

Finally, at 2030 hours on August 20, the day the Germans unleashed their counterattack against First and Second armies in Alsace-Lorraine, Joffre ordered Third and Fourth armies to attack on the following day. Convinced that he understood the German scheme of maneuver, he ordered Fourth Army to cross the Semois River and advance northeast toward Neufchâteau and Third Army to advance toward Arlon and protect the right flank of Fourth Army against a German counterattack. To facilitate the task of Third Army, Joffre split it into two armies, Third Army and Army of Lorraine. The latter unit consisted of that portion of Third Army south of Verdun; it had the mission of guarding against an enemy incursion from the vicinity of Metz. By forming the Army of Lorraine, Joffre simplified the task of the Third Army commander and left him free to concentrate on his mission in Belgium.

As Third and Fourth armies charged into Belgium on August 21, the French expected to outnumber the enemy, but this expectation proved false. While Fourth Army sent six corps into Belgium (including IX Corps, which advanced only a short distance) plus a cavalry corps, Third Army sent three corps plus a cavalry division. The Germans, however, had their Fourth and Fifth armies between Metz and the northern tip of Luxembourg; these armies included ten corps, two cavalry divisions, six reserve brigades, and the garrison of Metz. The Germans thus had ten infantry corps in this region while the French had nine. Since the German Fourth and Fifth armies were near the center of the gigantic sweep through Belgium, they had moved more slowly than First, Second, and Third armies, which were farther to the west. When they learned of the French advance into Belgium and Luxembourg on August 21, they prepared themselves for a significant encounter. In contrast, the French knew little about the enemy to their front, had inadequate maps, and remained overly optimistic about their chances of success. As the French moved forward on the first day of the offensive, Third Army encountered the Germans first, but the enemy consisted only of small detachments. Oblivious to what was about to happen, Joffre told the minister of war, "the moment of decisive action is near."[48]

On the second day of the offensive, August 22, the French encountered much stronger enemy forces and soon learned that the Germans had not denuded eastern Belgium of troops. In Third Army's center, V Corps, which had discovered the entrenched enemy the previous evening, attacked the solidly occupied enemy positions near Longwy at 0500 hours. Since a heavy rain and thick fog limited visibility, the attack order for one of the divisions did not even mention artillery support or preparation, and the infantry suffered heavy casualties. When the fog lifted, the French attempted to bring their artillery into the battle, but the lifting of the fog enabled the Germans to see the French guns in open terrain and to silence them quickly with heavy artillery. One division broke and ran when a German counterattack supported by heavy artillery struck it. The V Corps commander succeeded in reforming his units and at 1820 hours ordered them to hold their positions "no matter what the cost."[49] On Third Army's left, IV Corps performed poorly, too. Also moving in a thick fog, it was surprised when it encountered entrenched enemy forces in open terrain around Virton and was thrown back with heavy losses. As with V Corps, one of its divisions fled under heavy enemy fire. On Third Army's right, VI Corps performed better than the other two corps, but it too had to yield ground to the enemy. By the end of the day notions of an easy march to Arlon had vanished.

On that same day, August 22, Fourth Army's left moved much farther than its right, and some elements actually reached Neufchâteau. From left to right Fourth Army had IX, XI, XVII, XII, Colonial, and II corps. On Fourth Army's right, II Corps made heavy contact early with the enemy and could not move forward; it nonetheless remained on line with Third

Army's left. The Colonial Corps found itself in desperate circumstances, for 3rd Colonial Division on its right fought at Rossignol, fifteen kilometers south of Neufchâteau, one of the deadliest battles of the campaign. After French cavalry discovered enemy soldiers in a forest north of the small village, 3rd Division sent six battalions, one after the other, on a narrow front against solidly entrenched German troops and suffered more than 5,000 casualties. The Germans responded by going around 3rd Division's right flank and destroying all its cannon, caissons, and vehicles. By the end of the day 3rd Division and 2nd, which came to its assistance, had lost 11,648 soldiers. While 3rd Division suffered horrendous losses, 5th Colonial Brigade on the Colonial Corps's left moved "nonchalantly" toward Neufchâteau,[50] where it encountered a very strong enemy force and was driven back with heavy losses. By the end of the day a twelve-kilometer gap existed between the units on the Colonial Corps's right and left. To the left of the Colonial Corps, other corps continued moving forward. XII Corps was, as reported by Fourth Army, in a "good" situation at the end of the day, but to its left XVII Corps was in the worst situation of any of the corps on the left: its 33rd Division lost nearly all its artillery when an enemy attack swept around its flank into its rear. Joffre later identified this loss as the key action in the failure of Fourth Army's offensive. Farther to the left, the situation seemed favorable for the remaining two corps. Shortly after midnight the Fourth Army commander reported to Joffre, "All corps engaged today. On the whole results hardly satisfactory."[51]

Despite the poor results on the twenty-second, Joffre told the Third and Fourth Commanders to resume the offensive as soon as possible the next day. His entire offensive depended on the two armies' making successful attacks into Belgium. At 0925 hours the commander of Third Army, General Pierre Ruffey, informed Joffre he could not resume the offensive that day because the "reconstitution" of units was not yet finished. At 1300 hours Ruffey reported an improving situation, but just as Third Army prepared to resume the offensive, Ruffey learned that the Germans had driven V Corps (in his center) eight kilometers to the rear. This loss ended any hopes of Third Army's attacking on August 23 and soon resulted in Ruffey's entire army falling back on a line with V Corps. Fourth Army fared worse. In XVII Corps, elements of 33rd Division, which had lost almost all its artillery the previous day, had panicked and fled to the rear, and the entire corps had pulled back during the night of August 22–23. As for the Colonial Corps, 5th Colonial Brigade pulled back from Neufchâteau at 0500 hours on the twenty-third, thereby uncovering the right flank of XII Corps and forcing it to withdraw. By the end of the day Third and Fourth armies, except for IX and XI corps on Fourth Army's left, had withdrawn to the approximate positions from which they had begun their offensives.

Fifth Army on Joffre's far left fared no better than Third and Fourth armies on his left or First and Second armies on his right. Fifth Army's offensive, as well as its preparations, occurred at the same time as Third and Fourth armies', for Joffre considered the three armies' offensives inextricably linked. In his General Instructions No. 1 on August 8, Joffre had ordered Fifth Army to occupy a position on the left of Fourth Army and to attack any enemy force debouching between Mézières and Mouzon (thirty kilometers east of Mézières). Fifth Army also had to prepare to advance north through the very difficult terrain between those two cities. It used its four corps to cover this front until August 12, when it received permission to move I Corps north toward Givet so that it could oppose any attempts by the Germans to cross the Meuse between Givet and Namur (thirty-five kilometers north of Givet). This move extended Fifth Army's zone of responsibility eighty kilometers in a straight-line distance between Mézières and Namur. Meanwhile General Lanrezac, Fifth Army's commander, had become extremely concerned about German forces in central Belgium and about the security of his left. Joffre, however, did not want Fifth Army spread across the 110-kilometer-front between Namur and Mouzon. Instead he ordered Lanrezac to keep his forces assembled in the vicinity of Mézières and to remain ready for an enemy attack in the region between Namur and Mouzon. Joffre expected the Germans to attempt a deep envelopment through Belgium, but he did not know if the Germans would cross the Meuse between Namur and Givet on Fifth Army's left, near Mézières in its center, or near Sedan or Mouzon on its right. Yet he clearly did not expect the Germans to move north of Namur on the west bank of the Meuse-Sambre rivers.

As additional reports of enemy activity in central Belgium arrived, General Lanrezac concluded that the enemy would send strong forces

The German advance to the Marne

across the Meuse and advance on the west bank of the river. On August 14 he met with Joffre and expressed his concerns about Germans' crossing the Meuse and outflanking him. In his memoirs Joffre explained why he dismissed Lanrezac's concerns. The Germans, he said, seemed to be massing their main force between Liège and the northwestern corner of Luxembourg and had sent only a small force of cavalry and infantry across the Meuse. Additionally, the French had arranged for the British to move into the sector on Lanrezac's left between Hirson and Maubeuge, and Joffre did not want to upset those complicated arrangements. Lanrezac left disappointed, but upon returning to his headquarters, he received a copy of Intelligence Bulletin No. 38 of August 14, which identified eight enemy corps between Liège and the northern tip of Luxembourg.[52] He immediately sent a long letter to Joffre in which he cited this intelligence report and again emphasized the importance of shifting Fifth Army farther west toward Maubeuge, where it could respond more effectively against German forces advancing on the west bank of the Meuse. A note from GQG, which arrived on the morning of the fifteenth, gave Lanrezac permission to extend his disposition slightly to the left, and in a telephone message an hour later Joffre authorized him to prepare to advance north for operations on the west bank of the Meuse.

Though Lanrezac's influence is not completely clear, Joffre concluded on August 14–15 that the Germans would send their main force north of Givet. Intelligence arriving on the fourteenth—possibly including a more careful consideration of Intelligence Bulletin No. 38—apparently played a key role in changing the French commander's thinking. Joffre noted in his memoirs that he received "more serious" information about enemy troops north of Liège and about "large German units" using four bridges to cross the Meuse north of Liège. Moreover, the Belgian army had lost contact with its troops at Liège and did not know the number of enemy troops besieging the fortress.[53] Adding to Joffre's concern was a report on August 15 from the governor of Maubeuge that 200,000 Germans had crossed the Meuse north of Liège and 10,000 enemy cavalrymen were heading southwest. Additional information, however, soon revealed this report to be false. A more alarming message from Fifth Army on that same day reported German forces attacking French forces at Dinant (between Givet and Namur) but failing in their attempt to cross the Meuse. Over the next several days the French, after capturing the pilot of a shot-down enemy plane, obtained more information about the composition of the German Second Army and received a report from a liaison officer with the Belgians about several enemy infantry regiments' having crossed the Meuse. Joffre's Intelligence Bureau speculated on August 18 that the German First Army was "grouped" around Liège,[54] and another report from Belgium late on that same day reported at least two German corps across the Meuse.

Beginning on August 15, Joffre made adjustments on his left to respond to the "hypothesis" that large enemy forces were advancing on the west bank of the Meuse. Among these adjustments a formal order late on that day stated: "The enemy seems to be making his principal effort on his right wing north of Givet. Another group of forces appears to be marching toward Sedan, Montmédy, Damvillers." The order confirmed the telephone message to Lanrezac earlier in the day and authorized him to advance about fifty kilometers into Belgium toward Namur. The order also shifted XI Corps from Fifth to Fourth Army and thereby strengthened Fourth Army for its role in what was still Joffre's main attack.[55] To strengthen Fifth Army Joffre transferred XVIII Corps from Third Army to its control and made Lanrezac responsible for Maubeuge.

If the Germans did advance on the west bank of the Meuse and Sambre, the French would have to depend on the British, and some reassurance came from a meeting on August 16 of Joffre and Sir John French, the British commander, in which the two allied commanders discussed strategy and operations. Greater reassurance came the following day, when Joffre learned that the British would be ready for operations as early as August 24 and that British elements could possibly reach Mons as early as the twenty-first or twenty-second. The availability of the British meant that they could move into position on the left of Fifth Army. To extend the line of allied forces farther west, Joffre asked the minister of war to place three territorial divisions along the French border between Maubeuge and Dunkirk. Though the forces west of Maubeuge were extremely thin, the occupation of this sector resulted in French and British forces' occupying the entire Franco-Belgian frontier from the English Channel to Luxembourg.

As Joffre extended and strengthened his left, the last of the Liège forts fell on August 17, and General Helmuth von Moltke, the chief of the German General Staff, ordered his massive right wing forward. On August 18 First Army moved toward Brussels with four active and two reserve corps, Second Army toward Wavre (twenty kilometers southeast of Brussels) with three active and three reserve corps, and Third Army toward the Meuse between Namur and Givet with three active and one reserve corps. Second Army was less than thirty kilometers from Namur and Third Army forty kilometers from Givet. Strong detachments of German cavalry, supported by infantry, screened their advance. With Liège lost and huge German forces over the Meuse, the Belgian king ordered his army to withdraw. By August 20 the entire Belgian army, except for one division at Namur, had entered the fortifications at Antwerp.

On August 18, with the German threat becoming more obvious, Joffre modified the mission of Fifth Army and ordered it to prepare for two contingencies: first, a German advance between Givet and Brussels on both banks of the Meuse; and second, German movement of only small forces across the Meuse. In the first case Fifth Army would operate in conjunction with the British and Belgian armies and oppose the Germans while seeking to envelop their western flank. In the second case Fifth Army would remain on the eastern bank of the Meuse and would advance on the left of Fourth Army while the Belgians and British opposed the enemy on the western bank. Joffre also sent copies of this order to commanders of the British and Belgian forces.[56] As additional information arrived about the strength of the Germans in central Belgium, Joffre did not become alarmed; by the evening of the twentieth, just before launching Third and Fourth armies into eastern Belgium, he was convinced that he understood German intentions. With the Germans moving forces deep into Belgium, he expected Third and Fourth armies to face fewer enemy forces, and he had even greater hopes for their success. Even if Fifth Army and the British were outnumbered, they could delay the Germans' advance until Fourth Army dealt the coup de grâce from their rear. Subsequent difficulties stemmed less from the failure to comprehend the strength of the German right or the depth of its sweep into France than from the failure to anticipate the strength of the enemy facing Third and Fourth armies.

Beginning on August 19 Lanrezac moved Fifth Army toward Namur into the angle formed by the junction of the Meuse and Sambre rivers. In this sector the Meuse flowed north while the Sambre flowed from the southwest to the northeast, joining the Meuse at Namur. From the time Fifth Army departed from the vicinity of Mézières until it arrived at its new position, many soldiers had marched more than 100 kilometers. When Fifth Army arrived in its new sector, it was positioned far beyond the leftmost unit in Fourth Army. Lanrezac placed I Corps on his right facing east along the Meuse to protect his flank and to guard the crossing sites along the river between Namur and Givet, X Corps facing northwest on I Corps's left along the Sambre, and III Corps farther to the left along the Sambre opposite Charleroi. When XVIII Corps arrived, he placed it along the Sambre to III Corps's left. Fifth Army thus occupied a position shaped like an upside-down "V." A cavalry corps covered the French left and became involved in numerous small fights with German cavalry on August 20. Fifth Army reported the cavalry corps's loss of a sixth of its personnel and added, "Not a single wound from a saber."[57]

The following morning, August 21, Joffre ordered Fifth Army to advance and asked Sir John French to advance on Lanrezac's left. Since sizable German forces were on both banks of the Meuse, the situation corresponded to the first alternative included in the August 18 order, and French and British units were supposed to locate and strike the main enemy force west of the Meuse. To accomplish this, Fifth Army had to cross the Sambre River and march north on the west bank of the Meuse. Around noon, however, Lanrezac informed Joffre that the British would not reach Mons for two more days and that if Fifth Army crossed the Sambre the following morning, it would have to fight alone. Lanrezac asked Joffre if he should cross the Sambre without the British.

As Lanrezac awaited a response to his question, leading elements of the German Second Army struck the French along the Sambre midway between Charleroi and Namur. The Germans seized crossings over the river relatively easily, since Lanrezac had ordered his commanders to remain on the heights on the south bank of the river and to send only small forces forward to protect the bridges. Though the Germans had crossed the Sambre, Lanrezac did not realize the significance of their actions and informed Joffre only that some outposts were being engaged and that

Namur was being invested by the Germans. These reports raised no concerns at GQG, and Joffre told Lanrezac to begin his offensive without the British. Since I Corps, which guarded Fifth Army's flank along the Meuse, could not be relieved until the twenty-second, Lanrezac chose to delay the attack and not to cross the Sambre for two days. Not until 0330 hours did Fifth Army report the Germans' crossing the Sambre. Note that the exchange between Joffre and Lanrezac and the crossing of the Sambre occurred on the first day that Third and Fourth armies attacked into Belgium.

The following day, August 22, Fifth Army attempted to drive the Germans across the Sambre but failed. By midafternoon German attacks had pushed back the two corps in Lanrezac's center. By 2030 hours all three corps on Lanrezac's center and right had been driven from the Sambre, but the two corps in the center had been driven back farther than the one on the right. Hoping to strike the Germans in the flank, Lanrezac shifted General Louis Franchet d'Espèrey's I Corps on his right north toward Namur and the next day asked Fourth Army to advance and cover his right flank along the Meuse. Since Third and Fourth armies were heavily engaged in Belgium, they could do nothing to assist Fifth Army. After Lanrezac attempted to secure his right flank by stretching a reserve division along twenty kilometers of the Meuse, elements of the German Third Army forced their way across the river eight kilometers north of Givet. Franchet d'Espèrey's I Corps drove some of the enemy soldiers back, but by the end of the day the Germans still held several bridgeheads, including Dinant. Lanrezac thus faced the German Second Army on his front and the Third Army on his right rear. Also on August 23, the British came under heavy attack at Mons from the German First Army, and territorial divisions to the west of the British came under pressure. At 2130 hours Lanrezac, fearing an attack in his rear, informed Joffre of his intention to withdraw toward Givet. This withdrawal ended what became known as the battle of the frontiers and yielded the initiative completely to the Germans.

Joffre's main attack had lasted only a few days. On the right First and Second armies advanced into Alsace Lorraine on August 14, but a German counterattack on August 20 pushed them back toward their starting positions. On the left Third and Fourth armies, paying little attention to reconnaissance or security, attacked on August 21 but returned to their starting positions two days later. On the far left Fifth Army moved into position on August 19–20, came under pressure from the Germans on the twenty-first and even heavier pressure the following day. On August 23 Lanrezac informed Joffre of his intention to withdraw. None of the attacks accomplished its strategic or operational goals. The French had miscalculated German capabilities and had diffused their offensive capability across three widely separated battlefields.

The attacks failed for strategic and tactical reasons. Early on August 20 the French general-in-chief had reported to the minister of war that "the situation appears favorable to me."[58] Three days later he informed the minister that he had "terminated" his strategic maneuver. Refusing to acknowledge his own responsibility for the failure, he blamed others for "many individual failures." He insisted that he had placed the "main body of his army against the most sensitive point of the enemy" and had gained "numerical superiority at this point." French troops, he complained, had not demonstrated the "offensive qualities" expected of them despite "numerical superiority."[59] Perhaps more than anything else, these comments demonstrate that Joffre's later denial of his responsibility for the disastrous and costly tactical offensives is pure balderdash. In reality, he had not concentrated his army against the enemy's most vulnerable point, and his army had fought at a severe disadvantage. At the Ministry of War, Messimy accepted Joffre's explanation of the "failures" and reacted with an emotional telegram saying that the responsible officers should be shot.[60]

Tragically for France, many casualties suffered in the attacks from August 14 to 23 were unnecessary and came from foolish bayonet charges against an entrenched enemy. On the twenty-third, before Third Army completely abandoned its hopes for a successful offensive, General Ruffey told his corps commanders:

Yesterday's attacks failed solely because they were not prepared by artillery, or even by the fire of infantry. It is essential that the infantry never be sent in an attack without the artillery's having prepared this attack and [without] its being ready to provide support. We cannot allow bayonet charges [in the future] under the circumstances in which they have been conducted thus far most of the time.[61]

But France had already lost the initiative, and disastrously inappropriate tactics had magnified the destructive effects of a failed strategy. In his daily journal, Poincaré wrote, "We are facing the possibility of defeat."[62]

Despite the initial failures, the French were not yet beaten, and they now began to wage a much more sensible and effective campaign. Beginning on the morning of August 24 Joffre ordered his armies on his left to withdraw to new positions, generally along a line running between Maubeuge, Mézières, and Verdun. He also started shifting forces from his right to his left. Ironically, the first unit alerted for movement to the left was VII Corps, which had performed so poorly in the attack on Mulhouse. As the French left withdrew, Joffre ordered destruction of railways that could be used by the enemy. He told the minister of war, "We are condemned to a defensive supported by fortified places and large-terrain obstacles while yielding the least possible [amount of] terrain. Our objective must be to last as long as possible, while striving to attrit the enemy, and to resume the offensive when the moment arrives."[63] To reassure the government, Joffre sent a colonel to Paris with the message that the army remained intact and he remained confident.

Part of his confidence came from positive reports from Russia. On August 11 the French ambassador reported initial successes against the Austrians. On August 21, the day Third and Fourth armies marched into Belgium, Grand Duke Nicholas reported that his forces had seized the first German colors, and three days later, the day after French attacks into Belgium had collapsed, he reported that Russian forces were advancing "very rapidly."[64] Joffre believed the Germans had concentrated against the French, leaving the way open for the Russians, who were now advancing easily. Not until midnight on August 30–31 would he learn of the "catastrophe" at Tannenberg.

With the first part of the campaign behind him, Joffre had to devise a new strategy and organize new operations to support it. To regain the initiative, his staff presented two alternatives for his consideration: attack the inner (eastern) wing of Bülow's First Army on the extreme right of the German forces or envelop the right of the entire German force. Joffre chose the second alternative and on August 25 published his General Instructions No. 2, which outlined his new campaign strategy. Though Joffre initially wanted to withdraw on his left to Maubeuge-Mézières-Verdun, the new strategy envisaged a withdrawal to Amiens-Reims-Verdun, an additional 100 kilometers to the rear. Near Amiens, to the left of the British, he wanted to assemble two active corps and four reserve divisions and attempt an envelopment of the German wing. When this attack commenced, British, Fifth, and Fourth armies would also attack. Before resuming the offensive, the armies on the left would fight a delaying action and would launch quick counterattacks, primarily with artillery.[65] This delaying action would obviously compel the French to yield some national territory, but it would provide time to shift forces to the extreme left.

As Joffre adjusted his strategy, he told his army commanders to modify their tactics. In particular, he called for an "intimate combination of infantry and artillery." He was especially concerned about infantrymen: "Thrown in line in numerous and dense units, they are exposed immediately to the fire of the adversary which decimates them, halts their offensive, and often leaves them at the mercy of a counterattack."[66] Though his concerns were real, the need for even greater change would become obvious as the campaign continued.

For Joffre's new strategy to succeed, his entire line had to hold, and for several days he feared that Germans moving south toward Hirson between Fourth and Fifth armies would break through. To cover the sector between the two armies, Joffre formed a special detachment under General Foch. Initially placed under the control of Fourth Army, Foch's detachment consisted of two corps, three additional divisions, and a cavalry division. The two corps came from Fourth Army and two of the divisions from Fifth Army. In his usual energetic fashion Foch immediately took control of these forces and attempted to close the gap between Fourth and Fifth armies.

Joffre's greatest concern as he shaped his new strategy, however, was the British, for they had to help delay the enemy and support the maneuver of the forces assembling on their left. On the morning of August 26 he traveled to British headquarters at St.-Quentin to meet with Sir John French and Lanrezac. The meeting occurred while British II Corps was heavily engaged at Le Cateau and revealed bad feelings between Lanrezac and Sir John, who insisted that Fifth Army had not kept him informed about its withdrawals and had left the British isolated. When the British commander's ignorance of the new strategy of falling back on Amiens-Reims-Verdun became apparent, Joffre explained his new concept to him. During this explanation the British field marshal objected and said he desired to fall back farther than Joffre's new strategy permitted. After further discussions, Joffre left the meeting with the impression that Sir John had agreed to participate in the new maneuver, but he had grave concerns about the "fragility" of his left.[67] His fears worsened that night, when the French liaison officer to the British headquarters reported the results of the Le Cateau battle: "Battle lost by British army which appears to have lost all its cohesion. To be reconstituted, it will require strong protection."[68]

To avoid a disaster, Joffre strengthened his left. Later that night he issued orders for forming Sixth Army with General Michel Maunoury as its commander. Still clinging to the idea of enveloping the German flank, Joffre assigned to Sixth Army the four reserve divisions and the corps that had been shifted to the left for the maneuver. At the same time he abolished the headquarters of the Army of Lorraine and sent its divisions to Third Army and its staff to Maunoury. He also abolished the Army of Alsace, since he had transferred most of its units to Sixth Army.

To slow the enemy's advance on his left, Joffre wanted Fifth Army to launch a counterattack. At the meeting with Lanrezac and Sir John French on August 26, Lanrezac had expressed his intention to launch a counterattack against enemy troops pursuing him, but he had ordered units in Fifth Army to "break contact with the enemy" and march south prior to launching this counterattack.[69] At 0630 hours on the twenty-seventh, Joffre sent an urgent message to Lanrezac reminding him of his promise to counterattack immediately. To comply with Joffre's wishes, Lanrezac had to begin his attack from the vicinity of the Oise River between Guise and Hirson, but he preferred to withdraw another twenty kilometers and counterattack from the vicinity of Laon. After some tense discussions between the staffs of the two headquarters, Lanrezac relented and informed GQG of his intention to counterattack toward the north-west from the vicinity of Guise.

Throughout August 27 Joffre received increasingly pessimistic reports about the British. In the early afternoon GQG learned that the British had completely evacuated St.-Quentin and in doing so had uncovered the left of Fifth Army, making it extremely difficult for Lanrezac to launch a counterattack toward the northwest. At 1745 hours, the French liaison officer to the British conveyed concern that the British retreat might become a "rout" and described the situation as "extremely grave."[70] Another report later that night described the British as "beaten, incapable of a serious effort" and said that two of their divisions were "nothing more than disorganized bands incapable of offering the least resistance."[71]

To aid the British, Joffre attempted to reduce the enemy's pressure against them. At 2010 hours on the twenty-seventh he ordered Lanrezac to launch his counterattack toward St.-Quentin against the flank of the Germans pursuing the British. Since attacking toward St.-Quentin was a change in the direction of attack from northwest to west and would require Fifth Army to turn ninety degrees while confronting large enemy forces, Lanrezac objected strenuously. On the morning of August 28 Joffre traveled to Lanrezac's headquarters and had what both generals described as a tense and heated meeting. When Lanrezac complained about not receiving a written order, Joffre sat down immediately and wrote: "The Fifth Army will attack, as soon as possible, the German forces that were engaged yesterday against the British army."[72] Despite Lanrezac's complaints, he already had issued an order to his army, warning it of an attack on the twenty-ninth toward St.-Quentin. Late that afternoon he sent formal instructions to his corps commanders for the following morning's attack.

Several events on August 28 increased the importance of Lanrezac's counterattack. Shortly after midnight GQG informed Fifth Army that the enemy had crossed the Somme near where Sixth Army was detraining on the French left flank. If the enemy penetrated into the detraining area, Sixth Army could not assemble, and the French would have to establish another line farther to the rear. To avoid this strategic calamity, GQG asked Fifth Army to make its counterattack "as energetic as possible."[73] The French hoped the British would assist Lanrezac's counterattack by covering the left of Fifth Army, but late on the twenty-eighth Joffre received a message from a liaison officer conveying Field Marshal French's "regrets" at being unable to cooperate in this action because of the "excessive fatigue" of his troops.[74] Joffre later learned that Sir John had granted his I Corps a "complete rest" for August 29,[75] the day Lanrezac would finally deliver his counterattack in what became known as the battle of Guise.

On the morning of the counterattack, August 29, Fifth Army had, from left to right, Fourth Reserve Division Group, XVIII, III, X, and I corps. While Fourth Reserve Division Group and XVIII Corps faced west, III Corps faced northwest, X Corps north, and I Corps—protecting Lanrezac's right flank—northeast. The attack began at 0600 hours. As one participant later recounted, the overall battle degenerated into three distinct battles.[76] On the left Fourth Reserve Division Group and XVIII Corps moved west about four kilometers until they encountered strong resistance at around 1300 hours. The Germans were completely surprised by the attack, as is evident from one corps commander's driving up to a village occupied by the French and being wounded. Also attacking at 0600 hours, III Corps advanced toward the northwest but came under heavy enemy pressure on its right at around 1100 hours. On III Corps's right, X Corps, which had been attacked during the night, received another enemy attack at 0845 and came under heavier pressure at 1300. The strength of the German attack against III and X corps in the north forced Lanrezac to halt his move toward St.-Quentin. As his left withdrew under pressure, he moved General Franchet d'Espèrey's I Corps between III and X corps and launched a vigorous counterattack at 1700 hours toward the north. Assisted by III and X corps, I Corps drove the enemy back.

Although Lanrezac's counterattack slowed the Germans' advance, it failed to halt them completely and to restore the situation. After spending the morning at Fifth Army's headquarters and carefully monitoring the conduct of the battle, Joffre hurried in the afternoon to Sir John French's headquarters. He hoped to convince the British field marshal to return his troops to the battle line between the Fifth and Sixth armies and give Sixth Army time to assemble completely. If the British continued withdrawing, a huge gap would open between the French Sixth and Fifth armies, and Joffre could not hold the Amiens-Reims line or counterattack from it. Despite the French commander's most compelling arguments, Sir John adamantly refused to do anything for forty-eight hours. Joffre left the British headquarters extremely discouraged, convinced that he could not launch a counterattack near Amiens around the German right wing and certain that he would have to change his strategy. After returning to his headquarters, he received reports that Sixth Army was under heavy pressure and that Fifth Army's left was being pushed back. Though pleased that Lanrezac's offensive had slowed the German advance, he ordered Fifth Army to break contact and withdraw. He now focused his efforts on halting the enemy along a new line running between Compiègne, Soissons, and Reims, thirty to forty kilometers to the rear of the Amiens-Reims line.

Still hopeful about the British, he sent a message to Field Marshal French on August 30 asking him to remain in "constant liaison" with Fifth Army.[77] At noon, however, he received a message from Sir John saying that the British would not fill the gap between Sixth and Fifth armies and would not enter the front line for ten days. The next day Sir John refused Joffre's request to leave rear guards and keep the enemy from discovering the gap between Sixth and Fifth armies. That morning the French intercepted a German radio transmission ordering a cavalry corps to cross the Oise River south of Noyon and march east. The Germans had found the hole in allied lines opened by the British precipitous withdrawal, and that evening, August 31, enemy cavalry crossed the Oise, moved around the left of Fifth Army, and threatened to drive deep into its rear. Only some extraordinary luck and some fortuitous assistance from British cavalry enabled Fifth Army to escape its perilous situation. Adding to the bad news, Joffre had received word around midnight on August 30–31 about the defeat of the Russians at Tannenberg. The Germans clearly had the upper hand.

Facing a deteriorating strategic and operational situation, Joffre decided to pull back much farther than he initially thought necessary. In his General Instructions No. 4, published on September 1, he ordered Fifth and Fourth armies to withdraw as far south as the Seine and Aube rivers, 100 kilometers to the rear.[78] The instructions clearly stated, however, that the withdrawal could end before troops reached the Seine-Aube line.

Joffre also ordered Sixth Army to fall back toward Paris. When the Sixth Army commander, General Maunoury, proposed attacking the Germans in the vicinity of Compiègne, Joffre told him, "Your role is to cover Paris. Therefore, withdraw toward the capital and make contact with the military governor."[79] Amidst this turmoil Joffre learned that Field Marshal French intended to withdraw west of Paris, directly across Sixth Army's line of communications. After agreeing to withdraw east of Paris behind the Marne River, Sir John proposed halting the allies along the Marne and waging a defensive battle there. He suggested extending allied lines a few kilometers west or northwest of Paris. Although Millerand urged Joffre to accept the British field marshal's proposal, obviously because the Council of Ministers wanted Paris defended, Joffre refused. He doubted that his forces could hold the Marne River and then maneuver.

For the next several days the French fell back day and night, and their rear guards fought frequently with the Germans' advance guards. According to Lanrezac, his soldiers withdrew 140 kilometers from August 30 to September 5. As the French withdrew, discipline began to break down, and some soldiers deserted their units. A few began pillaging and terrifying civilians. The great majority of the French soldiers, however, maintained their discipline and their unit cohesion. Rumors of German atrocities—including shooting defenseless civilians, burning villages, and widespread raping and pillaging—strengthened the soldiers' resolve to continue marching until the time was right for them to turn on the enemy. They remained grimly determined to drive the German invaders from their country's soil, and that determination ultimately made the difference in the outcome of the battle.

As the Germans drew closer to Paris, the question of defending France's capital came to the forefront. Long before the failure of Joffre's offensive, Messimy had become dissatisfied with the efforts of General Michel, the military governor of Paris, to strengthen the city's defenses. That dissatisfaction eventually led him to dismiss Michel and replace him with General Gallieni, who had been designated on July 31 as the successor of Joffre, should one be needed. As a condition for accepting the position Gallieni demanded at least three active corps to defend Paris, and on August 25 Messimy ordered Joffre to place three corps around Paris. Joffre, however, viewed this order as "governmental inter-ference in the conduct of operations" and thought it hampered his free-dom of action at a time when he most needed the latitude to put together a powerful response to the advancing German armies. Believing that the defense of Paris had to be integrated into his overall conduct of the com-mand, the French general-in-chief decided to ignore the minister's order. Unaware of Joffre's refusal to provide three corps, the president of the Republic appointed Gallieni as military governor of Paris on August 26.

As the Germans approached Paris, Premier Viviani's government fell. Since early August French political leaders had discussed the advantages of broadening the representation of political parties in the Council of Ministers, and as the Germans marched south, Poincaré worked behind the scenes to form what became known as the Sacred Union. Viviani and Poincaré hoped to broaden the base of the government simply by having five members, including Messimy, resign and then appointing five new members to replace them, but Messimy refused to resign. In trying to convince him to resign, Viviani described the strong criticism of him in the Senate and Chamber of Deputies. Those criticisms included his be-ing responsible for the first defeats, issuing communiqués that were ei-ther excessively optimistic or pessimistic, and having chosen Joffre as the generalissimo. In reality Joffre could not be dismissed in this moment of crisis, but Messimy could. When he refused to resign, Viviani had no choice but to tender the collective resignation of the entire council. Poincaré immediately reappointed him president of the Council of Min-isters (premier) on August 26, and Alexandre Millerand joined the gov-ernment as minister of war. The new Viviani government would remain in power until October 29, 1915.

The day after the new government came to power, Millerand visited Joffre's headquarters to be briefed on the military situation. During that visit Joffre warned him that German cavalry would reach the gates of Paris in four or five days. When the two discussed Messimy's order to send three active corps to defend Paris, Joffre emphasized the need to have every available soldier participate in the forthcoming maneuver around the flank of the enemy at Amiens, and Millerand emphasized the importance of ensuring the capital's safety. Joffre expressed his confidence in General Gallieni's ability to organize the city's defenses, and he agreed to send three corps to Paris if the Amiens counteroffensive failed.

The approach of the Germans eventually resulted in the government's leaving Paris. As early as August 29 the Council of Ministers discussed the possibility of the enemy's investing Paris, and Millerand informed his fellow ministers that Joffre advised the government to leave the capital city and not be isolated from the country as in 1870. The following day, as the limited success of Fifth Army at Guise became apparent, Joffre informed the government that he was no longer certain he could keep the enemy from entering Paris, and he advised the government's leaders to leave the capital rather than draw the enemy toward them. Adhering to his agreement with Millerand, he also ordered Maunoury's Sixth Army to withdraw toward Paris. Over the next several days the Germans continued advancing toward Paris, and news of the Russian defeat at Tannenberg erased all hopes of a dramatic change in the strategic situation. When the Council of Ministers met on September 2, Millerand insisted that the time to leave had arrived. German planes had bombed Paris, killing a few civilians, and the minister of war knew the capital city would soon be within range of enemy artillery. After extended discussions, the president of the Republic and the council members concluded that they had no choice but to depart. The experience of 1870 had demonstrated the dangers of having the government cut off from France. That night, the forty-fourth anniversary of the fall of Sedan, government officials left Paris in several trains for Bordeaux.

Before leaving the city, the government published a proclamation explaining its reasons for doing so. The proclamation said: "to give this struggle all its spirit and all its effectiveness, it is indispensable that the government remain free to act. At the request of military authorities, the government thus momentarily transports its residence to a point in the territory where it may remain in constant contact with the rest of the country."[80] Though the government remained in Bordeaux until December 9, the subsequent battle of the Marne made the unfortunate move unnecessary. Some critics have argued that Joffre encouraged the government to flee Paris so that he would be free to conduct the war without its interference, but he did not yet know the outcome of the battle and could not risk having the Germans capture France's political leaders. Although several reports on August 31 and September 1 suggested that General Alexander von Kluck's First Army was turning away from Paris, the Germans remained very close to the city. Moreover, Gallieni demonstrated his recognition of the city's vulnerability on September 2 when he told the French general-in-chief that if three active corps were not sent to the capital, it would be "absolutely impossible to resist."[81] From Joffre's perspective the threat to Paris was real and the requirement to move the government urgent.

Despite the worsening situation, Joffre remained firmly in control and did not hesitate to relieve commanders who failed to meet his expectations. On August 30 he visited Third Army's headquarters and relieved its commander, General Ruffey. He found Ruffey "very nervous" and "bitter" about the performance of his subordinates, and he judged it "imprudent" to leave him in command. General Maurice Sarrail, a corps commander in Third Army, replaced him.[82] Four days later he relieved Lanrezac, commander of Fifth Army. The relief of Lanrezac was "intensely painful" to Joffre, who had known him for years and had great esteem for his intellectual gifts, but he had lost confidence in the Fifth Army commander and had tired of his challenging orders.[83] In contrast to his reservations about Ruffey and Lanrezac, Joffre had great confidence in his other army commanders (particularly Fernand de Langle de Cary, Dubail, Castelnau, and Foch, whose detachment would soon become a field army). In his memoirs Joffre described what he expected of his army commanders: "you can wage war only with men who have faith in their success, who by their mastery of themselves know how to impose their will on their subordinates and dominate events."[84] As events would demonstrate, Joffre had complete control of himself and no reservations about imposing his will on others. Those characteristics soon enabled him to be the victor of the battle of the Marne.

As the French continued withdrawing, intelligence reports provided information about the Germans' progress. On September 1 reports identified an enemy force near Compiègne (sixty-five kilometers north-north-east of Paris). That same day French and British aerial reconnaissance reported German columns moving east of Paris in a south-southeasterly direction. A captured German map revealed the objectives of Kluck's First Army and the change in its direction of march toward the east. Although these reports suggested an enemy turn toward the southeast, a radio intercept on the following day indicated that Kluck had sent strong cavalry forces toward Paris. To complicate matters the French did not know the exact location of the German Second Army on September 2. On September 3 Joffre learned that the entire German First Army was moving east of Paris in a southeasterly direction. The first report came from the British, and subsequent reports from Maunoury and Gallieni. Later that evening British aerial reconnaissance confirmed these reports and said that Kluck's First Army, after leaving one corps east of Paris, had moved southeast with three corps toward Château-Thierry, on the Marne River. Amidst hopes that the Germans would overextend themselves, Joffre also received reports from Belgium that the Germans were transporting troops from France and Belgium to Russia.

The operational concept of drawing the Germans into a salient between Paris and Verdun and then cutting them off with an attack on the neck of the salient coalesced slowly in Joffre's mind. The first hint of such a grand maneuver appeared late on September 2, when Joffre modified his General Instructions No. 4 slightly but significantly. After again specifying the deep concave line between Paris, the Seine, the Aube, and Verdun along which his forces would be stretched, he expressed his intention to resume the offensive along the entire front and added, "Simultaneously, the garrison of Paris will attack in the direction of Meaux."[85] Since Meaux lay thirty kilometers east of Paris along the Marne River, this attack would send Sixth Army against the flank of the Germans who had advanced into the salient between Paris and Verdun. Joffre's modification on September 2 was the first explicit expression of the operational concept that would prove to be the key to eventual French victory. Yet the opportunity for the Marne maneuver did not appear certain until the next day, when the movement of the Germans to the east of Paris became apparent.

Early on September 3, before knowing definitely the direction of the German advance around Paris, Joffre sent a personal note to Millerand summarizing the situation facing his army and suggesting the outline of future operations. After giving the location of the enemy's armies, he blamed the British for the failure of the Amiens-Reims flanking maneuver and for subsequently exposing Fifth Army's left flank and leaving him no choice but to continue withdrawing. He ruled out an immediate counter-attack with only part of his forces, since the "slightest check" could be transformed into an "irreparable rout." With his troops exhausted and his subordinate commanders recommending against an immediate coun-terattack, Joffre wanted to continue withdrawing and wait several days before beginning a major battle. In preparation for that battle he would strengthen his right with at least two corps and work diligently to recon-stitute his units. While the French became stronger, the Germans would become weaker, Joffre believed, because they had left substantial forces behind to besiege places such as Antwerp and Maubeuge and because they had to pass through a region in which roads, bridges, and railways had been partially destroyed. Though he did not reveal the shape of the coming counteroffensive, he intended to "prepare the approaching offen-sive in liaison with the British army and the mobile troops of the Parisian garrison."[86]

Late on September 3–4, as more information arrived about the Ger-mans' movements east of Paris, Joffre explained his concept in greater de-tail to Gallieni, who had asked for more information on the exact role to be played by the forces in Paris. In a handwritten note, Joffre explained to Gallieni that "part of General Maunoury's active forces can be pushed to-ward the east to threaten the German right."[87] To ensure that Gallieni had received and understood his General Instructions No. 4 and the modification of September 2, Joffre enclosed copies in his letter; he also included a copy of a letter he was sending Field Marshal French on the same subject. In the latter he told the British commander that if the Ger-mans continued moving toward the south-southeast, the British could act more effectively on the south bank of the Marne while forces from Paris operated on the north bank of the Marne and protected the British flank. None of the messages, however, specified a date or hour of attack.

From Gallieni's perspective the attack had to come as quickly as possi-ble. By his calculations the fast-marching Germans could reach the Seine and Aube rivers, the line along which Joffre expected to halt the enemy, by September 6. He also feared the French withdrawal to those rivers would leave Paris completely uncovered and particularly vulnerable to enemy attack. At 0910 hours on September 4 he ordered Maunoury to prepare Sixth Army to march east into the flank of the advancing Germans. Gallieni promised to provide the exact direction of march as soon as he knew the route to be taken by the British. Leading elements of Sixth Army would move that afternoon and the remainder of the army the following morning. Gallieni sent the order even though he knew little about British intentions and did not know if Sixth Army should attack north or south of the Marne. After dispatching the order, he notified Joffre that he had ordered Maunoury to begin moving east. Though the overall scheme of operations remained vague, Joffre approved Gallieni's order to Maunoury.

On September 4, at about the same time that Gallieni ordered Maunoury to prepare to move east, Joffre's staff engaged in a spirited debate over the timing of the attack. The debate focused on how far the Germans should be allowed to advance into the salient before the French unleashed their counterattack. If the French attacked immediately, then Sixth Army should remain north of the Marne and the British south; but if they waited for "five or six days," both Sixth Army and the British should attack south of the Marne. Joffre listened to his staff's opinions and concluded that the crucial variable was the condition of Fifth Army and its ability to halt its withdrawal, do an about-face, and launch an attack. Such an operation would be difficult even for a well-rested and confident army, but it would be particularly difficult for Fifth Army, since Joffre had relieved its commander, Lanrezac, the preceding afternoon. On September 4 Joffre sent General Franchet d'Espèrey, the newly appointed Fifth Army commander, a telegram asking him if his army would be ready to launch a counterattack "tomorrow or the day after tomorrow" with the British and Sixth Army against the First and Second German armies.[88]

Another crucial consideration for Joffre was the willingness of the British to participate in the counteroffensive. He had sent Sir John his General Instructions No. 4 and his modification of September 2, which had ordered the Parisian garrison to attack east toward Meaux, and at 0800 hours on September 4, he sent the British field marshal a letter asking him to participate in the attack with Sixth and Fifth armies. Before he received a response Gallieni (with Maunoury) visited the British head-quarters and met with Sir John's chief of staff, Sir Archibald Murray. After a tedious three-hour discussion, Gallieni left the meeting believing he had failed to convince Murray of the necessity to attack. Meanwhile, the ever-cautious Field Marshal French—using the French liaison officer—informed Joffre of his willingness to participate in the offensive *if* enemy forces were not too strong and Fifth Army covered the British right. In a subsequent telegram, Field Marshal French asked to meet with d'Espèrey that afternoon, evidently to ensure that his right would be covered.

As d'Espèrey waited to meet Sir John later that day in a small town midway between British headquarters and his own, he received Joffre's telegram asking him if Fifth Army could participate in an offensive with Sixth Army and the British. Before he could respond, the British deputy chief of staff, General Henry Wilson, not Sir John French, arrived for the meeting. The results were completely different from Gallieni's meeting with Murray. The two agreed that an offensive with French and British forces could occur on September 6, but Wilson insisted that Sixth Army cover the British left flank and launch an "energetic" attack north of Meaux. Wilson also wanted Foch's detachment to participate. D'Espèrey quickly informed Joffre of the results of the meeting and followed with another message about the condition of his army. The latter said: "My army can fight on the sixth but is not in a brilliant situation; the three reserve divisions cannot be counted on."[89] Joffre was immensely relieved when he received d'Espèrey's messages, for they indicated that the British probably would and Fifth Army definitely would participate in the offensive. D'Espèrey had distinguished himself as a corps commander in the fighting along the Sambre and Meuse early in the campaign, and his corps had performed superbly in the subsequent battle of Guise, but these were small accomplishments in the eyes of Joffre in comparison with what the future marshal of France had accomplished within twenty-four hours of assuming command of Fifth Army. In his memoirs Joffre wrote, "The role of Franchet d'Espèrey on September 4, 1914, merits being underlined in history: it is he who made the battle of the Marne possible."[90]

The date of the attack nevertheless remained undecided, for earlier in the afternoon Joffre had directed his staff to draft an order fixing September 7 as the date of the offensive. After d'Espèrey's messages arrived, the French general-in-chief modified the order to bring it into line with the arrangements made by the Fifth Army commander, but he did not change the date. That evening Gallieni called Joffre and demanded that the attack occur on September 6. Joffre had already approved Maunoury's moving into position on the evening of the fourth, and Sixth Army would probably, said Gallieni, make contact with the enemy on the afternoon of the fifth and alert the Germans to the threat against their flank. Recognizing the validity of Gallieni's concerns, Joffre changed the date of attack to the morning of September 6. In his postwar memoirs he expressed regret about this change and claimed that an attack on the following day would have found the enemy in a more "disadvantageous" position and produced better results.[91] Nevertheless, at 2200 hours on September 4, Joffre's staff published the order providing the details for the French and British attack on the Germans' extreme right.[92] Earlier that day Joffre had modified the organization of Third and Fourth armies and named Foch's detachment Ninth Army. Everything seemed to be in place.

Sir John French, however, had not yet formally agreed to participate in the counteroffensive. After returning to his headquarters on the afternoon of September 4, the British field marshal listened to Murray's and Wilson's accounts of their meetings with Gallieni and d'Espèrey and realized that the two French generals had asked the British to occupy two different positions, one facing north and the other east. He decided to withdraw southwest in consonance with arrangements made by General Gallieni (the British had to face toward the east and have their left join Sixth Army's right south of the Marne), but he wanted to analyze the situation before deciding on subsequent operations. Concerned about Sir John's continued hesitation, Joffre asked the minister of war on September 5 to use diplomatic channels and bring to the field marshal's attention the "decisive importance" of the counterattack.[93] An hour later a message from the French liaison officer with the British informed Joffre that Sir John would "conform" to the intentions expressed in the operations order but that his army would occupy a position to the rear of the one arranged by Gallieni.[94] Because the British had moved in accordance with Gallieni's design rather than Franchet d'Espèrey's, they spent the night twenty-five kilometers to the rear of where Joffre wanted them to be.

Reassured by Sir John's willingness to participate in the offensive, Joffre met with him that afternoon, September 5, ostensibly to thank him personally for his decision but in reality to reinforce in the mind of the British field marshal the importance of the operation. In an emotional presentation the French general-in-chief explained his strategy, provided a description of the coming battle, and emphasized that he was committing all his soldiers to the battle in order to achieve victory and save France. British forces, Joffre believed, would play a crucial role in the campaign, but if they chose not to participate, their absence would be "severely judged by history." Banging his fist on the table, Joffre concluded, "The honor of England is at stake, Marshal." Sir John's faced turned red, and after a short silence he tried to say something in French but then told one of the officers near him, "Damn it, I can't explain. Tell him that all that men can do our fellows will do."[95]

Throughout the campaign Joffre had remained in close contact with his subordinates. An advantage for the French came from their falling back on their lines of communications and their reliance on the telephone. Whereas Moltke issued no orders from September 5 to 9 and received no reports from his First and Second Army commanders from September 7 to 9, Joffre remained in constant contact with his army commanders via telephone (even though he preferred written messages). He also had frequent meetings with his subordinate commanders and Sir John French. These meetings enabled him to take careful measure of his subordinates, give them key instructions, and ensure that they followed his directions. Had he been as distant or detached as Moltke, he could not have coordinated the complex withdrawal of allied forces and remained in close touch with what was happening. More important, if Sir John French had had almost no contact with him (as did Kluck and Bülow with Moltke), there is little doubt he and his troops would have withdrawn past Paris and never played the key role they did in the Marne victory.

Two hours after learning that the British would participate in the counteroffensive, the French general-in-chief dispatched a message to

Fifth and Sixth armies telling them to strike the Germans' extreme right. Messages also went to Ninth, Fourth, and Third armies, notifying them of the decision to resume the offensive. In brief Joffre intended to attack the right flank of enemy forces in the salient between Paris and Verdun but also to maintain pressure on the remainder of the enemy forces in the salient to fix them and keep them from moving toward the threatened flank. To underline the importance of the battle, he sent a message to all French soldiers reminding them that the safety of their country depended on the battle and that every effort had to be made to attack and force the enemy back. The message concluded, "Under these circumstances no weakness can be tolerated."[96] On the eve of the battle he also sent a letter to the minister of war explaining his actions. Though he considered the strategic situation "excellent," he still had doubts about the British and noted that a failure would have the "gravest consequences" for the country.[97]

For the approaching battle Joffre had six armies, including the British, stretched from Paris to Verdun. From left to right were Sixth, British, Fifth, Ninth, Fourth, and Third armies. The five French armies that would participate in the battle of the Marne had fifty-one infantry and eight cavalry divisions. Additionally, the British had five infantry and one and a half cavalry divisions, giving the allies a total of fifty-six infantry and nine and a half cavalry divisions. According to French calculations, the Germans had forty-four infantry and seven cavalry divisions in the battle.

The first engagement in the battle began at 1300 hours on September 5 thirty kilometers northeast of Paris. Early that morning Sixth Army had marched east from Paris. Following Joffre's instructions, Maunoury intended to move his army into a position northeast of Meaux and have it attack the next day along the north bank of the Marne. Though Gallieni had warned Joffre of the possibility of an early engagement, Maunoury's forces did not expect to encounter any resistance on the first day of their march, since French cavalry had swept through the area where they were headed and had encountered no enemy. Unknown to them, the German IV Reserve Corps had moved south that morning to a new position just north of Meaux. When the German commander received reports from his cavalry that French forces were advancing, he made the bold decision to attack. The French learned of the enemy's presence only after two

77-mm guns opened up on their leading forces northwest of Meaux. The fighting continued until dark, and the French made no gains. When night fell, the Germans still held the heights north of Meaux, but IV Reserve Corps withdrew ten kilometers to the east that night to a stronger defensive position. Aerial observation the following morning revealed significant German forces being shifted from south to north into a position facing Sixth Army. As Gallieni had predicted, the engagement east of Paris had revealed Joffre's maneuver to the enemy.

The battle raged over the next four days, but in the first two days the Germans made several moves that had a significant effect on the outcome. When the German IV Reserve Corps first made contact with Sixth Army northwest of Meaux, Kluck's First Army had four corps south of the Marne (from the German right to left, II, IV, III, and IX). At 0300 hours on September 6, Kluck ordered II Corps to move north and assist IV Reserve Corps. As Maunoury's forces continued attacking, Kluck at 1630 hours ordered IV Corps to march north. After dark Kluck ordered IV Corps to march at night so that it could assist IV Reserve and II corps at daylight on September 7. At 2100 hours Kluck directed his III and IX corps to fall back ten kilometers, but the following night, after several confusing changes, he ordered III and IX corps to march to the north of the Marne with the remainder of the German First Army. Kluck expected two cavalry corps to cover the front vacated by First Army and justified his actions by reasoning that "the repeatedly beaten British will scarcely be quickly induced to come forward and make a powerful offensive."[98]

The rapid reinforcement of IV Reserve Corps prevented Sixth Army from crossing the Ourcq River and kept it under heavy pressure. Except for September 6, when the ten-kilometer withdrawal of the German IV Reserve Corps enabled Sixth Army to advance, Maunoury made little progress. In fact his forces struggled desperately to hold their positions. As evidence of the fragility of their situation, Maunoury sent instructions to his subordinate commanders on September 8 identifying a second line to which the army, if necessary, would withdraw. Since Sixth Army failed to advance deep into the German rear, the results of its attack were not what Joffre expected, but Kluck's decision to shift his corps north gave the allies another opportunity and eventually opened a gap between the German First and Second armies. In the decisive moment of the campaign, the British and Fifth Army would advance through this gap and compel the Germans to withdraw.

Fifth Army played a significant role in expanding the gap. On the first day of the attack, September 6, d'Espèrey's forces advanced four to five kilometers. With the German II and IV corps gone, his troops advanced easily on the morning of the seventh until they struck the enemy's rear guard. Toward the end of the morning they resumed their forward movement. On September 8, with the German III and IX corps gone, d'Espèrey's forces continued their advance, but after striking the right of Bülow's Second Army, French infantry had to fight their way across the Petit Morin River, which ran from the southeast to the northwest into the Marne. After Fifth Army crossed this small river, Bülow had no choice but to pull back the units on his right, pivot on his center, and refuse his right flank. This movement opened the way for d'Espèrey. On September 9 at 1430 hours French cavalry crossed the Marne five kilometers southwest of Château Thierry. They crossed easily because the British had seized the bridge there early that morning. Infantry crossed shortly thereafter, and by 1900 hours the French controlled Château Thierry.

The key advance into the gap, however, was made by the British. Though Kluck expected the British to remain out of the battle, Joffre had successfully induced them to march forward. Marching with three corps abreast, Sir John advanced easily but slowly toward the northeast on September 6 and 7. The British encountered no serious opposition until the third day, when they approached the Petit Morin River and the village of La Ferté-sous-Jouarre, which sat at the junction of the Petit Morin and Marne rivers. Early on September 9, British cavalry seized several bridges across the Marne between La Ferté-sous-Jouarre and Château Thierry, and by the end of the day the British held a bridgehead about eight kilometers deep on the north bank of the river. An analysis of German decisionmaking is beyond the scope of this study, but the crossing of the Marne placed the entire German position in jeopardy. By noon Kluck and Bülow had decided to withdraw, and shortly thereafter the Germans began pulling back.

While Sixth, British, and Fifth armies pressed forward on Joffre's left, Ninth, Fourth, and Third armies on the center and right struggled desperately to hold and not allow the Germans to open a large hole between them. Of these actions those on the right of Ninth and the left of Fourth were particularly difficult. On September 7 the German Third Army entered the breach between the two armies, and only desperate fighting and the arrival of French reinforcements prevented them from breaking through. The next day the German Second and Third armies struck the right of Foch's Ninth Army. When the withdrawal of Foch's right resulted in his center's falling back, Foch responded by ordering a counterattack. On September 9 he ordered another offensive. Although only a few battalions advanced, they encountered little resistance. Bülow's decision to retreat had compelled the German Third Army to withdraw and had opened the way for Foch.

Sarrail's Third Army also fought a desperate battle. Its situation was especially dangerous because as its left pivoted counterclockwise around Verdun, its front line came perilously close to the rear of French units occupying the line that ran southeast from Verdun. Beginning on September 8 the Germans, concentrating on Troyon, struck the heights of the Meuse, hardly fifteen kilometers behind Sarrail's right. Though overwhelmingly outnumbered, the French succeeded in holding the heights and halting the threat to Sarrail's rear. Another threat to Third Army came from strong German attacks on its left between Third and Fourth armies. A breakthrough in this sector could have had significant strategic effect, allowing the enemy to strike Second Army in the rear. Despite the consequences of a breakthrough on his left, Sarrail remained most concerned about Verdun on his right even though the fortress system had sufficient strength to fend for itself if it were cut off. At 2000 hours on September 8 Joffre authorized him to withdraw his right and relinquish contact with Verdun so that he could strengthen his left and maintain contact with Fourth Army. Sarrail, who was to become enormously controversial in subsequent months, refused to let Verdun be isolated and managed to maintain contact with it. Though he was later credited with having saved the fortress system, Verdun was never under serious pressure and was hardly at risk. By paying insufficient attention to the threat to his left, Sarrail subjected the French army to far greater risk than the loss of Verdun would have entailed. Sarrail thus caused Joffre some troubling moments, but his army maintained contact with Verdun on its right and Fourth Army on its left.

On Joffre's right, Second Army came close to falling back in the face of strong enemy pressure. On September 5, while Joffre was meeting with Sir John and pleading for British participation in the counteroffensive, Castelnau notified GQG that Second Army was under violent attack and might have to withdraw. Almost twenty-four hours later Joffre responded by informing Castelnau that his counteroffensive had begun and that he hoped Second Army could hold its position until the battle was decided. If Second Army had to withdraw, however, Joffre gave his approval. The situation of Second Army worsened the following day, and with his judgment clouded by the news of a son's death, Castelnau gave the order to withdraw. When Joffre learned about the impending retreat of Second Army, he telephoned Castelnau and ordered him to hold for another twenty-four hours. Fortunately for the French, Second Army held, and the crisis passed.

On the evening of September 9, with the British across the Marne, Joffre recognized the significant gains of the day, but he was not yet willing to announce a victory. Instead he sent the minister of war a brief note highlighting Maunoury's success in protecting Paris and halting German attacks against the French left. After mentioning the British crossing of the Marne and expressing confidence in a French crossing, the note said, "The enemy has thus withdrawn about forty kilometers."[99] Later that night Joffre sent instructions to his commanders for the following day and said, "the enemy appears to be withdrawing." He then assigned Sixth, British, and Fifth armies their objectives for the following day's attacks. While the British and Fifth armies drove north, Maunoury's Sixth Army would seek to envelop the enemy's right flank, and the cavalry to Maunoury's left would extend his operational effect by seeking the enemy's flank and rear.[100]

By the next afternoon the extent of the allied victory was clear, and late that day Joffre informed the minister of war. He had not wanted to send news, he explained, until he had "indisputable results." The same telegram included Joffre's name for the battle, the battle of the Marne. According to Joffre, this name "evoked at the same time the idea of a front and of a large region."[101]

Beyond a doubt credit for what came to be known as the "miracle of the Marne" belonged to Joffre. After the collapse of his attempted maneuver around the German flank at Amiens, he kept his forces under control and did not panic when the Germans moved around the flank and into the rear of Fifth Army. As French and British forces withdrew, he remained in constant contact with them and prepared a counteroffensive. Though he did not foresee the subsequent course of events and did not attempt to trap the Germans, he recognized the opportunity to strike the enemy forces in their flank when Kluck's First Army turned to the east of Paris. In reality, this opportunity resembled what he had tried to do with Sixth Army on the Amiens-Reims line. Additionally, as Sixth, British, and Fifth armies attacked the Germans' right flank, Joffre displayed strong judgment and a remarkable degree of composure in his calm response to near disasters on both flanks of Fourth army, the right of Ninth Army, the left of Third Army, and the front of Second Army. Perhaps his greatest achievement was his refusal to let these near disasters divert resources from the crucial actions on his left. Though he initially sought to envelop the enemy's flank with Sixth Army's attack from Paris, he reacted capably and appropriately when a gap opened between the German First and Second armies and gave him the opportunity to send forces deep into the enemy's position. Gallieni's role was important, but the key concept and decisions belonged to Joffre.

Despite the significance of the victory, the battle of the Marne did not end the war. Ordering his armies forward, Joffre said: "To affirm and exploit the success, it is necessary to pursue energetically and leave the enemy no respite: victory depends on the legs of our infantry."[102] As the allied armies on the left began moving forward, the Germans struck Third Army west of Verdun. This attack caused Joffre some concern because it threatened to unhinge his right, but by the end of the day Sarrail had the situation under control. The attack nevertheless was a clear signal that the Germans were not beaten.

For the next four days the French and British followed the enemy across terrain over which they had already fought. Though the Germans left behind stragglers, wounded, supplies, and munitions, as well as many empty wine bottles, they remained just beyond the reach of the pursuing allies and used rear guards to protect themselves. Joffre quickly recognized the advantages of using Sixth Army on his left and Third Army on his right-center to outflank the Germans. On September 11 and 12 he ordered the forces on his left to try to outflank the enemy in the west. He also ordered Third Army to use Verdun to cover its right and to attack energetically toward the north. Despite Joffre's prodding, his exhausted forces moved too slowly, and the Germans slipped out of their grasp. As the French marched forward Joffre feared that the German might advance from the vicinity of Metz and strike his right. To guard against such an attack, he ordered Second and Third armies to protect his right flank. By the fourteenth, however, the Germans had halted their withdrawal and occupied strong defensive positions north of the Aisne River. Instead of confronting rear guards, French troops now faced numerous enemy troops in fortified positions along a stabilized front. Acknowledging that the opportunity for decisive victory had slipped from his hands, Joffre complained that "the main cause of this stabilization was the slowness and the lack of skilled maneuvering displayed by the two flank armies and Fifth Army during the short period of our exploiting our victory."[103]

Joffre's initial instinct was to have his center continue driving forward while his left sought the enemy's flank. Late on the fourteenth he again ordered his armies forward, this time in an energetic attack that would "put out of action" the German First and Second armies on his left.[104] Attempts on September 15 and 16 by Fifth and Ninth armies to advance north of the Aisne River and by Sixth Army to advance on Joffre's left, however, made few gains. It was apparent that French forces were not equipped for a frontal assault against a prepared enemy position. Adding to Joffre's concerns, intelligence reported that the Germans were moving troops from east to west. Given this increasing threat, Joffre had no choice but to shift forces toward the west. In a telegram early on the seventeenth, he informed the minister of war that his forces had encountered strongly organized enemy positions, thereby deflating hopes of a rapid victory. After warning Millerand that the battle would not end quickly, he provided no hint about the course of future operations.

Although subsequent operations are usually categorized as the "race to the sea," no such race occurred from September 17 to October 17. Instead, the two sides launched a series of turning movements, resembling leapfrogging more than racing, seeking to go around their opponent's western flank. The shift of Second Army to the west was Joffre's first leap. After moving Second Army's headquarters and several corps from the east, Joffre placed Castelnau, the Second Army commander, in command of the units assembling on the left of Sixth Army and ordered him to strike the enemy's flank.

Throughout the battle of the Marne and the subsequent pursuit, Joffre had shifted forces from his right to his left. The first elements of IV Corps, for example, left the east on September 2, and the last elements arrived on Joffre's left four days later. XIII Corps departed on September 11, and its last elements arrived on Joffre's left five days later. IV Corps used 109 trains to make the move, and XIII Corps used 105. As the race to the sea began, units moving to the left still traveled by train. XIV Corps, using 109 trains, departed on September 18, and arrived five days later; XX Corps, using 118 trains, departed on September 9 and took six days.[105] If Joffre had a secret weapon, it was the highly efficient French railway system, which could move an entire corps from his right to his left in five or six days.

By moving units toward the west, however, Joffre risked denuding part of his front and giving the enemy an opportunity to make gains. In particular, the transfer of Second Army to the west left only Third Army and the depleted First Army on the French right. To protect his right Joffre placed the remaining units of Second Army in First Army and gave the latter army responsibility for the sector once belonging to First and Second armies, as well as the Army of Alsace. Beginning on September 20, the Germans struck Sixth Army along the Aisne, Fifth Army north of Reims, and Third Army on both sides of Verdun. The attack against Sixth Army caused particular concern because of the threat against the forces assembling on Joffre's left, but the Germans made their largest gains against Third Army, seizing the heights overlooking the railway west of Verdun and carving out what came to be known as the St.-Mihiel salient. Despite these gains, the Germans, according to French intelligence, focused their main attention on Joffre's left. Even though the French general-in-chief had received reports that the Germans were placing a new army on his extreme right, intercepts of enemy wireless transmissions convinced him that the real threat was to his left, and he proceeded resolutely to get Second Army into position.

As Castelnau assembled his forces and marched toward the German flank, Joffre increased the depth of Second Army's move on two occasions. On September 24 the Germans struck Castelnau's army, which—instead of turning the enemy's flank—found itself struggling to hold its position. Joffre responded by sending XI Corps, which was his only reserve, to Second Army. During the next week, in an attempt to enhance Second Army's chances of turning the enemy's flank, he pulled three other corps out of the line and sent them to Castelnau. Given the great length of Castelnau's front and the number of corps under his command—eventually eight—Joffre decided on September 29 to place General Louis de Maud'huy in command of the units on Second Army's left and have him report to Castelnau.

Despite the reinforcements sent to Second Army, the Germans gained the upper hand. The first "bad omen," Joffre's words, came when Second Army reported on October 2 that it could not detrain XXI Corps as close to Lille as the French general-in-chief desired. Even though Joffre ordered Castelnau not to lose Lille, the Second Army commander reported that he probably would yield the city and withdraw his left wing behind the Somme. Upon learning of this possible withdrawal, Joffre immediately traveled to Second Army's headquarters and told Castelnau he would not tolerate any thought of retiring. Despite Joffre's personal intervention, the situation worsened.

Thoroughly dissatisfied with Castelnau's performance, Joffre called on Foch to rectify the situation. On September 24 Joffre had asked the minister of war to name Foch (instead of Gallieni) as his potential replacement and expressed his intention to bring Foch to his headquarters to assist him. Though Millerand and the Council of Ministers approved Joffre's request, they asked that official notification of the change not occur until the end of the current operation. With this approval in hand, Joffre made Maud'huy's detachment an independent army (Tenth Army) on October 4. He also named Foch "assistant to the commander-in-chief" and gave him authority to "coordinate" the actions of Second Army and the newly formed Tenth Army.[106] Additionally, Joffre dissolved Ninth Army and split its corps between Fifth and Fourth armies. These changes placed Foch, who had started the war as a corps commander in Castelnau's Second Army, over Castelnau and made him the equivalent of an army-group commander. Joffre told Foch to envelop the enemy's flank but, if this proved impossible, to prevent the enemy from enveloping the French flank.

The situation of Second Army, however, did not improve. Late on October 6 Castelnau reported to GQG that his line might break. After informing Foch, Joffre asked the British to send two cavalry divisions, which were already in the region, to reinforce Second Army until additional French forces could arrive. Following Foch's visits to Maud'huy's and Castelnau's headquarters and the arrival of small reinforcements, the new commander of the Provisional Group of the North reported early in the afternoon of October 9: "Situation good on the entire front."[107] Though Joffre retained Castelnau as Second Army's commander, he relieved his chief of staff and appointed a successor without consulting him. Beyond a doubt, Castelnau, who would end the war as an army-group commander but never become a marshal, came perilously close to being relieved by Joffre. The results obtained by Foch more than justified his rapid elevation and the strong confidence Joffre had in him. Nevertheless, attempts by Maud'huy's Tenth Army on October 9 and 10 to roll up the enemy's flank failed.

While moving forces to his left and strengthening Second and Tenth armies during the first week of October, Joffre had to contend with an unexpected request from Sir John French. On September 29 the British field marshal asked to move the British army to the left of the allied line. Though Joffre had doubts about the wisdom of moving the British toward the English Channel, he did not object in his initial response. He thought the move could take place if the British, while maintaining the integrity of their front, shifted individual divisions to the left and landed newly arrived divisions at Dunkirk. Sir John French agreed and proposed that a corps in his center and a cavalry division move immediately, but Joffre said that the moves could not commence before October 5 because of existing demands on railway services.

Much to Joffre's dismay, only a few days passed before the British, showing little regard for his efforts to shore up Second and Tenth armies, said they wanted to move the entire British Expeditionary Force toward the Channel. He reluctantly agreed, but he insisted that newly arriving British troops not await the entire B.E.F. but enter battle as soon as they detrained. Any hesitation by the British could disrupt the transport of French troops to his left and dismantle his hopes of turning the enemy's flank. On October 6 Sir John French assured Joffre of his intention to act as quickly as forces arrived, but he again emphasized the importance of the entire B.E.F.'s moving to the left as quickly as possible. To the credit of the British, new units went into action immediately after arriving in the north and took positions on the left of Tenth Army.

While Joffre shored up Tenth and Second armies and arranged to transport the British to the north, he also had to address serious questions concerning the Belgian army. The first issue arose when the Belgians, who had withdrawn all their forces into fortified positions around Antwerp, came under heavy bombardment from the Germans on September 28 and appealed for help. When the minister of war indicated his intention, if Joffre did not object, to have a territorial division join the British in operations along the Belgian coast, the French general-in-chief insisted that he could not divert troops from ongoing operations. He suggested advising the Belgians to have their army withdraw from Antwerp, leaving only a garrison to defend the fortifications. A week earlier Joffre had appealed to the Belgians to leave their fortifications and attack the Germans' lines of communications, but they had remained at Antwerp. With the French attempting to maneuver around the German flank, the best way to assist the Belgians, Joffre now believed, was to assemble large forces on the French left and advance toward Antwerp. In early October Foch arranged an offensive toward Lille and Antwerp with the British and the Tenth Army, but the attack made only small gains.

Despite objections from Joffre and Sir John French, the British and French governments agreed to send a British and a French division to assist the Belgians. The French also sent General Pau to Belgium to provide advice and ensure cooperation between the Belgian and French armies. Though the French never sent troops, the British did, and it quickly became apparent that Antwerp could not be saved. As German pressure increased, Belgian forces withdrew from Antwerp on the night of October 6–7, leaving only a few troops in the city's fortifications and setting the stage for the city to surrender on the morning of October 10. As the Belgians retreated from Antwerp, they moved south along the coast and had to beat off attacks on their flank. On October 10 Pau informed Joffre that the Belgian king had decided to move to a position southwest of Calais behind allied lines and rest for a few days. Still concerned about his left, Joffre insisted that the Belgians accept his orders and participate in the defense of their territory. To Joffre's relief, the Belgian king decided on October 11 not to withdraw south but to keep his army on his nation's territory. The Belgian minister of war informed the French:

> The sovereign, acting in accord with the [Belgian] government, intends to retain command of the Belgian army, no matter what its numbers. But, deeply believing in the necessity of unity of action among the allied armies, he will be happy to have the [French] generalissimo act vis-à-vis the Belgian army as he acts vis-à-vis the British army and have him as a consequence communicate directly with its [Belgian military] commander.[108]

On the morning of October 15 the Belgian army, consisting of 50,000 troops, occupied a position behind the Yser Canal between Dixmude and the English Channel.

The arrival of the Belgians marked the end of the "race to the sea." On the allied left, from left to right, the allies had the Belgians on a fifteen-kilometer front; a mixture of Belgians, French, and British on another fifteen-kilometer front; the British on a forty-kilometer front; and Tenth Army on a twenty-five-kilometer front. With the appearance of the British I Corps, Sir John French's front temporarily extended a few kilometers farther to the north, covering most of the Ypres salient.

Despite the existence of a continuous front, neither the allies nor the Germans wanted the battle zone to remain static. Both launched offensives in an attempt to restore mobility to the war. When the drive by the British and Tenth Army toward Lille faltered in early October, Joffre sent Foch additional troops to continue the attack in the sector between the Belgians and the British. To provide better control of the jumble of French units in Belgium, Foch, with Joffre's approval, formed the Army Detachment of Belgium under General Victor d'Urbal and placed all

French units in Belgium under his control. This detachment later became Eighth Army. While Foch marshaled his forces, the Germans unleashed their offensive against the Ypres salient in what became known as the first battle of Ypres. They struck the British line northeast of Ypres particularly hard. The timely arrival of the British I Corps strengthened the northern face of the Ypres salient, but this corps in turn was replaced by the French IX Corps. As fighting continued, the Germans sent five ill-trained reserve corps against strong allied positions and suffered horrendous casualties in what has sometimes been described as the "massacre of the innocents."

Throughout the fighting Joffre continued to send reinforcements toward Belgium and the Ypres salient. By November 4 the British held only one-third of the Ypres salient. As the Germans continued their attacks, Joffre kept sending reinforcements, and by the time the fighting finally ended on November 12, he had committed his last reserves. On November 13 Foch reported to Joffre that the enemy had stopped attacking and apparently abandoned the idea of seizing Ypres.

With the conclusion of the first battle of Ypres and with some 400,000 French soldiers already dead, the opening campaign of the war on the western front ended. Although Joffre had not saved France from a long and bloody war, he had prevented the Germans from winning a decisive victory. Despite a bankrupt strategy, terrible losses because of poor tactics, and several crushing defeats at the hands of the Germans, the grim determination of French soldiers and the ability to move units rapidly from the eastern to the western flank had enabled Joffre to achieve success. By mid-November a long line of entrenchments ran roughly from Nieuport (on the English Channel) south to Noyon (ninety kilometers northeast of Paris), east to Verdun, and then southeast toward Belfort. Both sides now faced the prospect of a static battlefield on which methods for siege warfare were more appropriate than those for mobile warfare.

CHAPTER 3

Siege Warfare

1914–1915

A VISIT TO POINCARÉ on September 29 by the liaison officer from GQG marked the opening of a new phase in the war and the end of Joffre's hopes for continued movement and success. The colonel informed the president that French forces could not continue advancing. Aware of the significant change, Poincaré scribbled in his journal, "we are condemned to wage a long war of siege against the enemy's trenches."[1] Formal notice of the new situation came two days later, when Joffre sent the minister of war a telegram saying that a shortage of 75-mm rounds had forced him to halt his attacks. After the first battle of Ypres ended on November 12, French, British, and Belgian forces faced the Germans across a continuous front extending from the English Channel to Switzerland.

In the new strategic and operational environment, fighting on the Western Front entered a static phase that would last for almost four years and that demanded very different strategy, doctrine, and weapons than the French had anticipated. In his memoirs, Joffre claimed:

> before undertaking new operations, and after an uninterrupted battle of three months, it was necessary to proceed with the constitution of new reserves, the rebuilding of [the numbers of] our person-

The Western Front, 1914

nel, and the provision of munitions. It was equally necessary to develop the special equipment demanded by operations in siege warfare that we, from the first, were obliged to conduct before the mobile war began again.[2]

As Joffre's comment about mobile war beginning "again" suggests, he expected "siege warfare" to continue for a relatively brief period until he transformed the French army and restored mobility to the battlefield. He had no idea that the war would continue for four years after he halted his attacks in early October 1914.

Unfortunately for the soldiers in the trenches, Joffre resumed offensive operations before the "special equipment demanded by operations in siege warfare" became available and long before battlefield conditions favored a return to mobility. In mid-December the French attacked in Artois and Champagne, in mid-February in Champagne, and in late March against the St.-Mihiel salient. As a consequence of Joffre's premature resumption of the offensive and his soldiers' having to fight with inadequate weapons, particularly artillery, 268,000 men lost their lives from October through March. In reality, the French were less prepared for the grinding siege warfare that now began than the war of movement that had just ended.

In this period of transition and transformation France's grand strategy remained closely akin to that of the prewar period, since the strategic advantages arising from the Central Powers' having to fight a multifront war had not changed. By maintaining pressure on three fronts (Anglo-French, Russian, and Serbian), the allies could force—France believed—the Central Powers to spread their forces thinly and prevent them from concentrating overwhelming force against one of the allies. This grand strategy accorded not only with France's desire to concentrate its main efforts on driving the enemy from its soil but also with its prewar emphasis on Russia's placing pressure directly on the Germans and forcing them to divert forces from the west. When the French ambassador in Petrograd talked without authorization to the Russians in late 1914 about possibly making a separate peace with Austria-Hungary, the government acted swiftly to curtail his efforts. Such an initiative, Paris feared, could halt operations by the Russians, convince Italy and Romania not to intervene, and leave France and Great Britain facing Germany alone.[3] In the broadest sense France's grand strategy favored any state capable of placing direct pressure on Germany or Austria-Hungary, but especially Germany, and no state appeared more capable of that than Russia.

As in the prewar period, France's multifront strategy valued Britain's small army and large navy less than Russia's massive army. Britain's contributions early in the war were extremely small, and its willingness and ability to field a large, effective force on the continent uncertain. As the stalemate began, its forces occupied about 65 kilometers on the Western Front while the Belgians occupied 27 and the French 700. As far as the French were concerned, the British increased their contribution to the land campaign far too slowly. Much like the Americans later in the war, organizing, equipping, and training British forces required time, and until they fielded larger numbers and gained greater experience, French leaders did not expect powerful and well-organized offensives from them. Additionally, British actions in the Marne campaign, which at one point had opened a huge hole in allied lines, created strong doubts about not only their effectiveness but also their reliability. Only gradually, as British numbers and capability increased, did the French begin to expect more.

As part of its multifront strategy, France focused its efforts on its own soil. With the Germans occupying a significant portion of France and holding positions only eighty kilometers from Paris, notions of grand operations in distant theaters usually encountered deep-seated skepticism, as well as the hard logistical reality that France's forces were stretched thinly across the long Western Front. As France's political and military leaders confronted the stalemate there, however, suggestions surfaced about finding and exploiting a weak point somewhere in the Central Powers' perimeter. On October 6, 1914, when talking to Poincaré, Franchet d'Espèrey, who had served as an attaché in the Balkans, suggested sending eight divisions to Salonika (now Thessaloniki) and having them advance up the valley of the Vardar River and join with the Serbs. At about the same time, Castelnau, who considered Austria-Hungary the most vulnerable of the Central Powers, also advocated such an operation. He and Gallieni believed a strong expedition to Salonika could encourage Greece, Bulgaria, and Romania to join the allied powers and join an attack along the Danube toward Vienna.

On January 1, 1915, Briand, Poincaré, and Viviani had breakfast together and discussed sending an expedition to Serbia to strike Austria in the rear. The three men considered landing forces on the coast of the Adriatic Sea or at Salonika and then marching to Budapest and Vienna. They were intrigued by the strategic possibilities, and their interest was heightened by Franchet d'Espèrey's ambitious proposal for restoring movement to the war by attacking the enemy from the rear, cutting off the Turks from their allies, and going through Romania to join forces with Russia. Thinking in grand terms, the three political leaders also foresaw the possibility of provoking a revolt among the Slavs and Czechs under Austrian domination and drawing the Italians and Romanians into the war on the allied side.

When Joffre met with Poincaré and the Council of Ministers on January 7, he adamantly opposed operations outside France and objected to the politicians' grand scheme. First, the French did not have sufficient men to send a large force to the Balkans and could not provide leaders, artillery, or logistical support for such a force. Second, sending an army to the Balkans would require pulling units from France, prohibit any future offensives on the Western Front, and give the enemy an opportunity to make a breakthrough there. Third, France was the principal theater of operations, as was evident from Germany's having massed the majority and the best of its forces there. "It is not Austria that we must beat," said Joffre; "it is Germany." Finally, Joffre anticipated significant problems from Greece's neutrality and from inadequate rail lines from Salonika into Serbia. He explained that the Serbs had encountered difficulties trying to supply their army of 100,000 and that supplying a larger army would be even more difficult.[4] Despite Joffre's opposition, Briand brought the proposal to the Council of Ministers, but Millerand repeated Joffre's objections there. At this early point in the war Joffre's arguments easily overcame those of Poincaré, Viviani, and Briand.

As the French paused to make crucial adjustments and rebuild their forces, Joffre dominated not only the formulation of strategy and operations but also the development of doctrine. Even though he had led the French army to disaster in August 1914 with his unsuccessful strategy and mistaken faith in the offensive, his victory at the Marne made him invulnerable to those who wanted him replaced. His powers were particularly strong before the government returned from Bordeaux on December 22 and the Ministry of War resumed its duties in Paris on January 6, 1915, and some critics have maintained that he acted as the dictator of France in subsequent months. While such charges are exaggerated, the new minister of war, Millerand, did write a personal note to Joffre affirming his confidence in him[5] and soon made it clear that he accepted the division of responsibilities established by Messimy. That is, the government fixed the political objectives of the war and provided the "means of action," but as commander-in-chief of the only French front Joffre controlled strategy and operations. The strong-willed general officer bristled at any hint of Millerand's intrusion into strategic and operational matters. In mid-January 1915, after Millerand asked for information about methods being used in attacks, Joffre refused to provide the information and responded, "Any time the government or yourself no longer has complete confidence in what I am doing, I am completely ready to be relieved of the responsibilities you have confided in me."[6] Facing the enormous, unexpected demands of the Great War, the minister of war was overwhelmed with the challenge of providing the "means of action" and hardly had the time—even if he had had the inclination—to wrest control of strategy from Joffre.

Moreover, Joffre's powers over general officers in the army were now greater than in the opening days of the war. As he relieved dozens of generals, he tightened his control over the army. Of the ninety-three divisions mobilized in August 1914, only two commanders were still in command in November 1916. More than half were relieved, replaced, or "made available" for other assignments. One-third received commands of other divisions or were promoted to corps or corps-equivalent commands. One committed suicide, four were killed in action, one died of natural causes, one was captured, and two were placed on convalescent leave. The officers who succeeded these commanders also experienced considerable turbulence. The 12th Division, for example, had its first commander relieved, its second and third promoted to corps command, its fourth sent on convalescent leave, and its fifth killed. By November 1916 it had had six different commanders.[7] Corps commanders had a somewhat better record. Of the twenty officers who commanded corps in August 1914, one-third became army commanders, and one-third took over regions or other units roughly equivalent to a corps but probably a step down from their previous command. Another third became "available" for assignment but without any responsibilities, meaning they probably were relieved.[8] As documents in the French archives clearly demonstrate, however, the initiative for the reliefs came more from army commanders than from Joffre himself.[9] When a senior commander became dissatisfied with a subordinate, he quickly relieved him and just as quickly received Joffre's approval. Though the reliefs of Lanrezac and Ruffey had caused Joffre some personal discomfort, increasing the ranks of the *limogés* became a routine event for him. His senior commanders knew what he expected and moved quickly to reshape the corps of general officers. Only Gallieni had the stature to challenge him, but Joffre had ordered him on September 7 not to communicate with the government except through his headquarters, the GQG. Joffre was now—to use Gallieni's words— "all-powerful."[10]

Facing a front that extended from the English Channel to Switzerland, Joffre streamlined his span of control. Several key changes had occurred during the Marne campaign. At the end of September 1914 General Dubail became responsible for directing operations of the armies on the French right wing, and in early October 1914 General Foch began directing operations of the armies on the left wing. Foch, now bearing the formal title of assistant to the commander-in-chief, coordinated operations on Joffre's left with those of the British and Belgians. In this role, Foch worked closely with the British, a task that proved particularly complicated when the French asked their allies to extend their front. As the French gained more experience, Joffre formally specified the authority of Dubail and Foch on January 5, 1915. Both had responsibility for operations, but Joffre retained responsibility for administration and personnel as well as for strategy. Foch's headquarters referred to itself as Provisional Group of the North while Dubail's headquarters referred to itself as Provisional Group of the East. Nonetheless, both effectively functioned as army-group headquarters, and on June 13 Joffre formally designated them as Northern Army Group and Eastern Army Group respectively. In the same order he created the Central Army Group, but he did not formally "constitute" it until June 23.

While pausing to make crucial adjustments and to rebuild and reorganize his forces, Joffre refused to go on the defensive and halt all attacks. Believing such a strategy to be "absolutely negative," he would not surrender the initiative to the Germans or allow his forces to remain passive.[11] He indicated his preference for what he called "partial" offensives as early as September 17, just as the race to the sea was beginning, when he ordered his army commanders along the already-static portion of the front to "maintain an aggressive attitude" and thereby "prevent the enemy from disengaging and making lateral moves from one part of the front to another."[12] Subsequent messages reminded army commanders of the importance of partial or local offensives. In the middle of October, after recognizing the end of the mobile phase of the war, Joffre ordered his subordinate commanders to demonstrate the "vigor" and "will" of the French to fight. The purpose of this activity was to "maintain the spirit of the offensive among our troops and not let them lapse into inaction under the pretense that the enemy will not attack."[13] In explaining this effort publicly, Joffre said that he was "nibbling" *(grignoter)* at the enemy.

Despite the optimism Joffre conveyed in his messages to the army, he did not anticipate breaking through German lines until after he acquired sufficient heavy artillery and ammunition. As Sir John French reported to London, he hoped to achieve some success with "partial" offensives until the Russians could "finish the business."[14] Although reports of Russian success against the Austrians (despite defeat by the Germans at Tannenberg) engendered optimistic but unrealistic hopes, it soon became clear that the Russians faced enormous difficulties on the Eastern Front. In early December, Grand Duke Nicholas complained of inadequate pressure on the Western front and warned Joffre that if German reinforcements continued to arrive on the Eastern Front, he would give up his "current tactics and adopt the system of entrenchments used on the Franco-Belgian front."[15] To reassure the grand duke, Joffre told him that the French advance had halted only because the Germans had established a "continuous barrier of entrenchments" from the English Channel to the Swiss border. As soon as the French assembled the weapons required to wage "siege warfare," they would, he promised, resume the offensive.[16] Despite this reassurance, Russian doubts about the French failure to advance persisted, especially after intelligence reports confirmed the shift of German units from the Western to the Eastern Front. Meanwhile reports from Petrograd brought disturbing news to Paris about the condition and capability of the Russians. In mid-December the French ambassador, Paléologue, warned Paris that in "two or three months" the Russian army would be incapable of an offensive.[17]

As concerns about Russia mounted, Joffre became frustrated with his inability to communicate directly with Grand Duke Nicholas. In January 1915 he complained loudly about reports from the Russians or the French military attaché in Petrograd having to pass through the French ambassador, Paléologue. He demanded permission from the minister of war to communicate directly with Russian military leaders. Part of Joffre's concern stemmed from the Russians' mistrust of Paléologue; on several occasions the grand duke had expressed reservations about him and refused to deal with him. By early March 1915 Joffre had his own wireless telegraph communications link with the Russian commander, as well as a special cipher, and no longer had to bother with Paléologue. Within days of the establishment of this communication link, detailed reports about the condition and capability of the Russian army arrived from the military attaché and the grand duke.

Meanwhile Joffre's "partial" offensives continued in November and early December, producing thousands of casualties. Most of these attacks were not senseless frontal assaults. In addition to showing support for the Russians, many sought to give some local advantage to the French, usually by the seizure of a piece of key terrain. One example involved an assault by Third Army under General Sarrail against the heights west of Verdun in an attempt to open railway access into that city. The double-track railroad connected Paris, Châlons, Ste.-Menehould, and Verdun and passed through Aubréville, twenty kilometers west of Verdun. The Germans occupied the heights seven kilometers to the north of Aubréville and bombarded any train attempting to pass. Though a single-track railway entered Verdun from the south, the French concluded that the smaller railway could not carry sufficient traffic in the event of a major battle around Verdun. Using artillery and aircraft, Sarrail attempted to neutralize the threat to the railway, but the Germans continued to interdict movement along the track. With no obvious alternatives,

Third Army spent much of the winter of 1914–15 attempting to dislodge the Germans from the heights overlooking Aubréville. In these and other attacks, Third Army suffered almost 10,000 casualties during November.

While attacks such as the one north of Aubréville sought to provide tactical or operational advantages, others did little more than comply with Joffre's directive about maintaining a high level of activity. Second Army under General de Castelnau, which occupied positions north and south of the Somme River west of Péronne, made separate attacks with its XI, IV, and XVI corps. On November 19 two divisions of XI Corps launched an attack to "fix" the enemy. Nine days later XIV Corps attacked with two divisions along another portion of the line. In early December, IV Corps made several attacks. The attack by XI Corps failed completely, the one by XIV Corps gained 300–400 meters, and those by IV Corps gained 300–1,000 meters. As the French official history notes, Second Army had "fixed" the enemy to its front and advanced its front lines to the "immediate proximity of those of the enemy,"[18] but the attacking infantry had paid a high price for only small gains. In these and other local offensives, the French lacked sufficient artillery and machine guns and fought at a significant disadvantage.

As the French army made the painful adjustment to unexpected conditions, nothing was more complicated, or important, than mobilizing the industrial resources of the nation. During the mobile phase of the war, French industry had struggled to meet the army's needs, but France soon faced the more difficult challenge of manufacturing vastly greater amounts of ammunition, weapons, and supplies than previously anticipated.[19] During the initial chaotic months of adjustment, the director of artillery shaped the effort to mobilize France's industrial forces, since his office had responsibility for providing most of the equipment and munitions required by the army.

In the new age of industrial warfare, Germany had significant advantages, including its much larger population of 68,000,000 versus France's 39,000,000. Germany also had a significant advantage in its industrial and natural resources, for France, despite its cosmopolitan flair and its manufacture of luxury items, was much more an agrarian, rural society than Germany. In 1913, for example, France produced 41,000,000 metric tons of coal, while German produced 191,500,000, plus another 87,500,000 tons of lignite. Also, France produced 5,000,000 tons of steel in 1913 while Germany produced 17,000,000. As for railways, France had only 49,500 kilometers of single- and double-track lines while Germany had 61,000. As the economic and industrial requirements of the Great War became evident, so too did the weight of Germany's advantages.

Efforts to increase France's industrial production were hampered by several factors, including the Germans' having occupied the region that contained most of France's natural reserves of iron and coal, as well as much of its industrial capacity. Before being occupied by the enemy the regions in northeast France had provided most of its iron ore, steel, and cast iron. The French High Command paid little attention in its war plans before August 1914 or in its operations during the first months of the war to retaining control over critical resources such as those in the Briey basin, east of Verdun. After the Germans occupied the Briey basin, obtaining vast amounts of iron and steel proved to be one of the most complicated and expensive aspects of the war. France nonetheless was producing 1,710 tons of cast iron and 3,200 tons of steel daily by September 1915. Imports from Britain, the United States, and numerous other countries around the world met many of France's needs, but purchasing materials from other countries required an enormous expenditure of wealth and sapped the long-term economic health of France.

A shortage of workers, many of whom had been conscripted into the army, also hampered production during the first months of the war. Since the French had expected a short war, they had anticipated needing only a small number of workers and consequently had deferred only 50,000 skilled workers, 35,000 of whom worked in governmental arsenals and factories and 15,000 in private industry. When the requirement for skilled workers became apparent, the High Command returned many soldiers to their civilian jobs; by the end of 1915 about 500,000 former soldiers had returned. The number working in factories fell nonetheless from 1,500,000 before the war to 524,000 in December 1914 and did not approach the original number until January 1917. Without women, people from the colonies, and foreigners, the number of workers in January 1917 would have been even smaller. By November 1917 France had 1,663,820 workers, including 410,086 women, manufacturing military materiel.

The most immediate task in October 1914, however, was obtaining additional artillery ammunition. Within a week after the end of the battle of the Marne, the French had fired approximately 700 rounds per artillery piece and had only 695 rounds per piece remaining, including those held in reserve. On September 20, with stocks of 75-mm ammunition sufficient for only five weeks, Joffre wired the minister of war and told him that in order "to continue active operations," the army had to receive some 50,000 rounds per day.[20] The minister quickly responded that it was "impossible" to provide so many artillery rounds, but he hoped 30,000 per day could be provided in three or four weeks.[21] Problems also existed with heavy artillery ammunition. In December the French estimated that they needed production of 2,000 rounds per day but were producing only 300. To conserve ammunition, Joffre ordered his army commanders to choose targets carefully. Thus, "Artillery should never be fired without a well-defined target," and it should be used only "to facilitate the progress of our infantry or to halt enemy attacks."[22] The French quickly learned through bitter experience, however, that saving artillery rounds, as Joffre explained to the minister of war, "costs human lives."[23]

Before the war, French planners had assumed that the conflict would be brief and had anticipated the daily manufacture of 13,600 rounds of 75-mm ammunition within eighty-one days after mobilization. Though the French achieved this level of production within sixty days, such levels hardly met the vast needs of the army. Despite severe restrictions, production of 75-mm rounds gradually increased from 22,000 rounds per day in November, to 33,000 in December, to 42,000 in January.[24] As fighting continued, production requirements grew ever larger. In early January 1915, Joffre demanded production of 60,000 75-mm rounds per day for the French army.[25] Demands from allies complicated the task of providing additional artillery ammunition, for France provided munitions to Serbia, Romania, Belgium, and Russia. On January 4, 1915, the minister of war reported that France had to produce 83,000 rounds of all calibers each day in order to send 2,000 to Serbia, 3,000 to Romania, 1,000–2,000 to Belgium, and 12,000 to Russia. Joffre argued, however, that Romania should not receive any munitions until after it had joined the Entente powers and that Russia should not receive munitions until after the French army began receiving 60,000 rounds a day. Throughout the war the requirement for artillery rounds continued to expand, as did the ability to manufacture them. By August 1, 1916, French factories were producing 210,900 rounds each day, including 153,400 65-mm, 75-mm, 80-mm, and 90-mm, and 57,500 heavy. Production of 75-mm rounds peaked at 245,000 rounds per day in May 1917, but the numbers declined thereafter as the French gave higher priority to the manufacture of heavy artillery.[26]

While increasing the output of artillery rounds, French industry dramatically upped its production of explosive powder. In August 1914 the French produced 40 tons of powder per day, but daily production increased to 55 tons in January 1915, 110 tons in January 1916, 295 tons in January 1917, and 380 tons in October 1917. Though output increased almost tenfold during the first three years of the war, the most difficult increases came early in the war, when the French had to build new plants to manufacture the precious powder.

French industry also faced a substantial challenge in meeting the demand for artillery pieces. When the war began, the army had 4,076 75-mm cannon, consisting mostly of 1897 models with a few 1912 models. There were also 666 75-mm cannon in reserve. The cannon were organized into 1,019 batteries and provided almost all the artillery support to France's divisions and corps. By September 10, combat losses and equipment failures resulted in a shortage of 401 75-mm cannon, and that number rose to 805 by April 16, 1915. The French had not anticipated such losses and by the middle of November 1914 had submitted orders for forty complete batteries of 75-mm cannon. Since they had about 7,500 obsolete or near-obsolete de Bange and Lahitolle pieces in their arsenals or fortified positions, they replaced some of the missing 75-mm guns with these 90-mm and 95-mm guns. According to Joffre, these were "excellent" but had a slow rate of fire. Nevertheless, the French had 4,046 75-mm cannon in February 1916. As a result of combat losses and wearing of tubes, the French had to replace artillery pieces frequently and by the end of the war had manufactured 27,000 75-mm guns.

Additional problems with the 75-mm guns came from metal failure in some of the firing tubes. Given the insufficient number of French long-range cannon and the presence of such cannon among the Germans, artillery commanders often fired their pieces with a maximum charge in the early months of the war to attain the greatest range. According to Joffre, this practice ruined many artillery pieces and consumed great amounts of ammunition "without significant results."[27] The frequent bursting of 75-mm guns intensified the urgency of obtaining long-range cannon.

The French did have some heavy artillery at the beginning of the war and organized them into four artillery regiments. The regiments included 104 155-mm short-range, 84 120-mm short-range, and 120 120-mm long-range pieces. As with the 90-mm and 95-mm guns, the French began removing and fielding the heavier guns from the 7,500 pieces in their arsenals or fortified positions even though they considered them obsolescent. Before the outbreak of the war the French had ordered 36 105-mm guns, and these began entering service in the middle of September. On October 5 Joffre asked the minister of war for long-range 120-mm and 155-mm pieces. Numerous other requests for additional artillery followed, including one that came to be known as the "October 14 program" and that established overall requirements for heavy artillery. The enormity of the problem facing the French is obvious, but Joffre's request in the October 14 program that all artillery rounds be converted to smokeless powder rather than black powder perhaps illustrates it best. By late November the French had assembled sufficient artillery to provide each corps a battalion of heavy long-range pieces varying from 105-mm to 155-mm. They also provided each army group additional heavy artillery that could function as "reserve" artillery. Although the French lacked sufficient heavy artillery this early in the war, they would have almost equal numbers of modern 75-mm (or light) and heavy pieces by July 1918: 5,933 and 5,355, respectively. Manufacturing sufficient heavy artillery, however, proved to be one of the greatest challenges of the war.

French industry had to meet numerous other demands as the army adjusted to trench warfare. Providing machine guns proved especially important. On August 1, 1914, the French had 5,106 machine guns; of these, 2,020 were issued to units and 2,886 to fortified regions. Like the Germans and British, each infantry battalion had only two machine guns in the opening days of the war. Monthly production increased from 54 in

September 1914, to 283 in January 1915, 480 in August, and 1,199 in December. A similar expansion occurred in the manufacture of rifles. Most French soldiers carried the model 1886 M93 Lebel rifle, but the army lost 700,000 rifles in the first eight months. The Ministry of War briefly considered retooling some of the 1,260,000 obsolete Model 1874 rifles in arsenals but soon abandoned this project as impractical. Production of the more modern rifle increased from 20,000 a month in June 1915 to 58,000 in December.

Adding to the complexity of the challenges facing the French, the peculiar requirements of trench warfare forced them to improvise and develop completely new weapons and equipment. In the initial battles, the absence of barbed wire, hand grenades, and trench mortars handicapped the individual soldier in his effort to combat the German soldier on equal terms. The French had nothing similar to the German *Minenwerfer,* a trench mortar capable of firing a six-inch shell 200 meters. Despite crash production, they did not possess 1,000 large-caliber trench mortars until September 1915. In their search for completely new weapons, the French seriously considered mounting machine guns on armored vehicles and using them to restore mobility to the battlefield. On August 25, 1914, Jean Estienne, the "father" of French armor, predicted, "Victory will belong to the one who can first mount a cannon on a vehicle capable of moving in all types of terrain."[28] The French even built and tested small armored carts capable of protecting an infantryman as he knelt behind the bullet-proof shield and crawled toward enemy lines. Almost no idea seemed too outlandish to consider.

Whether in artillery, machine guns, rifles, or a host of other weapons, the French had little choice but to meet the needs of trench warfare. Their main difficulty was not an absence of ideas or an unwillingness to try new approaches but rather the challenge of finding weapons that would work and then manufacturing them. Industrial production had been thoroughly disrupted by the mobilization of workers into the army, the Germans' seizure of the Briey basin and numerous factories, and the lack of prewar preparation for economic and industrial mobilization. Adding to the complexity of the problem, when the Ministry of War moved to Bordeaux, according to Millerand it had only a "small room" in which to work.[29] The slow pace in the fielding of additional equipment, especially artillery and ammunition, soon enraged France's political leaders and engendered especially strong criticisms of General Louis Baquet, the director of artillery and the individual most responsible for providing the equipment and ammunition required by the army. While some of these criticisms may have had merit, the accomplishments of Millerand, Baquet, and others enabled the French to adjust to the unexpected demands of the war and to continue fighting. Given the enormous handicaps under which they worked, their accomplishments are truly remarkable, perhaps miraculous. Unfortunately for the soldiers in the trenches, however, launching wartime industrialization required time, and thousands of them suffered and died when Joffre resumed offensive operations prematurely.

As fighting continued along the front line, the French had to alter their organizations, equipment, and doctrine to meet the conditions of siege warfare. Changes in artillery best illustrate the challenges facing the French. At the beginning of the war, the primary mission of artillery had been to support the infantry during an attack, and the 75-mm gun's mobility, rapid fire, flat trajectory, and range of about seven to nine kilometers made it an ideal weapon for such a mission. Its severe limitations in trench warfare, however, quickly became evident. Its most obvious shortcoming was its short range, for its rounds could hit only the closest enemy positions and could not reach the enemy's second lines or longer-range artillery batteries. Also, because of flat trajectory, 75-mm rounds—even with fins added—could not hit enemy positions on the back side of hills, and the Germans quickly learned to protect themselves by placing their outposts or light defenses on forward slopes or crests and masking their main positions on reverse slopes. When the mobile phase of the war ended in late 1914, the artillery faced the difficult task of shifting its focus completely. It now had to fire preparatory rounds before an attack, destroy enemy positions with massed fires, win the counterbattery battle against enemy artillery (most of which had longer range), and disrupt or halt enemy attacks. Although the arrival of heavier long-range guns helped, these new tasks required a fundamentally different approach to the use of artillery.

The French also worked hard on achieving better coordination between the infantry and the artillery. The High Command quickly concluded, "Every time a strong point is to be taken, the attack must be prepared by artillery. The infantry should be held back and should deliver the assault only from a distance where it is certain that the objective can be reached."[30] In early January 1915 Joffre explained to his subordinate commanders that as a result of the increased effects of firepower and the strength of organized defenses, operations in the future had to be "slower" than those envisaged in the prewar doctrine. If an attack were to succeed, it had to be prepared down to "the smallest detail," and a large number of artillery rounds had to be concentrated on the objective to weaken the enemy and ensure the infantry could advance.[31] Joffre's memorandum clearly established the framework for fighting battles with artillery and infantry working in close coordination. Though rudimentary techniques for moving artillery and infantry enabled the French to provide some coordination between the artillery and infantry, ensuring proper coordination remained one of the most complex challenges of the war.

As the French adjusted their weapons and methods, Joffre maintained tight control over operational and tactical issues. The GQG collected reports from the field, sent out liaison officers to gather information, held meetings of large-unit commanders, and obtained after-action reports. Throughout this period of collecting information, the GQG continued making its own assessments of that information and providing guidance to the field. This centralizing of change and dispatching of instructions from "on high" produced anger and frustration in combat units. Some officers characterized the officers surrounding Joffre as "young Turks" and charged them with "ignoring the difficulties into which they cast combatants and making war on paper."[32] Messimy, the former minister of war, who was now a brigade commander in the trenches, complained bitterly about the lack of combat experience among the officers in Joffre's headquarters. Likening the GQG to an "ivory tower," he insisted that Joffre and his staff knew nothing about what was happening at the front.[33]

Many also complained that higher commanders did not visit the trenches, thereby providing ammunition for future critics of "château generalship." General Émile Fayolle wrote in his diary, "Instead of re-

maining in their offices next to their telephones, if the highest commanders would gather their impressions from the trenches, they would see
more clearly."[34] Notwithstanding such criticisms, commanders such as
Pétain and Fayolle remained in close contact with the men in the trenches
and—with some exceptions—did not command from afar. Four of the
thirteen division commanders who died in the first fifteen months of the
war were killed in action; three others were wounded. Also, in March
1915 a sniper seriously wounded General Michel Maunoury, commander
of Sixth Army, while he was visiting the trenches. Soldiers had particularly high esteem for those officers who led by example and who remained calm under fire, and they frequently repeated stories of officers
such as General Charles Mangin, who brazenly demonstrated contempt
for the Germans and their firepower. Some political leaders recognized
the importance of being seen by frontline soldiers. In his daily journal
and memoirs, Poincaré mentioned numerous visits to units, including
treks through the trenches. At one point he was only 130 meters from the
Germans.[35] Soldiers welcomed the president of the Third Republic,
though they feared his presence might attract enemy fire if the enemy noticed. Another political leader who made an exceptional effort to visit the
trenches and be seen by soldiers was Georges Clemenceau. In his biography of "the Tiger," Jean-Baptiste Duroselle observed that while he was
premier and minister of war in 1917 and 1918 Clemenceau spent about
one-third of his time visiting commanders and encouraging soldiers in
the trenches.[36] Yet the main reason for such visits pertained to leaders'
concern about the morale of their soldiers. While Joffre did pay attention
to questions of morale, he rarely entered the trenches and usually remained close to his headquarters. Even when he visited units, he did not
motivate soldiers with his charisma. After one such visit, Fayolle described him as "heavy, dull voice, mediocre appearance, not worth a
penny as a speaker, no appeal, no military bearing."[37]

Instead of receiving reports by telephone, Joffre preferred to receive
written reports from his subordinates and to send liaison officers to units
to gather information. A clear example of the process by which he gathered information appears in his assessment in early 1915 of French
trenches. His investigation of the state of the trenches began when he
sent several messages to his subordinate commanders ordering them to

complete a detailed study of the trenches in their sectors. The first message, sent on December 27, 1914, reminded French commanders of the "necessity" to organize the "first line of trenches in a manner to make them absolutely inviolable in order to reduce the [number of] personnel placed in the trenches" and to "permit the forming in the rear of important reserves required for future operations."[38] Two subsequent messages placed increased emphasis on the second line and its role in adding depth and halting an enemy breakthrough. After requiring detailed reports from subordinate commanders, the GQG soon received a wealth of information about the location, organization, and condition of trenches in each army's sector.

After the reports arrived, Joffre provided specific instructions to each army commander on what to do about the trenches in his area. In his letter to the Third Army commander, for example, he criticized a particular line for being too close to the crest of a hill.[39] The letter to the Fourth Army commander stated, "I draw your attention to the importance of forming to the rear of your actual second line a series of centers of resistance supported by natural obstacles."[40] Such comments endeared Joffre to no one, but they demonstrate clearly the extraordinarily tight control he maintained over every aspect of the French army. Additional evidence of his attention to detail and his tight control exists today in the numerous GQG staff studies, memoranda, and letters that remain in the archives and bear his personal signature or initials, especially when one compares them to those completed later in the war, when General Philippe Pétain commanded the French army. Whereas Joffre saw and approved almost every piece of correspondence, Pétain saw only the most important ones and left the remainder to his chief of staff.

Joffre also tightly controlled the effort to find a way of breaking through enemy lines. While French and British forces were still trying to maneuver around the enemy's flank, General Franchet d'Espèrey sent Joffre a thoughtful message on October 1 suggesting how to penetrate the enemy's lines. He explained that if strategic maneuver around the enemy's flank failed, it would be necessary to choose a point of attack along the front, concentrate sufficient troops and artillery, especially heavy artillery, and then drive through the enemy's position. D'Espèrey explained, "This procedure will require a preparation of many days for the coordination and accumulation of the means that only you [Joffre] can achieve."[41] Though Joffre approved d'Espèrey's proposal for an offensive, the deteriorating situation on his left compelled him to transfer two divisions from Fifth Army in his center and thereby disrupt d'Espèrey's preparations. As the situation worsened on his left, Joffre ordered d'Espèrey to launch his attack on October 12. When the attacks on October 12–14 failed, d'Espèrey blamed the failure on lack of artillery.[42] Joffre made his own assessment and sent d'Espèrey a caustic letter highlighting the mistakes made by Fifth Army, but the battle clearly revealed the difficulties of making a breakthrough and served as a warning about the material and doctrinal changes that had to be made.

Amidst the search for better methods, Joffre began reconstituting his reserves. He recognized that reserves were essential for future operations—whether offensive or defensive—and for providing troops the opportunity to recover from extended stays in the trenches. Since the French could not be strong everywhere on the Western Front, they had to have reserves that could participate in an offensive or rush to a threatened point. On November 12 Joffre ordered his army commanders to fortify their fronts and create small reserves. He explained that reserves could be created "only by reducing numbers in the first line and by decreasing the density of men on the firing line." He added, "An excessive density in the front line, without any depth, without small reserves in the regiments, presents the greatest danger from the tactical, as well as the hygienic, viewpoint."[43] In mid-November Joffre prescribed the size of reserves, ranging from a brigade to a division, for each of his armies. He ordered First Army, which covered a huge front on his right, to have larger reserves: five infantry brigades and three cavalry divisions. In only a few weeks, Joffre built up his own reserves to two infantry and two territorial divisions. Altogether the French had the equivalent of fifteen divisions in reserve by the end of November. To ensure that the reserves could be transported easily to any point on the front, the High Command placed them near railway centers.

In early November the GQG—under Joffre's tight control—began looking beyond partial offensives and considering possible strategies and operations. The first assessment by the Operations Bureau of the General Staff, which had responsibility for operations, was completed on November 15 but never formally approved. It included a general scheme for forward movement in the unlikely event of a German withdrawal.[44] Joffre obviously did not think the enemy would withdraw voluntarily, but he did think the situation required the French to attack. The Germans had halted their offensive in the west and apparently were moving as many as four to six corps by railway to the Eastern Front. Despite limitations in personnel and supplies, Joffre wanted to assist the Russians and concluded that an offensive would disrupt this shifting of forces and keep some of them on the Western Front.

In late November the Operations Bureau completed an extensive study on the possibility of an offensive. The study acknowledged the futility and cost of "partial" offensives in recent weeks and argued against a general offensive across the entire allied front. Instead, the bureau preferred attacks on several different portions of the front but only after extensive preparation and the "gathering of powerful means of action." The staff had learned from d'Espèrey's attempted breakthrough in mid-October that detailed preparation was essential to success in an offensive against strongly fortified and entrenched positions. After noting the importance of Belgium and analyzing the relative strength of German defenses across the front, the study concluded that an attack should be launched in Artois by the right wing of Tenth Army in the direction of Cambrai. The study also emphasized that a supporting attack could be launched in Champagne by Third and Fourth armies in the direction of Mézières. With attacks in Artois and in Champagne, the French would strike both shoulders of the huge salient in German lines (known as the Noyon salient) that protruded toward Paris. In the opinion of the Operations Bureau, however, the French lacked sufficient personnel and munitions to make both attacks simultaneously. A strong attack in Artois by Tenth Army, the bureau argued in late November, had the best chance of "breaking" the German position and forcing the enemy to pull his center back to the Meuse River.[45]

A week later, however, the Operations Bureau favored an attack in Champagne and published a detailed assessment of its "strategic consequences." The new assessment differed from the November study primarily in its emphasis on railways and lines of communication. Unfortunately for the French, the Germans could use the French and Belgian railway systems to move troops and materiel across the entire front, as well as from Germany through the Meuse-Sambre (Liège, Namur, Aulnoye), Moselle, and Rhine valleys. The Operations Bureau recognized that by driving to Mézières, the French could interdict the railways used by the Germans and sharply curtail their transportation of troops and equipment.[46]

Two days later the Operations Bureau, again changing its mind, favored two attacks: one in Artois and one in Champagne or near Verdun. A memo to Joffre explained, "Enemy forces within the salient pointing toward Paris will find themselves squeezed between the two jaws of a vise." The surprising aspect of this assessment is that it rested upon the assumption that France had sufficient resources to launch two major attacks. The only acknowledgment of insufficient resources came in the officers' comparison of an attack from Verdun or Champagne against the southern face of the salient. Attacking in Champagne, they argued, required the movement of fewer forces into the attack zone and offered less exposure to an enemy riposte against its flank.[47]

Although adequate weaponry and sufficient munitions had not yet arrived, Joffre had preparations for an offensive well under way by late November. In early December he told his subordinate commanders that the "moment" had arrived to resume the offensive. He also told Poincaré and Millerand that he would launch a series of small offensives but cautioned them that since "weapons of siege warfare" were "not yet ready," they should not expect "very great results." He could not, he explained, leave the Germans free to shift forces toward Russia.[48]

Joffre's offensive involved two "principal" attacks, one in Artois by Tenth Army and another in Champagne by Fourth Army. Tenth Army would drive from Arras toward Cambrai, and Fourth Army would drive from Suippes toward Rethel and then Mézières. Several supporting attacks would be made. Eighth Army (and the British if they participated) would attack south of Ypres, Second Army north of Péronne, Third Army between the Argonne Forest and the Meuse River, and First Army east of the St.-Mihiel salient. Joffre made the operational goal of the attacks clear in a message to Grand Duke Nicholas: "The objective of these actions is twofold: (1) hold the enemy in front of us in order to facilitate the general action of allied forces; (2) make a breach in one or more points on the front, then exploit this success with reserve troops by taking the enemy in the rear and forcing him to retreat."[49] He offered a grander goal in his formal order: "The moment has come to resume the offensive that will drive the enemy toward the northeast and prepare a subsequent action by us against his communications." A message to French soldiers added, "The hour of attack has sounded; after having contained the attack of the Germans, it is necessary now to smash them and liberate completely the occupied national territory."[50]

Despite the flowery language in the memoranda and high expectations in the trenches, Joffre and his staff knew that France did not have sufficient resources for two simultaneous attacks and that strategic requirements had overruled tactical considerations. He acknowledged the paucity of materiel in his message to the grand duke. If the attack did not succeed, he said, the failure would stem from its being launched "with still insufficient means." Evidence of inadequate equipment and supplies was apparent in numerous areas, including a message from 77th Division, the unit that would lead XXXIII Corps and Tenth Army in the attack toward Cambrai. Three days before the attack began, the division indicated it had only fifteen wire cutters but needed more than a hundred. General Fayolle, commander of a division that would participate in the Artois offensive, wrote in his diary: "This project appears stupid, insane to me. . . . Failure will not result in any catastrophe, since we will have our line of trenches from which the enemy will not chase us. But it will result in a terrible consumption of men without any gain."[51]

In Artois, Tenth Army's immediate objective was Vimy Ridge, just north of Arras. This was a long ridge that began near the small village of Souchez, ran southeast across hills 119 and 140, and extended to a point northeast of Arras. On the east side of the ridge the villages of Givenchy, Vimy, and Farbus sat on the edge of a large plain that extended twenty kilometers east to Douai, an important railway and road center. By seizing the heights overlooking these villages, the French could dominate the plain to the east and force the enemy to withdraw, perhaps beyond Douai. From left to right Tenth Army had XXI, XXXIII, and X corps. The main attack by XXXIII Corps, commanded by General Philippe

Pétain, would try to break through south of Souchez and seize the high ground dominating the village of Vimy. To its north in a supporting attack, XXI Corps would attack through Souchez and advance toward the heights overlooking Givenchy. A dozen kilometers to the south, X Corps would make another supporting attack, moving northeast out of Arras with the mission of protecting the right flank of XXXIII Corps against enemy counterattacks. All the artillery of Tenth Army would support the operation; by December 25 the army would have 632 artillery pieces, including 110 heavy guns. Though this amount of artillery seemed sufficient to France's military leaders, it was in fact woefully inadequate. To place the number in perspective, Tenth Army would make another attack on Vimy Ridge six months later with 1,160 artillery pieces, including 355 heavy.

A great deal of effort went into preparations for the December attack on Vimy Ridge. Prior to beginning the assault, the French pushed their trenches forward, using techniques common for centuries in siege warfare. On November 30 Joffre had ordered all his army commanders to advance their trenches to within 150 meters of the enemy to give attacking infantrymen a better chance of success as they charged across open ground toward the enemy's trenches. To deceive the Germans about the location of the main attack, he wanted digging to occur across the front wherever an offensive appeared possible. Shortly before the offensive began, Foch, who had responsibility for the overall attack in the north, became concerned that Tenth Army wanted to move too quickly, so he met with its commander, General de Maud'huy, and emphasized the importance of careful and thorough preparation. He described the upcoming battle as taking on the "character of a siege with its method and its slowness."[52] Maud'huy, who had already divided the attack into successive phases over several days, slowed the planned pace of the attack to ensure the best possible support for the assaulting infantry. Foch assured Joffre that the operation would not cost the lives of many soldiers but would consume large amounts of ammunition.

Despite the careful preparation and conduct of the battle, the attack on December 17 accomplished little at relatively high cost. Artillery fires proved insufficient, and rain turned the battlefield into a morass. XXI Corps made only small gains and seized less than a kilometer of the first

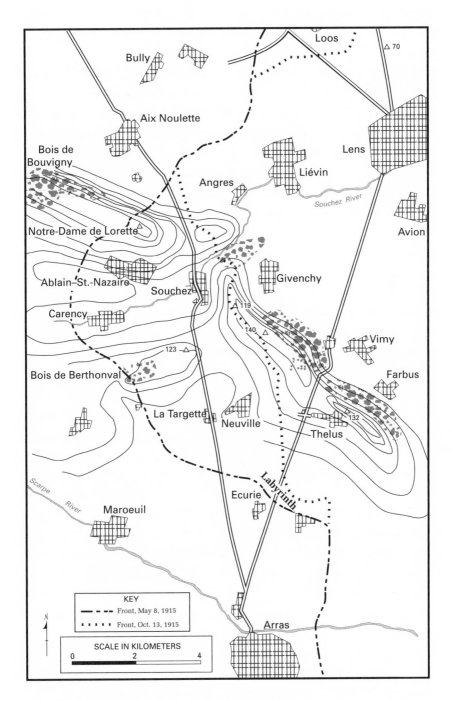

Artois, 1915

enemy trench immediately to its front. To the south X Corps made slight gains in its attack near Arras. To provide the strongest possible support, Maud'huy delayed the attack of Pétain's XXXIII Corps in the center until the following day, but the assault gained little. After failing to make progress on a broad front, XXXIII Corps concentrated its attacks on the small village of Carency, southwest of Souchez. Little progress was made until December 27, when XXXIII Corps managed to grab about 700 meters of enemy trenches but then lost most of its gains to enemy counterattacks. Continued bad weather delayed Tenth Army's preparations to renew the attack, and on January 5, 1915, Joffre notified Foch of his intention to shift fifteen infantry battalions out of Tenth Army to the Vosges Mountains. Along with the bad weather, this shift effectively ended the offensive north of Arras, and the High Command formally "suspended" it on January 13.

In Champagne Fourth Army performed only slightly better. Before formally issuing his attack order, Joffre had informed the Fourth Army commander, General de Langle de Cary, of the impending attack in Champagne. A very experienced officer who had been wounded in the Franco-Prussian War, de Langle issued his attack order on December 7. His order stated: "The purpose of the operation is to make a breach in the enemy line."[53] To make a breach forty kilometers east of Reims between Aubérive and Massiges, the Fourth Army had 258,000 soldiers and faced, it believed, between 153,000–168,000 enemy. From left to right, de Langle had the XII, XVII, I Colonial, and II corps. He expected the two corps on the left to make the main attack while I Colonial Corps made a supporting attack and II Corps remained on the defensive. I Corps acted as Fourth Army's reserve. The attack would concentrate along a front of twelve kilometers, with one assault being launched on the right of XII Corps and another on the left of XVII Corps. According to Fourth Army's staff, having two assaults would double the chances of success, permit both corps headquarters to control a separate action, and enable the army's reserve to move in support of either thrust. The attacking units had sufficient troops to provide several successive efforts. If an assault failed, fresh troops could enter the fight and launch additional assaults prior to the commitment of the army's reserve. In essence, by feed-

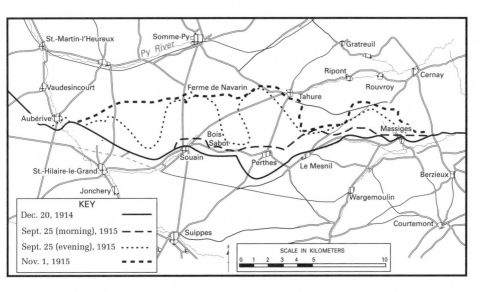

Champagne, 1915

ing new troops into the fight in what would become known as a "continuous battle," French commanders hoped to maintain the momentum of the attack.

For artillery support, the army had 488 75-mm, 144 90-mm, 16 65-mm, 14 80-mm, 30 long-range 120-mm, and 50 short-range 155-mm pieces. In comparison to what had been available six months earlier, this was a massive amount of artillery, and it more than doubled the artillery the British later concentrated at Neuve-Chapelle in March 1915. Fourth Army also seemed to have sufficient munitions for the attack, including 360 rounds for each 75-mm gun. On December 9 de Langle sent a letter to Joffre expressing his intent to use rifle and machine-gun fire, as well as 75-mm rounds, to make breaches in the enemy's barbed wire, and voicing no concern about inadequate preparation or support. Although the Fourth Army had ample artillery support by the standards of the day, events would prove that even greater amounts of artillery were necessary, particularly to cut enemy wire in front of attacking infantry.

As for the tactical conduct of the attack, the commander of XII Corps described what he wanted his units to do:

the attack will take the form of an assault preceded by eight batteries firing for an hour on the enemy barbed wire to create numerous passages. The breach fire of the batteries will commence at 0830 and will be suspended three minutes at 0900 hours and at 0915. Once the fire on the entanglements terminates, the breach batteries will increase their range 100 meters and then will fire 16 rounds from each piece toward the German trenches.

The fire will be conducted in a fashion so that the last burst should strike the trenches and terminate at exactly 0930.

Following this fire and exactly at 0930 hours, the first line of infantry will make the assault. In each battalion, the reinforcements and the reserves will begin moving at the same time as the first line, following them closely, and will complete their success.

The platoons in the first line will be provided destruction equipment and will be accompanied by sappers furnished with hand grenades. The last elements of the attacking troops will be amply provided with digging tools, defensive materials . . . and flares to enable them to proceed without delay in organizing the captured trenches and repelling a counterattack.[54]

Fourth Army divided its attack into phases so that XVII and I Colonial corps made their assaults on the first day and XII Corps on the second day. When the offensive began on December 20, XVII Corps made small gains, as did I Colonial Corps. The following day, XII Corps could not advance because flanking machine-gun fire covered most of the breaches in the enemy's wire. De Langle halted infantry assaults in XII Corps and had the soldiers conduct mining operations and fire artillery at known enemy positions. Following several days of minor gains, de Langle shifted the principal effort of his attack to his center in the vicinity of Perthes and inserted an infantry division from I Corps between XVII and I Colonial corps. On December 27 Joffre moved IV Corps to the vicinity of Fourth Army but kept it under his own control. This move permitted de Langle to insert another division from I Corps into the front line and thus the remainder of the corps into the battle. Having IV Corps nearby also permitted Fourth Army to begin a new series of attacks. In essence, both de

Langle and Joffre fed more troops into the battle in order to maintain pressure against the Germans.

On December 30, however, just as Fourth Army began its new attacks, the Germans launched a strong attack against II Corps on de Langle's right, captured three lines of trenches, and inflicted heavy losses on the defenders. The next day II Corps managed to recapture most of the lost terrain, but on that same day the enemy launched four major counterattacks across the front of Fourth Army. When the French attack threatened to degenerate into a series of small infantry assaults, de Langle forcefully reminded his subordinate commanders of the importance of artillery, and in subsequent days the French relied strongly on artillery to maintain pressure on the enemy. On the night of January 7–8 a German counterattack drove the French out of a salient just west of the village of Perthes in the center of the primary French objective, but a counterattack recaptured the trench and then flushed the Germans out of Perthes. Though the gain measured only a few hundred meters, it was one of the largest gains of the campaign. For the next two weeks the French kept pressing forward, occasionally repelling an enemy counterattack. They made few gains, and on January 13 active operations by Fourth Army ceased.

At the termination of the offensive, de Langle sent Joffre a letter analyzing the campaign. De Langle said his operation had adhered to the "principle" that his army should not launch a "general offensive" with masses of soldiers but instead should launch "an ensemble of prepared attacks against judiciously chosen points." He emphasized that once initial objectives were taken, it was necessary to repeat preparations for another attack, including digging approach trenches and methodically destroying enemy positions with artillery fire.[55] In essence, de Langle acknowledged the difficulties of achieving a breakthrough with "continuous" attacks and the advantages of making small gains and seizing key terrain with methodical, successive attacks, a technique whose value would only slowly become apparent to Joffre and his staff.

In Joffre's response to de Langle's note the French commander-in-chief said he had no objection to the methods used by de Langle. He curtly added that the failure of the attack came from two causes: "insufficient and too brief artillery support; too few personnel engaged on fronts that were too narrow."[56] His comment about inadequate artillery support agreed with those of the veterans of the front lines, but his comment about "too few" personnel on "too narrow" fronts came from his belief that even though the attack occurred over a front of twelve kilometers, the actual attacks often had a front of only a few hundred meters. Such attacks, Joffre believed, were particularly vulnerable to concentrated artillery fire. On the day he wrote de Langle, he also sent a letter to all his army commanders and cited the broader fronts of German attacks as evidence of a need to have greater breadth in French attacks. In closing his letter to de Langle, he ordered him to renew the attack as quickly as possible and said, "It is only by the shock of incessantly repeated blows against the enemy that you will be able to obtain the success that one has the right to expect of an army as powerful as Fourth Army."[57] Joffre admitted to Poincaré, however, "We must resign ourselves to accept a war of movement as impossible for a long time."[58]

The supporting attacks that occurred at the same time as the offensives in Artois and Champagne also yielded little. Most of the attacks sought to fix the enemy, prevent him from shifting forces laterally, and confuse him about the location of the main attack. Second and Eighth armies, as well as the Nieuport Group along the coast, supported Tenth Army's offensive, while First and Third armies, as well as the Army Detachment of the Vosges, supported Fourth Army's. Most of the supporting attacks had far less artillery than those in Artois and Champagne. In Second Army, XI Corps's attack on December 27 occurred without artillery preparation, and in the Vosges artillery did not open fire until two divisions advanced toward the enemy. Casualties were high even among Fifth and Sixth armies, which had defensive missions.

German attacks also created problems for the French. In mid-January the Germans struck north of Soissons, near the tip of the Noyon salient. Though a major attack could have threatened Paris, the Germans, who were beginning to look toward the Eastern Front, did not commit sufficient soldiers and resources to make significant gains. In the end the French held at Soissons, and as far as they were concerned, their successful defense had supported the offensives by Tenth and Fourth armies on the shoulders of the Noyon salient. In late January the Germans struck Third Army, which was clinging to part of the heights overlooking

Aubréville and the railway running into Verdun. After being driven back, the French counterattacked six times, losing 2,400 men, but failed to retake the position. General Sarrail, Third Army commander, complained that the Germans had gained "moral superiority" and said that the French could regain it only by attacking in the Argonne.[59] Though Joffre obviously wanted to control the heights overlooking Aubréville and the railway into Verdun, he had no desire to launch a large attack into the Argonne Forest and continued to focus on the shoulders of the Noyon salient.

Before ending the winter offensives of Tenth Army in Artois and Fourth Army in Champagne on January 13, Joffre initiated preparations for his next offensive. Some of the most important steps in this preparation concerned efforts to obtain more assistance from the British. Not surprisingly, the British had their own ideas about the conduct of the land campaign and their role in it. Evidence of their independent thinking appeared on December 9, when the British ambassador gave the French minister of war a memorandum formally proposing that British troops be shifted to the coast, on the allied extreme left, so that they could operate more closely with the Royal Navy. Such a move would permit the British to launch an offensive along the coast, free Ostend and Zeebrugge, and disrupt enemy torpedo-boat and submarine attacks against the fleet in the English Channel. Joffre had strong reservations, however, about the wisdom of putting the British on the coast.[60] Although he considered such a drive "interesting," he believed it was "secondary" and contributed little to the main French effort, which consisted of attacks in Artois and Champagne and sought to "render the enemy's line of retreat increasingly precarious." He told Sir John, "a movement up the coast, after meeting successive lines of enemy entrenchments, finishes only opposite Antwerp, which we have no intention of attacking."[61] Such a move would also distract the British from cooperating with the French and disrupt preparations for the coming offensive. Consequently, Foch treated the entire idea, said Sir Henry Wilson, with the "greatest contempt."[62] Additionally, Joffre had doubts about British motives, particularly with regard to their plans to move into Belgium. In a March letter to the minister of war he emphasized the importance of keeping French forces on the northern portion of the front in order to "conserve our influence in Belgium upon the conclusion of peace."[63]

From the earliest moments of the Artois campaign, the French had reservations about the British, even though they greatly appreciated their contributions to the war effort. Even Foch, who had especially good relations with the British and praised their courage, had complaints. "They seem to confuse war with a great sport," he told Poincaré, "and thus imagine that one is free to choose the hours of rest and the hours of combat."[64] Joffre's reservations about the British came from the significant problems he had had with them in the first weeks of the war. As the conflict wore on, he became even more frustrated, and in late October he suggested that Sir John be replaced by General Wilson.[65] Despite Joffre's discontent with Sir John, he preferred him to all other British officers except Wilson. On November 1 he defended the British field marshal when Lord Kitchener came to France to relieve him and replace him with General Sir Ian Hamilton. The British had performed well in the first battle of Ypres, Joffre explained, and Foch had developed a reasonably positive relationship with the field marshal.[66] Moreover, Joffre may have had reservations about Hamilton, who later came under sharp criticism from the French commander in the Dardanelles. He apparently concluded that unless Wilson became the B.E.F. commander, Sir John French offered the best chance of cooperation from the usually "slow and late" British.

Clearly, Joffre wanted the British under his direction, if not his command, and he wanted their operations to support the strategy he had devised. Since he had doubts about their offensive capability, however, his priority was getting them to occupy as much of the front line as possible and thereby free French troops for his reserves or for offensive operations. Even if poorly trained, the British reinforcements could occupy more of the front. In late December he decided that the British should retain responsibility for their existing front from La Bassée to the Lys River but should gradually stretch their front toward the north as reinforcements arrived on the continent. The proposed extension soon came to include having the British take over responsibility from the French Eighth Army for the Ypres salient. Extending the British front, Joffre believed, could take advantage of their "aptitude" for the defense and free at least two French corps for use elsewhere. As he planned a two-pronged offensive against the shoulders of the Noyon salient, he also wanted Field Marshal French to support Tenth Army's attack in Artois by making an attack north of the Lys River, perhaps in the Messines area. Yet he never expected the British to play more than a secondary role in the offensive. Despite Joffre's efforts, the British showed little willingness to occupy more of the front, and on January 15 he wrote to Foch telling him to delay Tenth Army's attack. A postponement, he explained, was necessary "above all" because the slow relief of French troops by newly arrived British troops had derailed the creation of new reserves required for an attack.[67]

A few days later Sir John informed the French liaison officer at his headquarters of his willingness to support a French offensive with an operation of his own. To halt attacks on the British fleet by German torpedo boats and submarines, London preferred an offensive along the coast toward Ostend and Zeebrugge, but such an operation could not be conducted until the arrival of at least two or three additional British corps and a large supply of ammunition. Hence, Sir John was interested in a combined offensive, with his forces attacking near La Bassée (and ultimately Neuve-Chapelle) and the French Tenth Army attacking near Vimy Ridge. Though pleased with Sir John's willingness to attack near La Bassée, Joffre still wanted the British to relieve French units around Ypres as quickly as possible. Writing to Sir John on January 19, he said, "to defeat the enemy, it is necessary for us to have reserves. These reserves, because of the extended front held by French troops, can be drawn only from the Ypres region and can be made available only by the arrival of British reinforcements."[68] Not until January 21 did Sir John formally agree to take over the Ypres salient completely and relieve IX and XX corps on the north face of the salient. In the negotiations, Joffre also agreed that French units would relieve a corps on the British right, thereby shifting the entire British line toward the north.

By the first week of February, however, Joffre's agreement with Sir John French had unraveled, primarily because of differences in France's and Britain's strategic thinking. While Joffre believed the war could be won only through victory on the Western and Eastern fronts, Kitchener had increasing reservations about prospects for victory in France and

preferred striking the Central Powers somewhere in the eastern Mediterranean. The sending of forces to the Dardanelles (discussed in a later
chapter) had slowed the arrival of British troops in France and had delayed the relief of IX and XX corps. Moreover, the arrival of additional
units in France resulted in only small increases in the British front line.
Joffre noted with dismay the British tendency to mass large forces behind
their trenches and their reluctance to consider a large offensive. With intelligence reports suggesting that the Germans were turning toward Russia in early 1915, he became more insistent about pressuring the Germans
on the Western Front. He explained to Sir John French, "it is important
to . . . take the offensive in our theater of operations, less to profit from
our numerical superiority than to hold the maximum [number] of enemy
forces before us." Joffre urged Sir John to attack north and south of the
Lys River, making one push on the British left south of Ypres and another
on their right near La Bassée.[69] Sir John also favored action in France
rather than in the eastern Mediterranean, and he responded quickly, explaining his preparations for an attack in early March near La Bassée. He
insisted, however, that if the British diverted forces to relieve IX and XX
corps, the attack could not occur before early April. In short, he was not
prepared to relieve the French corps at Ypres immediately.

Joffre's letter in response hardly concealed his anger. Once again he insisted that the relief of IX and XX corps in the Ypres salient was "absolutely indispensable to the success of our common operations" and that
IX Corps had to leave the Ypres salient and join Tenth Army for its attack. To demonstrate that the British had enough personnel and units to
assume responsibility for more frontage, he said that the British were
holding a front of 50 kilometers with the equivalent of twelve divisions
while the Tenth Army was holding a front of the same length with only
eight divisions. He added that the density of British forces was double
that of the French, for while the French had seven times as many personnel in the theater of operations as the British, they held a front fourteen
times longer, some 700 kilometers.

Despite the condescending tone of Joffre's letter, Field Marshal
French responded politely. He reminded the French commander that the
relief of IX and XX corps at Ypres could not occur until the arrival of reinforcements from Britain. He also objected to Joffre's comparison of the

density of French and British forces: "The number of troops necessary to hold a front depends not only on its length but also on the nature of the terrain, the size and condition of the enemy, the quality of available artillery munitions, and several other factors." Having to establish and operate a long line of communications also consumed numerous personnel. Sir John concluded by saying that the British expected to participate in the combined offensive with Tenth Army and launch their offensive at Neuve-Chapelle around March 7.[70]

Seeing no chance to change French's mind, Joffre asked the minister of war to appeal directly to Lord Kitchener. He suggested that the minister emphasize that French reserves, "far from being idle," were preparing for an "energetic offensive" in Champagne which would relieve enemy pressure on other parts of the front. He also said that a combined offensive with Tenth Army and the British could not be launched unless IX Corps was relieved by the British and made available to Tenth Army.[71] Despite increased political pressure, London showed no willingness to bend to Joffre's demands or to acquiesce to his strategic concept. As Winston Churchill had suggested in a meeting of London's War Council, the British refused to let the French have the "last word" on the employment of their forces.[72] Adding to Joffre's difficulties, Lord Kitchener had grave doubts about the wisdom of large offensives on the continent and had concluded that the war could last three more years and end only through attrition. Additional reservations appeared in a secret memorandum Kitchener wrote on March 16, 1915:

> It must not be forgotten that, after the conclusion of peace, old enmities and jealousies which have been stilled by the existing crisis in Europe, may revive. We have, in fact, to assume that, at some future date, we may find ourselves at enmity with Russia, or with France, or with both in combination, and we must bear this possibility in mind in deciding how, when the time for settlement comes and the question of the partition of Turkey in Asia arises, our interests can best be safeguarded.[73]

Thus, Britain would pursue its own interests and not follow Joffre's lead blindly.

Seeing no prospect that the British would relieve IX Corps, Joffre decided that Tenth Army would not attack in Artois. He wrote Field Marshal French on March 7 and informed him of his decision in a more conciliatory tone: "Since the beginning of the campaign, the British army has provided valuable collaboration to the French armies. Our complete accord is the guarantee of victory; only our adversaries can wish anything else." He then noted that the continued arrival of reinforcements had permitted the British to constitute "numerous reserves," and he encouraged Sir John to launch the planned offensive near La Bassée.[74] The next day he told Foch to cancel Tenth Army's attack and ordered him to assist the British attack (which would hit Neuve-Chapelle on March 10) by providing support with heavy artillery and covering its right flank. By delaying Tenth Army's attack on January 15 and then canceling it on March 7, Joffre had limited the French offensive to a single large attack in Champagne, rather than one in Champagne and another in Artois.

Preparations for the offensive in Champagne had proceeded while Joffre worked to obtain additional assistance from the British for the offensive in Artois. The High Command had issued the order formally on January 19 for Fourth Army's offensive in Champagne. Supporting attacks would come from the Nieuport Group along the coast, Third Army near Verdun, First Army near the St.-Mihiel salient, and the Army Detachment of the Vosges in its region. Notwithstanding the extended discussions with the British, reserves were surprisingly large, totaling twenty-one divisions, including seven cavalry divisions, and were expected to rise to twenty-six and a half divisions, including eight cavalry divisions. Joffre expected these reserves to parry a large German attack or to exploit the results obtained by the offensive.

On the eve of its attack, General de Langle's Fourth Army had 155,000 infantry, 8,000 cavalry, and 879 artillery pieces, 110 of which were heavy. From left to right, Fourth Army had XII, XVII, I, I Colonial, and II corps. De Langle ordered XVII and I corps to concentrate their attacks along a front of about five kilometers, centering on Perthes, and to seize an objective about 1,500 meters beyond their front lines. After they reached this objective, he expected them to turn right and left, attack the still-intact German defenses from the rear, and thereby enlarge the breach. He saw the need for a "series of successive efforts" and expected IV Corps

(Fourth Army's reserve) to move deep into the enemy's position when the breach opened.[75] The successive efforts would come primarily from waves of infantry, not from carefully choreographed movements of infantry and artillery that would later characterize such battles.

Although de Langle's attack should have begun on February 12, a snowstorm severely limited visibility and therefore the control of artillery, so he delayed the attack until February 16. The deepest advance on the sixteenth was no more than 500 meters, but XVII and I corps managed to capture several hundred meters of enemy frontline trenches along the five-kilometer front of the attack. Though the French continued attacking the following day, they captured less terrain. Over the next several days the battle became a fight for position, with the Germans launching, according to Joffre, twenty-five counterattacks. After neither XVII nor I Corps made appreciable gains, de Langle asked Joffre for reinforcements so that he could avoid "partial attacks" and instead make "one very powerful attack."[76] The Fourth Army commander told the High Command, "A vigorous attack, executed with fresh troops, may yield important results."[77] Joffre refused to release the entire IV Corps, but he eventually released a division and allowed de Langle to move a brigade from II Corps on his right and a regiment from I Colonial Corps, also on his right. When Joffre learned that it might take as many as three or four days for the new units to enter the battle, he sent de Langle a sharp rebuke, reminding him of the importance of acting "as rapidly and as energetically as possible."[78] Since the enemy could build new defensive positions faster than the French could fight through them, he feared a slow, step-by-step attack would never pierce enemy lines. He also reminded de Langle of the strategic importance of a "rapid and energetic action." Such an action was essential, Joffre believed, because the Germans would reduce their forces on the Western Front to the minimum and concentrate on the Eastern Front if they concluded that the French could not penetrate their defensive positions.[79]

As the number of units engaged in the bitter fighting increased, de Langle divided the narrow front into two parts. On his left were XVII Corps and part of IV Corps, and on his right I Corps and part of II Corps. Fourth Army eventually named the two portions of the front Sector 17-4 and Sector 2-1. Counting I Colonial Corps, de Langle had five corps involved in the fighting, and to provide better control, he gave the commander of XVII Corps command of Sector 17-4, and the commander of II Corps Sector 2-1. To add energy to Fourth Army's attack, Joffre made XVI Corps available to de Langle. On February 26 he approved de Langle's proposal to launch a surprise attack between Souain and Aubérive, some ten kilometers west of Perthes. The commander of this operation, General Paul-François Grossetti of XVI Corps, could attack only on Joffre's order. Grossetti's mission was to "break through" the enemy's line and then to advance north toward Ferme de Navarin.[80] De Langle expected the new attack to occur on March 3 or 4.

As fighting continued and Fourth Army made slow and bloody progress on both sides of Perthes, Joffre canceled Grossetti's attack farther west in order to reinforce this success. In his memoirs de Langle complained about this decision because he believed the attack could have achieved surprise. He had ordered Grossetti to dispense with the normal preparatory works, particularly the digging of approach trenches, and have the artillery move forward secretly at night.[81] With the surprise attack abandoned, the battle devolved into bloody assaults against specific pieces of terrain in an attempt to move forward step by step on the narrow front. As days passed and the fighting continued, de Langle reminded his corps commanders of the importance of continuing the offensive in a vigorous fashion once it had begun. He also reminded them that when a unit advanced and seized terrain, it would sustain fewer casualties by resolutely holding that terrain instead of fleeing back to its starting point.[82] To explain this, he used the locution *fuite en avant* (flee forward), a phrase used by Ardant du Picq that had provided much of the philosophical underpinning for the *offensive à outrance*.[83]

Believing that Fourth Army was on the verge of a breakthrough, Joffre told de Langle that the moment had arrived for a "brutal" attack. On March 8 he directed that XVI Corps's attack be different from the "succession of efforts" in previous attacks. Reinforced by 48th Division, XVI Corps would concentrate as many soldiers as it could along its front and make assaults as long as it could sustain them with fresh infantry.[84] In essence, Joffre wanted de Langle to end step-by-step efforts and maintain continuous pressure. On the evening of March 11, Grossetti assumed command of Sector 2-1 and directed that every "fresh" soldier entering the line participate in the attack. He wanted no soldiers left behind to occupy the trenches. He also ordered that every piece of terrain "seized" in the attack be consolidated "immediately" and used as a base for a new attack.[85]

On the following day attacks by XVI Corps, as well as other corps in Fourth Army, began. At the end of that day an observer from Joffre's headquarters reported that XVII Corps had made more progress than XVI Corps. Though the assaults continued, XVI Corps made little progress. On March 14 Grossetti reported to de Langle that his corps had made a small "crack" in enemy lines but that attempts to enlarge the crack had met intense flanking fire.[86] De Langle changed the direction of the attacks slightly and ordered them continued. After XVI Corps failed to make progress and sustained additional casualties, Joffre finally stopped the offensive. He told de Langle on March 16 to continue XVI Corps's attack with the remaining fresh troops and then to cease attacking. He also ordered de Langle to organize a strong defensive position and to pull all corps but three out of the front line. By March 20, Fourth Army's offensive had ended.

The massive offensive on a narrow front had failed to make a breakthrough and had advanced French lines, according to de Langle, an average depth of a kilometer across a front of about three kilometers. Fourth Army paid a high price—43,000 casualties between February 16 and March 20—for those three square kilometers of terrain. In a note to de Langle, Joffre expressed admiration for the "offensive capacity, warrior spirit, spirit of sacrifice, and devotion to country" of Fourth Army's soldiers.[87] In his postwar memoirs de Langle said, "Nearly forgotten today after the famous four years of gigantic battles which followed it, the first offensive in Champagne nevertheless marked an important phase in the history of the war."[88] The attack had demonstrated clearly that "rapid and energetic action" was no substitute for improved doctrine and weapons, especially artillery.

Prior to the Champagne offensive in mid-February, the French had started preparing a new offensive, an offensive that was probably the most poorly conducted operation by the French in the war. On February

12 the headquarters of the Provisional Group of the East had completed an analysis of possible operations on the two faces of the St.-Mihiel salient. In brief, the analysis called for attacks on the extremities of the bulge at St.-Mihiel. While one assault struck the eastern end of the southern face, just west of the Moselle River, another would strike the northern end of the salient's western face, east of Verdun. In mid-March, before ending the Champagne offensive, Joffre ordered General Dubail, commander of the Provisional Group of the East, to begin preparations for an offensive against the St.-Mihiel salient. He also ordered Dubail to precede this offensive with an attack against Vauquois (on the heights overlooking Aubréville and the railway into Verdun) and another attack in the Vosges. The attack against Vauquois was particularly important because of the need to protect lines of communication for the forces attacking the western face of the St.-Mihiel salient. The aim of the offensive was to "maintain the morale of the country and retain the initiative in operations." Seeing the coming battle as a partial rather than general offensive, Joffre hoped to surprise the Germans. On March 24 he informed Dubail that he would be reinforced with I, II, and XII corps, each of which had played a key role in the recent Champagne offensive; he also promised to send Dubail a cavalry corps. Two days later he canceled the operation in the Vosges because of insufficient resources.

The ill-fated attack against the St.-Mihiel salient began on March 30 with 73rd Division attacking along the Moselle River. On April 3, XII Corps attacked on its left; then on April 5, VIII and XXXI corps attacked on the left of XII Corps, resulting in pressure along the entire southern face of the salient. Support came from 376 artillery pieces, 107 of which were heavy. The French hoped these sequenced attacks would draw the Germans to the south, making them vulnerable to attacks farther north on the western face of the salient. In the supporting attack against Vauquois, Third Army, reinforced by a single division, began its advance on April 4.

To attack the northern end of the western face of the salient, Joffre formed Army Detachment Gérard, named after its commander, General Augustin Gérard, and assigned I and II corps to it, as well as I Cavalry Corps. Gérard concentrated six divisions, including a cavalry division, along a front of thirteen kilometers. Instead of assaulting the heights of

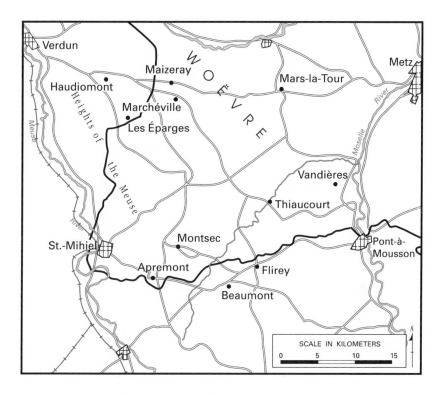

St.-Mihiel, 1915

the Meuse directly, his attack concentrated farther north, near Maizeray, and was supposed to drive deep into the rolling terrain of the Woëvre plain, northeast of the heights. The French intended to assault one hill in the heights, Les Éparges, on the southern edge of the zone of attack, since the Germans could overlook from this hill the French attack into the Woëvre plain to their north. The 12th Division, which was not under the command of Gérard, had responsibility for the attack on Les Éparges. The attack on the western face of the salient began on April 5, but heavy rain and poor visibility delayed the operation. As visibility improved, scheduled artillery fire began destroying enemy positions and cutting wire at 1100 hours, and the infantry assault began at 1415.

Though the French achieved surprise, the assaulting troops encountered numerous difficulties, most of which came from inadequate artillery support against well-prepared enemy defenses. The hasty preparation for the attack had not permitted sufficient preparation by the artillery, and the rolling terrain and the distance between the opposing lines severely limited the ability of artillery observers to adjust their fire and support the infantry. Also, the consistency of the soil, which was soaked from constant rain, reduced the effectiveness of the exploding artillery rounds, enabling enemy machine guns and wire to escape damage. Since the artillery cut only one breach in the wire, the attacking infantry had to cut their way through the unbroken wire with wire cutters. The attack made almost no progress, and many of the attacking French died without ever seeing an enemy soldier. To the south, bad weather and poor artillery support delayed the attempt to capture Les Éparges, and by the end of the second day the infantry had captured only 500 meters of trenches.

With the attack on the western face stymied, Dubail ordered a frontal assault on the southern face. In a swirl of attacks and counterattacks, both sides sustained heavy casualties. As the fighting took its toll, Dubail told Joffre that he needed infantry replacements and that he would attempt to make a penetration along a narrower portion of the western face of the salient. Recognizing that the French could not achieve the desired results and had lost the advantage of surprise, Joffre ordered Dubail on April 8 to transition to a "methodical but powerful attack, which will permit us to seize terrain where possible and which will maintain the attention of the enemy's reserves in this region."[89] Dubail quickly halted the broad-front attacks and made preparations for a new attack. Meanwhile, in the one piece of good news for the French, 12th Infantry Division captured Les Éparges on April 9, a task it had been pursuing since November.

On April 10 Dubail informed Joffre that he intended to make four assaults. Two of these would concentrate on the western face, one on a four-kilometer front (near Maizeray in the Woëvre plain) in the original zone of attack in the north, and another on the heights immediately south of Les Éparges. Two other assaults would concentrate on the southern face, both near its center. Artillery began firing on April 6 in an attempt to cut wire in front of Maizeray. After ensuring that breaches had been cut in front of the three attacking divisions, the infantry began its assault at 1000 hours on April 12. But the attack, which had a front of about four kilometers, failed. Gérard reported to Dubail that the results obtained by the artillery were "much less" than expected. Though artillery cut some breaches in the wire, it did not reduce the strength of enemy defenses or artillery barrages. Gérard, who had commanded Sector 2-1 in the Champagne offensive, reported that the German defenses were stronger than those in Champagne, primarily because the enemy had had six months of "stagnation" in which to strengthen them. He explained that the Germans had constructed wire barriers with a depth of 500 meters and protected their soldiers with concrete casemates. He concluded, "to continue to seek a penetration of the enemy line in this region with quickly prepared attacks, one risks . . . ruining an excellent infantry and destroying its confidence without [achieving any] results."[90]

Before receiving Gérard's report, Joffre reacted angrily to reports of inadequate preparation, for he had directed all his army commanders on April 10 not to make any attacks unless they had completed detailed and effective preparations. He had warned them that it was their personal responsibility to ensure adequate preparation. Dubail replied firmly but tactfully to Joffre's concerns and said that it was important to "profit from experience" and to continue with an even more methodical attack.[91] Joffre agreed to continue the attack, but on April 14 he pulled two corps and part of the cavalry corps from the operation. Though fighting continued through the middle of June, the removal of these forces effectively ended large attacks against the St.-Mihiel salient.

Much to the surprise of the French, on April 23 the Germans launched an energetic but limited attack against Les Éparges. Although the French succeeded in turning back this attack, the Germans attacked the next day southwest of Les Éparges and seized four kilometers of frontline trenches and two kilometers of second-line trenches; they also captured a battery of 75-mm guns and sixteen heavy pieces. Dubail reported that the Germans attacked with three divisions, and he credited their success to a "prodigality" of artillery and to their use of a "considerable number" of *Minenwerfer*.[92] After numerous counterattacks, the French regained some second-line trenches, but by May 1 the Germans still held the captured frontline trenches and all but 800 meters of the second-line trenches. This gain was larger than that of the French during the entire St.-Mihiel offensive. Counting the losses at Vauquois, the French had suffered 65,000 casualties, a figure 50 percent higher than the losses from February 16 to March 20 in the Champagne offensive. Joffre's quick shift from Champagne to St.-Mihiel had yielded nothing but high casualties.

As the French offensive against the St.-Mihiel salient ended, the Germans surprised the allies by using chemicals in an attack at Ypres. By this point in the war, all the belligerents recognized the extraordinary difficulty of overcoming an enemy's defensive position, and it is not surprising that the major industrial powers—France, Great Britain, and Germany—considered using chemicals to end the stalemate. Such efforts, however, were circumscribed by the Hague Conventions and Declarations, which sought to restrict the employment of asphyxiating gases. While France had signed the conventions of 1899 and 1907, as well as a separate declaration, and thereby declared that it would not employ "poison or poisoned arms" or use "projectiles" to spread "asphyxiating gases,"[93] it had accepted no such limitation on the use of noxious gases. Before the war France had developed *cartouches suffocantes,* which were filled with liquid noxious gases and fired as rifle grenades. Employed in the first months of the war against fortified positions, the shells had very limited effects. In April 1915 the French introduced a hand grenade filled with stronger noxious gases, but this, too, proved to have only limited effects. Although the Germans later accused the French of developing a 75-mm artillery shell filled with noxious gases and employing it in the Argonne in March 1915, a specialist who has examined the issue carefully found no evidence about such a projectile. The same specialist, however, concluded that it was only a matter of time before France began employing lethal gases.[94]

Since the French were experimenting with various gases, they should have been more attentive to intelligence reports about the possibility that the Germans might use asphyxiating gases. On the night of April 13–14 a German deserter, carrying a crude protective device, made his way across no-man's-land near Langemarck (northeast of Ypres) and informed the French that the Germans intended to use asphyxiating gases from batteries of twenty cylinders placed along every forty meters of the front. The commander of the division in that sector participated in the interrogation of the deserter and then informed his corps commander and a liaison officer from GQG. He also warned the Belgians, as well as the Canadians and British on his flank. During this same period the French discovered respirators on several dead German soldiers, and the Belgians warned of German preparations for a gas attack. The Belgian report on April 16 identified an enemy unit that had received special training in the employment of gas and that occupied a sector coinciding with the Ypres salient and Langemarck. Despite these reports, the French did not believe the Germans would employ asphyxiating gases. Staff officers suspected that the enemy had sent the deserter across the lines to give the allies false information, and they refused to believe that the Germans would violate the Hague Conventions and Declarations.

Part of the failure to prepare for the Germans' use of gas also came from confusion stemming from the rotation of units in the Ypres salient. After Joffre canceled Tenth Army's attack in Artois in early March, the entire northern portion of the front had remained relatively quiet except for fighting that flared up frequently near Vimy Ridge and except for the March 10 offensive by the British at Neuve-Chapelle. In the meantime, British relief of French units continued slowly, as did alterations in the chain of command. As the relief of units in Eighth Army proceeded, and as that army became smaller and smaller, Joffre renamed it the Army Detachment of Belgium. After the relief of IX and XX corps, 45th (Algerian) and 87th Territorial divisions occupied a front of eight kilometers between the British and the Belgians. The French organized the two divisions into an ad-hoc corps, naming it the d'Elverdinghe Group and providing it only modest artillery support. This group and the Nieuport Group along the coast constituted most of the Army Detachment of Belgium.

On April 22 at 1700 hours near Langemarck on the northern part of the Ypres salient, the Germans released chlorine gas from 5,830 cylinders along a front of six kilometers. Eighty-seventh Territorial Division received the brunt of the attack, but the yellow-green cloud also hit 45th Division. Soldiers from the two divisions fled in disorder toward the Ypres Canal, some four to five kilometers to the rear, while the Canadian Division on their right, hardly affected by the gas, moved a battalion up to St.-Julien to cover its exposed left flank. These movements opened a gap of three and a half kilometers in the line, with French and Belgians holding one shoulder and the Canadians the other. Fortunately for the allies, the Germans were as surprised as the French and did not have reserves available to exploit the gains. German troops in the gap halted at around 1930 hours and began digging in.

Almost immediately, the French and British began rushing reserves piecemeal toward the threatened sector. Early on the following morning the Canadians and the French reestablished contact, thanks to the Canadians' extending their left across the gap. That day the French launched two weak counterattacks, but neither made any progress. The Canadians eventually made some progress, as did an attack on the left of the gap after additional reinforcements arrived. On the night of April 23–24, the Germans made another gas attack and followed it with an infantry assault to push back the allies. Foch responded by bringing in IX Corps and its two divisions from Tenth Army. The British also responded by bringing in additional forces. On April 26 and 27 the French launched several attacks but made only slight gains. The Germans used gas on both days and nullified the gains made by the allies. Impressed by the valiant efforts of the British and Canadians in this fighting, the commander of one of the brigades in 45th Division later wrote: "the British troops, faithful to their ancient tradition, demonstrated that, when they must, they know how to die but not how to withdraw."[95]

Lack of effective protection against asphyxiating gases continued to hamper French efforts. Though they would eventually bring in respirators used by miners and firefighters, no protective devices had arrived by April 28. Soldiers were advised to protect themselves by breathing through water-soaked handkerchiefs, first-aid packets, or cotton pads. Even so, the Germans had the advantage only as long as the winds came out of the north; the French were well aware that prevailing winds came out of the west and thus favored them. By April 30 the winds had shifted to the southwest. An attack that day pushed back the Germans a few hundred meters in the center of the original three-and-a-half-kilometer gap. Throughout May the line remained stationary though active in the French portion of the Ypres front. No longer concerned about the enemy's making gains near Ypres, Joffre focused on preparing another offensive to the south and ordered the Army Detachment of Belgium to fix enemy forces to its front by launching "partial offensives." He wanted to prevent German forces in that region from moving elsewhere. What became known to the British as the second battle of Ypres did not end until May 25.

As casualties in Artois, Champagne, and Flanders mounted and as reports of the bungled operation at St.-Mihiel reached Paris, Joffre came under sharp criticism. From the first days of the war, soldiers had complained to political leaders about their situation and their commanders. By early December several political leaders wanted to replace Joffre with Gallieni. Some of Gallieni's supporters wanted him to be the minister of war, as well as the generalissimo. By March 1915 even Poincaré had lost patience with Joffre. He concluded that Joffre had no "overall concept" and persuaded Viviani to discuss Joffre's performance in a meeting of the Council of Ministers. At a meeting of the council on March 21, however, the optimistic, confident general described his efforts to "divert German forces from Russia" and deflected some of the criticisms.[96] A month later another influential politician, Abel Ferry, the undersecretary of state for foreign affairs, brought his concerns about Joffre to the Council of Ministers. A reserve officer who had joined II Corps in January 1915 but returned to Paris to attend council meetings, he had participated in the April offensive against the St.-Mihiel salient and was shocked by the poorly organized operation. At the April 27 meeting he presented a written report that scathingly criticized the officers who had organized the operation.[97] Although Ferry expressed disappointment in his diary about the response of the ministers, Poincaré noted a detailed discussion about the "incoherence" of Joffre's objectives. Only after Millerand vigorously defended the need to give Joffre "personal and undivided command" did the ministers reluctantly accept the "great authority" this gave him and agree to his having "complete" freedom to conduct operations. They insisted nonetheless that he consult with his major subordinate commanders and agreed to discuss the issue further if his next offensive failed.[98] In reality, France's political leaders had acknowledged the difficulty of

Joffre's task and accepted the division of responsibility and authority—and the civil-military relationship—that Messimy had arranged with Joffre shortly before the war began.

Resuming the offensive so soon after the Marne campaign thus proved costly and extremely disappointing. Instead of providing a ray of hope, the bloody failures in the Artois, Champagne, and St.-Mihiel offensives demonstrated that the war would be far more arduous and entail more suffering than anyone had yet imagined. Despite the high casualties and numerous mistakes, Joffre believed the army had learned a great deal, improved its operational methods, and acquired weapons more suitable for trench warfare. With the exception of the St.-Mihiel operation, he believed the offensives had progressively become better coordinated and more powerful.[99] The increased number of heavy artillery pieces gave him even greater confidence in France's eventual success. At a meeting of allied leaders, Joffre said, "The morale of the German army is very low. Ours is marvelous." He added, "We will be ready at the end of April to take the offensive and chase the G[ermans out of France]."[100]

CHAPTER 4

An Offensive Strategy

May–October 1915

B EGINNING IN EARLY April 1915, Joffre visited French units and spoke openly about a new phase in the war. At about the same time he informed Britain and Russia that his forces were ready to take the offensive. With the arrival of more heavy artillery and ammunition and with the formation of additional reserves, the French had made the difficult transition and improved their ability to fight on the World War I battlefield. Although Joffre resisted sending troops and resources to the eastern Mediterranean, his operations from May to October fitted within France's multifront strategy, for he attempted simultaneously to drive the Germans from France's territory and to aid the Russians and Serbs. Viewing the war more broadly than most allied generals, he saw his attacks within the context of similar attacks on the Russian, Serbian, and— eventually—Italian fronts. He explained: "With all these simultaneous attacks, each helps the others; it is not so much a question of one getting through, as of all pressing at the same time, and thereby increasing the chances that one or the other will achieve success."[1]

One development, which favored a French attack but which carried ominous indications about the effects of previous attacks, concerned reports of the Germans moving forces to the east.[2] The thinning of German lines on the Western Front created favorable conditions for an attack, but they also suggested that previous attacks had not tied the enemy's hands. Seeking to inform Grand Duke Nicholas of France's efforts and to quash any doubts about France's reliability, Joffre sent a long message on April 12 to Russia in which he described French efforts. He acknowledged that Germany had moved forces from west to east, but he insisted that France had used all available forces and done the best it possibly could. To increase forces available for an attack, the French were absorbing another class of conscripts, he said, and the British were extending their front, thereby freeing another French corps for a "strong offensive in no more than three weeks." The French commander also emphasized the importance of "simultaneous action" by the Russians, Serbs, and perhaps the Italians. Joffre concluded, "If we succeed in realizing the coordination of all our efforts, which appears to me to be clearly possible, it will result in a general offensive on all our fronts and will have considerable impact."[3]

Despite reports of enemy troops moving east, Joffre remained optimistic that Russia would hold against the Germans. A report on April 10 from Major Langlois, a Russian specialist who had arrived in Petrograd in December, provided some encouragement. The report included comments from the Russian chief of staff about his high regard for the French, as well as from Russian officers about their willingness to fight until the end of the war. The report concluded, "The only black mark is weakness in the production of munitions."[4] Nothing provided any hint of the disaster that would result from the Austro-German attack in Galicia near Gorlice and Tarnów on May 2. The breakthrough of the combined German and Austrian force and subsequent drive toward Przemyśl and Lemberg made French gains in their first offensives appear small and insignificant. As the Central Powers' advance accelerated, Joffre sent the grand duke a message describing preparations for an "energetic" attack by combined Franco-British forces. Hopes for allied success faded as the Russians fell back before the Austrians and Germans. With efforts on the Western Front having little effect on the Germans, the French military attaché in Petrograd noted a "growing anti-French attitude."[5] The best that Joffre could do was to inform the Russians on May 24, three weeks after the Central Powers began their offensive against Russia, that no large enemy units had moved "recently" from the Western to the Eastern Front. Unfortunately for the soldiers in the trenches, the Central Powers' success placed even greater pressure on Joffre to launch a large offensive as soon as possible.

Weeks before the Central Powers attacked at Gorlice-Tarnów, Joffre had begun preparations for another offensive. On March 17 he sent the minister of war two memoranda explaining his operations since the "race to the sea" and summarizing the not-yet-terminated operation in Champagne.[6] The next day Millerand discussed these memoranda at a meeting of the Council of Ministers. Although Poincaré and other political leaders considered the reports "very optimistic," they saw no need to end the "series of operations" aiming to "break" enemy lines and aid Russia. Neither they nor Joffre had any desire to go on the defensive and let the French army lapse into a passive role. The French people, they believed, would not tolerate a long period of inactivity in which military forces bided their time waiting for more favorable conditions. Political and strategic situations demanded a significant effort on the Western Front.

Foch spent March 19–21 at Joffre's headquarters at Chantilly and used the time to reinforce the commander-in-chef's desire for an offensive in Artois near Vimy Ridge. Foch brought along a handwritten note emphasizing that the war could be won only with an offensive. He wrote: "The *form* of this offensive always remains the same. It includes: a *general action* along the entire front; a *decisive action*, a central attack, on the portion of the front which provides the opportunity for the desired result, breaking through the enemy." The decisive action, said Foch, should take place on a portion of the front where the enemy could not reestablish his fortified position a short distance to the rear, and the general action should confuse the enemy about the location of the decisive attack, fix him in place, and take the form of an "aggressive defense." Foch recommended that the decisive action take place at Vimy and that the general action include attacks across the entire Western Front, including attacks by the British.[7] On March 23 Foch learned that Joffre had approved his proposal for an offensive, and the following day he submitted a detailed plan for approval. The objective of the operation was "seizing" Vimy Ridge. The proposal explained: "occupation of this crest will undoubtedly have a significant effect and will result in a breakthrough of the enemy line."[8]

Although Joffre and his senior generals believed the army was ready to resume the offensive and make a "breakthrough," the French had not yet perfected their methods. Many new weapons (especially heavy artillery) had not arrived, and debates continued within the army about the best way of fighting through the enemy's defenses. In the broadest sense, the French recognized two different methods, one employing the "continuous" battle and the other the "methodical" battle. The former, which was favored by Joffre, consisted of an unremitting, brutal thrust while the latter consisted of a succession of hammerlike blows.[9] In his cover letter on a memorandum published on April 19 about the conduct and purpose of an offensive, Joffre said, "Attackers at all echelons will be imbued with the idea of breaking through, of going beyond the first trenches seized, of continuing to attack without stopping until the final result [is achieved]." The authors of the memorandum used the word "ensemble" to describe a properly organized offensive, since it suggested a tightly coordinated action producing harmony, much as a conductor and a musical score produced harmonious music from the different instruments in an orchestra. Joffre and the staff officers nonetheless favored "systematic," rather than methodical, preparation and anticipated the "unceasing entry of fresh units" into the fighting to maintain the momentum of an attack seeking to break through enemy lines on a relatively narrow front.[10] Time and experience, as well as thousands of casualties, would eventually lead the French to seek a "rupture" on a broad front rather than a breakthrough on a narrow front and to favor the methodical rather than the continuous battle.

As part of the preparation for another offensive, Joffre sought assistance from the British. Though Field Marshal French's forces had performed well at Neuve-Chapelle and Joffre had sent Sir John a message describing the operation as "brilliant,"[11] his estimation of the British remained low. He told the minister of war on March 17: "Beneficiaries of our attack in Champagne, which attracted the German reserves, the English found in reality only inferior forces [at Neuve-Chapelle]. They were able to gain surprise . . . because of their preceding inaction."[12] Despite these reservations, Joffre thought the British could make a "partial" attack and thereby support Tenth Army, which would make the main attack north of Arras against Vimy Ridge. On March 24 he wrote to Sir John about the upcoming offensive and asked him to make an attack at the end of April. Partial offensives, Joffre explained, would weaken the enemy, prevent him from shifting forces to the Eastern Front or another part of the Western Front, keep him from launching an offensive on the Western Front, and leave him uncertain about allied intentions.[13] He also wanted to "space" British and French attacks so that the enemy would have to disperse his units and artillery, but the allied attacks would be close enough together to have a synergistic effect. To achieve the appropriate spacing and keep the enemy from concentrating against the main attack, Joffre wanted an attack north of Tenth Army. Only the British, he said, had the capability to make such an attack, since the French had only small elements in the north.

In a meeting on March 29 at Joffre's headquarters, Millerand, Joffre, Sir John French, and Lord Kitchener discussed Anglo-French cooperation. Kitchener, who was having increasing doubts about the value of massive attacks on the Western Front, focused on the question of sending troops to Holland if the Germans invaded that country, and Joffre attempted to get him to agree to a British attack on May 1, the same day the French intended to attack near Vimy Ridge. Joffre responded to Kitchener's doubts about the utility of "partial" attacks by insisting that they were "indispensable" in keeping the Germans from shifting troops from the Western to the Eastern Front. When Kitchener expressed doubts about making a breakthrough in France, Joffre cited British success at Neuve-Chapelle as evidence against such an argument. Kitchener finally agreed to send troops to relieve IX and XX corps in the Ypres salient, but he emphasized that he would not send additional troops until he had clear evidence of progress on the Western Front.[14] On April 1 Sir John confirmed his intention to relieve IX and XX corps and to attack at the same time as the French.

Despite outward signs of cooperation, the period from April 22 to May 27 was, as explained by the British official history, "one of the most difficult in the relations of the two allied headquarters."[15] Much of the friction came from disagreement about strategy, especially as it pertained to the Dardanelles campaign, but it also came from increased tension between the two allies. When the Germans employed gas at Ypres, the British had been surprised by French weakness in the sector to the north, and their confidence in them sagged. Shortly before the attack on May 9,

Sir John French wrote to Joffre asking him to place two or three divisions between the extreme left of the British and the extreme right of the Belgians. He added that he had replaced the Indian troops on his left with "white troops" and asked Joffre not to place colonial troops on his left. Reflecting heightened doubts about the French, he wrote: "It is particularly necessary that the front defended by French troops be completely organized with lines of defense reinforced by strong points in the rear." Not wishing to disrupt the combined offensive scheduled for early May, Joffre agreed to the field marshal's request and assured him that the position would be "solidly organized."[16]

As for the attack against Vimy Ridge, General d'Urbal, who assumed command of Tenth Army on April 2, had the mission of "breaking through enemy lines." To do this, he had six infantry and one cavalry corps, as well as three additional infantry divisions. He expected a seventh corps to move behind his army when the offensive began. From left to right the corps on the front line were IX, XXI, XXXIII, XX, XVII, and X. Three corps (XXXIII, XX, and XVII) would make the main attack along a front of ten kilometers and would attempt to seize the heights of Vimy Ridge. To the left of the main attack, XXI Corps would make a supporting attack with two divisions against the hill known as Notre-Dame de Lorette. The three corps in the main attack would seize the heights of Vimy Ridge and fortify their positions so that no counterattack could drive them off. Then the cavalry, as well as all infantry not involved in occupying the ridge, would pursue the enemy.[17] D'Urbal expected the cavalry to occupy Douai and then to conduct reconnaissance farther east.

To support the attack, Tenth Army had 1,075 artillery pieces, including 293 heavy ones. D'Urbal initially preferred an artillery preparation of no more than four hours in order to gain surprise, but the GQG overruled him in favor of a long preparation. Bitter experience, particularly in the abortive St.-Mihiel offensive, had convinced Joffre of the importance of an extended bombardment. According to d'Urbal's final plan, the artillery would pound the enemy for four days before the infantry assault.

Though Joffre scheduled the attack for May 1, the slow arrival of heavy artillery and other equipment delayed the operation. With the infantry assault delayed until May 7, preparatory fires began at 0530 hours on May 3, but bad weather intervened. Despite poor visibility, the artillery continued firing. On the day before the attack the artillery shifted to destroying strong points in the enemy's main position, reportedly with great effect. For four hours before the infantry assault, all the artillery in Tenth Army blasted the enemy's wire and his first and second trench lines. On May 9 at 1000 hours the assault finally began amidst beautiful weather.

Despite reassuring reports about the morale of the infantry, only XXXIII Corps, commanded by General Pétain, made a significant advance. With responsibility for the main attack in Tenth Army's center, Pétain used 70th Division to secure the corps's left flank, while the 77th in his center and the Moroccan Division on his right drove toward the heights of Vimy Ridge. Elements of the latter two divisions reached the top of Vimy Ridge at 1100 hours, and some soldiers actually moved completely across the heights. Tenth Army claimed that elements of XXXIII Corps had advanced almost four kilometers into enemy lines,[18] an astonishing distance in comparison to usual gains. The sudden success, however, quickly dissipated when Pétain could not get reinforcements forward. To remain outside the range of enemy artillery, his reserves were eight kilometers from the line of contact, and Tenth Army's were twelve kilometers. To make matters worse, the leading elements had lost many of their leaders, and when heavy machine-gun fire struck their flanks, French 75-mm guns could provide little support, since they had to fire almost to their maximum range. Strong German counterattacks between 1400 and 1500 hours finally drove the soldiers off Vimy Ridge. This withdrawal reduced the gains of 77th Division to 1,900 meters and the Moroccan Division's to 2,100. But Pétain's corps had captured 1,200–1,500 prisoners, several batteries of artillery, and "dozens" of machine guns. Needless to say, Pétain's remarkable advance demonstrated his talents to France's political and military leaders and accelerated his already rapid rise in the military hierarchy.

Other corps made only small advances. To the left of XXXIII Corps, XXI Corps advanced only a few hundred meters on Notre-Dame de Lorette. To the right of XXXIII Corps, one division in XX Corps advanced 1,500 meters, with a few elements moving 2,000, but the division to its right made only small advances after becoming entangled in a fortified position known as the "Labyrinth." Although d'Urbal had expected XVII Corps on the right of XX Corps to make the most significant advances, the lengthy preparatory artillery fire had not reduced German defenses, and the corps encountered heavy machine-gun fire. The leading regiment lost its regimental commander, known to his men as "the Invulnerable," and one of its battalion commanders; in all the regiment lost about thirty officers. Despite d'Urbal's high hopes, XVII Corps captured only a small portion of the enemy's frontline trench. To the right of XVII Corps, X Corps made no progress. Thus, by the end of the first day, only XXXIII Corps and one division on its right in XX Corps had made noteworthy progress.

Despite limited gains, the High Command remained optimistic. Joffre moved two cavalry divisions behind Tenth Army and had a cavalry corps move closer to its sector. On May 10 d'Urbal ordered his subordinate commanders to continue driving toward their objectives. The attacking troops, however, made few gains. Realizing that delays gave the Germans time to strengthen their defenses, d'Urbal ordered his corps commanders to advance with the "greatest speed." After reinforcing XXXIII and XX corps with additional divisions, he ordered them to attack on May 11 following two hours of artillery preparation. In a message to the soldiers of Tenth Army, he said, "The moment has arrived to deliver a great blow to the enemy and to liberate our soil completely from the detested presence of the invader."[19] Despite this optimism strong enemy defenses smashed several bloody frontal assaults. Pétain reported that machine-gun fire on his left and right had struck his advancing troops; enemy artillery fire also had increased and caused much damage. The other corps made no progress.

The failure on May 11 convinced d'Urbal that he had to reduce the enemy's defenses that were keeping his forces from advancing. After meeting with his corps commanders on the morning of May 12, he focused the efforts of Tenth Army on the villages of Souchez and Neuville. Pétain's XXXIII Corps would clear Carency before driving toward Souchez, and XX Corps would attack Neuville. Meanwhile XXI Corps would fight its away across Notre-Dame de Lorette. By the morning of May 14 the French had captured Carency and had driven the Germans from most of Notre-Dame de Lorette, but the enemy still held their positions between Carency and Notre-Dame de Lorette. Enemy fire from these positions into the flank of XXXIII Corps prevented Pétain from advancing toward Souchez.

Despite the limited gains, Joffre refused to quit. He provided Tenth Army two additional divisions and promised more if they became available. After the German breakthrough on May 2 at Gorlice-Tarnów on the Eastern Front, he was gravely concerned about the Russians' being knocked out of the war and wanted to maintain pressure on the Germans. Additional forces and a greater sense of urgency did not help Tenth Army's offensive. The attacking units had only two hours of preparatory artillery fire before the assault and failed to make any gains. It was clear that Tenth Army had to do something different.

The British began their attack on May 9, the same day that Tenth Army began its offensive against Vimy Ridge. In what came to be known as the battle of Aubers Ridge, they attacked north and south of Neuve-Chapelle. Enthused by their success at Neuve-Chapelle on March 10 but lacking the munitions of the French, they decided to rely again on surprise. Before the French infantry's assault on May 9, the British began their bombardment at 0500 hours and their infantry assault at 0540. This time, however, the Germans were ready and inflicted heavy casualties on them. After the attack stalled, General Sir Douglas Haig, who commanded the British First Army, ordered the attack renewed. When an assault at 1600 hours also stalled, Haig canceled any further attacks.

On May 12 Joffre and Foch met with Sir John French and complained about the halting of First Army's offensive. The two French leaders pointed out that after Haig halted his attack, the Germans had shifted two divisions out of that sector into the Vimy Ridge sector. Joffre wanted Haig to attack immediately or relieve a French division so that it could move south and reinforce the French offensive. On the night of May 14–15 a British division did relieve a French division south of La Bassée, and the following night Haig attacked south of Neuve-Chapelle after almost three days of preparatory fire. For the next ten days the British maintained pressure on the Germans as the French focused their efforts on capturing key terrain at Vimy Ridge prior to launching a new assault. When the French renewed their offensive again in mid-June, the British made two small attacks, one northwest of La Bassée with two divisions and one east of Ypres with one division. The weakness of Sir John

French's attacks, however, greatly displeased Joffre, and he scathingly criticized British "inaction" for letting the Germans concentrate their reserves against Tenth Army.[20]

As d'Urbal worked on the evening of May 15–16 to provide new instructions to his corps commanders, Foch arrived at his headquarters and altered Tenth Army's plans. His intervention began a new phase in the Vimy Ridge offensive. Foch explained that a week of attacks had failed to break the enemy's defenses and another poorly prepared frontal assault would not achieve the desired results. A new offensive, he said, should be launched only after "complete and minute" preparation similar to that preceding the attack of May 9. In essence, he directed d'Urbal to use a more methodical technique. He ordered him to seize a "base of departure" that included Souchez and Neuville before launching an assault on the heights of Vimy. Foch believed that capturing this base of departure could take as many as eight to ten days. After canceling plans for an attack on the following day, d'Urbal sent a new order to his corps commanders. His order envisaged a "series of operations" to seize points required for subsequent operations against the heights of Vimy. The various points constituted Foch's base of departure, and each corps had its own points to seize. For the attack on Souchez, d'Urbal identified five points for XXXIII Corps to take before assaulting the village. XXI Corps would assist XXXIII Corps in its assault on Souchez but not before conquering three other points.[21]

The first of the carefully prepared attacks seeking to seize specific points and establish a base of departure was set to begin on May 17, but heavy rains forced a delay. The attacks actually began three days later, with larger infantry assaults occurring the following night. Step by step the corps pushed forward, always preceded by a massive artillery bombardment and usually seizing only a few hundred square meters of terrain. D'Urbal then had XXI, XXXIII, and IX corps attack several key points simultaneously. Though preparatory fires lasted a day, the attacks on May 25 accomplished little. As attacks against individual points continued, d'Urbal decided to destroy the enemy in Neuville with a massive artillery bombardment. Artillery fire began on June 2, and three days later the infantry advanced. The soldiers seized the main road through the village, but Germans remained in the cellars and rubble and poured a murderous fire into them. The Germans also used their own artillery skillfully. From June 6 to 11 the French nevertheless advanced 500 meters into Neuville on a front of 300 meters.

Meanwhile Joffre closely watched preparations for Tenth Army's offensive, which was supposed to begin after that army seized a base of departure. He and Foch had anticipated seizing a base of departure at Vimy Ridge in no more than ten days, after which they expected a final assault to occur; but on May 25 Joffre agreed to delay the final assault until May 31. As heavy fighting in Souchez and Neuville continued, he delayed the operation several times, finally scheduling it for June 16. In the interim he added new divisions to Tenth Army until it contained twenty-four, including four infantry and three cavalry divisions in reserve. Behind these forces Foch had six infantry and five cavalry divisions ready to exploit any success achieved by Tenth Army. To avoid the problems that had occurred on May 9 after XXXIII Corps's remarkable advance, Joffre gave explicit directions about the role and placement of reserves. He wrote: "The main lesson [from recent combat] is the necessity to push reserves as far forward as possible."[22] Both Foch and d'Urbal followed Joffre's lead and emphasized the importance of reserves' entering battle quickly.

For the attack on June 16 Joffre shortened the front of Tenth Army and gave it more artillery. Tenth Army had 1,160 artillery pieces for the attack; of these, 355 were heavy. In an attempt to gain surprise, the French modified their use of preparatory fire. Tenth Army planned on commencing its artillery fire on June 10 but hoped to conceal its purpose by having the rounds concentrate on various targets whose destruction would not unmask the coming assault. At daybreak on the day of the attack, firing would commence at the same pace as the previous evening but would concentrate on destroying defenses prepared by the enemy during the night. To conceal the coming attack, French gunners also would fire at the enemy's second line and at artillery batteries. This firing would continue until the exact moment of the assault; then all of Tenth Army's artillery would concentrate on the enemy's forward line immediately in front of the advancing infantry. The infantry would thus leave their trenches just as a massive concentration of artillery struck the enemy. Planners hoped that by delaying final preparatory fires they would not alert the enemy's artillery and could avoid massive enemy barrages on their advancing infantry.

As the French executed their fire-support plan, the firing batteries expended a vast amount of munitions. In the days preceding the attack and on June 16, they fired 497,122 artillery rounds, almost double the number fired on May 9 and in the days preceding that attack. On the morning of the attack, however, they concluded that the destruction was "insufficient." D'Urbal ordered additional firing for three hours before the infantry assault began at 1215 hours. Then, as planned, the artillery and infantry went into action simultaneously. Whereas the French had fired 30,278 rounds of heavy artillery on May 9, they fired 63,557 on June 16.

Despite the careful preparation and methodical execution, as well as the much larger expenditure of ammunition, Tenth Army made smaller gains on June 16 than on May 9. For example, in XXXIII Corps the Moroccan Division (which had performed superbly on May 9) advanced one kilometer on a front of 300–400 meters. Other divisions made less progress. The failure of the attack was obvious in the army's heavy casualties (19,000) and in its capture of only 600 prisoners. The Germans responded quickly to the attack, neglecting counterbattery efforts and concentrating massive fires against exposed French infantry. They also launched several furious counterattacks, recapturing some of the terrain they had lost.

Even though Tenth Army failed to make significant gains, d'Urbal ordered his corps commanders to continue the attack "day and night with the greatest possible energy."[23] On the morning of June 17, Joffre, realizing how many soldiers were being consumed in the battle, visited Foch's headquarters at 0700 hours and directed continuation of the attack only where progress had been made. That evening d'Urbal ordered an energetic attack by the three corps in his center, but the attacks on the following day accomplished little. On the evening of June 18 Foch halted the attack. Tenth Army focused its efforts on conquering Souchez and establishing a new base of departure for a subsequent attempt to seize Vimy Ridge. On June 25 Joffre formally halted the offensive.

When Tenth Army attacked Vimy Ridge on May 9 and June 16, other armies launched secondary attacks to fix the enemy to their front. These attacks constituted the "general action" along the entire front that Foch had suggested in his late-March note and that sought to support Tenth Army's "decisive action." Thirty kilometers south of Souchez, Second Army attacked on June 7–13 and advanced 900 meters on a front of two kilometers while suffering 10,351 casualties, including 1,760 killed. Sixth Army attacked ten kilometers south of Noyon on June 6–16 and advanced 500 meters on a front of one kilometer, suffering 7,905 casualties. Other attacks occurred in the east. From May 1 to June 20, First Army attacked the St.-Mihiel salient and made only small gains, yet it lost 16,000 men. Seventy kilometers southeast of St.-Mihiel, the Army Detachment of Lorraine made two attacks from June 5 to 22; one advanced 1,000–1,500 meters on a front of five kilometers, the other 2,000 meters on a front of eight kilometers. Casualties numbered about 800. From May 5 to June 22, Seventh Army attacked twenty kilometers west of Colmar and advanced three kilometers on a front of four and a half kilometers; it lost 6,667 men. With Tenth Army having priority, the secondary attacks had minimal artillery support and usually captured areas smaller than that captured by Tenth Army at Vimy Ridge. Casualties from the secondary operations amounted to 40 percent of those at Vimy Ridge and did little to affect Tenth Army's operation.

As for the results of the main offensive, the French advanced about three kilometers at Vimy Ridge on a front of eight kilometers, but they failed to break through German defenses. From May 3 to June 18, they fired 2,155,862 artillery rounds in support of Tenth Army. The lavish use of ammunition did not reduce casualties; the French suffered 102,500 casualties, 35 percent of whom were killed. Counting secondary operations, Joffre's offensive resulted in the injury or death of more than 140,000 French soldiers.

The failure of the Artois attacks shocked France's political leaders and produced a tidal wave of complaints. On June 22, at a very "somber" meeting of the Council of Ministers, the politicians expressed deep disappointment at Joffre's halting the offensive in Artois. According to Poincaré, the ministers were "stupefied" by the bad news.[24] Their shock came not only from the shattering of their optimistic expectations but also from the contrasting German success in Galicia after the breakthrough at Gorlice-Tarnów on May 2. On June 5 the French military attaché in Petrograd reported that Przemyśl had fallen and that the Russians would have to evacuate Galicia. In a month the Germans had advanced 100 kilometers, and Warsaw seemed vulnerable. Meanwhile the French had made little progress.

Poincaré observed, "Everyone is complaining about Joffre and especially about his entourage." At a meeting in early July of the Army Committee of the Chamber of Deputies, critics angrily attacked Joffre and his staff. Among the evidence cited was a letter from a corps commander, later identified as General François Anthoine, who wrote anonymously: "Nothing but mistakes have been committed since October; men are being uselessly slaughtered; the troops have lost their spirit and have lapsed into gloomy resignation. . . . Time is on our side. Let us hold on; let us manufacture [the war materiel we need]; let us husband the men. Let us have a real army [for use] when other armies are worn out instead of wearing ours out for nothing."[25] Amidst all this criticism, Millerand's defense of Joffre made him numerous enemies. Many of his critics believed he was protecting Joffre and had allowed him too much leeway to run the war as he wished. Unable to get rid of Millerand without causing the government to fall, the politicians reduced his authority by appointing four assistant secretaries and giving them some of the powers of the minister of war. The Viviani government managed to survive, but support clearly was waning.

Concerned about strident criticisms of French strategy and operations, Poincaré, Viviani, and Millerand attended Joffre's meeting on June 23 with his army-group commanders. The meeting began on a negative note with Poincaré and Viviani criticizing Joffre for creating false hopes for a breakthrough. When Joffre denied having promised a breakthrough or a quick end to the war, Viviani and Poincaré sharply took issue with him. In the analysis of the conduct of the war, Joffre and Foch favored launching, after a "brief delay," large attacks such as the recent Artois offensive, while Castelnau favored resuming the offensive only after accumulating sufficient means for two large attacks. Without providing specifics, Dubail favored resuming the offensive in "two months, perhaps more."[26] Despite obvious differences, the senior generals supported Joffre's emphasis on the offensive and just as strongly rejected Kitchener's preference for the "passive defense." Poincaré reported: "All believed that if we remain on a pure and simple defensive, we will expose ourselves to massive and incessant attacks. Moreover, Kitchener, they say, can readily suggest this; he does not have occupied provinces to liberate."[27]

Despite support for Joffre at this meeting, strong doubts existed among some of his subordinates. General de Langle, one of Joffre's most experienced and capable army commanders, kept his thoughts to himself, but in his memoirs he complained bitterly about Joffre's interfering in operational planning and decisions. According to de Langle, Joffre controlled the most minute details of operations and "paralyzed the initiative of army commanders." Though decisions appeared to come personally from Joffre, de Langle believed he allowed a small group of officers on his staff to act behind the façade of his authority.[28] Pétain also voiced criticisms. Shortly before the June 16 offensive, he vented his frustrations privately by calling Foch and d'Urbal "fools."[29] In his memoirs Poincaré described a meeting with Pétain in which the future marshal disagreed with Joffre's assessment of the May offensive's failure against Vimy Ridge. The reason for the failure, said Pétain, lay not with the reserves' having been too far in the rear. Even if the reserves had come forward in time, the other corps had not advanced, and XXXIII Corps would have come under strong German counterattack. The root of the failure, Pétain explained, lay in "again starting an action without sufficiently consulting those who had to carry it out."[30] The commander of 70th Division, Fayolle, also had doubts. His division, which had 14,000 soldiers, including 8,000 infantry, had suffered 16,000 casualties between August 1914 and July 1915. He wrote in his diary: "Should we conclude that a penetration is impossible? It surely is [impossible] if the Boches have several lines of defense separated one from the other so [our] artillery cannot take them simultaneously under fire . . . The outcome of the war is in the hands of the Romanians and Bulgarians."[31]

Amidst the numerous criticisms and doubts, Joffre began using the word "attrition" *(usure)* in correspondence with the minister of war and the allies.[32] When he used the word, he had something in mind very different from and more costly than the "nibbling" *(grignotage)* operations of late 1914 or the breakthrough and exploitation he sought in early 1915. Yet he made no dramatic changes in his strategy or in his operational concepts to adjust to a war of attrition. He also refused to "husband" the lives of his men, as General Anthoine had suggested anonymously, and save the French army for use when other armies were "worn out." France could win a war of attrition, he reasoned, only by continuing to bear the heaviest burden of the war, maintaining its multifront strategy and breaking the Germans' defenses with large offensive operations.

Joffre clearly had not lost his faith in the offensive. In a memorandum written in June by the GQG staff on the conduct of an offensive, he carefully edited the first paragraph to read, "If our infantry is stopped, it is less because their offensive force is finished than because the exploitation of their initial success has not been pushed far enough and fast enough."[33] Several weeks later he told a British officer that the idea of abandoning the offensive was "unthinkable" and that the French people could not be expected to remain patient with the stalemate for another winter or docilely await the liberation of the occupied provinces. He emphasized, "We're not the people to let go."[34] When Sir John French asked whether he would consider adopting a "purely defensive position for the moment," Joffre replied that he "entirely and absolutely opposed" such an alternative and that such a strategy would result in the defeat first of the Russians and then of the French and British. He described a "passive defense" as a "wretched strategy, unfair to Russia, Serbia, and Italy, and therefore totally inadmissible."[35]

Events on the Eastern Front, Joffre believed, increased the importance of an offensive in France. As the Germans marched east and the Russians grew more desperate, another report from Major Langlois arrived, this time filled with Russian criticisms of the French.[36] Adding to the alarm signals, the military attaché in Petrograd warned Joffre on June 21 about the deteriorating situation and urged him not to leave the Russians alone to face the "ordeal."[37] To encourage the Russians, Joffre sent Grand Duke Nicholas a message describing French offensive efforts since December and assuring him that France was working toward the same goal as Russia: "never leave our adversary free to concentrate all his effort in a single theater of operations." By working together, France and Russia could "drain the enemy and attrit him."[38] Despite Joffre's reassuring words, the situation in Russia continued to deteriorate, and in mid-July the grand duke demanded strong action on the Western Front to halt the transport toward Russia of new enemy troops. A month later the French ambassador reported, "I fear this army will soon reach the limit of its endurance."[39] As Joffre noted in his memoirs, while some were criticizing him for launching too many large offensives, the Russians were criticizing him for not launching enough.

Ironically, Italy's entry into the war in late May on the side of the Entente added to the pressure on Joffre for an offensive. While the Italians could tie down Austrian forces and indirectly affect Germany's efforts, they did not pose a direct threat to Germany. Additionally, even though the Italians had thirty-eight infantry and four cavalry divisions, they faced very difficult terrain and had little chance of diverting significant forces from the east or achieving a decisive victory. Yet by adding a southern front to the already large Eastern and Western fronts, Italy's entry into the war created additional difficulties for the Central Powers and increased the importance for the allies of "simultaneously attacking on several fronts."[40] As Russia fell back and Italy made little progress, Joffre concluded that "the principal effort of the allies must be made in France."[41]

To shape that "principal effort," Joffre drew several key lessons about operations from the recent offensives. First, he believed it was necessary to attack on as large a front as possible. Enemy reserves, he reasoned, could halt advances on a narrow front easily, but they could not halt all advances on a broad front. Though he refused to rule out a "breakthrough" and insisted that Pétain's XXXIII Corps had "clearly" demonstrated on May 9 that enemy lines could be pierced,[42] he began favoring a different operational concept, one of "breaking up" *(rompre)* enemy lines and causing a "rupture." The idea of seizing enough of a defender's position to make his overall position untenable and thereby forcing him to withdraw probably came from Tenth Army, which had argued in early April that seizing the heights of Vimy Ridge would force the Germans to withdraw toward Douai.[43] The operational concept meshed nicely with the idea of attacking on a broad front, and by late May most orders and memoranda envisaged an attack on a broad front seeking a rupture rather than an attack on a narrow front seeking a breakthrough.

Joffre also favored attacks on several points along the Western Front. The May–June attacks in Artois had demonstrated, he believed, the disadvantages of a "single" attack and the advantages of "simultaneous and mutually supporting attacks on a large front."[44] In essence he had learned that a main attack required support from something other than what Foch had called a "general action along the entire front." A main attack required support from several other large attacks, not from numerous small assaults or raids. By launching several powerful attacks on broad fronts, Joffre concluded, the allies could tie down the Germans' reserves, keep them from concentrating against the main effort, and rupture their defensive lines.

Evidence of Joffre's thinking appeared in a meeting on August 11 with his army-group commanders. Before Millerand's arrival, Foch and Castelnau offered two very different operational concepts. Foch, who was doubtful about Joffre's notion of rupturing the Germans' lines and forcing them to fight in open terrain, favored a carefully prepared, methodical attack. Since the second and third lines of enemy defenses lay outside the range of preparatory artillery fire, an attacking force, he said, had to make a separate effort for each subsequent line and thus had to advance step by step from one trench line to another. In essence, Foch advocated the methodical method he had compelled d'Urbal to adopt in Artois on the night of May 15–16. Disagreeing completely, Castelnau argued that a methodical attack could never push through an enemy's lines, since a defender could rebuild his defenses as quickly as an attacker could renew his means of attack. Instead of a "toe-to-toe" fight with the enemy, he favored a continuous battle. A surprise attack with minimum preparatory artillery fire, he thought, could advance ten to twelve kilometers in twenty-four or forty-eight hours. Although such an attack could not break through all the enemy's defenses, it could rupture the enemy's front. That is, it could drive other opposing forces back sufficiently to create room for maneuver and create a "wing" in the enemy's disposition that would be vulnerable to a subsequent maneuver. The third army-group commander, Dubail, agreed with Castelnau. An attack, he explained, was no longer an attempt to "break through at one point" but instead was a "battle on a front." He also argued that the enemy did not have enough soldiers to man every position in the second and third lines of trenches. The result, Castelnau explained, would be "empty spaces" through which attacking forces could pass. Scoffing at this possibility, Foch insisted that a few enemy machine guns could block the sparsely manned spaces and keep attacking forces from passing through the second and third lines.

Not surprisingly, Joffre favored Castelnau's concepts of continuous battle and rupture and again revealed his instinctive preference for the offense. He told Foch: "If we adopt your system of methodical attack, which will require a month for the attack and a maximum expenditure of munitions, when will we be ready to attack? Perhaps not in the coming year, perhaps not ever. But it is necessary to act—for us and for our allies. As our regulations say, 'Only inaction is shameful.'"[45] France could not, he declared, rest with its "arms crossed" and leave the Germans free to concentrate against the other allies.

Aware of numerous doubts about him and his strategy, Joffre knew he had to convince France's political leaders, as well as his own subordinates, that he had made a careful assessment of his strategic alternatives before he launched another offensive. "The intention of the commander-in-chief," he wrote, "is to profit from the present circumstances, which have caused the Germans to thin their western front, by rupturing their lines of organized defenses and forcing them to accept battle in open country."[46] How to "profit" from the Germans' having shifted forces to the east and thinned their defenses, however, was not clear. On June 27 he asked Foch for his comments about a "larger" attack by Northern Army Group with thirty-five divisions and 500 heavy artillery pieces. On the same day he asked Castelnau for his assessment of an attack with thirty divisions and 450–500 heavy artillery pieces in Central Army Group's sector. He also sent Pétain a copy of his letter to Foch and asked for his views.

Foch sent two responses, a formal one and a long handwritten one, each of which had a different argument to convince Joffre to choose Artois as the sector for the next major offensive. The handwritten note included a long history "lesson" and reflected the academic background of the former École de Guerre professor. After invoking the experiences of Napoleon, the Franco-Prussian War, and the Crimean War, Foch advised Joffre to seize "certain important points of terrain" on Vimy Ridge.

Capturing these points, he said, would compel the Germans to withdraw, but no similar points, he insisted, existed in Champagne. Arguing for another attack by Tenth Army, Foch said the front of the attack had to be enlarged with an attack south of Arras by Second Army and an attack in the north by the British. He also acknowledged the difficulties of coordinating an action with the British and the uncertainty about how long they would continue their attacks.[47]

Just as Foch favored an attack in his sector, Castelnau favored an attack in his army group's sector. After analyzing the fronts (from left to right) of Sixth, Fifth, and Fourth armies, he favored launching an offensive in two sectors. The first was a ten-kilometer sector twenty kilometers west of Reims, near the Chemin des Dames and Aisne River. The second was in Fourth Army's sector. This thirty-kilometer front had Perthes in its center—exactly the same sector as the previous offensive in Champagne. Yet he acknowledged any attack in that sector would "inevitably run up against very serious difficulties."[48]

A very different assessment came from Pétain. Only an army commander and not an army-group commander, he told Joffre that neither a breakthrough nor a decisive battle was possible. He explained: "The war has become a war of attrition. There will be no decisive battle as in other times. Success will come eventually to the side that has the last man. The only objective we should seek is to kill as many Germans as we can while suffering a minimum of losses." Pétain argued that while it was still necessary to carry the battle to the enemy, attacks should take the form of a succession of assaults, each minutely planned and prepared and each coming several weeks after the previous assault. In essence, he favored several small battles or limited offensives rather than one gigantic battle. Joffre, however, saw no strategy for ending the war in Pétain's ideas and was unwilling to decrease pressure on the Germans or to leave them free to concentrate against the Russians. For the GQG staff the most useful part of Pétain's letter came from his analysis of a possible offensive against Vimy Ridge. Pétain had stated emphatically that troops north of Arras were exhausted. "All they are capable of doing at this moment," he said, "is to hold in front of them part of the troops they face."[49]

Despite Foch's desire to continue Tenth Army's attack and seize the heights of Vimy Ridge, the commander of Tenth Army, d'Urbal, agreed with Pétain and advised against renewing the offensive in Artois. He explained: "Fifty days of uninterrupted combat have resulted in a state of fatigue among the troops that does not permit the immediate renewal of the general offensive."[50] Joffre agreed with d'Urbal and abandoned hopes for an immediate renewal of offensive operations in Artois. He ordered Foch to have Tenth Army establish strong defensive positions and limit offensive operations to those absolutely necessary.

As the army-group commanders conducted their assessments, the GQG embarked on its own analysis of alternatives. In an attempt to consider the entire front, the staff divided the Western Front into two parts, with the dividing line running between the Meuse River and the Argonne Forest. An attack east of this line would encounter the Germans' defensive system in the valley of the Rhine River or the fortified barrier formed by Strasbourg, Metz, and Thionville. The staff believed that this sector held no strategic opportunities and that only local offensives such as the reduction of the St.-Mihiel salient should be conducted. To the west of the Argonne Forest, the front line had the shape of a giant salient, the Noyon salient. If a breakthrough were made, the staff believed, attacks on the south face of this salient could ultimately intersect with those on the west face. Converging attacks could thus isolate and destroy the German armies holding the forwardmost part of the Noyon salient. Moreover, the attacks would lead to "the region of Liège, Charleroi, and Mézières, which constitutes south of the Dutch enclave at Maastricht the node of all the communications of the German armies engaged in Belgium and northern France." France and its allies, the GQG staff believed, should concentrate their large offensives west of the Argonne.

The staff's assessment of possible locations for offensives represented a blend of Foch's and Castelnau's comments. The best and only real choices, they thought, were Artois and Champagne. Disagreeing with Foch's reservations, they identified the "incontestable strategic advantages" of rupturing enemy lines in Champagne. By seizing Mézières and cutting the important rail junction there, the French could disrupt the Germans' lines of communication and prevent them from shifting forces laterally in the Noyon salient or receiving assistance from east of Reims. After weighing the advantages of attacks in Champagne and Artois, the staff favored Champagne primarily because of terrain but also because of the significant concentration of German forces and artillery in Artois. They recommended that the principal effort be made in Champagne on "a vast front of more than thirty kilometers" and the secondary effort be made in Artois. If the French began their offensive in Artois with Tenth Army and the British attacking several days before Fourth Army's attack in Champagne, the enemy would shift his reserves from Champagne toward the secondary attack, and Fourth Army could face fewer enemy forces.[51]

After huge losses and several failed offensives, a careful strategic assessment by the GQG staff had returned to the same recommendation as that of December 6, 1914. The primary difference was the emphasis on attacking across a "vast front." Whether this recommendation came from a truly honest assessment or was predetermined to accord with Joffre's predilection is not clear.

In fact the GQG staff knew Joffre's preferences and sometimes presented him suggestions they knew he would favor. For example, when he opened the door in June 1915 to ideas about the best operational methods, two of the brightest people on the GQG and Ministry of War staffs, General Maurice Pellé and Colonel Edmond Buat, offered suggestions. Pellé, Joffre's chief of staff, favored powerful attacks on a broad front, and Buat, the minister of war's executive officer, favored a series of limited attacks similar to those favored by Pétain.[52] While Pellé's proposal did not differ dramatically from those previously preferred by Joffre, Buat suggested something very different. Aware of his commander's thinking, Pellé may have offered his proposal to curry favor with him. Ideas differing significantly from Joffre's came from Foch and Pétain, not from the GQG, and Castelnau's concept—which Joffre favored—corresponded neatly with Joffre's previously expressed idea of "rupturing" the Germans' lines and "forcing them to accept battle in open country." Another example of the staff's acquiescence to Joffre's preconceived ideas appears in an assessment of alternatives for the Central Powers. Completed on August 3, the twenty-seven-page document offered an intelligent, comprehensive assessment of Austro-German options on the Russian, Balkan, Italian, and French fronts. Anticipating an end "very soon" to the drive into Russia, the authors predicted a subsequent "vast effort" by the enemy either in the Balkans or in France. As for the best response by

France to this threat, however, the anonymous staff officers cavalierly concluded, "The simplest method is the attack."[53] Thus, the real problem of the GQG may not have been the influence of the "young Turks" but may instead have been their reluctance to offer ideas they knew Joffre did not favor.

Concurrent with the examination of strategy and operations came an effort to expand production of weapons and materiel. Although the French had vastly increased the manufacture of crucial items and the acquisition of additional resources, the burden and complexity of the effort continued to mount. Angered by Millerand's defense of Joffre and desiring to curb the powers of the minister of war, the government created a new position, assistant secretary for artillery and munitions, and identified Albert Thomas—a young Socialist deputy who was serving in the army on Foch's staff and had dealt with weapons and ammunition issues—for the position. Appointed on May 18, Thomas remained responsible to the minister of war and reduced the burden on him. Although some political and military leaders would have preferred the appointment of General Baquet, the director of artillery, Thomas was far less dependent on Joffre. Turning to his duties with energy and enthusiasm, he quickly uncovered numerous problems in coordination and planning. Ultimately his efforts improved French weapons and munitions even though army officers grumbled about his new role and the blurring of the distinction between civilian and military responsibilities. As a consequence of Thomas's important contributions, the government eventually created a new post, minister of armaments and manufacturing, in December 1916 and appointed him to the position. Thomas thus gained a seat in the Council of Ministers on a par with the ministers of war and navy.

Despite the rearrangement of responsibilities within the Ministry of War in May 1915, Joffre continued to establish requirements for new weapons and materiel, and in the wake of the failed offensive in Artois, he demanded additional artillery. The Artois offensive, he believed, had demonstrated the need for more powerful, long-range artillery that could support the infantry without having to displace forward. By July the French had 4,646 light (3,049 75-mm and 1,597 90-mm) and 3,538 heavy artillery pieces. Joffre considered only the 2,033 long-range 105-, 120-, and 155-mm to be adequate heavy pieces and aimed to have as many of the 120- and 155-mm pieces as 75-mm cannon. Consequently, Thomas placed particular emphasis on the manufacture of 120-mm howitzers. Joffre also demanded very long-range, large-caliber artillery. On July 3 the French had only one 305-mm and twelve 190-mm guns, all of which were mounted on railway platforms. As for munitions, he asked for 80,000 rounds per day for the 75-mm (not including supplies for allies), 9,300 rounds per day for 80- and 90-mm, and 21,250 per day for heavy artillery. Additionally, he asked for "large quantities" of artillery rounds filled with chemicals. Recent combat experience, he said, had demonstrated the importance of asphyxiating gasses in attacking fortified positions.[54] With the arrival of additional heavy artillery and munitions, the French infantry would receive better artillery support in the coming offensive than in past operations.

As Joffre prepared for the autumn offensive, he made a special effort to achieve some semblance of unity of command or direction among the allies. The Marne campaign had demonstrated the difficulties of coordinating allied operations in a fluid and unpredictable environment, and the debate with Sir John French in February over the British relief of two French corps in the Ypres salient, as well as their "inaction" during Tenth Army's offense in May in Artois, demonstrated the persistence of significant problems even in a much less fluid environment. As the British became more interested in the eastern Mediterranean and the Italians entered the war, Joffre perceived an even greater need for allied coordination. On June 24, the day before the Artois offensive formally ended, he wrote the minister of war three letters about the need for unity of command or direction. In the first letter he asked the minister to propose to the other allies that the conduct of the war be "centralized" at the GQG, "where overall plans and operational directives can be elaborated." If the other allies did not want him to give orders, the British and Belgian commanders, he suggested, should follow his instructions. "Only by doing this will it be possible to coordinate all our efforts and make them converge against our adversaries, for whom the conduct of the war is clearly in the hands of only one of the belligerents."[55] Two other letters dispatched that day demonstrated concern about specific issues pertaining to the lack of coordination among the allies. The first complained about the British sending additional troops to Gallipoli. Joffre argued that "English projectiles will be better employed against the Germans than against the Turks." He added, "If Germany is defeated, Turkey will have little weight in the balance, and its fall will be accomplished without difficulty."[56] The second, a personal letter to Millerand, revealed that Sir John French had reservations about possibly being ordered to remain on the defensive and that he was opposed to sending new British divisions to the Dardanelles.[57]

Finally, on June 29 Joffre wrote an even stronger letter to the minister of war and argued for a "common plan of action" among the allies. It began: "Never has the necessity for direction over the coalition appeared more evident than today." Citing the retreat of the Russians, the inactivity of the Serbs, the hesitation of the Italians, and the preference of Lord Kitchener for a passive defense, he argued that "an energetic, concerted offensive by all the allied armies, except Russia, is the only means of parrying the danger and defeating the enemy."[58] With Lord Kitchener scheduled to visit France in a week, he suggested a meeting of allied leaders at Chantilly, the location of his headquarters, to discuss the "best means of giving aid to Russia and interrupting the string of German victories against our eastern ally."[59]

Although many French political leaders deeply resented the power Joffre had, they supported his quest for greater influence over the allies. Clemenceau, for example, joined the chorus of those complaining about Joffre's refusal to subordinate himself to the government, and he insisted that the generals would revolt if Joffre continued his autocratic ways. Poincaré also complained to Millerand about general officers', including army-group commanders', not having the authority to make decisions. Whatever their reservations about Joffre, French political leaders welcomed the obvious influence he had at the first allied military conference in July 1915, which included French, British, Belgian, Russian, Italian, and Serbian representatives. Hopeful of greater cooperation among the allies, the GQG staff referred to Joffre as the "military director" of the coalition,[60] but the allies, particularly the British, refused to permit the emergence of a supreme allied commander. Until March 26, 1918, when Foch was charged by the French and British governments with coordi-

nating the action of allied forces on the Western Front, no allied commander rivaled Joffre's influence over the coalition.

On July 7 Joffre began the allied conference at Chantilly by looking at
the broader aspects of the war and explaining the importance of the allies' coordinating their efforts. After identifying three principal theaters
(Anglo-Franco-Belgian, Italo-Serbian, and Russian) and two secondary
theaters (Caucasus and Gallipoli), he argued: "A decision in the war can
be obtained and should be sought only in the larger theaters of operations. The most favorable conditions for a definitive victory can be established only if the allied armies launch at the same time in the three main
theaters a vigorous offensive against the Austro-German block."[61] If the
allies did not attack simultaneously, he said, the Central Powers could
shift their forces from one theater to another and defeat the individual,
piecemeal attacks.

In his analysis of the Anglo-Franco-Belgian front, Joffre indicated that
the French would launch a "large operation" in several weeks and that he
had delayed this offensive in order to permit new British forces to disembark in France. He believed this offensive would assist the Russians and
occur under the "most favorable conditions," since the Germans had
shifted substantial forces from the Western to the Eastern Front. Even if
the Germans transferred large forces from the east, they would not have
time to organize strong defenses, and thus the French still could attack
under favorable conditions. Sir John French agreed that the strategic situation compelled action and added, "The French soldier, more than any
other, has the necessary offensive qualities."[62]

In discussions at Chantilly, as well as those at Calais with the British
on the previous day, Joffre chose his words carefully. Wary of again being
accused of false promises, he cautioned his colleagues not to use the
words "breakthrough" or "decisive." A more careful use of terms, he suggested, would avoid the "disillusion" that had occurred after the Artois
offensive had failed to break through enemy lines. He also said, "The war
in which we are engaged is so vast that the most striking success will not
always have a decisive effect. It is better to say that the effort will be the
strongest possible given the means at our disposal."[63] Though not expecting a decisive victory over the Germans, he hoped the autumn offensive in France, along with those of the other allies, would yield significant

gains. Joffre's efforts at the conference thus ensured broader acceptance of the French view of the war and better coordination of the coalition's efforts, but they also demonstrated his evolving views on the nature of the war.

During this same period Joffre sought greater cooperation from the British. A month before the allied conference, he had sent Sir John French a draft concept for an attack in Artois and Champagne and asked for his support. After considering the proposal, Sir John accepted it, according to the British official history, "in principle."[64] With the requirements of the coming offensive in mind, the two leaders met on June 24, and Sir John revealed that London might order him to stay on the defensive (something that Joffre quickly communicated to the minister of war). Although many questions remained with regard to the coming offensive, the two agreed to devote their energies to ensuring that British reinforcements went to France rather than elsewhere. With Sir John French safely in his camp, Joffre turned to the more difficult task of convincing Lord Kitchener. Although the British secretary of state for war had reluctantly agreed at the March 29 meeting to send additional forces to France, the failure of the Artois offensive in May and June heightened his doubts about Joffre's operations and strengthened his resolve not to waste British lives in futile attacks on the deadlocked Western Front. He preferred delaying any offensive until the following year, when "all the allies can take the offensive at the same time."[65]

The day before the Chantilly conference, French and British political and military leaders met at Calais and discussed strategy. At the meeting Millerand argued that "prudence during the coming months is imperative, [but] we can never think [of assuming] a passive defense."[66] Also favoring offensive action, Joffre insisted that two large attacks, one with a front of twenty-five kilometers and the other with one of thirteen, would suffer fewer casualties than smaller attacks. He also insisted that the allies could not remain on the defensive; if they did, the Germans would attack "in a month." Given the Germans' significant advances in the east, the French general argued persuasively that the allies had to strike before the enemy shifted troops from the Eastern to the Western Front. After acknowledging that such attacks might not break through the enemy's defenses, he argued that Russia was being attacked "at this moment" and that the allies on the Western Front should assist it, as well as Italy and Serbia, by attacking. To increase the power of such an attack, he encouraged Britain to "give the maximum" and send additional divisions to France. He concluded, "It is necessary for each nation to fulfill its duty as an ally."[67] Despite Joffre's best efforts, Kitchener left the conference believing that the allies had agreed not to launch a "serious offensive" until all the allies were ready. In mid-August, with the situation much worse in Russia, Kitchener finally yielded and reluctantly accepted the launching of an offensive. When Churchill complained about this, Kitchener responded: "unfortunately, we have to make war as we must, and not as we should like to."[68]

Throughout July and August Joffre, who did not want British "inaction" to hinder another offensive, worked with Field Marshal French on the details of British actions in the coming offensive. By launching attacks in different regions, Joffre argued, the allies could prevent the Germans from concentrating all their reserves in a single sector, and by attacking on a broad front, the allies could avoid having enemy artillery on the flanks of an attack place enfilade fire across the entire front of advancing troops. The May and June offensives in Artois had failed, he said, because they were launched on too narrow a front. The two allied leaders agreed that the front of the next attack should be extended by having the English and French make separate attacks on the flanks of the main attack, but they disagreed on the location of the British attack. Joffre believed a British attack between the left flank of Tenth Army (which would strike Vimy Ridge) and La Bassée would widen the front of the general offensive but still permit Tenth Army and the British to cover each other's flank. An attack north of La Bassée would not have the same effect, he believed, since it would separate the two forces too far for them to provide such support. Joffre also wanted the British to relieve French troops on the right of Tenth Army south of Arras so that he could accumulate reserves for his offensive. Sir John French, however, refused to relieve French troops south of Arras, since his government preferred to extend the British front to the north. After Joffre insisted, Field Marshal French finally agreed to relieve the French Second Army south of Arras in time for the offensive. When he reviewed the minutes of the meeting, however, he asked for the text to be changed to indicate that the relief would be completed during the first week of August. His comments indicated some doubts about whether the British would be ready to attack on August 15.

Other problems immediately appeared. After the commander of the British First Army, General Haig, studied the possibility of an attack south of La Bassée, he strongly recommended against it. German defenses were too strong, the ground was too open, and parallel trenches could not be dug beforehand in the chalky soil without warning the enemy. Haig's doubts compelled Sir John French to meet with Foch on July 27 and propose an attack north of La Bassée. Foch acknowledged Sir John's concerns but insisted that if the British reached the heights overlooking Lens at the same time that the French reached the top of Vimy Ridge, the allies would dominate the entire plain of Douai. A British success north of La Bassée, Foch argued, would not have the same operational effect and would not contribute as much to the main offensive effort. More important, an attack at another point such as Ypres would not draw off the enemy's reserves and would have no effect on enemy artillery in the Vimy Ridge area. As for the La Bassée region's being strongly defended, Foch reminded the field marshal that the Germans had had months to prepare their position and that they occupied strong positions in the entire northern region.[69]

Sir John French remained unconvinced. In a letter to Joffre he objected to Foch's assertion that German defenses were no stronger south of La Bassée than anywhere else along the front. He insisted the numerous buildings, slag heaps, and mines in the Lens-Loos area offered many advantages to a defender. As for the operational importance of the region, he believed the capture of Aubers Ridge (near Neuve-Chapelle) or the Wytschaete-Messines Ridge (eight kilometers south of Ypres) would provide the greatest advantage for offensive operations in the spring. He nonetheless expressed a willingness to attack wherever Joffre desired. The area south of La Bassée, Joffre responded, was the best location for the British to attack. He explained:

> The experience of this war clearly confirms that it is best to attack on fronts as large as possible to avoid concentrations of enemy artillery fire [from both flanks]. This will be precisely the case for the at-

tack by the Anglo-French armies, who will mutually cover their interior flanks. Finally, I believe with the strongest conviction that an English action applied on another part [of the front] . . . will constitute a distinct effort and will diverge from the principal French effort in the region of Arras.[70]

In short, Joffre wanted him to attack south of La Bassée at Loos.

Sir John French's response on August 10 surprised Joffre. Though the field marshal agreed to attack, he said he would rely primarily on artillery and leave most of his infantry in the trenches. Joffre's quick response reminded the British commander that he had promised to help Tenth Army and that such help could come only from a "large and powerful attack."[71] In a note to Foch, Joffre complained that the British intended to make a "simple demonstration and not a serious attack."[72] Two days later Sir John French said that the role played by the British would depend on the quantity of munitions available to them. Since the British had previously used ammunition shortages as an excuse not to attack, this report was bad news. Good news, however, came on August 19 from the chief of the French military mission to the British army. He reported that Lord Kitchener had arrived that day (apparently at the bidding of the French), discussed the upcoming attacks with Field Marshal French, and directed him to support the French attack with all his available forces. On August 22 Sir John informed Joffre that the British would be ready on September 8 to attack south of La Bassée. Thus, as the British official history observed, Field Marshal French was "compelled to undertake operations before he was ready, over ground that was most unfavourable, against the better judgment of himself and of General Haig."[73]

After the Chantilly conference on July 7 and publication of the GQG's strategic assessment on July 8, Joffre published an order on July 12 providing the broad outlines of the autumn offensive, which would squeeze the Noyon salient in the "vise" of two large offensives coming from Artois and Champagne. According to this order, both Northern Army Group and Central Army Group would seek to "rupture" the enemy front, the former in Artois near Arras and the latter in Champagne. Eastern Army Group would remain on the defensive but would conduct local actions. When Joffre reviewed the various orders associated with the offensive he added the word "rupture" to Foch's instructions.[74] Additional directions from Joffre to Castelnau and Foch placed the responsibility for France's main attack with Castelnau's Central Army Group. While Castelnau had twenty-seven infantry divisions and two cavalry corps for the main attack in Champagne, Foch had twelve infantry and two cavalry divisions for his attack against Vimy Ridge. Joffre also allocated Castelnau 584 heavy artillery pieces and Foch 344 (these numbers would increase substantially by the date of the attack). Foch's and Castelnau's attacks would occur in the same sectors as the previous attacks in Artois and Champagne, but Joffre wanted Castelnau's main attack to have a front of forty kilometers, many times larger than the five-kilometer front of the Champagne offensive from February 16 to March 25.

To amass sufficient forces for the offensive, Joffre had to shift boundaries and move units. After the British assumed responsibility for part of Second Army's front in Artois and Sixth Army took over the remainder, he pulled the headquarters of Pétain's Second Army out of the line and sent it to Champagne. He also transferred command of Sixth Army from Central to Northern Army Group and Third Army from Eastern to Central Army Group. With these changes, Castelnau's Central Army Group had four armies: Second, Third, Fourth, and Fifth.

As Central Army Group planned its part of the autumn offensive, a key question concerned the placement of Second Army. After Fourth Army conducted a detailed terrain analysis and identified four operational sectors in the zone of the main attack, Castelnau decided to give Fourth Army the two sectors on the left and Second Army the two sectors on the right. The insertion of Second Army meant that Castelnau had from left to right Fifth, Fourth, Second, and Third armies. To conceal the transfer of Second Army to Champagne, the French named Pétain an assistant to Castelnau and spread false information that the army was being transferred to Italy or the Dardanelles. Not until August 10 did Pétain formally assume command of "Pétain Group," which initially included three corps, and not until September 20 did Second Army become the formal name of Pétain's command.

On July 21 Castelnau sent Joffre his concept for his attack. Using words he would use again in a meeting on August 11 with Joffre and other army-group commanders, he wrote:

> the essential objective of these operations is to create a wing in the disposition of the enemy. . . . Once this wing is created, reserve forces should intervene for the maneuver [phase] and inflict a severe defeat on a significant part of the opposing forces that operate on the Franco-Belgian front. To create a wing in the actual disposition of the enemy, one must rupture his front and drive back the remnants on a width and on a sufficient depth to assure a zone of free movement, a zone of maneuver, for the forces that are charged with attacking the rest of the opponent's disposition.

A depth of twelve kilometers seemed sufficient to Castelnau to provide this zone of maneuver.[75] The army-group commander proposed having Fourth and Second armies make the main attack, while Fifth Army on their left and Third Army on their right made supporting attacks. He intended to attack only after "particularly effective" preparatory fire from the artillery, and he anticipated needing sufficient artillery ammunition for ten days' firing, two in preparation, six in the assault, and two for the unexpected. He expected the mass of the French forces to move toward the northwest after rupturing the enemy's lines. On July 25 Joffre approved Castelnau's concept. His key change pertained to artillery; he considered stocks for only seven, rather than ten, days' firing sufficient.

With Joffre's approval Castelnau gave his army commanders his plan for Fourth and Second armies to make the main attack across a twenty-eight-kilometer front that centered on Perthes and extended generally from Aubérive to Massiges. Preparatory firing would begin three days before the assault, but, as in the June 16 attack north of Arras, massive fires on the enemy's forward position would not begin until the infantry assault. Such a tactic would not alert the enemy or "provoke" barrages on the assaulting troops. The French intended to use asphyxiating gasses and incendiary rounds in the offensive; they would use gas rounds primarily in counterbattery fires and incendiary rounds against wooded areas. Though Joffre's original intention was for Fifth Army to remain on the defensive, he approved Castelnau's proposal that Fifth Army attack in conjunction with the principal offensive in Champagne.

With Castelnau's concept in hand, de Langle (commander of Fourth Army) and Pétain proceeded with their planning. De Langle published a warning order for the attack on July 30 and an operations order on September 5. Between a point west of Aubérive and another west of Perthes, he placed four infantry corps in the front line (ten divisions, but one of these guarded the army's left flank). He also placed an infantry corps (two divisions) and a cavalry corps, plus two infantry divisions, in the second line. For the attack, de Langle's army had 1,212 artillery pieces, including 392 heavy ones. Evidently intending to make a breakthrough along a line between Suippes, Souain, and Somme-Py, he concentrated more of his front- and second-line forces on his right. Pétain did not formally assume command of Pétain Group until August 10, but he arrived in the area a week before this date and on August 6 published instructions for the attack of Second Army, which was temporarily called "N" Army. He distributed more detailed instructions on September 5 and on September 20 published the final order. Between a point west of Perthes and another east of Massiges, he placed four infantry corps in the front line (nine divisions) and an infantry corps (two divisions) and a cavalry corps, plus two infantry divisions, in the second line. For the attack, Pétain's army had 952 artillery pieces, including 336 heavy ones.

In accord with Joffre's order Fourth and Second armies, attacking on a front of twenty-eight kilometers, aimed to rupture the enemy's defenses. Eighteen divisions in Central Army Group (each with a front of 1,500–2,000 meters) would assault the German positions, while eight infantry divisions followed closely in the second line. Together, the two attacking armies had 2,164 artillery pieces, including 728 heavy ones. Though divisions in the second line could act as reserves, their actual role was to maintain the momentum of the attack by entering the front line at an appropriate moment to join in the attack or to assault a previously assigned objective. In essence, divisions in the second line would enable Fourth and Second armies to fight a continuous battle without having to pause for the shifts inherent in a methodical battle. As for Fifth and Third armies, their supporting attacks sought to keep the attacking armies advancing once the offensive began.

An important change of leadership within Central Army Group occurred on July 22, when Joffre relieved the commander of Third Army, General Maurice Sarrail, and replaced him with General Georges Humbert. Since the beginning of the war, Joffre had relieved 138 generals who had failed to perform to his expectations, but the relief of Sarrail proved particularly controversial because he was widely considered France's foremost republican general. The Germans had attacked in the Argonne on June 20 and 30 and July 12 and 13, and, according to Joffre, Sarrail's Third Army had performed poorly in the exchange of attacks and counterattacks and "yielded the initiative to the adversary." On July 16 Joffre asked Dubail, commander of Eastern Army Group, to investigate the causes of the "persistent lack of success" in the Argonne.[76] Hints of Dubail's reservations about Sarrail as a leader had appeared in a memorandum on July 16 from him to General de Castelnau. After Joffre transferred Third Army from Eastern Army Group to Central Army Group, Dubail had warned Castelnau about the condition, situation, and operations of the army and noted that the Germans—unlike Third Army—had maintained an "aggressive attitude" without considerable losses.[77] While eschewing a large offensive, Sarrail had launched many small attacks to gain and maintain "moral ascendancy" over the enemy, but these attacks had come at high cost in casualties and had contributed to Third Army's slowly being driven back several kilometers.

After conducting his investigation, Dubail sent the results to Joffre in two letters; one addressed operations and the other morale. The report on operations contained positive comments but damned Sarrail's operational concept for being "too simplistic" and keeping the divisions in "rigid zones." The report on morale emphasized the "lack of mutual confidence" between Sarrail and the commander of XXXII Corps and the presence of severe problems in Third Army's staff, including the sending of false reports to higher headquarters. Dubail concluded his report by emphasizing the "malaise" in Third Army and recommending Sarrail's relief.[78] With his reservations about Sarrail corroborated, Joffre relieved him and the commander of XXXII Corps; he also reassigned Sarrail's chief of staff. Accepting Dubail's recommendation, he named Humbert the new commander of Third Army.

As one historian has noted, Sarrail's relief brought the "first direct confrontation between the government, the parliamentarians, and the

High Command."[79] Yet it also created considerable concern about Third Army's performance in the coming offensive and compelled Castelnau to monitor Humbert's actions carefully. At one point Castelnau sharply reprimanded him and then identified "imperfections" in Third Army, including inadequate obstacles in front of trenches, poor shelters in trenches, and "defective practices" among the artillery. As Central Army Group prepared for the autumn offensive in Champagne, Castelnau wanted to avoid a disaster in Third Army that might place the entire offensive at risk.

Meanwhile Northern Army Group also prepared for the autumn offensive. On July 15 Foch informed General d'Urbal, the Tenth Army commander, of Joffre's plan for a "double" attack, one in Artois near Arras and the other in Champagne. Though only 800–1,200 meters separated d'Urbal's frontline units from the crest of Vimy Ridge, Tenth Army had fewer infantry than in its previous offensives, a reduction that greatly troubled its commander. At the end of a memorandum to Foch providing an initial concept for the operation, d'Urbal wrote: "it is my duty to call to your attention the reduction of means at my disposal. . . . But the task remains the same, an arduous effort against an enemy warned and on guard; this [situation] will necessitate considerable and prolonged efforts and will result in great losses among the attacking infantry." D'Urbal requested three additional divisions, but Joffre said no and wrote on his copy of d'Urbal's memorandum, "I do not want to sacrifice the infantry uselessly."[80] He then sent Foch a letter in which he said Tenth Army had sufficient personnel to perform its mission in the coming offensive. Thinking that d'Urbal wanted to launch an "uninterrupted succession of partial attacks," Joffre condemned such attacks and expressed his preference for operations "prepared by artillery concentrations, separated by delays during which enemy batteries will be discovered and destroyed." Though he had not yet moved into the methodical-battle camp, he recognized that such methods could be useful. Unaware of d'Urbal's letter to Foch, Fayolle damned the entire operation: "This is foolish."[81]

On August 23 Foch ordered d'Urbal to alter his plans, which had envisaged a methodical attack on a relatively narrow front. Attentive to Joffre's intentions, Foch wanted the front enlarged by an action south of Arras. D'Urbal completed a new plan on August 29, but Foch rejected the plan because the main attack still had too narrow a front. The Tenth Army commander completed another plan on September 4, and Foch accepted it. With six corps in the front line, the front of Tenth Army stretched across thirty-two kilometers from south of Loos to south of Arras. The four corps on the left would make the main attack north of Arras while the two corps on the right made a supporting attack south of Arras. To increase Tenth Army's chances of success, Joffre increased its allocation of heavy artillery ammunition. On the eve of the attack, Tenth Army had six corps with sixteen divisions in the front line and three infantry divisions, plus a cavalry corps, in reserve. It also had 1,090 artillery pieces, including 420 heavy ones. As in Fourth and Second armies, each of the three infantry divisions in de Langle's reserve waited closely behind a corps in the front line.

As the French prepared their offensive, local attacks and counterattacks proceeded. From the end of June until the end of July, the Germans attacked in the Argonne and in the St.-Mihiel salient. The French responded by attacking in the St.-Mihiel region, as well as in the Vosges Mountains. While making only small attacks on the Western Front, the Germans concentrated their primary efforts on the Eastern Front. On July 13 they renewed their offensive against the Russians. Warsaw fell on August 5, and the Polish salient ceased to exist by the middle of August. For the next six weeks the Germans and Austrians advanced relentlessly across Russia, finally halting at the end of September along a line that ran south from the Gulf of Riga to Dvinsk, Pinsk, and the northern tip of Romania. From Gorlice-Tarnów, the Central Powers had advanced more than 300 kilometers.

As the Germans marched across Russia, the scheduled date of the allied autumn offensive slipped from September 8, to 15, and then to 25. Constituting Second Army proved more complicated than expected, and Pétain demanded additional time to coordinate the actions of his army and become familiar with its commanders. General de Langle's Fourth Army, though in place for months, welcomed the delay. Joffre intended Northern Army Group to attack before Central Army Group, but after the first delay he decided to launch both attacks simultaneously. A study by the head of the Operations Bureau, Lieutenant Colonel Maurice Gamelin, convinced him that uncertainties in the weather could delay the first or second offensive and thus disrupt the operational effect of having two offensives. All the attacks in the offensive, Joffre decided, should occur on the same day.

Hoping to have the advantage of surprise, Joffre ordered local attacks and digging of parallel trenches along the entire front to keep the enemy confused about the location of the coming attack. The High Command also developed a deception plan to convince the Germans that the allies were going to attack on the Western Front between the Somme and the English Channel and that seven French corps were being transported to the Italian theater. When the French learned that the Germans were paying special attention to the activities of Pétain, Joffre had him make a well-publicized visit to Nancy, 120 kilometers to the east of his actual headquarters. Though an intelligence report on September 23 indicated heavy railway traffic near Douai, neither it nor reports on the following two days provided any evidence that the Germans expected a new offensive on the Western Front.

Doubts nonetheless existed about achieving complete surprise. In early September an intelligence report identified a second band of defenses four to five kilometers behind the enemy's frontline trenches in Champagne and a third band fifteen kilometers behind the second. Both Fourth and Second armies knew that these new trenches were "more than a simple line without depth."[82] Joffre's optimism nevertheless prevailed, and on September 15 he wrote to his army-group commanders: "The Germans have only a very few reserves behind their thin line of entrenchments." He added, "The simultaneity of the attacks, their strength, their width, will prevent the enemy from massing his infantry and artillery reserves on a point as he was able to do north of Arras [against the May 9 and June 16 offensives]."[83]

Hopes for an exploitation after the rupture of enemy lines caused the French to pay particular attention to the cavalry. According to General de Castelnau, the cavalry had failed in previous battles to move forward rapidly and take advantage of advances made by the infantry, so he directed more centralized control of squadrons within corps and numerous exercises in crossing trenches and battered terrain. He also directed the formation of special platoons on foot to open passages for the cavalry on horseback. The first objective of the cavalry was the enemy's artillery, the

destruction of which would ease the advance of the following waves of infantry and cavalry. Joffre directed that cavalry in the north drive toward
Mons and in the center toward Mézières. Everything was set for a vast
exploitation.

Confident of success, Joffre asked that the size of the coming attack be
explained to all soldiers. The explanatory note said: "Three-quarters of
all French forces will participate in the battle. They will be supported by
2,000 heavy [artillery] pieces and 3,000 field pieces for which the provision of munitions surpasses greatly those at the beginning of the war.
Every chance of success exists, particularly if one remembers that our recent attack near Arras was made by fifteen divisions and 300 heavy
pieces."[84]

For Central Army Group's attack, Second Army's frontline divisions
were in position by August 30 and the second-line divisions by September 21. Except for one frontline division, which did not arrive until September 16, Fourth Army's frontline divisions were in position by August
20 and second-line divisions by September 20. Preparatory fires began
on September 22, three days before the date of the infantry assault. The
frontline divisions initially kept only a small number of troops in the front
trenches, but on the night of 24–25 the remainder moved forward and occupied frontline positions a few hours before the assault. Unfortunately
for the French, heavy rain began on the night of 24–25. The rain continued with only short respites until September 29.

At 0915 hours on September 25, eighteen divisions in Central Army
Group assaulted the German positions. In Second Army, the most remarkable advance came north of Perthes from XIV Corps on Pétain's left.
With 27th Division on its right and 28th Division on its left, XIV Corps
had only 100–150 meters separating it from the German front line. Beginning at 0900 hours French artillery blasted the enemy's trenches to the
immediate front of the two divisions, and fifteen minutes later waves of
French infantry, organized in columns, left their trenches. The infantry
moved quickly, overrunning the enemy's first trench and crossing the
danger zone before German artillery fired barrages on the forward
trenches of the French. By 1000 hours 27th Division, moving more
quickly than the 28th because it had open terrain instead of woods to
cross, had overrun the three trenches of the first German line. The two

divisions continued attacking and by the end of the day had advanced four kilometers, halting when they encountered the enemy's second band of trenches.

In Fourth Army, the most remarkable advance came north of Souain from II Colonial Corps on de Langle's right; the corps pushed forward about three kilometers. Since II Colonial and XIV corps were side by side on the boundaries between Fourth and Second armies, hopes of a breakthrough soared. After ordering II Colonial to use all its reserves, de Langle moved VI Corps closer behind II Colonial and then at 1615 hours ordered VI Corps to enlarge the gain made by the colonial corps. By nightfall two divisions of VI Corps had entered the line. Later that night Castelnau placed another division at the disposition of Fourth Army. Other than the gains made by II Colonial and XIV corps, only two small gains were made on the first day, one in each of the armies.

On September 26 the French continued their attacks. German heavy artillery, which had fired only sporadically on the first day of the attack, massed rounds against the infantry. In Second Army, XIV Corps, which had moved forward rapidly on the first day, received strong enemy fire from a second band of trenches that sat on the reverse slope of a hill and had fields of intact barbed wire to its front. Against poor weather and bad visibility, XIV Corps tried to open breaches in the wire with 75-mm rounds but failed; it nevertheless made two attacks north of Perthes that morning. At noon Castelnau placed XVI Corps at the disposition of Second Army; he wanted XVI Corps inserted to the right of XIV Corps. Late in the afternoon a brigade in XIV Corps managed to fight its way through the second band of trenches, but a counterattack drove the soldiers back.

Fourth Army also continued to attack. On its right VI Corps advanced at 1430 hours in II Colonial's sector and suffered heavy losses. The corps commander explained that barbed wire in front of the German trenches had a depth of sixty to eighty meters and had not been destroyed by artillery fire. To the left of II Colonial and VI corps, VII Corps, which had been reinforced with a division, began moving forward rapidly in the morning and reached the second band of trenches at 1000 hours. As it attempted to fight its way through enemy defenses, it, too, suffered heavily. Nonetheless VII Corps's advance added significantly to French gains. At the end of the second day of the offensive, Fourth and Second armies had driven forward three or four kilometers, but the second band of German defenses had halted their forward movement. Fourth Army had captured 6,000 prisoners, Second Army 10,000.

The insertion of VI and XVI corps raised hopes for even greater gains on the third day of the offensive. To increase the chances of success, the French moved part of their heavy artillery forward, but when Fourth and Second armies attacked at 1600 hours on September 27, neither made significant gains. After halting Second Army, Pétain informed Castelnau that enemy defenses and barbed wire to his front could be destroyed "only by a meticulously detailed preparation like that executed on the first [enemy] position." Troops previously engaged in the battle could not participate in the attack because "their losses have been considerable, their leaders have for the most part disappeared, and their offensive value is greatly reduced."[85] The following day, Second Army did not attack, but Fourth Army did. A visit by Joffre to Pétain's command post that day resulted in a terse message from Pétain to his corps commanders saying that Second Army would continue attacking.

That night, September 28–29, Castelnau's headquarters received a report that VII Corps had broken through the second band of trenches west of Souain "at a depth that is not yet determined."[86] The breakthrough supposedly had occurred in the center of Fourth Army. Joy surged through Castelnau's headquarters when a subsequent report stated that the breach was 700 meters wide and that two or three brigades had passed through it. Castelnau quickly ordered Second Army to "support at any price the progress" of Fourth Army.[87] The next morning he sent another message verifying that Fourth Army had made a breach in the enemy's second band of trenches.

The report, however, proved false. In fact a brigade from 14th Division in VII Corps had captured what was known as the Trench of Tantes (500 meters west of Ferme de Navarin) and continued to advance, but it immediately encountered heavy machine-gun, gas, and artillery barrages and was thrown back. Within the enemy's second band of trenches, another trench lay a few hundred meters behind the Trench of Tantes. Though—as the French official history notes—the origin of the false information is "difficult to determine,"[88] an erroneous report of a breakthrough flashed from 14th Division to higher headquarters.

The false report resulted in several costly actions. Castelnau ordered Fourth Army to move all its available forces toward the "breach," and de Langle brought his cavalry corps forward. VII Corps made a night attack in an attempt to widen the breach, and on its right VI Corps launched a night attack. Both failed with heavy losses. The following day three infantry brigades attempted to pass through the breach and also suffered heavy losses. For reasons that are incomprehensible, the false information became even more exaggerated. After receiving reports that the breach had been enlarged, Castelnau reported to Joffre on the twenty-ninth that three infantry divisions had passed through the opening.

Later that afternoon, the disappointing truth became known. Attempts to open a breach had failed, and the attacking infantry had suffered terribly. Around midnight Castelnau told de Langle to halt the attack and devote the following day to restoring order. He wired Joffre's headquarters and informed him that the attack could not be renewed for several days. Second Army had prepared an attack for September 30, but at 0930 hours Pétain terminated it. The offensive had made its largest gains on the first day, and except for the advance of VII Corps on the second day, no other significant advances occurred. Though chances of further gains may have existed, the mixing of units and the disorder that arose from the false report of a breach ended any hopes of renewing the offensive quickly.

The supporting attacks on the left and right of Fourth and Second armies contributed little to the offensive. On the right, Third Army had the mission of covering the flank of the two armies in the main attack, but it failed to advance. Bad weather prevented the French from using aircraft and balloons for observation, and artillery had no effect on a second line of defenses that ground observers could not see. The infantrymen of 128th Division, who led Third Army's attack, advanced quickly until they struck this second line and came under heavy artillery and machine-gun fire. After three German counterattacks, they pulled back in disorder to their original line. In only a few hours the division lost 130 officers and 4,158 soldiers. Having little choice, Castelnau ordered Third Army to remain on the defensive. Changing commanders of Third Army—from Sarrail to Humbert—had not improved its performance.

On the left of the main attack, Fifth Army never moved forward. Since its attack was supposed to support Fourth and Second armies after they penetrated the main German defenses, Fifth Army began its artillery preparation but never moved out of its trenches. In the middle of the night on September 29–30, Castelnau stopped the preparatory firing.

After Castelnau suspended the offensive on September 30, he asked Joffre for a delay of several days before renewing the offensive. Though uncertain about the offensive, Joffre told Castelnau to proceed as if another attack were going to be launched. On October 2, after meeting with Foch to discuss the situation, he told Castelnau to make the attack and gave him the requested ammunition, emphasizing that "these munitions represent the totality of what I have at my disposal."[89] He also sent Castelnau his few remaining fresh divisions.

The next day Joffre sent the minister of war a long memorandum in which he described the planning and execution of the autumn offensive. Though he wrote the memorandum to convince the Viviani government to give priority to the Western Front and not shift forces and resources to the Balkans, he acknowledged that it had not been possible to break through the enemy's second band of defenses. Given the need for fresh troops and more ammunition, he expected to "suspend the attacks momentarily." He would launch another large offensive as soon as preparations were complete.[90] Thus, Joffre gave the green light to the final costly attacks of the autumn offensive. This time, however, he favored a methodical, rather than a continuous, battle.

Castelnau intended to concentrate his main attack along a front of twelve kilometers, two-thirds of which was on Fourth Army's right and one-third on Second Army's left. Preceded by two days of artillery preparation, the attack aimed—the formal orders stated—to rupture the Germans' second line by driving them back three kilometers behind the small Py River; but none of the senior commanders expected such grand results. Castelnau initially scheduled the attack for October 5 and then changed it to October 6. The only noteworthy aspect of the attack was that de Langle planned on using a rolling barrage. Adhering to a timetable, artillery batteries would fire their barrages automatically on previously designated objectives, and the infantry would move by "successive bounds regulated in advance by space and time."[91] The French had started using such techniques as early as May 1915.[92]

Artillery preparation began on October 4 even though the weather limited visibility. At 0520 hours on October 6, the infantry made its assault against trenches described by a liaison officer from Joffre's headquarters as "much less solid but less familiar than the position seized on September 25." Adding to the defense's strength, enemy artillery—more numerous than that of the previous attack—protected the trenches.[93] Fourth Army made almost no progress. Elements from two brigades in II Colonial Corps in de Langle's center initially made rapid progress, driving through the wire for more than a kilometer, capturing numerous prisoners, and destroying an artillery battery, but heavy enemy fire and counterattacks soon drove them back. In Second Army, XIV and XVI corps on Pétain's left made almost no gains. XIV Corps reported that artillery had cut the first line of wire but not the second. The corps commander estimated that it would take five or six days to make another assault, including four or five days to dig parallel trenches. Two of the three divisions in XVI Corps made no progress, primarily because enemy barbed wire barred their way, but the division on the right advanced 500 meters and captured the heights of Tahure. This gain was the most significant of the offensive.

At 1600 hours Castelnau ordered de Langle and Pétain to continue the attack the following day with the same objectives, but Pétain, concerned that his troops were "very tired," requested that only the two corps in his center continue the attack.[94] Castelnau relented and ordered his army commanders to secure the terrain they had seized and to conduct only those local actions necessary to consolidate their positions. He then informed Joffre of his actions and said: "the operation . . . has not succeeded. It can be resumed only after a new preparation, more complete than that which was accomplished on October 4 and 5."[95] Joffre had no choice; he approved Castelnau's actions and late on October 7 terminated the offensive.

The attack in Artois met with no more success than the one in Champagne. Following Foch's halting of the Artois offensive on June 18, the Germans had worked diligently to strengthen their position on Vimy Ridge. While the crest of the ridge near Souchez lay only 700–1,100 meters from French lines, the heights elsewhere generally lay 1,500–2,000 meters from friendly lines. The Germans filled this area with a vast array of trenches, making it a ghastly network of defenses looking down on the French and bristling with barbed wire and machine guns. Though the defenses immediately south of Arras seemed weaker than those to the north, the Germans skillfully placed reverse-slope defenses in the first band of trenches and gave their position additional depth by establishing a second band of trenches about four kilometers to the rear. Though previous attacks had established a base of operations for Tenth Army, defenses to its front now were stronger than ever. Tenth Army had more artillery than in previous attacks, but it had fewer infantrymen.

Preparations for the attack proceeded according to the plan. Artillery fire began on September 18 for III Corps, which was in the center of Tenth Army and faced some of the strongest defenses. Preparatory fire for the other corps began on September 23. On the same day, aircraft and dirigibles began striking railways running between Lille, Valenciennes, Douai, and Cambrai. When the weather turned bad the next day, Foch toyed with delaying the attack for a day.

The Artois offensive began, however, on the morning of September 25, the same day as the Champagne offensive. With the infantry in the trenches by 0430 and visibility sufficient, Foch scheduled the attack for 1225 hours. At the assigned minute the infantry climbed out of their trenches and quickly captured most of the enemy's front line. Much to Foch's dismay, rain began half an hour after the infantry started its assault. Water and mud filled the trenches and covered the battered terrain, making movement extremely difficult. Despite the bad weather Tenth Army made "appreciable gains"—the words of d'Urbal—north of Arras on the first day of the offensive. Since artillery preparation had done little damage to the enemy's wire south of Arras, attacks there failed to make any gains.

The next day d'Urbal decided to continue the attack where it had a "chance of success." Foch agreed and directed him to attack only after a "serious artillery preparation."[96] While the corps south of Arras remained in their trenches, the two northernmost corps launched another assault at 1310 hours. Foch and d'Urbal wanted to maintain enough pressure to keep the enemy from shifting forces to another portion of the front. Joffre, however, sent Foch a message saying that he should "not think of forcing the crest of Vimy," since the French did not have sufficient artillery ammunition to permit another prolonged preparation.[97] He also met with Foch that afternoon. The minutes of that meeting captured Joffre's primary concerns: "Stop the attacks of Tenth Army but avoid giving the British the impression that we are letting them attack alone. . . . The attack of Tenth Army may succeed, but this will be at the price of new quantities of munitions and new divisions that the commander-in-chief cannot provide now because they are needed elsewhere to exploit success."[98] In short, Joffre did not want attacks at Vimy to come at the expense of his attempt to break through enemy lines in Champagne, but he also did not want the British to think they were being sacrificed for nothing.

Despite limitations on artillery support, Tenth Army again made progress on September 26, capturing Souchez and advancing east. To the left of Tenth Army, the British First Army also made gains on September 25–26. Some British units drove forward three kilometers before being halted by the enemy's second band of defenses. Between the right of the British advance around Loos and the left of the French advance around Souchez, however, the Germans continued holding, forming a salient several kilometers deep and posing a threat to the British right flank. As the French prepared to renew their offensive, false reports late on September 26 of a breakthrough by XII Corps near Neuville—in a bizarre coincidence—caused considerable confusion and unnecessary moves and left the two corps in Tenth Army's center in such a "state of disorder," according to Foch, that the two corps could not participate in an attack the following day.[99] On September 27 the four corps on Tenth Army's right "reorganized" themselves, while the two corps on the left renewed their attacks. Sensing that the enemy was yielding on Tenth Army's left, Foch and d'Urbal hoped the attack would aid the British First Army. The attack, however, made almost no gains.

The British demanded more support. Late on September 27 the liaison officer to Foch's headquarters informed him that the British had expended a large amount of artillery ammunition and that without French assistance they would halt their offensive. Foch responded by sending eight batteries of heavy artillery. That same evening Sir John French sent a message to Joffre saying that his flank was exposed and that if Tenth

Army did not continue attacking, he would halt his offensive. At Joffre's direction, Foch met with the field marshal on September 28 and agreed to relieve the British division on Sir John French's right so that the British could use it as a reserve. Foch also assured Sir John that the three corps on Tenth Army's left would continue attacking. Later that day Foch decided to shift the entire IX Corps from the right of Tenth Army to its left and to extend the French boundary to the north. He wanted to support and enlarge the gains made by the British and for the moment did not anticipate any further action south of Arras.

Before Foch's meeting with the British field marshal, the French made an unexpected gain in the center of Tenth Army. During the night of September 27–28, the division on XXXIII Corps's right and the one on III Corps's left, neither of which had made significant gains thus far in the offensive, advanced rapidly. In an attempt to take advantage of these gains, d'Urbal attacked at 1340 hours on September 28 with his three left corps. Elements of III Corps made their way to the top of Hill 140, the highest point on Vimy Ridge, and elements of XXXIII Corps occupied the crest of Hill 119, just northwest of Hill 140. German counterattacks briefly drove the French off Hill 140 that night, but the French managed to regain the important hill the following morning until heavy artillery fire drove them off again. About 400 meters, nonetheless, lay between the French infantry and the sharp dropoff on the ridge's eastern edge. The French held their hard-won gains despite continued rain and numerous counterattacks, but the initiative would slip away from them over the next twelve days when they failed to renew their offensive quickly.

Foch recognized the importance of maintaining the momentum of the attack and met with Field Marshal French on September 29 to discuss a combined attack. The two agreed on a two-pronged attack, one made by the British from Loos and the other made by the French from the crest of Vimy Ridge. After returning to his headquarters, Foch notified d'Urbal of the coming attack and told him to be ready on October 1 or 2. Foch then met with Joffre, who approved the plan and allocated artillery ammunition. Had the two-pronged attack occurred on October 1 or 2, the Germans would have had time to bring up part of their reserves and improve their defenses somewhat, but the allies still would have had the initiative and the momentum of success behind them. Events, however, delayed the launching of the new attack and gave the Germans more than enough time to strengthen their defenses and ultimately to halt the October attack.

The first indication of problems appeared on September 29, when d'Urbal concluded that the relief of the British right could not be completed as quickly as anticipated. Bad roads and miserable weather slowed the movement of IX Corps from his right to his left for the relief. This delay forced Foch to change the date of the attack. At a meeting on September 30, Foch and Sir John French agreed to attack on October 3. The next day, in another meeting with Sir John, new problems surfaced. Though Haig's First Army would be ready to attack on October 4, the British field marshal wanted two pieces of key terrain captured prior to the general attack; he wanted the British to capture a mining pit on Haig's left and the French to capture Hill 70 (southeast of Loos) on Haig's right. Foch agreed that Hill 70 should be attacked but wanted it attacked as part of the overall operation, and Sir John relented. Foch had no choice, however, but to agree to the British making an attack against the mining pit on Haig's left on October 4, the day before renewing the offensive. A few days later, Sir John asked for another day's delay, thus pushing the general attack back to October 6. Then he asked for another delay, pushing the date back to October 10.

Amidst these several delays Joffre had notified the British field marshal of his intentions to launch the Artois and Champagne attacks simultaneously and had set October 6 as the date of the offensive in Champagne. When Sir John's memo asking for another delay arrived, artillery preparation had already begun in Champagne. Joffre nevertheless wrote a polite note to Sir John saying that he understood the reasons for the delay. Foch had already assured Joffre that the enemy would not be able to shift forces from Artois to Champagne, and on October 5 Foch visited the British headquarters and asked the British to accelerate their preparations. To achieve the greatest operational effect, he insisted that they be ready to resume operations on October 7 or 8 at the latest. Despite his efforts, the British continued moving at their own pace.

Developments within the Tenth Army then affected preparation of the offensive. During the night of October 5–6, General d'Urbal pulled III Corps, which occupied a position in the center of his army, out of the front line and shifted it south, just north of Arras. He believed the corps had been stretched to its utmost because of its especially heavy losses and the terrible weather, and he moved it to a "defensive sector." Even though this action effectively halted Foch's plans for an offensive, d'Urbal notified Foch only a few hours before he began pulling III Corps out of the front line. Foch was furious, but he did not countermand d'Urbal's order. He informed Joffre and then wrote a sharp letter of reprimand to d'Urbal in which he expressed astonishment at d'Urbal's action, which was "absolutely contrary" to all the directions he had received.[100] Though d'Urbal's action had delayed Tenth Army's attack until at least October 10, Foch left him in command of Tenth Army. D'Urbal's account of the battle, written in early November, offered no explanation for his actions other than "considerable losses" suffered by III Corps and frequent delays in the attack because of the British.

Foch and d'Urbal met on October 7 to discuss how to renew Tenth Army's offensive, since it had to attack on the same day that the British made their main attack—still planned by Foch for October 10. They devised a new plan, which had the three corps in the center of Tenth Army driving toward the crest of Vimy Ridge while IX Corps on the left pressed against Hill 70 and III and XVII corps on the right remained on the defensive. The two French leaders expected IX Corps to attack Hill 70 in close coordination with the British. Hopes for simultaneous attacks evaporated, however, after the Germans launched a strong counterattack on October 8 against the British First Army and French IX Corps. Preceded by a heavy two-hour artillery bombardment that included a large amount of gas, the counterattack captured a few hundred meters of trenches in the British and French sectors. This action "upset" British preparations and resulted in the date of their attack being pushed back to October 13.

Foch grimly insisted that Tenth Army attack on October 10, but heavy fog on October 9 disrupted plans for artillery preparation to begin that day. Despite poor visibility, artillery firing began on October 11 at 1400 hours, and the infantry assault occurred at 1615. The daily log in Foch's headquarters recorded the results: "progress was almost nil, and the attack did not yield the expected results. Preparation by heavy artillery insufficient. Attack conducted by exhausted or already sorely tried troops. Enemy forewarned and strongly reinforced with artillery, unleashing at the slightest indication of attack terrible [artillery] barrages."[101] General d'Urbal halted the attack four hours after the first infantry assault and told his corps commanders to prepare to resume the attack "when the vigilance of the enemy has eased."[102] In a letter to Joffre, Foch blamed the failure on "insufficient" preparatory fire. He explained that Tenth Army had fired 73,000 rounds of heavy artillery for the attack on September 24–25 but only 21,600 rounds on October 10–11.[103]

In a meeting with his subordinate commanders on October 13, Foch directed continuation of the attack after a brief delay. He told Joffre that Tenth Army could not remain "inactive" while the British attacked and that it could not remain entrenched only 100–150 meters from the crest of Vimy Ridge for the entire winter when "only a bound" would gain the crest. To make the attack, he asked Joffre to double Tenth Army's allocation of heavy artillery. Despite Foch's desire to continue the attack, Joffre ordered him to have Tenth Army consolidate its position on Vimy Ridge. The events of October 11 demonstrated, Joffre explained, that d'Urbal's army did not have the "capacity" for a new offensive and that a shortage of ammunition compelled him to halt the operations in Artois and Champagne. He nevertheless ordered Foch to have IX Corps participate in the British offensive as the French had promised. An entry in the log of Foch's headquarters noted: "This is the end of our offensive."[104]

The British First Army finally attacked on October 13, supported by IX Corps's artillery demonstration on Hill 70. After a two-hour bombardment, British infantry advanced. The results are noted in the British official history: "The fighting on the 13th–14th October had not improved the general situation in any way and had brought nothing but useless slaughter of infantry."[105]

The French had consumed vast quantities of ammunition in the September and October offensives. Second, Third, Fourth, and Tenth armies fired 4,369,900 rounds of 75- and 90-mm and 832,100 rounds of heavy ammunition. According to the French official history, the four armies also suffered 191,795 casualties, including 30,386 killed, 110,725 wounded, and 50,686 missing in action. Of those missing, many were killed, others were captured, and some were temporarily missing from their unit and eventually returned. As for gains, the French advanced in Champagne as much as four kilometers and in Artois as much as two kilometers. The key gains occurred in Artois, where the French cleared Souchez and advanced almost to the crest of Vimy Ridge. Despite the lavish use of artillery and loss of thousands of lives, Joffre's huge offensives in Artois in May–June and in Artois and Champagne in September–October had accomplished very little. French gains seemed minuscule in comparison to those of Germany and Austria in the east.

The failure of the autumn offensive forced Joffre to reconsider French strategy and operations and to reconstitute his forces. As part of this reconsideration, he sent a memorandum to his army-group commanders in early October asking them to assess the operation. After receiving their responses, he sent them a memorandum on October 22 in which he said that Franco-British forces had achieved "important tactical results," inflicted heavy losses on the enemy, and gained an "undeniable moral superiority" over the enemy. He insisted that the primary reason for not making a breakthrough and gaining the anticipated strategic results was insufficient artillery. Aware that his army had been pushed to the edge of exhaustion, he ordered a period of waiting in which the French could halt enemy attacks and launch counterattacks but in which the primary emphasis was on resting soldiers and reconstituting units. Since the French still had to keep as many German soldiers as possible on the Western Front and could do this only by keeping the enemy under the threat of attack, he told his army-group commanders to undertake local offensives that would facilitate future operations. Nonetheless, he wanted troops in the front line reduced to the absolute minimum, probably for the entire winter.[106] The year of numerous offensives on the Western Front had ended; France would now look for other strategic and operational alternatives.

CHAPTER 5

The Search for Strategic Alternatives

1915–1916

I N THE FIRST WEEKS of the war, France sought a quick victory and gave little thought to anything other than driving the enemy from its soil. While its grand strategy envisaged a multifront war (Anglo-French, Russian, and Serbian) against the Central Powers, its political and military leaders recognized that France did not have the resources to conduct large operations in distant theaters. After the victory of the Marne and the ensuing stalemate, however, other ideas on strategy and operations outside France emerged. While some of these ideas came from those seeking to expand French colonial possessions or to make strategic or operational gains in the Near East, most concerned alternatives to the stalemate on the Western Front.

When the Ottoman Empire entered the war on the side of the Central Powers, France began seriously considering operations in the Balkans and Near East. The Turks entered the war openly on October 29, 1914, when their armed forces sank several Russian ships and bombarded Odessa and Sevastopol on the coast of the Black Sea. After closing the Dardanelles, they restricted allied access to Russia and curtailed the flow of weapons, munitions, and equipment. They also posed a direct threat against the Suez Canal, a vital route through which supplies and people flowed toward the allies, particularly the British. In early February 1915,

Turkish troops attacked the Suez Canal. After repulsing the attack, the British left large numbers of troops (too many, the French thought) to protect the canal. The Turks also opened a new front in the Caucasus against the Russians, but they initially fared poorly.

With the Turks in the enemy's camp, officials charged with administering France's empire welcomed the opportunity to expand French colonial possessions at their expense. For decades France had helped prop up the "sick man of Europe" and prevent its collapse, and if the Ottoman Empire crumbled and was partitioned, the French aspired to control a large area on the eastern shore of the Mediterranean. The area they preferred extended across Cilicia, the Bay of Adana, Alexandretta, and Syria. Shortly after the Turks entered the war, French colonial officials in North Africa and the Near East asked Paris to send an expeditionary force to Syria. The officials wanted not only to engage the Turks but also to prevent the British from expanding into that area. A few military officials added their voices to those urging Paris to send forces to Syria. Amidst growing concerns about British aspirations, Viviani's government in early January 1915 authorized Millerand, the minister of war, to send troops to Syria. Seeking only to "show the flag," the French did not want to open a new theater of operations that would drain forces and resources from the Western Front, so Millerand planned on using only territorial or North African troops in the expedition. Unfolding events in the Near East, particularly landings in the Dardanelles, however, soon derailed plans for a Syrian expedition.

Other notions of operating outside of France came from those who saw strategic opportunities in the Balkans. Influential leaders favoring action there early in the war included Generals Franchet d'Espèrey, Gallieni, and Castelnau, as well as Aristide Briand (who replaced Viviani as premier on October 29, 1915). While Franchet d'Espèrey and Castelnau devised operational plans for landing and advancing in the Balkans, Briand and Gallieni pored over maps studying possible operations there. The first ideas focused on assisting the Serbs; later ideas envisaged a strong offensive against a weak point along the perimeter of the Central Powers. In a meeting on January 1, 1915, Briand, Poincaré, and Viviani discussed sending an expedition of 400,000–500,000 soldiers to Serbia to hit Austria in the rear. These initial ideas focused on landing at

Salonika and advancing up the Vardar River. The French foreign minister, Théophile Delcassé, even discussed with Sir Edward Grey, the British foreign minister, having France, Britain, and Russia each send a division to Salonika. The French also considered landing at Dede Agatch (now Alexandroúpolis), a port on the Aegean near the Greek and Turkish border, but abandoned this idea when it became apparent that the Germans were there and had mined the harbor. When Joffre met with Poincaré and the Council of Ministers on January 7, however, he adamantly opposed operations in the Balkans. Hoping to circumvent this opposition, Briand took the proposal to the Council of Ministers and there encountered Millerand's objections. With Joffre and Millerand opposing the diversion of scarce resources to the Balkans, there was little chance that France would seek an indirect path to Vienna and Berlin.

Amidst the debate over strategic opportunities in the Balkans, the French faced diplomatic challenges of Gordian knot complexity, for pre-1914 conflicts had left many grievances and great distrust among the Balkan states. While Greece, for example, initially favored the allies and sought to form a confederation with Serbia, Bulgaria, and Romania, Bulgaria demanded concessions from Greece and Serbia before joining. Like Turkey, Bulgaria had lost territory to the other Balkan states before 1914 and wanted its former opponents to make amends. To satisfy Bulgaria's ambitions, the allies secretly offered Thrace and Macedonia, Thrace to be taken from Turkey and Macedonia from Greece and Serbia, both of which opposed concessions. Even France's own political leaders could not agree on which states to favor, for while Briand favored Greece, Delcassé favored Bulgaria. Similarly, allied actions in the Balkans sought to open lines of communication with Russia, but the Russians trusted neither the British nor the Greeks to relinquish Constantinople if they seized it. Adding to the imbroglio, the French remained suspicious of British motives. As Millerand explained to Delcassé on January 5, 1915, "our traditional interests in Asia Minor demand that the English not land there by themselves."[1]

The impetus for operations in the Balkans came from Britain. Since the enemy was not eighty kilometers from London, the British could be more flexible in their thinking and studied carefully whether their troops could be better employed somewhere other than in France. Searching for

Europe and the Near East

alternatives to the high casualties of the Western Front, officials such as
Winston Churchill and David Lloyd George looked to theaters such as
Schleswig-Holstein, Syria, and the Dardanelles. In these early discussions Lloyd George appealed for an attack on Austria on the grounds
that "the moment Austria was knocked out, Germany would be entirely

isolated."[2] Interest in operations in the Near East heightened after January 2, 1915, when a telegram from the British ambassador to Russia arrived in London; the telegram included a request from the Russians for operations that might relieve Turkish pressure in the Caucasus. Though London did not know that before the arrival of the telegram the Russians had halted the Turkish advance and thereby relieved pressure in the Caucasus, the British War Council on January 8 and 13 discussed driving through the Dardanelles to the Sea of Marmora with a naval force and then bombarding Constantinople. When Churchill notified the French naval attaché in London of the plan, the minister of the navy reacted suspiciously, particularly when he learned of British ideas for attacking Alexandretta, ostensibly as a diversion. Before the war the British and French had completed naval agreements that gave France responsibility for the Mediterranean and the right to command any naval operations in that region. A quick trip to London by the French minister of the navy gained reassurance about French interests in the region and a promise from the British not to attack Alexandretta. On January 28 the British decided formally to launch the naval operation against Constantinople, and a few days later Lloyd George arrived in Paris to discuss the operation. France decided to participate in the operation and agreed to send a naval squadron, which would operate, despite the prewar naval agreements, under the orders of a British admiral.

Though neither London nor Paris thought the operation should divert troops from the Western Front, both soon made ground forces available for operations in the Mediterranean. Initial planning rested on the assumption that Greece would provide three divisions for use in the campaign. For a brief period the allies planned on sending a British and a French division to Salonika to protect the communications of Greece when it abandoned its neutrality and assisted the allies with an attack on the Dardanelles. Hoping that the landing of troops would sway the Romanians to join the Entente, the government of France formally decided on February 4 to send a division to the Balkans. The situation changed, however, when Russia refused to accept the presence of Greek forces at Constantinople and King Constantine of Greece decided not to participate in the campaign. Lacking faith in a purely naval operation, London decided to send a division to the theater in case allied land forces were required when naval forces attacked the Dardanelles, and Paris, following London's lead, decided on February 18 to send a division to the Mediterranean. Four days later the French minister of war directed the organization of an expeditionary corps consisting of two infantry brigades, a cavalry regiment, two battalions of 75-mm guns, and one battalion of 65-mm mountain guns. Somewhat larger than a division, the entire force would consist of 18,000 men and 5,000 horses and mules. Three of the four regiments would come from Africa or the colonies. Joffre ensured that none of the French troops came from the Western Front.

As preparations proceeded, the government considered arranging with Britain to have a French general officer control allied ground forces in the Dardanelles since a British admiral controlled naval forces. With the British sending more forces than the French, however, the government did not raise the issue with London and placed French expeditionary forces under the British ground force commander, General Sir Ian Hamilton. The minister of war appointed General Albert d'Amade as commander of the Expeditionary Corps of the Near East and ordered him to cooperate with the British in the attempt to force a passage of the Dardanelles. Planning for the operation remained firmly under British control.

On February 18 the naval attack began. Allied ships bombarded the forts at the entry of the Dardanelles, but bad weather interrupted the bombardment until February 25. With the outlying forts destroyed, naval attacks on the interior forts protecting the Narrows began anew on March 5 but ended the following day because of heavy Turkish artillery fire. The allies renewed the naval bombardment on March 18, but naval gunfire failed to silence the enemy's batteries and enemy fire disrupted efforts to clear the passageway of mines. Even worse, enemy mines sank three allied battleships and badly damaged several others. Within a week British leaders decided to use ground forces to push through the Dardanelles.

By the last week of March, the allies had 75,000 personnel en route to or present in the theater of operations. The first French transports had departed Toulon on March 4 and arrived on March 9 at Lemnos, a Greek island sixty kilometers from the Dardanelles. The last of twenty-two transports arrived on March 27. Bad weather and the absence of fresh water, however, forced the British to move most of the allied ground forces to Egypt. The last French transports arrived at Alexandria on March 31.

By the middle of April General Hamilton had completed his plan for an amphibious assault on the Dardanelles. He intended to make one landing on the southern extremity of Gallipoli Peninsula, near Cape Helles, and another twenty kilometers to the north at Gaba Tepe. Meanwhile, the British fleet, feinting another landing, would bombard the narrowest portion of the peninsula fifty kilometers to the north of Gaba Tepe. While the British forces landed on the European side of the Dardanelles, the French would land on the Asian side near Kum Kale. Hamilton directed d'Amade to make a "diversion" with a regimental-sized force and then to land the entire French force at Cape Helles.[3]

The initial fighting proved extremely difficult. For years before the outbreak of World War I, most European military authorities had little regard for the Ottoman Empire and its military forces, but combat in the Dardanelles revealed the real capabilities of the Turks. Aided by naval gunfire support, a French infantry regiment and a battery of 75-mm guns landed at Kum Kale on April 25. They occupied the village and took 600 prisoners. French casualties numbered a surprisingly large 190 killed and 588 wounded. As planned, the regiment departed the following night. On April 27 two battalions landed at 0500 hours on Cape Helles; they moved forward and relieved British troops on the allied right. The entire allied line extended five kilometers across the peninsula. The following morning, when the French had five battalions ashore, the allies attacked but encountered strong enemy resistance. In a day of heavy fighting the French lost 1,000 of the 5,000 soldiers participating in the battle.[4] Strong enemy counterattacks on the night of May 1–2 caused even heavier French losses. The enemy's main assaults struck first the French right and then their left. When a Senegalese battalion on the French left (near the allied center) panicked under heavy enemy fire and pulled back 800 meters, prompt action by a British brigade behind this portion of the line filled the gap. General d'Amade attempted to counterattack but made few gains despite heavy casualties. In less than a day the French lost 2,100 soldiers and the British 680.

Hopes for a simple campaign against a weak enemy had evaporated.

Warned by the allied naval attack in February and March, the Turks had strengthened their defenses considerably. Not willing to halt the campaign, Lord Kitchener decided to send reinforcements and asked the French on April 29 to reinforce General d'Amade. The British sent a territorial division from Egypt, and the French sent 156th Infantry Division. Lead elements of the French division departed for the Dardanelles on May 2. Over the next three months, the allies increased their forces to thirteen divisions, two of which were French. Despite this increase, the allies could not advance far beyond the beachhead, and the Turks could not drive them into the sea. In an attempt to outflank the Turks the British landed on August 8 at Suvla Bay but failed to make gains in what had clearly become a stalemate.

The French had their own ideas about how to end the stalemate. After General Henri Gouraud replaced d'Amade in mid-May as the commander of the expeditionary corps, he sent Hamilton a long letter in which he analyzed operational alternatives, including a landing three kilometers southwest of Kum Kale on the Asian side of the Dardanelles.[5] Following Gouraud's wounding by Turkish artillery, his replacement, General Maurice Bailloud, also called for a landing on the coast of Asia. Such an action required from the French five infantry and two cavalry divisions, including the two infantry divisions already in the theater, but landing on the Asian side of the Dardanelles would silence the long-range guns pounding allied forces at Gallipoli and provide an opportunity to advance against weaker enemy defenses. Gouraud and Bailloud agreed that the situation at Gallipoli could only get worse, especially if an epidemic of cholera swept through allied troops. At the end of July Bailloud sent Paris a thorough study of operational alternatives for operations along the Asian coast to silence the Turkish batteries bombarding the allies from the rear.[6]

Joffre used the first allied military conference, which took place at Chantilly on July 7, to ensure that the Gallipoli operation did not drain resources from the Western Front. As French, British, Belgian, Russian, Italian, and Serbian representatives discussed a wide variety of topics pertaining to strategy and operations, he argued that a "decision" could be obtained only in the principal theaters of operation (Anglo-Franco-Belgian, Italo-Serbian, and Russian): "The secondary action in the

Dardanelles does not have immediate military interest. Its success, nevertheless, will gain political and economic advantages. It will naturally draw into our orbit the hesitant Balkan people; by pushing Turkey aside, it will ease the task of the Russian army." He added, "Anyway, this question [of Gallipoli] is outside the purpose of this meeting." Sir John French strengthened Joffre's position by stating that he was "entirely in accord" with the French general.[7]

After being asked by the minister of war for his assessment of the situation in Gallipoli, Joffre advised against abandoning the operation but also thought it impossible to send additional troops to ensure its success. He explained that abandoning the operation could have significant strategic effects, particularly in the Balkans, where news of an allied defeat might convince Bulgaria, Romania, and Greece to remain neutral or, worse, join the Central Powers. As for shifting forces out of France, Joffre argued that to do so would be a "grave mistake," since the Germans could then move troops from the Russian front and attack in the west against weakened allied defenses. He nevertheless advised that a shift could be possible at the end of September, when the results of the German offensive in Russia were apparent, the French had remedied their shortcomings in artillery, and the autumn offensive had ended. At the conclusion of his memorandum Joffre volunteered to begin planning for operations in Turkey. Over the next few days, however, Joffre's attitude toward the Gallipoli operation became more negative. As pressure to send troops from the Western Front to Gallipoli increased and the demands of his autumn offensive in Champagne mounted, he sent the minister of war a strong letter on August 3 in which he warned him against being "lured by false hopes" and argued that conditions on the Western Front were "too uncertain" to shift forces from France to the Dardanelles. He cautioned the minister that France had attained its maximum size in military forces and could not generate additional forces for the Orient. He concluded, "before beginning a new operation of great energy in the Dardanelles, it is essential to establish an overall program, based on known information; such a program has been missing since the beginning of this adventure."[8]

The possibility of a French landing on the Asian coast of the Dardanelles became an important political issue when the Viviani government appointed General Sarrail, recently relieved from his command of

Third Army, commander of the Expeditionary Corps of the Near East. Although Joffre preferred Franchet d'Espèrey and knew that Sarrail had accused him of planning a coup d'état, he concurred with Sarrail's appointment.[9] Sarrail initially declined the appointment, asserting that commanding a corps was a severe demotion from commanding an army. After meeting with Millerand on August 3, however, he said he would accept the command if its name was changed to Army of the Near East, if he was not placed under the orders of British generals, and if he received reinforcements. Two days later Millerand informed him that he had been named commander of French forces in the Near East. When asked to make suggestions about military operations in the Near East, Sarrail responded with a memorandum that included a grand scheme for several landings on the Mediterranean coast (including Smyrna, Alexandretta, and Salonika) and for operations in Turkey.[10] Asked by the minister of war to critique Sarrail's proposal, Joffre responded with scathing comments, damning one of Sarrail's alternatives with the opinion that logistical support for the four divisions in the operation could be provided only by "Arabs and mules." Joffre characterized Sarrail's "solutions" as "incomplete, unrealizable, and disastrous."[11]

Throughout August, France's political leaders placed considerable pressure on Joffre to release divisions for operations in the Near East. When Poincaré, Viviani, and Millerand visited his headquarters on August 13, Joffre insisted that he could not release four divisions until the end of his autumn offensive, which was scheduled to begin in a month. He caustically asked, "What can we do in the Dardanelles? Launch an expedition for a factious general?" Viviani and Poincaré tried to convince him to release the divisions, but he remained intransigent. Poincaré concluded that if they pushed too hard, Joffre would resign.[12] On August 21 Joffre met with Poincaré, Viviani, Millerand, and Delcassé and promised that if he did not rupture enemy lines in September, he would release four divisions to the Dardanelles. A week later, fresh from a meeting of the Council of Ministers in which France's political leaders agreed that an expedition to the coast of Asia was necessary, Poincaré, Viviani, and Millerand again met with Joffre. Though more subdued than in previous exchanges, Joffre nevertheless insisted that he needed the four divisions for his autumn offensive and possibly for defense against a German attack. He kept repeating, "The battle that we are about to begin will be the great battle of the year." He pleaded with the president and premier of France to leave the divisions with him until October, when he would know the results of the offensive in Champagne. If this offensive failed, he anticipated going on the defensive and seeking a "diversion" elsewhere, such as in the Near East or Alsace.[13] Confident that an expedition would occur, the Viviani government notified the British of French plans to land somewhere in the theater other than Gallipoli and requested assistance with transporting additional troops.

Despite pressure from Poincaré and Viviani, Joffre continued to object to releasing divisions for service in the Near East. Recognizing that Sarrail's proposal lacked operational and logistical details, Joffre asked the Office of National Security Studies to analyze options in the Dardanelles. The recently formed office, which functioned under the minister of war and would eventually serve as the secretariat for the Council of National Defense, concluded that operations in Turkey would require 200,000 soldiers and eight additional divisions, as well as the equivalent of three divisions in support troops. It was "imprudent," the authors of the study concluded, to pull troops from the Western Front. They also deftly suggested asking the Italians to provide the required troops and hinted that it was foolish to launch an expedition on the coast of Asia.[14] Joffre used the study as a weapon against those desiring the Turkish expedition. France would "profoundly regret," he said, launching an operation that would require men and munitions "indispensable" for the defense of the nation. The expedition also would expose France to a failure of "disastrous consequences." In a handwritten note on the study, Joffre added, "It is the British who have led us to the Dardanelles. In reality halting the offensive will be a British defeat. Tomorrow, if we send reinforcements and assume command, we will find ourselves, in case of failure, facing a French disaster."[15]

Joffre's arguments did not sway political leaders. On September 7 Millerand directed him to identify four divisions plus supporting elements to send to the Near East; he subsequently ordered the divisions to leave Marseille on October 10. Refusing to bend, Joffre responded that preparations for the autumn offensive prevented him momentarily from identifying the divisions and that France was being drawn into an operation that it would "profoundly regret."[16] He later informed Millerand that his sending the four divisions remained dependent on the course of operations in France and that he could not promise that the four divisions would be at Marseille on October 10. After reminding Millerand of his previous objections, Joffre warned that sending additional forces to the Near East would "compromise" the safety of France.[17] When Millerand presented Joffre's latest objections to the Council of Ministers, Premier Viviani exclaimed, "You see. It's just what I told you. The expedition . . . will never occur."[18]

Changes in the strategic situation, not Joffre's objections, eventually ended plans for an expedition to the Asian coast. As the allies' campaign in Gallipoli faltered, as evidence of their weakness in the Balkans accumulated, and as the Central Powers raced across Russia after the Gorlice-Tarnów breakthrough, Bulgaria began negotiating with the Central Powers. In early August an intelligence report warned France that Bulgaria might abandon its neutrality, and the French military attaché in Serbia reported that King Ferdinand of Bulgaria had decided to attack Serbia. French diplomats attempted to influence Bulgaria by offering additional inducements, including territory from Serbia and Greece, for it to join the allies, but one of the diplomats eventually reported to Paris, "The cooperation of Bulgaria cannot be expected and should not be sought."[19] Meanwhile Bulgaria completed a secret agreement with the Ottoman Empire on August 22 and joined the Central Powers on September 6.

Bulgaria's entry into the war on the side of the Central Powers fundamentally changed the strategic situation in the Balkans and placed the Serbs in an extremely difficult situation. While still fighting the Austrians along the Danube on their northern frontier, the Serbs had to shift forces to their eastern border and thereby risk spreading their units too thinly to halt a simultaneous attack by Austria in the north and Bulgaria in the east. Bulgaria's entry into the war also threatened allied lines of communication through the region. To transport supplies to the Serbian army, the French used the railway network from Salonika in Greece, to Skopje (also called Uskub) in Serbia, to Nich (now Niš) in Serbia. They next

Serbia and Salonika

used the railway and trucks to transport supplies from Nich to Serbian forces along the Danube. With the Bulgarian border so close to Nich and the railway running from Salonika to Nich, however, the Bulgarians posed a strong threat to France's links with Serbia. As for the Central Powers, Bulgaria's entry into the war brightened their prospects, for it opened the possibility of the fabled Berlin-to-Baghdad railway. To establish railway links with the Ottoman Empire, Germany and Austria-Hungary could have passed through Serbia or neutral Romania, but they preferred the shorter route through Serbia along the railroad that went directly from Austria-Hungary to Belgrade, Nich, Sofia, and then Constantinople. If Serbia could be defeated or its forces driven back enough to open the railway from Belgrade to Constantinople, the Central Powers could easily provide much-needed supplies to the Turks and control a vast area from the North Sea to the Persian Gulf. Bulgaria's entry into the war thus altered the strategic situation considerably.

The specter of a disaster in Serbia compelled France to accelerate its preparations for an expedition and to shift its focus from the coast of Asia to the Balkans. Thinking ahead, the French had sent specialists to Salonika to study the railways from Greece to Serbia,[20] and on September 4 the Office of National Defense Studies completed an initial assessment of an intervention.[21] On September 20 the military attaché in Bulgaria notified Paris that Sofia had ordered its cavalry regiments to depart the next day for the Serbian frontier and that a general mobilization would occur on the following day. This mobilization occurred at about the same time that Viviani complained to the other ministers that the expedition to the Turkish coast would never occur. As momentum for an operation in the Balkans gathered, words of caution about establishing a "base" at Salonika came from General Bailloud, the commander of French forces at Gallipoli. What previously had seemed possible to him now seemed very difficult with Bulgaria's joining the Central Powers.[22] A few days later he wrote a private letter to the minister of war bitterly criticizing the British actions at Gallipoli and warning of troubles in the Balkans: "We cannot count on the help of the English, not only when their important interests are in opposition to ours but also when it is a simple question of pride or prestige."[23]

Other indications of future difficulties came from Greece. Since

Greece and Serbia had concluded a military convention in June 1913 pledging mutual support in the event of an attack by a third party, France hoped Greece would support Serbia even though Athens had refused to help Belgrade when the Austrians attacked in late 1914. In what should not have been a surprise, Greece again found a reason to refuse assistance. The prime minister of Greece informed Paris and London on September 21 that King Constantine had decided not to intervene, since Serbia had failed to provide the 150,000 men for operations against Bulgaria promised in the convention. The prime minister said that Greece would intervene if Romania joined the effort and provided the 150,000 men, but if it did not, he asked France and Britain to intervene and contribute the promised level of support. If the allies furnished the support, then Greece, he said, would act in accordance with the military convention.

France's political leaders recognized the challenges of conducting operations in the Balkans, and in meetings of the Council of Ministers on September 23 and 25 they sharply debated grand strategy and relations with Britain, Russia, and Bulgaria. After the council agreed to "go to the aid of the Serbs," Paris informed the Greek Government that it was ready to furnish the requested troops.[24] London also promised support but only after considerable disagreement between Lloyd George, who argued for sending troops, and Kitchener, who compared moving troops from Gallipoli to Salonika to "jumping out of the frying pan into the fire."[25] With the autumn offensive in Artois and Champagne about to begin, Millerand sent the French commander in Gallipoli a warning order on September 24 about sending a division to Salonika; the division would "cover the railway from Salonika to Nich."[26] On the same day he informed the British about French intentions.

Also on that day Joffre, who recognized the strategic importance of Serbia and Romania and the need for a Balkan expedition, provided his advice to the government on how to respond to the Serbian crisis. He advised sending two French and two British divisions from Gallipoli to the Balkans. Although the British had anticipated needing 300,000 Anglo-French troops against 450,000 Austro-German troops, he believed that the enemy did not have 450,000 men to spare for the Balkans. To him, four allied divisions seemed sufficient. As for the strategic effect of abandoning the Dardanelles operation, Joffre wrote, "We are simply changing the point of application of the forces we have in the Near East; we are ma-neuvering, not withdrawing." He added: "This maneuver is logical and necessary. The objective of the operation in the Dardanelles was to open communications with Russia. We have failed. It is now necessary to maintain the communications existing between Salonika and the Dan-ube; we can do this by transporting to Serbia the forces necessary to as-sure the effective defense of this country."[27] An operation in Serbia thus fitted within France's multifront strategy, but Joffre did not want to weaken the allied effort on the Western Front by sending a large force.

The allied situation became more complicated because of strained re-lations between the king and prime minister of Greece and because of Greek fears of a Bulgarian attack. The Greek prime minister asked to be notified twenty-four hours before the arrival of the first allied detach-ments so that he could lodge a diplomatic protest prior to the landing and thereby maintain an aura of neutrality. On October 1 he became alarmed at a speech by Sir Edward Grey, the British secretary of foreign affairs, and demanded that the landing be delayed until the allies made their intentions clear. The following day Paris and London assured Ath-ens that the Bulgarian mobilization had annulled all promises to Sofia and that their intention was solely to aid Serbia. The next day the Greek government went through the motions of formally protesting the allies' action but at the same time made final preparations for their troops to disembark at Salonika.

As the French and British prepared to land forces in Greece, key ques-tions remained on the objectives and role of those forces. On September 28 General Sarrail was notified that he would command French forces in the Balkans, not on the coast of Asia, and was asked by the minister of war, as was customary, to provide an operational assessment of alterna-tives in the Near East. Beginning by expressing his opposition to an evac-uation from the Dardanelles, Sarrail said that a withdrawal from the pen-insula would create a "dangerous situation" in North Africa and create doubts about the allies' military capabilities. He thought the British should have the entire responsibility for maintaining a presence in Gallipoli, since they had "decided, designed, and commanded" the oper-ation. As for the French, Sarrail thought that little could be done in the Balkans with the three brigades en route to Salonika. The brigades could

protect the railway running from Salonika into Serbia, but he did not
know whether this protection would occur north or south of Skopje,
which was 200 kilometers northwest of Salonika (Nich lay 300 kilometers and the Danube 450 kilometers north of Salonika). Looking more
broadly at the region, Sarrail, unveiling an ambitious plan, argued that
France could achieve its goals by defeating Bulgaria and driving it out of
the war. He suggested having 30,000 British soldiers defend Salonika
while three or four French corps drove toward Sofia. Because of the cli-
mate, terrain, and quality of the enemy, Sarrail thought the campaign
would require high-quality troops with an extremely effective supply and
support system.[28]

As one would expect, Joffre vehemently opposed sending three or four
corps to the Near East. His analysis of the strategic situation facing
France and its allies was one of the clearest and most effective of his command. He began by describing the autumn offensive and what it had accomplished. Though the final step in that offensive would occur five days
later, Joffre expressed doubts that the French armies would succeed in
forcing their way through the enemy's second band of defenses on the
Western Front. A new offensive could be launched only after the arrival
of fresh troops and the reconstitution of units, and he had no choice, he
said, but to suspend the offensive "momentarily" after the last Champagne assault in October was finished. No significant gain had occurred,
but Joffre insisted that "success in Champagne gives us confidence in the
final victory." He added: "it is in the principal theater of operations, that
is to say, in France, that we should continue to seek a solution. All our
efforts should seek to achieve a large strategic rupture [of enemy lines]
that will have as its first consequence the liberation of [our] national
territory."[29]

As for allied actions in the Near East, Joffre believed that the Central
Powers could not be allowed to crush Serbia. France should provide assistance, but only an absolute minimum, while Britain should assume
primary responsibility for supporting the Balkan states favorable toward
the allies. Joffre again criticized the Dardanelles operation, saying that the
allies could not conduct operations in the Dardanelles and the Balkans at
the same time. He explained, "Given the actual state of our resources,
this dispersion of our efforts will be true folly." He added: "Under these

conditions, supporting an excessively large expeditionary corps in the Near East will result in such a consumption of our resources in men and munitions that it will render uncertain the possibilities of decisive victory in the principal theater of operations and may even risk compromising the defense of the national territory." In sum, France could spare no more than one or two divisions beyond the two already in the Dardanelles. Sending more would reduce France's ability to launch offensives on the Western Front or defend successfully against an enemy attack.[30] Two days later Joffre again emphasized some of the same points, particularly the fact that France had limited resources and could not open a new theater of operations with large forces. He recommended that the mission of allied forces in the Balkans focus on covering the railway from Salonika to Serbia, but he did not indicate whether coverage should occur north or south of Skopje.[31] Nonetheless, Joffre thought France's contribution should consist of one cavalry and three infantry divisions, or 60,000 soldiers; the British should provide the remainder of the 150,000 soldiers requested by Serbia and Greece.

During this crucial period, however, Millerand and the Council of Ministers, not Joffre, controlled French strategy in the Near East. The limitations on Joffre's powers were most evident in the appointment of Sarrail on August 5 to command the Army of the Near East and then on September 28 to command French forces headed for Salonika. Despite the obvious limitations on his powers, Joffre continued to attempt to shape Balkan strategy by critiquing operational and strategic concepts and by slowing the flow of French forces to the region.

At a meeting at Calais with British officials on October 5 to discuss the Balkan operation, Millerand attempted to convince the British to shoulder the bulk of the burden. At the time of the meeting both France and Britain had an infantry division and a cavalry regiment en route to Salonika. Since Joffre had agreed to release another infantry brigade in the near future and an infantry and two cavalry divisions as soon as his autumn offensive was finished, the French had a total of 64,000 soldiers en route to or programmed to go to the Balkans. Lord Kitchener promised another infantry division and a cavalry division, plus three infantry divisions, once Joffre's offensive was finished. The British leader planned to pull these units from Sir John French's forces in France. When

Millerand asked Kitchener to provide an additional 20,000–22,000 personnel so that the allied forces would attain the promised 150,000-man level, the British leader insisted that this could be done only by taking additional troops from Sir John French. As for the arrival date of allied forces, the French expected their third division to arrive no later than November 12. Unlike in the Dardanelles, where a British officer commanded the entire operation, British and French commanders, Millerand suggested, should be coequals and should operate under the direction of the Serbian commander. When Kitchener asked about operational plans, Millerand said that the French had not yet completed any plans, but he acknowledged having ordered the French commander to defend the Salonika-Skopje railway and to send a division toward Nich if requested by the Serbs.[32]

One important result of the meeting at Calais was to demonstrate Lord Kitchener's reservations about the Balkan operation. He was concerned not only about sending troops far into Serbia at the beginning of winter but also about their role. He complained that the original purpose of the operation had been to encourage Greece to fulfill its obligations, but now the operation was being shaped to aid the Serbs. In any case, he did not believe that 150,000 soldiers would suffice if the Greeks refused to join the allies. He emphasized, "Me, I do not march without the Greek army. My troops will not go beyond Salonika if the Greeks refuse to march."[33] Kitchener's reservations about the operation resulted in an agreement that British forces would defend Salonika while French forces advanced into Serbia. Most British leaders shared Kitchener's doubts. The British official history noted: "Step by step, disputing every step but dragged irresistibly forward, we had engaged ourselves, probably 'for the duration,' in a venture which at the moment had scarcely a friend among our statesmen, our soldiers, or our sailors."[34]

Though not completely unexpected, new troubles for the expedition came from the Greeks. Since King Constantine's wife was the sister of the German kaiser, doubts about the king's loyalty to the Entente had existed among the allies for some time. Their distrust intensified, however, when Constantine dismissed his prime minister, who had favored the allies, on October 5, the same day as the Calais conference, the arrival of allied troops at Salonika, and the Bulgarian attack. The British ambassador to

Greece met with the king, who told him that the allies could continue to use Salonika to disembark troops en route to Serbia. In a later meeting the king added, in the words of the British diplomat, "He did not wish to fight against Germany and he did not wish to fight with her."[35] A few days later the new prime minister met with the French ambassador and told him that Greece's neutrality remained "benevolent."[36] Despite the favorable comments from the king and prime minister, the French and British recognized that the Greeks could become hostile.

From October 5 through 7 the French landed 12,000 and the British 3,000 troops at Salonika. The first French elements—two brigades and an artillery battalion from the French 156th Infantry Division—bivouacked near the port, but they initially lacked transportation and support units, particularly horses. Between October 12 and 23, 57th Division arrived, and between November 1 and 8, 122nd Division arrived. The British arrived more slowly; their second division did not begin disembarking until November 5. As units continued arriving, the difficult terrain in the Balkans compelled the French to modify the organization of their force. After the arrival of a cavalry regiment, they recognized that the mountainous terrain and the absence of fodder rendered mounted units useless in the Balkans. They had planned on sending two cavalry divisions, but they ended up sending only two regiments and one squadron to the region. Because of the extremely narrow roads, the French replaced some of the 75-mm guns in the divisions with 65-mm guns, which were much lighter and could be hauled more easily. In the subsequent campaign, even the infantry encountered difficulties moving and often had to advance single file on narrow mountain paths. It quickly became apparent that most operations would occur relatively close to railways.

On October 12 General Sarrail arrived and took command of the Army of the Near East. Before Sarrail's arrival, General Bailloud had acted as commander and had received a flurry of orders. On October 7 he was told not to go into Serbia, the next day to advance thirty kilometers into Serbia, and on the third day not to cross the frontier. Shortly after Sarrail arrived, Bailloud received a telegram saying: "Wait for new instructions before taking action."[37] That same day Millerand sent Sarrail and Bailloud orders to "cover the lines of communication between Salonika and Serbia against the advance of Bulgarian forces."[38]

Sarrail quickly ordered an infantry regiment and an artillery battalion to advance into Serbia; their destination was a railway station, Strumica Station, on the Vardar River 100 kilometers north of Salonika and 30 kilometers beyond the Greek border. The Bulgarian border protruded west 50 kilometers in this region, placing it a dozen kilometers from the rail line running from Salonika to Nich. On October 14 the French began arriving at Strumica Station but quickly found themselves under enemy artillery fire and then infantry assault. The Serbs had seven battalions in the area, and they and the French repulsed the enemy attack. Within a week the remainder of 156th Division had arrived at Strumica Station, relieved the Serb battalions, and extended its position toward the Bulgarian border. The French colonel who commanded French forces in the initial engagement reported the action to Sarrail and mentioned that relations with the Serbs were "excellent." He noted, however, that the Serbs wanted to engage the French "more and more in their affairs."[39]

As the Serbs fell back in the north in the face of Austrian attacks, they requested additional assistance from the allies. The Austrians captured Belgrade on October 9 and drove south, and on Serbia's eastern border the Bulgarians drove west toward Nich and Skopje. Believing that the seven Serb divisions in the north and northeast faced eleven enemy divisions, the Serbs asked the French to move their forces north and to concentrate them near Nich. After Sarrail refused to "hurl his forces into an adventure," the Serbian minister of war asked him to advance to Skopje and said, "Otherwise it will be too late and the catastrophe inevitable."[40] Though Sarrail again refused, he recognized that he had to do something, and on October 19 he sent an infantry regiment and an artillery battery (both were from 57th Division and had just arrived in Greece) to Krivolak, some 30 kilometers from Strumica Station and 130 kilometers from Salonika. Like Strumica Station, Krivolak was on the railway and next to the Vardar River. On October 20 the general officer commanding French troops at Krivolak reported to Sarrail that the Bulgarians held the east bank of the Vardar River just north of Krivolak and that trains could not pass.

Also on October 20, the Serbs again asked the French to advance farther north. The Bulgarians had attacked Veles, 40 kilometers from Krivolak, and the Serbs desperately needed French assistance. Veles, which fell that same day, was also on the railway and next to the Vardar River, but Sarrail could not and would not move north. His caution seems warranted, given that he had already had moved 156th Division and part of 57th Division 145 kilometers from Salonika and spread them across a front of 50 kilometers stretching from Krivolak to the Bulgarian border east of Strumica Station. Additional troops were not immediately available, since the last elements of the 57th had just finished disembarking at Salonika, and the third French division was en route. To make matters even more complicated, heavy fighting continued near Strumica Station, the loss of which would cut off French forces between there and Krivolak. Sarrail's explanation in his memoirs seems appropriate: "One cannot do something with nothing."[41]

Although British forces could have helped, London steadfastly refused to permit its troops to advance into Serbia, primarily because the British continued to have strong reservations about operations in the Balkans. Sending a large force into Serbia without the support of the Greeks seemed foolish to them. Debate between the French and British also continued about the number of forces needed. Kitchener met with Joffre at the GQG on October 8 and insisted that at least 250,000 soldiers would be required to help Serbia and 400,000 to attack Austria. Joffre knew that the allies could not send that many troops and insisted that 150,000 could protect the Serbs' communications. On the basis of studies done by the GQG staff, he believed that the British had far more troops available for use outside the Western Front than did the French. Hoping to convince the British to do more, Millerand traveled to London and discussed the situation in the Balkans, but British officials objected to the operation and defended their position with a "passionate tenacity."[42] Pulling out all the stops, Millerand warned British leaders that the fate of the French government and the alliance itself depended on British support for the Salonika operation. The British reluctantly agreed to send two divisions, but Millerand had to agree that if Sir John French objected, Joffre would replace two British divisions with two French divisions so that British units could go to the Balkans. After the enemy captured Skopje, however, the British decided that it was "too late" to assist the Serbs and said they preferred to send the two divisions to Egypt.[43] A few days later Joffre also traveled to London and delivered a message similar to Millerand's. On October 26 Kitchener finally permitted the British 10th Division to advance into Serbia to support the French. The division began moving on October 29, but it did nothing more than relieve French units in Sarrail's second line a dozen kilometers across the Greek border.

While the Serbs in the north and northeast withdrew slowly, the Serbs in central Serbia fared poorly against the Bulgarians driving southwest toward Skopje and Veles. On October 30 the Serbs evacuated Veles and withdrew southwest toward Prilep. After the Bulgarians crossed the Vardar River, they moved toward the southwest with the Tcherna (now Crna) River on their left and threatened to envelop the entire Serbian force and cut off its evacuation route through Albania. The Tcherna River (flowing from the southwest toward the northeast) joins the Vardar (flowing from northwest to southeast) fifteen kilometers northwest of Krivolak; their junction forms an upside-down "V." The French had troops along the Vardar from Strumica Station to Krivolak, and on November 2 Sarrail began preparations for an offensive by ordering his northern division, the 57th, to advance to the Tcherna and seize crossing points. The next day he ordered the division to cross the Tcherna and hit the Bulgarians in their flank. When a brigade of France's third division, the 122nd, arrived in Salonika in early November, Sarrail moved it north to participate in the attack.

Notions of a bold and easy maneuver, however, soon fell victim to the realities of the enemy and the terrain. As Sarrail pushed forces beyond Krivolak toward the Tcherna, the Bulgarians made strong attacks on Krivolak and east of Strumica Station on November 3. During the same period the situation of the Serbs in the north deteriorated significantly; Nich fell on November 5. Amidst these unfavorable developments, the commander of 57th Division, General Paul Leblois, submitted a pessimistic report about the number of troops required to hold the junction of the Tcherna and the Vardar. He believed that he required substantial reinforcement to hold the region, protect his line of communications, and advance across the Tcherna. Leblois reminded Sarrail that Napoleon had said, "a general who loses his line of communication merits death, for this loss will result in the total ruin of his army."[44] In a telegram to Sarrail, Leblois described the area west of the Tcherna as "without roads, without water, without woods. Only paths where we can be halted by a few men. Resupply here will be impossible."[45]

Despite this negative assessment, Sarrail pushed units forward as the Serbs, hoping to recapture Skopje and Veles, pleaded for French assistance. Between November 3 and 12, 156th Division attacked east of Strumica Station toward the Bulgarian border, while 57th and 122nd divisions guarded the railway near the junction of the Tcherna and Vardar rivers and attacked across the Tcherna. East of Strumica Station, the French advanced a few kilometers and captured the heights along the Bulgarian frontier. West of the Tcherna, the French advanced about five kilometers but soon encountered strong enemy resistance and heavy counterattacks. Sarrail had hoped that pressure against the Bulgarian border would draw the enemy to the east and facilitate the advance across the Tcherna, but the Bulgarians greatly outnumbered the 45,000 Frenchmen.

With Sarrail's offensive making only slow progress and with growing evidence that the Serbs had collapsed in the north, the minister of war, now Gallieni, ordered Sarrail on November 12 to halt his offensive, gather together as much of the Serbian army as he could, and—on the minister's order—withdraw to a fortified position at Salonika. In Paris a new Council of Ministers with Briand as the president of the council and Gallieni as minister of war had replaced the Viviani government on October 29, thereby providing the opportunity—because of Briand's long interest in the region—for Paris to give a higher priority to the Balkans. In response to Gallieni's telegram of November 12, Sarrail emphasized three points: first, the Greeks would interpret a withdrawal from Serbia as a French defeat; second, making a withdrawal would be difficult because the Greeks had halted the movement of allied troops in Greece along the railway from Salonika to Strumica Station; and third, Salonika was now occupied by a Greek division and elements of two corps. Paris immediately responded that Sarrail was the "best judge of military operations" and had "latitude" to be on the offensive or defensive as he sought to accomplish his mission. The same telegram reminded Sarrail of his mission: "come to the aid of the Serbian army while maintaining your [lines of] communication."[46] For the next week, the French held their positions, including the position across the Tcherna.

Recognizing that his mission was at risk and hoping for a higher priority from the Briand government, Sarrail appealed to Paris for reinforcements. When he first ordered his troops across the Tcherna River, he had requested an increase in his forces from three divisions to four corps. As the difficulty of the task became more apparent, Sarrail asked for reinforcements on November 9, 16, and 17. He also wrote to members of the government with whom he had personal influence. When Lord Kitchener visited on November 17, Sarrail said that he needed four French corps and a total of 300,000 British and French troops to occupy and defend Salonika. The commander of the Army of the Near East obviously hoped that the Briand government would be more sympathetic to his requirements, but a firm response from the new minister of war, whose view of the strategic situation was no longer favorable, dashed his hopes. "Your dispatches or reports," Gallieni wrote, "have repeated several times your requirement for four army corps, but the government has never consented to or discussed making your army this large." Gallieni added: "adapt your plans to the personnel at your disposal."[47]

Over the next few days Sarrail made preparations for withdrawing to Salonika but still hoped for reinforcements. On November 19 he sent General Leblois an order that made him the acting commander of 57th and 122nd divisions at the junction of the Vardar and Tcherna rivers and provided guidance about the conduct of a withdrawal. Sarrail explained clearly that no order for a withdrawal had been given but that when one arrived, the operation had to be conducted quickly. The next day Gallieni sent Sarrail a telegram notifying him that the Serbs would launch an offensive toward Skopje and that Sarrail had the authority to decide what kind of support to provide them. The minister of war also told Sarrail that he had to decide when the security of his force required a withdrawal to Salonika. Sarrail wrote in his memoirs: "after having been invited to return to Greece, I was free to remain in Serbia or to withdraw when the circumstances required it; everything was my responsibility."[48] A telegram from the minister of war on November 21 quashed Sarrail's hopes for something other than a withdrawal. Believing that Sarrail was "indecisive and not up to the task," Gallieni told him that the government had considered reinforcing the Army of the Near East and had decided not to send additional forces. Sarrail scribbled on the telegram that he had no choice but to withdraw.[49] The need to withdraw became even more apparent a few days later, when Serbian defenses collapsed and soldiers began fleeing across the mountains of Montenegro and Albania toward the Adriatic.

On November 23 Sarrail ordered the withdrawal of the three French divisions from Serbia. Three days earlier the commander of 122nd Division had pulled his troops back across the Tcherna and then notified Sarrail. When Sarrail expressed astonishment at the withdrawal, the general officer defended his actions by saying that his left was under heavy enemy pressure. Believing this was a lie, Sarrail relieved him. The subsequent withdrawal from Serbia occurred under Sarrail's tight control. The commander of the Army of the Near East first moved his supplies and then on December 3 marched his forces to the south in a step-by-step maneuver. Despite heavy pressure from the Bulgarians, the withdrawal went smoothly, and by December 12 all French and British troops had crossed the border into Greece. The time was ripe for a full reassessment not only of French strategy but also of the role of political and military authorities in making that strategy.

Discontent with France's conduct of the war had percolated through political and military circles for months. The first casualty of this discontent was the Viviani government, which fell on October 29. During the two months before the fall of Viviani, the Chamber of Deputies had voted twice and expressed its confidence in his government. The first vote occurred on August 21 in a session that consisted primarily of a defense by Millerand of his role as minister of war; at issue was his control of General Joffre. Millerand explained his concept of the government's control of Joffre: "The general-in-chief is responsible to the government, which can relieve him if it does not approve of his actions." He noted that he had stated in 1912: "Leave full and entire liberty of action to the military leader, [who is] responsible for operations in war."[50] Though some deputies believed that giving so much freedom to the general-in-chief was an abdication of the government's "authority and control," the Chamber overwhelmingly supported Viviani, and thus Millerand, by a vote of 535 to 1.

Another vote of confidence occurred on October 12, following the failure of Joffre's autumn offensive, Bulgaria's entry into the war on the side of the Central Powers, the dispatch of an expedition to the Balkans, and the resignation of the minister of foreign affairs, Delcassé. Though the Chamber of Deputies voted 372 to 9 to support the government, the large number of abstentions indicated that Viviani was in trouble. Hoping to rescue his government, Viviani considered replacing Millerand, but only after asking Joffre to recommend a general officer. The general-in-chief initially responded that nine out of ten generals would make poor ministers of war, but when Viviani asked whether Gallieni would be acceptable, Joffre said, "Perhaps," and then, after a moment's reflection, "Yes."[51] Despite Viviani's best efforts, he could not reconstitute a new council, since France's leaders, except for Gallieni, refused to join him. On October 29 Briand formed a new government; Viviani became the vice president of the Council of Ministers and Gallieni the minister of war.

One of the first questions faced by the new government pertained to Joffre's powers. For some time Joffre had argued for unity of command and for having a single commander over the three theaters in France, the Balkans, and the Dardanelles. When allied operations began in the Dardanelles and Balkans, Joffre had no authority in those theaters and acted only as a technical advisor to the government on issues pertaining to them. He and the commander of French forces in the Near East reported directly but separately to the minister of war. In a letter to the minister on July 29, 1915, however, Joffre had argued for having a single military commander over French forces in France and the Near East: "In every aspect of war, unity of command is required; it is an absolute prerequisite for success. Better to have a mediocre plan executed with coordinated actions than to have a better-conceived plan with divergent views among those who execute it."[52]

The liaison officer between Joffre's headquarters and the government told Poincaré that military leaders feared a catastrophe. Obviously expressing the ideas of Joffre, the officer added: "Of the two alternatives, choose one. Have the minister of war direct the conduct of the war as a whole, in which case it would be necessary to have near him a real chief of the General Staff, such as Castelnau. Or have Joffre—in my opinion, the best solution—become generalissimo of all the French armies and be responsible for operations in the Near East as well as those in France."[53] In his memoirs, Joffre argued that he opposed a "confusion of authority" that could weaken the French army. He explained, "It is often difficult to draw a line between the domain of politics and that of strategy." Such a line was especially difficult to draw, he added, when political and military interests clashed. As for the minister of war's having responsibility for directing operations, Joffre believed Gallieni could handle the task, but he knew that the government could fall and that a new minister might know nothing about military operations. Yet he did not favor appointing an army officer the minister of war. The possibility that the government might fall and the minister be replaced, he insisted, created the possibility of frequent changes in operations.[54] By the end of November Poincaré had decided that France needed a commander-in-chief, not a more powerful minister of war. Agreeing with Joffre, he wrote:

> No matter what the value of Gallieni, he is a member of the government, he shares the collective responsibility of the cabinet, [and] he is required constantly to provide explanations before the [parliamentary] chambers and commissions. If he was charged with overall command, he would risk, on the one hand, not having the requisite strategic independence and, on the other hand, involving the government in whatever action he took. . . . Finally, if we wish to lead the coalition, the authority of General Joffre, [with his] ascendancy over the allies, will be a great help to us.[55]

Despite Poincaré's support of Joffre, Briand hesitated before expanding Joffre's powers and making him commander-in-chief. Numerous politicians wanted him dismissed, not given additional powers, and Briand initially had his hands full defending his choice of Gallieni as minister of war. The new premier nonetheless offered strong support for Joffre. On the day the new ministry entered office, Briand asked Poincaré to convince Gallieni to give Joffre a free hand and full responsibility for directing operations. Gallieni readily agreed and showed the president a cordial letter to Joffre in which he had assured the general, "you can count on me." The minister of war did not send the letter to Joffre until after he had shown it to Briand.[56] The following day Briand met with Gallieni and Joffre and had them shake hands as evidence of their mutual good-will.

Despite such gestures, friendly relations between the two generals had long since dissolved, and the dividing line between Joffre's and Gallieni's powers remained uncertain. Joffre used a meeting of the Superior Council of Defense on November 24 to hasten Briand's addressing the issue. Before the meeting Joffre met with Poincaré and Briand and complained that Gallieni's staff was "trying to run the war." The two political leaders assured Joffre that they intended to safeguard his freedom of action and would soon address the question of who directed the conduct of the war.[57] During the subsequent meeting of the Superior Council of Defense, Joffre objected to the council's discussing an operational issue that he believed was his responsibility and threatened to resign if he did not have the "liberty" to fulfill his responsibilities.[58] After the meeting, Joffre emphasized to Poincaré and Briand the importance of having a single person direct operations in France and the Near East. Poincaré and Briand apparently agreed, but Briand indicated that he had not yet discussed the issue with Gallieni. Aware of Joffre's efforts to increase his power, Gallieni complained bitterly in his diary about the unwillingness of Poincaré and Briand to thwart Joffre.[59]

On December 1 the president and premier of France met with Gallieni and discussed what Poincaré called "the question of command." Gallieni's staff had completed a study that argued for placing the reins of command in the hands of the minister of war, but Briand rejected this proposal with the comment, "It would open the command and, consequently, operations to parliamentary discussions. The minister, [who is] responsible before the [parliamentary] chambers, can be questioned there on everything and does not have the right to ignore questions." Gallieni finally relented and agreed to make Joffre the commander-in-chief over all French forces.[60] The minister of war wrote in his diary: "Joffre will have [control of] all the fronts, with Castelnau as his chief of staff, and they will banish his crew [of 'Young Turks']. . . . He [Joffre] will be under the orders of the minister of war."[61] On December 2 Poincaré published a governmental decree stating: "Command of the national armies . . . is confided to a general officer who bears the title 'commander-in-chief of the French armies.'"[62] The president also announced that Joffre would occupy this position. As Jere C. King has observed, France now had a generalissimo.[63] Only the colonial forces in Algeria, Tunisia, and Morocco lay outside his authority. Though Joffre's appointment aroused considerable discussion in the Chamber of Deputies, a vote of 406 to 67 on December 9 supported his occupying the new position.

Before Joffre assumed his new position, the arrival of the Briand government on October 29, 1915, had brought renewed interest in operations in the Balkans. In his first speech to the Chamber of Deputies on November 3, Briand promised not to abandon Serbia, but unfortunately he had assumed power just as the Bulgarians began driving southwest toward Skopje and Veles and the Serbs began withdrawing southwest. Only two weeks after becoming minister of war, Gallieni had no choice but to order Sarrail to halt his advance north into Serbia and prepare to withdraw to Salonika. Despite Sarrail's strong demands for reinforcements, Gallieni refused, as mentioned above, and curtly ordered him to adapt his plans to the forces he had. As Sarrail withdrew toward Salonika, the Council of Ministers affirmed its desire to remain in the Balkans and asked Britain for additional troops to raise the total number to 300,000. Briand believed that such a force could keep Greece neutral and persuade Romania to join the allies. Abandoning Salonika, he thought, would result in enemy occupation or control of Greece, with disastrous consequences throughout the Balkans and the Near East.

Giving Joffre additional powers did not make it easier for Briand to realize his dream of attacking the Central Powers through the Balkans. While some historians have argued that Briand's elevation of Joffre was an attempt to reduce the general's opposition to sending significant resources to the Balkans, Joffre had fought too long and too hard to keep France focused on the Western Front for anyone to expect a sudden change in his beliefs. Just before his appointment, he again expressed his conviction to Briand and other members of the Council of Ministers that the war could be won only in one of the principal theaters, France or Russia, and not in the Balkans or the Dardanelles. In essence, the appointment of Joffre guaranteed the subordination of the Salonika and Dardanelles operations to those on the Western Front.

If Joffre's views had changed, those changes involved only the role to be played by the French army. Until the failure of his autumn offensive in 1915, he had believed that "only the French army can stand toe-to-toe to the German army and beat it."[64] This view had shaped his efforts to fight through German lines in the May–June and September–October 1915 offensives. Before his autumn offensive he had acknowledged that if this offensive failed, it would be necessary for France to change its strategy and perhaps remain on the defensive and seek a diversion elsewhere such as the Near East or Alsace. Hopes that Joffre would agree to focus outside France quickly evaporated, however, when he sent Millerand a letter shortly before his massive offensive ended and insisted that the war could be won only in the principal theater, France. While he did not recommend abandoning "secondary theaters," he thought Great Britain should bear most of the burden in them. He also thought the British should do more on the Western Front while the French rebuilt their forces.

On December 4, a few days after Joffre's appointment as commander-in-chief, French and British leaders attended a meeting at Calais in which the main point of discussion was Salonika. The meeting occurred at a time when the currents of the war seemed to be flowing against the allies. The Germans had broken through at Gorlice-Tarnów and driven the Russians back 350 kilometers; Joffre's autumn offensive had failed to make significant gains; the British were considering abandoning Gallipoli; the Serbs were fleeing across the mountains toward the Adriatic; and Sarrail's forces were withdrawing from Serbia toward Salonika. For more than three and a half hours, the British argued for leaving the Balkans, and the French argued to keep allied forces there. Lord Kitchener believed that the opportunity for accomplishing something in the Balkans had passed and that the Serbs could not continue to fight. He even threatened to resign if allied forces remained at Salonika. The British prime minister said that the retention of 150,000 troops at Salonika could result in a disaster, and he insisted on an immediate evacuation. Briand did most of the talking for the French. Still believing in the importance of the Balkans, the premier said that the allies had entered the Balkans to prevent the Central Powers from dominating the region and to keep Greece and Romania from joining the enemy camp. By maintaining forces at Salonika, the allies could still achieve these objectives, despite the defeat of Serbia, and could form the 100,000 Serbian soldiers into a force to assist allied efforts. He reminded the British that the Russians had concentrated some 400,000 men in the vicinity of the Balkans and that the Italians had agreed to intervene. Both Briand and Joffre argued that by keeping 150,000 soldiers at Salonika, the allies could tie down 400,000 enemy troops and prevent them from marching on Egypt.

French explanations did not change the minds of British leaders. When it became apparent that the British would not budge, Briand reluctantly said that if the British withdrew their troops, the French would have no alternative but to follow. The meeting concluded with British and French representatives agreeing to make immediate preparations for evacuation. Despite this agreement, France's political leaders did not favor departing, and when the Council of Ministers met the following day in Paris, they agreed unanimously to make another appeal to London and to ask Russia's assistance in convincing the British to stay. Briand even modified the wording of the minutes of the Calais meeting to make it appear that he had not agreed to abandon Salonika.

At the three-day military conference, which began the following day, the French hoped to gain greater coordination of allied actions and induce members of the coalition to accept France's proposals for allied strategy and for remaining at Salonika. One of the reasons for Briand's not firing Joffre was his great influence over allied military leaders, and Joffre more than met the premier's expectations. Before the meeting, Joffre completed a strategic assessment that he called a "plan of action," and he provided a copy to each representative attending the conference. The assessment viewed the war as a whole but, as one would expect, placed primary emphasis on the "principal" theaters. As for the "secondary" theaters, which included the Balkans and the Dardanelles, Joffre placed the needs of these theaters in the context of opposing the "imperialistic program" of the Central Powers. His main point was to argue that the Gallipoli expedition had failed and that the allies should continue to maintain forces around Salonika. He devoted an entire section to arguing against abandoning Salonika. Maintaining troops in Greece, he said, would end that country's "pusillanimity" and prevent Bulgaria from turning against Romania. Moreover, having troops at Salonika would "facilitate" Russian action against the Balkans and prevent the Germans from launching a winter campaign against Russia. The allied presence would also keep the Germans from using Greek ports to resupply their submarines and thereby dominate the Mediterranean. "In principle, the troops that are actually in the Near East should be sufficient," said Joffre, "to meet the indispensable needs of this secondary theater." Finally, he argued for economic and military assistance to Romania to help it resist German pressure to join the Central Powers.[65]

The representatives of the Russian, Italian, Serbian, and Belgian armies supported Joffre's "plan of action," while the British strongly objected to maintaining allied forces at Salonika. Before the conference, Tsar Nicholas II and the Russian chief of the General Staff, General Mikhail Alekseev, had complained bitterly to the French military attaché about British shortsightedness and lack of interest in the Balkans, so Russian support for Joffre's proposal was not unexpected.[66] On the first day of the conference, the Russian representative emphasized the advantages of having allied forces at Salonika threaten the flank of enemy forces in the Balkans, provide indirect cover for Egypt, and prevent the enemy from using Greek ports as submarine bases. On the last day of the conference, the Russian representative asked that his objections to the abandonment of Salonika be inserted into the minutes of the meeting. The Russian insertion warned, "The decision of the allies (to abandon Salonika) will worsen the strategic situation in the present and the future; it will complicate the political situation on the Turkish front and compel the Romanians to submit to the will of our adversaries."[67] Sir John French attended the meeting, but since he had secretly submitted his formal letter of resignation on December 4, Lieutenant General Sir Archibald Murray, chief of the Imperial General Staff, led the British effort to convince the other allies to withdraw from Salonika. Murray stressed the wavering attitude of Greece, he questioned the wisdom of leaving 150,000 men at Salonika to keep Romania from joining the Central Powers, and he emphasized the need to defend Egypt. But his comments did not sway the other participants. They agreed that allied troops should be maintained at Salonika, that Gallipoli should be evacuated "immediately and completely," and that Egypt should be defended with as small a force as possible.[68] The assembled allies thus offered strong support for the French, not the British, position. Frustrated by the turn of events, the British prime minister, Herbert H. Asquith, complained privately about what the "Frogs" had done.[69]

At a meeting of the British War Committee on December 8, London decided to send Sir Edward Grey and Lord Kitchener to Paris to confer with the French government and General Staff. Kitchener asked the French attaché to inform Paris that Britain would do its "duty" in this time of danger as French forces withdrew from Serbia.[70] Kitchener also informed Gallieni that "very grave" circumstances in the Near East required France and Britain to collaborate.[71] On December 9 and 11, British and French political leaders (including Kitchener, Grey, Briand, Gallieni, and Joffre) met in Paris and discussed the occupation of defensive positions around Salonika. Their main concern was whether the Greeks would remain neutral. Though the two allies did not resolve the question of whether they would remain at Salonika, the discussions lowered tensions between them and, as Lord Kitchener later reported, eased French "annoyance" with and "suspicion" toward the British.[72] During the meeting in Paris with the British, Joffre wrote to Sarrail and informed him the two allies had agreed to fortify Salonika. How long allied troops would stay, however, remained unclear.

Joffre had used the assistance of the Russians to batter down British resistance to remaining at Salonika, but he avoided being drawn into the ambitious operation desired by the Russians. In late November the Russian chief of the General Staff, General Alekseev, had sent the French, British, and Italians a proposal for coordinated action by the coalition. He suggested a grandiose operation in which the Russians would drive 500 kilometers west to Budapest while an Anglo-French army of at least ten corps drove north 800 kilometers from Salonika toward Budapest. The converging drives also would "open the way" for the Italians to advance toward Vienna.[73] A French officer in Russia during this period described the scheme as filled with "dreams and romanticism,"[74] and an analysis by the Office of National Defense Studies dismissed the proposal as "impracticable." If the allies advanced north, they would face at least 500,000 troops from the German, Austrian, Bulgarian, and Turkish armies; would have to clear the enemy from mountainous and difficult terrain in Serbia; would require more logistical support than could be provided by the port of Salonika; and would have to cross the barrier of the Danube River, a task requiring an enormous amount of heavy artillery and bridging materials. More important, launching the operation would require the weakening of the front in France, a front on which an allied withdrawal would give the Germans an opportunity for "decisive" action.[75]

In reality Joffre had no interest in Alekseev's proposal, but he had used the Russians to gain British cooperation. He had also used the question of Salonika to reassure the Russians and to ensure that they continued offensive pressure against the Germans. To increase Russian efforts, he continued sending messages to Alekseev summarizing actions on the Western Front and encouraging him to attack. His efforts were rewarded in January 1916, when the tsar informed a visiting French general officer of "his firm intention never to be separated from the allied cause" and by Russian preparations for a large offensive in mid-1916.[76] Keeping allied troops in the Balkans seemed a small price to pay for such cooperation, especially since the British seemed more willing to increase their efforts in France.

After France and Britain agreed in December 1915 to fortify Salonika, Gallieni asked Joffre whether it could be defended successfully by 150,000 allied troops. Joffre responded that 150,000 troops seemed adequate, but he then sent General de Castelnau to Salonika to verify the number. Castelnau submitted his report on Christmas Day, saying that he accepted the general dispositions made by Sarrail and that, once all promised reinforcements had arrived, the allies could defend Salonika. The French had three divisions in Greece, and the British had promised five. When Sarrail insisted that he needed two more French divisions, Joffre turned down his request. Refusing to accept no for an answer, Sarrail appealed to his political friends in Paris, and on January 18 Gallieni directed Joffre to send another division.

Despite this positive signal to Sarrail, Castelnau had delivered a strongly negative report about him to Joffre, Gallieni, Briand, and Poincaré. He criticized Sarrail for the same negative qualities that had resulted in his being relieved from command of Third Army, and he identified several "grave mistakes" he had made, including his remaining in Salonika far from the fighting in Serbia and his going forward to Krivolak only once. With Briand in power and with Sarrail's political supporters still willing to defend him, however, there was little chance that he would be relieved.

Meanwhile the allies evacuated the remnants of the Serbian army from Albania. The Serbs requested transportation on December 11, and a week later Prince Alexander of Serbia appealed directly to Joffre for assistance for his starving army. Joffre forwarded the telegram to Briand and suggested providing emergency supplies to the Serbs and transporting them from northern and central Albania to the port of Vlona (now Vlorë), in southern Albania. When the Italians objected to the Serbs' moving to Vlona, Joffre proposed moving the Serbs to the island of Corfu, off the western coast of Greece. This time the British objected, and the French decided to move them to Bizerte, in Tunisia. By the first week of January 1916, the French had overcome British objections, and the allies had agreed to transport the Serbs to Corfu. Though a few Serbs had already departed for Bizerte, the rest began landing on Corfu on January 18. The last contingent did not arrive until early April.

While evacuating the Serbs and fortifying Salonika, France reconsidered its strategic and operational alternatives in the Balkans. Some of the most important discussions occurred in the Superior Council of National Defense in February and again in March. On February 8 the council agreed that "the launching of offensive operations in the Balkans is and will be subordinate to circumstances."[77] By "circumstances," the council meant French and British preparations for an offensive on the Somme, an operation that would soon be transformed by the German attack on Verdun. In a meeting on March 10 the council again discussed the situation in the Balkans and agreed that General Sarrail should "manifest the level of activity requested in the directives of the general-in-chief."[78] The council thus ruled against assigning the Balkans a higher priority in France's strategy and against drawing resources and troops from the Western Front, and it kept the direction of operations under Joffre.

Focusing on the Western Front did not come at the expense of France's influence in the Near East. In March–April 1915 France and Britain had allayed Russia's suspicions about operations in the Near East by accepting Petrograd's claim to Constantinople and the Straits of Bosporus and Dardanelles, but discussions about spheres of influence and the eventual partition of the Ottoman Empire continued secretly among the three allies. In January 1916 France and Britain accepted the general outline of a partition, and after making modifications requested by Russia, they formally ratified on May 15–16 what became known as the Sykes-Picot Agreement. This agreement acknowledged France's control over a large area encompassing Cilicia, Alexandretta, Lebanon, and Syria.

As part of France's strategic reassessment and in preparation for an anticipated meeting of allied military leaders, in mid-February 1916 Joffre's headquarters prepared an assessment of the military situation facing the coalition. That assessment emphasized the importance of increasing allied influence in the Balkans by rallying Greece and Romania to the coalition and detaching the Ottoman Empire and Bulgaria from the enemy camp. The study acknowledged that during the meeting of December 6–8, 1915, allied military leaders had recognized the "impossibility of undertaking a grand offensive" in the Balkans, perhaps requiring as many as fifty divisions. With the advantage of central position and better lines of communication, the Central Powers could always concentrate superior forces against an allied offensive. The allies could do little more than strengthen the confidence of the "still hesitant" neutral powers and compel the enemy to maintain as large a force as possible in the Balkans. To do this, the allies had to maintain the threat of an attack in the Balkans and launch an offensive "if circumstances permit or require it." Maintaining the threat of an attack, however, required as many as 400,000 soldiers, most of whom would have to come from Britain and Italy.[79]

Even if Joffre had favored greater activity, the British adamantly refused to expand the war in the Balkans. In late 1915 London had reevaluated the conduct of the war and made significant adjustments. In addition to asking Sir John French for his resignation and replacing him with Sir Douglas Haig, the British appointed General Sir William Robertson chief of the Imperial General Staff and expanded his powers while reduc-

ing those of Kitchener, the war minister. Robertson's first act was to recommend evacuation of Gallipoli. After the cabinet approved the recommendation in late December, the British departed the battered area on
January 8. As part of this strategic adjustment, they also decided to concentrate their efforts in France and Flanders.[80]

Joffre nevertheless saw some benefits coming from allied offensive operations in the Balkans. In a meeting on February 15 with Robertson, he
identified Romania as the "grand prize" in the region. The French government thought, he said, that adding another 100,000 allied troops to
Salonika would cause Romania to join the allies. An offensive with
400,000 allied troops, he added, would make the Bulgarians reluctant to
attack Romania and would influence Bucharest to join the allies. To have
a significant strategic effect, however, the allies had to have 600,000–
700,000 troops. Not surprisingly, Joffre insisted that any additional men
had to come from the British, not the French.[81]

Most British political and military leaders did not understand why the
French wanted to stay at Salonika. The British sometimes attributed
their staying, in Robertson's words, to the Briand government's desire to
"find employment for General Sarrail, who was associated with certain
political leaders of the Left whom it was advisable to placate."[82] Although
Robertson became the most persistent critic of Salonika, London favored
abandoning the Balkans and, except for concern that a withdrawal would
undermine the French government, found few reasons to remain there. A
British General Staff memorandum of late November 1915 explained,
"The only argument for holding it that is worth considering is to deprive
the enemy of a submarine base. We cannot for a moment consider that as
sufficient justification for locking up an army of 150,000 men."[83] In other
communications with the French, however, the British acknowledged
that keeping allied forces in the Balkans would make Constantinople reluctant to send large forces to Egypt or Mesopotamia.[84]

The British remained concerned that the French might impulsively
expand the war in the Balkans. On March 4, 1916, after the Germans attacked Verdun, Joffre directed Sarrail to "study" the possibility of an offensive to prevent the enemy from withdrawing divisions from the Balkans and shifting them to the Western Front.[85] Two days later Joffre
received a letter from General Robertson complaining that it was "un-

sound to embark on offensive operations in the Balkans."[86] The British and French governments had agreed that no offensive would occur without approval by both governments, and Joffre responded that he had asked Sarrail for nothing more than a study of possibilities. Robertson's concerns proved superfluous, for Sarrail concluded that before the arrival of the Serbs from Corfu and the provision of additional allied reinforcements, only a "series of demonstrations" was possible.[87] Making even a limited offensive, Sarrail said, would require twenty-one divisions.

In a letter to Sarrail on March 10, Joffre acknowledged the limited role of the Army of the Near East: "Our military action [at Salonika] consists in retaining before us as many enemy forces as possible and giving them the impression by our activity that they are under the threat of . . . our passing to the offensive if circumstances permit or require it." Joffre acknowledged that this mission constituted a "bluff," but he insisted that this bluff had to be translated into "real preparation for an offensive."[88] The idea of a bluff at Salonika was repeated in a strategic assessment that his headquarters completed in preparation for allied conference scheduled for March 12. The authors of the study carefully considered alternatives in the Near East and recommended not withdrawing any French or British divisions from Salonika. Again repeating the goal of rallying Greece and Romania to the allied powers and drawing off the Ottoman Empire and Bulgaria from the Central Powers, they saw a force of 200,000 at Salonika as being nothing more than a "bluff of limited duration." Moreover, transporting the Serbs to Salonika would provide the allies sufficient forces to pose a threat against the enemy, possibly even to launch an attack.[89]

At the allied meeting on March 12, representatives from France, Britain, Italy, Belgium, Serbia, and Russia discussed a massive, coordinated offensive on all fronts and debated alternatives in the Balkans. The question of maintaining forces in Salonika proved far more controversial than launching a general offensive. The Russians and Serbs pressed for an increase in allied forces at Salonika and an attack toward the north. The Russian representative explained, "An offensive from Salonika can have significant results. If it advances to Sofia, it will cut the route between Germany and Constantinople. At the least it will retain important Bulgarian and Austrian troops on that frontier." The Russian added, "The presence of allied troops at Salonika will greatly influence decisions of Germany vis-à-vis Romania." Joffre and Robertson, however, opposed sending additional troops to Salonika for a large offensive. Breaking through enemy defenses around Salonika, Joffre said, would require a very large allied force, perhaps as many as 600,000. When Kitchener and Robertson proposed withdrawing up to three British divisions from the Balkans, Joffre angrily objected and said that if any country withdrew troops from Salonika, it "ought" to be France.[90] In the face of such opposition, Prime Minister Asquith did not support Kitchener and Robertson's proposal to withdraw three British divisions. The allies finally agreed not to reinforce or withdraw troops from the Balkans or to launch an offensive. They nonetheless agreed to transport the Serbian army as quickly as possible to Salonika and to reconsider alternatives in the Near East in the future.[91] In mid-July the Serbs moved into position at Salonika.

Despite the results of the allied conference, Sarrail continued preparations for an offensive at Salonika. In early March he had submitted plans for a massive offensive involving twenty-one allied divisions, and in early April he again requested additional troops for a large offensive. Joffre was struggling to meet the demands of fighting at Verdun, and on April 20 he reminded Sarrail that allied military leaders had decided in March to concentrate their efforts in the principal theaters and not to launch a large offensive in the Balkans. He told Sarrail not to expect additional resources but gave him permission to begin preparations for a "demonstration."[92] Not wanting to send additional forces to the Balkans and perhaps wanting the British to kill Briand's hopes for a large offensive in the Balkans, Joffre wrote to Robertson—only five days after telling Sarrail to conduct nothing more than a demonstration—and proposed an offensive. Counting the Serbs, Joffre anticipated having fifteen divisions available: four French, five British, and six Serbian. Such an offensive, he wrote, could draw Greece and Romania onto the allied side, but if it did not, it might make significant gains against the Bulgarians, who were growing "impatient" with the heavy burden of the war. If the offensive failed to make significant gains, then it would at least draw German and Austrian formations into the peninsula and away from the Russian front or the deadly battle going on around Verdun.[93] On May 15 Joffre met with

British officials to discuss the proposed offensive, and one of them observed, "Joffre was not at all keen about the proposal, but appeared as if he had to make the best of it." In reality the French general did not expect a large offensive, but he believed firmly that "it was impossible that this force [at Salonika] should remain there doing nothing while the allies were engaged in big operations elsewhere."[94]

As expected, the British War Committee objected even to a limited offensive, insisting that "it is not feasible to undertake such a stupendous task as that involved by a campaign in the Balkans at a time when the Entente forces are so vitally committed to fighting on the main fronts." The War Committee concluded: "From every point of view the weight of argument is in favor of the Entente trying to re-establish their influence in the Balkans by direct attack on the Austro-German armies [outside the Balkans], instead of seeking a means of defeating those Powers indirectly by attacking the Bulgarian army."[95] This conclusion amounted to a British veto of any offensive in the Balkans.

Despite the firm no from London, Briand tried to convince the reluctant ally to participate in a Balkan offensive. At a conference in London on June 9, he argued for an offensive in the Balkans that would create a favorable environment for Romania's entry into the war. A French memorandum explained, "Romania will enter the line only if our Army of the Near East delivers it from the Bulgarian peril."[96] Once again Joffre supported Briand's demand, but Lloyd George noted the "incomprehensible" and "cynical" performance of the French general: "He was urging an attack with forces devoid of the armament necessary to achieve their purpose, and he made no suggestion that the equipment should be strengthened up to the point of effectiveness."[97] To what Lloyd George called the "secret satisfaction" of Joffre,[98] the British again responded firmly that "an offensive at Salonika cannot be taken at present with any prospect of success, and . . . will probably lead to grave embarrassments that must be prejudicial to the offensive in France, and may even be fatal to the Allied chance of success in the whole war." Despite this strong objection, the British government stated that it would "not refuse at a future date to examine the question of an offensive from Salonika as soon as circumstances and the condition of the troops and material allow."[99] Joffre wired Sarrail that the French and British governments had decided to "defer" the offensive until "circumstances and the state of troops and materiel permit."[100] In other words, he would not send additional units to the Balkans.

Meanwhile Romania edged closer to the allies, and the Russians routed the Austrians in Galicia. Bucharest had negotiated with the allies for more than a year and previously had indicated a desire to enter the war at the same time as Italy, which declared war on Austria-Hungary on May 23, 1915. After the Germans and Austrians broke through at Gorlice-Tarnów in that same month and drove east quickly, the Romanians had second thoughts about joining the Entente. The launching of General Aleksei Brusilov's offensive in Russia on June 4, 1916, and its great success against the Austrians, however, reassured Bucharest and revived its interests in joining the Entente.

As the extent of the Austrian collapse became apparent, Joffre went from being a lukewarm supporter in early June of an offensive in the Balkans to being a strong supporter in late June. By launching a limited offensive against the Bulgarians, the allies, he thought, could bring indirect pressure on the Austrians and assist the Russians and, eventually, the Romanians.[101] He had previously used British objections to deflate the desire of French political leaders for a grand offensive in the Balkans, but he now asked for Briand's assistance in overcoming those objections. Briand needed no prodding, since the Council of Ministers had watched Romanian actions anxiously and hoped Bucharest would join the allies and enable them to seize the initiative in the Balkans.[102] Unwilling to let the British kill any possibility of an offensive and miss the fleeting opportunity for strategic gain, Joffre also asked Sarrail if he could attack with only French and Serb forces. After Sarrail affirmed that French and Serbian forces could fix the Bulgarian forces along their front, Paris reopened the question of an offensive at Salonika, and on July 10 London reiterated its objections to such an operation. London's response, however, added that the British would cooperate in an offensive if Romania joined the Entente. On July 14 Joffre received additional information from the Russian chief of staff about a military convention between Russia and Romania, and on the following day he ordered Sarrail to plan an operation to tie down the Bulgarian army along the Greek frontier and keep it from launching a strong action against Romania. Although Joffre intended, if necessary, to attack without British assistance, General Robertson was aware of developments in Romania and assured him on July 18 that British forces would cooperate in an offensive at Salonika "commensurate with the strength and equipment of their forces in that area."[103] Both Joffre and Sarrail nonetheless remained skeptical about British participation in an offensive.

Doubts about the possibility of success against the Bulgarians came from Salonika and London. A French liaison officer at Salonika warned Joffre that French troops were "fatigued" from "very hot weather, uninterrupted work, poor rations without vegetables, general weariness resulting from the absence of regular leaves, and incomprehension among the troops about the role they play far from France."[104] A letter from General Robertson on July 19 expressed doubts about every aspect of the operation. He wrote that "a decisive result such as will cause Germans to ask for terms can only be reached by achieving success on one or both of the main fronts." He asked that requirements for "secondary" theaters such as the Balkans be subordinated to those of the main fronts, and he expressed doubts about the allies' "forcing the Bulgarian lines" and accomplishing anything other than "holding" the Bulgarians and preventing them from attacking Romania. He asked Joffre not to make a large attack seeking a breakthrough until later and not to commence operations until Romania "definitely enters the field."[105]

On July 23 military representatives of France, Britain, Russia, Italy, and Romania met in Paris to discuss strategy and operation in light of the anticipated entry of Romania into the war. The delegates agreed that Romania would begin its operation on August 7 and that the allies would begin offensive operations on August 1 "with all the forces at Salonika" to "restrict the freedom of action of Bulgarian forces." The allies expected an attack at Salonika to prevent the Bulgarians from shifting forces northeast against the Romanians. The representatives also agreed that the objective of allied forces at Salonika and of Russo-Romanian forces on the Danube was to "destroy the enemy's forces and achieve a link-up after only a brief delay." Britain and France agreed to provide weapons, munitions, and equipment to Romania.[106] On the same day Joffre wired Sarrail that the purpose of the offensive by allied forces at Salonika, as agreed upon by the French and British high commands, was to "cover" the mobilization and concentration of the Romanian army against an attack from the south by Bulgaria.[107] Though Joffre's message mentioned the "destruction of enemy forces," it said nothing about linking up with the Romanians, a mission that would have required Sarrail to drive 500 kilometers to the northeast across most of Bulgaria. In reality, given British reluctance and the state of allied forces, the troops at Salonika could do little more than launch a limited offensive and thereby fix the Bulgarians to their front. Yet this assistance was important, since Romania faced a very difficult strategic situation, and fixing Bulgarian troops around Salonika would give Bucharest's forces a better chance of success.

In the message to Sarrail on July 23, Joffre also informed him that he would command allied forces in the Near East. A memorandum from London had agreed that the British commander at Salonika would "be placed upon the same footing with regard to General Sarrail as that of Sir Douglas Haig in regard to General Joffre."[108] Joffre informed Sarrail that he must "consult" the British commander on the employment of British forces but that after this consultation Sarrail had the "latitude to decide missions, objectives to be gained, zones of action, and dates on which every operation is to commence."[109] The Serbs accepted a command relationship for their forces similar to that established for the British. As for the Italians, whose troops had boarded ships in the first week of August for transport to Salonika, they accepted a relationship similar to that established for the British and the Serbs and agreed to operate under the command of Sarrail. After the tsar expressed an interest in sending troops to Greece, a Russian brigade began disembarking at Salonika on August 1. Sarrail placed the Russian brigade with French forces on the west bank of the Vardar.

By early August 1916, allied troops at Salonika included 115,396 French, 119,176 British, 122,596 Serbs, 16,000 Italians, and 9,560 Russians, a total of 382,728 soldiers. These numbers closely approached the 400,000 Joffre considered necessary for anything other than a demonstration. As the size of the allied force increased, and as the allies agreed formally to Sarrail's controlling their contingents, Joffre became concerned about Sarrail's simultaneously controlling the complex allied force and the operations of French forces. Hence he ordered Sarrail, while retaining his position over the coalition's forces, to yield command of French forces to another general officer. Joffre gave him a choice of three French generals from whom to choose. Sarrail's choice, Émilien Cordonnier, arrived at Salonika on August 11.

From December 1915 to late March 1916, Sarrail had kept most of his forces in defensive positions near Salonika. Beginning in late March, he moved allied forces toward the north. In preparation for an offensive in August, Sarrail distributed his forces in July 1916 along a front 60 kilometers north of Salonika. Along the arc-shaped front, which extended 275 kilometers, the British occupied the right, the French the center, and the Serbs the left. The French held both banks of the Vardar but kept most of their forces on the eastern bank. Given uncertainty about British participation in an offensive, Sarrail planned on the British defending while the French and Serbs attacked. The main effort would occur along a front of 50 kilometers on both sides of the Vardar.

Sarrail expected to launch his offensive on August 1, but on July 25 Romania requested a week's delay. Three days later the allies learned that Romania intended to declare war solely against Austria-Hungary, not against Germany, Bulgaria, or the Ottoman Empire. Romania planned on defending in the south along the Danube against Bulgaria while making an attack in the northwest against Austria-Hungary. Though the allies wanted Romania to declare war against more of the Central Powers, Bucharest adamantly refused. As negotiations continued, Joffre notified Sarrail of another delay in the date of the allied attack. Finally, on August 17, France, Britain, Russia, Italy, and Romania signed the military convention and promised to attack Austria-Hungary on August 28, eight days after the allies began their offensive at Salonika. Joffre immediately notified Sarrail to begin his offensive on August 20. He also encouraged the British to do everything possible on the Western Front to keep the Germans from helping the Austrians by shifting forces to the east against the Russians and Romanians. With the strategic situation apparently favoring the allies, optimism prevailed at Joffre's headquarters, and the GQG staff brashly predicted the Austrians' "inevitable collapse" before the winter and the "irremediable ruin" of the Central Powers in the campaign of 1917.[110]

The Romanians, however, had waited too long. On August 18 the Bulgarians attacked, striking the two wings of the allied front at Salonika. While the British on the right held, the Serbs on the left gave ground. As Bulgarian forces overran all of Greece east of Sarrail's forces, the Romanians charged into Austria-Hungary at the end of August. A counteroffensive, which the Central Powers had devised beforehand, quickly drove the Romanians back. With Brusilov's offensive stalled and only uncoordinated Franco-British actions occurring on the Somme, Austria and Germany shifted large forces toward Romania, and on December 6 German troops entered Bucharest. By mid-January enemy troops occupied two-thirds of Romania, including the important oil- and wheat-producing areas. Brusilov offered a simple explanation for the Romanian defeat: "the Romanians demonstrated no understanding of modern war."[111] Whatever the Romanians' level of competence may have been, allied operations had provided them very little help.

Six weeks before the Germans entered Bucharest, French and British leaders met at Boulogne to discuss the situation in the Balkans, and they agreed to reinforce allied forces at Salonika. The French eventually sent another colonial division and two battalions of heavy artillery. Though willing to send reinforcements, they acknowledged their inability to help Romania directly. The Superior Council of National Defense met on October 26 and concluded: "The Romanian military question is now a Russian military question." The council added: "The Russian army should first halt the enemy on all fronts and then undertake an offensive into Bulgaria, an offensive that operations by the army of Salonika will assist."[112] On December 6 Joffre ordered Sarrail to establish and occupy strong defenses around Salonika.

To Joffre's dismay, the ill-fated Romanian campaign added to Russian discontent toward France, especially in perceptions of their usurping Russian influence in the region. Since the Romanians distrusted the Russians, Joffre had sent General Henri Berthelot to advise them on the conduct of the campaign and to encourage them to work more closely with the Russians. Despite this effort, the Romanians refused to subordinate themselves to the Russians, and the Russians concluded that the French had been "stingy" with their weapons when giving them to the Russians but generous when giving them to the Romanians. The French military attaché summarized the Russian view: "Russia sends soldiers to Romania to be killed, and France sends them to entertain themselves."[113]

Although Sarrail eventually regained the terrain lost on his left, the strategic prize had slipped from allied hands. Allied troops at Salonika would launch other attacks before the war ended, but no one except Sarrail had serious hopes for significant gains. Russia could not provide assistance in the Balkans, and France and Britain refused to send substantial reinforcements. Paris and London agreed that "the mission of allied forces in Salonika is to hold the enemy forces presently there and attack the enemy if an opportunity appears."[114] The Germans derisively referred to Salonika as a large "internment camp" and noted the advantages of keeping thousands of allied troops in the Balkans, not in France. Similarly, Sarrail remained sensitive to being compared to Marshal Achille Bazaine, who had locked his army in the fortress at Metz during the Franco-Prussian War and lost it to the Prussians. If France and its allies had had an opportunity to gain strategic advantages in the Near East, that opportunity had vanished. With the collapse of Romania France insisted on keeping a sizable force at Salonika, but it accepted the conclusion of the allied conference in Petrograd in February 1917: "the Balkan theater has lost its importance."[115]

CHAPTER 6

A Strategy of Attrition

1916

D URING THE MAY–JUNE 1915 offensive in Artois, Joffre began using the word "attrition." In a letter to the minister of war on May 27, he mentioned the "struggle of attrition . . . we are already waging."[1] A month later in a message to Grand Duke Nicholas he said that France and Russia should work together to "drain the enemy and attrit him."[2] Despite his recognition that the war had become one of attrition, in September–October 1915 he launched his huge offensive in Artois and Champagne and attempted to rupture the enemy's defenses. As his offensive faltered, he warned the minister of war on October 3, 1915, that his attacks would not get through the enemy's second band of defenses. He could launch a new offensive, he said, only after the arrival of fresh troops and the reconstitution of units and thus had no choice but to suspend offensive actions "momentarily" after the last assault in Champagne. Yet France could not remain completely passive, for, as he later explained, "if we ourselves do not attack, we will be attacked."[3] To provide time for France to rebuild its forces, Joffre wanted Great Britain to bear the main burden of future attacks on the Western Front. He wrote on October 7, "Since the beginning of the campaign, France has borne the heaviest burden of the war. It has given without reservations the best of its blood for the triumph of the common cause. . . . It is the allies, who still have considerable forces at their disposal, who have the duty henceforth to provide the principal effort that will result in the definitive attrition of the adversary."[4] Poincaré noted: "Joffre thus proposes, for the moment, a war of attrition that will be waged primarily by our allies, British, Russian, and even Italians."[5]

At the allied military conference at Chantilly of December 6–8, 1915, Joffre sought to induce members of the coalition to bear a larger share of the war's burden. Before the meeting he completed a strategic assessment, titled "Plan of Action," and provided a copy to each representative attending the conference. The assessment viewed the war as a whole and, as one would expect, placed primary emphasis on the "principal" theaters: Franco-British, Italian, and Russian. Joffre had changed his designation of the Western Front from the Franco-Belgian to the Franco-British front not only to acknowledge the increasingly large role played by the British but also to encourage them to assume an even larger role. He had included Italy as a principal theater, even though he considered its possibilities to be less than those in France and Russia, because he did not want to offend the Italians by appearing to disparage their contribution. "Britain, Italy, Russia will intensify their efforts," his "plan of action" said, "and do everything they can to attrit the adversary. France will collaborate in this attrition as much as its resources in men will permit."[6]

Still favoring a multifront strategy, Joffre sought simultaneous, coordinated offensives on the Franco-British, Italian, and Russian fronts. By making attacks on the west, south, and east of the Central Powers, the allies could wear down the German and Austrian forces and eventually prevail against their strong defenses. No more than a few weeks should separate offensives on the different fronts, Joffre said, since the Germans and Austrians could use their interior lines to shift reserves from one front to another and to halt allied efforts. Coordinated offensives, he believed, would eventually yield a "strategic rupture" of enemy lines.[7] Unlike a narrow penetration or a breakthrough in the manner of 1940, a strategic rupture would occur suddenly when the enemy could no longer endure losses and his defenses crumbled, much like the collapse of a building or bridge after the weakening of its load-bearing structure. With as many as 110 German divisions in France and their occupation of newly strengthened defensive works, Joffre thought achieving a rupture would be "easier" on the Eastern than on the Western Front. Hence he believed that France, Britain, and Italy should provide supplies and equipment to Russia in order to revive its army's offensive value.

Joffre presided at the allied conference, and the representatives of the British, Russian, Italian, Serbian, and Belgian armies unanimously accepted his "plan of action." They agreed that a decision in the war could be obtained only in one of the "principal" theaters, where the enemy had the largest portion of his forces. They also agreed that a decision should be sought through "coordinated offensives" in the principal theaters and that these offensives should occur as soon as possible after March 1916. If the enemy attacked one of the allied powers, the others would provide as much assistance as they could. The representatives also agreed that "attrition of the enemy should be pursued with partial and local offensives, above all by the powers that still have abundant resources in men." With the inclusion of this final idea, Joffre obtained allied agreement on France's temporarily reducing its offensives and on the other powers' placing greater pressure on the enemy.[8]

Thus the conference established the outlines of allied strategy and operations for the coming year, and for the moment allied strategy was also France's strategy. While evacuating the Dardanelles and maintaining a relatively small force at Salonika, the allies would launch coordinated offensives in the spring of 1916. In France, Britain would bear the primary burden of an offensive. Joffre nonetheless recognized that getting the allies to agree was one thing and getting them to launch more offensives was another.

As the French moved toward a strategy of attrition, the hard reality of combat pervaded operational assessments. An April 1915 memorandum by the GQG on offensive action had stated: "The participants, in every echelon, are imbued with the idea of penetration, of going beyond the first trenches seized, of continuing the attack without halt until the end."[9] After the failure of the autumn offensive, assessments from the GQG and the army-group headquarters emphasized the "fragility of the infantry."[10] The GQG's formal assessment of the autumn offensives conceded that "in front of an enemy infantry that is entrenched and protected by barbed wire, the infantry alone is powerless." The assessment added, "The notion of 'succeeding no matter what happens,' 'succeeding at any price' is erroneous."[11] No longer portraying battle as "glorious," doctrine rested upon the fundamental belief that "one does not fight with men against materiel."

In the context of this more realistic approach, Joffre worked to improve the operational methods of the French army. A memorandum written on October 7 began: "Despite considerable tactical success, we have not been able to achieve a strategic penetration, which was the objective of our offensive."[12] Earlier in the war, the French had attempted to break through enemy defenses primarily with a single, continuous thrust, but they faced even stronger defenses in late 1915 after the Germans had replaced lines of defenses with deeper and more elaborate belts and had improved their ability to concentrate reserves quickly on any threatened point. The failure of the autumn 1915 offensive, as Foch had predicted in August, demonstrated conclusively that the enemy's defensive system could not be penetrated completely with a continuous thrust. Instead the French had to advance step by step and fight their way through each successive belt with a series of "powerful, slow, methodical, repeated" attacks. By advancing methodically, an attacking force could launch organized assaults against each successive position, destroy the enemy's reserves piece by piece, and initiate a battle of rupture just as the enemy's defenses began to crumble.[13] Such methods, Joffre believed, would enable the French to chip away at enemy forces and hammer their way into the Germans' elaborate defenses without incurring huge losses. In essence, he shifted the focus of French doctrine from a battle seeking penetration and breakthrough to a battle seeking attrition and then rupture. By abandoning hopes for a breakthrough and accepting battles of attrition, Joffre rendered moot his previous reservations that the methodical battle was too slow and incapable of breaking through an enemy's defenses.

The organization of successive actions in an attack received special emphasis in a directive on offensives by large units (division, corps, and field army). The directive, which the GQG published on January 26, 1916, explained that corps and army commanders must begin "new preparation" when a second or third enemy position was encountered. The directive stated: "A specific number of attack zones will be identified, including clearly identified successive objectives, where operations will be conducted by a single leader who controls the means [of attacking] and

[is] aware of the objective being pursued."[14] With belts of enemy defenses to cross, an offensive, Joffre believed, should consist of a series of carefully controlled attacks, advancing from objective to objective after preparatory fires by the artillery. As the infantry moved by bounds, artillery batteries would displace forward to ensure continued firing against enemy positions. The launching of successive attacks thus presented the characteristic of preparatory fires, followed by an infantry attack, followed by forward displacement of artillery batteries to provide preparatory fires against the next German positions, followed by another infantry attack. Though such methods had been used in Artois and Champagne by some units, Joffre wanted the entire army to understand and use them. After subsequent adjustments, the methodical battle became the "usual" method for the French army.

Joffre's "new methods" also included changes in defensive doctrine. One doctrinal publication noted: "Diminishing density, augmenting depth, these characterize the procedures of combat today."[15] Abandoning any notion of neat, linear trenches, the French emphasized defense in depth with a mixture of noncontinuous trenches and strong points, strengthened by numerous machine guns. No longer focusing on holding specific terrain, doctrine strongly emphasized the effectiveness of "rapidly executed and energetically conducted" counterattacks.[16] Such methods accorded smoothly with battles of attrition and rupture. Yet getting the army to understand and apply them took time. Pétain complained after the war that French defensive tactics in February 1916 still emphasized holding every "inch of ground."[17]

As Joffre modified French doctrine and worked to get the army to accept new methods, he devoted considerable effort to adjusting training and command philosophy. In his formal assessment of the autumn offensive, he said that many troops had not been adequately trained and that some commanders had not organized their "means" effectively when they attacked a second band of enemy defenses. To remedy these shortcomings, he issued new instructions on the training of cadre and troops. Insisting that units in the second line do more than rest, Joffre wanted continuous training and improvements in units' offensive capabilities. In a later document that specified training tasks, he said that the army's equipment had improved since the beginning of the war, but that commanders and troops still lacked an understanding of "methods of combat appropriate for modern offensive battle."[18] Among the practices condemned by Joffre were leaders' failures to command their units directly; in particular, he damned division commanders' delegating their responsibilities to brigade commanders. Rejecting what became known as "château generalship," Joffre said, "It is necessary that the division commander be at the center of his forces and displace with them."[19] With these and other directives, he attempted to improve the performance of combat units.

To ensure a higher level of training Joffre pulled General Pétain and the staff of Second Army out of the front line and gave him the mission of training large units, including artillery, in Sixth Army's sector. The idea was to rotate three corps at a time through a training camp, instructing them in new methods of war. The choice of Pétain was significant, particularly given his reluctance to continue attacking during the Champagne offensive in October; but he was considered one of the best trainers in the French army. He also had added significantly to his reputation when he offered critical assessments of the Artois and Champagne offensives. In the view of many soldiers, he, not Joffre, was the architect of the new methods.

While modifying doctrine, training, and command philosophy, Joffre also sought to improve French armaments. Since August 1914 the army had contended with a shortage of ammunition, for consumption of munitions had increased faster than their manufacture. The French used the relatively quiet period after the autumn 1915 offensive to replenish their stockpiles. With 9,000,000 rounds of 75-mm and 2,800,000 rounds of heavy artillery on January 1, 1916, the French aimed to boost their stocks to 17,000,000 rounds of 75-mm and 4,500,000 rounds of heavy artillery. To place these figures in perspective, the French had expended 6,000,000 rounds of 75-mm and 1,200,000 rounds of heavy artillery during the autumn offensive. Expecting a huge increase in stocks, logisticians arranged for army groups to store rounds in their sectors instead of placing all the ammunition in depots.

To improve the performance of artillery, the French tried to replace missing field pieces in divisions and corps. They needed only 94 pieces in early February to have four 75-mm cannon in each battery. Beyond this, they wanted an additional 592 75-mm pieces for 146 newly created batteries. By February 20 the GQG reported having 4,046 75-mm cannon. Counting another 2,373 65-mm to 90-mm cannon, most of which were not rapid-firing, the French had a total of 6,419 light pieces.

As for heavy artillery, the army had by the first of February 3,376 heavy artillery pieces, most of which were modern and rapid-firing. Joffre paid particular attention to heavy artillery because of its demonstrated effectiveness in counterbattery fire and against enemy fortifications. The French organized their short-range heavy artillery into battalions and placed one in each division, and they organized their long-range heavy artillery into twenty horse-drawn and five tractor-drawn regiments and spread them across the Western Front. Dispersing heavy artillery assets across the entire front not only made them available for local requirements but also ensured they could be shifted relatively quickly and easily to any threatened sector. For an offensive the French anticipated providing each corps with a regiment of long-range heavy artillery and at least two battalions of short-range heavy pieces. Beyond these, the entire army had 157 very powerful long-range artillery pieces, known as *artillerie lourde à grande puissance.* Stripped from the navy or coastal artillery, most of these fired from railway platforms and sent huge projectiles across vast distances. In contrast to what had existed in August 1914, the French had made great progress in heavy artillery.

As Joffre improved the capabilities of French forces, he paid close attention to aviation. At the beginning of the war France had possessed a modern air fleet and used its aircraft primarily to observe the enemy and fight for control of the air. With very limited range and bomb loads, aviators also bombed enemy troops and transportation assets in western and southwestern Germany and attacked some military targets such as a factory producing aircraft engines. In the spring of 1915 they continued bombing military targets, but they also dropped bombs in Ludwigshafen, Mannheim, and Karlsruhe in reprisal for German attacks on Verdun and Nancy. Though they primarily hit industrial or chemical factories, they also struck civilian residential areas. By late 1915 advocates of airpower championed the advantages of an aerial fleet of 1,000 planes flying over German lines and bombing targets in the Rhineland.[20] In November 1915 the French established a new aviation program envisaging some 1,300 modern aircraft divided into fighters, bombers, and artillery spotters. Although the new aircraft had greater range and larger bomb loads, the Council of Ministers, fearing enemy reprisals, refused to give Joffre free rein to bomb German cities. Not until May 25, 1916, did the council approve Joffre's bombing of German cities, and even then the ministers carefully monitored and restricted the selection of targets. As the war proceeded the minister of war would limit the targets French aircraft could attack by carefully defining "industrial objectives," "communications," and "military objectives."[21] Political authorities refused to make the war total and give the military free rein to attack targets in Germany.

Improved aircraft also gave the French the opportunity to wage bacteriological warfare, but political leaders refused to approve such an escalation. They ruled out the use of some chemicals as well. After technicians increased the army's chemical-warfare capabilities and conducted tests of new chemicals, political leaders refused to permit the use of artillery shells filled with phosgene and hydrogen cyanide because of their great toxicity. They later relented and agreed to the use of phosgene. Thus, France was completely mobilized and committed to the war effort, but some options remained unavailable to Joffre.

Preparations for an offensive on the Western Front began shortly after the autumn offensive in Champagne. On October 27 Joffre directed his army-group commanders to examine the possibility of an offensive, either alone or in conjunction with another army group, but he did not indicate any strategic goals. The memorandum said, "The scale of the envisaged offensive will be at least equal to that of the last offensive in Champagne." Foch wrote on the memorandum, "An offensive to do what?"[22] After the Chantilly conference in early December, Joffre sent his army-group commanders the results of their analysis, including a list of the regions deemed most appropriate for an offensive. The area identified in the Northern Army Group's sector was south of the Somme River. Joffre expected an offensive to occur early in the spring, but he included no strategic goals. A few days later his staff completed another assessment, this time analyzing alternatives for a British offensive. The study, which asserted that the British could attack only on a narrow front, considered the three British armies' sectors and concluded that the British Third Army's sector north of the Somme provided the best opportunity for a successful attack. The two staff studies thus suggested possible offensives on both sides of the Somme.

Though such an offensive made sense to Joffre and his staff, Foch, who would direct the combined offensive on the Somme, believed an offensive in that region would not yield important strategic results. An attack into compartmented terrain and numerous villages in the region, Foch argued, would require enormous amounts of heavy artillery, and an advance of ten to fifteen kilometers would bring the attackers to a new and difficult line of natural obstacles. Thus, the efforts and costs of such an offensive seemed too great for any results that could be obtained. The commander of the Northern Army Group favored a demonstration south of the Somme and a larger operation elsewhere. Foch's objections were not short-lived; as late as May 31 he advised against an offensive on the Somme in 1916. Despite Foch's reservations, Joffre decided to launch a combined offensive on both banks of the river. He doubted that the British would launch a major offensive without French participation, and since the Somme marked a boundary between the French and British, he saw the region as the only place where the two allies could join forces and launch a combined offensive. Thus the choice of the Somme was driven primarily by Joffre's desire to shift the burden of the war to France's allies and by the coincidence of where British and French forces were.

To avoid having the British back out of the Somme offensive, Joffre's initial efforts to induce them to participate did not emphasize attrition. On December 26, 1915, he wrote to General Sir Douglas Haig, who had replaced Sir John French a week earlier, and informed him of French preparations for an offensive. Among the regions being considered, Joffre said, was the sector south of the Somme. He added, "Without preselecting the regions where our principal attacks will occur, a French offensive will be greatly assisted by a simultaneous offensive [north of the Somme] by British forces between the Somme and Arras." He did not use the word "attrition" but noted that this region had been inactive for "long months" and had "very favorable" terrain for a strong offensive.[23] On January 20 he visited British headquarters and again raised the idea of a combined Franco-British offensive. Having identified five areas for possible offensives (three in the northeast, one in Champagne, and one along the Somme), he wanted the British to attack north of the Somme in late

April. A few days later he introduced the idea of attrition and placed a British offensive north of the Somme in the context of a "decisive offensive" by the French and British. As part of the preparation for this offensive Joffre wanted a British attack in April to wear down the enemy.[24] He expected the British to accomplish this goal with several "large and powerful offensives such as those the French army had conducted in the course of 1915." Following the British attack in April, he wanted them to launch another offensive in late May or early June. These attacks would use up the enemy's reserves prior to a general offensive by French and British forces. If the Germans began a large offensive in the spring against the Russians, Joffre intended to launch his general offensive earlier and asked the British to participate with at least twenty-five divisions.[25]

In a carefully crafted response on February 1, Haig informed Joffre that the British had initiated preparations for an offensive north of the Somme and that he agreed on the need to wear down the Germans and reduce their strength before the general offensive. He had reservations, however, about Joffre's methods. He insisted that the preparatory battles sought by Joffre would not keep the Germans from bringing up reserves in front of the allied general offensive, because they would have two or more months to replenish their reserves. Instead, such battles would weaken the morale of friendly troops and have an unfortunate effect on public opinion, since the real allied objective would not be generally understood. Launching "two isolated offensives by large forces," Haig said, would also "reduce considerably the striking power of my armies in the subsequent general offensive." The British commander preferred raids, artillery bombardment, gas attacks, and small attacks over costly preliminary battles of attrition.[26] Joffre insisted, however, that although British raids and artillery bombardments would inflict casualties, they would not drain the enemy of his reserves or prevent him from concentrating reserves at points where allied attacks had the best chance of success.

After the exchange of several letters, Joffre, Haig, Castelnau, and General Sir William Robertson (the chief of the Imperial General Staff) met on February 14, a week before the Germans began their offensive at Verdun. At the conclusion of the meeting Haig summarized its results: "Decisive attack on the Somme with the French taking the two banks. This attack will be preceded by one or two weeks with a partial attack in

northern France. The relief of Tenth Army [by the British] is acknowledged in principle, but the date remains in question, [since] the relief will
be accomplished successively according to the availability of British
troops."[27] The allied leaders also agreed that the attack would take place
around July 1. In his diary Haig celebrated having achieved "quite a victory."[28] In essence, he had foiled Joffre's efforts to have the British launch
a relatively large preparatory attack. Joffre knew, however, that there was
little chance of an important gain on the Somme without a significant
weakening of German reserves before the offensive. Even though he told
his army-group commanders he was seeking a "rupture" of the enemy's
position with his general offensive, he knew the Somme offensive would
not cause a collapse of German defenses. Since the offensive would occur
simultaneously with similar operations on the Russian and Italian fronts,
he nonetheless could hope for a significant gain by the Russians.

As Joffre prepared for the campaign of 1916, he recognized the possibility
of a German attack on the Western Front. Following Franco-British attacks in the autumn of 1915, the Germans had not shifted substantial
forces from the west as they had done in the summer of 1915 for their offensive against Russia. Instead, they had kept most of their reserves (one
cavalry and sixteen infantry divisions) in the west. The absence of any
large allied offensive over the winter of 1915–16, Joffre believed, had left
the Germans free to prepare an offensive in the west. Though he did not
expect a large enemy offensive before the first of April, he believed the
Germans could undertake a limited operation against Verdun or Nancy
to weaken the morale of their adversaries. To take advantage of a German
attack, Joffre favored a defensive-offensive strategy. Instead of the allies'
wearing down the enemy with preparatory attacks, the Germans could
weaken themselves with an attack, enabling the allies to launch their general offensive. He told an officer on January 8, "I ask only one thing, that
the Germans attack me and, if they attack me, that it be at Verdun."[29] He
continued to believe, however, that the Germans would not make Verdun
their primary objective, since he could discern no strategic results to be
obtained from such an attack. An attack on Verdun, he thought, would
most likely be a diversion.

While Joffre improved the army's combat capability and convinced the allies to modify their strategy, the Germans carefully considered their alternatives on the Western Front and adopted a strategy of attrition. The German chief of the General Staff, Erich von Falkenhayn, believed the Germans could not break through allied lines and win the war with a decisive battle but had to act before the British mobilized completely and sent a massive army to France. Remembering the huge French offensives and staggering losses of 1915, he favored an operation that would place the French in unfavorable operational circumstances and cause them to launch numerous offensives and suffer huge losses. In essence, Falkenhayn wanted France to impale itself on Germany's sword. Beginning in late November the German General Staff started its planning. After ruling out operations in Champagne or along the Aisne, the Germans identified two objectives that the French would never abandon willingly: Belfort and Verdun. They did not favor Belfort because of its close proximity to the Swiss border and the limited opportunity for maneuver. They preferred Verdun, since German railway communications ran to within twenty kilometers of the fortified region and the terrain offered numerous advantages. If the Germans quickly seized the hills east of the Meuse, the French, the staff officers concluded, would use desperate measures to retake them and would suffer immense losses. Verdun seemed ideal for inflicting the most damage on the French at the least possible cost.[30] Unfortunately for German soldiers, the planners did not anticipate a change in French strategy or operational methods or foresee that Pétain would husband the lives of his men.

Shortly before Christmas 1915, Falkenhayn met with Kaiser Wilhelm II and presented an assessment of the strategic and operational situation. His presentation, which he revamped for his memoirs, began with a political and strategic assessment ruling out the possibility of a ground attack against Britain. To defeat British forces the Germans would have to do "nothing less than drive the English completely from the Continent," but even this defeat might not result in the British quitting the war, since the French would remain strong. Defeating Britain required an unrestricted campaign by German submarines against allied shipping and the defeat of London's allies on the continent. Furthermore, since Austria-Hungary could take care of Italy, and a campaign against Russia might not yield a decision, only France remained a strategic target. Even though Falkenhayn believed France was near the "breaking point," he did not advocate a massive offensive to smash its defenses. He proposed instead an operation to "bleed to death" its army and ultimately to force it to sue for peace.[31] With the Kaiser's concurrence Crown Prince Wilhelm, commander of Fifth Army, received orders shortly before Christmas to attack French positions north of Verdun on the east bank of the Meuse. Five German corps began moving toward Verdun at the end of December. On January 27 the Germans issued orders for preparatory artillery fires to begin at 0700 hours (French time) on February 12.

Throughout December the French received information from a variety of sources suggesting a large German offensive in the near future, but the reports were contradictory and hinted at the possibility of an offensive on both wings of the allied front. Though other conflicting reports appeared in early January, the first report of an attack on Verdun arrived at the GQG on January 10. A French diplomat in Denmark provided information about a German deserter who said the Germans were preparing an attack at Verdun. During the same period several reports identified German troops and artillery moving into the Verdun sector. One of the earliest appeared on January 9 and indicated the movement since late December of enemy troops into the Montmédy-Longuyon sector northeast of Verdun. Subsequent reports identified German units moving into the general vicinity of Verdun and posited the possibility of an attack to seize the eastern bank of the Meuse. As information accumulated, General Frédéric Herr, commander of the Fortified Region of Verdun, conveyed his concern to General Dubail, commander of Eastern Army Group, about the numerous indications of heavy enemy activity near Verdun. These indications included the arrival of heavy artillery, statements by deserters about Verdun's being an enemy objective, and construction of new cantonments behind enemy lines.

Beginning in the last week of January the number of reports multiplied. Several German deserters reported suspensions of leaves and warnings being issued about "difficult days." Other reports said that Crown Prince Wilhelm was preparing an offensive on Verdun and the emperor desired a huge review at Verdun after the signing of a peace treaty. At the end of the first week in February an intelligence bulletin described traffic on one railway line in the vicinity of Verdun as double its usual volume. On February 11 an intelligence assessment from the GQG declared: "From a source normally very reliable, we learn that the Germans will try a large offensive in the region of Verdun. A large concentration of troops . . . should be established behind the [enemy] front. . . . The source also indicates a considerable concentration of heavy artillery. . . . The Crown Prince will direct the operation."[32]

The Germans intended to begin their attack the day after publication of this intelligence assessment, but bad weather forced them to delay it until February 21. On February 12, the day the attack was originally scheduled to begin, General Herr wrote to his subordinate commanders: "The latest enemy intelligence considers as probable an attack on the northern front of the F[ortified] R[egion of] V[erdun] accompanied undoubtedly by an intense bombardment of long duration and a demonstration more or less violent on the rest of the front."[33] During the next week intelligence specialists at Verdun tracked enemy activities carefully. On February 15 Herr notified his subordinate commanders that an enemy attack would probably concentrate east of the Meuse on the northern face of the salient. Five days later, the day before the enemy attack, Herr concluded that the Germans would use massive amounts of gas and would hit his northern front with at least four corps. On the eve of the German attack the Council of Ministers was informed of the threat against Verdun. French intelligence thus provided an extremely accurate and timely portrayal of enemy capabilities and intentions.

Despite this information, Joffre could perceive no strategic result to be gained by the Germans with such an attack. Consequently, when the attack on Verdun began, he considered it a diversion and expected a larger attack elsewhere on the Western Front. In a letter to Sir Douglas Haig on February 22, the day after the enemy attack, he said it was difficult to predict the form the Germans' offensive would take but he expected them to launch a series of preliminary attacks before unleashing elsewhere "one or two principal attacks with large forces." Preliminary attacks on places such as Verdun, Joffre believed, would capture the attention of the allies and hamper their reaction to the enemy's main offensive elsewhere.[34] In essence he projected onto the Germans a mirror image of the offensive he had attempted to organize and conduct. As the scale of the German action became apparent, however, Joffre recognized the threat to Verdun and to France as a whole. On March 7 in a memorandum to the Superior Council of Defense he asserted that the Germans had a "precise objective" at Verdun: "attack the principal enemy [France], not with the hope of putting it out of action but with the thought of beating down the nation's morale."[35] Unfortunately for France, Joffre's previous reservations about the strategic consequences of an attack on Verdun resulted in his not strengthening the region in the weeks before the attack and in his failing to recognize until early March what the Germans were doing.

In the months before the attack on Verdun, considerable controversy swirled through Paris about the state of Verdun's defenses. This controversy appeared at an awkward time for Joffre, since his autumn offensive had just failed and the allied position in the Balkans was unraveling. Moreover, after the last Serbian troops withdrew into Greece on December 12, the French and British had engaged in an acrid debate over maintaining forces at Salonika. Additional discord arose after Briand named Joffre commander-in-chief of all French forces on December 2. In an environment of dissension and recrimination, an officer, Émile Driant, who had served at Verdun and was also a member of the army commission in the Chamber of Deputies, corroborated reports of inadequate preparations along portions of the Western Front. The Council of Ministers discussed these reports, and Poincaré asked the minister of war, Gallieni, to draw Joffre's attention to deficiencies in the defenses. On December 16 Gallieni wrote to Joffre about these weaknesses. He noted that the networks of trenches near Toul and Verdun were not as complete as they were on other parts of the front.

Irritated by the rising crescendo of criticism in Paris, Joffre responded indignantly to the letter. After informing the minister that he had ordered army-group commanders to repair first and second lines along the entire front and to establish a system of fortified positions behind their second line, the French commander-in-chief said, "I believe that nothing justifies the fears you expressed in the name of the government." He then demanded to know the names of individuals who had sent reports to political authorities. As far as Joffre was concerned, he had taken adequate steps to prepare Verdun for an attack, and those officers who complained to Paris were undermining discipline and morale.[36] Given his refusal to believe that the Germans could make strategic gains with a major offensive against Verdun, however, he had measured the region's readiness against a secondary or diversionary attack, not against a huge offensive. And even if the Germans launched a huge offensive, he saw no need to risk a loss like those the Austrians and Russians had suffered at Przemyśl.

In fact some of the complaints about Verdun stemmed from deliberate alterations made by the French High Command beginning in August 1915. Verdun's defenses consisted of a ring of forts built after the Franco-Prussian War by General Raymond Séré de Rivières around the citadel of the city. With the example of Przemyśl and its loss by Austria in March and by Russia in June 1915 fresh in their minds, the GQG staff recommended avoiding unnecessary losses by abandoning Verdun and emptying it of inhabitants.[37] After further study, Joffre informed his army-group commanders on August 9, 1915, that fortified places such as Verdun had lost their importance as "independent" positions of resistance and had value only if they facilitated the operations of field units. He directed that permanent fortifications around Verdun not be defended by themselves but be integrated into successive lines of defense.[38] He also designated Verdun a "Fortified Region" and ordered it to report directly to the commander of Eastern Army Group, General Dubail. Changing the role of Verdun from a fortress system to a "normal" portion of the front with trenches and barbed wire also opened the door for removing numerous artillery pieces from its forts. After Verdun became a Fortified Region, the first communication from the Eastern Army Group commander to Verdun ordered a list to be compiled of "resources" that could be removed from the forts. An analysis of available resources quickly identified 237 cannon and 647 tons of ammunition, as well as other supplies. These materials came from forts outside the new zone of defense.

As one would expect, transforming Verdun into a network of trenches and barbed wire required considerable time and effort. The commander of the Fortified Region of Verdun, General Herr, began reorganizing the region's defenses and was making progress until the autumn offensive in Champagne began draining resources from his command. Though some of the units moved to Champagne were replaced, work schedules were disrupted, and the cohesion, efficiency, and readiness of the fortified region declined. Not until the latter part of October did units levied from the fortified region return. As work continued, Herr followed instructions given by Joffre on October 22 and began organizing first, second, and third positions in the Verdun region. He had made some progress in improving the state of Verdun's defenses when Gallieni's letter of December 18 to Joffre arrived expressing concern about the network of trenches at Verdun, as well as other places on the front. Thus Joffre's indignant response was at least partially justified, especially since on December 26 Dubail reported excellent progress in improving the defensive works.[39] When Joffre and Dubail met with Poincaré and Briand on December 29, they reported that the second line of defenses at Verdun was complete and the third line being constructed. Herr personally assured the president of the Republic that the region's lines of defenses were "very solid."[40] When a German attack became likely, however, he reversed his thinking about the strength of Verdun's defenses, and the tone of his appeals to Dubail became more insistent.

As the French worked more energetically to improve defenses around Verdun, Joffre detached the Fortified Region of Verdun from the Eastern Army Group on February 1 and attached it to the Central Army Group. In a meeting with Dubail on January 19 Joffre informed him of the change and said that Verdun should be removed from the control of Eastern Army Group because the most important part of its front faced north and because the Central Army Group could provide better logistical support. In his memoirs Joffre added that a defense of Verdun had to encompass the sector west of the Meuse toward the Argonne Forest and that communications favored placing Verdun under Central Army Group. When told of the change, Dubail warned Joffre that he had chosen a bad time to change the region from one army group to another, since the change would disrupt preparations for Verdun's defense. The French commander-in-chief, however, declined to reverse an already-issued order.

Obviously concerned about Verdun, Joffre sent Castelnau to inspect its defenses. Castelnau's report gave no cause for alarm, saying only that the defenses complied with Joffre's instructions except for deficiencies in three small sections of its front. The commander of the Central Army Group, General de Langle de Cary, arrived at Verdun on February 1, the day the Fortified Region of Verdun came under his control, and spent three days reviewing its defenses. Agreeing with Castelnau's assessment, he provided Herr additional men for labor. Between February 3 and 20 he visited Verdun several times, thereby showing much more energy and interest than Dubail. In his memoirs de Langle blamed Dubail for many of Verdun's deficiencies and claimed that Joffre shifted the fortified region out of Eastern Army Group because of his dissatisfaction with Dubail's performance. Though de Langle softened his criticism by conceding that preparations for a French offensive had diverted Dubail's attention, he insisted that Dubail had failed to organize a solid defense for Verdun despite having had the region under his command for fifteen months. De Langle asked, "Could I do in a few winter days, under rain and snow, that which had not been done in fifteen months?"[41]

Throughout most of January Herr had only two corps in the Fortified Region of Verdun, but on the morning of February 21 he had three. VII Corps, which had been ordered by Joffre on January 23 to move to Verdun, occupied the northern face of the salient west of the Meuse. East of the Meuse, XXX Corps (previously known as the Northern Sector) covered the northern and northeastern face of the salient, while II Corps covered the heights of the Meuse on the eastern face. Herr had eight and a half divisions in his front line and two and a half in immediate reserve. De Langle kept control of other reserves: XX Corps with two divisions, I Corps with two divisions, and most of 19th Division. In addition to these divisions Joffre had some twenty-five divisions in his general reserve, but he intended to use these in the Somme offensive. As additional units arrived and doubled Verdun's infantry, de Langle ordered Herr to echelon his forces in depth and not to place too many in the front lines. The Central Army Group commander expected these forward positions to come under heavy artillery fire, and he did not want to have them filled with troops who would do little more than become casualties.

The French thus took numerous steps between January 10 and February 21 to strengthen the Fortified Region of Verdun. Given the significant improvements made by de Langle and Herr after the twelfth, the French were fortunate that weather delayed the German attack until the twenty-first. Nevertheless, the divisions in the region occupied relatively large fronts, and according to the German official history, French artillery, including mortars, was outnumbered almost four to one. On the day of the enemy's attack XXX Corps—which occupied the twenty-five-kilometer

Verdun, 1916

sector east of the Meuse on the northern face of the salient and would be assaulted by five German corps—had 340 artillery pieces, 120 of which were heavy. The other French corps had less support. Additionally, second and third positions were not as strong as they needed to be; in his memoirs de Langle described the third position as "almost nonexistent."[42] The consequences would become apparent in the first days of the battle.

At Verdun the German artillery bombardment began unevenly between 0600 and 0730 on February 21. Most rounds landed on the front lines of the 72nd and 51st, two divisions east of the Meuse on the left of XXX Corps. Beginning around 0800 hours enemy rounds struck other portions of the fortified region, including the two divisions on the west bank. Verdun soon came under long-range enemy fires, as did the bridges over the Meuse. To deceive the French about the location of the main attack, enemy fires struck French trenches east and west of the fortified region. The heaviest fires, however, landed in XXX Corps's sector and eventually struck in depth through its position. One officer reported, "The violence of the fire was such that when we left our shelters we could not recognize the countryside in which we had lived for four months."[43] The devastating artillery fire continued until 1600 hours, when enemy infantry from four corps assaulted the 72nd and 51st divisions. As the Germans captured portions of the first line, their artillery continued pounding the second line. By the following morning the enemy had made a two-kilometer advance on the right of 72nd Division and small gains elsewhere, but the first wave of attacks was only a reconnaissance in force designed to probe French positions.

The main assault began at 0730 on the second day. Preceded by massive artillery fire and armed with flamethrowers, the German infantry advanced, more than doubling the gains made on the first day. The French launched battalion-sized counterattacks but did not roll back the enemy. As the Germans continued pushing the defenders back on the third day, French artillery had to displace to the rear, thereby disrupting or delaying much of its support to the hard-pressed infantry. At midday de Langle told Herr, "Hold, hold no matter what the cost."[44] The Germans continued advancing on the third day, however, and by its end had made a three-kilometer advance across an eleven-kilometer front in the 72nd's and 51st's sectors. The two French divisions had been driven from the first position and were now in the second position. The following day the Germans again made significant gains, forcing the French to displace their artillery and abandon some of their heavy pieces. At the end of the day on February 24, the 72nd and 51st, plus other reinforcing units, were in the third position, but they were significantly weakened by numerous losses in the infantry and the disruption of supporting artillery fire.

During the first four days of the German attack, the French rushed reinforcements forward. XXX Corps sent regiments and battalions from its reserves forward one by one into 72nd's and 51st's sectors. The Fortified Region of Verdun also sent its reserves forward piecemeal. Central Army Group's reserves arrived more slowly. With these reinforcements Herr had VII Corps with four divisions (29th, 67th, 48th, and 39th) on the west bank and XXX Corps with five divisions (72nd, 37th, 51st, 153rd, and 14th) on the east bank, plus II Corps on the east face of the salient along the heights of the Meuse. Meanwhile the enemy continued to press the hardest against XXX Corps on the east bank.

Although German units drove forward no more than five kilometers on the northern face of the Verdun salient, their advance threatened to cut off the two territorial brigades holding the salient's northeastern face in the Woëvre. With defenses weak and resupply difficult, the territorials, de Langle feared, might panic and flee toward Douaumont. Such a calamity could cause a complete collapse of defenses on the east bank of the Meuse. At 1900 hours on February 24 de Langle called the GQG and informed Joffre that he was withdrawing all troops from the Woëvre and pulling them back toward the heights of the Meuse. Recognizing how controversial the order would be, de Langle said that he was not asking for permission to make the withdrawal but was ordering it on his own responsibility. Joffre approved the order and explained, "You are the sole judge of the necessities of combat." Despite Joffre's willingness to abandon the Woëvre, he refused to abandon the east bank of the Meuse and told de Langle, "You must hold, facing to the north, the front between the Meuse and the Woëvre with every means at your disposal."[45]

After sending this message, Joffre discussed the situation with

Castelnau, his chief of staff, and decided to send Pétain and his Second Army headquarters to Verdun. At 2145 hours the GQG sent a message to Pétain to meet with the French commander-in-chief the following morning at the GQG, and shortly after midnight Castelnau left for Verdun to assess the situation. In his memoirs Joffre stated that he gave Castelnau the authority to make whatever decisions were necessary but warned him to order a withdrawal to the west bank only if a defense on the east bank was impossible. Additionally, the real possibility that the Germans would drive Herr's forces from the east bank led Joffre the following day to give Pétain a restricted mission: "(1) Rally the troops of the F[ortified] R[egion of] V[erdun] . . . if they are compelled to withdraw to the west bank; (2) Prevent the enemy from crossing the [Meuse] river."[46] Thus Joffre ordered neither Castelnau nor Pétain to hold the right bank, and a more ambitious mission for Second Army appeared only after Castelnau arrived on the scene.

After meeting with Castelnau, Joffre went to bed, but he was awakened later that night when Briand, the premier of France, arrived at the GQG. Fearing that the fall of Verdun would crush France's morale and destroy his government, Briand had traveled to Chantilly to ensure that Joffre did everything possible to defend the region. When members of Joffre's staff explained the advantages of abandoning Verdun and organizing a more easily defended line along the river, Briand lost his temper and threatened to relieve everyone present if Verdun fell. After listening quietly to this rancorous exchange, Joffre interrupted and expressed his agreement with Briand: French forces would remain on the eastern bank and defend Verdun. In his study of civil-military relations Jere C. King implies that Briand's intervention kept Joffre from abandoning Verdun, but the precise effect of Briand's visit is impossible to gauge. Although the GQG had analyzed the possibility of relinquishing the east bank, Joffre had not ordered the evacuation of Verdun and had told de Langle to use "every means" at his disposal to maintain troops on the east bank. Additionally, he had sent his chief of staff, Castelnau, to Verdun to assess the situation and to initiate any necessary changes.[47]

Poincaré later said that even though several GQG staff officers had expressed doubts to him about the wisdom of holding Verdun and remaining on the east bank, Joffre had never expressed such doubts. The politically astute Joffre knew how controversial the abandonment of Verdun would be and never openly suggested such a course of action. Nevertheless rumors continued to circulate in Paris that he had ordered the abandonment of that region. Seeking to verify what had happened, General Gallieni, the minister of war, asked for a copy of all orders he gave during the battle. Since he never ordered the evacuation of Verdun, copies of his orders provided no ammunition for his critics. Instead of issuing the controversial order or meekly acceding to Verdun's loss, Joffre had cagily sent his chief of staff into the hornets' nest.

Before Castelnau's departure for Verdun and Briand's arrival at the GQG, de Langle and Herr prepared on their own on the twenty-fourth to abandon the east bank. After de Langle prohibited the movement of troops across the Meuse to the east bank, Herr ordered all support troops to move to the west bank and directed that forts and casemates on the eastern bank be prepared for destruction. However, Joffre's conversation on the telephone with de Langle around 2100 hours, before Briand's visit, halted these preparations. At 0230 hours on the twenty-fifth XXX Corps published a new operations order for defending the Bras-Douaumont-Vaux-Eix line, a semicircular position six to eight kilometers northeast of Verdun. As XXX Corps struggled to hold this position, elements in the Woëvre retired in the night to the heights of the Meuse, leaving only advance posts behind. At 2230 hours on February 25 the Fortified Region of Verdun reported the evacuation of the Woëvre complete.

On February 25 Castelnau arrived at de Langle's headquarters at 0400 hours. In a long discussion with Joffre's chief of staff the Central Army Group commander expressed doubts about holding the east bank. Given the substantial reinforcements moving toward Verdun, Castelnau thought otherwise. He telephoned Herr and ordered him to hold the east bank of the Meuse "no matter what the cost."[48] Herr reacted by moving a division from the west to the east bank and ordering XXX Corps to defend the Bras-Douaumont-Vaux-Eix line, including the forts, "to the utmost."[49] A few hours later Castelnau arrived at Herr's headquarters, which was in the midst of a move from the east bank to the west bank, and found Verdun's commander depressed and suffering from lack of sleep. After visiting several units and gaining a better assessment of the situation, he made several changes, including having the XX Corps commander take control of XXX Corps's sector.

At 1530 Castelnau telephoned Joffre's headquarters and proposed that Pétain be given command of the Fortified Region of Verdun and all reinforcing troops arriving in the region. He also suggested that Pétain be ordered to halt the enemy north of Verdun. Joffre, who rarely spoke on the telephone, approved the recommendations an hour later, but before this formal approval arrived at Verdun Castelnau notified Pétain of his new mission and authority. Pétain arrived at the Fortified Region's headquarters at 1900 hours and assumed command of the region at 2300. Unfortunately for Pétain, the first piece of news he received was that Douaumont, the "best and most modern" of the French forts at Verdun, had fallen. In the confusion of XX Corps's moving into position and the territorials' pulling out of the Woëvre, the French had failed to send infantry to reoccupy the fort, and commanders on both sides of the fort had erroneously assumed that it could defend itself. As a consequence a handful of German soldiers easily captured Fort Douaumont, a loss that would eventually cost the French thousands of casualties in attempts to recapture it.

Back at the GQG, Joffre finally acknowledged the strategic advantage the Germans could gain at Verdun. He wrote to General Robertson that the fighting at Verdun could "influence the outcome of the war."[50] He sent a similar message to Haig and added that the enemy had committed large forces in an attempt to "penetrate" the French front.[51] After less than a week of fighting the French had lost 25,000 soldiers, most of whom came from the divisions in XXX Corps on the northern face of the east bank.

After assuming command Pétain ordered his subordinate commanders to defend the terrain occupied by their units. A formal operations order stated: "The mission of Second Army is to stop at any price the enemy effort on the Verdun front. Every time the enemy wrests a parcel of terrain from us, an immediate counterattack will take place." Pétain also specified the defensive position of his army. He divided the troops in his front line into "groups," each of which was the rough equivalent of a corps. Each group contained divisions and brigades from several corps and was named after the corps commander in charge of it. One group occupied the west bank, a second group occupied the east bank in the sector between the Meuse and Douaumont, a third group defended from Douaumont to Eix, and a fourth stretched along the heights of the Meuse to a point a few kilometers northwest of St.-Mihiel.[52] The headquarters of XX and I corps, as well as their divisions, had arrived from February 24 to 26, giving Pétain fourteen and a half divisions on the twenty-sixth. Other corps ordered toward Verdun by Joffre were XIII, XXI, XIV, and XXXIII. By March 6 Pétain had twenty and a half divisions. In his history of the battle Pétain said the GQG had so many large units moving toward Verdun that he asked that no more large units be sent and requested heavy artillery instead.

Though Pétain launched a few minor attacks, he devoted most of his attention between February 27 and March 6 to strengthening defenses. He sought an organized defense in depth and ordered the establishment of four lines. He also ordered units to offer strong resistance along their front line and to launch counterattacks even though this exposed them to massive concentrations of enemy fire. To reduce casualties, he eventually decided to place an "advanced line of resistance" 300–500 meters in front of a "principal line of resistance" and to place only a small number of soldiers in the forwardmost line. Holding a strong line of resistance, however, remained difficult, and he later compared it to "balancing on a tightrope."[53] As part of his effort to strengthen Verdun's defenses, Pétain paid particular attention to the artillery, especially in its demonstrating to the infantrymen that they had support. To increase the use of artillery, he ordered his commanders to establish daily firing plans and to use artillery fire not only defensively but also offensively. On the twenty-ninth he ordered units on the west bank to keep the enemy on the east bank under constant fire. As the Germans advanced on the east bank, they exposed themselves to enfilade fire from the west bank, and French artillery began taking a heavy toll. Slowly but surely French defenses stiffened, but the enormous pressure on Pétain exhausted him and caused him to develop a nervous tick in his face.

As the tactical organization of Pétain's forces improved, so did their logistical system. Always attentive to logistics, Joffre placed Third Army under Pétain. This arrangement enabled Pétain to simplify support services by combining supply and transportation assets of the two armies, both of which had located many of their support services in Bar-le-Duc.

Desiring to provide a continuous flow of supplies to his units, Pétain created depots behind Second Army for each of his groups. To ensure the flow of supplies, he ordered these depots to carry three days of ammunition and four days of rations. To reduce traffic and thus targets on the east bank, he moved most support services to the west bank, permitting them to come forward only to accomplish their mission, usually at night. Supplies normally flowed from Bar-le-Duc to distribution points on the west bank, and thence to the groups' depots.

Transporting supplies to Verdun proved particularly difficult, for the two main rail lines to the beleaguered region were unusable. While the railway from the south was cut off by the St.-Mihiel salient, the one from the west had to pass under German guns at Aubréville. The only railway remaining was the narrow-gauge line from Bar-le-Duc to Verdun, and the French quickly took advantage of it. By the end of March thirty-two trains a day traveled from Bar-le-Duc to Nixéville. Since the narrow-gauge railway could not handle alone the vast transportation requirements of Verdun, the French had to use the only road into Verdun from Bar-le-Duc, a simple country road not designed for heavy traffic. Despite the road's limitations the French moved numerous personnel and vast amounts of supplies over it. In their initial planning the French expected to transport each day 2,000 tons of ammunition, 100 tons of food and supplies, and 15,000–20,000 soldiers. Between February 22 and March 7 transportation units carried to Verdun 22,500 tons of ammunition, 2,500 tons of food and supplies, and 190,000 men. During that same period they also evacuated 6,000 civilians from Verdun. With an average of 1,700 trucks making a round trip each day, a vehicle passed a point on the road every twenty-five seconds; during peak periods the average number of trucks doubled. For obvious reasons the road became known as the "Sacred Way."

After the German attack on the east bank slowed, the crown prince shifted his efforts on March 6 to the west bank in an attempt to silence the French batteries firing across the Meuse onto the east bank. The Germans preceded their attack with a heavy artillery bombardment, causing the French group on the west bank to report, "All of the second position and the zone of the batteries behind it look like foam. Shell holes overlap one another."[54] The Germans made their deepest advance along the

Meuse, but after a month's fighting on the west bank they had gained only three kilometers on a front of twelve kilometers. Despite numerous assaults the French kept troops atop two important hills on the west bank: Hill 304 and Mort Homme. On the east bank the Germans launched few large infantry assaults in March, but they continued bombarding French lines, inflicting numerous casualties, and launching small attacks. They did advance to the edge of the village of Vaux, but they failed to capture Fort Vaux.

The fighting in the vast battle of attrition bore no resemblance to the combat envisaged by Ardant du Picq and others. Most battles began with an artillery bombardment that smashed the opponent's forward position and killed numerous defenders. As the attacking Germans pushed infantry forward, the defenders concentrated huge barrages in front of their defensive position and rushed reinforcements toward the threatened point. Many of these reserves never arrived at the forward trenches, since enemy shells and bullets pounded them unceasingly as they advanced. Whether attacker or defender, those who successfully made their way to the contested point fought from demolished trenches and shell holes with grenades, trench mortars, machine guns, or anything else available. A battle was thus nothing more than a brawl that consumed almost everything thrown into it.

One French veteran described his company's nighttime move into the front lines:

> [Advancing] by successive bounds we reach the Ravine of Bazil, also known as the "Ravine of the Dead". . . . In groups of five or six men under a rain of bullets and shells we have to cross the Ravine of the Dead, which is under [enemy] enfilade fire. . . .
>
> . . . the terrain is completely churned by shells, filled with craters into which groups can fall at any instant under frightfully violent bombardment. We cross painfully, always bent double under the harsh light of German flares. . . .
>
> Under these conditions our losses increase with each step. But where the carnage is the most hideous is at the bottom of the Ravine of the Dead—well named—where we step literally on bodies into which our feet sink. . . . An odor of rotting bodies floats in the air.

We step on bodies.

We brush past bodies.

We lean against bodies [with] green faces or exposed skulls. Bodies everywhere . . .

Have we arrived alive in the land of the dead?

No. It is simply the hell of Verdun.[55]

Beginning in early March Pétain sought an uninterrupted supply of replacements. Instead of leaving units in the trenches until casualties rendered them ineffective, he rotated units through the trenches, replacing them before losses drained them of their combat potential and will to fight. In his account of the battle Pétain described this as a *"noria"* system, named after a mill's unending chain of buckets, which rotated through water and then emptied before returning to water.[56] Though this system made sense from Pétain's perspective, the constant rotation of units through Verdun's trenches threatened to drain the combat capability of units that Joffre wanted to use in his Somme offensive. Pétain's insistence on replacements thus endangered Joffre's overall strategy.

As Verdun began consuming troops and materiel, Joffre attempted to maintain a large reserve and thus to preserve his freedom to attack on the Somme or to defend against a German attack on another portion of the front. For the March 10 meeting of the Superior Council of National Defense Joffre, as was customary, prepared a paper for discussion and included an account of his reserves. With Haig having agreed "in principle" to relieve Tenth Army, he expected to have twenty-seven or twenty-eight divisions in his reserves, seven of which were in the Verdun region.[57] In order to keep his reserves this numerous, he pulled divisions from the army groups and held them in the rear, and he established a process for replenishing the corps that had fought at Verdun and then rotated to the rear. When Pétain requested another corps on March 7, Joffre agreed, but he insisted that other corps pulled out of the front line be returned to him as soon as possible. When Pétain requested another corps on March 9, however, Joffre refused. Instead, he left XX Corps with Pétain on the grounds that the corps's losses had not been so great that it had to stay out of the line after being filled with replacements.

Joffre was not alone in his desire to slow the flow of replacements to

Verdun. In a carefully worded letter to the French commander-in-chief Foch explained the dangers of reducing Sixth Army by compelling it to send units to Verdun. That army, which was supposed to attack south of the Somme in Joffre's general offensive, held a front of 105 kilometers with only twelve divisions, nine of which were in the front line. Reducing it any further, Foch said, would compromise its ability to participate in the Somme offensive.[58]

For the next month, however, Pétain continued requesting reinforcements and Joffre reluctantly sent them. Pétain normally requested one or two divisions at a time and less frequently asked that a corps headquarters be replaced. Joffre's response to Pétain's requests occasionally contained comments about the effects of this rotation on the entire army and included complaints about Second Army's not returning corps and divisions fast enough to the GQG's control. The quick return of units to the GQG facilitated their replenishment with troops and equipment and their transfer to other portions of the front, and Joffre suspected that Pétain purposely delayed returning units so he would have more reserves at his disposal. Pétain had his own complaints. In addition to protesting the sending of green recruits into the trenches, he objected to Joffre's sending units to Verdun for a second time and insisted that the terrible bombardments, awful existence in the trenches, and significant losses should be experienced only once. Divisions, Pétain believed, could normally endure eight to ten days in the trenches before losing much of their combat effectiveness. He usually relieved a division on a regularly scheduled basis or immediately after it suffered heavy losses. In reality, Joffre had no choice but to accede to Pétain's requests, since he could not risk a collapse of French forces at Verdun. Reluctantly accepting the rotation of divisions, Joffre limited the number of divisions in Second Army to twenty-four.

While trying to conserve his reserves, the French commander-in-chief worked diligently to ensure that the British would replace the French Tenth Army in the Vimy-Arras sector between the British First and Third armies. Although Haig had strong reservations about the readiness of his forces to assume responsibility for a larger portion of the front, he had agreed "in principle" on February 14 to do so. On February 20, however, the day before the Germans attacked Verdun, the French liaison officer to British headquarters told Joffre to expect the relief of only two to four divisions. After the German assault began, Joffre insisted that the British relieve Tenth Army quickly and also move some of their reserves behind Sixth Army, which occupied the sector south of the Somme, so that he could move French reserves currently in that region. On February 27 Haig notified Joffre that he would replace the entire Tenth Army with British forces. By March 14 the British Third Army had slowly extended its front toward the north and replaced the French units.

While arranging the relief of Tenth Army and attempting to restrict Pétain's use of his reserves, Joffre asked France's allies to press the Germans on their fronts and thereby prevent the enemy from shifting forces toward France. Russia expressed its willingness to aid the French army and said it could commence operations in the middle of March, but Italy said it could not launch an attack before the end of May because of ammunition shortages. Haig responded that he could attack in six weeks but hinted that the size of the attacking force would not be large. A franker assessment of the British came from the French liaison officer to Haig's headquarters. If the British attacked before April 15, the colonel reported, the number of divisions would be no more than twelve to fifteen, and an offensive would lack power because of a deficiency in reserves, heavy artillery, and munitions. Thus, after more than two weeks' fighting at Verdun, Britain had provided important assistance with the relief of Tenth Army, but only Russia had expressed willingness to launch an early attack.

Joffre used the allied conference on March 12 to pressure France's allies for assistance. With representatives from Britain, Italy, Belgium, Serbia, and Russia attending, he presided over a wide-ranging discussion. The participants did not question the need for a massive, coordinated offensive and agreed that the Russians would attack on May 15 and the remainder of the allies on May 30. The question of maintaining forces in Salonika proved far more controversial than launching a general offensive. The conference nevertheless set the framework for allied strategy for the next few months. While France continued to resist German attacks at Verdun, members of the coalition would prepare major offensives. At a date still to be determined simultaneous offensives would occur on the Russian, Italian, and Franco-British fronts.

As for the Franco-British offensive on the Somme, French planning for the operation had begun in mid-February, when Joffre sent his concept for the attack to Foch, commander of Northern Army Group. When Foch submitted his proposal on March 16 for the French portion of the offensive, he anticipated employing three armies on a fifty-kilometer front south of the Somme. Of the three armies expected to participate in the operation, Sixth Army was already in position, and Tenth Army had been relieved by the British and moved south of the Somme. Second Army, however, was now deeply involved in the Verdun battle, as were many of the corps and divisions earmarked for the operation.

Despite the diversion of French forces, Joffre thought that French and British forces—in conjunction with attacks by other allies—could make significant gains on the Somme. Since the Germans had concentrated large forces at Verdun and were not expecting a massive offensive on the Somme, an attack there, he thought, should encounter relatively weak enemy defenses. On March 27 he wrote to Haig about his intentions to "rupture" the enemy front between Hébuterne (twenty-five kilometers north of the Somme) and Lassigny (forty kilometers south) and then drive east. The French would be responsible for two-thirds of the sixty-five-kilometer front. With the French committing thirty-nine and the British twenty-five divisions, the offensive, Joffre told Haig, could overwhelm the German defenders and achieve "important strategic results."[59]

The bloody toll at Verdun, however, forced him to modify his thinking. As the Germans continued pressing Verdun and Pétain continued demanding new reserves, he had to lower his sights and seek relief for the hard-pressed soldiers at Verdun. In his letter on March 27 to Haig, Joffre had warned that demands at Verdun could compel the French to attack only south of the Somme, and at the Paris conference of March 27–28 the French again warned that they might have to reduce their level of effort. A month later Joffre informed Foch that he had no choice but to reduce the number of French divisions in the offensive from thirty-nine to thirty. Haig, however, had long recognized that the fighting at Verdun could compel the French to reduce their forces in the Somme offensive. In an entry in his diary in late March he noted an acrimonious exchange between General Robertson and Briand at a Paris conference. The French premier had said that "it was now time for the British to play their part." On May 20, after a meeting with Clemenceau and learning more about doubts in Paris concerning Joffre's offensives, Haig wrote in his diary, "Indeed, it almost seems likely that the French may give up the idea of an offensive, while doing all in their power to induce *us* to attack."[60] Yet French and British leaders knew, as Robertson admitted candidly in a meeting of the British War Committee, that Haig would not attack "if the French intended to leave all the fighting to him."[61]

On May 22 Joffre officially informed Haig that because of the desperate struggle at Verdun the French had to reduce the number of divisions scheduled to participate in the upcoming offensive. Instead of thirty to thirty-nine divisions, Joffre could promise only twenty-two, but if events permitted, three or four more divisions might be available. Hints about more significant changes appeared in a paper prepared by the GQG for Joffre's use in a Franco-British conference on May 26. The paper analyzed possible courses of action for the allies if the Germans intensified their assault on Verdun, and it acknowledged that the British might have to attack alone during the summer. The French gave a copy to the British.

Another sensitive point pertained to the starting time for the Somme offensive. In early May Haig had suggested starting the offensive in August. He thought that a thoroughly prepared offensive could achieve "decisive results" while a "hasty" attack would achieve much less.[62] Though Joffre's staff thought a later offensive would give the French more time to recuperate from Verdun, the French commander-in-chief knew that his army needed assistance sooner rather than later. As he explained in a letter to General Haig, the French had suffered many losses at Verdun and could not endure losses there indefinitely. Any further delays could result in a severe reduction of French forces participating in the Somme operation. In several letters to Haig and Robertson Joffre emphasized the need to coordinate the Somme offensive with a Russian attack on the Eastern Front.

On May 26 French and British commanders met to discuss the timing of the Somme offensive. Joffre set the tone for the meeting when he said, "To allow its allies to be prepared completely, France has resisted alone violent enemy assaults for three months. The enemy probably sought to hinder the general offensive. . . . It would be vain to deny that he has succeeded." Acknowledging 150,000 casualties, Joffre added that fifty-two French divisions had fought at Verdun and two-thirds of his reserves were engaged in that battle. To prevent a further weakening of the French army, the Somme offensive had to begin soon.[63] When Haig started explaining the advantages of delaying the offensive until August 15, Joffre lost his composure and shouted that the French army would "cease to exist" if the British did nothing until then. Haig calmed Joffre by saying he was prepared to commence operations on July 1.[64] The two quickly agreed to begin the offensive on that day.

A few days later the French finally spelled out the small role they would play in the Somme offensive. At a conference attended by Haig, Joffre, Foch, Poincaré, and Briand, Castelnau read a memorandum prepared by the GQG staff and given beforehand to the British. The memorandum acknowledged that the Germans had succeeded in disrupting French participation in the allied offensive. If the Germans intensified their efforts or opened a new front, the memorandum said, the French would reduce their participation further. The memorandum also described the British attack as an "absolute necessity," since it fulfilled the Franco-British obligation to support the Russian offensive on the Eastern Front.[65] To ensure that Haig did not back out of the Somme offensive, French representatives emphasized that Verdun could fall if the offensive did not occur. French and British leaders thus acknowledged the shifting of responsibility to the British for the main attack. Haig objected to only one statement in the memorandum: "The British have not been attacked."[66]

Despite several meetings with Joffre, the British commander still did not know the size of the French effort, and the two generals had different conceptions of what would happen on July 1. The two allied leaders had agreed to begin their attack on that date, but they had not discussed whether the infantry assault or artillery preparation would begin then. The misunderstanding surfaced when Joffre asked the French liaison officer at British headquarters to determine when Haig wanted the artillery preparation to begin. The request angered Haig, who thought the allies had agreed to start the artillery preparation on July 1, but he used this opportunity to ask how French units on his right would be employed.

When Joffre responded on June 6, he sent Haig a copy of the instructions Foch had given the Sixth Army commander, General Fayolle. Written on May 25, before the key meetings with Haig, those instructions stated: "The principal offensive will be executed by the British armies; the task of Sixth Army is to support them in this offensive." The instructions also indicated that Sixth Army would have three corps (eleven divisions) for the attack and one corps in reserve.[67] Thus the French intended to have far fewer divisions participate than the forty-two planned in January, the thirty-nine in February, the thirty in April, or the twenty-two in May.

While Joffre and Haig coordinated the Somme offensive, brutal fighting continued at Verdun. On April 9 the Germans began a large offensive, striking first the west bank and then the east. For four days enemy forces alternated their attacks from one bank to the other. The attacks ended on the twelfth and were replaced by continuous artillery bombardments. Modifying their tactics, the Germans ended broad-front attacks and began concentrating their efforts on narrow portions of the front. Though most of their subsequent attacks came after massive artillery barrages, the French successfully fought off their efforts to seize key points such as Hill 304 and Mort Homme. A soldier on Mort Homme described a German attack on April 16:

> The first assault wave is annihilated by our fusillade; a second wave is launched, and it receives the same treatment. A third and then a fourth wave leave their trench, but this time in columns of four. We have the impression the Germans do not want to leave their trench and their leaders have to put them in formation and threaten them. The last two waves are also halted by the fire of our rifles and machine guns. During the two hours of the attack, we fired continuously. . . . We were no longer men, we were demons intoxicated by the powder. Our losses were heavy: the company commander, several officers and noncommissioned officers, and numerous men.[68]

Throughout this period of frequent German assaults the French did not remain passive. In addition to frequent counterattacks, the French launched carefully coordinated offensives, most notably the attempt by

General Robert Nivelle to seize Fort Douaumont at the end of April. Like the Germans, however, the French made only small gains. Pétain believed the French suffered more casualties than the Germans, since the latter could spread their units in a "fan-shaped formation over a larger territory with well-constructed shelters and wooded zones . . . to conceal their concentration of men."[69] Such a distribution of soldiers and artillery provided the Germans some protection against French artillery. In contrast, the French had 500,000 men concentrated in the small "handle" (or area) at the base of the "fan-shaped formation" with few or no trees to conceal them.

Throughout April Joffre demanded that Pétain be more aggressive. Though France had already suffered 90,000 casualties, including 11,000 known dead, by the end of March the French commander-in-chief believed Second Army had more troops than the enemy and insisted that Pétain exploit the advantages he had. Instead of fighting to retain every square meter of terrain, Joffre wanted him to launch immediate counterattacks at favorable points. Sitting in the quiet safety of his headquarters, the French commander-in-chief wrote on April 1, "This is the only way you can impose your will on the enemy, maintain the high morale of your troops, and close with success the final part of the operation that the enemy began at Verdun."[70] A week later he was even more insistent that Pétain mount strong offensive operations when fresh troops entered the front. Such active operations, he contended, could halt the enemy completely, while "successive, passive positions of resistance" could not.[71] To prod Pétain into action, Joffre praised the "aggressive attitude" of General Nivelle, a corps commander at Verdun.[72] While pressing Pétain to be more aggressive, Joffre simultaneously restricted the flow of reserves to Verdun. Not surprisingly, the relationship between the two became very strained.

The opportunity for Joffre to make changes at Verdun occurred after General Pierre Roques succeeded Gallieni as minister of war. Since the first turbulent days of Verdun, discontent in Paris with Joffre and his senior commanders had mushroomed, and Gallieni, who had defended Joffre several times in the past, became particularly critical of him. Incensed by events at Verdun during the first few days of the battle, Gallieni wrote an extremely critical report on the High Command and presented it to the Council of Ministers on March 7. As Poincaré observed, Gallieni sought to "discredit Joffre and force him to resign."[73] Instead of heightening criticism of Joffre in the council, however, Gallieni's report caused the ministers, particularly Briand and Poincaré, to rally to the French commander's defense. Both knew that publication of Gallieni's report would bring down the government and seriously affect the army's morale and will to fight. Dissension between Gallieni and Joffre had already risen to the Council of Ministers several times, and in this case, as in most of the others, the ministers sided with Joffre. Terminally ill from prostate cancer and frustrated by his inability to make changes in the High Command, Gallieni tried to resign but agreed to remain in office until a replacement was found. Several names surfaced, including Joffre's, but General Roques was appointed on March 16 after Briand made sure that Joffre had no objections.

Within a week after entering office Roques bent under the pressure of criticism aimed at Joffre and his senior commanders. On March 23 he wrote Joffre and asked him to remove Dubail and de Langle de Cary, as well as two other officers, from their commands. A few days later de Langle and Dubail received courteous letters from Joffre notifying them that since they had passed the age limit recently fixed by the government, they would have to give up command of their army groups. Age obviously was not the real reason for their removal, since de Langle had received much blame for the bad news coming from Verdun, and Briand had considered relieving him as early as March 4 and replacing him with Pétain. As for Dubail, even though he had been considered a possible replacement for Gallieni, members of the Council of Ministers had complained about his "foolish" partial offensives. Even more intriguing, Roques had served under Dubail as commander of First Army immediately before becoming minister of war, and one of his first significant acts was removal of his former boss. Whatever the reasons for removing the two generals, Joffre expressed greater concern in his memoirs about the government's "interference" in the assignment of general officers than with losing two experienced army-group commanders.[74]

No neophyte with regard to underhanded maneuvers, Joffre used de Langle's removal to promote Pétain and move him from Verdun. Though crediting Pétain with many of the tactical innovations that saved Verdun,

Joffre objected to his not looking beyond Verdun and comprehending the broader French strategy. In essence, he saw Pétain as a tactical rather than a strategic thinker. By giving him command of Central Army Group, Joffre expected him to gain a broader perspective on the strategic situation and thus to understand and support the GQG's efforts. In mid-April Joffre notified Pétain that he would be commander of Central Army Group and that Nivelle would replace him at Second Army. On May 1 the two generals assumed their new responsibilities. At the same time General Franchet d'Espèrey became commander of Eastern Army Group. Joffre now had Castelnau as his chief of staff and Foch, Pétain, and Franchet d'Espèrey as his army-group commanders. Only Castelnau had begun the war as an army commander. Despite his poor performance in the first weeks of the war, Joffre had gradually gained great confidence in him. When asked in May 1916 about their relationship, Castelnau replied, "Except for sleeping together, we could not be closer."[75]

Once promoted to his new position as commander of Central Army Group, Pétain proved as obstinate as before and frequently visited Nivelle's headquarters, thereby ensuring that no major changes occurred in the conduct of the battle. On May 7 he wrote to Joffre and offered his views on strategy and operations. He began his letter with a description of the improved tactics the Germans had used recently at Verdun. Instead of bombarding and attacking on broad fronts, Pétain said, the Germans had started concentrating their fires on narrow zones, destroying defenders throughout the depth of these zones, and thereby opening corridors for the infantry to advance. Defending against such tactics proved extremely difficult, since the time of an enemy's attack was never known beforehand and since sending reinforcements forward exposed them to devastating concentrations of enemy fire. He added, "In effect, ignorant of the points threatened by attack, the defenders are obliged to be strong everywhere and to place in the front line increased numbers of personnel who must be replaced often."[76]

As for allied planning, Pétain complained about the resemblance between the coming Somme offensive and the attacks launched in Artois and Champagne in late 1915. That is, he did not believe the allies should make successive thrusts at the same point on the front line or seek a rupture of enemy lines. Such attacks, he argued, would be disastrous, since they would seize only a few kilometers of terrain and would last for a long period. Even worse, the enemy could mass artillery around the battle zone after the first French thrust and inflict heavy losses on subsequent thrusts. Though a series of successive attacks would wear down the enemy, it would not compel the Germans to halt their efforts at Verdun. Thus the results of such an attack would be "almost nil." Pétain thought it wiser for the British not to attack at all than to suffer huge losses and be unavailable for subsequent operations. He preferred massing forces along three or four points on the Western Front and launching a series of brief, limited drives. By surprising the Germans and attacking with enormous concentrations of artillery and small numbers of infantry, the allies could keep their losses small while inflicting larger casualties on the Germans. By initiating such battles on all fronts, the allies could drain the enemy of soldiers and equipment. In such a campaign, Verdun would be France's contribution.[77] In essence, Pétain proposed the adoption of limited offensives, an operational method that he would perfect after he became general-in-chief in May 1917.

Ignoring most of Pétain's suggestions, Joffre responded to his letter and ended with a subtle warning that the French commander-in-chief was counting on him to "conform" to the GQG's directives.[78] Those directives were clear: hold Central Army Group's front and retake Fort Douaumont. Holding the Verdun front proved particularly difficult in Pétain's first month as commander of Central Army Group. Using even more artillery than in the past, the Germans renewed their assaults on Hill 304 and Mort Homme on the west bank and finally occupied the crests of both hills. Though the French clung to trenches barely a hundred meters below the crests, the German could now observe many of the defenses on the west bank. In contrast to this German success, Pétain failed in his attempt to seize Fort Douaumont. Supported by fifty-five batteries of heavy artillery that began firing on May 17, 5th Infantry Division under General Charles Mangin attacked on May 22. Though a few infantrymen fought their way into the galleries of the fort, German artillery and counterattacks drove them back on the twenty-fourth. Pétain later blamed the failure on his shortage of troops and his inability to enlarge the attack's front.

With the Germans' morale heightened by the successful seizure of Hill

304 and Mort Homme and defense of Fort Douaumont, they launched a major offensive on the east bank in June. After a long bombardment with heavy artillery, including a giant 420-mm mortar, they attacked Fort Vaux on June 1 and after a week's fighting seized the demolished but important structure. They then tried to expand control over the area around Vaux. On June 9 Nivelle warned his subordinate commanders that the Germans were closely coordinating their artillery and infantry and using "infiltration" and "encirclement" to make their way through French defenses.[79] It is not clear whether the Germans developed these tactics on their own or learned them from a study written by Captain André Laffargue,[80] but it is clear that Nivelle's warning about German infiltration tactics did not aid the defenders. The Germans seized terrain around Vaux and renewed their offensive on June 23. Attacking on a front between Douaumont and Vaux, they captured the village of Fleury and continued their advance until the end of June. Since the Germans had captured key terrain on both banks of the Meuse and had driven a salient three kilometers wide and two kilometers deep into French lines, they seemed poised for a final decisive thrust. Pointing toward Verdun, the tip of the salient was only four kilometers from the citadel.

After the Germans captured Vaux, Pétain sent an alarming message to the GQG. Complaining that the enemy possessed twice as much artillery as the defenders of Verdun, he said that his troops had hardly any terrain to yield. Any further gains by the Germans would place the Meuse bridges at risk and disrupt the flow of supplies and replacements across the river. Even worse, the French might have to abandon the east bank. He begged Joffre to set a date for the Somme offensive and asserted that any losses incurred from launching the offensive prematurely would have a smaller effect than the loss of Verdun. Joffre acknowledged Pétain's letter but offered no concessions. Instead of promising an early offensive, he said, "Every step has been taken so that the offensive on the Western Front will be unleashed on a date as early as possible and with carefully calculated preparations without which the attack is certain to fail."[81] By June 23 the situation at Verdun was desperate. After the enemy captured Fleury, Pétain telephoned the GQG and talked with Castelnau. He warned Joffre's chief of staff that he had committed his best troops and had only demoralized troops remaining. If the enemy advanced much farther, he would have to evacuate the east bank. Though Pétain's chief of staff later said that his commander was exaggerating in order to gain reinforcements, the French had reached the limit of their resistance. At the moment of Verdun's greatest crisis, Nivelle issued one of the most famous orders of the war: "Comrades, they will not pass!"[82] Only an attack on the Somme, Pétain believed, would save the positions on the east bank of the Meuse.

Of France's most senior military leaders, Foch remained the main critic of an attack on the Somme. In a meeting on May 31, 1916, Joffre, Castelnau, Haig, and Foch discussed the Somme operation with Poincaré, Briand, and Roques (the new minister of war). During the meeting Foch remained silent until Poincaré asked his advice. He responded by saying that France should concentrate on rebuilding its forces and should wait until the following year to attack. Castelnau disagreed and responded sharply, "That's an option when there is no opponent. You must suppress the enemy! He will continue to operate and will not leave you free until the coming year."[83] In response to pressure from Roques, Foch relented and agreed to support an offensive designed to assist Verdun but not to break through enemy lines. Privately with Joffre and Castelnau, however, he continued to express reservations about sending French troops into another large offensive or getting the British to cooperate.[84] Despite Foch's doubts, Joffre was certain that the defensive attitude of the allies over the winter had left the Central Powers free to seize the initiative and to launch offensives at Verdun in February and from the South Tyrol against the Asiago plateau in Italy in May. He insisted that planning continue for the Somme offensive.

Though Joffre and Haig had accepted July 1 as the date of the infantry assault on the Somme, on June 11 Joffre asked Haig to begin the infantry assault on June 25. After Fort Vaux fell and the situation worsened at Verdun, he thought an offensive on the Somme would compel the Germans to shift troops from Verdun. In his letter to Haig, however, he did not mention the desperate circumstances of Verdun's defenders; instead, he emphasized taking advantage of the Germans' having levied forces from other portions of the front for the Verdun drive. Although the

French request meant that artillery preparation had to begin on the twentieth, Haig readily agreed. A few days later, as German pressure subsided momentarily at Verdun, Joffre informed Haig that the infantry assault could begin on June 29 or July 1. In several subsequent exchanges the two allied commanders agreed that the attack could be delayed one or two days if bad weather intervened.

In the weeks before the opening of the Somme offensive, Joffre worked to coordinate Italian and Russian offensives with the Franco-British offensive. An unexpected attack by the Austrians against the Italians on May 14 made the Russian offensive especially important. The Russians intended to begin their offensive on June 15, but Austrian gains against the Italians forced Rome to ask the Russians to begin their offensive as soon as possible. On June 1 Joffre encouraged the Italians to hold against the advancing Austrians and assured them the Russians would attack on June 15. Later that day Joffre learned that Tsar Nicholas II had decided to aid the Italians by beginning immediately a secondary offensive in Galicia with Brusilov's army group. The main attack, which extended north from the Pripet Marshes to the Gulf of Riga, was supposed to begin on June 14. Thus, despite the unexpected Austrian offensive, the coalition's plans remained on track. If the Russians made any gains, the Germans, Joffre hoped, would shift forces from the Western to the Eastern Front to meet the Russian offensive and thereby increase the chances of success for the Franco-British offensive. Though the Russians made few gains in their center and right, General Brusilov's forces on their left made spectacular gains against the Austrians and thereby raised Joffre's hopes for success on the Western Front. The possibility of even greater Russian success caused him to host a conference in late June on providing additional support to them.

On June 21 Joffre sent Haig instructions for the attack on the Somme. The objective of the attack, he explained, was to place allied forces on the junction of the enemy's lines of communication in the area between Cambrai and Maubeuge. To accomplish this, the British would advance along an axis extending from Bapaume toward Cambrai. Joffre offered two hypotheses about the campaign: first, the enemy would yield after an attack of a "few days" and pull back along the entire breadth of the allied attack; or second, the allies would rupture the enemy front quickly. Though

Joffre did not acknowledge the possibility of failure, he did say the allies would have to fight a "long and hard battle" on the Somme.[85] A more detailed and frank assessment of allied prospects came from Joffre's staff, which considered several hypotheses, including the Germans' reestablishing their front after the allied attack. This would result, the staff explained, in "the continuation of the battle of attrition on other terrain."[86] Another staff study, which was simply an elaboration of the first, began: "If, during the first phase of the battle, the Franco-British armies seize the successive positions of the enemy. . . ."[87] Earlier in the war the ever-optimistic staff would have said "when" instead of "if." An even more cautious assessment came from General Fayolle, commander of Sixth Army, which would play the largest part in the French portion of the offensive. On May 21 he wrote in his diary: "The approaching battle will cost 200,000 men, and I wonder if there is any interest in admitting it. Attrition, is it such that we can hope for a decisive success? I don't think so. . . . Will it be necessary to spend another year in the trenches? Yes." After the battle began, he wrote: "This was always a battle without a purpose. There was no question of breaking through."[88]

As for the actual attack, the mission of Sixth Army was to "support" the British offensive. To provide this support, General Fayolle placed XX Corps north of the Somme (as Joffre and Haig had agreed on February 14), I Colonial Corps south of the river, and XXXV Corps to its right. Located on the northern bank of the Somme, XX Corps had responsibility for covering the British right and attacking in close coordination with it. Northern Army Group kept one corps in reserve for Sixth Army for use on either bank of the Somme; instead of passing this corps to Fayolle, Foch kept control of it himself. Fayolle had eleven divisions, four in each of the two corps on his left and center and three in the one on his right.

The Sixth Army commander preached a new philosophy about the relationship between the infantry and artillery: "The artillery devastates, the infantry overwhelms."[89] A note from Fayolle to his corps commanders described the methodical battle he anticipated:

> It is not a matter of rushing across enemy lines, of a general assault
> resulting in a loss of breath [because of the distance traveled], but of
> a battle organized and directed from objective to objective, always

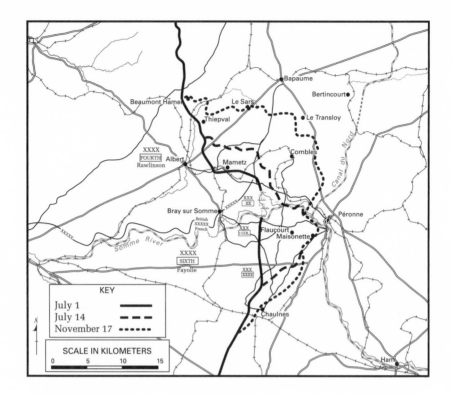

The Somme, 1916

with an exact and consequently effective artillery preparation. It is the commander who has the responsibility for determining the successive objectives; that is his principal task. Some officers have feared that this method will break the spirit of the infantry. In reality, that which breaks the spirit of the infantry is the presence of intact [defensive] networks where enemy machine guns intervene on the flanks. This is why the desired goal is to destroy the enemy's defenses before each attack.[90]

To ensure destruction of the enemy's defenses Foch provided Sixth Army with 552 pieces of heavy artillery in addition to the artillery organic to the army and its corps. Since the British Fourth Army and its five corps had 467 heavies, Sixth Army and its three corps had almost 100 more heavy artillery pieces than the British main attack.

Neither Foch nor Fayolle intended to waste the lives of his infantry. Foch addressed the role and methods of the infantry in a note he sent to each battalion in Northern Army Group. After insisting that the infantry advance only after artillery fire had destroyed the enemy's defenses, he said, "The infantry, not having any shock action, cannot attack in a mass formation. The number [of the infantry] is no indication of the power of its action." To ensure success, commanders had to abandon frontal assaults and not send waves of infantry against objectives. The infantry would advance in small groups, arrayed in depth, using machine guns and hand grenades. Foch concluded, "Real combat is a struggle of long duration. To conduct it to the decisive result, the infantry must be able to endure." Commanders had to employ their infantry "with a strict economy" and ask their soldiers to do only what they were capable of doing.[91] In retrospect French methods contrasted starkly with the archaic methods used by the British in the Somme offensive. British infantry would advance in waves of massed infantry, moving forward no faster than 100 meters every two minutes.

Expecting the infantry assault to occur on June 29, the French launched preparatory artillery fire on the morning of the twenty-fourth. After bad weather commenced on the twenty-sixth, Foch and the British Fourth Army commander, General Sir Henry Rawlinson, agreed to delay the assault forty-eight hours. At 0730 hours on July 1, XX Corps (on Fayolle's left north of the Somme) attacked simultaneously with the British. Its infantry easily overwhelmed the first German lines, capturing within an hour the objectives fixed for the first phase of the offensive. South of the Somme, I Colonial Corps left its trenches and attacked at 0930. It, too, advanced easily, making contact with the enemy's second position by 1100 hours. Beginning at 1615 the colonial corps continued its attack but made only small gains. To the right of I Colonial Corps, XXXV Corps also attacked at 0930, but it had only one division in its first line and made less progress than the colonial corps. Nevertheless, the French seized all objectives identified for the first day. In addition to capturing 4,000 prisoners they advanced one and a half kilometers on the north bank of the Somme and two kilometers on the south. As for the British, only the two corps on Rawlinson's right made any progress; these two corps advanced about as far as XX Corps on Fayolle's left.

As the British struggled to continue their offensive, Haig shifted the weight of his attack to the right, where he had made the most gains. In the middle of this shift, Joffre visited Haig's headquarters on July 3 and emphasized the importance of seizing Thiepval on the British left and thereby attacking on a broad front rather than a narrow front. When Haig explained his reasons for shifting the weight of his attack to the south, Joffre exploded in a rage, said he would not "approve" the change, and told Haig to press the attack in the British left and center. Maintaining his composure, Haig calmly explained that he was responsible to the British government, not to Joffre, for the actions of his army. The French general immediately relented and acknowledged that this was an "English battle."[92] The following morning Foch nonetheless met with Haig's operations officer to discuss the British concept of operations. Though the exchange between Haig and Joffre ended with assurances of mutual friendship and goodwill, its occurrence underlined continued French reservations about the British, as well as British unwillingness to follow French orders or even to learn from them.

A report from the French liaison officer to British headquarters outlined many of the concerns the French had about the British. The officer, who had recently been promoted from colonel to brigadier general, reported that the British had "dispersed and wasted" their artillery in preparatory firing for the Somme offensive. Moreover, they had passed into a period of "almost complete inactivity" following the terrible losses of July 1. After subsequently narrowing their attack zone, they had only three of their twelve divisions in the front line "engaged." According to the liaison officer, such actions left the enemy free to concentrate against the few points at which the British attacked. The French general attributed the "minimal results" obtained by the British to their lack of heavy artillery and their being a "new army in which the commanders lack experience, decisiveness, and above all firmness."[93] The liaison officer was not the only French soldier critical of the British; staff officers at Sixth Army openly complained about having to participate in an offensive organized "for amateurs by amateurs."[94] Fayolle noted in his diary that British tactics were "infantile."[95]

While the British struggled to renew their offensive, the French continued to make progress south of the Somme. By the end of the third day

Sixth Army had captured 8,000 prisoners, 6,000 of whom were taken by I Colonial Corps. To assist the attackers on the north bank, Foch ordered Fayolle to capture the plateau of Flaucourt, which lay directly ahead of I Colonial Corps. After capturing this plateau, Foch wanted to move heavy artillery forward and provide assistance to XX Corps on the north bank. The colonials continued advancing and by July 9 had reached Maisonette, a small village eight and a half kilometers from their starting point. Though the French had achieved a penetration, they could not exploit it: priority of effort went to units north of the river, and the French could not shift forces fast enough to the south to take advantage of the hard-won gain. One analysis of the battle concluded that the possibility of exploitation existed on July 3 and 4 but soon slipped away. By July 12 the French had captured more than 12,000 prisoners and seventy cannon. Fayolle noted in his diary, "The Boche front is broken open for eight kilometers, and we cannot exploit it." He added, "The Senegalese kill everything."[96]

As I Colonial Corps advanced on the south bank, Foch endeavored to shift the weight of the French attack behind it, but he did not send his reserves into the narrow breach made by the colonials. On July 8–9 he ordered Fayolle to defend north of the river and attack south of it. While XX Corps remained on the defensive on the north bank (until the British began another offensive effort), I Colonial and XXXV corps would attack south of the river. Fayolle, however, could not attack until the twentieth, since he had to transfer artillery to the south. When the British made gains on July 14, Foch met with Haig, and the two decided that XX Corps should attack on the twentieth. Fayolle thus prepared an attack north and south of the river with all three of his corps (XX, I Colonial, and XXXV), but by shifting his heavy artillery to the south, he gave priority to the southern attack. To the right of Sixth Army, Tenth Army, reinforced by a corps, prepared to attack after its neighbor advanced a few kilometers. Despite expectations of great success, only XXXV Corps made appreciable gains, and Foch reported, "Losses appear not to have been high."[97] In fact the colonial corps suffered nearly 8,000 casualties between July 15 and 21.

Despite these losses Foch pressed another attack forward on July 30, this time north of the Somme. With the addition of a new corps, Sixth

Army had two corps north of the river, and the French advanced simultaneously with the British. Though the infantry made gains in the morning, enemy counterattacks, bombardment, and machine-gun fire forced them to pull back. The French lost 3,600 men.

An unexpected benefit of French success on the Somme was the capture of German equipment and documents. Intelligence specialists studied captured materials very carefully and distributed translations of documents, as well as assessments, throughout the army. Many of these publications included a cover letter from Joffre highlighting the most important ideas. One particularly interesting assessment concerned German use of the elastic defense. A Sixth Army report that the GQG distributed throughout the army stated: "In its most recent orders the German command constantly revisits the necessity in the defensive of occupying the first line with small numbers of troops and of placing units in echelon and in depth in order to reserve the means of making local counterattacks."[98] Another report concerned German offensive methods. French intelligence noted the Germans' desire to achieve surprise and have combat engineers very far forward (often following immediately behind the first wave). Though the French often copied Germans ideas or equipment, they did not always want to acknowledge this. After capturing some German flamethrowers, for example, the French improved their own flamethrower and then provided instructions to units in the field. Yet someone at the GQG lined out the following sentence in these instructions: "The Germans have utilized similar devices successfully more than once."[99] The document included a translation of a German report on use of the *Flammenwerfer*.

As French operations on the Somme continued, Joffre's mood shifted from optimism to pessimism. On a visit to Fayolle's headquarters on July 6, the French commander-in-chief anticipated victory and considered bringing the cavalry closer so it could begin an exploitation more quickly, but a week later in another visit with Fayolle he was discouraged. Two weeks later, having failed to convince the British to increase their level of effort and attack on a broad front, he called Foch to his headquarters and lectured him on the fundamentals of offensive operations. Attacks on a broad front minimized the effect of enemy action on the flanks, he said, and prevented defenders from easily concentrating fire and reserves against the main offensive effort. If French attacks occurred simultaneously with those of the British, the allies could gain the best possible benefits of attacking on a broad front and could provide better assistance for the Russians, who still were making gains against the Austrians.

Joffre's main point, however, was expressed in a message that Foch sent to the commanders of Sixth and Tenth armies when he returned to his headquarters: "The fundamental intention of the Somme offensive must continue to be supporting the British attack in the north; our offensive in the south must remain secondary or subordinate to the results obtained in the north."[100] In reality, Foch and Fayolle had lost sight of the original purpose of the Somme offensive and because of their frustrations with the British had shifted the focus of their efforts south of the river. Though none of the French leaders expected much progress from the British, they could not allow themselves, Joffre insisted, to be drawn into a series of small battles destined to be costly and indecisive. He was well aware that continued fighting at Verdun prevented the French from playing the primary role in the Somme offensive, and he insisted that Fayolle's army provide significant assistance to the British.

Throughout the Somme offensive the French and Germans remained locked in battle at Verdun. Before preparatory artillery fires began for the Somme attack, Joffre instructed Pétain on June 19 to maintain an "aggressive attitude" and to seize several key positions around Verdun. In launching these limited operations, however, Pétain had to "economize" and use his resources judiciously. Joffre had high hopes for the Somme offensive and counted on Pétain to retain large numbers of enemy troops on his front, but he did not want Verdun to drain resources from the Somme, since the latter operation stood first in his priorities. In an indication of his priorities Joffre notified Pétain of his intention to shift units from Central Army Group to the Somme operation. As Joffre undoubtedly expected, Pétain objected to this loss and complained about its effect on his operations, but one corps and four battalions of heavy artillery nevertheless went to the Somme. These levies contributed to Pétain's warning to General de Castelnau on June 23 that Second Army might have to withdraw from the east bank. Such dire prospects forced Joffre to return two divisions recently transferred from Verdun.

What infuriated Joffre, however, was Pétain's appealing to the minister of war, Roques, about the transfer of artillery from Verdun to the Somme. Joffre vehemently objected to a subordinate's going over his head and wrote a caustic letter to Roques in which he complained about "needless" appeals to governmental authorities. Also, in a letter to Pétain he demanded that the Central Army Group commander inform him "directly" of his army group's needs. Despite Pétain's appeal to the minister of war, Joffre prevailed, and he withdrew artillery from Verdun. While personal pique played a large role in this incident, it illustrates the complex and difficult task Joffre faced in his attempts to balance the needs of Verdun and the Somme.

Maintaining an aggressive attitude at Verdun proved a challenging and costly task. French soldiers at Verdun faced an unfavorable situation, for the Germans were only four kilometers from the citadel and held several important pieces of terrain (Fleury, Fort Douaumont, Fort Vaux) overlooking much of the battlefield. Joffre explicitly directed Pétain and Nivelle to focus their efforts on seizing this key terrain on the east bank. When preparatory artillery fire started on the Somme on June 24, Nivelle began his counterattacks around Fleury. With Mangin directing operations, French soldiers attacked eight times over the next ten days. Under constant German bombardment the infantry suffered heavy losses during these attacks; some frontline regiments were reduced to half-strength. In an effort to support the infantry, commanders used thousands of artillery rounds, thereby causing consumption of munitions to rise dramatically. In the last week of July the French fired an average 77,000 rounds of 75-mm and 24,000 of heavy artillery daily. Some 75-mm cannon fired as many as 900–1,000 rounds each day. As the attrition toll grew, Pétain continued rotating divisions through the front lines; by early July sixty-eight divisions had served at Verdun. Meanwhile, despite Joffre's clear instructions, Pétain continued delaying the release of divisions and occasionally kept their artillery after releasing them.

The Germans did not passively await the French. With preparatory fire beginning on July 9, the enemy drove forward east of Fleury on the eleventh in what would be their last attack until the beginning of August. They pushed toward Fort Souville, which dominated the crest of a hill one kilometer southeast of Fleury. Since capture of Souville would enable the Germans to control the heights overlooking Verdun, Pétain feared that its loss would compel him to withdraw from the east bank of the Meuse. French infantry, however, lost only a small amount of ground and retained Souville. After an immediate counterattack failed to push the enemy back, Nivelle ordered a larger counterattack. Mangin again organized the operation, which started early on the fifteenth but which failed to drive the Germans back. For the remainder of the month, the French launched only small attacks.

As Franco-British operations on the Somme exacted a high toll from the Germans and the Russians inflicted heavy losses on the Austrians in the Brusilov offensive, Nivelle sensed a change at the end of July in the situation at Verdun. With less artillery fire, reduced counterattacks, and fewer aircraft flying overhead, the enemy had obviously moved units out of the sector. The French commander-in-chief also recognized the changed situation and moved artillery and infantry from Verdun. A surprise attack on August 1, however, demonstrated the continued existence of strong German capabilities. Attacking east of Fleury toward Souville, the enemy advanced 800–900 meters. Subsequent efforts by the French made some gains, but after two weeks of uninterrupted combat, the Germans still held most of what they had seized.

With French casualties mounting, Nivelle appealed to Pétain on August 9 for fresh troops, and the Central Army Group commander in turn appealed to Joffre. Since the enemy contested every foot of terrain and launched strong attacks, Second Army had to maintain an aggressive attitude, Pétain argued, but could not do this without fresh troops. He explained, "The experience of several months proves that a unit that has lost a third of its combatants no longer offers sufficient resilience to resist an attack or, as a minimum, to maintain the integrity of the front."[101] Though aware of the serious situation, Joffre insisted on subordinating the needs of Verdun to those of the Somme and denied Pétain's request. Since the Germans faced strong pressure at the Somme and on the Eastern Front, he doubted the enemy could send additional troops to Verdun. Having no choice, Pétain moved three divisions from Fourth and

Fifth armies to Second Army, and Nivelle transferred individual cannon between artillery batteries to ensure that each battery had enough workable guns.

While fighting continued at Verdun and on the Somme, Joffre had to contend with political challenges on the conduct of the war and attempts to replace him or reduce his authority. A few days before the Germans began their attack at Verdun, the Chamber of Deputies had discussed and rejected a motion asking "the Government to respect the exercise of its [the Chamber's] right to control all mobilized, national forces."[102] Beginning on June 16, the Chamber of Deputies met for seven days in secret session and fiercely debated the conduct of the war. André Maginot, a highly respected deputy who had been crippled at Verdun in the early months of the war, began the session with a virulent attack on Joffre: "Verdun proves that the Commander lives from day to day. He yields the initiative to his adversary instead of imposing his will on him. He has neither method nor energy. He counts on a miracle. He has shown us what he can do. It is necessary to replace him."[103] During the week of debates there were several fights in the Chamber, one of which, according to the minutes, produced an "indescribable uproar." Fortunately for Joffre, Briand and Roques sprang to his defense, and the Chamber supported the government. Other secret sessions of the Chamber, however, occurred on November 21 and November 28–December 7 of that year. The Senate had similar sessions on July 9 and December 19–23. Joffre's liaison officer to the government summarized many of the harsh comments made privately to him: "The commander is not up to the task, and the government does not know how to impose its will on the command. It is necessary to change one or the other."[104] As Albert Thomas, who served as the minister of munitions, noted, an "atmosphere of intrigue" was engulfing the capital city.[105]

As the political cauldron approached the boiling point, Joffre became increasingly concerned about the performance of the British Expeditionary Force and the effectiveness of its commander, Haig. He had begun the year hoping, as the allies had agreed in the December 1915 conference, that the British would "intensify their efforts" and do everything they could to "wear down the adversary" while France only "collaborated" in this attrition.[106] After the disastrous failure at the Somme on

July 1, however, he saw little evidence that the British were expanding their effort and allowing the French to recuperate. His concerns became greater after the French liaison officer to the B.E.F. submitted a disturbing report on August 10 that the British headquarters was "disoriented" and lacked confidence. "Disarray" in the British headquarters, the liaison officer explained, had exacerbated its "traditionally" slow pace and resulted in the shifting of command authority from Haig to corps commanders. "Practically speaking," he said, "as far as the English are concerned, the battle of the Somme is dead."[107] A later report disclosed rumors that Haig would be relieved if his offensive in September failed. Other reports criticized the British for making only "small, distinct attacks" and achieving nothing but "rare and weak" progress.[108] Joffre concluded, as he explained to Foch, that the British would not become more energetic on their own and that the French had to "support and activate" them by becoming more active themselves.[109] In one of his letters to Haig, Joffre assured the British commander that the French were prepared to increase their efforts on the Somme even though they had "borne at Verdun, for more than five months, the weight of the German push." The same reasons obliging the French to increase their efforts, Joffre wrote, also applied to the British.[110] Despite such messages, Haig continued launching small attacks and justified them by saying he was seeking to weaken the Germans and enable a later attack to succeed.

After receiving a very favorable intelligence assessment at the end of July that the Austrians were running out of resources and the Germans were being compelled to use "expedients,"[111] Joffre made a special effort throughout August to get the British to participate in a "great battle" against the Central Powers and to launch another offensive on the scale of the July 1 effort. To obtain a "concordance of effort in all theaters," he urged Haig to attack with greater "vigor." Such an effort, he explained, would facilitate the "victorious advance" of the Russians, aid the Romanians, and prevent the Germans from shifting troops from the Western to the Eastern Front or from the Somme to Verdun. He asked Haig to launch a large offensive even though he thought the bungled offensive of July 1 on the Somme had demonstrated that the British had neither the staff nor the experience to conduct large-scale operations with several field armies.[112] To convince Haig to abandon small attacks, he warned him of the dangers of prolonging secondary operations and providing the enemy time to reinforce his defenses. Despite Joffre's best efforts, Haig continued making small attacks, and on August 20 the French liaison officer to Haig's headquarters informed Joffre that the British did not envisage a large offensive until September 10.

By late August Joffre believed the strategic situation overwhelmingly favored the allies and demanded a powerful offensive on the Western Front. Although the Austrians had made gains against the Italians in the latter half of May, Brusilov's success after June 4 against the Austrians had forced Field Marshal Franz Conrad von Hötzendorf to suspend the South Tyrolean offensive on June 15 and shift forces from Italy to Galicia. As the Austrians continued to suffer severe losses, a strategic assessment completed by the GQG staff on August 20 opined that Romania's entry into the war would increase pressure against the Austrians and magnify the effects of ongoing Russian and Italian efforts. By October, the assessment stated, the Austrians would be "incapable, without the help of Germany, of offering serious resistance to a Russian and Italian attack." The "inevitable collapse" of the Austrian army would have "incalculable consequences" on the German army and lead to the destruction of the Central Powers. The "annihilation" of the Austrians could conceivably occur before the winter and would compel the Germans to wage a defensive campaign in 1917. The memorandum brashly concluded that the campaign of 1917 would destroy the Central Powers' "defensive capacity and seal the irremediable ruin of their military power."[113] Reports of Austrian peace feelers heightened French optimism.

On August 27, the day Romania declared war on Austria-Hungary, French political and military leaders met to discuss strategic and operational alternatives for the coming winter and spring. Haig also attended the meeting. Convinced that the Austrians were "tottering," Joffre used the meeting to pressure the British commander to launch another offensive on the scale of the July 1 effort. Despite the importance of pressuring the Germans on the Western Front and preventing them from sending forces to aid the Austrians, Haig insisted that the British could not attack before September 15. Joffre responded, "That's too late. It's death."[114]

The French commander-in-chief nonetheless had no choice but to accept the delay, and he complained bitterly and openly that the British "as usual" were not doing what they had promised.[115] Meanwhile Brusilov's offensive, which had begun on June 4, had stalled by August 14. While the Central Powers had rushed units to Galicia to slow Brusilov's advance, the other Russian army groups had done little to help him. Brusilov now faced defenses he could not break. Also, the Romanians initially drove easily into Transylvania, but Austro-German forces drove them back with a counteroffensive in late September and entered Romania in late October. Reports from Italy, however, that the Austrians had lost 100,000 men on the Isonzo between September 14 and November 5 suggested continued Austrian vulnerability.

Not wanting to miss the fleeting opportunity for significant gains, Joffre informed political leaders that British attacks were "too limited and too fragmentary."[116] As concerns about the British reverberated through political circles, visitors to Haig's headquarters encouraged him to be more aggressive and to attack on as wide front as possible. At the end of August, Robertson provided a summary to the British War Committee of French complaints that the British were "going too slowly."[117] Despite such complaints British leaders supported Haig's limited actions. General Robertson wrote Haig: "Several hints have reached me that Joffre and Co. think you are going too slowly. I spoke to Mr. Lloyd George [the secretary of state for war] about this the other day and he repeated what he has said many times lately, that he thinks you are playing absolutely the right game, and doing your job in absolutely the right way."[118] Protected by British political and military leaders, Haig continued launching fragmented attacks and ignoring French pleas. In the end, the British participated in a combined offensive with the French, but their effort was only distantly connected to that of France or their other allies. While the operation was not as large or as well coordinated as Joffre had hoped, it was the best he could arrange. His frustration with Haig surfaced in a meeting of the Superior Council of National Defense when he said, "Do not count on the English. . . . count only on us."[119]

With Joffre still optimistic about the strategic situation, preparatory artillery fire for the French offensive south of the Somme began on August 28. Bad weather, however, forced Foch to delay the infantry assault until

September 3. With two corps attacking, Sixth Army initially achieved considerable success north of the Somme; the northernmost corps advanced the farthest and captured 2,000 prisoners, twelve cannon, and numerous machine guns. The attack nevertheless soon stalled. Farther south, Tenth Army did not do as well. Attacking on September 4 with three corps in its front line, Tenth Army failed to seize key defensive positions in the German first line. By September 7 both armies had halted their attacks. Sixth Army renewed its offensive on September 12, this time with three corps in its front line. Fayolle's forces made enough progress for Foch to alert II Cavalry Corps for a possible exploitation, but the infantry's advance eventually slowed even though Fayolle inserted another corps into the front lines. Infantry assaults by Sixth Army ended on the fifteenth. Tenth Army attacked on the fifteenth but ended its efforts on the nineteenth. When the British finally began their offensive on September 15, Haig launched his main attack in the sector to the north of Sixth Army with three corps from Rawlinson's Fourth Army and made his supporting attack with two corps from the British Reserve Army. Though the British continued fighting for a week and advanced more than two kilometers, soldiers of Sixth Army remained in their trenches and provided assistance only with artillery. The attacks in early and mid-September thus occurred sequentially (Sixth, Tenth, and then British), and French efforts had little or no operational relationship with British efforts. Joffre's hope for a vigorous, coordinated Franco-British offensive in early September never materialized.

With diminished expectations, Joffre insisted that the offensive on the Western Front should continue as long as weather permitted, and Robertson and Haig agreed. During the remainder of September and October the French attacked frequently but in the same fragmented fashion as the British. Sixth Army, after being increased to five corps, drove forward on September 25–27 and October 7, 12–13, 15, and 18. Tenth Army, still with three corps, attacked on October 10–11, 14, and 21–22. Despite several attempts, the French made only small gains, and the fighting gradually diminished. As the days became shorter, rain and fog limited visibility, soft soil absorbed the impact of exploding artillery rounds, and mud demoralized and immobilized the infantry. Such conditions favored the defenders over the attackers, and "the battle of the Somme," as Joffre explained in his memoirs, "slowly died away during November."[120]

While Joffre tried in August and September to get the British to launch a large offensive, the French launched numerous small attacks at Verdun. Most of the bloodiest fighting occurred around the periphery of the Fleury salient. After capturing the destroyed village of Fleury on August 18, Mangin's group continued attacking and by the end of the month had rolled back many of the enemy's gains in July and August. During the first three weeks of September, the attacks continued. On September 3, the same day Sixth Army attacked on the north bank of the Somme, Mangin hit both flanks of Fleury and advanced the front lines a few hundred meters. After German counterattacks failed on September 4–5, Mangin attacked at three points on September 6. On September 9 and 13 he attacked two different points just east of Fleury. Other attacks in the same vicinity occurred on September 15, 16, and 17. Though entire divisions nominally participated in these operations, only one or two battalions usually left the trenches, and thus the operations seized only small bits of terrain, and the attackers suffered few casualties. The worst losses occurred on September 4–5, when a fire broke out in a railway tunnel in which several staffs and support services were sheltered, and 474 soldiers died. Despite the relatively light casualties during the period of small attacks, Joffre had to continue rotating divisions through Second Army. The number of divisions that had served at Verdun rose to seventy-eight.

On September 13, two days after saying at a meeting of the Superior Council of National Defense, "Do not count on the English. . . . count only on us," Joffre initiated preparations for an offensive at Verdun. Along with the Somme offensive, which began on August 28, this operation was part of his "great battle" around the perimeter of the Central Powers. In a meeting with Nivelle and Mangin, he emphasized the importance of their maintaining an offensive attitude. Two days later he sent a liaison officer forward to meet with Pétain and Nivelle and discuss an operation that would push the Verdun front line forward on the east bank, perhaps as far as forts Douaumont and Vaux. Though both commanders supported the proposal, Pétain emphasized more than Nivelle the importance of Joffre's providing three or four additional divisions to Second

Army. When Joffre asked the two generals to supply him with a concept for the attack, the Central Army Group commander quickly responded with a proposal for an "offensive of great energy" on a front of five kilometers with three divisions in the first line and three others in the second. Joffre approved this proposal and promised to send fresh infantry and additional artillery.

As Pétain and Nivelle began preparing the offensive, they carefully coordinated the replacement of weakened divisions in Second Army and the husbanding of whatever resources already existed at Verdun. To ensure a vigorous offensive Joffre replaced two trench-worn divisions with two new ones, and he replaced five others (out of a total of twenty-two in Second Army) by mid-October. As part of the preparation for the offensive, Pétain and Nivelle paid particular attention to strengthening artillery. They also looked at improving the performance of artillery with the rolling barrage, a technique championed by Nivelle since mid-1915. Combat at Verdun and the Somme had demonstrated clearly the importance of having the infantry follow the artillery as closely as possible, and technical trials of the rolling barrage confirmed that infantry could follow as close as 50 meters behind artillery bursts. Experience taught the French to have 75-mm barrages advance in 50-meter bounds every two minutes with the infantry following 75 meters behind. The French also learned to advance heavy artillery rounds at the same pace but to move their barrages in 500-to-1,000-meter bounds and keep them at least 150 meters beyond the 75-mm barrages. In another aspect of Pétain and Nivelle's preparation for an offensive, Second Army reconsidered the organization of its infantry platoons; the resulting mixture of riflemen, grenadiers, and machine gunners would remain standard in the French army through the 1930s. While these changes strengthened Second Army, they also demonstrated Pétain's and Nivelle's faith in firepower and their intention to blast their way through the enemy's defenses, not push their way through with infantry.

As for operational planning, Mangin framed the early concepts, but Pétain and Nivelle remained deeply involved and insisted on considering and approving every aspect of the operation. In the early phases of the planning Mangin aimed for nothing more than improving French defenses by seizing key terrain immediately forward of the front lines, but his commanders forced him to craft a much more ambitious operation. On October 9 Mangin, repeating the mission given him by Nivelle, said: "Group D. E., under the order of General Mangin, has the mission of assuming the offensive on the right [east] bank of the Meuse to drive the enemy beyond Fort Douaumont."[121] To accomplish this, the French would have to advance more than two kilometers, a vast distance in comparison to the 100-meter advances of the past. Mangin expected strong resistance, since French intelligence reported that the Germans had moved forces from Verdun but had not reduced the density of troops in the Fleury sector.

Though the offensive was scheduled to begin in early October, bad weather delayed it. Starting on October 21, more than 700 cannon from Second Army pounded the Germans. Against Fort Douaumont the French concentrated two 270-mm, two 280-mm, one 370-mm, and two 400-mm pieces, plus numerous smaller guns. From October 20 to 27 the French fired 855,264 rounds in support of Mangin's attack, including 532,926 75-mm, 272 370-mm, and 101 400-mm. At 1140 hours on October 24 infantry from three French divisions, protected by a thick fog, climbed out of their trenches and raced forward. By the end of the day they had captured Fort Douaumont and advanced to the edge of Fort Vaux with only light casualties.

An attempt to seize Fort Vaux on the following day failed, but the French shifted their heaviest rounds toward the fort and pounded it for the next week. On November 2, after a 220-mm mortar shell produced a huge explosion inside the fort, the French intercepted a German radio message announcing its evacuation. Late that night a company entered the fort without having to fire a shot. In a message to the soldiers of Mangin's group, Nivelle explained the significance of the battle:

> In four hours, in a magnificent assault, you seized from a powerful enemy in a single blow the terrain northeast of Verdun, which bristled with obstacles and fortresses and which had torn you to shreds for eight months and demanded desperate efforts and considerable sacrifices. You have added new and brilliant glory to that which already covers the flags of the army of Verdun. In the name of that army, I thank you.[122]

Though Mangin's soldiers had earned great praise, their success had come less from the stellar performance of the infantry than from the crushing power of the artillery. Additionally, Mangin's soldiers captured Vaux because the Germans had shifted significant forces from Verdun and no longer sought to "bleed" France's forces to death there. After the resignation of Falkenhayn on August 29, the new German commander, General Paul von Hindenburg, had abandoned Falkenhayn's strategy of attrition and lowered the priority of Verdun.

With Douaumont and Vaux secured, the French expected a vigorous German counterattack. Such ripostes had occurred frequently in the past, and they had no reason to expect anything different. Additionally, since the October operation had consumed vast quantities of artillery ammunition, the French feared shortages when the German attack occurred. After the Germans failed to counterattack, the French reduced the scale and pace of their operations to conserve ammunition for another drive. Except for some minor actions almost no infantry combat occurred on the east bank of the Meuse from November 5 to December 15.

Before the capture of Douaumont, Mangin and Nivelle had considered subsequent operations that could drive the Germans farther from Verdun. After the French captured Vaux, Nivelle planned an operation to seize the next line of hills beyond the two forts and ensure their security. When the proposal arrived at the GQG, the Operations Bureau recommended disapproval, but, as will be explained in the next chapter, Joffre insisted on maintaining pressure on the enemy during the winter and approved Nivelle's request. To conduct the operation, however, he promised no more than one or two fresh divisions.

Preparatory artillery fire similar to that of October 24 began on December 10, and five days later four infantry divisions under General Mangin attacked north. The French encountered little enemy resistance in the first lines, which had been devastated by artillery. Except for one of the divisions on the left, the French seized their assigned objectives in the two-day attack. Second Army's after-action report gave special credit to rolling barrages and noted the Germans' surprise at the French infantry's arriving in their trenches so closely behind the artillery. On the night of December 16–17 the French established new defensive lines two to three kilometers beyond Douaumont and one kilometer beyond Vaux. The Germans were no closer to Verdun than seven and a half kilometers.

Though casualty figures are not exact because of the huge number of missing soldiers (some captured, some separated temporarily from their unit, some left wounded or dead on the battlefield), the French claimed 377,231 casualties at Verdun between February 21 and December 20. Some historians have criticized these figures and cite the larger one of 442,000 that Winston Churchill gave for French losses. Churchill's figures, however, are inflated, since he erroneously included losses along the entire front, not just those at Verdun.[123] Second Army reported 89,367 casualties from February 21 to March 30, 42,186 in April, 52,000 in May, 66,632 in June, 31,212 in July, and 28,601 in August. Of these casualties, 16 percent were confirmed killed, 56 percent wounded, and 28 percent missing. Many of the missing would eventually be declared dead. The heaviest losses occurred in the first forty-five days of fighting and in the months of May and June, when the Germans made a concerted effort against Vaux and Verdun on the east bank. Casualties dropped significantly in July and August, when the Franco-British offensive began on the Somme, and they averaged about 20,000 a month in the final two months of the campaign, when the French recaptured Douaumont and Vaux.

Considering the small gains, losses on the Somme were surprisingly high. The French claimed 202,567 casualties on the Somme between July 1 and November 20, or about 54 percent of those suffered at Verdun. The heaviest casualties occurred in July (49,859) and September (76,147), when the French launched their largest attacks. The British, according to their official history, suffered 419,654 casualties in the fighting along the Somme.

Though the French suffered 579,798 casualties in both battles, they actually suffered fewer deaths in 1916 than in 1914 and 1915. According to data accumulated after the war (the figures do not agree precisely with those above), 350,200 soldiers died (or were missing in action) in the entire French army from February to December 1916; 454,000 from August to November 1914, in the mobile phase of the war; and 391,000 from February to November 1915, when Joffre attempted to rupture German lines in Artois and Champagne. While the casualties at Verdun and the

Somme were high, they were less than those in the early months of the war or in the failed offensives of 1915. Thus, Falkenhayn succeeded in bleeding Joffre's forces severely, but the French suffered fewer casualties at Verdun and the Somme than they did in the bungled operations of 1914 or the incessant offensives of 1915.

Whatever the casualties, France's defense at Verdun and allied offensives on the Somme and at Verdun had not altered the strategic equation. Despite the surge of optimism in late 1916, the year ended with Brusilov's offensive stalled, the Romanians driven out of Transylvania, Sarrail sitting still at Salonika, and the Italians stymied on the Isonzo River. Additionally, the Austrians no longer seemed to be "tottering," and the Germans showed no signs of abandoning their defensive positions in France. Nivelle's victory at Verdun on October 24 provided encouragement, but the optimism of late August had yielded to the reality of at least another year of war. For French political leaders, the most noteworthy development was the contrast between Nivelle's quick thrusts at Verdun on October 24 and December 15 and Joffre's slow, repetitive battering-ram attacks on the Somme. The capture of forts Douaumont and Vaux with light casualties contrasted sharply with the heavy casualties and small advances on the Somme and convinced political leaders not to let France become involved in another battle like that of the Somme. Though political leaders had not lost their confidence in the offensive and in France's multifront strategy, they had lost faith in Joffre.

CHAPTER 7

A Strategy of Decisive Battle

Early 1917

A S PART OF THE preparation for another year of war, France invited its allies to a conference on November 15–16. To provide the "French view," on October 15 Joffre sent the participants a strategic assessment in which he said: "To prevent the enemy from accomplishing any of his objectives, the Coalition should continue to exert pressure during the winter on all fronts where climactic conditions permit and to prepare for coordinated offensives in spring 1917 similar to those undertaken in 1916 but which will be more powerful and more fruitful." He called for attacks on the Italian and Russian fronts, and he proposed continuing attacks "on the Somme front to achieve the withdrawal, perhaps the rupture, or at least immobilizing the enemy's active troops." He also called for enlarging the French position at Verdun to prevent any enemy threat against it.[1] In short, he anticipated no change in France's multifront strategy and expected another year of allied offensives larger than those of 1916.

Getting the British to cooperate in a combined offensive on the Western Front remained difficult. After concluding that another offensive on the Somme would not yield decisive results, the British War Committee asked for a meeting of allied political leaders to examine strategy and operations for the coming year. The British suggested delaying the conference of allied military leaders until after the political leaders had met. Since Russian leaders could not travel to the west, the British wanted French, British, and Italian representatives to travel to Petrograd and meet with Russian policymakers. The proposal came from David Lloyd George, the secretary of state for war, who argued in the War Committee that questions of policy and strategy "should be first discussed by the statesmen, who had the real and ultimate responsibility for the whole conduct of affairs."[2] Lloyd George also wrote a long memorandum that summarized the current military situation and scathingly criticized the failure of military leaders to end the stalemate. Among his assertions were, "Still the same old obsession has taken a firmer grip than ever of the military brain."[3]

Despite the British request for a delay, the allied military conference opened on the scheduled date, and the political conference began at the same time. On the morning of November 15 the British prime minister, Herbert H. Asquith, and Lloyd George met with Briand at the Quai d'Orsay and presented a heavily edited version of Lloyd George's memorandum calling for political leaders to take control over the direction of the war. The British prime minister had revised the first draft substantially to avoid offending military leaders in both countries. Arriving late from having been grilled by Clemenceau in the Chamber of Deputies on the conduct of the war, Briand appeared distracted during the discussion of the paper but asked for a copy before the British representatives departed. That afternoon, when the political conference began officially, Briand opened the meeting with a speech in which he called for the allied governments to "take the initiative in regard to operations," since they "bore the whole responsibility for the conduct of the war." Reflecting his long-term interest in the Balkans, he insisted that the most effective allied efforts would involve putting Bulgaria out of action. Russian and Romanian offensives, supported by allied troops in Salonika, could defeat Bulgaria and thereby sever links between the Austro-German armies and Turkey. Asquith spoke next and emphasized the importance of sending political and military leaders to Russia to determine what could be done on the Eastern Front and what help the Western Powers could provide Russia and Romania in their campaign against Bulgaria.[4] For the French, none of the topics were new, including the idea of political leaders' playing a larger role in the conduct of the war, and Briand said nothing to suggest that he would soon make significant changes in the relationship between French political and military leaders.

The allied military conference also began on November 15 and opened with the reading of a memorandum prepared by Joffre's staff. The memorandum praised allied offensives of 1916 for having "shaken" the Central Powers and expressed regret that the Romanians had entered the war so late; had they entered earlier, they could have caught the Austrians "demoralized by recent bloody defeats." The allies could take advantage of the strategic situation, the memorandum said, by launching an attack of "grand style" on the Western Front in the spring and a "large-scale action against Bulgaria." The memorandum also suggested helping the Russians "reconstitute" their forces by providing them additional weapons, munitions, and equipment. Such an effort could enable the Russians to devote significant forces to a campaign against Bulgaria and conceivably drive them out of the war. With Sofia "out of action," Berlin and Vienna would lose their links with Constantinople, and Turkey would be vulnerable.[5] When Joffre spoke, he argued before the assembled military representatives for "coordinated" offensives on all fronts in the spring of 1917. In particular, he argued for a "powerful offensive" on the Western Front. After Haig insisted that the British could not make their maximum effort until early May, the Italian and Russian representatives said that they, too, would have to delay their operations. To avoid an attack by the Germans and a "repeat of what happened in 1916," Joffre urged the allies to launch attacks in the first half of February "if circumstances permitted." At the end of the meeting, the representatives agreed on a "plan of action" that would make the campaign of 1917 "decisive." They also agreed that "to keep the enemy from regaining the initiative in operations, the armies of the coalition will be ready to undertake combined offensives in the first half of February 1917 with all the means at their disposal."[6] The discussion had made it clear, however, that France would attack alone in early February and the others would attack later.

The military representatives spent most of their time discussing the Balkans. They finally agreed to put Bulgaria "out of action" as soon as possible by attacking from the east with Russo-Romanian forces and from the south with allied forces at Salonika. The representatives also agreed to raise Sarrail's forces to twenty-three divisions—seven British, six French, six Serbian, one Russian, and three Italian. Joffre's staff had studied possible operations in the Balkans and had concluded that difficulties of transportation, logistics, and terrain limited the allies to twenty-three divisions at Salonika. With eighteen divisions already in place, the Italians and French would each send another one and a half and the British two. As with previous analyses, Joffre refused to consider letting the additional forces for Salonika come from metropolitan France. As the GQG staff explained in a memorandum, "the Anglo-French armies have the heavy task of defeating Germany." Without identifying from where the French troops should come, the officers recommended that British troops come from Mesopotamia or Egypt.[7]

After this meeting ended, political and military leaders assembled to discuss the results of the military talks. The main point of contention pertained to the deployment of twenty-three divisions at Salonika. At the end of the meeting Briand emphasized that the conclusions of the military conference coincided with those from the political authorities. Despite this positive spin, Lloyd George later insisted that the conference was "little better than a complete farce." As far as he was concerned, the campaign of 1917 would repeat "all the bloody stupidities of 1915 and 1916" and "the old fatuous tactics of hammering away with human flesh and sinews at the strongest fortresses of the enemy."[8] In short, he believed there had been no real reconsideration of allied strategy and operations.

Notwithstanding Lloyd George's criticisms, Joffre had a different assessment. As he stated in his memoirs, "the fruits we had let ripen in 1916, we would gather in 1917."[9] In reality, what Joffre had in mind for the Western Front was large attacks on both sides of the Noyon salient, followed by a surprise attack between Soissons and Reims. While combining French and British efforts had appealed to him in the past, he now wanted to separate the British and Northern Army Group's attacks. Counting only on the French on the Western Front, he did not plan on letting the "usual" British delays hamstring the entire offensive, but he had not lapsed into thinking that the French could win the war alone. Instead, he expected coordinated attacks by the Russians, Romanians, and

Italians, as well as allied forces at Salonika, to place massive pressure on the Central Powers.

Preparation for the offensive in France began long before the allied conference in mid-November. On September 23 Generals Joffre and Robertson had met and discussed future operations. Planning proceeded in October, and by the end of the month Joffre's staff produced a proposal for a combined Franco-British offensive. The British would attack with two armies north of the Somme on the two flanks of the salient between Vimy Ridge and Bapaume, and Northern Army Group would attack with three armies between the Somme and Noyon. The proposal also called for a surprise attack by Fifth Army between Soissons and Reims. After discussions between British and French staffs, Joffre wrote to Haig on November 1 and formally proposed the offensive. To ensure that Haig understood the operational concept and did not revert to small attacks, he sent Foch a separate letter with even greater detail and asked the Northern Army Group commander to discuss the key points with Haig. He asked Foch to begin the attack south of the Somme around February 1. Joffre also wrote to Pétain, the Central Army Group commander, and confirmed his intention to have Fifth Army attack fifteen days after the offensive opened south of the Somme. Fifth Army's sector included Reims and the heights north of the Aisne River known as the Chemin des Dames. If Northern Army Group ruptured enemy lines, Fifth Army would cooperate in the subsequent exploitation; if Northern Army Group failed to fight its way through enemy lines, Fifth Army would attempt to rupture enemy lines on its own. In either case Fifth Army would benefit from the Germans' having to shift forces and munitions to the sectors threatened by attacks from Northern Army Group and the British.

On the same day that he wrote to Pétain, Joffre published his last formal statement about operational methods. In a letter to all division, corps, army, and army-group commanders, he emphasized that attacks had to occur on fronts as broad as possible to prevent the enemy from concentrating fire on attacking troops or bringing reserves easily into play. Attacks also had to reach the enemy's artillery in order to disrupt its support of the infantry. To enable the artillery to accompany the infantry closely, commanders had to push batteries as far forward as possible. Since the enemy occupied several zones of defenses, commanders had to proceed methodically; they had to divide their attacks into different phases and fight a series of battles with delays between each successive battle being as short as possible. Additionally, to ensure immediate availability, reserves had to remain close to the assaulting troops. Such methods would enable commanders to exploit their gains "to the utmost." Joffre closed his letter by saying:

> Attacks prepared and conducted in this manner will always succeed if those making the attacks have confidence in their success. Results will be obtained if the troops are trained and disciplined; if leaders at all echelons are actively involved in the preparation [of the attack] and carefully pay attention to every detail; if, finally, these same leaders, ardently convinced of success, seize every opportunity to convey the faith that motivates them to the hearts of their subordinates.[10]

Though more than 1,000,000 French soldiers had died or disappeared by November 1916, Joffre had not lost his faith in the offensive.

Joffre's faith in the offensive also shaped his response to Nivelle and Mangin's proposal in November for an offensive at Verdun. When the project arrived at the GQG, the Operations Bureau recommended disapproval, saying it was "neither necessary nor even desirable" and would disrupt preparations for a spring offensive and consume resources needed for subsequent operations. With winter approaching, the staff officers believed the army needed rest and training. After Joffre considered the recommendations of the Operations Bureau, Castelnau, his chief of staff, wrote on the back of the paper: "The general-in-chief has decided that during the winter we will not let up on the pressure we have placed on the enemy during the summer. This pressure will be placed at Verdun and on the Somme." In this way, Castelnau wrote, the French could prevent the enemy from shifting forces to the east.[11] While this document and the notes on it do not explain Castelnau's role in making this significant decision, it demonstrates clearly that Joffre wanted to continue the attacks and the "young Turks" in the Operations Bureau did not. Aside from his faith in the offensive, the reasons for Joffre's decision are clear. He had encouraged the allies to maintain pressure on the Central Powers over the winter and keep the Germans from making another offensive like the one at Verdun in February 1916, and he could not let French troops hibernate in their trenches.

Joffre chose continued action even though he knew the morale of French soldiers had dropped considerably. To remove classified information from soldiers' letters, postal authorities began censoring letters early in the war and quickly recognized that the letters provided valuable information about morale. By late 1916, formal reports on morale indicated a "crisis" stemming from the Romanian defeat, German willingness to continue the war, political turbulence in Paris, and concerns about families. Soldiers had concluded, postal authorities reported, that the costs of the war greatly exceeded any potential gains. They wanted Britain and Italy to make an effort "proportional" to that of France, and they believed Britain had "duped" France. Many wanted an immediate end to the war or a "partial" victory in which "appearances" could be maintained.[12] Many also were saying, "we do not want responsibility for continuing the slaughter; we want peace, nothing more."[13] Clearly, the stage was set for the mutinies and acts of indiscipline that would begin in April 1917.

Amidst preparation for another offensive, Joffre anticipated a marked reduction in 1917 in the number of riflemen in tactical units. To rectify this situation he intended to reduce the number of infantrymen in divisions and to augment their firepower. A division would have three regiments (instead of four) with three battalions in each regiment. Each battalion, in turn, would have three infantry companies and one machine-gun company. Each regiment also would have nine 37-mm accompanying guns. To add firepower, Joffre expected the heavy artillery to increase from 4,200 pieces on August 1, 1916, to 6,100 on January 1, 1918. In a significant blind spot in his analysis, ironically bearing a strong resemblance to that of Falkenhayn in Christmas 1915, he expected attrition to reduce the offensive capability of the enemy, but he acknowledged no serious effect on his own forces.

As Joffre prepared a huge offensive, important changes in the strategic situation occurred. With surprising ease and speed, the Germans propped up the tottering Austrians and redressed the unfavorable strategic situation. When the conferences of allied political and military leaders ended on November 16, Romanian forces, despite some losses, still occupied positions along the Austrian frontier, but within a week Austro-German forces were deep inside Romania. The fall of Bucharest on December 6 demolished any hopes of a combined Russo-Romanian offensive driving Bulgaria out of the war and thereby rendered irrelevant one of the strategic goals established at the allied conference. Romania's fall also created the possibility of strong enemy attacks against Salonika. On December 11 Joffre, in one of his last official duties, suspended Sarrail's offensive action against Bulgaria and directed him to establish a solid defensive position that could serve as a base for future offensive operations. He promised to accelerate the transport of new divisions to Salonika. Instead of worrying about the Balkans, the French now feared a German advance through neutral Switzerland. While the Germans could not cross Switzerland and march toward Italy in winter, they could attack into France in winter or wait until the summer to attack Italy. As part of a broad shakeup of the High Command that will be explained below, Foch was relieved of command of the Northern Army Group but instead of being sent to Limoges was given responsibility on December 24 for planning possible operations if Germany violated Switzerland's neutrality.

Disappointment with the unfavorable strategic situation and frustration over the turn of events caused discontent with Joffre's performance to boil over in Paris. Much of the pressure against Joffre came from the Chamber of Deputies, which met in closed session from November 28 to December 7 to discuss the High Command. Several factors led to the closed session, including a report from General Roques, the minister of war, about his visit to Salonika. Roques had traveled to Salonika on a fact-finding mission after Britain, Russia, and Italy had pressed for Sarrail's dismissal. Much to Briand and Joffre's surprise, Roques returned with a favorable report acknowledging the requirement for thirty divisions at Salonika before the allies could advance to Bulgaria. Though Roques did not praise Sarrail in his formal report, he was clearly impressed by what he had seen and thought that Sarrail's achievements in a very difficult environment reflected favorably on him. Roques also returned from Salonika believing that control of Sarrail's army should be withdrawn from Joffre. His report discredited Joffre and Briand and, when coupled with the failure of the Somme campaign and the imminent collapse of Romania, contributed to the deputies' demand for a closed session to discuss the conduct of the war.

The day before the closed session began, the Council of Ministers met to discuss Roques' proposal for modifying the decree of December 2, 1915; that decree had placed Sarrail's army under Joffre's control. Roques proposed abolishing the position of commander-in-chief, reducing Joffre to his former status as commander of the armies in northeastern France, and giving the minister of war power to apportion resources and approve plans for operations. If implemented Roques' proposal would have placed the minister of war firmly above theater commanders and made him the final arbiter of strategy and operations. After Joffre objected vehemently and threatened to resign, Briand supported him, and Roques withdrew his proposal. Though Briand would soon dismiss Roques and name a new minister of war, the damage was done, and the Chamber of Deputies began its closed session the following morning.

During the closed session, Briand realized he had to reorganize the High Command or his government would fall. On November 29 in a speech before the Chamber of Deputies he promised to abandon the decree of December 2, 1915, and separate control of the Balkan front from that of the French front. A general, serving as a "technical advisor" to the government, would ensure unity of direction and maintain harmony between the two fronts. Pressed to define the powers of the technical advisor, Briand waffled and said the government would retain control over the "political conduct of the war" and the technical advisor would supervise its execution. On December 3 Briand met with Joffre and asked him to accept the changes embodied in his presentation in the Chamber. According to Joffre, Briand proposed making him a marshal of France and giving him responsibility for overall "direction of the war." With one general officer commanding the armies of the northeast and another commanding the army in the Balkans, Joffre would have his own staff in Paris and work with representatives of the allied armies. Though suspicious Joffre accepted the proposals, and the following day Briand described the reorganization in vague terms to the Chamber. At the end of the closed session the government survived a vote of confidence, 344 to 160,

but its support had dwindled. Six months earlier, following another secret session, the government had won a vote of confidence by a more
comfortable margin, 444 to 80.

To remain in power, Briand began making significant changes in the
leadership of the army. On December 10 he sent General Hubert Lyautey,
the resident general in Algeria and one of France's most distinguished
soldiers, a telegram asking if he would accept the position of minister of
war. Apparently surprised by the question, Lyautey expressed interest
but reserved the right to decline until Briand told him more about the authority he would have and the bureaucratic structure within which he
would work. Without revealing what was happening with Joffre, Briand
responded that the government would control the overall direction of the
war through a War Committee with five members, including Lyautey.
The committee would provide "supreme" direction on all matters of
manufacture, transport, and supply pertaining to the war. He explained,
"Having in your hands the driving motor, possessing extensive powers
and unity of action your predecessors have not had, you will have the
means to render to your country the services it requires of you."[14]
Lyautey soon wired Briand, "I will answer your call."[15]

On December 13 Briand formed a new government, reducing the
Council of Ministers from twenty-three to ten and replacing Roques,
who was sent to command Fourth Army, with Lyautey. On the same day
his new government survived another vote of confidence, but this time by
only thirty votes. Also on that day, the president of the Republic published a decree announcing Joffre's appointment as "general-in-chief of
the French armies, technical military advisor to the government, consul-
tative member of the War Committee." Another presidential decree appointed General Robert Nivelle commander of the armies of the north
and northeast. Though the evidence is not completely clear, Briand apparently changed his mind in these crucial days about the role Joffre
would play. On the morning of the thirteenth, while reading a newspaper,
Joffre concluded that something was amiss and commented, "This is not
what they promised me." He immediately departed his headquarters for
Paris.[16] Despite Joffre's doubts, Briand convinced him to accept the new
position. Having previously been "commander-in-chief of French armies," Joffre recognized the significance of his being only the "general-in-

chief," but he proceeded with preparing himself for his new duties and organizing his staff. He told a British officer, "I am the commander-in-chief and I intend to command effectively."[17] Before Lyautey arrived in Paris from North Africa, however, the minister of the navy, who was the acting minister of war, sent Joffre a letter and told him he would only prepare studies and render advice to the War Committee. Another letter said that the new commander of the armies of the northeast, General Nivelle, would report "exclusively" to the minister of war.[18] The limitations on Joffre's power became even more apparent when the acting minister of war refused to grant him permission to approve units' receiving the *fourragère*. In reality, Briand did not want to dismiss the victor of the Marne, but he had changed his mind about the powers Joffre would have as technical advisor. Joffre's elevation to the position became nothing more than a façade intended to satisfy the army, the country, and France's allies. On December 26, the day he was appointed a marshal of France, Joffre asked to be relieved of his responsibilities.

Easing Joffre out of his position as commander-in-chief did not end Briand's troubles. The new minister of war, who arrived in Paris from Morocco on December 22, had spent most of his military service in France's colonies and had served in Morocco during the first twenty-nine months of the war. Since Lyautey knew little about the strategic, operational, or tactical aspects of the war, he initially devoted most of his time to visiting units and acquiring information about the issues pertaining to his new responsibilities. Despite the changes made by Briand and despite his having chosen a distinguished soldier as the minister of war, many political figures had doubts about the government's competence.

The situation in late 1916 thus differed markedly from that of early autumn. In late November Poincaré noted, "New wave of pessimism in Paris. Bad news from Russia. Bad news from Romania."[19] In an ominous portent, the morale of French soldiers dropped to its lowest point since the great retreat of 1914.[20] The negative shift in the strategic situation also created considerable unease among political leaders. As discontent with conduct of the war accumulated, the political scene in Paris became more unsettled, and support for Briand's government weakened even though it had a new minister of war and a new commander on the northeastern front. To add to the difficulties, both Lyautey and Nivelle had responsibilities far beyond those to which they were accustomed, and Nivelle lacked Joffre's personal prestige and influence among the allies. Time would prove that he also did not understand the limitations of the French army.

When France's political leaders chose a new commander of French forces in north and northeastern France, they had about a dozen officers from whom to choose, including the chief of staff (Castelnau), army-group commanders (Foch, Pétain, Franchet d'Espèrey), and army com-manders (Gérard, Nivelle, Humbert, Gouraud, Mazel, Fayolle, Villaret, and Micheler). Though one would expect the chief of staff and army-group commanders to be among the finalists, all had faults of one type or another that led to their not being chosen. Castelnau and Foch suffered from their long association with Joffre, as well as from their being devout Catholics. Briand had especially strong doubts about Castelnau's abili-ties. Since Foch had recently been injured in an automobile accident, questions also arose about his health. Franchet d'Espèrey, though hugely successful in the early part of the war and a confidant of Briand on strat-egy in the Balkans, had done nothing extraordinarily special since be-coming an army-group commander and was not highly regarded by his peers.

Of France's most senior army leaders, only Pétain seemed a viable can-didate to replace Joffre. While Pétain was a Catholic, he did not attend mass regularly and thus encountered few objections from the radical ele-ments in French political circles. Yet he had not curried favor with peo-ple such as Briand and Poincaré and had surprised some with his com-ments about French politics. At one point he had told Poincaré that he did not "give a damn" about the French constitution. On another occa-sion he had complained sharply about politicians' visiting his headquar-ters and insisted that they present their questions to him in writing.[21] Ad-ditionally, Joffre did not have great confidence in Pétain, believing that he lacked strategic vision and was too pessimistic. At the moment Briand chose Nivelle, he wanted to appoint a general officer with whom the new technical advisor could work smoothly.[22] Neither he nor Joffre found

Pétain's pessimism appealing, and neither relished the prospect of contending with his obstinacy.

Of the army commanders only Nivelle had the reputation and political support to merit serious consideration. While treating visiting politicians courteously and warmly, he had caused a sensation throughout France with his successful capture of forts Douaumont and Vaux. Among his supporters, for example, was André Maginot, who told Poincaré that Nivelle would make a superb commander-in-chief. Also, since Nivelle was a Protestant (his mother was English), anticlerical politicians found him more appealing than a Catholic candidate. The most important supporter of Nivelle, however, was Joffre. Joffre had long been impressed with Nivelle's optimism and his "can do" spirit and had frequently communicated directly with him, bypassing Pétain, when he sought greater offensive energy at Verdun. In early November 1916 he had told Nivelle he intended to make him an army-group commander, and on December 10 he told Nivelle he had recommended his appointment as commander of the armies of the north and northeast.[23] Shortly before Nivelle's formal appointment, the two dined together, and Nivelle showed great deference toward the soon-to-be-shelved commander-in-chief. At this dinner Nivelle told Joffre he owed his promotion to him and thanked him. At about the same time, however, he sent the acting minister of war a private note insisting that Joffre have no link with Haig or with any army-group commander.[24]

Nivelle had risen in rank remarkably quickly since August 1914. Beginning the war as a colonel in the artillery, he became a brigade commander on October 27 and received command of a division on February 19, 1915. His technical competence as an artillerist enabled him to coordinate infantry and artillery better than most officers, and he proved to be an innovative and inventive officer with his development of the rolling barrage. His great success as a division commander resulted in his becoming a corps commander on December 25. After distinguishing himself at Verdun, he became commander of Second Army on May 1, 1916. Six months later, after capturing forts Douaumont and Vaux, he received a telephone call from Briand on the night of December 12 and quickly drove to Paris. On December 13 a presidential decree made him commander of the armies of northern and northeastern France. With the outcome of the war at stake, France's political leaders had placed all their bets on an officer with no experience as a strategist, little understanding of how to work with allies, and only six months' experience as an army commander.

Nivelle nonetheless brought new ideas and great energy and optimism to his new position. Shortly before becoming general-in-chief, he told a French officer, "We now have the formula."[25] Some political leaders such as Paul Painlevé have insisted that Nivelle was chosen because of "doctrine" rather than "personality," since he represented the swift, sure methods of Verdun (in particular the capture of Fort Douaumont) instead of the slow, costly, methodical methods of the Somme. Nivelle's new "formula" resembled the method employed by the Germans at Verdun when they had concentrated their fires on narrow zones, destroyed defenders throughout the depth of these zones, and thereby opened corridors for the infantry to attack. His method relied on an extraordinarily high concentration of artillery fired in depth throughout a carefully chosen zone. Though the French had tried such tactical methods in the past, they had lacked sufficient long-range artillery. By October 1916, however, they had ample artillery—particularly long-range heavy artillery—to devastate entire zones of the enemy's defenses and open routes for the infantry. With accompanying batteries following as closely as possible, infantry, Nivelle believed, could drive quickly and relatively easily through the enemy's devastated defenses until they reached his artillery. After the successful attack of December 15 at Verdun, Nivelle bade farewell to Second Army by saying, "The experience is conclusive; our method has proved itself."[26]

Nivelle's operational and tactical ideas resembled Joffre's, but there were important differences. At the end of December, when Nivelle distributed new instructions on offensive methods, he did not write a new document and instead modified one that had been written and signed by his predecessor. Instead of emphasizing successive efforts in a methodical battle, however, Nivelle emphasized continuous thrusts. He believed the intervals required for artillery movement and preparation between successive assaults provided the defense with time to bring up reserves and strengthen defenses. He also abandoned the idea of "rupturing" an enemy position and instead favored penetration and breakthrough. When he distributed the new instructions, he attached a cover letter identifying the "directing principles" that would guide the preparation and execution of his 1917 offensive. He insisted that an attacker could penetrate a defense in twenty-four to forty-eight hours and advance as deep as the enemy's heavy artillery batteries in a single, continuous thrust. To achieve a breakthrough, he wrote, an attacker had to concentrate an unparalleled amount of heavy artillery fire throughout the enemy's position—as deep as eight kilometers—and then push the infantry through German defenses in one rapid, continuous move. To keep the attack moving, the heavy artillery—as Nivelle explained in one of his later publications—had to be employed as if it were a 75-mm cannon. After achieving a breakthrough, an "audacious lateral exploitation" would destroy the enemy's remaining batteries and cut his lines of resupply. For the final phase of the battle, additional forces would flow through and destroy the enemy's reserves. As he told Lyautey, the minister of war, in a handwritten note, "Objective: Total destruction of active enemy forces by maneuver and battle."[27]

Nivelle did not formally take over the full responsibilities of his new position until December 17, but thereafter he wasted no time revising French plans. On the eighteenth he halted preparations for Joffre's offensive and on the next day provided his chief of staff a rough outline of his operational concept. Two days later he sent a letter to General Haig with a more fully developed concept. First, he intended to fix the enemy's forces in the Noyon salient with two large attacks, one by the British north of the Somme between Arras (rather than Vimy) and Bapaume and the other by Northern Army Group south of the Somme. Next, he intended to have Central Army Group make a surprise attack on another portion of the front (the Aisne sector, which included the Chemin des Dames) and break through the enemy's defenses. Finally, after enlarging the breach by pushing forces forward and turning them laterally, he intended to send large forces through the breach. These "maneuver" forces would fight the "decisive battle" beyond the breakthrough. He wrote: "The success of our operations will thus depend essentially on the maneuver force."[28]

In those first few days Nivelle also revealed other aspects of his intentions and character. In a remarkably frank discussion with Haig on December 20, he spoke openly about his having sole responsibility for operations and about Joffre's loss of influence over the army. He also revealed to Haig his intentions to get rid of Foch, Castelnau, and Franchet d'Espèrey.[29] While Joffre and the three other general officers had made enough mistakes to deserve criticism and perhaps relief, Nivelle's frankness with Haig so soon after his appointment revealed his poor judgment. More egregious examples would appear in the coming months.

Through a series of decisions, Nivelle altered not only Joffre's concept but his own initial concept for the offensive. One particularly important decision occurred on Christmas Day after he conducted a reconnaissance of the future zone of attack. Since Pétain's Central Army Group had responsibility for the Aisne sector, Pétain and General Olivier Mazel, who commanded Fifth Army, accompanied him on the reconnaissance. During the discussions Pétain expressed doubts about attacking the Chemin des Dames between Reims and Soissons and suggested changing the zone of attack. He preferred making an attack farther to the east on both sides of Reims and then driving north. Unwilling to tolerate any doubts, Nivelle decided to form another army group under General Alfred Micheler and have it conduct the offensive. He chose Micheler, he explained later, because of Joffre's praise for him.[30]

Nivelle's new campaign plan included attacks by Micheler's newly formed Reserve Army Group and the Northern Army Group, as well as the British. While two armies in Northern Army Group attacked south of the Somme, three armies in Reserve Army Group would attack on the Aisne. The three armies in Micheler's Reserve Army Group included Fifth Army, which was already on the Aisne front, and Sixth and Tenth armies, which came from Northern Army Group. Fifth and Sixth armies (each with twelve to fourteen divisions) would lead the attack and make the breach on the Chemin des Dames. Tenth Army (with twelve divisions) would follow the two leading armies. Nivelle expected Micheler's Reserve Army Group to fight its way through enemy lines in the Aisne sector in twenty-four to forty-eight hours and then destroy the enemy's reserves in the open. He wrote: "The objective is the destruction of the principal mass of the enemy's forces on the Western Front. This can be attained only by a decisive battle, delivered against the reserves of the adversary and followed by an intensive exploitation."[31]

*   *   *

The first and most significant opposition to Nivelle's offensive came from the British. In early December Robertson had informed Joffre that he wanted to launch an offensive in 1917 along the coast and capture Ostend and Zeebrugge. Such an offensive, he believed, would end German use of the ports for submarines and ease the threat to allied shipping. Although Joffre did not object to a British attack, Nivelle considered the operation a distraction and believed it would do nothing more than drive German submarines "a little farther east." Such an operation, he insisted, would be "isolated" and "lose the benefit of the French attack." Additionally, he viewed the idea of driving along the coast and simultaneously attacking near Arras as "unsound."[32] Even more significant, Nivelle knew he could not launch his offensive unless the British relieved French forces and freed them to participate. Despite a personal appeal from Nivelle on December 21, Haig refused to accept any proposal depriving him of his offensive capability. Since he could relieve French units only if new British divisions arrived, he sent Nivelle's request to London and asked the War Committee to provide the divisions requested by the French.[33] After further pressure, Haig yielded and agreed to relieve the French on thirteen kilometers of front, but he refused to take over the entire thirty-two kilometers desired by Nivelle.

Other problems with the British appeared after Nivelle wrote to Haig on January 2 and provided more details about the coming offensive. With nearly one hundred divisions participating, including thirty-five British, the offensive would have a "prolonged duration" and consist of several phases.[34] Though most of Nivelle's letter focused on defining the different phases of the battle, Haig reacted strongly against the possibility of a prolonged battle. In his response he expressed his unwillingness to participate in such a battle and insisted, "If these [first] two phases are not so successful as to justify my entering on the third phase, then I must transfer my main forces to the north."[35] Haig did not want Nivelle's offensive to restrict his drive toward Ostend and Zeebrugge in what would become the Passchendaele offensive in Flanders. In a subsequent letter Nivelle allayed Haig's concerns about a prolonged battle but insisted on having "one single, grand battle." As for Haig's pulling out of the battle and following his own strategy, Nivelle insisted that both armies engage all their forces until the battle ended. He wrote: "It would be criminal to engage in a battle under other conditions." Nivelle closed his letter by commenting on the disadvantages of beginning the battle after the first of May, the date Haig said his army would be ready. He observed, "the earlier the date of our offensive, the more we will benefit from the relative inferiority of the forces opposing us."[36]

Meanwhile a change in the British government brought a more sympathetic ear to power in London. After the fall of the Asquith government on December 5, 1916, Lloyd George had become prime minister and presided over the London conference in late December. During the conference the new prime minister viewed an extension of British lines favorably but insisted on discussing the issue with British commanders. At his insistence the allies met again in Rome in early January to examine possible methods for focusing allied efforts in 1917 and defeating the Germans. During the discussions Lloyd George favored an allied offensive in Italy. He opposed sending additional troops to Salonika, but he insisted, "We can put the Germans out of action just as well on the Italian as on the Western Front."[37] Objecting strongly to the effects of such an offensive on Nivelle's preparations, Briand suggested referring the proposal to military leaders in the allied countries. In his memoirs Lloyd George said that Briand, who had long championed attacking Austria through the Balkans, became a "rancorous Westerner" when the British prime minister proposed making Italy the scene of the main allied attack in 1917.[38] Yet Lloyd George acknowledged that Briand had made a strong case during the Rome conference for focusing on the Western Front. On the second day of the conference Lloyd George said, "if eloquence could transport troops across the seas, [Briand's] would have done it [yesterday], no doubt about it."[39] Despite the unlikelihood that French and British military leaders would support Lloyd George's proposal, the conferees agreed to refer the question of "a combined offensive by the three Western Allies" to their military advisors.[40] Such a referral, of course, killed the idea of Britain and France's sending troops to Italy and forced Lloyd George to give serious attention to Nivelle's plan.

On the way back from the conference, the British delegation met General Nivelle at a railway station near Paris, and Lloyd George invited him to come to London and explain his campaign plan to the War Cabinet. In preparation for the conference in London, Nivelle met with France's political leaders on January 15. Before the parley he completed a note summarizing French strategy and describing the different phases of his upcoming offensive. Not surprisingly, the note emphasized the importance of the Western Front. It began: "Among the immutable principles of war, the most important, never contested, is that the destruction of the principal mass of the enemy's forces will lead to a decision in war." Nivelle labeled the transport of important forces from France "utopian" and objected to sending Franco-British forces to Italy. He added, "A general-in-chief, conscious of his responsibilities, would never accept such a strategic error." By destroying the principal forces of the enemy on the Western Front, he insisted, France and its allies could emerge victorious. As for the means of putting the enemy "out of action," Nivelle believed that his operations at Verdun on October 24 and December 15 had demonstrated the power of his methods. His success there convinced him he could break the enemy's front in one or two days. After describing his coming offensive, he concluded by calling it a "splendid harvest of glory for the British and French armies."[41] Nivelle had held his new position for less than a month, and his note exuded confidence and certainty, two qualities desperately sought by an exhausted France. He had seduced French political leaders with his self-confidence, and he soon did the same with Lloyd George.

On January 15–16 Nivelle and Haig traveled to London to meet British political leaders and discuss extending the British front and specifying the date of attack. With the British prime minister presiding, Nivelle explained his campaign strategy and appealed for an extension of the British front farther to the south and for an early beginning of the offensive. After the French ambassador to London emphasized his government's support for Nivelle's proposals, British leaders responded favorably to Nivelle's comments but asked how he could be so certain of achieving a penetration. Nivelle responded with a description of France's improved artillery and its ability to fire throughout the depth of an enemy's position. He insisted that his methods were new and had resulted in the loss of only 1,550 soldiers at Verdun in the December 15 attack. As for his campaign strategy, he summarized it in one sentence: "it is necessary to fix the enemy at one point and then to attack another point where we will penetrate and will march toward his reserves in order to destroy them."[42] On the second day Lloyd George questioned Nivelle carefully about his strategy and about his actions in the event of an attack against Salonika, Russia, or Italy. Nivelle replied that he would not hesitate to attack on the Western Front and thereby take advantage of the enemy's shifting forces to the other front. He insisted that such an attack was the best way to assist an ally, but his comments revealed his lack of interest in a true multifront strategy.

Those attending nevertheless spent most of their time discussing the extension of the British front and the date of the attack. Haig invoked several arguments against Nivelle, including effects of weather, questions about the Russians and Italians, and the British need for additional divisions. Despite Haig's reservations, Lloyd George found Nivelle's arguments appealing. Before the conference the British prime minister had told Haig that the French army was "better all around" and was "able to gain success at less cost of life" than the British army.[43] The British finally agreed to give "all the assistance in their power by attacking with all the means at their disposal." They also agreed to relieve French forces by the first week of March as far south as the Amiens-Roye road, in other words for the entire thirty-two kilometers desired by Nivelle. Since the British relief would not release French forces as early as Nivelle had originally hoped, both allies agreed to take the offensive no later than the first of April.[44] Except for the offensive's being delayed from early February to early April, Nivelle accomplished everything he desired in the London meeting.

The day after the London conference Lloyd George directed Robertson to ensure that Haig abided by the "letter and spirit" of the agreement, and during the next few weeks the French and British worked energetically to get ready for the offensive. The inability of the rail network to transport all supplies demanded by the British, however, soon engendered a complex and controversial confrontation over unity of command. The root of the problem was the British demand for many more locomotives and railcars than the number customarily used by the French. Even though the British had half as many troops engaged in the offensive, they demanded 8,000 railcars a day, a requirement far larger than the 2,800 used by the French to support their seventy divisions preparing for the offensive. After several complaints about inadequate transportation support, Haig notified Nivelle on January 24 that the failure to move troops and equipment on time could affect his operational preparations. Nivelle insisted that transportation shortcomings not delay the offensive, and in a meeting on January 29 he and Haig discussed methods of increasing the tonnage of supplies delivered to the British. When the transportation situation did not improve, the two met at British headquarters on February 16. At the conclusion of this meeting Nivelle wired the minister of war that the date of the attack was delayed and that it was "impossible" to fix a new date.[45] A few days later he notified his army-group commanders that the attack would be delayed until April 10.

As Haig continued frustrating Nivelle's efforts to arrange a coordinated Franco-British offensive, Lloyd George became impatient with British delays. At a meeting on February 13 of the British War Cabinet, Robertson objected to launching "such an important and vital offensive" before British troops were completely ready. Over his objections, the War Cabinet, as the minutes state, "laid it down" that "on no account" should the British delay the French. The minutes observed, "Sir William Robertson said that he interpreted these instructions as meaning that Sir Douglas Haig is expected to attack whether he be ready or not."[46] Despite this interpretation, Haig and Nivelle met on February 16 and agreed that "the attack is not to be made until preparations for attack are completed on British front."[47]

On February 27 political and military leaders of the two countries conferred in Calais. Haig had requested the meeting in the middle of February, when he became dissatisfied with the railway situation. The British also wanted to discuss "means of action," preparation of forces, "intentions" of French and British commanders, and "establishment between the two commanders of a complete unity of views."[48] Briand, Lyautey, and Nivelle attended, as did Lloyd George, Robertson, and Haig.

During this meeting Nivelle gave Lloyd George a paper in which he requested that the British army in France be placed under him on March 1. Nivelle asked for authority over "the planning and execution of offensive and defensive actions; the dispositions of the forces by Armies and Groups of Armies; the boundaries between these higher formations; [and] the allotment of material and resources of all natures to the

Armies."[49] To facilitate planning Nivelle also wanted the British to place a chief of staff at his headquarters. In essence the British commander would function as an army-group commander. Early the next morning Robertson and Nivelle met privately, and Robertson complained that Nivelle had not raised the issue with him before placing it in front of the civilian ministers. Nivelle replied:

> But the idea of placing the British armies under my command did not originate with me. It was the subject of communication between the two Governments before we came here, and I was instructed to work out the details of the scheme and lay them before the conference for your consideration, the understanding being that it would receive the support of your Prime Minister. Naturally, therefore, I assumed that you knew as much about it as I did.[50]

Also blaming others, Lyautey later told Haig that he had not seen the paper until he had boarded the train for Calais. The proposal apparently originated in a discussion between Lloyd George and the French military attaché in London. After the British prime minister said it was necessary for Nivelle to have all troops operating on the Western Front (including British) available to him, the French officer notified Paris of Lloyd George's desire for the French to take a strong position on the subject. Seizing the opportunity, French political authorities directed Nivelle to prepare such a proposal. According to Robertson, Nivelle never dreamed the British would consider such an arrangement without informing the chief of the Imperial General Staff.[51]

Robertson and Haig's adamant opposition compelled Lloyd George to compromise. The conference concluded with an agreement that "the general direction of the campaign should be in the hands of the French commander-in-chief." Unless the safety or success of the British were endangered, Haig would conform his operational plans to the campaign strategy of the French commander. The British commander, however, was free to choose the methods he would use and to determine how he would employ his troops. The agreement, and thus Haig's subordination to Nivelle, would terminate when the operation ended.[52]

Despite the Calais agreement, considerable friction continued between Nivelle and Haig. In his memoirs Lloyd George blamed Haig and Robertson for "viciously" resisting "unity of command" and thereby obstructing Nivelle's efforts to begin the offensive early. According to Colonel Maurice Hankey, who participated in many of the discussions with the French, however, Nivelle's "tactlessness" caused most of the problems.[53] The first correspondence from Nivelle to Haig raised considerable umbrage at the British headquarters, for it not only provided directions on operations and transportation but also asked for the British operations officer to be attached to the GQG and for General Henry Wilson to be assigned as the liaison officer. Moreover, Nivelle asked to be informed about the directives Haig issued to his forces and the "dispositions taken by them to execute" his orders.[54] Within days Haig, feeling that Nivelle was treating him as a subordinate, complained to Robertson.

While allied generals squabbled, the Germans improved their operational situation. On February 4 they issued orders for a withdrawal from the Noyon salient against which Nivelle had intended to make two supporting attacks. Beginning with the small salient in allied lines between Arras and Bapaume, created by the Somme offensive of the previous year, the Germans intended to conduct a series of withdrawals and to occupy a new position that extended from Arras through St.-Quentin to a point ten kilometers east of Soissons. According to Hindenburg the Germans withdrew from the Noyon salient because of its vulnerability to attacks on its northern and southern shoulders and because of the need to create additional reserves through the occupation of a shorter line. The withdrawal shortened the German front by forty kilometers and enabled them to pull as many as thirteen or fourteen divisions out of the front line. The Germans began pulling back from the small salient between Arras and Bapaume as early as February 24; their withdrawal from the Noyon salient began formally on March 16.

Although the Germans spent months building new positions to the rear along what they called the Siegfried Position, most of the preparations escaped the allies' notice. In early January the British had sufficient indications of defensive preparations behind German lines to convince Nivelle to direct closer coordination between French and British aviation in the reconnaissance of enemy activities. A month later the GQG had considerable evidence that the Germans were preparing positions behind their front lines. By February 25 the allies could plot the course of the entire position between Arras and Soissons. Since the Germans also constructed several interim positions between their front line and the Siegfried Position, the French viewed the preparations as the construction of a defense in depth. They doubted that the Germans would voluntarily give up positions so close to Paris. By the end of March the allies had tagged the vast fortified zone between Arras and Soissons the Hindenburg Line. The word "line" was inappropriate, however, since the defensive system consisted of a very deep fortified zone.

Despite attempts to gain unity of command, relations between Nivelle and Haig worsened in early March as more evidence suggested a German withdrawal. After the Germans pulled out of the small salient between Arras and Bapaume, Haig concluded that they were shortening their front so they could accumulate reserves for an offensive near Ypres. On March 4 he proposed attacking only with his First and Third armies near Vimy and Arras and not attacking with his Fifth Army near Bapaume. This change would enable him to shift forces from Fifth Army to Second Army at Ypres in the event of a German attack; it would also shift the center of his attack farther north. The French liaison officer reported that Haig considered his forces endangered and therefore—under the provisions of the Calais agreement—believed he could refuse Nivelle's demands. Only a week after the agreement at Calais on unity of command, Haig appeared ready to disregard the French commander's instructions. Recognizing that his entire offensive was at stake, Nivelle sent Haig a "directive" in which he announced his decision to make no fundamental modification of his plan. While accepting the cancelation of the attack by Haig's Fifth Army, the French commander expected the British to use reserves created by this cancelation to augment the offensive by the British First and Third armies in the Vimy-Arras sector. In blunt terms he ordered Haig to make an attack on as large a front as possible. Almost simultaneously, Briand complained to London about Haig's refusal to cooperate, making "unity of command impossible."[55]

With the two allied generals at loggerheads, Lloyd George proposed another conference in London. Held on March 12–13, the meeting began with the British prime minister's complaining about the "tone" of the communications sent to Haig, and it ended with a new agreement on relations between French and British forces. The agreement stated: "All the British troops stationed in France remain in all circumstances under the orders of their chain of command and of the British commander in chief." Nivelle would communicate with British forces only through Haig, and the British would provide Nivelle information about their operations orders and measures taken to execute them. As for the role of the British liaison officer at French headquarters, he would have normal liaison duties and keep Nivelle and Haig informed about key issues pertaining to both commands.[56] In essence Haig would be treated as a fellow allied commander and not as a subordinate, and the French would not usurp planning responsibilities or disrupt command relationships. Although this modification to the Calais agreement fixed relations between Nivelle and Haig, the weeks of bickering had exacted a high price. Nivelle, as well as Joffre, had hoped to begin the offensive in the first half of February, but the two allies were still wrestling with preliminary arrangements.

While Nivelle sparred with Haig, he made other decisions that altered his offensive. One of the most important occurred after March 4, when General Franchet d'Espèrey, who had replaced Foch as commander of Northern Army Group, suggested modifying plans for the offensive because the enemy to his front was preparing a withdrawal. He proposed beginning a surprise offensive in ten days. Following two days of artillery preparation, including the day of attack, French infantry would advance. Once they encountered strong resistance d'Espèrey would unleash a large mass of tanks in a surprise attack. Though Nivelle acknowledged on March 7 that the enemy had pulled back slightly from the small salient between Arras and Bapaume, he saw no "concrete" evidence that they intended to withdraw elsewhere and expressed doubts that the Germans would abandon their position closest to Paris without fighting. Insisting that he could not "base a decision on hypotheses," he foresaw no need to alter his plan of attack.[57] He nonetheless had his staff consider alternatives for the possibility of a German withdrawal.

A few days later, after the German intention to withdraw became obvious, Nivelle adjusted the mission and composition of his army groups. Shortening of the front line, he later stated, enabled him to have sixteen additional divisions, including artillery. Although he made only a few changes in his instructions for Micheler's Reserve Army Group, he strengthened Pétain's Central Army Group and ordered it to participate in the main offensive by attacking twenty-five kilometers east of Reims. Nearly fifty kilometers would separate Pétain's and Micheler's attacks. As for Franchet d'Espèrey's Northern Army Group, Nivelle reduced it to a single army with three corps and ordered it to maintain "energetic and continuous" pressure on withdrawing enemy forces. After reaching the Hindenburg Line, d'Espèrey would launch only local attacks. The reduction of his army group to a single army meant, however, that it could do little more than follow the Germans as they pulled back to the Hindenburg Line and could not place heavy pressure on that line once Nivelle's offensive began. In response to the German withdrawal Nivelle thus increased the main attack's power by adding Central Army Group's efforts (soon called "auxiliary" rather than "subordinate" or "supporting") to those of Reserve Army Group and practically eliminating Northern Army Group's supporting attack. Through a series of incremental changes, he had transformed Joffre's concept of sequenced attacks (two large attacks followed by a surprise attack) into a powerful frontal assault, and he now had only the British making a large supporting attack.

After the Germans began their withdrawal on March 16, the allies moved forward cautiously. In his diary Fayolle wrote: "If we follow them, we play their game by entering a devastated zone without resources and with lines of communication cut. If we do not follow them, we lose contact with them and they maintain their freedom [of action]."[58] Some of the French caution came from the small number of forces involved, but some also came from a lack of aggressiveness. Franchet d'Espèrey relieved one corps commander who moved too slowly. As Cyril Falls noted in the British official history, d'Espèrey might have won a "sensational victory" if Nivelle had accepted his proposal of March 4 for a surprise assault with tanks,[59] but instead Northern Army Group did little more than maintain contact with the Germans as they withdrew.

As the Germans pulled back from the Noyon salient, the Briand government fell. The incident provoking the fall occurred during a mid-March session of the Chamber of Deputies when Lyautey refused to discuss military aviation during a closed session and insisted on speaking when the session became public. He then surprised the deputies by insisting that discussion of a military topic even in closed session would place the national defense at risk. His comments provoked an outcry in the Chamber and his immediate resignation from the Briand ministry. After several leading politicians refused to become minister of war, Briand resigned, and a new government was formed on March 20.

The new president of the Council of Ministers, Alexandre Ribot, had held the position twice before the war and had served as minister of finances since August 26, 1914. Briand described Ribot to Poincaré as "an excellent patriot, resolute partisan of all-out war, a very honest man who will remain out of suspicious affairs and intrigues."[60] For minister of war, Ribot considered two individuals, Albert Thomas and Paul Painlevé. Roques, who had frustrated Joffre so much, was not a candidate because both Nivelle and Pétain wanted him relieved for incompetence from his duties as an army commander. Since Thomas, a Socialist, did not express interest in the position and Ribot needed the parliamentary support from the political left that Painlevé's appointment would bring, the new premier quickly focused on Painlevé. Knowing that Painlevé had reservations about Nivelle, however, Ribot did not choose him until the aspiring war minister expressed his willingness to work with Nivelle. Despite this concession the new minister of war soon revealed that he, unlike Ribot, would become involved in "suspicious affairs and intrigues."

A mathematician who had previously served as minister of public education and minister of inventions during the Briand ministry from October 1915 to December 1916, Painlevé had solid credentials to be the minister of war. While serving as minister of inventions, he used his knowledge of science and mathematics to support the war effort, and he worked closely with the army's senior leaders in the development of weapons such as the tank. With science becoming more and more important in the war effort, making a mathematician with experience in technical military developments the minister of war appealed to the Chamber of Deputies. Painlevé, however, brought to his new office strong ideas about the conduct of the war. When Briand had formed his new government in December 1916, he had asked Painlevé to remain part of his ministry, but Painlevé had declined because he did not wish to be associated with Lyautey, an individual strongly disliked by the left. He also objected to Joffre's elevation to technical advisor and to Nivelle's appointment as general-in-chief. Painlevé viewed Nivelle as an "unknown" who had commanded an army for a brief period and who had no experience at higher levels of command. In contrast to his reservations about Nivelle, Painlevé had great confidence in Pétain. He had developed a friendly relationship with Pétain in 1916 when he visited Verdun several times to discuss technical issues. Though Pétain's brusqueness and pessimism often irritated politicians, Painlevé found his operational and tactical ideas appealing. In March 1917 Painlevé still had misgivings about Nivelle, high regard for Pétain, and doubts about the wisdom of a large offensive.

Two days after the new government came into power Painlevé met with Nivelle. Though the two men later offered different summaries of their conversation, the meeting marked the beginning of a difficult relationship. Despite the demands of preparing a large operation, Nivelle had to allay Painlevé's concerns about the offensive, for the new minister of war had hardly entered office when complaints came pouring—from "twenty different directions," according to Painlevé—into his office.[61] Though some have described Painlevé as an "incompetent ideologue" whose meddling unleashed the "jealous animosities" of Nivelle's subordinates,[62] the new minister of war did not have to plant seeds of doubt in the minds of Nivelle's lieutenants. Numerous doubts about the operation already existed throughout the army, including at Nivelle's headquarters. The operations officer at the GQG, for example, had written a letter to Nivelle and formally expressed concerns about the coming operation.

Among the key leaders having reservations about the offensive was General Micheler, commander of Reserve Army Group, whom Nivelle had personally chosen to command the huge force on the Aisne. As early as March 22 Micheler suggested to Nivelle that he modify his plan. In a letter to the French general-in-chief, Micheler argued that conditions favoring an offensive in December 1916 had changed. First, the withdrawal of the Germans from the Noyon salient had enabled them to increase their forces in the Aisne sector. The Germans now had sufficient troops to occupy their positions in depth, including third and fourth positions. Second, the scheme of operations initially envisaged by Nivelle no longer matched the operational situation. With the withdrawal of the Germans

Nivelle had changed both the mission of Northern Army Group and the nature of the supporting attacks. Instead of having several large attacks precede the assault of Micheler's Reserve Army Group, only the British would make a significant effort before Micheler's advance and thus divert enemy troops from the Aisne sector. Consequently Micheler saw little chance of penetrating the enemy's deep defenses quickly or easily.[63]

After learning of Micheler's concerns, Painlevé summoned him to Paris on March 28. Micheler repeated the ideas in his letter of March 22 to Nivelle and emphasized the unlikelihood of a breakthrough. Despite these concerns, he did not want the offensive abandoned, since such a decision would free the Germans to attack elsewhere. Micheler was even more frank when talking to other general officers. When Fayolle visited Reserve Army Group's headquarters, Micheler gave him a list of reasons for not attacking. Fayolle noted in his diary, "He is not a partisan of the attack."[64]

The next criticism came from Pétain. Painlevé visited Pétain's headquarters on April 1 and devoted most of the afternoon to discussions about the offensive. Not surprisingly, Pétain was brutally honest and expressed grave doubts, most of which he had already communicated to Nivelle. In essence, Pétain rejected Nivelle's method or "formula" for using artillery to destroy the enemy throughout the depth of a defensive position. While such methods had worked on relatively narrow fronts at Verdun, he thought they would not work on the broader front in the Aisne sector. He explained, "Even the waters of Lake Geneva would have but little effect if dispersed over the length and breadth of the Sahara Desert." Rejecting the possibility of a breakthrough, Pétain preferred concentrating all French artillery on the first two enemy positions and seeking only limited gains.[65] The following day Pétain dined with Franchet d'Espèrey and the minister of war. Though d'Espèrey proved circumspect, Pétain blasted Nivelle's plan and said it was rash to expect a strategic breakthrough and exploitation.

As doubts about Nivelle's planned offensive mounted, events in Russia altered the strategic situation profoundly. In mid-January 1917 the French military attaché in Petrograd warned, "Political situation absolutely alarming." He also expressed reservations about the Russians' readiness for another offensive.[66] In late January General de Castelnau arrived in Russia for an allied conference and met with Russian leaders. Oblivious to the tidal wave about to engulf Russia, Tsar Nicholas II assured him several times that he would launch a "decisive" offensive in the 1917 campaign.[67] After returning from the conference, Castelnau reported, "If the French army has a value of twenty, the Russian army has a value of only eight or nine."[68] During the next few weeks the value of the Russian army dropped even more. In early March riots broke out in Petrograd, and a widespread mutiny of troops followed. On March 12 the Russians established a Provisional Government, and three days later Tsar Nicholas abdicated in favor of his brother, Michael, who soon abdicated in favor of the Provisional Government. As disorder spread, General Alekseev sent a telegram to Paris in which he acknowledged the disarray of his army and said the Russians could not attack for three or four months. Expecting the Germans to shift divisions from the Eastern to the Western Front, Alekseev advised the French to "advance slowly and prudently and occupy a new and strong line of defense."[69]

As bad news came from Russia, good news came from across the Atlantic. On March 29 the French military attaché informed Painlevé and Nivelle that the United States would soon declare war against Germany. On April 2 President Woodrow Wilson addressed a joint session of Congress and asked for a declaration of war. The Senate passed the war resolution on April 4, the House of Representatives on April 6, and Wilson immediately signed it. A telegram in late March from the French military attaché in the United States, however, had underlined America's military weakness. The U.S. army had only 125,000 soldiers scattered through the United States, Philippines, Hawaii, Puerto Rico, China, and Alaska. As for combat troops, the United States had no divisions and only twenty-four infantry, fourteen cavalry, and six artillery regiments. Despite this military weakness, Ribot noted in his diary that America's entry into the war "excited great enthusiasm."[70]

An opportunity for France's leaders to discuss the new strategic situation came on the evening of April 3, when Painlevé held a meeting at the Ministry of War. Among those attending were Ribot, Painlevé, and Nivelle, plus the ministers of navy, armaments, and colonies. Painlevé opened the meeting by suggesting that the German withdrawal from the Noyon salient, the Russian revolution, and American entry into the war compelled a reexamination of France's conduct of the war. He then focused on criticisms of Nivelle's plan and expressed his own reservations about the offensive's chances of success. Responding confidently and assertively, Nivelle assured his listeners that he could drive through the enemy's third and fourth positions and would not be halted by additional forces the Germans moved into the Aisne sector. He boldly predicted that Micheler's and d'Espèrey's army groups would meet north of Laon within three days after the offensive began, and he promised to halt the offensive if it did not succeed within twenty-four to forty-eight hours. Under no circumstances, he assured his audience, would he repeat the mistakes of the battle of the Somme and fight a series of successive battles. When queried about possibly waiting until the United States could play a role, Nivelle reminded his audience of the Americans' military weakness and how long it would take for them to arrive in France in large numbers. As for the Russians, he said he would not be surprised if they made peace with the Germans by July. He also expressed doubts about the willingness of the Italians to attack and their ability to withstand a large Austro-German offensive. From Nivelle's perspective these factors argued for a Franco-British offensive as soon as possible.

Nivelle played his trump card when he discussed the British. He reminded his audience that postponing the offensive would dismantle all arrangements Briand had completed with the British. For the first time French and British forces had some semblance of unity of command and were about to embark on a vast combined offensive. By not attacking, the allies would allow the Germans to seize the initiative or concentrate against the Italians. After answering a few additional questions, Nivelle left the meeting confident that he had won the argument.

Despite Nivelle's optimism an even more uncomfortable meeting for him soon occurred. The impetus for the meeting came from several sources. First, the presidents of the Senate and Chamber of Deputies had visited Micheler's army group and received pessimistic appraisals from several general officers. Second, Messimy, the former minister of war and now commander of 46th Infantry Division, sent Ribot a letter in which he decried preparations for the offensive and rejected the possibility of any strategic gains. After predicting failure and heavy losses, he said, "I summarize here the opinions of the most highly regarded leaders of our

army and most notably the leader himself who will direct the approaching offensive, General Micheler."[71] Finally, after Painlevé asked Pétain for
his advice, the highly respected general told him the attack had "no
chance of success" and would result only in "useless casualties."[72] At a
meeting on April 5, France's political leaders decided to meet the following day with Nivelle and his army-group commanders.

From the earliest days of the war, political authorities had met with
military leaders, but those meetings differed substantially from the one
on April 6. Political leaders, for example, had attended meetings on June
23 and August 11, 1915, when Joffre met with his army-group commanders to discuss strategic and operational issues. In the meeting on April 6
Nivelle was treated much more roughly than Joffre had been, and he had
to offer a much more energetic defense of his plans. Among those attending the meeting in a railway car at Compiègne were Poincaré, Ribot,
Painlevé, Nivelle, Castelnau, Franchet d'Espèrey, Pétain, and Micheler.
Coincidentally, they met on the day the United States declared war on
Germany, and two days after the British began their artillery bombardment in preparation for the Arras offensive. Though the conference
proved to be one of the most controversial of the war, the details of the
discussions remain vague, since no formal minutes were taken. Several
participants nonetheless later provided summaries of what happened.

When the meeting began at 1030 hours, Painlevé spoke first and summarized the government's concerns and the reasons for having the meeting. The minister of war explained that the government did not intend to
intrude into the execution of operations, which was the responsibility of
the general-in-chief, but since the government was responsible for the
general conduct of the war, it had to ensure that all factors were considered before Nivelle launched a new offensive on which the safety of the
country could depend. After acknowledging unfavorable circumstances
in Russia and Italy, Painlevé said the entry of the United States into the
war would enable the allies to endure and eventually emerge victorious.
Given the depletion of France's manpower, he saw no reason to gamble
France's last reserves in an operation in which possible losses outweighed any conceivable gains. Painlevé thus argued for delaying the
offensive.

Nivelle spoke next and offered his analysis of the strategic situation. After acknowledging that Russia was in "anarchy" and that problems would continue in Russia and Italy, he emphasized the long period required for the United States to play a significant role. To await the arrival of American troops, he said, would require giving up all hope of ending the war in 1917. With unrestricted submarine warfare taking a heavy toll, he believed that time, which previously had favored the allies, now favored the Central Powers. He then reminded everyone that recent allied conferences had called for offensives by each of the Entente powers and that the French government had never ordered him to remain on the defensive. If the allies abandoned the offensive, the initiative would pass to the Germans, who had forty-three divisions available for an attack. From Nivelle's perspective, then, the risks entailed in canceling or delaying the offensive were much greater than those associated with an immediate offensive. At this point Ribot banged his fist on the table and said, "The offensive! The offensive! The defensive always leads to defeat!"[73]

As for Nivelle's concept of operations, the French general-in-chief insisted on the importance of a large offensive. By having numerous forces available he might achieve a breakthrough and exploit his success. He observed that "the objective of the battle is not to conquer this or that fortified position, [or] to gain a geographic objective, but to beat and, if possible, destroy the enemy army." He added, "there is no such thing as a half battle, neither in time nor in space. If one is considering a deliberate halt in the middle of the effort, on routes already opened through bloody sacrifice, it is better to cancel the offensive at the beginning."[74] He objected strongly to a partial offensive.

The army-group commanders also spoke. Expressing his views cautiously, Franchet d'Espèrey emphasized the significance of the agreements reached with the British and the folly of canceling the offensive three days before the British made their infantry assault on Arras. Micheler and Pétain also advised against canceling the attack, but both had doubts about a breakthrough. While Micheler thought he could capture the enemy's first and second positions, he did not believe he could penetrate the third and fourth. Pétain doubted that the offensive would achieve any strategic success, and he preferred a limited attack to capture the first and second positions. Of the four generals, Castelnau, who had just returned from Russia, was the most circumspect, but he advised the political leaders to replace Nivelle if they lacked confidence in him.

Toward the end of the meeting, Nivelle sensed the government's, as well as his army-group commanders', lack of confidence in him and offered his resignation. This unexpected turn of events surprised everyone, and a general chorus of objections came from around the table. Pétain said, "You cannot submit your resignation at this moment; that would have a very bad effect in the army and on the country." With Nivelle momentarily mollified, Poincaré summarized the results of the meeting: "An offensive battle followed by the prudent engagement of the reserves if a rupture of the enemy front is obtained, or the halting of the battle if a wide breach is not made in the enemy front in the first efforts." Ribot added, "if the desired results are not attained after a brief period, we will not stubbornly continue the battle indefinitely as we did on the Somme."[75] Poincaré then closed the meeting.

Though Pétain had participated in the criticism of Nivelle's plan, he later said the Compiègne meeting weakened the authority of the High Command and was a "huge mistake." It would have been wiser, he said, not to have voiced doubts about the plan's success.[76] Immediately after the meeting, however, Pétain unleashed a torrent of criticism. He described Nivelle as an arrogant individual who was inadequate intellectually and blinded by his passion. Since Nivelle had commanded only relatively small operations, he did not possess, said Pétain, an understanding of the situation France now faced. Micheler vented his own frustrations. It was foolish, he said, to expect a penetration and a strategic exploitation. He expressed strong doubts about Nivelle and Mangin and complained that Mangin, who commanded Sixth Army, was bypassing him and communicating directly with Nivelle. The day after the conference the liaison officer between Nivelle and the government noted Nivelle's nervousness. The officer observed, "the damage is done and cannot be undone."[77]

While Nivelle wrangled with the British and faced challenges from his political superiors and military subordinates, the French lost one of the most crucial elements needed for success—surprise. Throughout the preparation for the offensive, Nivelle paid insufficient attention to information security. He sometimes discussed his plan with visiting dignitaries and even showed them maps of his dispositions. During a visit to London he shocked his British hosts by discussing his plans in the presence of civilians who had no need to know the information. In the middle of February the Germans captured an order from an infantry division that revealed French plans for an offensive on the Aisne in April. On the night of April 4–5 a sergeant carrying a copy of his battalion's operations order, which included summaries of the missions of the three corps on Fifth Army's right, disappeared during a German attack. By the time word reached Nivelle the attack was a week away, and he refused to alter his scheme of maneuver.[78] His arrogance partially explains his violation of fundamental tenets of information security, but a more complete explanation comes from his having to do battle with the British, his political superiors, and his military subordinates in order to apply his "formula" and launch his offensive. As Lloyd George wrote, "General Nivelle in December was a cool and competent planner. By April he had become a crazy plunger."[79]

German commanders in the Aisne sector initially thought the information they received about the offensive had been planted to deceive them, and they refused to accept the possibility of a French offensive. After withdrawing from the Noyon salient and shortening their line, however, they recognized the possibility of a French offensive and increased the number of their forces in the Reims-Aisne sector. The Germans also transferred labor units into the Aisne sector to accelerate the completion of rear trenches. French intelligence assessments recognized that the Germans had strengthened the sector in front of Micheler's army group. A report on April 14 indicated that since February 15 the Germans had increased their strength from four to six divisions in front of Sixth Army and from five to nine or ten divisions in front of Fifth Army. The report also acknowledged that five to seven divisions were immediately available to the Germans in the Aisne sector and six more would be available after "a short delay." During the same period the French count of enemy artillery "emplacements" increased from 39 to 180–200 in front of Sixth Army and from 53 to 320 in front of Fifth Army.[80] Even though Nivelle

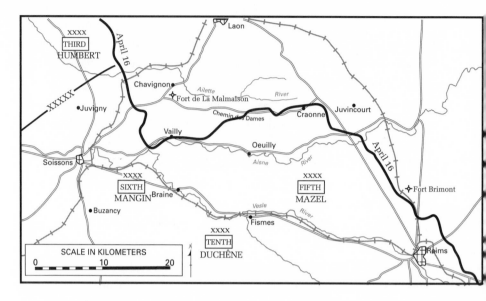

The Nivelle offensive, April 1917

knew the Germans had increased their strength in the Aisne sector to forty-one divisions and east of Reims to fourteen divisions, he refused to change his plan. He dismissed the importance of the increase and said the French could now capture a larger number of prisoners.

Nivelle's final plan had Reserve Army Group making the main attack, Central Army Group making an "auxiliary" attack, Northern Army Group playing a minor role, and the British conducting a supporting attack near Arras. Of the three army groups participating directly in the offensive, Reserve Army Group had the largest role. On April 1 Nivelle wrote to Micheler and told him that nothing had changed with regard to the methods and conditions necessary for a breakthrough. He then quoted his letters of December 30, 1916, and January 29, 1917, about the importance of "violence, brutality, and speed" in the coming offensive.[81] To make his attack Micheler had Sixth Army on his left and Fifth Army on his right. Tenth Army followed closely and expected to pass between the leading two armies as soon as a breakthrough occurred. Behind Tenth Army Nivelle held First Army and its two corps under his own control; he intended to commit First Army after the breakthrough.

In Reserve Army Group Mangin's Sixth Army had seventeen divisions grouped into five corps; it also had one territorial and one cavalry division. Its sector extended around an "elbow" in the front line, northeast of Soissons, which had one face running south to north (formed by the German withdrawal to the Hindenburg Line) and the other running west to east. Mangin placed one corps on the face running south to north and three others on the face running west to east. While two corps pinched off the elbow, two others would drive north. After a short advance, a fifth corps would insert itself between the two corps moving north. Mangin expected the corps moving north to advance three kilometers in the first three hours and six kilometers after six hours. He requested tank support, but all French tanks went to Fifth and Fourth armies.

To the right of Sixth Army, Mazel's Fifth Army had sixteen divisions plus a Russian brigade, grouped into five corps. Mazel placed all five corps on the front line. He also had three divisions, plus a second Russian brigade, in his reserves. He expected his frontline units to advance four kilometers in the first four hours and eight kilometers after six hours. To assist the assaulting infantry, Fifth Army had eight battalions of Schneider tanks (about 128 tanks). Expecting the tanks to be slow, Mazel warned his corps commanders that while the tanks could provide "serious support" to the infantry, units had to adhere to the timetable even if the tanks could not keep up. "The tanks," he said, "must conform to the conditions of combat established by the infantry."[82]

In Tenth Army, General Denis Duchêne had the mission of passing through the breach made by Sixth and Fifth armies. Consisting of four infantry and one cavalry corps, Tenth Army was organized into four lines, with four divisions in the first, three in the second, and four in the third. One cavalry division was in the second line, and another in the fourth. The army would begin moving three hours after the attack started and pass between Sixth Army's right and Fifth Army's left. The mass was supposed to advance in three bounds through the breach. By the end of the second day Tenth Army expected to be twenty-five kilometers beyond the original front line.

As for Central Army Group, Nivelle wanted Pétain to "profit" from Micheler's attack, but he expected the "principal" battle to occur across Reserve Army Group's entire front and the left of Central Army Group.

Pétain's army group consisted of two armies, with Fourth Army on its left and Second Army on its right. After the relief of General Roques on March 23, General Anthoine had taken command of Fourth Army and completed planning for its participation in the main battle. In the first draft of his plan, Anthoine said the mission of his army was to "support" Reserve Army Group's attack,[83] but Nivelle immediately informed him that Fourth Army had responsibility for an "auxiliary" not a "subordinate" attack and directed him to redo his plan.[84] Calling the attack "auxiliary" instead of "supporting" meant that Fourth Army had to penetrate and not just put pressure on enemy lines. Though Pétain tried to limit the power and scope of Anthoine's attack, Nivelle demanded a more energetic effort, and Anthoine quickly published another plan calling for a "frontal attack" by two corps along a front of eleven kilometers. With the center of this attack twenty kilometers east of Reims, Fourth Army aimed at breaking through the enemy's position on the first day and beginning an exploitation on the second day.

In Northern Army Group, which was on the left of Reserve Army Group, Franchet d'Espèrey had only Third Army and its three corps, and Nivelle expected him to do nothing more initially than maintain pressure on the Hindenburg Line. On March 29, however, d'Espèrey suggested modifying his army group's mission. Recognizing that the enemy had excellent observation points and strong artillery to his front, he proposed having Third Army seize the enemy's observation points near St.-Quentin before the attack by Micheler's Reserve Army Group. After Micheler advanced far enough north to threaten the enemy's artillery opposite Third Army, d'Espèrey would make a stronger attack. Nivelle approved this suggestion and ordered the attack to commence five days after Reserve Army Group started its offensive.

As Nivelle added other operations to his offensive, the final pieces of his plan came together. Among the additions were an attack by the Belgians and an artillery demonstration by Seventh Army in the Vosges Mountains. An important part of the final preparation pertained to the expected exploitation. The French general-in-chief ensured that Sixth, Fifth, Tenth, and Fourth armies had detailed plans, and his final instructions on April 4 dealt primarily with the movement of French forces after they broke through the enemy's defenses. "The objective," he reminded his army-group commanders, "remains the destruction of the principal mass of the enemy forces on the Western Front."[85] Such instructions did not mean that Nivelle's operational concepts had regressed to the blind charges of the *offensive à outrance*. A few days before the offensive began, his headquarters published operational and tactical guidance that warned, "the spirit of the offensive is not incompatible with caution."[86]

As with previous offensives, the date of attack underwent several revisions when weather and minor changes in plans forced delays. Because of these modifications Northern Army Group began its attack against the enemy's observations points near St.-Quentin on April 3 and 10, and the British began their infantry assault on April 9. For the main attack Micheler's army group sent its infantry forward on April 16 and Pétain's army group did likewise on April 17.

Before the assaults by Reserve and Central Army groups, the French pounded the German defenders with artillery. Though registration and counterbattery fires began on April 2, the French tried to conceal the registering of artillery until the fifth and sixth, when firing greatly increased in intensity. Beginning on the sixth, artillery fires concentrated on enemy defensive positions, and on April 9 the preparation began in earnest. On April 15 the artillery fired numerous chemical rounds. While Sixth Army concentrated its efforts along a fifteen-kilometer front, Fifth Army concentrated along a twenty-five-kilometer front. Fifth and Sixth armies had 5,350 cannon, including 2,000 field, 1,650 heavy, 1,500 accompanying, and 160 long-range heavy pieces. Between April 1 and May 5 Micheler's army group would fire more than 11,000,000 rounds of artillery, including 2,500,000 heavy rounds.

Despite this mass of artillery, its effectiveness was limited by weather, enemy air superiority, and supply difficulties. In his after-action report, General Micheler wrote: "During the preparation and the day of attack, the observation of fires, either by aerial observers or even by ground observers, was impeded considerably by very unfavorable atmospheric conditions." Between April 6 and 18, only the fourteenth was free of fog, rain, snow, or strong winds. To make matters worse, the Germans dominated the air over the Aisne sector, and French aerial observers could not adjust artillery. Since much of the enemy's position sat on the rear slope of the Chemin des Dames and could not be seen by ground observers, many defenders remained untouched by preparatory fires.[87] Compounding the problem was an unexpected shortage of ammunition at the firing batteries. In addition to the absence of well-trained ammunition specialists, who could have overcome some of the difficulties, cycles of freezing weather followed by heavy rains destroyed roads, and railways in the region lacked the capacity to transport the huge amounts of ammunition required by Reserve Army Group. Three days before the infantry assault a liaison officer to one of the assaulting corps reported that "the preparation is not what we hoped, what we expected." He added, "The infantry will find itself facing strong resistance. They will find the breaches not made or [already] repaired."[88]

When the infantry of Sixth and Fifth armies advanced at 0600 hours on April 16, they encountered uneven resistance. Atop the Chemin des Dames the two armies made only small gains. For Nivelle's offensive to succeed, II Colonial Corps, which occupied a position on the right of Sixth Army and had the mission of advancing over the top of the Chemin des Dames, had to advance six kilometers in six hours on the first day of the offensive. Tenth Army was immediately behind it and expected to pass on its right. The commander of II Colonial Corps described what happened to his unit on the first day:

> At H-hour, the troops approach in order the first enemy positions. The geographic crest is attained almost without losses; the enemy's artillery barrage is not very brisk and is sporadic. Nevertheless, our infantry advances with a slower speed than anticipated. The rolling barrage is unleashed almost immediately and steadily moves ahead of the first waves, which it quickly ceases to protect. A few machine guns on the plateau do not halt the . . . infantrymen, who are able to descend the northern side of the plateau to the edge of the steep slope descending into the valley of the Ailette [River]. There, they are welcomed and fixed in place by the deadly fire of numerous machine guns that, located on the [reverse side of the] slope, outside the reach of our projectiles, have remained undamaged.
>
> A few groups utilizing the approaches incompletely covered [by fire] succeed in descending the slope. But in general, the troops suffer considerable losses in a few minutes, particularly in leaders, and

[after] not succeeding in crossing this deadly zone, halt, take cover, and at some points withdraw to the first trench to their rear.

They are joined by the battalions [from increment] B, which depart at the scheduled hour and dissolve on the line of combat. The battalions [from increment] C, conforming to the combat plan, advance in their turn. A few of them . . . occupy the first German trenches or our jump-off trenches. In less than an hour, the fighting is stabilized. All attempts to regain forward movement fail as soon as they arrive on the line covered by enemy machine guns. The only possible movement is through . . . trenches using grenades, and [soon] this encounters growing resistance.

The enemy's reserves are in effect almost intact. Well protected in holes on the northern slope or in very strong dugouts, they have not suffered from the bombardment.[89]

Most units in Fifth and Sixth armies had the same experience as II Colonial Corps. A liaison officer reported: "The day has not yielded the results that we expected." He blamed this failure on enemy reinforcements, the strength of the enemy's defenses, defects in artillery preparation, bad weather, and difficult terrain. Of the two armies the only significant gains occurred in the center of Fifth Army (ten kilometers to the east of II Colonial). Sensing stronger resistance in front of Sixth Army and hoping for a penetration by Fifth Army, Nivelle tried to shift Fifth Army's axis of advance toward the northeast, but neither army made much progress on the seventeenth. During the night of April 17–18, however, Sixth Army pushed forward when the Germans began pulling out of the elbow in the front lines. By the time Sixth Army reached the new enemy position on the twentieth, its left had advanced six to seven kilometers, and it had captured 5,300 prisoners and vast quantities of equipment. This was the largest gain of the entire campaign. Meanwhile, Sixth Army's center, including II Colonial Corps, hardly moved. In an attempt to get Reserve Army Group moving, Nivelle ordered Tenth Army into the battle on April 19.

When Central Army Group attacked at 0445 hours on April 17, it made more progress than the centers of Fifth and Sixth armies, but its advance halted after only one or two kilometers. Aware that Micheler's army group had not broken through and that Fourth Army's flank would be exposed if it advanced too far, Pétain ordered the Fourth Army commander five hours after the beginning of the attack to proceed "methodically" and consolidate the captured terrain. Later that day he wired Nivelle and said he needed three new divisions to replace his frontline units. Unwilling to let Pétain halt Fourth Army's advance completely and thereby virtually guarantee the failure of the offensive, Nivelle quickly responded by sending another corps to Pétain and ordering him to continue advancing. Though Fourth Army advanced about one kilometer in its center the following day, gains on the next two days were extremely small.

By April 20 everyone knew the offensive had failed. On that day Nivelle met in Paris with Poincaré and Ribot. After the two political leaders asked him to avoid further losses, Nivelle said he envisaged "for the moment" nothing more than a series of small operations preceded by heavy artillery bombardment. He had inserted Tenth Army between Sixth and Fifth armies, he said, as an attempt to relieve some of the exhausted divisions. Subsequent operations would drive the enemy back from Reims, he thought, and complete the occupation of the Chemin des Dames. As for other efforts, he mentioned operations in Alsace and the Woëvre and expressed a willingness to support British efforts to seize Ostend on the coast. The following day Ribot, Painlevé, and Nivelle met with Lloyd George and agreed to continue the offensive in order to keep German reserves from shifting toward Haig's front.

To ensure that his army-group commanders understood the change in operational concept from all-out to limited offensives, Nivelle visited Micheler's and Pétain's headquarters on April 22 and directed them to drive the enemy back from Reims and complete the occupation of the Chemin des Dames. Though Nivelle had lowered his sights, his subordinate commanders had lost all confidence in him. On April 23 Poincaré sent Nivelle a message critical of preparations for a new operation. Since Nivelle had not yet decided the date or the details of the operation, it was clear to the French general-in-chief that someone was providing erroneous information to the president of the Republic. Suspecting that one of his subordinates had complained to the president, Nivelle exploded. He demanded severe punishment for this violation of military discipline. But despite Nivelle's objections the damage was done.

On April 24 Poincaré, Ribot, Painlevé, and Admiral Lucien Lacaze, the minister of the navy, met and discussed replacing Nivelle. The strongest criticisms came from Painlevé, who thought Nivelle had lost his authority over the army. Recognizing that Nivelle's dismissal would have negative effects on the army and public opinion, the political leaders hesitated and decided to have Nivelle appear before them and defend his operational plans. Nivelle appeared the following day. According to Painlevé the French general-in-chief said he intended to launch four separate operations at the end of April. A key component of his plan was Fifth Army's seizure of Brimont, the heights six kilometers north of Reims. During the discussion Painlevé informed the group of Pétain's and Mazel's reservations about the operation. The Central Army Group and Fifth Army commanders had termed the operation "hazardous, difficult, and bloody."[90] Though the politicians supported Nivelle's plans "in principle," they insisted that he return with more fully developed plans. Shortly thereafter, Painlevé met with Nivelle and discussed the possibility of his being replaced. After Painlevé promised not to embarrass him, Nivelle said he would submit his resignation if the government requested.[91]

For the next several days France's political leaders debated the fate of Nivelle and the High Command. Political leaders met again on April 26, but only Painlevé wanted Nivelle relieved immediately. In his diary Ribot noted the contradictory and shabby role played by Mazel. Though the general had assured Nivelle he could attack and seize Brimont, he had told Painlevé that the operation would fail and result in 60,000 casualties. Ribot noted in his diary, "The deputies and the minister of war are destroying discipline by provoking such critiques."[92] Two days later political leaders accepted an idea proposed by Painlevé: Pétain would be Nivelle's chief of staff and his designated successor. Ribot discussed this alternative with Nivelle, who had already discussed it with Pétain. Though Nivelle liked the idea, Pétain refused. Finally, on April 29, the politicians decided not to relieve Nivelle but to keep him as general-in-chief and appoint Pétain chief of staff of the army. Poincaré made the appointment that day.

Except for bureaucratic scuffling, most of the fighting associated with the Nivelle offensive had ended by April 25, and a sense of failure swept over the army and the government. Between April 16 and 25 the French suffered—according to estimates by French historical services—134,000 casualties on the Aisne, including 30,000 killed, 100,000 wounded, and 4,000 captured. Though more soldiers had died in Joffre's offensives in 1915, the casualties in Nivelle's offensive occurred over a relatively brief period and exceeded those of any month since November 1914. The French did make some gains. From April 16 to May 10, Fourth, Fifth, Sixth, and Tenth armies captured 28,500 prisoners and 187 cannon, and Sixth Army's advance proved to be one of the largest made thus far by the French in the war. Beyond a doubt the combination of French gains and German losses in the Nivelle offensive would have been trumpeted as a major achievement earlier in the war. The sense of failure came less from the casualties inflicted on the Germans and the terrain gained than on the deflating of extravagant hopes for success. Shortly before the offensive, morale had soared amidst expectations of success; the failure of the attack caused morale to collapse. In the end, the important facts were the frailty of the French army and the collapse of its morale, not the losses suffered in the operation. The army was very fragile when it undertook the Nivelle offensive; it was even more fragile when the operation ended.

Though Nivelle's enthusiasm and confidence had briefly infected the entire French army, his failure to break through German defenses yielded one of the worst disasters of the war. The offensive had done little more than demonstrate how the power of French artillery had increased since August 1914. The effect of Nivelle's offensive was not yet apparent, but the appointment of Pétain as chief of staff marked the beginning of new strategy and operational methods for France.

CHAPTER 8

A Strategy of "Healing" and Defense

Late 1917

W HEN POLITICAL AUTHORITIES appointed Nivelle general-in-chief in December 1916, they opted for an offensive strategy and a powerful attack. After they appointed Pétain chief of the General Staff on April 29, 1917, they adapted France's efforts to a new strategic and operational environment and opted for a defensive strategy. The revival of Austria-Hungary, increase in British operational capabilities, collapse of Russia, entry of the United States into the war, and weakness of the French army compelled them to make significant adjustments. Even though Pétain initially had only limited power, he quickly garnered enough power and influence to reshape France's efforts in the war. As General John J. Pershing said after the war, Pétain's appointment "had as important an effect on the outcome of the war as the later appointment of a supreme commander for the Allied armies."[1]

Before August 1914 no one would have expected Pétain to play a crucial role in the history of France. Born on April 24, 1856, he began the war as a fifty-eight-year-old brigade commander who had distinguished himself in his military service primarily by his thorough understanding of the relationship between artillery and infantry and by his willingness to disagree with his superiors. An efficiency report in 1903 mentioned him as one of the top two or three authorities in France on infantry tactics and added, "He defends his views with the power of a debater and the ardor of a champion."[2] By May 1917, political and military leaders knew him as an ardent critic of ambitious offensives aiming at a breakthrough and an effective proponent of carefully planned attacks with limited objectives.

When Pétain became chief of the General Staff, France's political leaders initially envisaged his having only a limited role. The president of the Council of Ministers, Ribot, wanted him to act under the authority of the minister of war and become involved only in those military affairs in which the government was involved. In other words, Pétain would not direct operations. In essence, the politicians revived the post that Messimy had suppressed in the reforms of 1911 when he combined the responsibilities of chief of staff and vice president of the Superior Council of War and gave them to Joffre as chief of the General Staff.

During the two weeks Pétain served as chief of the General Staff, however, he played a larger role than politicians envisaged for him. On the day of his appointment, April 29, Painlevé called Nivelle and informed him of Pétain's new duties. Given Pétain's reservations about Nivelle's operational plans, Painlevé asked that a soon-to-be-unleashed attack be delayed until the two military leaders discussed the plans. Nivelle reacted angrily to what he deemed interference in his conduct of operations and demanded a written confirmation of this order from Painlevé. Then, after discussing the operation with Pétain, he told Micheler to launch the attack in the vicinity of Reims but to make it more limited than initially planned. Thus, as Stephen Ryan has noted, Pétain, not Painlevé, put the "halter" on Nivelle on April 29 and thereby saved Fifth Army from suffering additional casualties.[3]

The British dreaded the prospect of Pétain's replacing Nivelle and changing French strategy. General Sir Henry Wilson, the British liaison officer to the GQG, wrote in his diary: "Three schools—Somme, Verdun, Pétain. . . . Somme was *usure* [attrition]; Verdun was a whirlwind and a crash through; Pétain was squat, do little and have small losses."[4] At a meeting of the War Cabinet on April 25, British leaders discussed the possibility of France's adopting a defensive strategy and awaiting the arrival of American forces. Concerned about the effect of such a change, they asked the French for a conference to discuss the conduct of the war. In preparation for that meeting, the British War Cabinet met on May 1 and considered a memorandum from Robertson. The allies faced a "drastic change in the military situation," Robertson insisted, because of France's reluctance to "continue serious offensive operations" and its preference for only "local offensive operations." Allied inaction, he said, would leave Germany free to attack Russia and Italy, provide the Germans time to recover from recent French and British offensives, hand the enemy a propaganda bonanza, and let the Central Powers take advantage of their gains in the east, particularly in their obtaining food from Romania.[5] Ironically, Joffre had used variations of these points in 1915 and 1916 to argue for greater efforts from the British.

When the conference began on May 4, military authorities (Robertson, Haig, Pétain, Nivelle) met in the morning and then presented their conclusions that afternoon to political representatives (including Lloyd George, Ribot, and Painlevé). The afternoon session began with Robertson's reading a document summarizing the results of the morning's discussions. After explaining that the generals had agreed to maintain an offensive strategy but change their methods, Robertson added:

> It is no longer a question of aiming at breaking through the enemy's front and aiming at distant objectives. It is now a question of wearing down and exhausting the enemy's resistance, and if and when this is achieved to exploit it to the fullest extent possible. In order to wear him down we are agreed that it is absolutely necessary to fight with all our available forces, with the object of destroying the enemy's divisions. We are unanimously of opinion that there is no half-way between this course and fighting defensively, which, at this stage of the war, would be tantamount to acknowledging defeat. We are all of opinion that our object can be obtained by relentlessly attacking with limited objectives, while making the fullest use of our artillery.[6]

The British had come to the conference intending, Lloyd George later said, to "press the French to continue the offensive,"[7] and Pétain had readily agreed to do so, since he had no intention of remaining solely on the defensive. Without fully informing Lloyd George, Robertson and Haig had worked out a *modus vivendi* with the French military leaders according to which the British would carry the main burden of offensive operations during the summer. This arrangement ended Haig's subordination to the French under the Calais agreement and ensured that the British would make the main attack and the French the supporting attack for the coming campaign. Pétain and Haig also agreed on another point: "Plan to be kept a secret. Governments," Haig wrote in his diary, "not to be told any details concerning the place or date of any attack."[8]

The conference on May 4 thus established the broad framework of French strategy for the remainder of the year. Yet that strategy would become more conservative and cautious in coming weeks as mutinies engulfed the army. While Pétain quelled unrest, restored the soldiers' fighting spirit, and initiated a broad program of rearmament, he had no choice but to limit the scope and number of operations. Not until the mutinies subsided and order returned did he devise a more aggressive strategy. Within the defensive strategy he preferred, however, he envisaged nothing more aggressive than limited offensives.

Following the Paris conference, additional changes occurred in the French High Command. On May 11 the government clarified the role of the chief of the General Staff and modeled the position after the British chief of the Imperial General Staff. A presidential decree identified the French chief of the General Staff as the "delegate" of the minister of war, who would "study" all technical questions pertaining to military operations and support services. He would advise the minister of war on the overall conduct of the war, cooperation of allied armies, planning of operations by theater commanders (who would be responsible for executing plans), construction of military equipment and weapons, allocation of resources in the theaters, and transportation of troops and equipment.[9] Though these powers were substantial, they fell short of what Pétain desired. Shortly after leaving Central Army Group, he had submitted a proposal to make the chief of the General Staff the "delegate" of the War Committee, not of the minister of war. Had political authorities accepted Pétain's proposal, they would have made the chief of the General Staff the most powerful individual in France's defense establishment and would have transformed the minister of war into nothing more than a "purveyor" of personnel and equipment.[10] The May 11 presidential decree, however, made the chief of the General Staff subordinate to the minister of war and only slightly more powerful than the pre-1911 chief of staff.

After quarreling between Nivelle and three of his subordinates (Micheler, Mangin, and Mazel) worsened, Ribot told Poincaré that replacing Nivelle with Pétain was "inevitable." Painlevé preferred having Pétain become general-in-chief and work beside the minister of war while another general commanded the armies in north and northeastern France, but Ribot considered this a "dangerous" solution and objected to it. Desiring a chief of the General Staff who was not as well known as Pétain, Painlevé then suggested Fayolle, and Ribot countered by nominating Foch. Ribot had discussed with Pétain the possibility of Fayolle's becoming chief of the General Staff and knew Pétain preferred Foch.[11] On May 10 the Council of Ministers supported Painlevé's request for Nivelle's resignation, but to everyone's surprise the beleaguered general-in-chief refused. Nivelle told the liaison officer to the government, "They want my hide. . . . But neither my dignity, my conscience, nor my sense of what I owe my country permits me to play their game."[12] On the morning of May 15 Nivelle met with Poincaré and Painlevé, and in a farcical display of political faintheartedness, neither politician had the nerve to dismiss him.[13] That same day the Council of Ministers made Nivelle an army-group commander, thereby salvaging some of his pride, and had Pétain replace him as general-in-chief. When Pétain formally took command of the armies of the north and northeast on May 17, Foch became chief of the General Staff. As for Nivelle's command prospects, there were no vacancies at the head of the army groups, since Fayolle had assumed command of Central Army Group in early May. Without an army group to command, Nivelle went on leave, and on June 29 Pétain placed him at the disposition of the minister of war after annulling his status as an army-group commander. Nivelle eventually became commander of French forces in North Africa. The leading military actors now had the parts they would play in the final act of the war.

Luck played an important part in Foch's appointment as chief of the General Staff. In December 1916, as criticism of the French High Command escalated, Joffre had removed Foch, who had directed the battle on the Somme, from command of Northern Army Group. Joffre told Foch,

"Poincaré called me and ordered me to relieve you."[14] Foch objected strongly and complained so loudly that his voice could be heard in neighboring offices. Fortunate not to be forced into retirement, he was appointed to lead a small planning cell that analyzed courses of action should the Germans violate Switzerland's neutrality. Though his new duties seemed minor in comparison to those of the past, he—unlike Pétain—had time to rest and recuperate for the final phase of the war, and he gained important insights into the relationship between the Italian and French fronts. At the end of January he replaced Castelnau temporarily as commander of Eastern Army Group when Castelnau traveled to Petrograd for an allied conference. In early April Painlevé ordered Foch to Italy to coordinate plans for reinforcing the Italians with French and British troops if the Germans combined with the Austrians and launched a powerful attack. During the crucial discussions in Paris on the appointment of a chief of the General Staff, Pétain's support for Foch probably kept him from being relegated to a secondary role, far removed from real power.

After assuming his new duties, Foch continued to play a smaller role than Pétain. His understanding of the strategic importance of Italy and Switzerland and his experience with the British, however, enabled him to see the war more broadly than any other French officer. That vision, as well as his language skills, enabled him to curry favor with Lloyd George, especially when he supported the British prime minister's interest in an attack in the Italian theater against Austria. Foch also customarily attended all the meetings of the War Committee, while Pétain attended only the particularly important ones. Those meetings provided Foch the opportunity to demonstrate his many talents, especially his ability to reduce complex concepts into simple phrases or ideas. In the end, he took advantage of the opportunities afforded him and skillfully maneuvered through the complex obstacles of domestic and allied politics to emerge from Pétain's shadow.

In May 1917, however, Pétain dominated the army. While he had less legal authority than Joffre at the height of his powers, he was highly regarded by the officers and soldiers of the army. Much of his influence came from the fact that all of France knew how sincerely and deeply he cared about and for his soldiers. Though his influence over soldiers played no direct role in his selection as chief of the General Staff, his reputation for husbanding the lives of his men proved invaluable when mutinies broke out in late April 1917. French soldiers knew Pétain would not waste their lives and limbs, and they responded reluctantly but positively to his leadership and his efforts to restore order. Pershing later said, "no other officer in France could have performed the task so well."[15]

The mutinies began in the wake of Nivelle's offensive. In *Les mutineries de 1917*, which stands as the standard work on the subject, Guy Pédroncini divided the mutinies into four phases. In the first phase, which occurred between April 16 and May 15, twenty-six incidents of "collective indiscipline" occurred. In the second phase, between May 16 and 31, disorder spread, and forty-six incidents occurred. More of the French army, including entire divisions, became involved in incidents during this period. In the third phase, which extended from June 1 to 6, incidents became more violent and threatened the functioning of the army. For the first time soldiers beat to death or shot their fellow countrymen, perhaps as many as six. Most of the acts of indiscipline that resulted in court-martial convictions occurred during this brief period. In the next phase, which extended through the end of June, the number of incidents declined, and order returned.[16] Though acts of indiscipline occurred in July, including refusals to enter the trenches, most incidents involved drunken soldiers at railway stations yelling "Vive la paix! Vive la Révolution!" Whether mutinous or only expressions of discontent, incidents after April 16 affected fifty-four divisions. Sixth Army was the most gravely affected, but Fourth, Tenth, Fifth, and Second armies—listed in descending order of effect—also experienced significant turmoil. Except for Second Army, the units most affected were involved directly or indirectly in Nivelle's offensive.

Most of the incidents, as the French official history notes, involved demonstrations against the war: "revolutionary slogans and songs, throwing of stones, breaking of windows, destruction of materiel. Several fires were set, and a few assaults on officers occurred. The indiscipline took the form of refusals to enter the trenches, above all to attack." Referring to the incidents as "collective acts of indiscipline," the official history avoids using the term "mutiny" even though the soldiers refused orders, encouraged resistance among others, and occasionally demanded revolutionary change.[17] During the crisis, however, Pétain described the incidents as "mutinies" to the War Committee.[18] In one example of the incidents, two regiments from 5th Infantry Division, yelling "Down with the war, and long live the Russian revolution," decided to march on Paris and send a delegation to the Chamber of Deputies; they wanted an immediate end to the war. Other regiments from the same division refused to enter the trenches. In the end, however, officers of 5th Division, as in other units, convinced the soldiers to return to their duties and gradually reestablished control.[19]

On May 30, just before the period of the most extreme incidents, Pétain's staff offered an explanation of the causes of the mutinies. After acknowledging that "indiscipline in the army comes from a variety of sources of which the relative importance cannot be ascertained," the report broke the causes down into two categories: "those which come from the conditions on the front, [and] those which are the result of external influences on this life." Among the causes associated with life on the front were weakness of the military justice system, inadequate number of leaves, lack of rest between battles, and drunkenness. Among the external causes were pacifist propaganda, unfavorable orientation of the press, and ideas about peace stemming from the Russian revolution.[20] In 1926 an aging Pétain published an account of the mutinies and cited three main causes: a pacifist propaganda campaign in the winter of 1916–17, exhaustion and grievances among frontline soldiers, and false optimism and imprudence among high-ranking leaders. Of these three causes Pétain gave first place to pacifist propaganda, the effects of which were worsened by the government's complacency and by the publications of an irresponsible press. He argued that propaganda flowed from the interior to the front.[21]

Recent historical studies cast doubt on the effects of subversion from the rear. According to Pédroncini, the protests did not stem from pacifist propaganda but instead came from exhaustion at the front and dissatisfaction with the conduct of the war. Leonard V. Smith, while offering new ideas about the relationship between soldiers and their commanders in his study of the 5th Infantry Division, has presented additional evidence demonstrating that mutinies originated in units in or near the front lines, not with civilians in the rear.[22] Adding to the weight of evidence about dissatisfaction in frontline units, Nivelle told army commanders a month before the offensive that a review of soldiers' correspondence revealed unsatisfactory morale in some units. Complaints gleaned by postal authorities included "bad food, lack of clothing, sustained fatigue, unskilled or indifferent leaders, length of inaction." Nivelle added, "Responsibility for this situation falls entirely on commanders."[23] In the weeks preceding and following the April offensive, biweekly reports on morale by postal authorities catalogued hopes rising dramatically before the attack and crashing with its failure. Even the entry of the United States into the war did not give soldiers hope. Postal authorities on May 1 reported, "Many [soldiers] think that the entry of America into the war, while giving us numerous advantages, will prolong the war at least a year and, by the relief of workers [who will be replaced by Americans], send thousands of Frenchmen to their deaths."[24] Two weeks later postal authorities included words used commonly by soldiers to describe the failed offensive: "fiasco, lynching, botched, misfire, massacre, butchery, failure." The report said soldiers blamed "indiscipline" on the command, "harshly" criticized their leaders, and hoped for "immediate peace."[25] Clearly, the bursting of inflated expectations caused morale to plummet even lower than the "crisis" level of December 1916.

To restore discipline among the rebellious soldiers, Pétain relied on a combination of carrot and stick. Recognizing that many of the soldiers' complaints were valid, he acted energetically to increase leaves, improve food, make transportation more available for soldiers on leave, establish rest camps, and end drunkenness. Among other measures, he authorized soldiers to take ten days' leave every four months, and he ordered the provision of fresh fruits and vegetables and the placement of field kitchens closer to frontline troops. As for the stick, Pétain established procedures on June 1 to accelerate the judicial process, but he did not compromise the judicial process or conduct "kangaroo courts." Despite the swiftness of judgment for some soldiers, most courts-martial did not take place until the mutinies were essentially over. Pétain also did not resort to the "decimation of regiments"—that is, the execution of one of ten mutineers. Instead of overwhelming the courts with thousands of cases, he sought to make examples of a few soldiers in each of the mutinous regiments and executed one soldier on June 6—after a court-martial—despite the objections of representatives in the Chamber of Deputies. During the height of the mutinies about 50 percent of those tried and executed had their court-martial within three weeks of the incident. According to Pédroncini's statistics, the army convicted 3,427 soldiers of offenses committed during the mutinies and sentenced 554 to death. Only 55 were executed, said Pétain, including 7 who went before the firing squad "immediately."[26] After a careful review of the records Pédroncini concluded that the French executed 52 and may have executed 10 others, for a total of 62.[27] More recently Nicolas Offenstadt counted "about forty" soldiers executed for offenses associated with the 1917 mutinies, a number significantly lower than the 600 or so executed during the entire war for a variety of offenses.[28] Pétain thus used punishment sparingly and avoided a wholesale execution of convicted soldiers, but he acted firmly and swiftly against carefully selected individuals. On June 18 he wrote, "I have pressed hard for the repression of these grave acts of indiscipline; I will maintain this pressure with firmness but without forgetting that it is applied to soldiers who, for three years, have been with us in the trenches and are 'our soldiers.'"[29]

Pétain's most significant steps aimed at restoring the confidence of soldiers in their leaders and in themselves. Knowing the importance of having soldiers see and trust their commanders, he prescribed weekly meetings on the grounds that "by explaining, one achieves understanding and arrives quickly at a community of ideas, the basis of cohesion." He also directed general officers and members of their staffs to "show themselves frequently in the trenches" and promised harsh punishment to officers who did not do their duty and restore order.[30] To reassure soldiers, he personally visited numerous units, supposedly seeing and speaking to the men of ninety divisions. During these visits he described the strategic situation and emphasized the enormous resources of the United States and the inevitability of France's victory with America as an ally. He also explained what was happening on other portions of the front in France and Italy, thereby ensuring the soldiers understood how they fitted within the broader sweep of the war. In numerous presentations he convinced his listeners that the safety of France depended on their resolve and that the sacrifices of their predecessors should not be in vain. Through other actions, such as visiting mess halls and rest billets, he demonstrated his concern for the well-being of the soldiers. He also published a series of articles titled "Why We Fight" and distributed a memorandum on the strategic situation that ended: "France can expect with reasonable confidence a victorious peace that is indispensable to it and that it deserves because of its heavy sacrifices."[31] Given Pétain's enormous credibility among French soldiers, one cannot overstate the importance of his words and actions. No other officer—including Joffre, Nivelle, and Foch—could have accomplished what he did.

Throughout the months of disorder, the French feared that the Germans would learn of the mutinies and take advantage of the opportunity to make large gains. Adding to their worries, they intercepted a German radio-telegram message in mid-May that included information about three French battalions calling for an end to the war and refusing to leave their trenches in an attack. Also, they knew that at least one German newspaper had published comments from a French soldier about two infantry regiments' refusing to enter the trenches.[32] Pétain later told Painlevé that his moment of greatest fear during the war was during this period. Though he initially did not provide France's political leaders with a candid assessment, they quickly learned of the army's "malaise" through numerous letters from soldiers at the front. On May 30 the GQG completed a report on discipline indicating that the first incidents had occurred at the beginning of May, and Pétain sent the minister of war a summary of the "collective acts of indiscipline" during the past "several days."[33] The next day he formally warned political leaders of the great "danger" associated with the "demoralization" of the army.[34] As mutinies increased in the last week of May and reached their high point in the first week of June, the High Command limited communications between frontline units and the rear and told British officials almost nothing. On June 2 Pétain's chief of staff gave Haig brief information about the unrest but avoided using the word "mutiny." Yet he made it clear that French soldiers needed rest and would not be ready for a "real" offensive for at least a month. Other British liaison officers were told of "some insubordination" among French troops behind the front lines. British political leaders first learned of the unrest on June 6 and received a more complete report on June 11.[35]

Fortunately for France, Pétain's emphasis on limited offensives strengthened soldiers' confidence in their leaders and encouraged rapid "healing" of their will to fight. Unlike Nivelle, he did not promise a quick ending of the war. The war, he believed, could be won only after a series of limited offensives, not after one single battle. In response to a question from the minister of war, he wrote:

> In the actual state of equilibrium existing between the [opposing] forces, [a breakthrough] is not possible. Experience—and reason— prove this. The capacity of resistance provided by modern fire permits personnel already in place to hold a continuous front between the sea and Switzerland. Railways facilitate the convergence of reserves on any point in minimum time (seven days to go from the Russian front to the French front). A breach can be envisaged only when successful pushes or attrition have created intervals in the enemy's line or have diminished German reserves considerably.[36]

Neither Pétain nor anyone else knew how long it would take before "intervals" appeared in the enemy's lines.

On May 19 Pétain published Directive No. 1 and provided the entire army a clear explanation of his operational concept. The directive repeated the idea of an "equilibrium of opposing forces" that would prevent an attacker from rupturing an opponent's defenses and conducting a strategic exploitation. To function within this equilibrium, the French could not remain passive and yield the initiative completely to the enemy; they had to attack. Instead of seeking a breakthrough, however, Pétain intended to launch limited offensives that would incur "minimum losses" but attrit the enemy. To lessen casualties he planned on massing artillery on the enemy's forward positions and then sending infantry into the destroyed trenches. Rather than fire into the huge area between the enemy's front and rear lines and thereby dilute the artillery's effect, he preferred concentrating all French rounds on the enemy's forward positions and having the infantry advance only a short distance. He also ruled out a series of successive attacks like those in the Somme offensive of 1916 or the coming Passchendaele offensive. Once in place the infantry would consolidate their gains and not have to endure a second or third advance with inadequate artillery support.[37]

Pétain's limited offensives thus differed from continuous and methodical battles and in the simplest terms consisted only of the first step in the methodical battle. The infantry would advance a short distance and not attempt continuous or successive movements. Since attacks focused only on immediate objectives, the artillery did not have to displace forward, and commanders did not need to organize tightly sequenced, step-by-step operations. Limited offensives also did not require days of preparatory fires and used far less artillery. Since attacking forces did not have to accumulate huge ammunition stockpiles or construct railways and roads for transporting ammunition, they had a better chance of surprising the enemy. The exhausted French soldiers welcomed Pétain's new methods; they knew their lives would not be squandered in pointless operations.

Reforms associated with limited offensives also strengthened French defenses. That is, by improving his forces' ability to move units from one point to another in order to make a surprise attack, Pétain improved their ability to respond to an enemy offensive. In fact his concept of limited offensives blurred the distinction between offense and defense. A memorandum on the application of Directive No. 1 included an entire section on "defensive organization," most of which focused on a "reinforcement plan" that was "simple" and "flexible."[38] Nivelle's previous efforts to reduce the number of troops in the trenches in order to mass sufficient forces for his offensive facilitated Pétain's efforts. Nivelle had emphasized placing only a few troops in forward trenches, spreading machine guns in depth throughout a position, and preparing minutely detailed plans for rushing reinforcements to threatened sectors. A week before the April offensive, Nivelle had appointed General Roques, who had been relieved from command of Fourth Army, to inspect defenses along the French front. Published after Nivelle's relief, Roques' report provided useful information to Pétain in his efforts to ensure that no weak points existed in the long front line. Other improvements, which originated during Joffre's reign but came to fruition in the summer of 1917, pertained to the French shift in some sectors from a continuous line of trenches to centers of resistance. Linked by communications trenches, the centers increased the solidity of the front and required fewer soldiers than lines of trenches. With these and other ideas shaping their efforts, French commanders spent much of May and June improving their defenses.

The harsh realization that France was running out of men added to the urgency of Pétain's reforms. On June 20 the General Staff in Paris published a study analyzing the effects of France's looming shortage of soldiers. The study stated:

> It is not necessary to deny that after three years of war and after having supported until now the greater part of the common effort, the French army has lost many of its offensive qualities. The crisis of personnel, which can only become more acute with each passing day, can only aggravate the situation. Consequently, the day is approaching when a large offensive by us must be curtailed because we cannot fill the vacancies in our units.[39]

The French had tried to keep their ranks filled by bringing "classes" of conscripts into the army before they turned twenty-one, compelling military service through age forty-nine, lowering physical standards, and rushing wounded back into the trenches as quickly as possible. Heavy losses compelled them to reduce their divisions from four to three regiments and their infantry companies from 250 to 200 riflemen. They also eliminated one infantry company in each battalion but added a machine-gun company. Although the number of artillerymen and other specialists increased, changes in the organization of infantry units reduced the typical division from 15,000–16,000 to 13,000 soldiers. Despite these adjustments, the French still did not have enough men to fill their infantry companies and battalions. To fill units, Pétain faced the unwelcome prospect in May 1917 of having to disband some infantry and cavalry divisions. To avoid this, he could ask the Italians to send workers to France, the British to extend their front, and the Americans to amalgamate infantry companies into French battalions and regiments. Yet the only sure option was to conserve soldiers' lives.

In a quest for better methods, Pétain directed his staff on June 23 to review operational and tactical methods. The "most likely" course of action for the Germans, he said, was a "combination of a frontal attack and a maneuver through Switzerland against France." It would be "difficult," he said, to find sufficient soldiers to oppose such an invasion, and it would be "impossible" for the French and British armies to halt such an attack on their front and remain in their "first" position. To hold until the Americans entered the line, the French had to develop better methods and assemble a mobile reserve of at least forty divisions.[40] The quest for new methods included a close examination of the failed offensive in April. Several studies carefully analyzed the employment of tanks on the Chemin des Dames and emphasized both their fragility and the significant assistance they provided the infantry. One study looked at artillery and compared its employments in Champagne on September 25, 1915, the Somme on July 1, 1916, and the Chemin des Dames on April 16, 1917. Open to any option that might provide an advantage, the French considered several new technologies, including a "ground torpedo" and a British "projector" that shot "gas bombs."[41]

Pétain also initiated a massive rearmament program that favored materiel over manpower. The four major components were aircraft, heavy artillery, tanks, and chemicals. The goal of the aircraft program, as Painlevé said, was to make the French "masters of the air."[42] Germany's control of the air over the Chemin des Dames in April had severely disrupted artillery preparation and underlined the importance of air superiority. Accordingly, the French sought to improve the quality and increase the number of their aircraft. In January 1917 French armies in north and northeast France had 1,420 aircraft; by June they had 2,100, 700 of which were fighters and 300 bombers. Counting those in training schools, reserves, and Macedonia, the French had about 6,000 aircraft, many of which were obsolete. Insisting that aviation was "indispensable" to success, Pétain initiated a program on September 6 aiming for 2,870 modern aircraft.

The main thrust of Pétain's artillery program was to achieve the goals of the May 30, 1916, program, which had sought a great increase in heavy artillery. French factories focused on manufacturing 155-mm short-range cannon and soon raised their monthly production from 82 on May 31 to 180 on August 31. During the same period factories decreased monthly production of 75-mm cannon, reducing their average from 316 in the first quarter of 1917, to 241 in the third quarter, to 150 in the fourth quarter. The new program thus shifted priority from 75-mm to 155-mm cannon, which had greater effect against entrenchments. A second aspect of the program made French artillery more flexible and more mobile. The idea of a mobile general reserve of artillery had surfaced in January 1917, when Nivelle had established such a reserve and incorporated tractor-drawn regiments into it. A mobile artillery reserve also appealed to Pétain, since it accorded completely with his operational concept of moving artillery quickly and easily and catching the enemy by surprise with a strong but limited attack. As part of the overall program, Pétain sought ten regiments of tractor-drawn artillery; he also attempted to resolve questions about control of this general reserve.

To complement the artillery program, the French ordered what Painlevé described as an "enormous" number of chemical and smoke rounds. In previous battles chemicals had proved particularly effective in counterbattery fires and against bunkers and underground shelters. Instead of squandering the infantry's lives in vain charges against fortified positions, Pétain intended to neutralize the enemy with chemicals. He also intended to cover the advance of infantry and tanks with clouds of smoke.

Pétain placed special emphasis on increasing the number of French tanks. On the eve of Nivelle's offensive the French had 256 tanks, including 208 Schneider and 48 Saint-Chamond. These tanks entered combat on April 16 and again on May 5. Though they proved useful in the first attack, they performed far better in the second one. Those who witnessed the performance of the tanks agreed with an officer who described them as a "precious aid for our infantry."[43] With the experience of two battles behind them, the French recognized the advantages of tanks that were lighter and more mobile than the Schneider and Saint-Chamond models. Fortunately for them, General Jean Estienne, who had conceived and developed the first French tanks, had already recognized the advantages of a light tank capable of accompanying the infantry and providing support with 37-mm cannon and machine guns. The first prototype of a light tank, the Renault FT-17, arrived on April 9, 1917, for trials. Before its arrival, Estienne increased the order from 150 to 1,150. Thus, when Pétain became chief of the General Staff and then general-in-chief, the French tank program was already well under way, but on June 20 Pétain increased the order for light tanks to 3,500. He also increased the order for Schneider tanks from 400 to 600. The French expected 80 FT-17 tanks to arrive in July and 110 in August. To ensure that French soldiers gained the maximum benefit from these weapons, as well as from new aircraft and heavy artillery, Pétain placed a special premium on training and on combining all combat arms into a tightly functioning team. To avoid unnecessary losses, he knew he had to do far more than just "wait for the Americans and the tanks."

As Pétain worked tirelessly to "heal" French soldiers and provide them the best possible weapons and doctrine, General Pershing arrived in Paris on June 13, and a U.S. infantry battalion marched through the city on July 4. The psychological effect of the Americans' arrival could not have been more opportune, for the French army was on the edge of disintegration and defeat. When Pershing arrived in Paris at 1830 hours on June 13, Painlevé, Foch, and Joffre, as well as several other dignitaries, met him and his staff at the Gare du Nord. Outside the railway station thousands of French citizens awaited the Americans. Pershing described the tumultuous welcome: "Men, women, and children absolutely packed every foot of space, even to the windows and housetops. Cheers and tears were mingled together and shouts of enthusiasm fairly rent the air. Women climbed into our automobiles screaming, 'Vive l'Amérique,' and threw flowers until we were literally buried. Everybody waved flags and banners."[44] One of the U.S. officers with Pershing wrote, "This country is well nigh bled white . . and our coming is hailed as the coming of the Lord."[45] When Pershing met Pétain on June 16, the French general-in-chief emphasized the importance of the American presence and said, "I hope it is not too late."[46]

A mission headed by Marshal Joffre had accomplished much of the initial coordination pertaining to the entry of the Americans into the war. Joffre had arrived in Washington on April 26 and participated in discussions about shipping thousands of troops and tons of equipment to Europe. While in the United States, he met with Secretary of War Newton D. Baker and U.S. Army Chief of Staff General Hugh L. Scott; he also met with President Woodrow Wilson. The meeting with Wilson proved particularly interesting in that Joffre advised him to select a commanding general who had the "aptitude for training troops rather than according to his aptitude for conceiving strategic plans and preparing vast enterprises of war."[47] He wanted the French to do the strategic thinking and high-level planning for the Americans, but he recognized the American desire for autonomy. Consequently, he urged Paris not to press for the amalgamation of American companies and battalions into French regiments, and he remained a firm opponent of amalgamation for the remainder of the war.

From the moment Joffre first arrived in the United States, he lobbied for the Americans to operate in the Lorraine sector and to use ports on the Atlantic coast. When he met with President Wilson, he advised him not to land American troops in Britain but to land them directly on the soil of France. On May 14 he and Secretary of War Baker signed a convention in which the Americans pledged to send an expeditionary force to France and to have the first troops depart the United States around June 1. This convention identified the Atlantic coast of France as the probable location of the American base. U.S. officials quickly recognized the merits of using the excellent ports near Bordeaux, La Rochelle, and Nantes in the estuaries of the Loire and Garonne rivers. Rail lines ran from these ports toward Nancy and Épinal in Lorraine without passing through the bottleneck of Paris. Moreover, the ports were outside the area normally patrolled by German submarines seeking to blockade the British Isles.

Shortly before his departure from the United States, Joffre met with General Pershing and suggested having the Americans occupy part of the front in Lorraine. To encourage the newly appointed American commander to accept the offer, he emphasized that "all the elements of the American army will remain constantly under the direction of General Pershing."[48] Joffre was willing to offer autonomy because the French did not want the British to convince the Americans to take over part of their front. Before Pershing's departure for Europe, British officials asked him to send 500,000 men to Britain for training, adopt British rifles and artillery, and occupy a portion of the front between the British and French. When Pershing stopped in London en route to France, General Robertson and other officials urged him to have the Americans serve "with or near" British forces.[49] The British wanted the Americans not only to operate close to their forces and to use the same ports and railways already used by the British Expeditionary Force but also to amalgamate small tactical units into larger British ones. In addition to turning a blind eye to the American desire for autonomy, the shortsighted British approach ignored significant operational and logistical questions about inserting American units into the front line and displacing forces whose main purpose was the defense of Paris. The British proposal also ignored their own complaints about the inadequacies of French railways in their sector. Pershing quickly recognized the limitations of French ports and railways and, with French encouragement, looked toward northeastern France for a U.S. sector.

On June 26, after arriving on the continent, Pershing met with Pétain and agreed to occupy a sector in northeastern France and to use the Atlantic ports and the railways from the coast. Strategically, the Lorraine region appealed to Pershing because of enticing objectives behind the St.-Mihiel salient. These objectives included the Briey iron basin and rail communications linking Metz with German armies farther to the west. By advancing in the St.-Mihiel–Verdun–Argonne region, the Americans could pose a significant threat to the enemy's natural resources and lines of communications. Pershing's proposal accorded easily with French strategy, for since the earliest days of the war the French had recognized the operational and strategic value of cutting the German railway in that sector. Yet Pétain had another goal in mind. He wanted the Americans to replace his Eighth Army, which occupied a sector east of the St.-Mihiel salient. If the Americans occupied this sector or extended farther to the west toward Verdun and the Argonne, the French could divide their front into two grand sectors. One would extend from the British right across the Noyon, Aisne, Reims, and Champagne sectors, while the other would extend from the American right to the Swiss frontier. Units in the first sector would act in concert with the British and Americans, while those in the second could guard against a German incursion through Lorraine, Alsace, or Switzerland.

French political and military leaders eagerly awaited the arrival of American forces. To reassure French soldiers and sustain their will to fight, they wanted an American unit to enter the trenches as quickly as possible. They also sought a sizable American presence—some 300,000–400,000 men, or fifteen to twenty divisions—by the spring of 1918. When elements of the U.S. 1st Infantry Division arrived at St.-Nazaire on June 28, however, both the French and the Americans knew that these first troops were not ready for the trenches. The question was whether the Americans could organize and transport hundreds of thousands of soldiers to France and be ready for a serious offensive effort by the spring of 1918. Despite the unpreparedness of the Americans, Pétain ensured that the French army knew the U.S. Congress had approved sending 500,000 men. He told his soldiers, "The Americans know that the French have contributed the greatest part of the effort that has saved civilization; they openly proclaim their gratitude to the soldiers of the Marne, Yser, Verdun, Somme, and Aisne and their willingness to shoulder a notable part of the burden."[50] The eagerness of the Americans to enter the fray in full force became apparent in early July, when Pershing wired Washington and asked for 1,000,000 men by May 1918.

While the French awaited the arrival of the Americans, the Russian army disintegrated. Following the revolution in March 1917 and the establishment of the Provisional Government, the situation in Russia became increasingly bleak. Only a few days after Pétain became general-in-chief, the French military mission in Russia transmitted a message from General Alekseev describing his assembling his army-group commanders for a meeting with representatives of the Provisional Government and a committee of workers and soldiers. The military mission also reported that the Germans had sent emissaries to talk to Russian soldiers about peace. A report one week later described the situation as "calm anarchy" and said, "The officers remain passive; the men do whatever they want."[51] In mid-July Brusilov reported difficulties with continuing a prolonged campaign and attributed the weakening of his army to an erosion of morale and to economic and political factors. Two weeks later the French mission described the situation as a "débacle."[52] On July 29 the Russians, pleading for an attack on the Western Front, described the situation in somber terms, including the collapse of morale, the breakup of units, and the retreat of units that had lost all cohesion. As the situation worsened, a report in early August acknowledged that Russian soldiers had abandoned their defensive positions and the Germans had made deep advances into Russia. On September 5 the French mission informed Paris of the "débacle of Riga" and said, "The infantry is nothing but a mob that blocks the roads."[53] Clearly, the foundation of French strategy for almost three years had crumbled.

Despite the alarming news from Russia, Pétain refused to launch a large offensive to relieve pressure on the Eastern Front. While Foch had an optimistic view of Russia's remaining in the war and striking Austria-Hungary, Pétain held out little hope for the Russians. He did not want to sacrifice the lives of his soldiers in a desperate attempt to keep the Russians in the war. On July 26 Pétain and Foch met with allied military leaders in Paris, and Pétain's views prevailed. Pershing reported to Washington:

> Steps to be taken in case Russia should be forced out of war considered. Various movements [of] troops to and from different fronts necessary to meeting possible contingencies discussed. Conference also weighed political, economic, and moral effect both upon Central and Allied powers under most unfavorable aspect from Allied point of view. General conclusions reached were necessity for adoption of purely defensive attitude on all secondary fronts and withdrawing surplus troops for duty on western front. By thus strengthening western front [those attending] believed Allies could hold until Americans forces arrive in numbers sufficient to gain ascendancy.[54]

Though Pétain dreaded the shifting of German forces in the future from the Eastern to the Western Front, he had no desire to sound a clarion call for offensive action to assist the Russians.

As the strategic situation changed, Pétain remained preoccupied with "healing" the army, but he did not—as General Wilson feared—"squat" and "do little." He nonetheless welcomed Haig's eagerness to "smash" the German army and thereby carry the main burden of fighting on the Western Front, for, like Joffre and Nivelle before him, he thought the British should be doing more. At the Paris conference on May 4—which occurred during the period between April 29, when Pétain became chief of the General Staff, and May 17, when he became general-in-chief—Haig and Pétain had agreed that the British would make the main attack during the summer and the French the supporting attack. On May 5 Haig sent a letter to the GQG describing his upcoming operations. The goal was to clear the Germans from several key ports along the Belgian coast from which they could launch submarine attacks against allied shipping. While continuing to press along the Arras-Vimy front, the British would first attack the Messines-Wytschaete Ridge (eight kilometers south of Ypres) in early June and then launch a larger attack closer to Ypres. Pétain told the field marshal that the French would assist with supporting attacks. He assured Haig that he was preparing four attacks "on a considerable scale" near the Chemin des Dames, Reims, Verdun, and Alsace.[55]

In a meeting with Haig on May 18, Pétain questioned plans for clearing the Belgian coast and insisted that such a deep drive violated the conclusions of the Paris conference of May 4 about seeking only limited objectives. The newly appointed general-in-chief conveyed his strongest criticism on May 20, the day after publishing Directive No. 1. General Wilson, the British liaison officer, recorded the key points of a discussion with Pétain:

> He said that he could not attack like Haig, because he was already holding far too long a line and we were holding far too short a line; that he entirely disagreed with any idea of distant objectives; that he was opposed to the Somme procedure [of successive attacks]; that he would make three or four small attacks for strictly limited objectives, and when the objectives were reached fighting would cease. . . . He told me that, in his opinion, Haig's attack toward Ostend was certain to fail, and that his effort to disengage Ostend and Zeebrugge was a hopeless one.[56]

Despite reservations about British plans and methods, Pétain favored some sort of British offensive, and on May 23 he confirmed his willingness to support Haig's offensive in Flanders. That support included not only First Army's participating in the Flanders offensive in mid-July but also Sixth Army's attacking in the Aisne sector on the Chemin des Dames around June 10 and Second Army's attacking near Verdun in mid-July. Pétain expected the June 10 attack against the Chemin des Dames to correspond with Haig's drive against Messines Ridge and the mid-July attack to correspond with Haig's subsequent offensive in Flanders. As for French forces attacking alongside the British in Flanders, his willingness to participate came at least partially from long-term suspicions of British motives. Since the early days of the war the French, refusing to relinquish the coastal position to the British, had maintained a corps at Nieuport, on the coast of the English Channel. Pétain told the French liaison officer with the Belgians, "The French will participate [in this operation] as much for its special interests in the region of the North Sea as from its desire not to be excluded from any military action that could have a decisive influence over the destiny of Belgium."[57] Though the French had initially planned on having only one corps with two divisions participate, Pétain told Haig he would contribute two corps with six divisions and pass the Nieuport sector to the British for the duration of the operation. He wanted the British, however, to return control of Nieuport once the operation ended.

As the mutinies spread in late May and early June, Pétain concluded that he could not send six divisions to Flanders and also attack on the Chemin des Dames. In Northern Army Group, Sixth Army had begun planning for the Chemin des Dames offensive while Nivelle was still general-in-chief, but the turmoil of the mutinies engulfed Sixth Army—more so than any other field army—reaching their peak on June 2. With regiments threatening to march on Paris and refusing to enter the trenches, General Paul Maistre, Sixth Army's commander, asked Franchet d'Espèrey, Northern Army Group's commander, on June 3 for a month's delay. Understating the effects of the mutinies, Maistre said, "We risk having the men not leave the trenches." D'Espèrey supported Maistre's request by saying, "In an offensive preparation of morale is as important as preparation of materiel."[58] Pétain formally canceled the operation on June 4.

Two days before the formal cancelation of the Chemin des Dames operation, General Eugène Debeney, Pétain's chief of staff, met with Haig and informed him that the French would participate in the Flanders offensive but could not launch the infantry assaults planned for the Chemin des Dames. Debeney emphasized the long period of preparation for Nivelle's offensive and the lack of opportunity for leave or rest for French troops, both of which were needed to maintain morale. When Haig asked when the French could resume large offensive operations, Debeney estimated a delay of at least a month. He did not, however, anticipate a delay in Second Army's attack north of Verdun, which was scheduled to begin on July 15.

Despite the effect of the mutinies and the cancelation of the Chemin des Dames operation, the French did not stand idly by and watch the British attack. Three of the armies most affected by the mutinies—Fourth, Tenth, and Sixth—managed to launch small operations in June and July. In Central Army Group, one corps in Fourth Army attacked on June 18 and 21, and two corps launched a spoiling attack on July 14 to disrupt German preparations for a small offensive. In Northern Army Group Tenth and Sixth armies launched local attacks on June 25–26 and July 1–3. Also, numerous artillery barrages, mine explosions, and small raids ranged across the front from Lorraine through the Argonne. The French gains, however, were small, and the Germans maintained a much more aggressive attitude.

As promised, the French also participated in the Flanders offensive. Beginning on July 7 the French moved First Army into position north of Ypres for what would become known as the Passchendaele offensive. Commanded by General François Anthoine, the army consisted of two corps and had 260 light, 298 heavy, and 76 long-range heavy artillery pieces, plus 300 accompanying guns. It was supposed to cover the left flank of the British Fifth Army, which would make the main attack. Haig expected artillery preparation to begin on July 15 and the infantry to attack ten days later, but for a variety of reasons, including Anthoine's request for a delay, he had to postpone the infantry assault until July 31. Concerned about the morale of his soldiers, Anthoine wanted to prepare the attack thoroughly and do everything possible to give his infantry a good chance of success. On the first day of the infantry assault, the British and French made significant advances. Beginning their attack at 0445 hours on the thirty-first, the French advanced about two kilometers and captured their objectives easily. Like the British, most casualties came not in the assault but during enemy artillery bombardments after units reached their objectives.

Had Field Marshal Haig adopted Pétain's methods, he would have halted his attack after making this easy gain, but he continued to push forward. As allied soldiers struggled under unusually heavy rains, he attempted to renew his attack on the thirty-first and then again on August 10 and 16. Subsequent efforts by the British and French consisted primarily of long artillery preparations followed by infantry assaults. In the middle of October, Anthoine wrote to Pétain and suggested terminating French participation in the offensive. He explained that the final assault on Passchendaele was nothing more than a "local and limited operation" and did not require a "vast combined operation" of French, British, and Belgian forces. Haig refused, he said, to acknowledge his "failure" and would deplete First Army "uselessly."[59] Well aware of Haig's frustration over the canceling of the Chemin des Dames operation, Pétain disapproved Anthoine's request and said he did not want the "halting of the offensive or the limiting of its gains" blamed on the French.[60] In early November the British—with First Army still on their left—finally captured Passchendaele, a destroyed village eight kilometers from their July 31 line of departure. First Army had suffered 1,625 killed and 6,900 wounded in the operation.

Pétain had also promised Haig in late May that he would support the Flanders offensive by having Second Army attack near Verdun in mid-July. On June 5, however, the new Central Army Group commander, General Fayolle, informed Pétain that he could not begin the operation on July 15 and two weeks later said he could not attack before August 15. In fact the infantry assault north of Verdun did not begin until August 20. The delay from July 15 to August 20 came from a variety of factors associated with the mutinies. Measures taken to restore order to units and provide rest to soldiers complicated the movement of units, and further delays came from the chain of command's insistence that every aspect of the operation be prepared completely. Given the low morale of French soldiers, no senior leader wanted to leave anything to chance.

German counterattacks also disrupted French preparations. An enemy attack at Verdun on June 28–29 had a particularly significant effect, since it seized terrain west of Hill 304 on the west bank of the Meuse that was part of the base of departure for the upcoming offensive. Second Army Commanding General Adolphe Guillaumat intended to counterattack on July 3 but postponed the operation several times, finally beginning it on July 17. With nine heavy batteries firing direct support, the infantry attacked on a front of 1,500 meters and advanced 1,000 meters. On August 1, however, the Germans counterattacked and regained the terrain. Still worse, they attacked on the east bank on August 16 and achieved small gains. The enemy's successes created great concern in Fayolle's headquarters, since the French had a huge amount of heavy artillery and should have repelled the attacks easily. Guillaumat attributed the enemy's successes to his soldiers' fatigue, defective communications, and poor liaison. His explanation, however, did not keep Fayolle from sharply rebuking him for letting the Germans delay preparations for the offensive.

For his much-delayed offensive, Guillaumat planned on attacking with four corps in the front line (from left to right, XIII, XVI, XV, XXXII). With two corps on the west bank of the Meuse and two on the east bank, he sought to capture Hill 304 and Mort Homme on the west bank and push toward Talou Hill and Beaumont on the east bank. Advancing on a front of ten kilometers on each bank, he hoped to move one kilometer forward on the west bank and two kilometers on the other bank. He told each corps commander to place two divisions in the first line and two in the second, but he ruled out trying to maintain momentum in the offensive by inserting second-line divisions into the forward line. Such procedures had been the rule in the past and had often produced high casualties when succeeding waves of troops launched frontal assaults on enemy strong points. Second Army would employ only a minimum of infantry, Guillaumat insisted, and second-line divisions would do nothing more than relieve first-line units after the leading units had seized their objectives.[61]

Artillery preparation began on the morning of August 11. Using 3,000 pieces, the French initially fired counterbattery missions and on August 13 began destroying enemy positions. From August 11 to 20 they fired 3,000,000 rounds of artillery, including more than 1,000,000 rounds from heavy guns. Using a technique borrowed from the British, the French also used machine guns to fire indirectly toward passage points, crossroads, supply lines, and enemy artillery batteries. The Germans responded with their own artillery fire and chemicals, but the French maintained control of the air with their fighters and obtained better results. As part of the final artillery preparation the French fired chemical rounds for six hours during the night of August 19–20.

The infantry assault began at 0430 hours on August 20 and advanced quickly. With the exception of XIII Corps's failure to seize Hill 304 on the west bank, Second Army seized most of its objectives by the end of the day. As an example of the battle's conduct, 31st Division on XVI Corps's left had responsibility for Mort Homme and climbed out of its trenches at 0440 hours. The leading battalions encountered little resistance at first but did come under light artillery and machine-gun fire. By 0520 hours the infantrymen had reached their first objective, a line of trenches one kilometer from their starting point. Their biggest difficulty in their advance was orienting themselves and moving across the "lunar terrain." Around 0700 hours, after bringing forward accompanying guns to destroy several enemy machine guns, 31st Division moved toward its final objective, a line of trenches 500 meters to the north. Encountering more resistance this time, the infantrymen had to fight their way forward and clear several enemy trenches. They used grenades to clear centers of resistance across most the division's front. Meanwhile German machine guns on Hill 304 fired into their left flank, forcing the division commander to echelon his left. German aircraft also gained control of the air and hampered the forward movement of accompanying guns. By 0915 hours 31st Division held most of its second objective. Another artillery preparation enabled the infantry to seize the remaining portions of the division's objective on the 31st's left and right. The Germans did not accept their losses passively. Between 1945 and 2100 hours they launched two counterattacks, but prompt artillery fire drove them back. Though the battle seemed easy in comparison to numerous others, it had its costs: 31st Division lost 200 killed, 810 wounded, and 100 missing in action.

During the next six days the French launched several small attacks at Verdun. On August 24 XIII Corps captured Hill 304 on the west bank. Though the gain was not easily made, the French pushed forward more than one kilometer on a two-kilometer front. On August 26 XXXII

Corps attacked on the east bank to seize terrain overlooking its position. The fighting was hard, as is evident from one division's losing 3,000 men, but the French advanced one kilometer along a three-kilometer front. By the end of that day Second Army had attained all its operational objectives.

Paris enthusiastically applauded the success at Verdun. On August 25, with the approval of Poincaré and the Council of Ministers, Painlevé conferred the Grand Cross of the Legion of Honor on Pétain. Four days later Poincaré and Painlevé traveled to Verdun, and Poincaré presented the award to the general. In his speech the president of the Third Republic expressed the thanks of the country and emphasized the importance of Verdun. In a setting that encouraged hyperbole, Poincaré did not mention the mutinies but said, "Never has the army demonstrated more courage and more spirit. Three years of hard combat have neither altered its strength nor cooled its ardor."[62] Given the depths from which the French army had risen, Pétain and his soldiers more than merited Poincaré's effusive praise.

Meanwhile Second Army continued advancing at Verdun even though Pétain's concept of limited offensives envisaged no subsequent attacks after the first forty-eight hours. On August 27 Fayolle asked Guillaumat to consider capturing several trenches and some high ground that would strengthen his position. Guillaumat, concerned about the weakened capability of his infantry, had reservations about launching too ambitious an operation. Nevertheless Fayolle ordered him to seize several trenches to his front and to plan a more ambitious operation to seize the last observation point from which the Germans could see Verdun. When Pétain learned of the preparations, he asked Fayolle and Guillaumat to explain their purpose. In a brief response Fayolle identified three alternatives, including remaining in place or withdrawing, and said he preferred to take advantage of the artillery that was already in place and launch a small attack that had a high probability of succeeding. Guillaumat provided a lengthier response that emphasized the "precarious" nature of the existing line.[63] He argued for a small advance to make enemy counterattacks more difficult, improve life in the trenches, and give the enemy the impression the French were going to continue their offensive. On September 1 Pétain approved the operation.

With Pétain's approval in hand, Guillaumat expanded the scope of the operation and had both corps on the east bank launch small attacks. XV Corps attacked on September 7 but failed, and XXXII Corps attacked on the eighth and succeeded despite heavy losses. After gaining Fayolle's approval, Guillaumat pressed forward again and succeeded. His gains were small in terms of territory and did not include the last observation point from which the Germans could see Verdun, but they included several trenches deemed essential to Second Army's defenses. Subsequent pushes, however, provoked strong enemy counterattacks and heavy artillery fire. The German response underlined the wisdom of Pétain's desire to halt attacks after forty-eight hours, before the enemy could concentrate reserves and artillery against an offensive.

Following the Verdun offensive, the French launched no major operation until late October. According to the British official history, Pétain visited Haig's headquarters on September 19 and supposedly told the field marshal that he did not have a single soldier in the front line upon whom he could rely. Discipline was so bad in the French army, Haig noted in his diary, that Pétain believed the French "could not resist a determined German offensive."[64] Given Pétain's desire for a larger effort from the British and Haig's desire to justify his grand offensive at Passchendaele, one can only surmise what the French general actually said, but political turmoil in Paris raised additional concerns in London. In early September, amidst great controversy over attempts by Socialist deputies to meet with German delegates at a conference in Stockholm and over German bribes to the editor of the left-wing journal *Le bonnet rouge*, Ribot had submitted the collective resignation of his ministry, and Painlevé established a new government. At a hastily called meeting with Lloyd George on September 25, the new premier opposed a negotiated peace with the Germans but said the French could replace only a third of their losses suffered that year. The effect of such information is apparent in Lloyd George's agreement that the British should take over more of the front. The French army nonetheless had passed through the worst part of the mutinies and, though still fragile and suffering from low morale, had regained enough of its confidence and effectiveness to participate in the Flanders offensive and to launch the Verdun operation in early September.

Not everyone agreed with Pétain's cautious approach. At a meeting of the War Committee on October 1, a future president of France, Paul Doumer, pleaded ignorance about strategy but insisted on resuming the offensive as quickly as possible. Though acknowledging France's shortages of personnel, artillery, and aviation, he saw no reason to remain passive. At another War Committee meeting on October 5, Doumer again pleaded for an offensive. Pétain responded by describing the best way to conduct operations on the Western Front. If the allies had two or three active sectors on the French front and two in the British, he explained, they could ensure that two attacks were always occurring at different sectors at the same time, and the Germans would find it difficult to handle two simultaneous attacks. Despite his earlier plea of ignorance about strategy, Doumer complained that he found no "strategic idea" in Pétain's concept.[65]

Additional criticism came from those who believed Pétain's limited offensives yielded the initiative to the Germans and left them free to conduct minor attacks. On the Chemin des Dames and the sector to its west, for example, German attacks occurred on June 3, 15–16, 22–23, 24–25, 29, and 30 and July 3, 8, 9, 11, 12, 18, 19, and 22. The largest of these attacks, on July 19 and 22, involved two German divisions on a front of three kilometers. Primarily as a result of frequent enemy attacks, Tenth and Sixth armies, two of the armies most affected by the mutinies, suffered 5,500 killed, 17,000 wounded, and 5,300 missing in action between May 15 and July 15.[66] Clearly, remaining on the defensive did not prevent casualties, and the units most affected by the mutinies continued to suffer losses.

Pressure for more aggressive operations came from General Franchet d'Espèrey, commander of Northern Army Group. Concerned about heightened enemy activity and greater French losses on the Chemin des Dames in June and early July, he complained about the "attitude" adopted after the "incidents" and the "renouncing" of offensive operations in the region. To force the enemy to halt his attacks, the French had to regain the initiative, d'Espèrey suggested on July 18, by launching more offensives. He proposed that his army group make three minor attacks—one in two or three days, one in a week, and one at the end of

July—and a large offensive against Fort La Malmaison, at the western end of the Chemin des Dames. The latter offensive could take place at the end of August.[67] Two days after d'Espèrey's request, Pétain approved the three minor operations but ordered only "active preparation" for the Malmaison operation. To make the minor attacks, d'Espèrey told the Tenth Army commander that his army should remain on the defensive and limit offensive activity to local attacks and raids. He also directed Sixth Army, the unit most affected by the mutinies, to begin preparation for an offensive at the end of August toward Malmaison. Anxious to avoid another débacle on the much-bloodied ground, he insisted that the operation be well planned.

On July 22 the Sixth Army commander, General Maistre, informed his corps commanders about preparation for an attack on the western end of the Chemin des Dames ridge. On a front of eight kilometers, he expected to advance two kilometers. Capturing this terrain would enable the French to see and fire down most of the valley of the Ailette River (in fact a small stream), which ran through a valley along the northern face of the Chemin des Dames ridge. Maistre expected three corps, each with four infantry divisions, to participate. After Pétain approved "active preparation" for an attack on the Chemin des Dames, planning for the operation proceeded slowly. Concerns about inadequate artillery support caused the first delays. Early in the planning Maistre asked for an additional nineteen 75-mm and thirty-six heavy battalions of artillery, and d'Espèrey supported his request. Instead of providing the additional artillery Pétain warned d'Espèrey not to plan an extended preparation that would result in the loss of surprise. He wrote: "do not lose sight of the fact that the operation is an application of Directive No. 1. It is necessary to make a surprise attack in which we endeavor to keep our losses to a minimum. This calls for the rapid placement and quick entry into action of units and weapons, as well as a reduction to the minimum of artillery preparation."[68] For the next several weeks, staff officers studied and debated the amount of artillery Sixth Army needed.

During this period the staff at the GQG completed a study that examined the possibility of enlarging Sixth Army's objective. Since the new objective apparently required no more units and artillery than the original objective, d'Espèrey found the idea appealing and agreed that the terrain favored expanding the operation and seizing a larger objective. While the eastern portion of the Chemin des Dames consisted of a long narrow ridge running on an east-west axis, the western portion was broader and contained several smaller ridges extending north from the main ridge. Fort La Malmaison sat on a small plateau where one of the smaller ridges joined the Chemin des Dames. If the French dominated the heights of the Chemin des Dames and captured Malmaison, planners noted, the Germans would occupy a poor position on the small ridges extending toward the north and would have insufficient room for launching powerful counterattacks. Although enemy soldiers could operate from this poor position, they would probably withdraw to a stronger position to the north of the Ailette River.

The enlarging of Sixth Army's objective raised anew the question of artillery support. The argument for more artillery became stronger after Sixth Army did a thorough analysis of Second Army's artillery in the successful attack at Verdun. The study emphasized the importance of heavy artillery and concluded that in several key categories Second Army had had almost double the heavy artillery of Sixth Army. With this study in hand, Maistre appealed to Franchet d'Espèrey, saying, "if we want to conduct the operation at Malmaison with speed and a minimum of losses, it is necessary to envisage an allocation of artillery much greater than that initially provided to Sixth Army."[69] On September 12 Pétain notified Northern Army Group that he would provide three additional regiments of heavy artillery (representing thirty-eight batteries). He also approved d'Espèrey's transferring five battalions of heavy artillery from Tenth to Sixth Army. D'Espèrey informed Maistre and told him not to ask for additional artillery; if Maistre thought additional artillery was required, he should reduce the size of his attack.

Throughout the careful preparation for the Chemin des Dames operation, Pétain did not press his subordinates for quick action and ruled out several ambitious proposals. In late August and early September his concerns about casualties increased when a lengthy study by the GQG staff concluded that France could not win a war of attrition against the Germans. To keep casualties low, he vetoed a proposal that Tenth Army participate in the offensive on the Chemin des Dames. He explained that the cost of Tenth Army's operation would be far greater than any conceivable gain. Instead, he directed a vigorous counterbattery action on the left of Tenth Army.

The delays frustrated Haig, who wanted energetic action from the French. On September 30 a liaison officer at Haig's headquarters informed Pétain that the field marshal believed the enemy was sufficiently weakened that the British could make large gains after two or three more "pushes." He quoted Haig: "The campaign of 1917 has reached its decisive phase. The British army, which is waging the principal battle, is on the edge of achieving important success, but to do that, it is necessary for the secondary attacks forecast for the French front to be launched at the agreed time (before October 10) to prevent the flow of [enemy] reserves into Flanders." The field marshal compared the existing situation to that in April, when the British had begun their supporting attack for Nivelle's offensive even though preparations were not complete.[70] Despite this request and others, the French continued their leisurely preparation of the Malmaison offensive. After the British requested an artillery bombardment simulating the beginning of an attack, Pétain directed Northern Army Group to fire the bombardment on October 6 and 7, but he took no steps to hurry his subordinates. When Haig and Pétain met on October 6, the French general expressed his "regrets" for not having "satisfied" the British commander.[71] Whether he gained some satisfaction from the fact that the French, and not the British, were now being "slow and late" is not known. Whatever his private thoughts may have been, Pétain had resuscitated the French army. On October 15 the British liaison officer to the GQG reported to the British War Committee that French morale had improved and that "discipline was now good."[72]

In mid-September Maistre published his order for Sixth Army's operation. Aiming to seize two successive objectives, Maistre planned on capturing the first objective in one bound and the second in the next bound. To capture the second objective Sixth Army should advance, he said, two kilometers four hours after commencing its move toward its first objective. As in the limited offensive at Verdun, each corps would advance with two divisions in the first and two in the second line. The second-line divisions would enter the line after the leading divisions had occupied the second objective.[73]

Preparatory fire for Sixth Army's offensive finally began on October 17, more than four months later than Pétain had promised Haig. Although Maistre had planned four days of firing, bad weather disrupted the destruction of long-range targets, and the French delayed the infantry assault until the twenty-third. He initially ordered his infantry to leave the trenches at 0545 hours, but after deciphering a German telegram ordering the defenders to be ready for an attack at 0530, he changed the time to 0515 hours, more than an hour before sunrise. Numerous difficulties surfaced early in the attack. With reduced visibility in the dim light hampering movement, rain started falling at 0600 hours and made conditions worse. Of the sixty-three tanks that were supposed to accompany the infantry, twenty-seven never moved beyond the muddy French lines. Fifteen broke down or became mired in the first enemy position, and only twenty-one advanced with the infantry toward the second objective. Though the weather did not halt the flight of French aircraft, pilots could see very little and thus contributed little. Despite the unfavorable beginning, the attack accomplished all its goals.

The experience of 38th Division illustrates the operation's progress. From left to right Maistre had XIV, XXI, and XI corps. As directed, XI Corps had two divisions in its front line, 38th Division on its left and 66th on its right. The division's first objective included Fort La Malmaison, one kilometer from its starting point, and the second objective included the outskirts of Chavignon, a small village two kilometers north of the first objective. Advancing with four battalions on its front, the division charged forward at 0515 hours on October 23 despite an enemy artillery barrage. Though tanks were supposed to support the division's left, they became mired in the mud or had mechanical problems and could not help. By 0615 the infantry held the fortress, a key portion of the division's first objective. After fresh battalions replaced those that had led the initial move and artillery struck the second objective, the division moved forward again at 0915. When the infantry entered the woods on the northern end of the small ridge extending north from the Chemin des Dames, they captured numerous prisoners and encountered machine-gun fire. As the soldiers pressed forward, increasingly heavy enemy artillery fire rendered their movement more difficult. When the division entered Chavignon, the Germans used grenades and flamethrowers against them, but the French held the village by 1145 hours. Advancing three kilometers, the division captured 2,000 prisoners, thirty-seven cannon, and 100 machine guns, but it had lost more than 700 killed and 2,000 wounded. While such losses were heavy for a single division, overall losses were small, since the French had not fed a series of divisions into 38th Division's zone of attack. In previous battles, two to five divisions would have fought successively in 38th Division's zone, and each would have suffered losses comparable to 38th's casualties.

On October 24 and 25 the two corps on Sixth Army's left pressed forward, gaining several kilometers of terrain. The rapid pace of the advance led Maistre, hoping for an exploitation, to place I Cavalry Corps in close contact with XIV Corps on his left, but the grounds for optimism soon disappeared. Maistre and Franchet d'Espèrey later lamented not having foreseen and prepared for the possibility of an exploitation. The French nonetheless had made one of their largest and most important gains of the war and had demonstrated the merits of limited offensives. While advancing as much as six kilometers and capturing 11,000 prisoners, 200 cannon, 220 heavy mortars, and 700 machine guns, the French had lost 2,241 killed, 8,162 wounded, and 1,460 missing in action from October 23 to 26. The remarkable aspect of the campaign was the capture of the heights of the Chemin des Dames, the ridge along which 30,000 French soldiers had died in Nivelle's offensive. At a price less than one-tenth that paid by Nivelle, Pétain had made far larger gains. The price he paid for those gains also compared very favorably with the price paid by Haig's forces at Passchendaele.

Though news of these gains caused France's hopes to soar, events in the summer and early fall had forced Paris to consider a compromise peace and caused Pétain to reconsider his strategy. Beginning in February 1917, several peace feelers had circulated through Europe's capitals.[74] The first occurred when Prince Sixtus of Bourbon-Parma, the brother-in-law of the Austrian emperor, Karl, arrived in Paris with a letter from the emperor exploring the possibilities of a separate peace between Austria and the allied powers. Hopes for peace, however, foundered when Italy refused to relinquish its claims to Austrian territory and when Germany objected to the Austrians' efforts. Another peace effort came in mid-June when Baron von Lancken, the German governor of Brussels, used Belgian intermediaries to communicate the possibility of a negotiated peace with Germany. Even though Briand, the former premier, strongly supported France's participation in negotiations, suspicions about German motives and Paris's unwillingness to conclude a separate peace without its allies scuttled the negotiations. A strong opponent of a separate peace, Ribot, who was premier at the time, insisted that France enter negotiations only if accompanied by its allies: "We can do nothing without them, and we will never do anything without them."[75] An attempt by Pope Benedict XV to mediate a peace also failed. After carefully considering the papal proposal, France's political leaders rejected a compromise peace and decided to continue the war. In his memoirs Poincaré noted the politicians' sentiment: "If Germany senses that Russia is weakened, it is unlikely that it would offer us an acceptable peace, or even that it would accept one today."[76]

The possibility of a negotiated peace initially had no effect on Pétain's strategy or his interest in Alsace. In November 1916 Joffre had begun to consider an offensive there, and Nivelle had continued those efforts. Shortly after becoming commander of French forces Pétain transformed the planned operation into a limited offensive. A few days later he ruled out the possibility of an operation by Eastern Army Group in June or July but nonetheless directed General de Castelnau to continue preparations. Even though the GQG identified an operation in Alsace as one of seven possible sites for attacks by the three army groups, Pétain emphasized in early June the unlikely chance of an offensive there. In early August he anticipated only one small offensive in Lorraine by Eastern Army Group in 1917, and he noted that the attack in Upper Alsace would occur only "when circumstances are favorable."[77]

New interest in Alsace appeared in mid-August as rumors of a negotiated peace swirled through Paris. On August 15 Pétain's chief of staff directed the GQG's Operations Bureau to study possible operations for 1918. The staff officers finished a strategic assessment on September 17 and for the first time explicitly considered territorial gains *(gages territoriaux)* that would enhance France's position in negotiations with Germany. Pédroncini called this a *"stratégie de gages"* or "bargaining-chip" strategy.[78] Like planners in the Korean War in the 1950s, staff officers suggested holding part of "occupied" France or, even better, part of Germany to facilitate negotiations and produce "honorable conditions" for France.

In their assessment the staff officers considered the entire French front and identified eighteen possible locations for French attacks in 1918. These locations included one site in Lorraine and another in Alsace big enough to support a large offensive. As the planners narrowed the range of choices, they foresaw a possible German withdrawal in 1918 from the broad Noyon salient facing Paris and the smaller salient at St.-Mihiel and concluded that such a withdrawal would eliminate eight of the eighteen possible locations for an attack. Nevertheless, they provided Pétain three alternatives: one assuming no German withdrawal, another assuming a withdrawal from the St.-Mihiel salient, and a third assuming a withdrawal from the Noyon salient. Each alternative proposed French attacks on different portions of the front in May, June, and July 1918; a combined Franco-American attack near Verdun in August; and a large French attack in Alsace in September. Each alternative assumed that in May the British would make only a single attack. Regardless of location, the first four attacks would be limited offensives and would occur sequentially, and the fifth, a large offensive in Alsace, would seek a rupture of enemy lines. Although the planners recognized the absence of any strategically important, war-winning objectives in Alsace, they concluded, "In 1918 with an offensive activity comparable to that of 1917, we can place the Germans in a critical situation because of the attrition of their human resources: this is a new situation in the war and very favorable for us."[79]

The Operations Bureau published a more succinct assessment on October 9. Again concerned about bargaining chips in a negotiated peace, the staff foresaw a battle of attrition followed by a strong offensive to rupture enemy lines. They rejected a quick battle like that of April 1917 and favored instead an extended battle over five or six months with three or four "methodical" attacks along different portions of the front. A strong offensive to "rupture" enemy lines would follow. If the initial attacks did not drive the Germans back, the rupture attack, said the planners, should focus on the eastern end of the Chemin des Dames. If the initial attacks did drive the Germans back, the final, strong offensive should strike in Alsace.[80]

An interesting aspect of the staff's assessment pertained to their perception of the Americans and the British. In the assessment of September 17, the officers anticipated that the Americans would have fifteen to sixteen divisions in France by May 1, 1918, and twenty-two divisions by August 1. Of the twenty-two divisions present in France on August 1, they anticipated that only twelve would be ready to participate in a limited offensive, and they recognized the need to support these with artillery from three to four French divisions. In contrast, the planners expected twenty-five British and fifty-four French divisions to participate. Expecting the British to object to having such a large force participate in an offensive, the planners noted that the French would have 3,204 infantry companies in September 1917 and the British 3,024. They advised Pétain to encourage the British to participate by emphasizing the large number of French units taking part in the offensives. The planners nonetheless anticipated greater cooperation from the Americans than from the British.

Notwithstanding Pédroncini's claim that Pétain approved the strategic and operational concepts in the September 17 and October 9 studies, neither Pétain nor his chief of staff preferred launching a large offensive in Alsace. Like Joffre before August 1914, they recognized that terrain in Alsace did not favor a large French offensive and preferred attacking elsewhere. On October 9 Pétain's chief of staff, General Debeney, formally expressed his reservations about the Operations Bureau's proposal. He wrote: "As for the French front, the final push in the direction of Mézières will always be the most fruitful. . . . In this case, British attacks in Flanders, Franco-American in Lorraine should be the prelude." He added: "The opposite solution—initial attacks in the center, final pushes on the wings (Flanders and Alsace)—is the worst alternative."[81] Pétain's preference for something other an Alsatian strategy was apparent in a note he gave Haig in a meeting on October 18. The note summarized allied alternatives on the Western Front, first, if Russia forged a separate peace and Franco-British forces had to remain on the defensive or, second, if Russia remained in the war and Franco-British forces returned to the offensive. In neither case did Pétain anticipate an offensive into Alsace.[82] Additionally, a handwritten note in the Operations Bureau's files changed a key sentence in a memorandum summarizing the Alsatian operation from Pétain's having "approved" it to his having "accepted" it "in principle."[83]

When Pétain met Haig on October 18, he emphasized the possibilities that the Russians would make a separate peace and that the Germans would increase their forces on the Western Front by as many as fifty divisions. Without larger reserves, Pétain feared that the allies could not defend successfully. To assemble reserves of at least forty divisions, he tried to convince Haig to extend his right boundary fifty kilometers south and relieve Third Army. Though Haig reluctantly agreed to extend his right thirty kilometers to the Oise River, he refused to relieve the entire Third Army. Taking over more of the front would divert units from his Flanders offensive, he said, and thereby reduce its scale and chance of success. The two leaders also discussed the possibility of allied offensives. With allied attacks possible only if the Russians remained in the war, Pétain proposed an offensive with British, French, American, and Belgian participation. He expected the French to make several successive attacks along different portions of the front early in 1918 and suggested a British attack from the vicinity of St.-Quentin toward the north. After these attacks, Pétain expected to make his main attack east of Reims, "probably about August."[84] If he had any hopes that the British would accept his suggestion, they were dashed when Haig presented him a paper proposing large but separate offensives by the British and French in 1918. Haig insisted that the allies could not wait until August 1918 to "try to obtain a decision."[85]

The two allied leaders had completely different strategic and operational concepts. While Haig expected large allied offensives to retain the initiative and compel the Germans to yield eventually, Pétain foresaw large offensives only after the Germans had weakened themselves with attacks or the allies had bled them with limited offensives. Haig obviously did not understand why Pétain preferred limited offensives or why he rejected continuous, successive attacks such as the Franco-British offensive on the Somme in 1916 or the Franco-British offensive at Passchendaele in 1917. And neither did Robertson, who in an analysis of "future military policy" for the British War Cabinet described the French as racked by a "succession of acute political crises," weakened by years of war, torn by "pacifist and socialist intrigues," and incapable of a "sustained offensive in 1918."[86] By highlighting these factors in their communications with British political leaders, Haig and Robertson brushed over differences in strategy and operations with the French and ignored the factors actually influencing Pétain's choices.

On October 23 Pétain informed Haig that he had abandoned all hopes of an offensive. Given the disintegration of Russia, he expected the Germans to shift large forces to the west. With these additional forces, the Germans could launch a large attack on the Western Front and simultaneously advance through Switzerland against France or Italy. Consequently, Pétain would concentrate on the defensive and form reserves that could move to threatened points along the front. He explained, "After having determined the disposition required to execute our defensive plan, we will establish our offensive plan. We will then study the means of passing from one to the other."[87] As for an Alsatian strategy, the GQG maintained its interest in an operation near Mulhouse and had Eastern Army Group plan an attack in that region for 1918. An offensive in Alsace, however, remained nothing more than a contingency for seizing bargaining chips in the event of a negotiated peace. Preparation for an attack into Alsace also provided the additional benefit of enhancing defenses against a German attack coming through Switzerland.

In the end, events on the Eastern Front and in Italy had a larger effect on French strategy than the possibility of a negotiated peace. Of these factors, the disintegration of Russia had the largest impact. The key strategic assessments of September 17 and October 9, both of which considered an offensive strategy in 1918, had rested on the assumption that the Russians would remain in the war but do little. In response to the worsening situation on the Eastern Front in September and October, Pétain's staff produced a pessimistic assessment on October 24 of the implications of Russia's making a separate peace. Specifically, the officers expected the Germans to move forty-five divisions from the Eastern to the Western Front and the Austrians to move twenty-three divisions from the Eastern to the Italian Front. Although the study did not weigh the relative merits of an offensive or defensive strategy for the allies, its authors clearly foresaw the Germans' having the initiative on the Western Front. They also foresaw France's needing larger reserves and not launching an offensive into Alsace. They recognized the strategic vulnerability of Italy if Russia left the war. Ironically, the study was completed the day after Pétain informed Haig that he would place first priority on preparations for the defense. That same day, October 24, the Italians reported a vast enemy offensive near Caporetto.

Before the Caporetto disaster, the French had resisted sending resources to Italy. They believed the Italians could hold out long enough for the allies to rush—if needed—to their assistance, and they completed plans for sending a contingent to Italy in case of an emergency. Of the leading French authorities, only Foch favored direct assistance. When Russian forces began to disintegrate on the Eastern Front, the French became more concerned about Italy, but they did little to help their ally other than send a few artillery batteries. In June, July, and August the Italians requested additional artillery, and in late August, faced with the allies' apparent reluctance, the Italian chief of staff, General Luigi Cadorna, announced the suspension of offensive operations until mid-September. This decision galvanized the French into action, and they quickly arranged to transfer 100 heavy guns from First Army, which was involved in the Passchendaele offensive, to Italy. By early September the French had 30 heavy pieces in Italy and the British 40, and the French had alerted two artillery regiments with a total of 104 heavy pieces for movement to Italy. By September 25 the French had fifteen battalions of heavy artillery, plus one 370-mm piece, in Italy.

Despite this assistance, Cadorna decided not to attack. After being warned that six German divisions were moving toward Italy, he ordered his troops to brace for a strong Austro-German counteroffensive. His decision to stay on the defensive led the French to pull back all but four battalions of their artillery, but after the Caporetto offensive began on October 24, the French War Committee approved returning the artillery and sending Tenth Army to Italy. When the British objected to sending troops to Italy, Foch responded, "It is in the interest of the allies to keep— at all costs—the Italian disaster from getting worse. It is necessary to support the Italian army morally and materially without delay."[88] If Robertson had doubts about the wisdom of intervening in Italy, Lloyd George

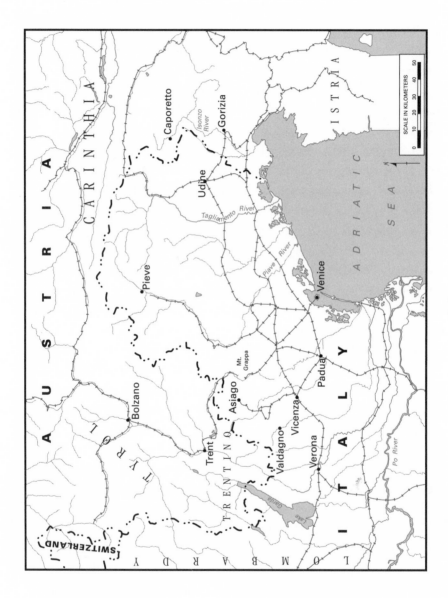

Italy

did not, and that same day Robertson notified Foch that the British would send two divisions. Beginning on October 28, four French divisions departed for Italy. Two divisions, plus a corps headquarters, had arrived by November 5; all four divisions had arrived by November 14. Two British divisions had arrived by November 22.

Arriving in Italy on October 30 before the first French troops, Foch met with Cadorna to discuss campaign strategy. Though Cadorna planned on withdrawing only sixty kilometers from the Isonzo to the Tagliamento River, he wanted to place French and British units along the Piave River, another forty kilometers to the rear. He did not expect to hold along the Tagliamento and wanted the French and British to occupy a position behind retreating Italian forces. He wanted them to act as his general reserve and guard his rear against an enemy advancing east from the Trentino. Cadorna's plans seemed reasonable to Foch, and he relayed them to the Tenth Army commander, General Duchêne. Later that day, however, after further discussions with Cardona, Foch shifted Tenth Army farther to the west, to the Lake Garda–Verona region. This move provided security against an enemy advancing south from the Trentino. On October 31, when Foch and Robertson met with Cadorna, who now wanted twenty allied divisions, they told him, "The Italian armies are not beaten; only one, the Second, has been attacked." They also emphasized that only the Italian army could ensure the defense of Italy.[89] During the next few weeks, however, the French and British increased the size of their contingents, the French from four to six divisions and the British from two to five. The last French units arrived on December 2, the last British in the middle of December.

A few days after Foch and Robertson met with Cadorna, the situation appeared to worsen. During the night of November 2–3, enemy soldiers forced their way across the Tagliamento and forced the Italians to withdraw. On November 6 the Italians fell back to the Piave. By November 11, after Italian units organized positions along the river, the situation appeared more favorable. With no threat appearing in the Lake Garda region, Foch, after discussions with the Italians, shifted French forces farther to the east (between Valdagno and Vicenza and behind the Piave) to act as a reserve. In early December the French and British relieved Italian units along twenty-eight kilometers of the Piave–Mount Grappa front and placed about half their forces in the front line. Despite strong pressure from the Central Powers, allied defenses held. On December 24 the allies agreed that the crisis had passed in Italy and they need not send additional reinforcements. They also saw no reason to begin an offensive there.

Throughout November and December, the question of command on the Italian front remained contentious. After Duchêne's Tenth Army began moving to Italy in late October, Pétain energetically sought to get Duchêne under his command. In phrases reminiscent of those used by Joffre in his attempt to gain control over Sarrail at Salonika, he demanded the subordination of French forces in Italy to him. The French had constituted their forces in Italy by taking units and artillery from his forces in north and northeastern France, and he insisted that the "consumption" of men, materiel, and munitions on either the French or Italian front would have a direct effect on the other. Despite Pétain's best efforts, the government sent General Fayolle to Italy to command French forces (Duchêne remained in command of Tenth Army) and to maintain contact with the Italian High Command. Fayolle was placed under the minister of war's control. In reality, subordinating Fayolle to the minister of war enabled Foch, rather than Pétain, to exert great influence over the Italian theater, and Fayolle's appointment marked an important point in the expansion of his powers.

Although Foch succeeding in keeping Pétain from commanding French forces in Italy, he failed to convince the British to place their forces under Fayolle. On November 27 Fayolle had asked that British forces in Italy be placed under him and that the arrangement be similar to that of the French First Army in Flanders, which functioned under the command of Haig. When Foch raised the issue with Robertson, the British chief of the Imperial General Staff refused. The British commander, Major General Sir Herbert Plumer, was an extremely capable officer, Robertson said, who had commanded an army brilliantly in Flanders, and the British did not want to place him in a subordinate position. Although British political and military leaders held Plumer in high esteem, continuing problems with Sarrail had influenced the British decision more than their regard for Plumer. Additionally, none of the British commanders relished working under French command. To limit French influence in Italy, the British also asked Painlevé to order Foch to return to Paris.

The combined effects of the Russian and Italian crises pushed the allies toward better coordination of their efforts. Now free to move large forces from the Russian front, the Central Powers could concentrate and gain numerical superiority at any point on the Western or Italian Front. To respond to this threat, the allies needed, French leaders believed, some means of concerting military policy and strategy and directing the rapid movement of troops from one theater to another. In early August Painlevé had met with Lloyd George and proposed that Foch be named chief of an allied general staff, but the British prime minister objected. He wanted to form an allied council where strategic issues could be analyzed by technical experts from the allied nations and advice be given to the governments. He wanted political, not military, authorities to have the real power. According to Robertson, Lloyd George did not accord his own military leaders a great deal of freedom and had no interest in the appointment of a powerful allied military leader who would be completely outside his control. Upon returning to Paris, Painlevé presented the idea of an allied council to the French Council of Ministers, which preferred having an allied generalissimo, and he defended it as an important step toward establishing allied unity of command under Foch. After further discussions, on October 30 Lloyd George formally proposed the creation of a "joint council" to "work out the plans and watch continuously the course of events for the Allies as a whole."[90] Though this proposal bore little resemblance to the Council of Ministers' desire for a generalissimo, Painlevé told Lloyd George that the British proposal was in "complete accord" with ideas previously presented by the French. The only modification he proposed was the creation of an allied general staff. Despite the persistence of several unresolved issues, the two governments finally accepted the proposal for the creation of an allied council on November 1 and thereby took an important step along the long road toward unity of command.

A few days later allied leaders met in Rapallo, Italy, just as the Italians pulled back from the Tagliamento. Among those attending were Painlevé, Foch, Lloyd George, Robertson, and Wilson. The Italian president of the Council of Ministers and the minister of foreign affairs also attended. The participants focused first on the military situation in Italy and then on the creation of an allied war council, or Supreme War Council. The meeting proved opportune, since Painlevé and Lloyd George had already agreed on the main features of an allied "joint council" and the Italians' presence created the impression of a more broadly based allied effort. The most contentious issue proved to be Foch's being dual-hatted as France's chief of the General Staff and its representative on the council. Facing strong objections from Lloyd George, Painlevé yielded and agreed to Foch's giving up his position as French chief of the General Staff when he became a member of the council. Another contentious issue concerned the location of the council's meetings. Lloyd George insisted on a location other than Paris to ensure that national influences did not affect the council's deliberations. After much wrangling, the allied leaders accepted Versailles as the appropriate location. As allied political leaders shaped the Supreme War Council, British military leaders, especially Robertson, adamantly opposed the entire idea. At one point he stood up when the subject came up for discussion and, after asking the secretary to record his departure, stormed out of the room. He insisted, "I do not quite see how a British Commander-in-Chief can be made, constitutionally, to obey the orders of an allied body."[91]

Despite Robertson's antics, France, Britain, and Italy signed the Rapallo pact on November 7 and created the Supreme War Council. The pact stated: "The Supreme War Council has the mission of watching over the general conduct of the war. It prepares recommendations for the decisions of the governments, assures the execution [of these decisions], and renders reports about them to the respective governments." Each of the "great powers" involved in the war was represented on the council by the president of its Council of Ministers (or its equivalent) and another member of the government. The "great powers" also had a permanent military representative on the council. Since the "exclusive function" of these representatives was to act as technical advisors, officers such as Foch could not have other responsibilities.[92] The real power of the council thus remained with the political leaders of the coalition, and the permanent military representatives fulfilled only an advisory role. As David Trask noted, the council in reality was a "political organization designed to concert inter-Allied strategy."[93]

After reaching agreement on November 7, the French, British, and Italian political leaders converted the fifth session of their Rapallo conference into the first meeting of the Supreme War Council and directed the permanent military representatives to consider the assistance the French and British should provide the Italians. Though real unity of command remained elusive, the allies had at least established an arena for discussion, and perhaps coordination, of their efforts. In reality Painlevé, who lacked the confidence, conviction, and character of Lloyd George, had withered before the objections of the British prime minister and had accepted a small gain in hopes of achieving a larger one later.

A week after the signing of the Rapallo pact, the French government fell. Throughout 1917 the French political situation had become increasingly turbulent. Briand's second wartime ministry survived from December 12, 1916, until March 20, 1917; Ribot's ministry from March 20 until September 7; and Painlevé's from September 13 until November 13. Though the army's leaders appreciated Painlevé's good intentions, they grumbled about his inability to dominate his own government,[94] and they were disappointed in early October when he had to plead for his fellow ministers to support his watered-down proposal for an allied war council. With several scandals weakening public confidence and discontent in the Chamber and Senate mounting, Painlevé's government fell on November 13. His was the first and only government to be overturned during the war by parliamentary vote. His government's fall marked the low point of France's political vitality during the war, a situation underlined by the British ambassador's reporting to London the possibility of civil war.

To avoid a collapse of its republican government, France required firm leadership, and the president of the Republic, Poincaré, had two clear choices: Joseph Caillaux and Georges Clemenceau. Caillaux had served as president of the Council of Ministers before the war, and some suspected that his return to power would result in his negotiating an end to the war. Known as "the Tiger," Clemenceau had also served as president of the Council of Ministers before the war and had made bitter enemies throughout France because of his vehement denunciation of numerous political and military leaders. No one, however, expected him to seek a quick end to the war. Given Poincaré's strong desire for victory over the Germans, his only real choice was Clemenceau.

On November 16 Clemenceau formed his new government with himself as the minister of war. In his ministerial declaration before the Chamber of Deputies on November 20, Clemenceau promised a "redoubling" of France's efforts and an end to political intrigues and crises: "Neither personal considerations, nor political passions will turn us from our duty. . . . No more pacifist campaigns, no more German intrigues. Neither treason, nor half treason. War. Nothing but war."[95] To galvanize the will of the French people, he acted quickly to quash defeatism and punish traitors. The former premier, Caillaux, was arrested, as was Jean-Louis Malvy, who had served as minister of the interior from the beginning of the war until August 1917. Even the former premier Briand came under suspicion and scrutiny. Among those accused of spying and executed were Bolo-Pacha and Mata Hari. Such actions demonstrated clearly Clemenceau's determination to continue the war and his refusal to accept anything other than victory. To strengthen the will of soldiers, he spent almost a third of his time visiting units and talking to commanders. Not one to avoid danger, he frequently went into the trenches and at one point was only 200 meters from the enemy. At a time when the French were faltering, the Tiger's fierce determination proved invaluable to sustaining their confidence and reviving their hopes of victory.

Though numerous political and military leaders had serious doubts about Clemenceau's ability to direct the war, his position on the Chamber of Deputies' Army Committee provided him a thorough understanding of France's army and its leaders and of the complexity of the Great War. Therefore his assumption of power produced none of the turbulence associated with Painlevé's tenure as minister of war and then premier. After assuming power Clemenceau clarified the relationship between political and military authorities. He shifted power from the parliament to the government by quickly ending the closed sessions of the Senate and Chamber of Deputies that had eroded previous ministers' authority. He also invigorated the War Committee, which had not played an important role since its establishment by Briand. During its seven sessions in December and January, the War Committee proved to be a useful forum for the discussion of strategic issues and for ensuring coordination among the various ministries.

Clemenceau gradually increased Foch's influence even though he had long thought that Pétain was the "best" of France's leaders.[96] As the first step, he removed Foch from the allied Supreme War Council. Painlevé had appointed Foch to the position of permanent military representative even though the appointment—in accord with the agreements with Britain—meant that Foch had to relinquish his position as chief of the General Staff. On November 29 Clemenceau appointed General Maxime Weygand, Foch's longtime chief of staff, as the French military representative. This action freed Foch to return to his duties as chief of the General Staff but ensured that his views would be faithfully presented in the Supreme War Council.

Clemenceau also pruned the chain of command. A week after entering office he firmly denied Pétain's request that French forces in the Italian theater be placed under his command. Like Salonika, the Italian theater would remain, Clemenceau said, an "entirely distinct" command under the minister of war.[97] As for Salonika, the Tiger moved rapidly to dismiss Sarrail. At his first meeting of the War Committee, he asked that the main topic of discussion be the question of command at Salonika and said, "Sarrail cannot remain there." The committee quickly approved dismissing Sarrail and sending a new commander.[98] When the committee discussed Sarrail's replacement, Clemenceau and Pétain preferred Franchet d'Espèrey, but Foch said General Guillaumat was more capable and should be sent. Clemenceau agreed, but only after Pétain shifted his support to Guillaumat. On December 10 Clemenceau informed Sarrail of his dismissal.

At a meeting of the War Committee a week later Clemenceau explained his view of French strategy and his relationship with senior military commanders. The opportunity arose from the presence of the presidents of the Senate and Chamber of Deputies, both of whom expressed concerns about the Germans' moving large forces from the Eastern to the Western Front. When one of them expressed doubts about limited offensives, Pétain responded strongly and offered to resign if anyone knew of a better method. Clemenceau quickly leaped to his defense and assured him that there was no question of resignation. "I am not for an offensive," he said, "because we do not have the means. It is necessary to hold; it is necessary to endure." He added, "I do not want to risk today the outcome of the war on an offensive. General Pétain is under my orders; I support him entirely."[99] For the moment the only things Clemenceau and France could do were to defer to Pétain and support his strategic and operational concepts.

Despite Clemenceau's determination, prospects for victory were not good. Although the arrival of the Americans gave the French some reason for hope and initially improved morale, soldiers became more critical, uncertain, and discouraged as the unpreparedness of the Americans became obvious. They knew novices when they saw them. One soldier wrote, "It is true that we have the Americans, but they have seen the war only in the movies, and it will be two years before they are ready."[100] In a report on soldiers' morale, postal authorities said an official statement from the government that the Americans would not be completely ready until 1919 had had a "deplorable" effect.[101] By mid-December the French High Command noted a "crisis of pessimism" among the soldiers.[102] A dismal assessment from the GQG staff catalogued the uncertainty of the future, weakness of the Italians, and dangers of even a "minor check."[103] Pétain concluded that "the situation . . . is less favorable than it was at the beginning of 1917."[104]

CHAPTER 9

Responding to a German Offensive

Spring 1918

I N THE LAST THREE months of 1917 and the first three months of 1918, the menace of a massive enemy attack weighed heavily on the French. In early December, about the time the Russians and Germans began discussing an armistice, Pétain's headquarters completed several assessments of the Central Powers' situation and identified the enemy's "most likely" courses of action. The GQG staff identified four variants in a massive German offensive: an attack on the Western Front, a maneuver through Switzerland against France, an attack against Italy, or an attack against Salonika. With additional forces available to the Central Powers as a result of Russia's collapse, the staff officers believed the enemy could combine options by, for example, attacking allied forces on the French front and simultaneously attacking through Switzerland against France or Italy. Whichever variant the Germans chose, the officers expected them to deliver their "decisive blow" on the Western Front.[1] In meetings of the War Committee on December 6, 10, and 12, Pétain discussed the strategic situation and France's options against a massive German offensive. After emphasizing the importance of keeping casualties low, he insisted that the situation imposed a "tactic of waiting" to permit the reconstitution of the Italian army and the transportation and organization of American forces. While waiting, the French could improve their defenses; create larger, more mobile reserves; gain additional cooperation from the allies, particularly the British; and achieve unity of command.[2]

Before the German offensive in March, French intelligence provided a reasonably accurate portrayal of enemy capabilities. As part of this effort, analysts carefully tracked the number of German divisions on the Western Front. On December 1 they counted only 151, about the same as the numbers of September 1 and November 1. On January 6 they counted 157; by February 3 the count had increased to 171, and by March 3 to 179. On March 14, a week before the German attack, analysts identified 188 enemy divisions on the Western Front and surmised that there might be as many as 193. After carefully studying the German offensive at Riga and counteroffensive at Cambrai, they concluded that the enemy could launch a large attack anywhere along the Franco-British front. In early March, as indications of an impending offensive multiplied, intelligence reported that the Germans were prepared to launch a large offensive after the middle of the month and identified the two most likely zones of attack as in the British sector between Arras and the Oise River and in the French Sector on a sixty-kilometer front centered on Reims. The most likely zone of attack appeared to be the British sector between Arras and the Oise. Except for the region east of Reims, both sectors corresponded roughly with the first and third of the coming German offensives. French intelligence thus provided ample warning of a massive operation and a reasonably accurate picture of German capabilities.

Despite the well-heralded threat of an enemy offensive, the allies moved slowly and hesitantly toward the formulation of a common strategy. Much of this hesitation came from the absence of any allied command structure, for after Joffre had left the scene in December 1916, no one had filled the vacuum in allied leadership caused by his departure. France had hoped the Calais agreement of February 1917 would result in Britain's tying its strategy and operations more closely to France's, but the failure of Nivelle's attack unraveled those arrangements. After allied leaders created the Supreme War Council in November 1917, the French again hoped for better coordination of allied strategy and operations, but progress came slowly. At the second meeting of the Supreme War Council, on December 1, Clemenceau insisted that the permanent military representatives study the situation and advise the political leaders on the council on the conduct of military operations. On December 13 the military representatives—Maxime Weygand from France, Henry Wilson from Britain, and Luigi Cadorna from Italy—suggested that the council adopt a "well-coordinated defense plan" for the front extending from the English Channel to the Adriatic.[3] In reality, the French and British had no "well-coordinated defense plan," and over the next three months they did little more than coordinate the employment of their reserves.

Many of the difficulties initially encountered in establishing a common strategy came from Pétain's and Haig's having fundamentally different strategic concepts in the autumn of 1917. Though Haig's views eventually changed, at the time he favored an offensive strategy for 1918 while Pétain favored a defensive strategy. On October 19 the field marshal notified Pétain that he intended to continue his offensive in Flanders during the coming year. In his discussions with Lloyd George and Robertson, Haig ruled out any possibility of a large French attack and painted the French army as incapable of an offensive, rather than as having chosen to remain on the defensive. He insisted that the British had to carry the burden of an immense offensive effort. An even more negative assessment of the French came from General Robertson, who also argued for a British offensive in 1918: "we ought not to be surprised if we find next year that, notwithstanding the splendid fortitude it has hitherto displayed, the French nation gives but comparatively feeble popular support to the continuance of the war."[4] Not until early December did Haig abandon his plans for an offensive. With the permanent military representatives recommending a defensive strategy to the Supreme War Council, he called together his army commanders and directed them to prepare for a powerful enemy offensive. His about-face came not from Pétain's persuasiveness but rather from the hard reality of enemy capabilities and his own limitations in terms of weapons, munitions, and personnel.

Although Haig's about-face promised better cooperation among the allies, nothing promised better cooperation between Pétain and Foch. Conflict between the two French generals was almost unavoidable, since their powers were not clearly defined and one was not under the command of the other. When Foch became chief of the General Staff,

Painlevé's confidence in Pétain had deflated his ambitions, but the arrival of Clemenceau and the French quest for allied unity of command gave Foch the opportunity to expand his powers. Fayolle, who distrusted Foch, said, "He wants to direct the war and be the generalissimo." He also wrote, "It is apparent from his conversations that he wants to replace Pétain, or in any case be the director of the war." In addition he noted that Pétain "shares my opinion of Foch."[5] For the first time in the war France had two generals who aspired to dominate the military effort and who competed to do so.

The first salvo between Pétain and Foch came in the form of a memorandum from Foch on January 1, 1918. Writing to General Weygand, one of the permanent military representatives at Versailles, Foch outlined a plan for the coming year and proposed a flexible allied strategy with a distinct offensive flavor. While acknowledging that the allies had to prepare for a strong German offensive, he advocated counterattacks against enemy attacks and "counteroffensives for disengagement" elsewhere on the front. The allied armies should "seize every opportunity to impose their will on the adversary by resuming as soon as possible the offensive, the only means of obtaining victory."[6] Foch also addressed the possibility that the enemy would launch another battle of attrition similar to the battle of Verdun. He reasoned that the Germans had halted their attack at Verdun only after the allies began their offensive on the Somme, and he called for preparations for a similar counteroffensive in 1918. To ensure sufficient power, Foch called upon the Supreme War Council to direct the French and British armies to plan for a combined operation. Less than a week later a proposal from the General Staff in Paris, which worked under Foch, suggested the appointment of a "temporary agent of superior command" who would direct a Franco-British counteroffensive.[7] Though the second memorandum did not bear Foch's signature, his desire to be the allied supreme commander and his role in crafting the missive were obvious.

When Pétain received Foch's first memorandum, he read it carefully and wrote his objections in the margin. Alongside Foch's comment about the allies' having the resolution to impose their will on the adversary, he wrote, "The period of waiting will last throughout 1918." Alongside Foch's comment about launching powerful "counteroffensives for disengagement," he wrote, "With what?" The most damning comment, however, came when Pétain compared Foch to a person who had little money but wanted to dine at an expensive restaurant.[8] Though Pétain did not disagree with all aspects of Foch's proposal, he responded with a memorandum that forcefully expressed his objections to an excessive emphasis on the offense. He argued that the Americans could not play an important role before 1919 and that allied soldiers should be used cautiously until then. The French did not have sufficient forces, he said, to rotate units through another battle of attrition or to launch a "counteroffensive for disengagement." The French, he insisted, had barely enough forces to do anything other than bar the advance of the enemy or come to the aid of allies, and these actions could occur only if French commanders succeeded in distinguishing enemy main attacks from secondary attacks and did not make any mistakes. "In summary," said Pétain, "the battle of 1918 will be defensive on the Franco-British side, not by the absolute will of the command but by the necessity of the situation. The absence of means imposes this on us."[9] Despite Pétain's emphasis on the defense, he did not favor a passive defense and worked diligently, as will be explained below, to assemble large, powerful reserves and to develop doctrine and train commanders for counteroffensives.

A meeting on January 24 between allied chiefs of staff and commanders provided an opportunity for Robertson, Haig, Foch, Pétain, and Pershing to discuss strategic and operational concepts for the coming campaign, but it also furnished an arena for continued sparring between Pétain and Foch. After Robertson opened the meeting, the discussions began:

> General Pétain . . . states that the French army because of its limited means will await the German attack while remaining on the defensive. The reduction of our personnel has already obliged us to suppress five divisions. Even without combat, our resources in the interior do not permit us to replenish our front until the month of April. In the future we will be constrained by new suppressions, so many that at the end of 1918 it will be necessary to envisage the dissolution of twenty divisions. To this reduction in personnel, it will be necessary to add the losses resulting from combat.

As a consequence, we will remain on the defensive while maneuvering on prepared successive lines. Meanwhile, we have organized four offensive battlefields that we will use if circumstances permit.

Furthermore, we have arranged the movement of available reserves by railway; they will be employed either on the French front or the British front to relieve units or to halt the enemy in a threatened sector.

In an indication of how things had changed since October, Haig indicated that "the English had adopted the same line of conduct as the French." In addition to conducting similar defensive operations, Haig and Pétain had agreed to discuss the employment of their reserves "on a common battlefield."[10]

The only discordant note in the meeting came from Foch's comments about offensive operations. The minutes recorded the exchange between Foch and Pétain:

> General Foch says that the best means of halting a powerful and persistent enemy offensive, an offensive of attrition and fury, is to launch a powerful offensive. The German offensive at Verdun was halted not by our resistance at Verdun but by our offensive on the Somme. But such an operation is possible only if it is anticipated and prepared. . . .
>
> General Pétain observes that in 1916 the Germans attacked only one point and had only 125 divisions. Now they will dispose of 170, 180, perhaps 200 divisions, and they will attack three points at the same time or successively, and on each point the attack will be more violent than at Verdun.
>
> General Foch responds that . . . the attack at Verdun commenced on February 21 and the offensive on the Somme was not launched until July 1. But it is clear that this offensive, which had a decisive effect on the campaign of 1916, could not have taken place if it had not been anticipated and prepared for several months. This is what is important to remember for 1918.
>
> General Pétain declares himself in accord with this principle but observes again that the suppression of twenty French divisions in

1918 means that we will not have the troops available to take the offensive.[11]

Later in the discussion, Foch emphasized that he was speaking of a counteroffensive, not an offensive. Foch and Pétain thus used the meeting to debate their conflicting ideas. The raw relationship between the two became apparent when Foch expressed ignorance of some of the logistical and transportation difficulties encountered by Pershing, and Pétain caustically commented, "One should not wait until such things are brought to one's notice but should look around and find them."[12]

The next arena in which the two clashed was the meeting of the Supreme War Council from January 30 to February 2, but this time Foch, not Pétain, gained the edge. When the council met, the assembly included not only the allies' political leaders but also their most senior military leaders. Discussions began with an analysis of the current situation. When Foch repeated the ideas in his memorandum of January 1, Pétain, Robertson, and Haig expressed strong reservations about the utility or possibility of a "large offensive." Though acknowledging the importance of combining defensive and offensive actions, Pétain and Haig insisted that they did not have the requisite troops and materiel for significant offensives. The bleak assessments of the two commanders-in-chief—Pétain expected to suppress twenty-five divisions in the coming year and Haig thirty—aroused the doubts and ire of Clemenceau and Lloyd George, but neither political leader sided with Foch's call for more aggressive operations.[13] Among the general officers only Foch anticipated the allies' having an opportunity for an offensive in 1918.

Most of the discussion on strategy focused on the permanent military representatives' Collective Note No. 12, which ruled out the possibility of a decisive action against the enemy on the Western Front in 1918 and recommended offensive operations against Turkey to take advantage of recent allied success. Given the likelihood of a massive German offensive in France, Pétain and Haig opposed transferring troops and equipment from the Western Front and suggested that only minor reinforcements be sent to the Near East. When Lloyd George suggested having the allies make their principal effort in 1918 against Turkey, Clemenceau demonstrated that he was a far tougher opponent than Painlevé. The Tiger emphatically opposed the proposal and insisted that any operation against Turkey be conducted only with British forces. Clemenceau's objections prevailed, and the formal adoption of Note No. 12 occurred only after the British agreed not to divert forces from the Western Front.

The allies also discussed Collective Note No. 14, which focused on establishing an allied general reserve. Pershing observed, "The discussion of this question became rather acrimonious."[14] Foch began the discussion with an explanation of the need for reserves. Since the allies could not predict where the enemy would concentrate his attacks, they needed, he said, to constitute reserves and to give an "inter-allied organ" the authority to make all preparations for their employment. In late January Pétain had formally expressed his concern about having inadequate reserves, and he feared that a general reserve would end up under Foch's control and be wasted in futile and costly "counteroffensives for disengagement." During the meeting, Pétain and Haig cited anticipated reductions in their forces to argue strongly against the formation of a general reserve. Neither of them concealed their disgust at the possibility of their reserves' being placed under another commander. Both maintained that a commander's freedom of action depended on the use of his reserves, and neither could conceive how someone else could control a portion of their forces. Despite objections from Pétain and Haig, the political leaders agreed with Foch, and the Supreme War Council approved the creation of a general reserve for the "Western, Italian, and Balkan Fronts."

After much debate, the council also created an Executive War Board to control the general reserve. The board included the permanent military representatives of Britain, Italy, and the United States and General Foch, who was designated its president after Lloyd George proposed his appointment. Until the board ordered the commitment of the general reserve, units in the reserve remained under the control of their respective commanders-in-chief. Despite this approval, significant obstacles still had to be overcome before the allied general reserve actually came into being and unity of command was established.

Foch turned eagerly to his new duties as president of the Executive War Board. On February 6 he informed the commanders of the French, British, and Italian armies that the board had decided to form an allied general reserve of approximately thirty divisions, thirteen or fourteen

from France, nine or ten from Britain, and seven from Italy. Foch heard
first from Pétain, whose long letter objected to the board's actions and
complained that it was disrupting his carefully arranged plans. With a
German attack imminent, Pétain believed he might have to commit his reserves rapidly, but the creation of a large allied general reserve could keep
him from responding quickly and would deprive him of any means of action on most of his front. He insisted that fourteen divisions (six French,
four British, four Italian) would suffice for the general reserve.[15] A week
later, for reasons that are not clear, Pétain relented and said he was willing
to provide eight but could not provide ten. Even stronger objections
came from Haig, who did not receive the message from Foch until February 27. The British commander argued that he had "already disposed" of
all the units under his command and having to "earmark six or seven divisions" would force him to revise all his preparations. He concluded, "I
therefore regret that I am unable to comply with the suggestion conveyed
in the Joint Note."[16]

While resisting the formation of the allied general reserve, Pétain and
Haig created reserves under their own control and arranged for recipro-
cal support should the need arise. Beginning with a careful analysis in
December 1917 of reserves available for "different offensive and defensive
alternatives," Pétain moved some of his reserves in late January to the
Oise region, near the boundary between French and British forces. The
next step came after the British extended their right and relieved Third
Army. As will be explained below, convincing the British to relieve Third
Army proved difficult, but once the relief occurred the French immediately began preparing for the contingency of Third Army's relieving a
portion of the British right or coming directly to its aid. After Pétain and
Haig decided to cooperate and agreed that only the British should come
to the aid of the Belgians, French and British representatives met on February 21 and 22 and coordinated possible reliefs, defenses, and counteroffensives. They selected three areas (west of Arras, around Amiens, and
around Montdidier-Noyon) in which the French could concentrate before intervening in the British sector and one area (south of Soissons) in
which the British could concentrate before intervening in the French sector. While the French anticipated sending as many as twenty divisions
into the British sector, the British anticipated sending as many as eight

into the French sector. On March 17 the French published a detailed summary of the Franco-British agreement.

In the end the existence of these plans and the opposition of the two allied commanders dismantled the general reserve. Before the Supreme War Council's meeting in London on March 14–15, Clemenceau and Lloyd George decided to support their commanders, Pétain and Haig, rather than the board. In his memoirs Lloyd George asserted that Clemenceau's anticlericalism caused him to distrust and ultimately to decide against Foch, but the French premier did not reject Foch because of his strong Catholic faith. The Tiger changed his mind about the general reserve after meeting with Pétain and Haig and confronting Haig's adamant opposition to providing divisions for the general reserve. Before meeting with the two allied commanders, Clemenceau saw himself as the arbiter between Foch and Pétain: "At the moment of attack, I will be there. If there is a clash, I will take care of it."[17] Late on the evening of February 23, Clemenceau met with Pétain, listened to his criticisms of the general reserve, and told him he wanted no more conflicts with Foch. The following evening Clemenceau met with Haig. The stubborn British commander told him, "I will never give up my reserve divisions to form a reserve army; I would rather resign immediately."[18] The Tiger recognized that he had no way to overcome this opposition and no authority to arbitrate a confrontation between Foch and Haig.

With key political leaders (Poincaré, Alexandre Millerand, and Charles de Freycinet) imploring Clemenceau to support Pétain, the Tiger met with his military assistant, General Henri Mordacq, on the evening of February 27 and discussed the issue of the High Command thoroughly. The complexity of the situation was obvious: Clemenceau could arbitrate between Foch and Pétain but not between Foch and Haig, and the concept of the general reserve had several key flaws, including its being controlled by a committee. Yet Clemenceau saw reasons for hope in Pétain's and Haig's having the same ideas about the conduct of the campaign, their having a cordial relationship, and Haig's having promised to come to Pétain's assistance in case of attack. On the following morning Clemenceau met with Pétain, who reported the results of the encounter to Poincaré: "The reserve army is dead."[19] Clemenceau's quest for unity of command, however, was not dead, and he told Mordacq: "It is necessary that we have it, no matter what the cost. Foch is ready to take the helm, and my having obtained the presidency of the Executive War Board for him a few weeks ago is very significant progress on this issue [of unity of command]. We will resolve this issue, but with Lloyd George, it will not be easy."[20]

The fourth meeting of the Supreme War Council began with Lloyd George's declaring that he had accepted Haig's advice and explaining why he believed Haig's and Pétain's reserves should not be touched. When Clemenceau spoke, he expressed his agreement with Lloyd George and noted Haig and Pétain's arrangements to provide mutual aid if needed. After considerable discussion, the council agreed to maintain the general reserve "in principle," but it included in this reserve only a handful of divisions. With the exception of one division, all were on the Italian front. The council expected additional divisions to join the general reserve once the arrival of new divisions from the United States freed units for such use. Although Foch complained that the council had deprived the Executive War Board of all executive power, the council retained the board and directed it to consider several strategic questions. As part of these discussions Foch provided a brief summary of the allies' situation and the functions of the Executive War Board. After emphasizing the importance of having an "agent" who could coordinate activities between the allied armies, he insisted that his remarks be included in the minutes of the meeting. Clemenceau eventually grew impatient with Foch's objections and told him, "Shut up!"[21] With a German attack imminent, the allies had taken two steps toward establishing unity of command but then had taken one step back.

Clemenceau's decision to favor Pétain and not insist on a viable general reserve kept the reins of military power in Pétain's hands. Although the Executive War Board provided the platform for a much greater expansion of Foch's authority, the French responded to the German attack on March 21 in consonance with the preparations made primarily by Pétain. That is, they remained on the defensive and relied on the arrangements made between Pétain and Haig for mutual support. Despite Lloyd George's complaint that these arrangements were "vague, loose and dilatory" and Foch's criticism that they were "weak and absolutely insufficient,"[22] Pétain's personal control over French reserves and his ability to employ them quickly provided the allies the edge they needed during the first German attack. In fact there is no evidence to suggest that an allied general reserve under Foch's control would have arrived more quickly or been more effective.

As Pétain continued preparations to defend against a massive German attack, a severe shortage of personnel continued to shape his actions. An assessment in early October 1917 anticipated that the army would receive 110,000 new recruits every month until September 1918 but still be short 100,000 soldiers at the end of that period. Such a shortage would require the French to suppress twenty-four battalions, the equivalent of six divisions. As shortages began hampering operations, Pétain dissolved three divisions in November 1917. That same month, another study anticipated a shortage of 200,000 men by November 1918 and the suppression of nine divisions. Mid-December 1917 brought a more extreme assessment of France's personnel situation. The study assumed the French would lose 920,000 soldiers between October 1, 1917, and October 1, 1918; this figure matched the losses suffered from July 1, 1916, to July 1, 1917. The study also said that the army required an additional 158,000 men if it was to increase its artillery, engineers, aviation, and antiaircraft units. The combination of projected losses and anticipated additions meant that the army required 1,078,000 recruits. Since the army expected to receive only 750,000 new recruits during this period, the study projected a deficit of 328,000 men. This deficit equaled twenty-five divisions (including three already dissolved), the figure cited by Pétain at the Supreme War Council meeting on January 30, 1918. With six divisions in Italy and eight in Macedonia, Pétain expected to have only seventy-seven divisions in France in October 1918.[23] Though one could quarrel with the assumptions and conclusions of this bleak assessment, the specter of a crisis in personnel continued to influence Pétain's preference for limited offensives within a defensive strategy. Similarly, many of his criticisms of Foch's ideas came from his fears that the French would run out of men.

The crisis in personnel also heightened Pétain's desire to have the British extend their front. Such an extension would enable him to assemble larger reserves and respond more effectively to the anticipated German offensive. His goal, as he explained to Foch on September 22, was to have the British relieve—"as a minimum"—Third Army. This fifty-four-kilometer extension of the British front would free six or seven divisions for inclusion in French reserves. Although Pétain and Haig soon agreed that the British would relieve four French divisions and extend their right to the south, on November 25 Haig proposed having the British extend their front only half the distance previously promised. In the ensuing quarrel over the length and timing of the extension, Pétain emphasized the importance of constituting reserves for the coming campaign and noted: "It is no longer a question of British forces or French forces; the battle must be fought with the entirety of British and French forces on that portion of the front where the decision is at stake. We can do this only if we constitute, as soon as possible, reserves prepared for combat. Holding the Western Front should thus be envisaged in its entirety without any selfish considerations."[24] When Clemenceau entered the fray, he informed Lloyd George that he intended to submit the question to the Supreme War Council; he also threatened to resign if the British did not relieve Third and Sixth armies. Meanwhile Pétain and Haig met on December 17, and Haig agreed to extend his right ten kilometers south of the Oise to the right boundary of Third Army. With the relief of the first French units commencing on January 10, Pétain expected the relief of Third Army to be completed by February 20.

Though the two allied commanders had ironed out most of the wrinkles, the permanent military representatives examined the question and published their recommendations in Collective Note No. 10 on January 10, 1918. They recommended that the British extend their right to a point twenty-five kilometers south of the Oise, fifteen kilometers beyond the right boundary of Third Army. When the Supreme War Council discussed Collective Note No. 10 on February 2, Clemenceau insisted that Haig extend his front the full twenty-five kilometers south of the Oise as recommended by the permanent military representatives. After much wrangling, the council adopted Note No. 10's recommendation to extend the British front beyond Third Army's right and asked Pétain and Haig to work out the details pertaining to time and method. The two commanders, however, declined to take any further action on the controversial issue. In fact Haig never extended his right farther than ten kilometers south of the Oise, and Pétain was content with the relief of Third

Army. This extension of fifty-four kilometers coincided exactly with what he had told Foch on September 22. Unfortunately for the British, the new front corresponded closely with the front of General Oskar von Hutier's Eighteenth Army, the German force that would make the deepest advances on March 21.

As Pétain sought additional reserves, his eyes fell on the six French and five British divisions in Italy. In November–December 1917 the French had contemplated an allied offensive from Italy if the Central Powers attacked France, but in early January Pétain wrote to the minister of war: "Important actions in the immediate future can no longer be envisaged in the [Near] East or Italy while a powerful enemy offensive appears imminent on the French front. . . . Under these conditions all our effort should be concentrated in the principal theater of operations." He then asked for the return of XII Corps from Italy.[25] Speaking on behalf of the minister of war, Foch refused to move the corps. He explained: "The reserves at your disposal, combined with the English reserves, are sufficient to support the battle initially; your reserves can be strengthened only slightly by the arrival of two divisions from Italy. These divisions will have plenty of time to [move to France and] take part in the battle when they are needed."[26] The disapproval of Pétain's request also rested on Foch's preference for an allied counteroffensive, probably in Italy. Pétain's desire to bring some of the French divisions back from Italy thus momentarily fell victim to Foch's designs.

Questions about the place of Italy in allied strategy surfaced in a meeting on January 24 among Foch, Pétain, Haig, Robertson, and Pershing. Robertson argued that since an enemy offensive in Italy could not occur before May and since an enemy offensive in France probably would occur before May, it seemed wise to move allied forces from Italy to France. After acknowledging the validity of Robertson's point, Foch argued for keeping some Franco-British forces in Italy to strengthen the Italians and assist their training. The movement of forces from Italy to France, said Foch, could occur more rapidly than movement from France to Italy, since logistical support and supplies were already in place in France. Three weeks later the changing strategic situation and increasing opposition from Haig and Pétain to losing divisions to the allied general reserve compelled Foch to withdraw his opposition to shifting forces from Italy.

Acting on his own initiative and going beyond his authority as president of the Executive War Board, Foch sent a telegram to London on February 13:

> The equilibrium of opposing forces on the Franco-British and Italian fronts is clearly in favor of the enemy on the first of these fronts and [in favor] of the allies on the Italian front. Thus it appears essential to bring back without delay from Italy part of the allied forces that are there. Since English reserves are actually less numerous than French reserves and the English front appears menaced more immediately, two English divisions should be brought back at once from Italy. French troops will follow.[27]

As for the French, Foch and Pétain quickly agreed to recall Fayolle and his army-group headquarters from Italy and to place Fayolle in charge of Pétain's Reserve Army Group. The French also prepared to move infantry and artillery out of Italy. When the Supreme War Council met on March 14, it approved having British and French divisions in Italy, as well as some Italian units, form the nucleus of the allied general reserve. In the end, these decisions added only modestly to allied reserves in France, for only one of the British divisions had returned when the Germans began their offensive.

While trying to convince the British to extend their front and Foch to withdraw French forces from Italy, Pétain struggled with another contentious issue, the amalgamation of U.S. army units. Shortly after Pershing arrived in France, he and Pétain had agreed that American divisions would concentrate in northeast France. The first U.S. division to enter the line would occupy a position on the east bank of the Moselle, the second on the west bank, and subsequent divisions on the east bank. This sequence would extend U.S. forces toward the east and place them in a position to participate in an offensive near St.-Mihiel. Despite Pershing's desire to create an independent American army, the French, as he later said, "continually argued" for integrating or amalgamating American companies and battalions into French units.[28] Pressure for amalgamation increased substantially after the Caporetto disaster and the beginning of armistice talks in Russia between the Bolsheviks and the Central Powers. On December 6 Pétain told the War Committee, "As for the Americans, it is absolutely necessary to achieve amalgamation."[29] Though American leaders had clearly stated that questions about amalgamation should be addressed to Pershing, Clemenceau, using the French ambassador, urged Washington to accept amalgamation. Pétain also met with Colonel Edward M. House, a close friend and adviser of President Wilson, and proposed having American battalions and regiments train with French divisions. He assured his American visitor that such a procedure would accelerate the training of Pershing's forces and thus American divisions and corps would be ready for operations earlier. When Pershing learned of these efforts, he complained to Clemenceau and Pétain about "back door methods."[30]

As pressure from France and Britain mounted, President Wilson consented to amalgamation but left the final decision to Pershing. For the French, this decision did not represent progress, since the American general clearly had no interest in amalgamation. Poincaré and Clemenceau considered trying to convince Washington to replace the difficult and obstinate officer, but a letter from Joffre reminded them that shortly after entering the war the Americans had expressed their intention to keep U.S. forces in France independent and autonomous. He also warned that too much pressure by France would "gravely compromise" the United States' willingness to cooperate with the allies.[31] The field marshal's intervention angered Clemenceau, but he would have been much angrier had he known that Joffre had advised Pershing to resist amalgamation.

While Poincaré and Clemenceau worked diplomatic fronts in Washington and Paris, Pétain led the effort to convince Pershing to accept amalgamation. On December 23 the two generals met and discussed the training of American troops. Pétain offered two alternatives: first, continue training the first two U.S. divisions in France in accordance with the program established by Pershing but amalgamate subsequent divisions with French units; second, conduct an experiment by having the U.S. 1st Division continue training under Pershing's program but have 26th Division (the second unit to arrive in France) send its regiments to train with French divisions. The French, Pétain said, would accept handling subsequent divisions according to whatever program proved most effective, but Pershing insisted that amalgamation should be used only if the situation became "very grave." He withheld his response to Pétain's proposal until he had additional time to consider it.[32] In a letter to Pershing a few days later Pétain explained the importance of accelerating the training of American units:

> The menace . . . of an enemy offensive of large energy on the French front compels us to call upon all our resources, including American troops. . . . we must presume that we cannot wait until [American] troops are formed and trained as we would have desired if we had . . . a great deal of time. The problem of training these troops thus is posed in a form different from that of six months ago when the first contingents arrived in France.

Pétain then proposed training the first divisions in France with Pershing's program but preparing subsequent divisions by temporarily assigning their regiments to French divisions. American units prepared in this manner, said Pétain, could come together "progressively" and occupy an increasingly large sector.[33]

Pershing responded to Pétain's desire for compromise by agreeing that newly arrived U.S. regiments could serve for at least a month in French divisions. He also offered the "temporary service of a certain number of indigenous regiments." These were African-American regiments, and Pershing added, "It is possible that circumstances will permit leaving them with you indefinitely." Pershing's offer obviously served to appease the French desire for soldiers to fill their ranks. As for other American regiments, he refused to leave them indefinitely with the French. In addition to difficulties caused by differences in "language, methods, and national temperament," Pershing believed the American people would object to dispersing them in the French and British armies.[34] He evidently believed the American people would not object to loaning the African-American regiments to the French.

Pétain responded immediately, saying, "We are entirely in accord on principles." Those French divisions that had U.S. regiments attached to them, Pétain promised, would not be thrown into a battle hastily and thus have their training interrupted. As for the African-American regiments, he was "very willing" to accept their attachment to French divisions, since black soldiers had served superbly in French units from the beginning of the war. His only disagreement pertained to Pershing's proposal for splitting the U.S. 42nd Division into two brigades and having one complete the American training program while the other served with the French and received instruction from them. Pétain thought this would create a "troubling disequilibrium" between the two brigades and weaken the performance of the division.[35] With the major issues resolved in their written correspondence, the two met on January 11 and established the new program. Pershing described the program on January 17 in a letter to Newton D. Baker, the secretary of war:

> It has been agreed, then, that we should go on as in the past, aided by French instructors and a more limited number of French units, following such courses of training as we should prescribe, and that later, our regiments should go into French divisions, posted in a quiet sector, for experience in the trenches, the generals and staff officers to have service with corresponding grades and commands in French units. This duty with the French divisions is to be for training only, and when finished the elements of our divisions are to be reunited under our own officers. I think the plan is the very best we could adopt and the French seem equally satisfied.[36]

Pétain and Pershing thus reached a compromise which improved training and accelerated the entry of U.S. divisions into the front line but which also retained the goal of having the Americans establish an autonomous force with their own sector.

Despite this compromise, the issue of amalgamation remained controversial, since the French and British still wanted to use U.S. companies and battalions to fill their thinned ranks. When the British asked Pershing to attach battalions to their divisions and offered to provide transportation across the Atlantic, Pershing refused. In a clever bureaucratic maneuver, he asked that shipping identified as available for transporting U.S. battalions be used instead to ship six divisions. Although

Pershing had initiated the assignment of African-American regiments to French divisions, he would not approve any additional attachments for reasons other than training. Pétain nonetheless argued in late January for additional concessions. He said:

> The American army will be no help if it wants to conserve its autonomy in 1918; even if its soldiers and lower ranks are excellent, it will not have commanders and staffs this year. Not having the nucleus that the English had [when they expanded their army], it will take longer for the American army to be constituted. The Americans cannot participate in battle [as an autonomous force] until 1919. While waiting, amalgamation is imperative; if we do not take these measures, the war will enter an extremely critical period.[37]

Despite such appeals, Pershing refused to let the diversion of companies and battalions disrupt his efforts to create an independent, autonomous force.

By March the French anticipated only modest support from the Americans in 1918. Pétain expected one U.S. corps of four divisions to be ready to enter the battle line in May. Hopes for more American divisions had collapsed when Pershing announced that he would have only eighteen divisions in France by July. As for the Americans' capabilities, Pétain thought the sole U.S. corps could participate in a defensive operation in May but not an offensive; he knew that other divisions would not be ready for combat for several months. His hands tied, Pétain complained bitterly to Poincaré that if the coming battle lasted longer than a month, the French would not have enough reserves. The general insisted, "There is only one remedy: the rapid arrival of the Americans and amalgamation."[38] Clearly, the issue of amalgamation would arise again.

Meanwhile the French looked at other alternatives. The options considered included having the Chinese provide 50,000 soldiers, the Czechs a brigade, and the Poles a division. Early in the war the French had attempted unsuccessfully to convince the Japanese to send troops to France. As in the case of the Japanese, there was little chance of getting the Chinese to send a large contingent to Europe, but the Czechs had a brigade ready in October 1918 and the Poles had a division in France in November 1918. No contribution was too small for France to consider.

While Pétain negotiated with the British to extend their front and the Americans to accept amalgamation, he revamped French doctrine. Since de Langle's innovations at Verdun in early 1916, the French had trumpeted the merits of a defense in depth, and in their numerous offensives they had recognized the Germans' defensive skills, including their fighting throughout the depth of a position and using counterattacks to disrupt the momentum and progress of an attack. Despite the obvious advantages of a defense in depth, some French commanders still placed large numbers of their troops in front lines and instructed their soldiers to hold every foot of terrain. Pétain understood the weaknesses of a linear defense against more modern methods and massive firepower, and he attempted to convince his officers to abandon their obsolete and vulnerable practices. A note from his headquarters in late November observed: "Recent operations of the British army in the region of Cambrai have demonstrated the possibility of launching an offensive operation of great energy while maintaining the benefit of surprise up to the last moment."[39] In the face of a well-prepared surprise attack, defenders could not always prevent enemy gains, but they had to do more than prepare successive lines behind the front. Commanders had to organize their positions so that the enemy could not move and exploit laterally, and they had to prepare their reserves to intervene rapidly. In short, the French had to be more flexible in their defensive operations.

In late December Pétain published two documents articulating the new defensive doctrine. The first, "Defensive Actions of Large Units in Battle," appeared on December 20 and the second, Directive No. 4, two days later. Both documents emphasized establishing a "position of resistance" and retaining large reserves. Instead of commanders' placing their strongest defenses along the forwardmost line, Pétain told them to spread their forces throughout the depth of their defensive position. He wanted them to place sufficient forces in their forward positions to weaken the enemy but to keep the bulk of their forces in the rear, where they could not only halt the enemy but also launch counterattacks. Forward of the position of resistance, commanders should place "islands of resistance," which would break up the enemy's assault, separate the enemy's infantry and artillery, and facilitate French counterattacks. By placing only small forces forward, commanders could reduce casualties, since enemy mortars and short-range artillery could not reach the main position of resistance. Rejecting a passive defense, Pétain instructed his subordinates to maintain an "aggressive" attitude in their operations and to locate reserves so that they could either strike the enemy's flanks or shift to another nearby part of the front. The two documents also emphasized the importance of reserves held by Pétain. Like the reserves of corps, armies, and army group, these would intervene at an opportune moment in a judiciously chosen location.[40] The similarity between the new French doctrine and the Germans' flexible defense did not escape the notice of senior leaders.

Although the British had adopted a three-zone defense-in-depth system, they did not fully understand Pétain's move away from lines of trenches and toward positions of resistance. When the British extended their front and Fifth Army relieved French units on both banks of the Oise in January 1918, commanders were appalled at the absence of a "continuous line" of trenches and complained angrily about the work involved in improving "very poor defenses."[41] Reporting to the British War Cabinet that the French "had not kept up their defensive lines" as well as the British, Haig complained about the "great need for improvement."[42] Since the French had done little to fortify the region, British complaints had some validity, but many of the criticisms came from their expectation of finding neatly arranged trenches, not haphazardly located centers of resistance. British commanders also did not understand completely how to conduct a defense in depth. Haig's headquarters, for example, expected Fifth Army to fall back rather than offer resistance throughout the depth of its defensive position, but Fifth Army concentrated its strongest efforts in the forward zone. As Tim Travers has argued, the British defensive system in the region of the March attack "was not understood, did not work, and did not properly exist at all."[43] The Americans also did not understand Pétain's new defensive doctrine. When they translated "Defensive Actions of Large Units in Battle," they left out the concept of centers of resistance.

In January 1918 Pétain met with his corps, army, and army-group commanders to ensure that they understood his new doctrine. He spent much of his time explaining why the French could not fight to retain every foot of soil. When he spoke to commanders in Second Army, he said, "We will lose terrain; that is understood." Recognizing that the loss of terrain could weaken French morale, he emphasized the importance of explaining to soldiers why they had to yield terrain and how to withdraw while fighting. He also said, "The best method of being victorious in battle is to economize our forces at the beginning."[44] When he met with the leaders of Fourth Army the following day, he said, "If we place everyone in the first line (as the Germans did at Malmaison) on a position known by the enemy . . . we will lose everyone." He added, "It is not possible to maneuver if everyone defends the first position." Also, "We do not have enough infantry divisions to accept a defensive battle on the first position. It is necessary then to maneuver and make the terrain work for us."[45]

After finishing his round of visits, Pétain sensed continued reservations among his senior commanders and sent them additional instructions about implementing the new defensive doctrine. He also provided them a detailed analysis of German operations on the Eastern Front at Riga in September 1917. This study emphasized the German practices of providing detailed training for their infantry, seeking surprise, and using brief artillery preparations. For their operation against Riga, the Germans had assembled their forces 120 kilometers from the point of attack and then had concentrated 157 artillery batteries and 550 *Minenwerfer* along a front of 4.5 kilometers. If French commanders doubted the Germans' ability to launch a massive surprise attack, the Riga example provided ample evidence of the enemy's capabilities and furthered Pétain's goal of ensuring that his subordinates understood the demands of the new operational situation.

As Pétain worked tirelessly to reeducate the officer corps, Clemenceau left him alone to prepare for the coming campaign, but prior to the German offensive the Tiger pressured him to redirect some of his efforts. In late January he wrote to Pétain and criticized the lack of progress in preparing four defensive lines along the entire front. Clemenceau derived his observations from a report written by General Roques about defensive preparations across the French front. Not one to tolerate political intrusion into technical military matters, Pétain responded, "The battle of 1918 is not being prepared solely by the organization of terrain." Preparations for the battle, said Pétain, involved numerous complex efforts, and the completion of defenses in depth was only one of these. Unwilling to be dismissed lightly, Clemenceau sent a more strongly worded letter that criticized Pétain's willingness to abandon terrain too quickly, his lack of emphasis on defensive preparation in forward positions, and his failure to communicate his ideas more clearly to his subordinates. The Tiger also noted that some units had halted work in their forwardmost positions and had suspended preparations for any offensive operations. Pétain quickly responded by not only renewing his efforts to educate his subordinates in the new defensive doctrine but also ensuring that preparations for an offensive or counteroffensive occurred. A memorandum from the GQG on February 11 explained that the French could not defeat the Germans without a counteroffensive and that Pétain's "freedom of action" in the coming battle depended "primarily on the results obtained in preparations on the front for an offensive." The memorandum also prescribed locations for which each of the armies would prepare offensives.[46] French commanders, however, overreacted to this new guidance, and on February 23 Pétain had to remind his senior commanders to prepare for a counteroffensive, not for an offensive.

Pétain also sought to clarify his guidance about the conduct of the battle forward of the position of resistance. Some officers believed that forward units should do nothing more than offer token resistance and then withdraw to the rear, but Pétain insisted that forward units fight as tenaciously as units on the position of resistance. He told his army and army-group commanders, "the covering-force mission which is fulfilled by troops in the first line . . . can be accomplished only by an all-out defense in the combat position assigned to every element by the commander."[47] Pétain also ruled against local counterattacks in the forward zone unless they sought to retain points essential for the subsequent success of the defense. The infantry, he insisted, had to compensate for its numerical inferiority by making the enemy pay a high price for any gains. Thus Pétain established doctrinal guidelines for yielding terrain in the face of a massive attack, and he never contemplated retiring or withdrawing without inflicting heavy losses on the enemy.

Throughout the winter of 1917–18 the French conducted only small operations, for Pétain wanted to avoid casualties and insisted on nothing larger than local attacks. On November 7 Seventh Army attacked in Alsace; two battalions advanced about 500 meters and captured some high ground that enabled the French to see to Mulhouse and Altkirch. Two weeks later Sixth Army attacked north of Soissons with two battalions and advanced 600 meters. On November 25 Second Army assaulted Hill 344, on the east bank of the Meuse north of Verdun; four regiments advanced several hundred meters and suffered 1,800 casualties. When the British attacked at Cambrai in late November, the French had one corps in the region, but it played only a minor role. In December French operations became even more conservative. Most operations were nothing more than raids designed to gather intelligence and prisoners. In the largest of these, two regiments from First Army charged forward east of the St.-Mihiel salient on January 8 and grabbed 188 prisoners. On February 13 two battalions from Fourth Army captured 196 prisoners east of Reims. On February 20 Eighth Army launched two small raids east of Nancy. One, involving four battalions, captured 357 prisoners; the other, involving three battalions, failed and suffered heavy losses. In early March the enemy made several small raids or attacks. In one raid the Germans captured 56 prisoners, and in another they killed 267 French soldiers. The French responded with several raids, capturing 50–125 prisoners. The pace and scale of operations thus remained markedly lower than in the previous winter.

On the eve of the German spring offensive the French High Command had done everything in its power to prepare for the approaching battle. When the British extended their front line 10 kilometers south of the Oise River, they—along with the Belgians—occupied 200 kilometers of the Western Front while the French occupied 530. Pétain divided his front into two sectors, with Northern Army Group under Franchet d'Espèrey on his left and Eastern Army Group under Castelnau on his right. From left to right Northern Army Group had Sixth, Fifth, and Fourth armies, and Eastern Army Group had Second, First, Eighth, and Seventh armies. Behind these seven armies Pétain placed Fayolle's Reserve Army Group. He had dissolved Central Army Group when Fayolle went to Italy in mid-November 1917 and established the new army-group headquarters when he returned. Pétain had great confidence in Fayolle and knew he and his army-group headquarters could handle the enormously complex operational and logistical challenges of responding to a massive German attack or even a breakthrough. He also assembled substantial reserves, including five corps with thirty-nine infantry and two cavalry divisions. He placed two infantry divisions behind the Belgian army near the coast, nineteen behind Northern Army Group, and eighteen behind Eastern Army Group. The reserves also included thirty-five regiments of heavy artillery, seventeen with Northern Army Group and eighteen with Eastern Army Group. Additionally, Pétain held ten regiments of 75-mm cannon in reserve. Altogether, his forces had 6,519 light, 5,853 heavy, and 417 long-range heavy artillery pieces.

With powerful reserves, Pétain expected to fight an active defense and to keep the Germans from making a breakthrough. He intended to receive the "first shock" of the enemy attack and to fight the defensive battle with "strict economy." To compensate for French numerical inferiority, he organized defenses in depth and arranged for his reserves to arrive quickly and in time. He also organized his front so that he could transition to the offensive quickly. After halting the Germans, he intended to launch a counterattack with the minimum possible delay.[48] All in all, he improved considerably the ability of his forces to move to a threatened region and attack. Yet he still refused to consider Foch's "counteroffensives for disengagement" or do anything that would fritter away the lives of France's dwindling number of soldiers. His greatest fear was that the Germans would launch another battle of attrition and drain the French of all their reserves.

On March 11 French intelligence reported that the Germans had changed their codes for encrypting wireless transmissions. In the past the Germans had changed their codes about a dozen days before an offensive. On March 20, the day before the German offensive began, intelligence identified 182 German divisions on the Western Front and, though not ruling out the possibility of an attack on either side of Reims, expected the enemy's main effort to strike the British sector between Arras and the Oise. On the night of March 20–21 enemy artillery fire and infantry raids occurred along the fronts of Sixth, Fifth, and Fourth armies, which stretched from Soissons, to Reims, to Ste.-Menehould. The following morning the German Seventeenth, Second, and Eighteenth armies struck between Arras and the Oise. Although Seventeenth and Second armies in the north made the main attack and Eighteenth Army in the south made a supporting attack, the Eighteenth Army achieved more success in the south than the Seventeenth in the north and drove the British Fifth Army back with a violent, massive attack.

On the first day of the enemy offensive Eighteenth Army advanced quickly through the sector originally held by the French Third Army but occupied by the British Fifth Army since mid-January. At 2015 hours, a liaison officer at Haig's headquarters informed the GQG of the "bad situation" developing on the right of British Fifth Army. Two hours later the GQG alerted V Corps that it might be moved to aid the British.[49] Shortly after midnight Haig asked formally for assistance. During the Franco-British negotiations in February on mutual assistance, the two allies had identified three alternate locations where the French could assemble reserves in the British sector in the event of an enemy offensive and had established two levels of priority for regulating the size of the forces moving to the three locations. Haig asked for Hypothesis A, First Priority. This translated into an army headquarters, three corps headquarters, six infantry divisions, and seven regiments of heavy artillery assembling near Noyon. The first elements were supposed to arrive no later than the evening of the fourth day and the last by the morning of the ninth day. Pétain quickly ordered Third Army with V Corps and II Cavalry Corps, including six divisions, to the north. Haig wanted Third Army to relieve part of the British Fifth Army and occupy a fifteen-kilometer sector north of the Oise along the Crozat Canal. Officers in the Operations Bureau of the GQG viewed the British request with dismay. One of them told an American officer, "It is well enough to help our allies, but when they call for help the first day, what can you expect by tomorrow?"[50]

With only eight divisions in his GHQ reserve on March 21, Haig had placed two behind each British army. Before the enemy attack, General

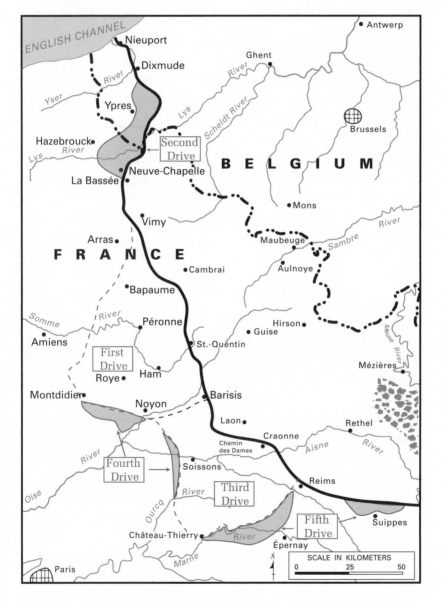

The German spring offensive, 1918

Sir Hubert Gough, Fifth Army commander, appealed to the GHQ to move two divisions in the reserve behind his army closer to his front lines, but the GHQ refused. Haig remained preoccupied with the junction between his First and Third armies near Arras rather than the front or boundaries of Gough's Fifth Army. After the battle began, Haig visited Fifth Army's headquarters and responded to Gough's appeals for assistance by saying, "Well, Hubert, one can't fight without men."[51] In contrast, the French had amassed considerable reserves, thirty-nine infantry and two cavalry divisions, and had carefully reviewed their procedures for assisting their ally. Although Pétain complained to officers in the GQG that the British were "playing a dirty trick" on him, he responded rapidly and effectively to Haig's request for assistance. On the second day of the German offensive, March 22, the V Corps commander met with the British III Corps commander a few kilometers north of the Oise River and coordinated the movement of French units into a sector just north of the river. That same day elements of 125th Infantry Division, which was not part of V Corps but was sent by Sixth Army, moved into position just north of the Oise to assist the British. As these efforts proceeded, Haig asked for the relief of all British forces south of the Oise.

Until midnight on the twenty-second, arrangements for providing mutual support seemed to be working, but the Germans' dramatic gains caused Haig to ask for assistance beyond that envisaged in the Franco-British agreements. Around 0100 hours on March 23 he asked for the relief of all British forces between the Oise and Péronne, an extension of the front twenty-five kilometers beyond what Pétain already had accepted. Despite troubling indications of German preparations for an attack in Champagne east of Reims, Pétain agreed to take responsibility for the much larger sector and, with Third Army already commencing its move, decided to send First Army, as well as Fayolle's Reserve Army Group headquarters. Counting units in Third Army that already had orders, twelve infantry divisions, five cavalry divisions, and twelve regiments of heavy artillery were ordered to move to the threatened sector. Pétain also told Fayolle to take command at 2300 hours of all French and British forces between Barisis (Sixth Army's northern boundary, ten kilometers south of the Oise) and Péronne. With Haig's blessing, two corps of the British Fifth Army came under Fayolle's control. Additionally,

Pétain arranged for French aviation to fly hundreds of sorties and drop thousands of pounds of bombs on the enemy between Péronne and the Oise.

In the Operations Bureau of the GQG officers harshly criticized British commanders and staffs for not being "efficient" or "highly trained." They also criticized Gough's handling of the British Fifth Army and his "indecision." An American liaison officer to the GQG reported that French officers believed the British "quit too soon and retired too soon." Despite doubts about British leaders, they remained impressed with the combat qualities of British soldiers. One said, "they are not like the Italians you know."[52]

The head of the British mission to the GQG, Brigadier General G. S. Clive, aptly summarized the operational situation when he told an American officer, "It is a race. We [the British] cannot stand it much longer. The question is can the French arrive in time to save the day. It will be a close race."[53] Though the French did their best to rush troops toward the threatened sector, they were hampered by a temporary shortage of cavalry. To quell strikes and riots, the government had sent five cavalry divisions and several regiments to Lyon and other industrial centers, and thus some of the most mobile units in the French army were not immediately available. By 1500 hours on the twenty-third, however, three divisions in V Corps were heavily engaged north of the Oise. That night three divisions in II Cavalry Corps attempted to move into position on the left of V Corps. As the Germans advanced, they kept the arriving divisions and the remnants of Fifth Army from establishing a new defensive line. When French units disembarked in the widening hole, usually without artillery and with only ammunition carried by individuals, they went into action immediately. Such piecemeal commitment of units resulted in high casualties, but the Third Army commander continued feeding them into the battle.

When Pétain met Haig at 1600 hours on March 23, he insisted that the enemy was "trying to drive a wedge between the two armies" and emphasized the importance of maintaining contact along the Franco-British boundary.[54] He warned Haig that it would take six days for all the elements of First and Third armies to arrive in their new positions. The British commander agreed to order his Fifth Army to "hold the line of the Somme at all costs" and to maintain contact with the French on its right.[55] When Haig asked Pétain to concentrate twenty divisions around Amiens, the French commander said he could not because of his limited reserves and his concerns about an enemy attack in Champagne. Pétain left the meeting worried about the outcome of the battle. An intelligence report that evening from Fourth Army added to his worries, for it affirmed the enemy's preparations for an attack "after March 26" in Champagne.[56] Pétain knew that halting an attack in Champagne of the same scale as the one on the Somme would be extraordinarily difficult.

Earlier on March 23 Pétain had dispatched a liaison officer to Paris to ask Clemenceau to meet with him to discuss "responsibilities and contingencies."[57] That night he gave the premier an update and harshly criticized the British. According to General Mordacq, Clemenceau's military assistant, no one at the GQG—including Pétain—had any confidence that the British would offer serious resistance. Returning to Paris by car, the Tiger said, "After a meeting like that, it's necessary to have ironclad resolution to have any confidence." The following morning he met with Poincaré and warned him of Pétain's extreme pessimism.[58] With rounds from German long-range artillery pounding Paris, he then met with the Council of Ministers. After describing the situation as serious, he told the ministers they might have to move the government out of the capital city and instructed them to begin preparations for moving out key resources and people.

The situation worsened considerably that day. In his formal report on the campaign Pétain wrote: "already on the twenty-fourth the British right wing was considered incapable of serious resistance; the hole opening at the junction of Franco-British [forces] was enlarged by the marked tendency [of the British] to pull back [toward the northwest] in the direction of Amiens and not toward Montdidier [in the west]."[59] That afternoon Clemenceau again met with Pétain after the general-in-chief requested his assistance in convincing the British to stop withdrawing. Pétain warned him of the "great danger" that the Germans might separate the two armies completely and then defeat the "weakest," the British. He insisted that he could not remain in position with his left uncovered and might have to withdraw to Paris or even beyond.[60] Although Haig later accused Clemenceau of ordering Pétain to "cover Paris at all costs," the Tiger gave no such order.[61]

On his own, Pétain took steps on March 24 to preserve the integrity of French forces and protect Paris. After the Germans crossed the Somme, which ran north-south between Ham and Péronne, he ordered First Army to establish a north-south defensive line in the vicinity of Montdidier, thirty kilometers to the rear of the Somme, and Third Army to delay the German advance "no matter what the cost." Third Army was supposed to hold along the Oise (east-west) and to establish a defensive line ten to fifteen kilometers behind the Somme between Noyon and Roye (north-south). Pétain told Fayolle to keep French forces intact and "if possible" maintain contact with British forces. He also gave French cavalry the "principal mission" of covering the left of Reserve Army Group and the "secondary mission" of maintaining contact with the British.[62] A late-night order reminded Fayolle that he should pay attention to his right.

In one of the most controversial moves of the war, Pétain had given first priority to preventing the Germans from driving west through Noyon and Montdidier and reaching Paris and second priority to maintaining contact with the British and protecting Amiens. In doing this, he did not order a withdrawal toward the southwest or accept the possibility of the Germans' driving northwest and splitting the French and British, but he did decide that defending Paris was more important than maintaining contact with the British. Under ordinary circumstances he would never have considered such a choice, but as he told the minister of armaments, he had never anticipated the Germans' "annihilating" the British.[63] Despite his concern for Paris, he did not abandon his efforts to reach out toward Haig. The British field marshal did not reach out to the French, however, or to his crumbling Fifth Army on his right but instead gave first priority to his left. In a meeting at 2000 hours, Haig directed his Third Army commander—in the words of the British official history— "to cling with his left to the First Army near Arras."[64] With few allied forces to their front, the Germans had the opportunity to split the two armies.

When Pétain and Haig met at 2300 hours on the twenty-fourth, the two discussed the possibility that the Germans might split their forces, and Pétain advised Haig not to "refuse the hand I am holding out to you." He also gave the field marshal a copy of the order he had given Fayolle. When Haig asked Pétain if he might lose contact with the British right flank, the French general nodded yes and said, "it is the only thing possible if the enemy compels the allies to fall back still further." Notes from Haig's chief of staff, Lieutenant General H. A. Lawrence, who attended the meeting, confirm Pétain's acknowledgment that French forces were authorized to pull back "in case of necessity." The same notes confirm that Pétain warned Haig that the British would be in a "difficult" situation if they were "cut" from the French.[65] Another British officer at the meeting, Brigadier General Clive, believed that Pétain was encouraged when he departed. Of those attending the meeting only Haig viewed the French commander as "much upset, almost unbalanced and most anxious."[66] In fact Haig was probably more shaken than Pétain and thought the British were on the edge of a disaster. The morning after meeting with Pétain, Haig gave General Weygand, France's permanent military representative at Versailles, a memorandum in which he stated that it was only a "matter of time" until "the French and English armies are driven apart." To restore the situation he asked Pétain to launch a counterattack with "at least twenty divisions" against the flank of the Germans who were attacking the British. He also said the British would continue fighting but would withdraw "slowly while covering the Channel ports."[67] Thus Haig had no intention of reaching out toward Pétain and expected him to counterattack and relieve pressure on the British. As Tim Travers has suggested, Haig was contemplating breaking contact with the French, and to conceal that fact and to protect his reputation he later doctored his account of the meeting on the twenty-fourth to make it appear that Pétain was the one refusing to "keep in touch" with his ally.[68]

Pétain was extremely worried, but neither he nor his subordinate commanders were "unbalanced." To strengthen Fayolle's Reserve Army Group, he sent additional units on the twenty-fourth: two corps headquarters, six more infantry divisions, and a regiment of heavy artillery. With twenty-three divisions ordered to the battle, he hoped his troops could halt the Germans and maintain contact with the British right. Furthermore, orders from him and other French commanders on March 23,

24, and 25 continued to emphasize holding, not withdrawing, and thereby buying time for reinforcements to reach the threatened sector. Even in 125th Division, the first to enter the battle, the commanding general continued to tell his men to resist the Germans strongly and to withdraw "only in case of absolute necessity."[69] Additionally, Pétain took special steps to ensure that his forces remained in contact with the British. That is, he tried to "buckle" the French and British together by moving French troops south from Nieuport to Amiens. At 0110 hours on March 25, long before Foch was charged with coordinating the action of the allies' armies, a telegram from the GQG alerted XXXVI Corps for a move south. When 133rd and 29th divisions moved a week later into position southeast of Amiens on the British side of the salient, their presence, as Auguste Laure and Guy Pédroncini have argued, offered tangible proof of Pétain's efforts to prevent the Germans from driving a wedge between French and British forces.[70] The allies nevertheless came perilously close to being separated and fighting two distinct battles, a British battle for the ports and a French battle for Paris.

Out of this near disaster came an important step toward allied unity of command. Three hours before meeting with Pétain on March 24, Haig wired Sir Henry Wilson (who had replaced Robertson as chief of the Imperial General Staff) and asked for a conference with the French as soon as possible. When notified of the meeting, Clemenceau foresaw the possibility of establishing a unified command and promised Poincaré he would devote all his energies to this long-sought goal. Allied leaders subsequently met at Compiègne on the twenty-fifth and Doullens on the twenty-sixth. At 1700 hours on March 25 Poincaré and Clemenceau met Lord Milner, a member of Lloyd George's War Cabinet who would soon be secretary of state for war. Foch and Pétain also attended the meeting, which took place at Pétain's headquarters. The conferees reached no conclusions, since Milner had not yet met with Haig. The following day, allied leaders met at Doullens.[71] If Pétain had had any chance of being the allied generalissimo, he lost it when he told Clemenceau, "The Germans will defeat the English in open country; after that, they will defeat us, too."[72] Nor did Pétain endear himself to the British; at one point he interrupted Haig's comments about the British Fifth Army and compared General Gough's troops to the Italians at Caporetto. Recognizing the opportunity, Foch exuded great confidence and conviction and, unlike Pétain, tried to maintain a cordial relationship with the British. Before the meeting, Foch had given Clemenceau a memorandum in which he emphasized the importance of common Franco-British action and called for the appointment of an "agent" to give orders to allied forces and ensure that they were executed. In this memorandum he described the area south of Péronne, where Pétain and Fayolle had struggled desperately to shore up the British Fifth Army and halt the Germans, as "easy to defend" and the area to its north as requiring substantial reinforcement by the French and British.[73] In his typically optimistic fashion, he argued during the meeting for not withdrawing any farther. Though Clemenceau bristled when he read Foch's self-serving memorandum, Foch's optimism proved far more attractive to the grizzled politician than Pétain's pessimism.

Without consulting their American, Belgian, Italian, or other allies, Clemenceau and Milner, after making several changes to a draft, signed an agreement charging Foch with "coordinating the action of the allies' armies on the Western Front."[74] Although Foch's powers were limited, the pressure of battle had finally produced some semblance of unity of command. After the meeting, French leaders celebrated with a luncheon in Doullens. According to General Mordacq, Clemenceau viewed the agreement as the equivalent of a victory over the Germans.[75] The Doullens agreement, however, affected only the British and French armies and did not extend to the American, Belgians, or Italians even though those signing the document had scratched out the words "British and French" and replaced them with "allies."

As soon as Foch had his new powers, he entered the fray by bypassing Pétain and Haig and talking directly to key commanders. At 1600 hours on March 26 he met with General Gough, who later complained that Foch was "amazingly ignorant" of how well Fifth Army had fought. Gough also said, "Foch was peremptory, rude, and excited in his manner."[76] After ordering Gough to defend "at all costs," Foch sent written instructions to the commander of Reserve Army Group, General Fayolle, to protect Amiens and to hold "at all costs" the position occupied by Fifth Army.[77] He also told Fayolle first to support and then to relieve British troops from Gough's army south of the Somme. Foch then telephoned General Debeney, commander of First Army. He directed Debeney not to remain in position near Montdidier and wait for the enemy but instead to move forward and support the British on Gough's right. Although these actions did not change the conduct of the battle completely or provide Haig with the twenty divisions he wanted, they did energize French actions and strengthened defensive efforts.

Pétain did not resist Foch's intrusion into what was his legitimate area of responsibility. Instead, late on the twenty-sixth he sent Fayolle a message that annulled his orders of March 24 and corroborated Foch's orders. On the morning of the twenty-seventh, however, he telephoned Fayolle and told him to give first priority to protecting Noyon, and thus Paris, and second priority to protecting Amiens. As Fayolle noted in his diary, Foch wanted him to give first priority to Amiens and second to Noyon. Elevating Foch to his new position obviously had not ended friction between the two generals.

Pétain's worst fears began to subside on the twenty-fifth. That day he received a report that the Germans had withdrawn troops from the Champagne front and thereby "renounced" their attack in that region. Late that night, Pershing drove to his headquarters and volunteered to relieve individual French divisions. Though Pétain had doubts about the Americans' readiness to assume responsibility for a sector, he sent out a message providing for the entry of four U.S. divisions into different sectors in the front lines. The reduced threat in Champagne and the availability of American divisions enabled Pétain to accelerate the move of additional forces to Fayolle's sector. According to Pétain's report on the campaign, the French had sixteen divisions participating in the battle on March 26 and twenty-seven en route. By then the worst of the crisis had passed, and on the evening of the twenty-seventh an American liaison officer to the GQG reported to Pershing, "The British and French flanks join." The same officer also reported that dinner with the GQG's Operations Bureau on the evening of the twenty-eighth was "almost like a congratulation party."[78]

Heavy fighting nevertheless continued south of the Somme in the French sector. The situation of Debeney's First Army was particularly difficult, since only part of it had arrived near Montdidier. Though the allies had halted the enemy almost completely by March 30, the Germans renewed their attack against First and Third armies, which occupied a front that stretched across sixty-two kilometers. By this time, however, Pétain had ample divisions to offer a strong defense, and the arrival of French artillery meant that the infantry no longer fought without adequate support. When German attacks on the thirtieth failed to make significant progress, soldiers in the front lines knew that the gravest danger in the Somme sector had passed.

The last spasm of the first German offensive occurred on April 4, when the enemy struck between the Somme and Montdidier. Though the Germans had sixteen divisions in their front line and the French only seven, the French had eight divisions in reserve, and they intervened rapidly. The French also had ample artillery, 588 75-mm and 378 heavy pieces. Showing little interest in infiltration tactics, the Germans attacked in dense formations and suffered heavy casualties. The following day First Army counterattacked. Instead of a tightly coordinated offensive, its individual corps launched separate attacks after brief artillery preparation, but the corps advanced as much as one and a half kilometers.

As the German offensive ground to a halt, Foch sought an extension of his powers. In his memoirs Pershing described the problem: "It was the prevalent British view that General Foch was simply a liaison officer between the two armies, with advisory and coordinating authority only."[79] On March 31 Foch wrote to Clemenceau and proposed that his powers be expanded from coordinating the actions of the allied armies to directing them. The next day Clemenceau met Foch and listened carefully to his proposal. The Tiger had long favored greater unity of command, but he was not certain that the time was right for giving Foch additional authority. Following this meeting, Foch sent him two letters, both of which argued for a "superior direction of the war."[80] Ostensibly bowing to Foch's advice, Clemenceau invited Lloyd George to France to discuss the situation.

At the Beauvais conference on April 3, which was attended by Clemenceau, Foch, Pétain, General Tasker H. Bliss (U.S. permanent military representative to the Supreme War Council), Pershing, Lloyd George, Wilson, and Haig, Foch appealed for greater authority. Although

Clemenceau strongly supported Foch, Lloyd George maintained that the British Parliament would never approve having a French general act as commander-in-chief over British forces. After Bliss and Pershing supported Foch's proposal, Haig expressed his willingness to follow the strategic guidance of the French commander-in-chief. Seizing the opportunity, Clemenceau produced a proposal drafted by his military assistant, Mordacq. That proposal gave Foch responsibility for the "strategic direction of military operations" but said nothing about his commanding British forces. Lloyd George quickly accepted the proposal, as did General Bliss, subject to the approval of Washington. In addition to giving Foch responsibility for the strategic direction of military operations, the agreement charged him with coordinating the action of allied armies on the Western Front and conferred upon him all the powers necessary to accomplish this coordination. For the first time in the war, the allies had unity of command on the Western Front. That evening, General Weygand, Foch's longtime protégé, cornered the liaison officer to the government and suggested that it was "natural and opportune" to name Foch a marshal of France as quickly as possible.[81]

Immediately after the Beauvais conference, Foch issued strategic guidance to Pétain and Haig. Though expecting a major enemy offensive in the British sector, he directed Pétain to attack "as soon as possible" in the region of Montdidier and Haig to attack "astride" the Somme while defending between the Somme and Arras. He also directed Pétain to assemble reserves south of Amiens and prepare them for employment in the British sector. Pétain faced an especially difficult task, for the French front had increased by ninety kilometers since the Germans began their offensive. Nonetheless, the day after receiving Foch's directive, he issued orders for assembling new reserves and launching several small limited offensives. South of Amiens he placed two infantry and one cavalry corps under Tenth Army (which had been withdrawn from Italy), and in the Oise valley he placed two infantry and one cavalry corps under Fifth Army. While Tenth Army could cross the Somme and support the British, Fifth Army could assist Reserve or Northern Army Group. In case of extreme need, Fifth Army could also assist Eastern Army Group. Pétain's reserves thus could intervene anywhere on the front, but their placement was particularly appropriate to counter an enemy offensive in the British sector or in the French sector near Paris. As Pétain's letter to Foch indicated, however, the last reserves would not arrive in their new positions until April 10.

Meanwhile Haig grew increasingly concerned that the Germans might renew their offensive and attempt to destroy the British army. On April 6 he asked Foch to assist the British by launching a large offensive in the French zone, relieving four British divisions south of the Somme, or moving a reserve of four French divisions farther toward the north in the British zone. A subsequent letter from General Wilson emphasized the importance of French assistance, for the British expected the Germans to attack with forty to fifty divisions between the Somme and La Bassée. Foch agreed with the British assessment, and he directed Pétain to send an infantry corps with four divisions and a cavalry corps with three divisions to an assembly area west of Amiens instead of south. That evening, April 7, Pétain sent instructions for Tenth Army to move farther north.

Despite indications of a coming enemy offensive, Foch insisted on a limited offensive by the French First and British Fourth (Fifth Army was redesignated the Fourth) armies south of the Somme. In a meeting with Haig on April 7, he said that such an offensive would bar the route to Amiens and create the opportunity for a larger counteroffensive. Foch initially wanted Pétain to attack with his First and Third armies, but when Pétain insisted that doing this would require forty-one divisions, Foch relented and agreed to an offensive only with First Army. He also relented when the British Fourth Army commander said he required additional divisions to participate in the limited offensive. In the end, only First Army planned on participating in the offensive, which was scheduled to begin on April 12. On April 8 Haig appealed again to Foch to relieve British divisions so that he could amass reserves for the anticipated enemy offensive, but Foch steadfastly refused and insisted on doing nothing more than pushing French reserves toward Amiens.

On April 9, as Pétain proceeded with preparations for a limited offensive by First Army, the Germans resumed their offensive. Instead of striking between La Bassée and the Somme, they struck north of La Bassée in Flanders. Aiming toward Hazebrouck, the important rail junction whose capture would sever Haig's lateral communications, the Germans assaulted the center and left of the British First Army and made particularly large gains against the Portuguese 2nd Division near Neuve-Chapelle. By the evening of the second day, the Germans had advanced eight kilometers and threatened to capture Hazebrouck. General Wilson met with Clemenceau on April 10 and emphasized the seriousness of the situation, but the two could not agree on an appropriate response.

Believing that the Germans aimed to destroy the British army, Haig wrote to Foch on April 10 demanding "that the French army begin steps immediately to relieve part of the English front and take an active part in the battle."[82] Before receiving Haig's note, Foch visited Pétain's headquarters and ordered him to hasten Tenth and Fifth armies' move north, but he did not foresee these reserves' being employed in Flanders. The German attack in Flanders, Foch believed, sought to divert allied reserves from the Somme-Arras region so that the main attack could break through allied lines and drive toward Abbeville and the coast. He also traveled to the British field marshal's headquarters and informed him of the movement of French reserves toward the north to protect the Somme-Arras front.

Furious at Foch's refusal to insert French troops into the fight, Haig complained in his diary that Foch was "afraid" to put French divisions into the battle because of their unwillingness to fight.[83] On April 11 Haig issued his famous "backs to the wall" order in an attempt to motivate his tired soldiers, but he also demanded that the French intervene with four divisions and assist the British in Flanders. The Germans made their largest gains (fifteen kilometers) in the first five days of the offensive, and the situation appeared even more desperate to Haig when he again met with Foch on April 14. He insisted that Tenth Army be deployed farther north so that it could reinforce the British in Flanders and that Fifth Army be deployed farther north so that it could reinforce the British between Arras and the Somme. As far as Haig was concerned, the British were bearing the entire burden of the German offensive and receiving no assistance from the French. He wrote, "If the necessary measures are not taken, the British army will be sacrificed and sacrificed in vain."[84] Foch refused to have French reserves relieve frontline British units, but he did move Tenth Army farther to the north and removed it from Pétain's control. He still believed the Germans intended to renew their offensive in the Somme-Arras region.

When the Germans launched another attack north of the Hazebrouck salient, Foch yielded to Haig's demands. With the battle of Flanders clearly shifting north rather than south, he had no choice but to direct the relief of British divisions and arrange for the transportation of additional French divisions to the north. To this end the French formed the Army Detachment of the North with XXXVI and II Cavalry corps. Beginning on the night of April 18, four divisions in the detachment entered the front lines in the Mount Kemmel sector, north of the Hazebrouck salient. Although the Flanders front remained quiet after the eighteenth, the enemy launched a strong attack on April 25, striking the newly formed Army Detachment and the British to its north. Though some soldiers fought very well, the French lost Mount Kemmel, and the British scathingly criticized them for losing that important observation point. After an attempt to regain Kemmel the following day failed, British criticism of their ally escalated. When the Germans attacked the French west of Kemmel on April 29, rumors that the French had again failed circulated widely through the British army even though the French repulsed the attack.

By the end of April the second German offensive had ended, but the allies' success had not engendered closer relations between the French and British. In fact the bloodied and battered British, seeking to place blame on someone other than Gough's Fifth Army, castigated the French and complained loudly about their ally's willingness and ability to fight. Many of these doubts came from the fact that the British suffered 259,779 casualties between March 21 and April 30 while the French lost only 92,004. The British believed that they had borne the heaviest burden of the two German offensives and that the French had done little to assist them. The British had no sympathy for the fact that the French had had to extend their front 92 kilometers (including the south bank of the Oise) and occupy 580 kilometers of front while the British occupied 135 and the Belgians 35. They ignored the fact that the *new* front occupied by the French after March 21 equaled two-thirds of the entire front occupied by the British on April 30. Despite this significant effort, the British remained suspicious about Foch's having delayed the entry of French troops into the front lines in Flanders and unimpressed by the performance of French soldiers, particularly at Mount Kemmel. Meetings of allied staffs revealed simmering anger and increased doubts among the British about the French.

The French had their own reservations about the British. At the GQG a staff officer told an American liaison officer that the "British custom" was "to get someone else to do the work and make the sacrifice."[85] In the past the French had compared the British favorably to the Russians and Italians, but as a morale report in mid-May emphasized, "The precipitous recoil of the English, and in particular of the Fifth British Army, has completely changed this view." The same report included bitter complaints that the British had pillaged French villages through which they had withdrawn.[86] In contrast, the French estimation of the Americans improved. As the soldiers watched the number of Americans increase and as they watched them enter battle eagerly, they became more optimistic about the outcome of the war. The soldiers were also proud of having halted the first German attack even though they had been greatly outnumbered. One report noted, "The German offensive and its initial success, far from demoralizing our troops, was a stimulant for the soldiers."[87] For the first time in a long while, many of the soldiers entertained hopes of a favorable and quick ending of the war.

As the German second offensive unleashed its last efforts, the amalgamation of Americans into French and British units resurfaced as an important issue. Given the large number of casualties in the first two offensives, the allies demanded greater assistance from the Americans. With General Bliss's support, in late March the permanent military representatives of the Supreme War Council recommended "temporary service" of American units in allied corps and divisions; they also recommended transporting "for the moment" only American infantry and machine-gun elements to Europe. Discussions continued on May 1, when the Supreme War Council met at Abbeville. With substantial pressure also coming from Lloyd George and Milner, Pershing finally relented and offered a compromise. Though wanting much more, the council accepted a formal resolution committing the British to transporting 130,000 American troops in May and 150,000 in June. At the time of the meeting there were 429,375 Doughboys in France but only four divisions in the front lines.

Pershing promised that two more divisions would be ready in a week and another two shortly thereafter.

The accelerated arrival of U.S. units did not alleviate Pétain's concerns about the long front for which he was responsible. On May 7 he met with Foch and emphasized the considerable extension of his front and the large number of divisions transported north of the Oise River. He asserted that "the French have reached the limit of their effort in sending divisions north of the Oise."[88] Foch, however, refused to permit the shifting of French forces toward the south. He explained, "On the front between the Lys [south of Hazebrouck] and the Oise, a German attack of great energy can come at any moment and achieve results that will have the gravest consequences because of the proximity of important objectives."[89] With the front line only eighty kilometers from the coast, an enemy advance along the Somme could split the allies and yield the Germans important strategic advantages. Consequently, Foch insisted on maintaining a large French force north of the Oise River; he wanted to retain Tenth Army north of the Somme and Fifth Army south of the Somme.

Foch's plans for transferring exhausted British divisions to a "quiet" sector on the French front caused additional concerns for Pétain. Foch proposed this transfer after forming the Army Detachment of the North and inserting it into the front line in Flanders. The transfer of British divisions to a quiet sector, he believed, would enable them to relieve French units, which then could move to the north and form reserves behind British front lines. Certain that the Germans would attack again in the north, Foch envisaged exchanging ten to fifteen divisions between Flanders and a quiet French sector. Pétain completed the logistical arrangements necessary to exchange four divisions, but he objected to reducing his operational capability. He had sent forty-seven divisions to "relieve or support" the British but was receiving only four divisions. He added sternly, "the British High Command seems to forget, despite a great deal of evidence, the past effort of the French army and underestimates its present effort."[90] Notwithstanding Pétain's complaints, the idea for the exchange of divisions came from Foch, not from Haig. Unfortunately for the allies, the four British divisions subsequently involved in the exchange ended up going to the Chemin des Dames, the site of the third German offensive, rather than to Lorraine or the Vosges, as Foch had initially envisaged.

Though expecting another enemy onslaught, Foch insisted that the allies prepare a counteroffensive. In essence, he sought an attack on both shoulders of the Hazebrouck and Montdidier-Amiens salients. In Flanders he wanted the Army Detachment of the North to attack toward Mount Kemmel while the British attacked from Béthune toward La Bassée. South of the Somme he asked the British and Reserve Army Group to strike east of Amiens while other units in Reserve Army Group hit the Montdidier-Noyon region. These attacks would cut off most of the gains made by the Germans in their March 21 and April 9 offensives.

Pétain, however, doubted that the French had the resources or opportunity for a large operation. He objected when Fayolle submitted his operational plans for approval and Foch responded with a detailed critique demanding more energetic and ambitious operations. Ignoring Foch's guidance, Pétain directed Fayolle to launch more restrained operations. When Foch learned of Pétain's intervention, he demanded that the attacks be "pushed as quickly and as far as possible with every available resource."[91] On May 15 Foch met with Pétain and Fayolle and explained his strategic concept, but Pétain refused to budge and insisted on written orders from Foch. True to his academic roots, Foch responded with an essay that argued, "Only the offensive will permit the allies to terminate the battle victoriously and regain, along with the initiative in operations, moral ascendancy."[92] If the Germans did not attack, the allies could surprise them with an offensive; if the Germans did attack, the allies could respond in a like manner. Pétain answered by complaining to Poincaré when he visited the GQG that an allied offensive would be "very dangerous" and waste allied reserves without achieving any results. The troops in Flanders were under Foch's orders, not his, and according to Pétain they were being thrown into poorly prepared attacks. With Pétain increasingly despondent and considering resignation, the long-simmering conflict with Foch remained very much alive.[93]

By May 26 Foch's focus on the north had greatly reduced Pétain's ability to respond to a German offensive south of the Oise. According to Pétain the allies had two-thirds of their sixty reserve divisions between the Oise and the Channel and one-third between the Oise and Switzerland. The day before the third German offensive Pétain had sixty-three French divisions (including three cavalry) between the Oise and Switzerland; he also had five British, three American, and two Italian divisions. Of the twenty-two allied divisions not in the front lines in this long sector, Pétain had four immediately behind Sixth Army, which occupied a long section of the front stretching from the Oise to Reims, including the Chemin des Dames. Behind the left of Sixth Army another four divisions, protecting Paris, occupied positions in the Oise valley, and behind the right of Sixth Army one infantry and two cavalry divisions occupied positions near Reims. To ensure that additional reserves were available, Pétain arranged to transport infantry and artillery from Reserve Army Group to the other two army groups. In essence he foresaw a complete reversal of what had happened after March 21; instead of French forces rushing to the north, he foresaw French forces rushing to the south. Pétain apprised Foch of his preparations and a week before the German offensive asked the allied commander for permission to include the Army Detachment of the North in his plans.

In the weeks before the Germans struck the Chemin des Dames, French intelligence discerned few indications of an impending attack in that region. The GQG did note that the Germans had seventy-five to eighty divisions available in their reserves on the Western Front in late May, a number comparable to the seventy-four available on March 21 and greater than the forty-six available on April 9. Aware that the Germans could attack anywhere along the front, on May 14 French intelligence calculated how long it would take the Germans to concentrate thirty-eight divisions in Champagne (between Reims and the Argonne) and in Lorraine. The specialists concluded that it would take a week to do so in Champagne and three weeks to do so in Lorraine. The assessment ignored the region west of Reims, which included the Chemin des Dames. Most intelligence reports suggested that the Germans would again attempt to separate the British and French.

After the Germans attacked along the Chemin des Dames, the Intelligence Bureau in the GQG carefully reviewed all indications of an offensive available to the French before May 27. This review included an analysis of the normal sources of information (such as prisoner interrogations, reports of escaped French prisoners, enemy infantry and artillery activity, railway traffic, road traffic, and aerial surveillance). The analysis concluded, "The meticulous camouflage of [enemy] preparations rendered illusory or misleading a very large number of sources of intelligence upon which we previously had relied."[94] Indications of an offensive had nonetheless come from a German aviator captured on May 19 and from five French soldiers who had escaped from the enemy on the twenty-second. The five soldiers reported having heard talk of a large attack to seize the Chemin des Dames. Not until 1500 hours on May 26, following the interrogation of prisoners captured that day, did the French have a clear indication that the Germans intended to attack the Chemin des Dames. At 1620 hours Sixth Army notified its corps of the impending offensive, and at 2100 hours it notified them that the enemy's artillery preparation would commence at 0100 and the infantry assault at 0330 hours. Thus the Germans did not achieve complete surprise.

When the Germans attacked on May 27, Sixth Army's main position of resistance lay along the crest of the Chemin des Dames rather than along the Aisne River to the rear. In mid-April Foch had directed allied forces north of the Oise to offer maximum resistance as far forward as possible, since only eighty to ninety kilometers separated the allies from the Channel. South of the Oise, the allies had more room for maneuver, and Pétain directed French forces to abide by his doctrinal guidance of December 1917 and establish a defense in depth. In early April, however, General Duchêne, Sixth Army's commander, decided not to establish a position in depth on the Chemin des Dames. When the Northern Army Group commander, General Franchet d'Espèrey, learned of Duchêne's decision, he warned him not to disregard Pétain's guidance. Pétain responded similarly when he learned of Duchêne's action. Duchêne nevertheless refused to yield and sent a note to d'Espèrey giving his reasons for placing his main defenses atop the Chemin des Dames. A defense along the heights, he argued, would be much stronger than one along the Aisne to the rear, and the abandonment of the Chemin des Dames, the capture of which had cost the French dearly, would have a negative effect on public opinion. Moreover, holding the Chemin des Dames would enable the French to keep the Germans as far as possible from Paris.[95]

In his postwar report on the battle, Pétain said that he had been aware of Duchêne's violation of his guidance but did not wish to force a change because it would have required relieving the Sixth Army commander. With an enemy attack imminent, he thought it wiser to leave Duchêne in command and to accept the situation.[96] Whatever the merits of this post-war explanation, Pétain, though insisting on obedience, did not compel his army commanders to follow his instructions to the letter. As an army commander, he had bridled under the tight restrictions imposed by Joffre and, after becoming general-in-chief, had given his senior commanders leeway to disregard his instructions if they believed a different action was necessary. By encouraging his senior commanders to think independently, he hoped to avoid placing them in impossible circumstances.[97]

As a result of Pétain's acquiescence, on May 27 Sixth Army had its position of resistance in the Aisne region along the crest of the Chemin des Dames. To hold a ninety-kilometer front, Duchêne had eleven divisions, plus four divisions in reserve, on the morning of the attack. Of these divisions, three in the front line and one in reserve were British. When the Germans attacked, they concentrated along a fifty-kilometer front, most of which was held by six allied divisions: from left to right, French 61st, 21st, and 22nd; British 50th, 8th, and 21st. Each of the three French divisions had a front of ten kilometers while each of the three British held seven. Behind the Chemin des Dames Duchêne had four divisions (74th, 39th, 157th, and British 25th), and late on May 26 he ordered them toward the Aisne. He planned on their holding the second line along the Aisne, sending reinforcements forward to the main position of resistance, counterattacking in sectors where the enemy made gains, or relieving forward divisions. Duchêne told his commanders, "Except for a formal and exceptional order from a commander (general of division or higher), each element, no matter where it is placed, will remain in place until overrun."[98]

When the Germans attacked on May 27, they aimed only to destroy allied reserves and compel the French to transfer units from Flanders to Champagne. Though conditions appeared favorable, General Erich Ludendorff did not expect to advance more than twenty kilometers. The Germans began their artillery preparation at 0100 hours. Using more than 4,000 artillery pieces, they bombarded allied positions to a depth of twelve kilometers. This massive fire overwhelmed allied artillery in Sixth Army's sector. Shorter than the preparation of March 21, which had lasted five hours, the bombardment on May 27 lasted only two hours forty minutes. At 0340 hours the infantry assault commenced. Of the forty-two German divisions involved in the operation, three struck the 21st, five the 22nd, and four the British 50th Division in the center of the Chemin des Dames. In the first few hours of the assault, the enemy almost annihilated the 22nd Division and inflicted heavy losses on the British 50th. General Wilson, chief of the Imperial General Staff, later blamed the poor performance of the 50th on the French, but the British division performed poorly for the same reasons the French divisions on the crest of the Chemin des Dames performed poorly: their forward position proved vulnerable to a massive artillery bombardment and infantry assault. Pushing forward rapidly in the sector occupied by the 22nd and British 50th, the Germans swept across the center of the Chemin des Dames, but they moved more slowly on the wings.

Back at Sixth Army headquarters, General Duchêne received reports that the enemy was making progress along the boundary between 21st and 22nd divisions. Seeking to strengthen his main line of resistance, he ordered units from the second line forward. At 0655 hours he authorized XI Corps to move 157th Division forward of the Aisne and to block the gap between the two frontline divisions. Similarly, at 0725 he authorized the British IX Corps to move a brigade of the British 25th Division north of the Aisne to assist the 50th. Unfortunately for the allies, the Germans had crossed the Chemin des Dames and were descending toward the Aisne. In his report to the commission investigating the subsequent disaster on the Chemin des Dames, Pétain explained what happened:

> The general commanding XI Corps gave the order to send north of the Aisne four battalions of the 157th Division that were holding the second position south of the Aisne. This order came at an inopportune moment, for it was executed just as the mass of enemy infantry descended the Chemin des Dames toward the river. The four battalions of the 157th, plus a fifth battalion that also moved forward because of an error, were thrown head over heels without ever being

deployed. Subsequent operations were dominated until June 1 by the rupture of Sixth Army's center, which upset the defensive system completely.[99]

At 0940 hours the Germans seized the bridge across the Aisne at Oeuilly (nine kilometers north of Fismes); they had advanced six kilometers in six hours.

Though Duchêne tried to retrieve the situation, the Germans had the initiative and continued advancing. With elements of the 157th Division already moving forward, at 0830 hours Duchêne ordered the 39th and 74th divisions to occupy positions along the Aisne to the left of 157th. Meanwhile Pétain and Franchet d'Espèrey ordered six additional divisions, as well as more heavy artillery, toward Sixth Army. Later that afternoon d'Espèrey also ordered three cavalry divisions forward. Between 1500 and 1600 hours the first of these reinforcements, 13th Division, moved into position at Fismes and came under heavy pressure after 157th Division collapsed and fled around 1700 hours. By the end of the day the Germans had crossed the Aisne, an advance of sixteen kilometers, and they pressed hard against 13th Division and other units thrown into the twelve-kilometer gap in allied lines.

In subsequent days the Germans advanced rapidly toward Paris. In the Operations Bureau of the GQG, officers initially did not view the situation as serious, but by May 30 they considered it the "gravest of the war."[100] By the evening of June 1 the Germans had captured Château-Thierry and advanced fifty-five kilometers from their line of departure on May 27. As additional French divisions rushed toward the expanding salient, Duchêne threw them piecemeal into the battle. On June 1 Pétain described the situation in a letter to Foch: "Since May 27 the battle has absorbed thirty-seven divisions, including five British. Seventeen of these divisions are completely exhausted; of these two or three may not be able to be reconstituted. Sixteen have been engaged for two, three, or four days. Four were engaged yesterday. Five others are arriving or will be engaged between May 31 and June 2."[101] Foch had already agreed to release his general reserves, Fifth and Tenth armies, from behind the British front. Fifth Army had arrived, and Tenth Army was expected to arrive between June 1 and 5. Five other divisions, including Pétain's reserves for a possible enemy attack through Switzerland, were scheduled to arrive between June 3 and 10. Pétain had no other divisions available, and he asked Foch to release divisions from the Army Detachment of the North and to dispatch U.S. divisions training with the British. Shortly after making this appeal, Pétain sent Foch a copy of a letter from General de Castelnau, commander of the Eastern Army Group; Castelnau said he had no reserves to use in the event of an enemy attack. When Foch refused to release additional reserves, Pétain insisted on receiving a written rather than telephonic message. He was furious at Foch and blamed him for depriving the French of sufficient reserves south of the Oise to halt the Germans sooner. With the situation appearing more ominous than at any other time in the war, Foch eventually sent Pétain two divisions from the Army Detachment of the North and asked the British to place three divisions in reserve south of the Somme.

Believing the outcome of the war was at stake, the GQG began considering "radical actions," including withdrawing completely from northern France and defending along the Somme or pulling twenty-four of the thirty-four French divisions out of the front lines east of Reims and ultimately abandoning northeastern France. As part of what it called the "big plan," the Operations Bureau suggested abandoning the front from Verdun to Switzerland and assembling two large masses of troops, one at Châlons (southeast of Reims) and the other at Beauvais (southwest of Montdidier). Pétain accepted the unwelcome option, which was little more than a final desperate counteroffensive before almost certain defeat, but he waited for the situation to worsen before asking for political approval and implementing it.[102] In preparation for this drastic move, Pétain ordered the Northern and Eastern army-group commanders to study a general withdrawal of their forces to the west. One officer in the Operations Bureau told an American liaison officer, "The war will be over in about two weeks."[103]

Not surprisingly, Pershing became the focal point of Franco-British anxieties, for the Americans had 650,000 troops in France but only a few divisions in front lines. On May 28 and 29 Pétain had arranged with Pershing for the U.S. 3rd Infantry Division to guard bridges across the

Marne in the vicinity of Château-Thierry; orders for the U.S. 2nd Division to move toward the Marne came on May 30. That same day Foch placed even greater emphasis on amalgamating American units. Meeting with Lord Milner and Pershing before the sixth session of the Supreme War Council, scheduled for June 1, Foch proposed shipping only U.S. infantry and machine-gun units in June and July and increasing the projected shipment from 150,000 to 250,000. When Pershing expressed reservations, Foch replied, "The battle, the battle, nothing else counts." At the meeting of the council the next day, Lloyd George proposed raising the question of U.S. troops with President Wilson. On June 2 Clemenceau added his weight to the pressure on Pershing, but the American commander escaped some of this pressure when Clemenceau queried Lloyd George about how many divisions the British intended to maintain in France. According to Pershing, a "lively tilt" ensued between the French and British. Adding to the friction, Haig described French troops as coddled, lacking in discipline, and refusing to fight. With Pershing doggedly refusing to bend, the conferees finally agreed to ask Washington to send 250,000 troops in June and July, 140,000 of whom would be combatant troops and not auxiliary or support units. Pershing cabled Washington on June 3: "The attitude of the Supreme War Council . . . is one of depression."[104]

But the tide of the battle had turned while the council met. On June 1 Pétain halted the throwing of individual divisions into the battle and directed Duchêne to have arriving divisions occupy a line north of Château-Thierry. He told Duchêne, "Do not voluntarily yield an inch of terrain. Retake by counterattacks all terrain momentarily lost."[105] In another fortunate development, the arrival of U.S. forces strengthened the resolve of the sorely tried French infantry in the Marne sector. A French officer described the arrival of "swarms" of Americans and said,

> The spectacle of this magnificent youth from across the sea, these youngsters of twenty years with smooth faces, radiating strength and health in their new uniforms, had an immense effect. They offered a striking contrast with our regiments in soiled uniforms, worn by the years of war, with our emaciated soldiers and their somber eyes who were nothing more than bundles of nerves held together by an he-

roic, sacrificial will. The general impression was that a magical transfusion of blood was taking place.[106]

At the GQG, officers in the Operations Bureau, as an American liaison officer reported, were "wildly enthusiastic" about the "splendid demeanor and fighting qualities" of the new arrivals. One officer said, "the American entry upon the battlefield is the key to the situation."[107]

The favorable turn of events on June 1–2 nonetheless came from more than the arrival of two U.S. divisions. Four other French infantry and cavalry divisions had arrived during the same period to strengthen defenses north of Château-Thierry. As these units arrived, the German drive toward Paris began losing momentum and stalled. From June 4 through 6 several uncoordinated enemy assaults struck closer to the Oise, the first immediately south of the river, followed by others south and southwest of Soissons. On June 6 the Germans struck along the Marne east of Château-Thierry. After encountering solid defenses along the entire front of the Marne salient, the Germans halted their attacks.

The German advance between May 27 and June 6 placed them only sixty kilometers from the capital and created considerable political discontent. On May 31 Pétain had advised Clemenceau to move the government from Paris, and for the second time in two months France's political leaders had to face this drastic prospect. In contrast, Foch refused even to consider advising the government to move and confidently insisted that the attack was nothing more than a feint. He told one officer, "The gusts strike all sides of the house, the tiles on the roof are blown off, the walls shake, but the foundation holds and will hold. That's all that matters."[108] Once again Foch's optimism and confidence contrasted sharply with Pétain's pessimism. When members of the Chamber of Deputies demanded the relief and court-martial of Foch and Pétain, as well as others such as Duchêne, Clemenceau toyed with the idea of relieving Pétain. On June 4, however, he defended the two generals before the Chamber, saying, "These soldiers, these great soldiers, have good leaders, great leaders, leaders worthy of them in every respect."[109] The Tiger's eloquent and firm defense saved Foch and Pétain from embarrassment or worse and ended in a vote of confidence, 377 to 110, for his government. The crisis nonetheless heightened Clemenceau's esteem for

Foch, and the Tiger told Poincaré, "Pétain, who has his faults, belongs more in the second rank than in the first."[110]

Scarcely had the enemy's attack stalled when another offensive began on June 9, this time north of the Oise between Noyon and Montdidier. This attack was in reality part of the offensive that began on May 27. The Germans had intended originally to strike across a vast front north and south of the Oise, but shortages of artillery had made such an attack impossible. Consequently, the Germans had decided to attack in two phases, with the first effort striking south of the Oise along the Chemin des Dames on May 27 and the second striking north of the Oise between Noyon and Montdidier on June 7. Unfortunately for the Germans, they were unable to conceal their preparations for the second effort as completely as they had those for the first. As early as May 28 the French had received reports of a possible enemy offensive near Noyon, and on May 30 Reserve Army Group, which occupied the Noyon sector, reported preparations for an enemy attack along the front west of the city. The following day Reserve Army Group, relying on aerial observations, noted "feverish activity" west of Noyon that was "characteristic of preparations for an attack."[111] Enemy prisoners and deserters soon confirmed the reports of aerial observers, but the French remained uncertain about German intentions. On June 2 Captain Georges Painvin, a brilliant cryptologist who had played a key role in breaking the various codes used by the Germans in wireless transmissions, broke the Germans' new "ADFGVX" code and uncovered a message about "hurrying" the delivery of ammunition in the Compiègne region. Known as the "radiogram of victory," this decoded message provided the final bit of key intelligence. On June 6 the commander of Third Army, which occupied the Noyon-Montdidier sector, reported that "the offensive is imminent."[112]

Though warned about the impending offensive, Foch remained concerned that the enemy would strike farther north and asked Haig to place three divisions in reserve astride the Somme west of Amiens. By placing divisions in this location, Foch could employ them in the French or British zones. Although Haig agreed to send the divisions, he formally protested to his government under the provisions of the Beauvais agreement, and on June 8 Clemenceau and Foch met with Lord Milner, Wilson, and Haig in Paris. Since Foch had done nothing more than move Haig's reserves to the south, the British government let his order stand. More important, Lord Milner agreed that Haig had to obey Foch's directives but demanded that any orders for the movement of British troops go through Haig. In reality, this meeting firmly fixed Foch's control over allied reserves, and in a demonstration of evenhandedness he sent Pétain a message informing him that French reserves might be transferred to the British zone.

On the morning of June 9 Pétain had five armies on the front that stretched from Amiens (the Franco-British boundary) to Reims. From left to right he had First, Third, Tenth, Sixth, and Fifth armies. First Army occupied the northern shoulder and nose of the Montdidier-Amiens salient; Third Army occupied the southern shoulder of that salient; and Tenth Army held the front to its south and the northern shoulder of the Marne salient. With twenty-five divisions in the front lines of these three armies, Pétain had twelve infantry divisions in reserve in the Oise valley, plus three cavalry divisions and five exhausted infantry divisions. Anticipating an opportunity for counterattacks, Pétain coordinated with Foch the use of some of the reserves against the flanks of an enemy advance.

Unfortunately for the French, Third Army, which would bear the brunt of the coming offensive, had no defense in depth. Once again, Pétain was aware that defenses along that portion of the front did not accord with his guidance, but with Foch's concurrence he specifically exempted Third Army from establishing a defense in depth. During the March 21 offensive, he had rushed Third Army into position along the southern face of the German advance, and no one wanted to relinquish territory in that region again. After the German offensive halted, Third Army devoted more effort preparing to retake lost terrain than preparing to defend against another enemy offensive, and it paid scant attention to digging defensive works behind the front line. When the Germans attacked, "the first position," as the army commander later explained to Pétain, "was barely finished, the second only roughly laid out."[113]

Between Noyon and Montdidier on June 9, artillery preparation for the fourth drive in the Germans' spring offensive began at midnight, but the French, amply warned, began their counterpreparation ten minutes earlier. Though opportune, this fire did not disrupt the enemy's infantry assault, which occurred between 0300 and 0430 hours. Striking the left-center of Third Army, which occupied a forty-five-kilometer front, the Germans advanced seven kilometers on the first day and five on the second across a front of twenty-five kilometers. By the end of the second day, June 10, however, five reserve divisions had arrived and halted the enemy's advance. Unlike on May 27, the Germans had failed to achieve surprise, and French reserves had entered the battle early and solidly.

For some time the French had anticipated launching a counterattack and striking an exposed enemy flank, but Pétain refused to release the divisions requested by General Fayolle, commander of Reserve Army Group, for such an operation. Using the forces available to him, Fayolle assembled five divisions under General Mangin, who would take command of Tenth Army a week later, and ordered him to attack between the Aisne and Ourcq rivers near Soissons. Mangin's attack began on June 11 at 1100 hours, but German artillery and machine-gun fire halted his forces around 1500–1600 hours. His attack nonetheless shook the Germans, and when the enemy resumed their fourth drive in Tenth Army's sector on June 12, the attack stalled after advancing only a few kilometers. To avoid further casualties, the German High Command halted the offensive.

Just as the German operation ended, the Austrians attacked in Italy. Early in May, Foch had attempted to convince the Italians to launch an offensive, but the Italians refused because they had noticed preparations for an enemy offensive. The Austrians struck on June 15, with one drive advancing from the Trentino toward the Asiago plateau and Vicenza and the other crossing the Piave River northeast of Venice. The British had three divisions in the Asiago sector and the French two. When the Austrians struck the French and British, they made some gains in the British sector, but a counterattack drove them back. In the Piave operation, the Austrians initially succeeded in crossing the river, but Italian reinforcements kept them from expanding their bridgehead. On the night of June 23–24 the Austrians withdrew across the Piave. Their offensive had failed completely.

The May 27 offensive by the Germans and its continuation on June 9 did not alter the strategic situation. Neither had the Austrian offensive. The Germans had hoped to drain the French of their reserves, but thanks to Pétain's careful husbanding of his soldiers' lives, casualties were modest in comparison to those of 1915 and 1916. During the two phases of the offensive the French suffered 98,160 casualties between May 27 and June 6, and Third Army lost 39,466 between June 9 and 16. Altogether the French had 200,000 casualties between May 1 and June 15. Knowing that increasing numbers of American troops inevitably tilted the balance against the Germans, Pétain said during the height of the German offensive, "If we can hold until the end of June, our situation will be excellent. In July we can resume the offensive. After that, victory is ours."[114]

After the German offensive at Noyon-Montdidier ended in mid-June, the French prepared feverishly for another enemy attack, but an unfortunate clash between Foch and Pétain threatened to disrupt these preparations. The spark producing the clash came from Foch's concluding that the Germans would strike next in the British zone north of the Somme. After identifying thirty-five to forty German divisions available for an offensive between the English Channel and the Somme and ten to twelve between the Somme and Switzerland, Foch informed Haig and Pétain of the enemy's disposition and told them to prepare contingency plans for sending their reserves to assist their ally. A subsequent message directed Pétain to replace a British division occupying a position in the Oise valley on the left of First Army. Pétain strongly objected to this directive, as well as to one telling him to send additional artillery to the Army Detachment of the North, and he countered that the British had had two months to rest and could provide for themselves. In a note to his chief of staff, Pétain said, "I continue to refuse [to give] Ypres the same value as Paris and to think that we should not weaken ourselves on the Oise and Marne to the benefit of the Belgians."[115] He told Fayolle that Foch's plan for sending French reserves north would result in France's "ruin."[116]

During this same period Foch dispatched a note to Haig and Pétain that outlined a new doctrine for responding to a massive German attack. Foch's message described German infiltration tactics and said that such tactics worked best against "weak resistance." In essence he thought a defense in depth with centers of resistance was vulnerable to infiltration techniques. To foil enemy tactics, he directed strengthening of forward defenses.[117] This note provoked another angry response from Pétain. In his written response to Foch's directive, he insisted that French doctrine had proved itself appropriate for the battles of March 21, April 9, May 27, and June 9, and he pointedly criticized several aspects of Foch's doctrine, particularly those he deemed more appropriate for units north of the Somme, where no room for a defense in depth existed. Pétain closed by saying, "I am informing you that I have no intention of communicating your note of June 16 to the armies under my orders."[118] That same day Pétain sent his army-group and army commanders a reminder about the guidance he had given them on doctrine.

When Pétain sent Clemenceau a copy of his correspondence with Foch, the Tiger did not respond as he had expected. At a meeting of the War Committee on June 26, Clemenceau discussed the clash between Foch and Pétain and received unanimous support for his proposal that Pétain obey Foch's directives. During the discussion Clemenceau mentioned an ongoing investigation of the Chemin des Dames disaster and hinted about possibly replacing Pétain. The Tiger's reservations about Pétain seem surprising given that he also believed that Foch was devoting too much attention to the British sector, and he had recently informed Foch and the Council of Ministers of this disagreement. Whatever reservations Clemenceau may have had about Foch's strategy, he had no doubts about subordinating Pétain to Foch. His decision had more to do with his personal assessment of the two generals than with his opinion of their strategic outlooks.

June 27 thus marked the final step in Foch's rise to power. Like previous selections of Joffre, Nivelle, and Pétain, Foch's elevation had a profound effect on French strategy, operations, and doctrine. The day after the War Committee met, Foch sent Pétain a letter that began, "It is important to envisage henceforth the resumption of the offensive by the allied armies in 1918 as soon as means permit."[119] Bowing to Foch's new powers, on July 2 Pétain sent his army-group commanders a copy of Foch's memorandum of June 16 on doctrine. Neither Foch nor Pétain realized how close they were to the end of the war.

CHAPTER 10

A Strategy of Opportunism

FOCH'S MOST IMPORTANT service to France came after he became supreme allied commander. He brought to his new position a talent for getting French and British troops to work together. He also brought his gifts as a writer and thinker, qualities that had been honed during his service at the École de Guerre and not allowed to atrophy during the war. Yet his strongest attribute may have been what B. H. Liddell Hart characterized as "opportunism."[1] The term applies to Foch in the same way that French historians have applied it to Léon Gambetta, the political leader in the late nineteenth century who believed politics was the art of the possible and who referred to himself as an "opportunist" to underline his belief that successful advances could occur only at the opportune moment. In that same sense, Foch recognized that military advances could occur only when the opportunity for action appeared. As a strategist, Foch revealed himself to be a man who lacked any grand strategic theories but who had the vision, energy, and knack for seizing the opportunity for action when it appeared.

The great advantage Foch possessed in June 1918 concerned unity of command. Allied political leaders had established some semblance of a unified command at Doullens on March 26, when they gave Foch the authority to "coordinate the actions of allies armies on the Western Front";

and they strengthened his powers at Beauvais on April 3, when they gave him responsibility for the "strategic direction of military operations." Other important steps toward unity of command occurred on April 17, when he received the title "general-in-chief of the allied armies in France," and on June 26, when the War Committee compelled Pétain to obey his directives. Although Foch's power to give orders remained restricted and he usually had to rely on persuasion, he gained sufficient authority between March and July to exert considerable influence over allied strategy and operations. This expanded authority enabled him to seize the initiative from the Germans in July 1918 and to drive them out of France with a series of relentless attacks.

Foch also brought a thorough understanding of operational methods. He had learned in the Artois and Champagne offensives of 1915 that a breakthrough was impossible, and he had learned on the Somme in 1916 and at Passchendaele in 1917 that a series of massive blows against the same point on the front would result only in high casualties. He understood the importance of destroying the enemy's reserves and recognized that Pétain's limited offensives could inflict high casualties on the enemy while keeping friendly casualties low. He also recognized, however, that Pétain's slow and methodical offensives promised no quick end to the war. Foch's staff reflected their boss's view of Pétain when they referred to him as the "great grub."[2] By the spring of 1918 Foch had added his own twist to Pétain's methods by insisting on a rapid series of blows to keep the Germans off balance and prevent them from shifting reserves. He illustrated his method by punching with his right fist, then his left, and then again with his right and following these blows with a vigorous kick.

In mid-June 1918 Foch still expected the final campaign of the war to occur in 1919, and he based his strategy on that expectation. Envisaging sequenced actions, he foresaw, first, halting the coming German offensive; second, launching a counteroffensive; third, advancing on all allied fronts with a series of relentless attacks; and finally, ending the war with a decisive kick, a massive general offensive. Although Foch did not adopt an offensive strategy immediately after he acquired his new power, he began the transition from a defensive to an offensive strategy the moment the opportunity appeared. In doing so, he enabled allied armies to fight the final, decisive campaign in 1918, not 1919.

As Foch prepared for the summer's campaign, he gave highest priority to repulsing the approaching German attack, the fifth in their series of drives. In a memorandum on July 1 to Haig and Pétain, he emphasized the importance of holding the Franco-British front. An enemy advance of forty kilometers toward Abbeville or sixty kilometers toward Paris, Foch recognized, could decisively affect the outcome of the war by splitting the French and British armies or threatening Paris. The allies had to prevent the enemy from advancing to these two cities and could do so only by concentrating their reserves between Arras and Château-Thierry and preparing them to intervene in either the French or British zones. The renewed emphasis on mutual support encountered opposition from Pétain, who complained about the "extreme fatigue" of his troops and about the British having a "density" of infantry and artillery that he could never attain in his zone.[3] To provide some relief for French units, Foch shifted the Army Detachment of the North and its six divisions from Flanders to the French zone. He also transferred the battered British IX Corps and its two divisions out of the French to the British zone. By late June Pétain and Haig had agreed on the procedures for dispatching forces to the other's zone.

After halting the next enemy attack, Foch expected the allies to seize the initiative and resume the offensive with a counterattack. He recognized that the Germans had moved out of their strong defensive positions, advanced beyond the reach of their logistical infrastructure, and extended their fronts, thereby making themselves vulnerable in the Marne and Somme salients. Rejecting the notion of a small operation with only a few divisions, he sought to have about thirty (twelve French, twelve American, and seven or eight British) divisions prepared for a much larger attack. To heighten readiness for resuming the offensive, he told Pétain to compose a directive that would "augment the offensive value of troops called to take part in the [coming] battle."[4] Though Foch's emphasis on the offensive differed markedly from Pétain's previous inclination, Pétain willingly composed the missive, since he had already anticipated that the allies would resume the offensive if they endured the German attacks through June. On July 12 Pétain published Directive No. 5, which stated: "Henceforth the armies should envisage the resumption of the offensive. Commanders at all echelons will prepare for this; they will focus resolutely on using simple, audacious, and rapid procedures of attack. The soldier will be trained in the same sense and his offensive spirit developed to the maximum."[5] The directive also included information on training staffs and troops, achieving surprise, and conducting an exploitation. After four years in the trenches and a year of preparing only for the defense, the French army required much coaching before it could conduct a large offensive operation.

After thousands of Americans arrived in France and the numerical balance tilted against the Central Powers, Foch anticipated making limited attacks on each of the allied fronts (Western, Italian, and Balkan) in order to gain ascendancy over the enemy and keep him off balance. Following the arrival of even more Americans, the allies might be able to launch a strong general offensive in September 1918 and wage a final decisive campaign in 1919. Within that offensive strategy, he remained concerned about the willingness of the British to operate closely with the other allies. As he told Pershing's liaison officer, "When you and we go forward, we will pull the British along with us. If we are not near enough to do that we run the risk of leaving them behind. Guide left, then, is the command."[6]

Foch's strategy thus resembled Pétain's previous strategy in its reliance upon the arrival of numerous American forces. He told Clemenceau, "To launch an offensive in the spring of 1919 with a sufficient numerical superiority, it is necessary for us to have a minimum of 215 to 220 divisions at the end of 1918."[7] Only by having four U.S. divisions arrive each month (beginning in August 1918) could the allies attain this number. On June 23, when Clemenceau, Foch, and Pershing met to discuss the arrival of American forces, the two French leaders pressed Pershing to transport 100 U.S. divisions to France by July 1919. At the Supreme War Council's meeting on June 2, Foch had asked for "no less" than 100 U.S. divisions, and the three prime ministers at the session (Clemenceau, Lloyd George, and Vittorio Orlando) had supported this request. Though Pershing had concerns about overtaxing transportation and supply facilities, he accepted the "goal" sought by Foch and

Clemenceau. He agreed to have 46 U.S. divisions in France in October 1918, 64 in January 1919, 80 in April, and 100 in July. The American commander, however, refused to place regiments—other than African-American—permanently in French divisions. When the Supreme War Council met in early July, allied leaders again supported the 100-division program. As David Trask noted, "After the seventh session ended [in July 1918], the controversy over amalgamation faded into the background."[8] Only Pétain's complaints about having to dissolve French divisions if American regiments did not join them marred the otherwise favorably viewed agreement of June 23.

In late June the French began receiving information about a twin-pronged attack on both sides of Reims. Initial intelligence reports, primarily from prisoners and deserters, suggested an offensive east of Reims, but later reports suggested a crossing of the Marne River twenty-five kilometers southwest of Reims. Foch and Pétain reacted cautiously to these reports, for they feared a feint followed by a strong attack toward Paris or Abbeville. By July 7 the French anticipated a formidable offensive on July 9–10 in Champagne on both sides of Reims, but they viewed this operation as a diversionary attack prior to a larger drive toward Paris or Abbeville. Despite concerns about a German attack elsewhere, Foch approved Pétain's making changes in the general disposition of his reserves to respond to the threat in Champagne. In the first week of July the French had shifted their reserves north to cover the front between Château-Thierry and Arras, but from July 7 through 9 they shifted five infantry divisions into the threatened sector east of Château-Thierry. As part of these changes, the Northern Army Group was redesignated the Central Army Group, and the Army Detachment of the North became Ninth Army. General Maistre, who had succeeded Franchet d'Espèrey as commander of Central Army Group, commanded (from left to right) Sixth, Fifth, and Fourth armies across the threatened sector.

Foch's and Pétain's doubts that the Germans would make their main attack in Champagne vanished on July 10–12, when new intelligence confirmed German preparations for a large offensive in Champagne. On July 11 Foch acknowledged the likelihood of the enemy's weakening his effort north of the Somme, and he permitted the shifting of additional French reserves from north of the Oise to Champagne. Additionally, the French learned from prisoners and from the placement of the enemy's reserves that the attack would occur around July 14. On the eve of the German attack, Pétain had plenty of combat power for halting the enemy. He later wrote:

> The month's respite, which had followed the battle of Matz [between Noyon and Montdidier], had enabled us to train and rest our reserve divisions. . . . In materiel, our superiority had become undeniable; we had sufficient artillery and munitions; we could count on our heavy tanks and especially our light tanks against an adversary lacking similar weapons; our aviation incontestably dominated that of the adversary.[9]

With the Germans having lost operational and tactical surprise and with Pétain's reserves poised for action, the situation favored the allies.

The situation also provided an opportunity for a counteroffensive against the Marne salient. Although some American historians have given Pershing credit for suggesting the Soissons attack, the possibility of attacking the western shoulder of the Marne salient at Soissons and thereby cutting off the bulge in French lines was apparent long before Pershing suggested such an attack to Clemenceau and Foch on June 23. As early as May 30, staff officers in the GQG had begun studying a counterattack on the shoulders of the Marne salient. On June 14 Foch had directed Pétain to bombard the railway center in Soissons and thereby disrupt the flow of German supplies into the salient. He also told Pétain to consider mounting a limited offensive toward Soissons in order to bring French cannon closer to the railway center. Pétain's staff viewed Foch's demand for a limited operation with concern, since the Germans might consider it a prelude to a larger attack against the vulnerable shoulder of the Marne salient and strengthen their defenses around Soissons, thereby reducing French chances of achieving surprise in a real counteroffensive. Despite these concerns, Tenth Army attacked toward Soissons on June 28, advanced several kilometers, and captured several thousand prisoners. More important, the attack revealed the enemy's disorganization and weakness near Soissons but did not alert the Germans to the possibility of a larger attack.

On July 5 General Mangin, who had received command of Tenth Army on June 16 after his counterattack on June 11, proposed a more ambitious operation. A large attack on Soissons, Mangin said, had an excellent chance of success and could conceivably result in the reduction of the Marne salient. Pétain responded enthusiastically to Mangin's proposal: "Beyond a doubt this operation presents not only the best chance of success but also the opportunity for a fruitful exploitation; additionally, it constitutes the most effective parry to the imminent German offensive."[10] With Pétain's approval Tenth Army began preparations for an offensive at Soissons, on the western shoulder of the Marne salient. Pétain anticipated launching this counterattack only after halting the coming German offensive on both sides of Reims.

Foch and Pétain had met frequently in early July, so Foch was aware of Pétain's preparations for a counteroffensive near Soissons and concurred with them. The allied commander offered several suggestions, such as combining Tenth Army's operation with that of Sixth Army (which was to the immediate right of Tenth Army) and having Fifth Army strike the eastern face of the Marne salient. Initially, however, Foch was unwilling to commit his reserves to the operation because of his continuing concern about Flanders. His attitude changed on July 11, when he concluded that the German operation in Champagne was not a diversion. To make more forces available in Champagne, he released French reserves north of the Oise and asked Haig to send two divisions to replace them. He also warned Haig that if the operation consumed all of Pétain's reserves, he would be obliged to call upon British reserves. The next day Foch asked Haig to send four divisions to the French zone and warned him that he might be asked for four more. The British did not welcome the transfer of their reserves south, and on July 15, the day of the German attack, Haig met with Foch to voice his objections. British reserves, Haig insisted, should assist the French only if massive enemy forces advanced toward Paris. Foch reassured the field marshal by saying the British divisions could return immediately if the British front was threatened.

On the eve of the German attack, Foch and Pétain were prepared for a two-phased battle: first halting the German attack, then unleashing the counterattack at Soissons. Pétain expected the counterattack to reduce the Marne salient and hoped to begin it on July 18. In addition to Tenth Army's attack toward Soissons, he planned other counterstrokes. He prepared an assault against the east shoulder of the Marne salient to correspond with Tenth Army's assault on the west shoulder, an attack south of the Marne if the enemy succeeded in crossing the river, and an advance by Eastern Army Group near the Argonne. The most important operation, however, was Tenth Army's advance—with Sixth Army assisting on its right—against the western face of the Marne salient. A think piece from Pétain's chief of staff, General Buat, noted: "No matter how you view the question—defensive, counteroffensive, offensive—there are always advantages to be gained with the attack by Tenth Army."[11]

The French, as Pétain noted in his formal report, committed everything to the battle. Although Pétain's reserve in Champagne contained thirty-eight infantry (including four British and five American) and six cavalry divisions, he had only one division in reserve behind the entire front between the Argonne and Switzerland and only one British division in reserve on the front covering Paris. His flexibility came from his having prepared several counteroffensives. At a time when the situation called for decisive measures, Foch and Pétain bet everything on the outcome of this battle. With all the chips on the table, Foch would demonstrate stronger nerves and steadier composure than Pétain when the Germans revealed a surprisingly strong hand on the eve of Mangin's counteroffensive.

Expecting the Germans to begin their offensive in Champagne on the night of July 13–14, the French occupied their battle positions in anticipation of the assault. When the Germans failed to attack that night, Fourth Army launched a raid the following day and captured twenty-seven prisoners. The captured Germans revealed that the attack would occur that night and that artillery preparation would commence at ten minutes after midnight and last for three or four hours. Consequently, French artillery began counterpreparatory fire that night shortly before the Germans began their bombardment east and west of Reims.

The enemy infantry assault began unevenly between 0415 and 0530 hours on July 15. East of Reims, the Germans struck Fourth Army on a forty-kilometer front and advanced two to three kilometers. At several points enemy soldiers pushed into the main defensive position, but they failed to break through. By noon Fourth Army had halted the Germans east of Reims and inflicted heavy casualties. Subsequent attacks by the enemy failed to make any gains against Fourth Army, and around noon on the sixteenth the Germans suspended offensive operations in this sector. Southwest of Reims along the Marne, the Germans struck Fifth Army and made progress. French commanders had placed too many men along the river, rendering them vulnerable to massive artillery bombardment. Fighting their way across the Marne, the Germans drove the French out of their main position of resistance. Only the French 39th Infantry and U.S. 3rd Infantry divisions, which occupied positions near Château-Thierry, west of the German crossing, held their positions along the Marne.

As Fifth Army's situation worsened, Pétain diverted forces programmed to participate in the counteroffensive, and at 0930 hours he suspended preparation for the operation. Fearing large enemy gains across the Marne, he began assembling additional forces for a strong counterattack against the German bridgehead. When Foch learned around noon of Pétain's actions, he immediately directed him not to halt preparation for Tenth Army's counteroffensive. If Pétain needed additional forces, Foch promised to obtain them, probably from the British, but he did not want them taken from Tenth Army. To obtain reserves for Fifth Army, Pétain drew divisions from the right of Sixth Army and left of Fourth Army, but the situation did not improve. At 1645 hours, Pétain asked Foch to release the U.S. 2nd Infantry Division from its planned participation in Tenth Army's counteroffensive and send it toward the Marne. Such a move would require delaying Mangin's attack for a day. Half an hour after making the request, the situation seemed to improve, and Pétain canceled the request. Hard fighting nonetheless continued along the Marne. In several days of bitter combat, the Germans advanced five kilometers on a thirty-five-kilometer front, but on July 17 French counterattacks finally halted them.

Foch's intervention on July 15 was crucial, but it was also crucial the following day, when Pétain became concerned about the lack of reserves behind Third Army, the army protecting the most direct route to Paris north of the Oise. In a letter to Foch Pétain emphasized his lack of reserves and said, "It is necessary to guarantee the solidity of our front north of the Oise."[12] Although Tenth Army was adjacent to Third Army, Foch refused to permit the weakening of Tenth Army and its counter-offensive and instead diverted two British divisions, which were en route to positions behind Fifth Army, to Third Army. On the eve of the counteroffensive that would give the allies the initiative, Foch refused to let the tactical or operational demands of the battle subvert his strategic design and rejected all thoughts of diverting forces from Tenth Army. In contrast, Pétain's pessimism colored his assessment of the situation, and had Foch not intervened, he might have delayed, weakened, or canceled Tenth Army's operation. In the final analysis, Foch's optimism and his willingness to take a calculated risk earned him the credit for the subsequent victory.

On July 17 Pétain issued the final order for what had become Foch's counteroffensive. Since Ninth Army had taken command of the two corps on Sixth Army's right and thus assumed responsibility for the sector east of Château-Thierry between Sixth and Fifth armies, the offensive involved (from left to right) Tenth, Sixth, Ninth, Fifth, and Fourth armies, all of which would take part in the operation on July 18. Advancing south of Soissons, Mangin's Tenth Army had responsibility for the main attack. With ten divisions in the first line and six in the second, Mangin had I, XX, XXX, and XI corps from left to right. He also had a cavalry corps in reserve, and 1,545 artillery pieces and 301 tanks supporting his attack. The U.S. 1st and 2nd divisions fought as part of the French XX Corps, the unit Foch had commanded at the beginning of the war. In his memoirs Pershing said, "The [XX] corps, which was four-fifths American, had the honor of being the spearhead of the thrust against this vulnerable flank of the salient, an honor which it gallantly sustained."[13]

With the enemy's drive across the Marne halted, Mangin's counterattack on July 18 caught the Germans almost completely by surprise even though a deserter had warned them on the eleventh or twelfth about a large offensive southwest of Soissons. Striking first, Tenth Army advanced at 0435 without any artillery preparation. Preceded by tanks and a dense rolling barrage, Mangin's infantry advanced quickly and easily. The U.S. 2nd Division advanced eight kilometers, the deepest gain achieved by any unit on the first day, and the U.S. 1st Division interdicted

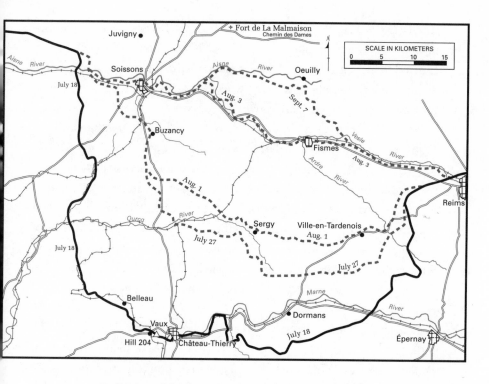

Reduction of the Marne salient, July–September 1918

the route at Buzancy from Château-Thierry to Soissons and thereby threatened the entire German position in the salient. By the end of the day Tenth and Sixth armies had achieved considerable success: Tenth Army captured 10,000 prisoners and 200 cannon, Sixth Army 2,000 prisoners and 50 cannon.

A colonel in the Operations Bureau of the GQG cheered, "This is the greatest day since the Marne." According to an American liaison officer, staff officers in the GQG celebrated the victory by pretending to be Ludendorff and Crown Prince Wilhelm complaining about the attack: "And between laughs they would read the latest message, mark it on the map, shake my hand and utter eulogies about the Americans. Such words as *superbe, magnifique, épatant* were used many times in talking about the 1st and 2nd divisions U.S." Several of the officers acknowledged, "Without the Americans this would never have been possible." That night the staff officers drank champagne with their dinner and toasted the

Americans.[14] After the war, the U.S. 1st Infantry Division placed a monument near Buzancy alongside the Château-Thierry–Soissons road. Erected to memorialize the Americans who participated in the campaign, the monument also marks the spot where the allies seized the initiative on July 18 and began their march toward victory.

Though other French armies made only small gains, at 1145 on July 18 the German commander ordered the evacuation of the bridgehead over the Marne. The Germans got most of their troops across the Marne in two nights, but the French did not clear the south bank until the end of the day on the twentieth. Meanwhile Tenth and Sixth armies, having lost the advantage of surprise, continued their pressure on the western face of the salient. While Tenth Army made only small gains, Sixth Army moved forward more rapidly and liberated Château-Thierry on the twenty-first. By July 22 the Germans had strengthened their defenses and offered stiff resistance.

During the fighting Foch had to contend with Haig's demands for the return of the four British divisions that had moved south to augment Pétain's reserves. When Foch and Haig had met on July 15 to discuss the status of these divisions, Foch had promised to return them if the British front was threatened. After the British XXII Corps and two of its divisions arrived, Pétain sent them to Fifth Army to relieve the Italian II Corps. When the other two divisions of the corps arrived, Foch placed them behind Third Army to ensure the security of Paris. The British thus had two divisions on the eastern and two on the western face of the Marne salient. On the morning of July 18 Haig, who expected little of the French counterattack and feared an attack on the Ypres front, demanded in writing the return of the four divisions. He qualified his written message with an oral message saying that the British divisions could remain in the French zone if they were needed to exploit a success. Foch immediately responded that the operation near the Marne prevented the enemy from making a large attack on the British front "for the moment" and that British troops should be levied from quiet portions of the front if needed.[15] The four British divisions eventually entered the front lines and contributed to pushing the Germans out of the Marne salient, but Haig's insistence on the return of the divisions on the crucial first day of the counterattack highlights his failure to comprehend the changing strategic situation. Neither Haig nor Pétain recognized as fully as Foch the strategic opportunity opening before the allies.

With Foch urging Pétain to strengthen Tenth Army's attack, the French renewed their offensive efforts, and the Germans considered their alternatives. Believing the continuation of the battle would cost excessive casualties, on July 24 Crown Prince Wilhelm ordered a withdrawal from the Marne salient, but Ludendorff canceled the order because he favored an attack ten kilometers west of Soissons. Objections from the crown prince and from the army commander charged with making the attack west of Soissons soon forced Ludendorff to accept withdrawal from the salient. Under constant pressure from the allies, the Germans pulled back skillfully and evacuated most of their supplies and equipment successfully. By August 3 they had withdrawn to a strong position at the base of the salient behind the Aisne and Vesle rivers. Upon reaching the Vesle, French forces halted.

Foch's counteroffensive proved to be one of the most important operations of the war. It drove the Germans from the Marne salient, lowered their morale, raised the morale of allied troops, and gave the allies the initiative. While shortening the front line by forty-five kilometers and removing the threat against Paris, Pétain's forces captured 29,000 Germans, 612 cannon, 221 *Minenwerfer,* and 3,330 machine guns. Casualties in Tenth, Sixth, Ninth, and Fifth armies totaled 95,165. In recognition of Foch's important role in the counteroffensive, Clemenceau informed him on August 5 of his appointment as a marshal of France. The presidential decree read:

Paris disengaged, Soissons and Château-Thierry reconquered by force, more than 200 villages freed . . . the high hopes proclaimed by the enemy before his attack shattered, the glorious allied armies advanced with a single victorious will from the edge of the Marne to the banks of the Aisne: those are the results of a maneuver admirably conceived by the high command and superbly executed by incomparable leaders.[16]

The failure of the German spring offensive and the success of the allies' counteroffensive against the Marne salient began the disintegration of the German army. With an influenza epidemic making matters worse, German soldiers began abandoning their positions and slipping away to the rear. Despite reports from commanders such as Crown Prince Rupprecht about worsening morale and discipline, Ludendorff refused to concede defeat. He told Kaiser Wilhelm II: "During the world war, so far I have had to withdraw my troops five times, only to beat the enemy in the end after all. Why should I not bring this off a sixth time?"[17] Ludendorff's optimism contrasted sharply with Pétain's pessimism. Though pleased with the progress of his troops, Pétain foresaw numerous difficulties, foremost of which was his shortage of 120,000 infantry. Of Pétain's 103 divisions, 71 were on the front and 32 in reserve. In his entire force he had only one fresh division on July 31. He told Foch, "We are at the limit of our effort."[18]

Before the fighting in the Marne salient ended, Foch had set in motion the operations that would crush Ludendorff's optimism, accelerate the disintegration of the German army, and end the war. On July 24 he met Pétain, Haig, and Pershing at his headquarters, and his chief of staff, Weygand, read them a long memorandum on the conduct of the war. The main thrust of the memorandum was contained in one sentence: "The moment has come to abandon the general defensive attitude imposed upon us until now by [our] numerical inferiority and to pass to the offensive." Though Foch still did not expect the final campaign until 1919, he called for quick, successive blows to keep the initiative on the side of the allies and establish the best conditions for the final victorious campaign. The first of these operations consisted of attacks against the three large salients protruding into allied lines: Marne, Montdidier-Amiens, and St.-Mihiel. With the Marne operation already under way, a combined Franco-British army would attack the Montdidier-Amiens salient, and American forces would attack the St.-Mihiel salient as soon as they had the "necessary means." By clearing these salients the allies would secure rail lines that were indispensable for later operations. Next, the allies would clear the mining region in northern France and drive the enemy from the vicinity of Dunkirk and Calais.[19] By leaving only brief intervals between operations, the allies could prevent the Germans from using

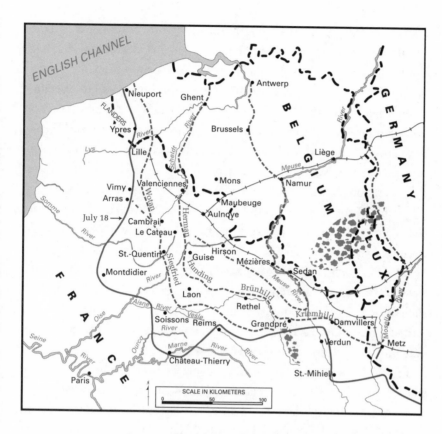

German defensive positions, July 1918

their reserves in counterstrokes and from rebuilding their depleted units. Foch's strategic concept became the basis of action for the next month.

The first step in Foch's strategy of July 24, repelling the Germans from the Marne salient, was accomplished by August 3. It was followed by the second, an attack against the Montdidier-Amiens salient, an operation for which preparations were already under way before Foch met with Pétain, Haig, and Pershing on July 24. The idea for this operation had fermented long in Foch's mind. As early as May 20, 1918, he had told Pétain and Haig to prepare a Franco-British limited offensive against the shoulders of the Montdidier-Amiens salient to "disengage" the railway line from Paris to Amiens.[20] Following the German attack against the Chemin des

Dames on May 27, he momentarily abandoned the idea of attacking the Montdidier-Amiens salient, but he returned to this idea when Haig, seeking to obtain the release of the British XXII Corps from the French, wrote to Foch on July 17 and identified the Montdidier-Amiens operation as the most fruitful in which his forces could participate. Three days later Foch proposed having the commanders of the British Fourth and French First armies meet and work out the details of such an operation. As planning proceeded, Foch wrote to Haig on July 28 specifying the purpose of the operation: "disengage Amiens and the Paris-Amiens railway" and "drive back" the enemy from the sector in front of Amiens.[21] To increase the chances of success and to ensure unity of command, Foch placed the French First Army under Haig and provided it with four additional divisions. After Foch urged Haig to "hasten" the date of the attack and possibly catch the enemy unprepared to respond, Haig changed the scheduled date from August 10 to August 8 and on July 29 sent a formal order to the British Fourth and French First Army commanders, General Sir Henry Rawlinson and General Eugène Debeney.

First Army's role in the operation changed considerably in the week before the offensive. After receiving Haig's order, Debeney envisaged First Army's doing little more than covering Rawlinson's right, but on the same day that he published his order, General Fayolle, commander of Reserve Army Group, passed XXXV Corps to him and extended First Army's front eight kilometers. Other changes occurred after Foch perceived signs of increasing enemy weakness and directed a deeper advance in the Montdidier-Amiens attack and an extension of French operations south toward the Oise. A message from Fayolle on August 5 pushed Debeney toward a two-pronged attack, one driving southeast and the other northeast, to bite off a large segment of the German salient. Fayolle also directed Third Army (on the right of First Army) to provide considerable support so that Debeney could advance more rapidly and deeply. A "mass" of Third Army's artillery, Fayolle promised, would cover Debeney's right, and the two corps on Third Army's left would participate in the assault. Thus, during the week before the attack, Debeney's forces increased from twelve infantry divisions to fifteen infantry and three cavalry divisions, and his front grew from twenty-six to thirty-four kilometers.

For First Army's attack, Debeney had, from left to right, XXXI, IX, X, and XXXV corps, but he had only two light tank battalions to support his attack. Instead of making a massive frontal assault, Debeney intended to strike first on his army's left (near the British Fourth Army's zone of attack) with two corps driving southeast; these corps would seize high ground in this sector and destroy the equilibrium of the enemy's defenses. As the enemy sent reinforcements toward the First Army's left and toward Rawlinson's Fourth Army, Debeney intended to strike on his right with X and XXXV corps. These two corps would drive northeast on the second day of the offensive,[22] as would two corps from Third Army on the third day. With artillery preparation commencing at H-hour, XXXI Corps would attack at H + 45 minutes, IX Corps at H + 4 hours, and X and XXXV corps late on the following day. By using sequenced attacks, the French could take advantage of the Germans' having shifted forces to the point of initial attack.

At 0420 hours on August 8, the allied attack began. Rawlinson's Fourth Army attacked with three corps supported by 430 tanks. Because of this strong tank support, Fourth Army did not use preparatory artillery fire; instead, its tanks and infantry advanced at once behind a rolling barrage. The Canadian Corps on Rawlinson's right (adjacent to the French) progressed more rapidly than any other unit on the first day and advanced ten kilometers. As Debeney had planned, First Army attacked on the first day with two corps, and despite difficult resistance, these units pushed back the enemy. Though the French advanced quickly, their left ended the day two kilometers behind the Canadian Corps's right.

On the second day the allies initially did not press their attacks vigorously. Although X Corps joined the attack at dawn, First Army's left did not advance as fast as Foch desired. Twice during the day he telephoned Debeney and urged him to accelerate the pace of his advance. When XXXV Corps attacked as planned at 1600 hours, the sudden commitment of forces on Debeney's right caught the Germans off guard, and the corps captured 1,300 prisoners in half an hour and advanced five kilometers before the end of the day. When Third Army's two corps attacked on the right of First Army on August 10, they also made rapid progress, as did Debeney's other corps. The third day witnessed the largest French gains, eight kilometers across a twenty-five-kilometer front. On the eleventh, however, enemy resistance stiffened, and the offensive stalled. First Army, which had six corps in the operation, had captured almost twice as much terrain as the British Fourth Army, which had three corps, but Debeney's less aggressive soldiers had captured about two-thirds as many prisoners. By the end of the month the three British armies involved in the offensive would capture 34,618 prisoners and the three French armies 31,453.[23]

In his memoirs General Ludendorff called August 8 the "black day" of the war for the German army.[24] Losses were so heavy, including 29,000 captured in the first four days, that the Germans faced the prospect of dismantling additional divisions. Though the great majority of German soldiers had fought bravely, a debilitating spirit of insubordination and a rising tide of indiscipline gnawed at the army's combat readiness. At a conference on August 14, Hindenburg and Ludendorff, who expected the allies to continue their attacks, informed the kaiser, "We have reached the limits of our endurance." Yet, in what Fritz Fischer called an "incomprehensible contradiction,"[25] the assembled group believed Germany still had the capacity to make the Entente accept a negotiated peace on Berlin's terms. After Hindenburg insisted that the army could "make a stand on French soil," the kaiser authorized the secretary of state for foreign affairs to initiate peace feelers through diplomatic channels.[26] The allies held the initiative, but Germany was not yet defeated. Some hard fighting remained before the Germans accepted peace on allied terms.

When Clemenceau asked Foch on August 11 what he intended to do, the marshal responded, "Enlarge the battle, go forward as much as I can."[27] Unlike Ludendorff in his spring offensive, Foch did not intend to give the enemy time to recover between attacks and would not unleash huge, costly operations. Instead he planned a series of punches to keep the Germans off balance before he delivered his final kick. He also sought to maintain constant pressure on the Germans so they could not break contact, counterattack, or reform their defenses on a line farther to the rear. As Tim Travers has argued, Foch, not Haig, was the "principal strategist of the moving warfare that developed after Amiens."[28] Neither Pétain nor Haig sensed as clearly as Foch that the opportune moment had arrived for resuming the offensive with attacks against carefully chosen points along the enemy's line.

On August 10 Foch issued orders for enlarging the battle and clearing the Germans from the Montdidier-Amiens salient. While the French First and British Fourth armies advanced east astride the Somme toward St.-Quentin, the French Third Army to the south would move along the Oise, and the British Third Army to the north would advance toward Cambrai. Haig saw this as little more than a frontal assault and objected strongly. Foch responded:

> In confronting the resistance offered by the enemy, it is not a question of obtaining results by pressing uniformly across the entire front; this would result only in [our] being weak everywhere.
>
> On the contrary, it is a matter of aiming concentrated and powerful actions at important points in the region; that is to say, [to strike] those [points] whose possession will increase the disorganization of the enemy, especially by compromising his communications. These actions should be quickly and strongly mounted.[29]

Two days later Haig postponed the drives by the French First and British Fourth armies along the Somme. Foch had hoped that these two armies would advance immediately and that operations on their flanks would commence as soon as possible thereafter. After Rawlinson and Debeney emphasized the strength of enemy defenses to their front and expressed doubts about their readiness to continue attacking, the British field marshal delayed their operations. He refused to launch frontal assaults with inadequate artillery support. Meanwhile he transferred his reserves to the north behind the British First and Third armies, where he expected less enemy resistance. Foch objected to the delay but yielded when Haig insisted that he was responsible for the handling of British forces. Subsequent discussions with Haig and Debeney convinced Foch that attacks by Rawlinson's and Debeney's armies would have resulted in heavy losses and that Haig's intervention had avoided unnecessary casualties. He nevertheless removed the French First Army from British control and returned it to Fayolle's Reserve Army Group.

General Fayolle did not require coaching on the value of successive rapid blows against the enemy. He captured Foch's intent in a message to his army commanders: "In the present situation, in which we find ourselves facing forces essentially equal to ours, parallel attacks made with equal energy across the entire front cannot produce large results. It is indispensable to concentrate our efforts on particularly important points whose possession will result in the general recoil of the enemy."[30]

As part of Fayolle's army group, First (which returned to Fayolle's control on August 16), Third, and Tenth armies pressed forward in subsequent days by attacking specific points in the German lines. The key action occurred on August 20, which Ludendorff described as "another black day."[31] Mangin's Tenth Army drove the enemy back between the Oise River and Soissons and advanced 12 kilometers in two days. On August 27 and 28 First and Third armies, profiting from Tenth Army's advance, pushed forward a dozen kilometers and by the twenty-ninth had seized Noyon. The British, who began their attack on August 21, made similar progress in the north; by September 1 they had seized Bapaume and Péronne. Thus, in about ten days the allies had advanced a dozen kilometers along a 110-kilometer front. With an "I told you so" tone, Foch wrote to Haig: "Through this increasing extension of the offensive, of an offensive nourished from the rear and pushed forward strongly toward carefully selected objectives without excessive regard for alignment or for close liaison, we will gain the largest results."[32]

As Foch's offensive continued, the British First Army struck the Wotan Position, near Cambrai. More a system of defensive belts than a line, the Hindenburg Line, as it was known to the allies, consisted of numerous fortified positions stretching from the North Sea to Metz. One belt stretched between Nieuport, Lille, Quéant, St.-Quentin, Laon, and Metz. Behind it another stretched between Valenciennes, Guise, Rethel, Grandpré, and Damvillers. Farther to the rear, a third belt ran between Valenciennes, Hirson, Mézières, and Montmédy. Portions of these belts had a depth as great as fifteen kilometers. The segment known to the Germans as the Wotan Position and to the British as the Drocourt-Quéant Switch stretched across the large plain east of Vimy Ridge and protected the crucial communications center in Douai. On September 2

Canadian infantry fought their way through enemy defenses twelve kilometers northwest of Cambrai and advanced as much as five kilometers. Once the Canadians broke through the Wotan Position, German units in the salient to the south withdrew toward the Siegfried Position between Cambrai and St.-Quentin. Near Péronne the Germans pulled back twenty kilometers and near Noyon twenty-five kilometers. This withdrawal resulted in the Germans' abandoning the last portion of the huge salient they had won in March–April 1918. The German withdrawal proved fortunate for the French. Fayolle had told Pétain on September 3 that his First and Third armies could advance only if British attacks north of the Somme had "sufficient effect" south of the river.[33] After the Germans began their withdrawal, Fayolle immediately pushed his armies forward to pursue them.

As allied units advanced, Foch devised an offensive strategy to enable the allies to maintain the initiative and drive the Germans back. His strategic concept strongly resembled Joffre's strategy of December 1914, when the French had attempted to squeeze the Germans "between the two jaws of a vise" by attacking the two faces of the Noyon salient.[34] As late as October 1917, the French had revisited Joffre's strategy and reaffirmed the importance of cutting the Germans' lateral lines of communication and making the "final push in the direction of Mézières."[35] Ignoring the deep roots of the concept, Haig prodded Foch into adopting twin drives by suggesting in a letter on August 27 that Foch distribute American divisions so that the British could drive toward Cambrai and the Americans toward Mézières in converging attacks. Foch responded the next day: "The final objectives that you indicated in your letter are the very ones that I myself have envisaged and toward which I have set the actions of the allied armies." The distribution of U.S. divisions, Foch said, depended on subsequent events.[36] The following day Clemenceau met with Foch and reinforced the idea of an American drive toward Mézières. Before meeting with Foch, the Tiger had had a long discussion with General Mordacq, who thought an offensive at St.-Mihiel could yield only tactical results and who argued for using the Americans in a decisive attack. In his memoirs Foch did not mention Haig's suggestions or Clemenceau's comments but said that at the end of August the time was ripe for envisaging something far more ambitious than simply clearing the St.-Mihiel salient.

Foch revealed his new campaign strategy on August 30, the day he met with Pershing. In a letter to the American leader he stated:

> It is important to exploit the advantageous situation to the utmost by pursuing and extending this battle to the Meuse and pushing [toward that river] all the allied armies in a converging action.
>
> Toward this objective:
>
> (1) The English armies, supported by the left of the French armies, will continue to attack in the general direction of Cambrai, Saint-Quentin.
>
> (2) The center of the French armies will continue its energetic actions to drive the enemy beyond the Aisne.
>
> (3) The American army and the right of the French armies, acting on the Meuse and to the west [of the river], will attack in the general direction of Mézières.[37]

According to an officer in the GQG's Operations Bureau, news of the new strategy was a "revelation" at Pétain's headquarters, which was still expecting the Americans to attack on the east bank of the Meuse and then drive toward Metz.[38] The new strategy expected much more from the Americans than French leaders had foreseen only a few weeks earlier, but it provided the main framework for allied operations until the war's end.

Though Foch's offensive would extend from the English Channel to the Meuse, the French viewed Mézières as the most important operational objective. Capturing Mézières would disrupt German use of the three main rail lines running from Germany to France. In the northwest a line ran from Köln to Liège and then followed the Meuse and Sambre rivers to Aulnoye. In the center a line ran from Koblenz to Luxembourg and thence to Longuyon. In the east a more circuitous route ran from Mainz to Mannheim, Strasbourg, Sarrebourg, Metz, and Longuyon. Running from northwest to southeast behind German lines, another railway connected Lille, Aulnoye, Mézières, Montmédy, and Longuyon. Numerous smaller lines connected the main lines.[39] By cutting the line between Montmédy and Mézières, the allies could significantly reduce the Germans' ability to transport supplies and equipment between Mézières and the English Channel and thereby force them—if they withdrew—to abandon huge stocks of arms and ammunition stockpiled in France and Belgium.[40] Capturing Mézières, however, depended on a high level of performance from the still-inexperienced and struggling Americans. It also demanded an entirely new plan for the employment of U.S. forces.

On August 30 Foch met with Pershing and presented his new strategic concept. He wanted Pershing to reduce the St.-Mihiel operation and allow American forces to participate in two subsequent operations, both of which would be commanded by French generals. One attack would occur between the Meuse and the Argonne Forest and the other to the west of the Argonne. Pershing objected vehemently: "This virtually destroys the American army that we have been trying so long to form." When Foch asked if he would take part in the battle, Pershing responded, "Most assuredly, but as an American army and in no other way." After an acrimonious discussion, the meeting closed with Pershing's refusing to accept Foch's plan and the French marshal's leaving exhausted and pale.[41] The next day Pershing wrote to Foch and indicated his willingness to attack in the direction of Mézières, but he refused to divide American forces.

Pétain, who foresaw no quick end to the war, played the role of peacemaker when he met with Pershing on August 31. The two generals had much in common, since they commanded national armies under Foch and agreed that Foch should determine strategy but leave operations to the commanders of the national armies. When the two pored over their maps, Pétain said he favored having the Americans retain responsibility for the St.-Mihiel sector while extending toward the west. He envisaged the Americans' eventually replacing the French Second and Fourth armies and—in a sequence of operations that would take months to execute—delivering the final blow against the Germans. When Pershing insisted on attacking toward Metz, a region strongly defended by the Germans because of the numerous mines in the Briey and Saar basins, Pétain pointed out that an attack toward Metz could occur only after the Germans were cleared from the Meuse-Argonne sector and posed no threat to the flank of an advance toward Metz. After additional discussion, Pétain proposed giving the Americans the entire front between the Moselle River and the Argonne Forest, an idea Pershing found appealing, since he had suggested it to Foch the preceding day.

On September 2 Foch, who had already agreed to the establishment of an American zone, met with Pershing and Pétain. The allied commander let Pershing choose whether he would attack through the rough terrain and strong enemy defenses between the Argonne and the Meuse or through the easier terrain and defenses west of the Argonne. Pershing chose the difficult Meuse-Argonne sector, and Foch accepted the expansion of the American front, which was eventually extended to the western edge of the Argonne Forest. After attacking the St.-Mihiel salient on September 10, the Americans would attack in the Meuse-Argonne sector between September 20 and 25.

Foch's decision to shift the Americans' focus from St.-Mihiel and Metz to the Meuse-Argonne and Mézières later produced sharp criticisms from American officers who believed U.S. forces could have advanced easily and quickly to Metz after overrunning the St.-Mihiel salient. One brigade commander, Brigadier General Douglas MacArthur, argued that Metz was "practically defenseless" after American forces pushed through the salient.[42] A more reasoned assessment came from General Hunter Liggett, who commanded a corps and a field army during the war. He said that U.S. forces were not functioning as smoothly as they needed to be for such an ambitious operation. More important, the Germans had sufficient reserves available to reinforce Metz, and the Americans could have advanced only by exposing both their flanks. Additionally, to cut the German railway the Americans had to advance thirty-five kilometers beyond the base of the salient, but this advance would cut only one of the three main rail lines used by the enemy and leave the Köln-Liège-Aulnoye and Koblenz-Luxembourg-Longuyon lines open. Liggett concluded, "Marshal Foch was exceedingly wise to limit us to the immediate task of flattening out the salient and protecting our rear for another attack to the westward."[43]

Though the decision to modify the St.-Mihiel operation was sound, Foch risked a great deal when he asked the inexperienced Americans to make the complex transition from the St.-Mihiel to the Meuse-Argonne offensive and then advance quickly through some of the most difficult terrain and strongest defenses on the Western Front. He accepted this risk because he could not convince Pershing to divide American forces and allow French generals to command them. He also may have suspected that the French army was no longer capable of undertaking such an arduous campaign on its own.

On September 3 Foch published a directive summarizing the operations aiming to drive the enemy back from the Hindenburg Line. According to the new campaign plan, the British, supported by French forces, would attack toward Cambrai, and the French would continue their advance between Soissons and Reims toward Laon. Meanwhile the Americans would first reduce the St.-Mihiel salient and then—after shifting west—advance, supported by the French, toward Mézières. French forces thus would assist the British on the left and the Americans on the right while simultaneously driving forward in the center.

Seeking to expand the allied attack even farther and prevent the Germans from shifting troops out of quiet sectors, Foch asked the Belgians and British to attack in Flanders. In a meeting with the Belgian king on September 9 he proposed a drive north of the Lys River into Belgium. He envisaged nine Belgian and two British divisions breaking the enemy's defenses and the entire Belgian army, British Second Army, and six French divisions participating in the exploitation. The Belgian king agreed to command the operation with the assistance of a French general and his staff. With Haig's and Pétain's concurrence Foch designated General Jean-Marie Degoutte to direct the overall operation. After the headquarters of Degoutte's Sixth Army was withdrawn from the front line, it was redesignated the Flanders Army Group, and on September 18 Degoutte and his headquarters arrived in Flanders. Combat units arrived later.

Believing the situation was ripe for a general offensive, Foch also sought attacks on the Italian and Balkan fronts. Because of logistical difficulties, the Italians refused to attack, and because of British opposition, prospects for an offensive in Macedonia appeared bleak. In late June, without the approval of the Supreme War Council, Clemenceau had ordered preparations for an offensive in Macedonia, but staunch opposition from Lloyd George disrupted these efforts. For more than a month the permanent military representatives to the Supreme War

Council studied the possibility of an offensive in the Balkans and on August 3 concluded that "it is necessary to push with all speed the preparations for an offensive in Macedonia." Such preparations, however, had to occur without diverting troops and materiel from the Western Front.[44] When the British continued dragging their feet, Clemenceau sent General Guillaumat, who had commanded allied forces in Macedonia until Franchet d'Espèrey replaced him in June, to London to persuade Lloyd George to accept an offensive in the Balkans. In a meeting with British leaders on September 4, the French general offered an optimistic report on the condition and outlook of allied forces in the Balkans. To illustrate the probability of victory, he emphasized the surprising success of a limited offensive on May 30 that had advanced two kilometers and captured 2,000 prisoners. Even though General Wilson doubted that any benefits could come from an offensive in the Balkans, Lloyd George consented to the operation. A quick trip by Guillaumat to Rome gained Italy's consent on September 9. Thus, in early September the allies anticipated offensives on the Western and Balkan fronts.

As the allies prepared these operations, the French continued to believe that the war would not end until 1919. Reflecting his usual pessimism, Pétain expected the enemy to continue fighting and withdraw toward the German frontier; he anticipated strong resistance on the Hindenburg Line and then on other, less-well-prepared lines. Adding to expectations of a series of withdrawals and hard fights, French intelligence identified five major lines between the Franco-Belgian border and the Rhine River. Of these successive positions, a defense along a line connecting Antwerp, Brussels, Namur, and the Meuse River offered considerable possibilities, and a rapid withdrawal to the German frontier, followed by an energetic defense of the national soil, was not out of the question. By taking advantage of the winter's interruption of operations, the Germans could reconstitute their reserves and be prepared in the spring for a hard fight, whether on one of the several positions in the Hindenburg Line or on one of the other lines to its rear or the German frontier. "When the battle commences again in 1919," Pétain wrote on September 8, "our adversary undoubtedly will be established behind a strongly fortified front, abundantly supplied with means of defending against tanks and covered either by a deep zone of advance posts or by lines of water." He anticipated several preliminary actions—limited offensives designed to weaken the enemy's reserves—followed by a "principal action" seeking a decision. "The battle of 1919," Pétain observed, "will be a battle of aviation and tanks."[45]

In preparation for the general offensive at the end of September, the organization of the French zone between the British and American zones underwent considerable change between August 30 and September 26. At the beginning of this period Pétain had Reserve and Central Army groups occupying a 240-kilometer sector while Eastern Army Group covered the eastern frontier. On September 26 the two army groups occupied a 160-kilometer sector between the British and American zones. Reserve Army Group, consisting of First and Tenth armies, held a 60-kilometer front, while on its right Central Army Group, consisting of Fifth and Fourth armies, held a 100-kilometer front. To take advantage of this shorter front, Pétain reorganized the two army groups and reduced the number of French corps in the front lines. Meanwhile, Pershing and the U.S. First Army came nominally under French control, and Eastern Army Group continued to occupy the long front between the American right and Switzerland.

Pétain planned on the main attack's being made by the French Fourth and the U.S. First armies. The Americans would reduce the St.-Mihiel salient and then drive toward Mézières through the Meuse-Argonne region. In Central Army Group, which was on the Americans' left, Fourth Army would drive toward Rethel and Mézières, while Fifth Army attacked west of Reims across the Chemin des Dames. To maintain the momentum of the attack Pétain planned on introducing Third Army between Fifth and Fourth armies. As for Fayolle's Reserve Army Group, Tenth Army would maintain pressure on the enemy to its front and march toward Laon while on its left First Army (and the British Fourth Army) drove toward St.-Quentin and Guise.

On September 23 Foch set the timing of the operations. Though he preferred unleashing all the attacks of his general offensive simultaneously, logistical constraints compelled him to phase the operations. He scheduled the U.S. First and French Fourth armies' advance toward

Mézières for September 26, the British move toward Cambrai for the twenty-seventh, and the combined Belgian-British-French advance in Flanders for the following day. He also ordered the British and French attack toward St.-Quentin to begin "without delay" after the British began their advance toward Cambrai;[46] these attacks actually would begin on the twenty-ninth. Additionally, the attacks by the French Tenth Army toward Laon and Fifth Army across the Chemin des Dames armies would begin on September 28 and 30, respectively. The operations thus would commence over five days and stretch from the English Channel to the Meuse.

Of all these offensives, Foch continued to believe that the drive toward Mézières could have the greatest strategic effect. On September 5 he wrote to Pétain:

> The nature and importance of the operation scheduled for the twenty-sixth require us to take advantage without delay of all the advantages gained, that the breaking of the line of resistance be exploited without interruption as deeply as possible, and that all halts be avoided. This especially applies to the advance of the American army between the Meuse and the French Fourth Army. Since the strength of this army relieves it of all risks, it must, without additional instructions and upon the initiative of its commander, push its advance forward as far as possible.

Foch added that the role of the American army could be "decisive."[47]

Despite this expectation, the British, not the Americans and French in the drive toward Mézières, made the most important advances in the first phase of the offensive. Attacking on the morning of September 27 toward Cambrai, the British First and Third armies, led by the Canadian Corps, advanced as much as seven kilometers on the first day. By the end of the third day the British were on the outskirts of Cambrai. The British also achieved considerable success ten kilometers north of St.-Quentin. On the first day of their attack in this region, September 29, the British Fourth Army advanced five kilometers. After two more days of heavy fighting, the British pushed their way through German defenses. Though the density of enemy divisions between Arras and Soissons was almost double that between Soissons and Verdun, the British made rapid progress south of Arras while the French and Americans made only small progress between Soissons and Verdun.

Farther to the north, the Flanders Army Group achieved surprising success. To protect Cambrai Ludendorff had shifted troops from Flanders, and the British and Belgians on that portion of the front advanced quickly against relatively weak enemy forces. With French divisions following as reserves, the British and Belgians advanced seven kilometers the first day, September 28, and swept across Passchendaele within the first forty-eight hours. By the end of the third day they had advanced a total of fourteen kilometers. On October 1 two French divisions entered the front lines, but the advance halted on October 3.

Elsewhere on the front, the French initially made only small gains. To the south of St.-Quentin, Debeney's First Army, which had the mission of supporting the British Fourth Army's operation, did nothing more on the twenty-ninth than provide assistance with artillery and launch a small attack on an enemy strong point ten kilometers south of St.-Quentin. After visiting Haig's headquarters on September 30, Foch ordered First Army to concentrate its attack north of St.-Quentin, but the shifting of its focus failed to quiet British complaints that the French were "hanging back."[48] On October 1 the French pressed forward and encircled St.-Quentin, occupying the city the following day. After hard fighting they crossed the canal to the east of the city, but strong enemy resistance soon halted their advance. Foch was pleased with British gains and incensed at the lack of French progress. First Army's slow movement toward St.-Quentin resulted in Foch's ordering it on October 4 to "support at all costs the right of the British Fourth Army."[49] To accelerate the drive, he admonished Debeney directly.

Foch's criticisms extended to other French armies, all of which made only small gains between September 26 and October 3. To the right of First Army, Tenth Army advanced four kilometers northeast of Soissons. The advance came, however, not from an energetic assault but from the enemy's withdrawal. To the right of Tenth Army, Fifth Army encountered strong resistance west of Reims when it attacked on the thirtieth, but the enemy's withdrawal behind the Aisne River permitted Fifth Army to advance thirteen kilometers until it reached the water obstacle on October 3 and halted. To the right of Fifth Army and left of Pershing's First Army, General Henri Gouraud's Fourth Army also advanced slowly and did not push ahead of the Americans. On September 26 Fourth Army, which had seven corps, all of which were in the front line, moved forward four kilometers and captured 7,000 prisoners. On subsequent days the army made less progress, and on October 3, which was marked by the U.S. 2nd Infantry Division's capture of Blanc Mont, Gouraud's attack stalled. Although Pétain had already reinforced Gouraud with this U.S. division, the Central Army Group commander requested two more American divisions on October 3 so that Fourth Army could continue its attack.

Foch believed that Gouraud's forces had performed poorly even though Fourth Army had advanced twelve kilometers and captured key terrain in several places. To get the French moving faster, he sent a scathing note to Pétain. "Yesterday, 3 October . . . we witnessed a battle that was not commanded, a battle that was not pushed, a battle that was not brought together . . . and in consequence a battle in which there was no exploitation of the results obtained." He added, "It should not escape your notice that the considerations I have identified with regard to the Fourth Army apply to several other [French units]."[50]

As Foch sought more energetic action from French forces, the offensive in Macedonia achieved great success. The gains in the Balkans came after the French obtained the reluctant approval of the British and Italian governments for an offensive in Macedonia and after Franchet d'Espèrey boldly attacked on September 15. Since Austria had concentrated most of its strength on the Italian front, enemy forces along the Macedonian front consisted primarily of Bulgarians, who suffered from shortages of food, clothing, and munitions and whose morale had plummeted. Preceded by a twenty-one-hour artillery and aviation bombardment, two French divisions, aided by a Serbian division, assaulted the heights west of the Vardar River at 0530 hours. By the end of the day additional Serbian forces had passed through the French and charged forward into Serbia. By the evening of the eighteenth, the Serbs had advanced 30 kilometers. When the British and Greeks attacked east of the Vardar River on September 18, they initially encountered strong resistance, but the relentless allied advance west of the Vardar soon undermined Bulgarian resistance east of the river. By September 23 allied forces, led by the Serbs, had advanced 65 kilometers, split the Bulgarians, and opened the road to Sofia. Although the Germans diverted six or seven divisions to the Balkans in a desperate attempt to buttress the Bulgarians, the king's abdication and the complete collapse of the Bulgarian army made the situation irreparable. On the twenty-fifth the British entered Bulgaria, and the next day the Bulgarians asked for an armistice. When hostilities ended at noon on September 30, French cavalry occupied Skopje in Serbia, 115 kilometers northwest of the original allied front line.

As Joffre had hoped early in the war, the multifront strategy finally yielded success. The collapse of Bulgaria created insurmountable strategic problems for the Central Powers, particularly since the allies had the initiative on the Western Front and were continuing their relentless attacks. In addition to concerns about losing contact with Romanian oil fields, the German High Command worried about protecting Austria from allied forces advancing up the Danube toward Vienna and feared the Austrians might collapse in front of the Italians. The downfall of Bulgaria also caused Germany and Austria to lose contact with the Ottoman Empire, which soon fell before General Sir Edmund Allenby's British forces. The Germans did not have enough resources to hold the allies in France and simultaneously shore up defenses in the Balkans.

On September 28, the day of Bulgaria's collapse, Hindenburg and Ludendorff concluded that the strategic and operational balance had shifted decidedly against the Central Powers. The following day the two military leaders, insisting on peace "at once,"[51] met with senior government officials and then on the thirtieth with the kaiser. In this time of crisis the chancellor, Count von Hertling, resigned, and the Germans formed a new government. When the newly identified but not yet appointed chancellor, Prince Max of Baden, expressed doubts about the wisdom of seeking an armistice, Hindenburg insisted that a peace offer be dispatched at once. On the night of October 3–4, shortly after being appointed chancellor, Prince Max sent a message to President Wilson proposing an immediate armistice with the Fourteen Points as the basis for peace. At about the same time Austria dispatched a note to the allies requesting an immediate armistice.

Despite these encouraging signs, the allied offensive in France slowed in early October. Hampered by the Germans' destruction of the country-side as they withdrew, allied armies devoted considerable time and re-sources to rebuilding their lines of communication. Soldiers required considerable amounts of ammunition and supplies if they were going to continue to advance, but these could not arrive until roads and railways were restored. In Flanders the allies did not begin moving again until Oc-tober 14. The British did not capture Cambrai until October 9 and did not advance toward Douai until the tenth. Debeney's First Army did not drive beyond St.-Quentin until October 8, and Mangin's Tenth Army did not launch a large attack until the twelfth and Fifth Army until the tenth. The largest gains came when the Germans withdrew north of Reims, and the right of Fifth Army and the left of Fourth Army followed them.

The slow progress of the Franco-American drive toward Mézières frustrated Foch greatly, for he believed this operation had the potential for the greatest strategic effect. In the Meuse-Argonne offensive, Pershing expected to make a rapid, deep penetration of German defenses before the enemy could shift reinforcements into the sector. In his initial attack the American commander sought to drive forward fifteen kilometers to the main German defenses in the Kriemhild Position (between Grandpré and Damvillers). After seizing this position and consolidating gains, he expected to drive forward another fifteen kilometers. These operations would clear the way for a final American advance toward Mézières. De-spite Pershing's optimism and confidence, the offensive, which began early on September 26, quickly bogged down and had stalled by the twenty-ninth. Officers in the Operations Bureau of the GQG criticized the Americans for using twice as many troops as needed in the attack, taking heavy casualties, and not being able to coordinate the complex maneuver. The situation was so bad that Foch believed the Americans had to "restore order in their units before resuming their operations in the direction of Mézières."[52] Pétain relayed to Pershing the French mar-shal's impatience with American efforts. The failure of the French Fourth Army to race ahead of the disorganized Americans did not help Foch's gray mood. His scathing note to Pétain on October 4 about Fourth Army's battle not being "commanded," "pushed," or "exploited" none-theless demonstrated that the allied commander neither blamed only

Pershing for the slow Franco-American advance nor accepted Fourth Army's excuse of having slowed its advance so that it would not move ahead of the Americans.

Unfortunately for Pershing, Clemenceau chose to make a visit when the American rear was—in Pershing's words—"hopelessly swamped."[53] Accompanied by General Mordacq, Clemenceau visited the American headquarters on September 29 and then tried to travel to Montfaucon, but the road was jammed with units and equipment. Convinced that the Americans were paralyzed by the inexperience and incompetence of their higher-level staffs, Clemenceau finally abandoned his attempt to reach Montfaucon and traveled instead to the French Fourth Army's headquarters on Pershing's left. Its commander, General Gouraud, complained that he could not risk advancing ahead of the Americans and exposing his flank to an attack from the Argonne Forest. Unlike Foch, Clemenceau accepted Gouraud's excuse for the slow progress of Fourth Army. With Bulgaria collapsing in front of allied troops, he thought that the war could end in 1918, perhaps in a few weeks, and he had grave concerns about the Americans. If the Germans launched a vigorous counterattack, they could disrupt the U.S. offensive and delay the allied victory. More important, the Tiger believed the Americans' ineffectiveness could cost the French "much blood."[54] Blaming Pershing, he questioned Foch about the American general's performance.

Foch was not blind to the strategic awkwardness created by the failure of the Americans to advance. On September 30 he sent a proposal to Pershing in which he suggested placing the French Second Army between the U.S. First and the French Fourth. The idea came from Pétain, who had complained that same day about the performance of the American headquarters and its inability "to move or supply troops." To remedy the situation, Pétain proposed having General Auguste Hirschauer's Second Army take command of a French corps on the right of the Fourth Army and an American corps on the left of the U.S. First Army.[55] Agreeing that Pershing and his First Army headquarters could not handle the complex Meuse-Argonne operation, Foch suggested reducing the size and span of control of the U.S. First Army and limiting its operation to both banks of the Meuse. The French Second Army, he said, should direct the operation in the Argonne. Not surprisingly, Pershing refused on the grounds that the change would delay rather than accelerate the allied advance. Foch yielded but only on the condition that "American attacks begin without delay and, once begun, continue without pause."[56]

Appalled at the "extraordinary disarray" in the Meuse-Argonne offensive, Clemenceau became increasingly dissatisfied with Foch's gentle handling of Pershing. On October 1 the Tiger told Poincaré that he would demand that Foch take the situation "in hand." Three days later Clemenceau again met with Poincaré and expressed even greater dissatisfaction with Foch's failure to correct the disorder in U.S. forces. After calling President Wilson a "Buddha" and describing his entourage as "zero," the Tiger demanded that Foch report Pershing's poor performance to Wilson.[57] On October 6 Clemenceau sent his military assistant, General Mordacq, to meet with Pétain, who had recently submitted a report highly critical of Pershing and recent American operations. According to Mordacq, Pétain's conclusion was clear: "If General Pershing continues along his current path, he is risking a disaster."[58] Pétain blamed the Americans for the lack of progress in the offensive and for the high casualties suffered by Fourth Army. Pershing had come under Pétain's control when he assumed command of the U.S. First Army and launched the Meuse-Argonne offensive, but Pétain found the relationship with Pershing unsatisfactory, particularly since Pershing had maintained his responsibilities as the senior American military officer in Europe.

By October 7 Clemenceau was furious about Foch's not handling the Americans more firmly. In a meeting with Poincaré, he complained about Foch's increasing independence and his siding with Lloyd George in a recent discussion about operations against Constantinople. He also expressed great concern about the "fatigue" of the French army.[59] In the meantime, Pétain had become even more critical of Pershing and the staff of the U.S. First Army and more concerned about the demands of supporting incompletely organized U.S. units. On October 8 Pétain opposed forming another American field army and suggested placing newly arrived units in French corps and armies. On October 11 Clemenceau showed Poincaré a draft of a letter to Foch that, in the Tiger's words, was "'harsh' to Pershing, who did not want to obey, and to Foch, who did not want to command." Poincaré advised him to revise the letter completely or not send it, and the next day Clemenceau circulated another draft.

Poincaré again expressed reservations; among his suggestions was deletion of a sentence that read, "Your country commands you to command."[60]

Undoubtedly aware of the Tiger's rising anger, Foch sent General Weygand to Pershing's headquarters on October 11 to deliver a letter, the content of which remains uncertain. Foch wanted to insert the French Second Army headquarters into the Argonne and may have directed Pershing and his staff to move to the Moselle valley and prepare for an offensive into Lorraine. Whatever Foch ordered, Pershing refused to obey, and the following day, October 13, the two met. After an extensive discussion Pershing agreed to form the U.S. Second Army, and Foch agreed to elevate him to the same status as Pétain and Haig.[61] Foch's order explained that the Americans had created the U.S. Second Army and that Pershing was now an army-group commander. In his memoirs Foch said nothing about sending Weygand to Pershing's headquarters, but he did observe, "Having a more complete appreciation of the difficulties faced by the Americans, I could not support the radical solution envisaged by Mr. Clemenceau."[62] Whatever Foch's "solution" may have been, he forced Pershing to reorganize American forces and pressed him to get the Meuse-Argonne offensive moving.

By October 21 Clemenceau's anger toward Pershing and Foch had reached a boiling point, and he sent Foch the letter that Poincaré had advised him not to send. He insisted in the much-modified letter that it would be "criminal" for him to allow attrition of the French army to continue "indefinitely" without doing something about it. "It is not necessary to be a [military] technician," he wrote, "to understand that the immobility of our right wing is not part of your plans and that you have lost—no matter how favorable the other circumstances—the benefit of movements that, through lack of organization, have not been accomplished." After reminding Foch of Pershing's refusal to obey orders and his "invincible obstinacy," Clemenceau urged the French marshal to provide President Wilson with "the truth, the whole truth" about Pershing's shortcomings. He asserted that Wilson would accept Foch's advice on "all questions of a military nature" and, without using the word "relief," urged Foch to make a "final decision" about the American general.[63]

Foch ignored Clemenceau's letter and compared it later to Don Quixote's charge at a windmill, but the disagreement between the two leaders set the stage for a larger clash. Already inclined to act independently, Foch tried to use his position as supreme commander to shape not only the armistice but also the peace. This effort brought a swift response from Clemenceau, who had the minister of foreign affairs write to Foch: "Your business is war, and everything that pertains to the peace . . . belongs to us and only us."[64] With some semblance of allied unity of command finally established, Clemenceau wanted Foch to give orders to Pétain, Haig, and Pershing and to bring the war to an end, not become involved in larger political issues. After the war he credited Foch with making a "very large" contribution to winning the war but added, "Fame is a troublesome temptress, especially when strutting reveals unattractive features."[65] Had Clemenceau asked, Pétain would have concurred with this assessment, but neither his pen nor his wit was as sharp as the Tiger's.

As Clemenceau criticized Foch and the Americans and fretted about the loss of French lives, the Germans attempted to negotiate an armistice through the "intermediary" of the American government.[66] On October 6 the German chancellor sent a message through the Swiss government to President Wilson asking for negotiations based on the Fourteen Points. After Wilson responded politely two days later with a request for additional information, the French military feared the worst: they knew the French could not continue the war on their own, and they feared the Americans would impose an armistice on France. One officer asked an American liaison officer, "Does your President realize with what swine he is dealing? They'll fool him if he is not very, very canny." Another commented, "Once you cease fighting I doubt that it would be possible to resume operations." Another said it was "unthinkable" to treat with the Germans as long as they occupied French or Belgian soil.[67] The French were greatly relieved when they received a copy of Wilson's reply of October 14 to the German request for an armistice, and they welcomed his insistence on leaving the "process of evacuation" and the "conditions of an armistice" to the "judgment and advice of the military advisers of the Government of the United States and the Allied Governments."[68] After learning of Wilson's response, the officers in the Operations Bureau of the GQG celebrated. An American liaison officer reported, "We drank toasts to America, France, President Wilson, General Pershing and Illinois (my native state)." The head of the Operations Bureau reflected the views of many French officers when he said, "the German army is not defeated now. The prospect is bright for their defeat next year."[69] Desiring an unambiguous defeat of the Germans, France's military leaders had no desire to accept a negotiated settlement.

As the head of the Operations Oureau feared, the German High Command became less pessimistic after Foch's offensive slowed in early October. Prince Max met with Ludendorff on October 9 and noted his more optimistic mood. When the German chancellor asked how long the army could keep the Entente's forces beyond the German frontier, Ludendorff replied: "Frontier a long way behind Western front, we can protect it for a long time yet. Attacks in Lorraine possible, I see no danger for Lorraine frontier. I see no danger from Holland, since troops who might cross the frontier would be interned."[70] Though Ludendorff did not recommend ending armistice negotiations, the momentary respite had enabled him to regain his composure. By mid-October he no longer feared a military catastrophe and believed the army could retire to the Meuse or to the German frontier. In a crucial meeting of the War Cabinet on October 17, Ludendorff observed that the strength of the enemy's attack was "falling off."[71] Although the chancellor had doubts, Ludendorff believed Germany could continue the war another year by withdrawing to new defensive positions when necessary and eventually could obtain a more favorable peace in 1919.

To keep the Germans from pulling back and reorganizing along their frontier, Foch realized, the allies had to continue their forward movement and increase the disorganization of the enemy. After considering ways of raising pressure on the enemy, he chose to continue the strategy he had followed in September. On October 10 he published a directive that identified three "converging" attacks being made by allied forces: the Flanders Army Group's drive toward Ghent, the British advance toward Maubeuge, and the Franco-American move toward Mézières. Of these three, the marshal identified the drive toward Maubeuge as "the most advantageous to exploit," because of the British success.[72] His directive included only two changes from his previous statements about strategy. First, and most significantly, he broadened his definition of the advance on the right from a relatively narrow one, involving the French Fourth and U.S. First armies, to a broader one in which the four French armies, plus the Americans, would move toward Mézières. Second, he directed Pétain to give Debeney's First Army more tanks. His operational goal was to have First Army flank the Germans' Hunding Position, which extended from Guise to Rethel.

In a sense Foch's directive was an acknowledgment of the significant gains made by the British and the lesser gains made by the French and Americans. In response to Foch's highly critical letter of October 4, Pétain had complained to the Central and Reserve army-group commanders about the lack of "energetic drive" in some divisions and corps,[73] but he did not push his forces forward and continued his cautious and deliberate advance. He insisted on careful preparation of all attacks and refused to rely on anything other than firepower to blast the enemy back. Similarly, on October 9 Pétain noted the importance of "giving no respite to the enemy,"[74] but not until two days later, after he received a new directive from Foch, did he publish an operational scheme for pressing forward. Hoping the thrusts toward Mézières and Maubeuge would rattle the Germans' defenses, Pétain saw no reason to incur high casualties, particularly since he believed the French had borne the heaviest burden of the war and would encounter several enemy defensive lines between the French and German frontiers. In short, he continued the cautious operations that had been his trademark since mid-1917.

As allied forces pressed forward, Ludendorff avoided placing his forces at a disadvantage. When the Flanders Army Group attacked on October 14, the combined French, Belgian, and British forces made steady progress, but then, as Foch noted in his memoirs, "the enemy gave way."[75] Abandoning the entire Belgian coast, the Germans withdrew toward the Scheldt River and, to its southeast, the Hermann Position, which stretched from Valenciennes south toward Guise. Though incomplete, this position barred a quick advance from Cambrai or Douai toward Maubeuge. To the south the Germans also withdrew and occupied new positions along a line stretching from Guise to Rethel and then along the Aisne River to Grandpré. This line included the Hunding and Brünhild positions. The Germans also held the strong Kriemhild Position, which stretched east between Grandpré and Damvillers and gave the Americans so much trouble. The Germans thus pulled back toward a new defensive line running initially along the Scheldt and then through Valenciennes, Le Cateau, Guise, Rethel, Grandpré, and Damvillers.

Debeney's First Army made the key assault against German defenses between Guise and Rethel. As directed by Foch's order of October 10 and Pétain's on the following day, First Army struck midway between St.-Quentin and Laon on October 15. The French fought their way across the small Serre River and two days later attacked across the front of the entire army with five corps. Even though the operation accomplished little, that night the Germans withdrew a few kilometers to the main defenses of the Hunding Position. On the twenty-fourth, after two French corps failed to break through the position, Debeney renewed the attack. By the evening of October 26 the French had driven through the enemy's defenses. Following this significant penetration First Army was poised to outflank German defenses in the Hunding Position, and on the night of October 26–27 the enemy pulled back five kilometers along most of First Army's front.

Other important allied advances occurred around the key date of October 17, when the German War Cabinet met and Ludendorff insisted on continuing the war. The British First Army reached the Scheldt River near Valenciennes on October 24. On its right, the British Third Army crossed the Selle River north of Le Cateau on the twentieth and pressed forward for the next five days. On Third Army's right, the British Fourth Army fought its way through the Hermann Position east of Le Cateau on October 25. At about the same time the French Fifth Army succeeded in capturing the last part of the Hunding Position (between Guise and Rethel) remaining in German hands. Thus by October 26 the allies had broken through enemy defenses in the Hermann and Hunding positions. In the same period the Americans succeeded in breaking the Kriemhild Position. On October 14–16 they captured the key heights anchoring German defenses and by the end of the month finally attained the main objective of their September 26 attack. This advance permitted American heavy artillery to strike the enemy's railway communications northeast of the Meuse River and provided irrefutable proof of the Germans' desperate situation.

Convinced that the situation was hopeless, the German government formally asked Wilson for an armistice, but his firm response on October

23 erased all hopes of a negotiated peace and convinced Hindenburg and Ludendorff to keep fighting. On October 24 Ludendorff published an army order that stated: "Wilson's answer is a demand for unconditional surrender. It is thus unacceptable for us soldiers. . . . Wilson's answer can . . . be nothing for us soldiers but a challenge to continue our resistance with all our strength."[76] On October 25 Prince Max demanded that Kaiser Wilhelm dismiss Ludendorff but induce Hindenburg to remain. The following day the kaiser accepted Ludendorff's resignation. As Berlin agonized over the kaiser's possible abdication, the German government informed President Wilson on October 27 that it was making "far-reaching changes . . . in German constitutional life" and was awaiting "proposals for an armistice."[77]

As German resistance weakened, Foch published a new strategic directive on October 19; this document maintained the campaign strategy established in September and modified on October 10. While the Flanders Army Group marched toward Brussels, the British Fifth, First, Third, and Fourth armies would march beyond Maubeuge and drive the enemy back on the Ardennes. Meanwhile, to the right of the British Fourth Army, the French First Army would march toward Hirson and the Chimay Gap. Farther to the east, the French Fifth and Fourth armies and the U.S. First Army would drive toward Mézières.[78] The directive of October 19 thus provided the outline of allied actions for the drive toward the Meuse River.

Though the operation never took place, the French also prepared an offensive in Lorraine. Initial planning began in early September, when Pétain asked the Eastern Army Group commander, Castelnau, to study an attack by thirty divisions across a front of sixty kilometers. As the German situation deteriorated in mid-October Foch recognized the operational advantages of launching an offensive through Longwy into Luxembourg or through Morhange into the Saar. With the Germans still forward of the Antwerp-Dyle-Meuse line, such an operation could drive into the enemy's rear and have considerable effect. On October 20 Foch directed Pétain to prepare such an offensive. Since Pétain had anticipated a drive by Eastern Army Group, he sent Foch a proposal the following day for an attack into Luxembourg and the Saar using forty divisions, including fifteen to twenty American divisions. After receiving Pétain's proposal, Foch decided against an operation on the west bank of the Moselle toward Luxembourg because it could not be launched in the immediate future. He chose instead to initiate preparations for an operation east of the Moselle near Nancy. Such an operation, Foch said, could be launched immediately with limited resources and achieve "important results."[79] On October 27 Pétain gave Castelnau detailed guidance for preparing the offensive. Using twenty infantry divisions, a cavalry corps, an "aerial" division, three regiments of light tanks, and two battalions of medium tanks, Pétain expected to "rupture" the German front northeast of Nancy. He anticipated inserting Tenth Army between the U.S. Second and French Eighth armies and having it attack with four corps (fourteen divisions) on a twenty-seven-kilometer front. The U.S. Second Army would protect the left flank of the attack against an advance from the vicinity of Metz. By advancing from Nancy toward Morhange and then northeast toward Sarreguemines (fifteen kilometers south of Saarbrücken), the French hoped to drive deep into the German rear and make significant gains.[80]

Final preparations for the Lorraine offensive occurred in early November. General Mangin and his Tenth Army's headquarters arrived south of Nancy on November 6 and began assembling units for the operation. Of the units programmed to participate in the operation, the French had five of the six corps and eighteen of the twenty divisions in the immediate vicinity of the planned offensive on November 11. Castelnau expected the attack to begin on November 14.

In the final weeks of the war, France did not focus solely on the Western Front. Shortly after the armistice with Bulgaria at the end of September, Franchet d'Espèrey responded to a request from Clemenceau for suggestions about the allied plan of action for the Balkans. The principal objectives of the allies in southeast Europe, said d'Espèrey, were to liberate all of Serbia and to threaten Austria-Hungary. He anticipated seizing important points in Bulgaria and stretching toward Romania in order to cut communications between the Central Powers and the Ottoman Empire. Additionally, d'Espèrey foresaw freeing the Dardanelles and driving enemy forces from Albania and Montenegro. The only development in the Balkans causing Clemenceau concern pertained to Lloyd George's decision to remove British forces from d'Espèrey's command and transfer them to General Allenby, the British commander in Palestine, for an attack on Constantinople. Seeing this as a flagrant grab for postwar influence, the Tiger reacted angrily and told the British ambassador that it was a "veritable denunciation of the Anglo-French alliance."[81] Foch's support for Lloyd George's action added to the Tiger's fury. Clemenceau nonetheless responded to Franchet d'Espèrey's telegram by encouraging him to "carry the war to the very frontier of Austria and extend allied military and maritime actions toward Romania and southern Russia."[82] A legend appeared after the war concerning d'Espèrey's supposedly having proposed in early October a march on Munich, but the French general focused only on the Balkans and did not propose a drive toward southern Germany. On November 5 Paris informed him that the allies had decided to concentrate an army, predominantly Italian, on the Bavarian frontier and march toward Munich.

Foch was particularly attentive to the Italian front. After the Italian commander, General Armando Diaz, refused to attack in mid-August because of logistical difficulties, the Italians sought additional divisions from the allies. When Diaz asked Pershing in early September for twenty-five U.S. divisions, the American commander refused, and the Italian prime minister, Orlando, then asked Foch for a dozen allied divisions. In a polite response on September 28 Foch declined and closed his letter by saying: "There is no war without risks. The question today, given these risks amidst the moral collapse and disorganization of the Austrian army, is to know if the Italian command is disposed to accept them."[83] After the Austrians asked Wilson on October 4 for an armistice, the Italians, fearing the war would end without their achieving a decisive victory, decided to attack. Assisted by three British and two French divisions, plus one U.S. regiment, Diaz's forces assaulted the Austrians on October 24. The first few days of the battle proved reminiscent of the battles fought earlier in the war along the Isonzo River, but the Italian Tenth Army, which included two British divisions, crossed the Piave River and broke through enemy defenses. As the Italians advanced, the Austrians offered half-hearted resistance and then collapsed completely on the night of October 30–31. On November 3 the Italian commander, General Diaz, acting on behalf of the allies, signed an armistice with Austria-Hungary.

As the war rushed to a close Foch and Pétain clashed over operational methods. The opening salvo came from Foch, who wrote to Pétain on October 25 criticizing his use of successive objectives, which he considered more appropriate for static than for mobile warfare. Having lost patience with Pétain's slow, methodical advance, he wrote:

> Troops launched into an attack should know only their direction of attack. In this direction they should go as far as they can, attacking and maneuvering [around] the enemy who resist without any concern for alignment, the units most advanced working to the advantage of those momentarily halted. They operate in this manner not according to lines established beforehand based on terrain, but according to the enemy.[84]

Pétain responded with a note lecturing the supreme commander on operational methods. Without using the term "methodical battle," he described an operation with "successive objectives" and a "main direction" in a "zone of action." After saying that these procedures could be used in a "fortified zone" or "open terrain," he insisted that a "series of efforts" ensured close liaison between artillery and infantry and guaranteed a "continuity of effort" far better than "simple" directions of attack. He added:

> I believe that the method which consists of defining an offensive mission by successive objectives with a principal objective and directions of exploitation responds to the real character of the struggle. The enemy is undoubtedly very exhausted, but his resistance rests on extensive echelons in depth and a multitude of machine guns. Consequently, he yields only to coordinated attacks, relying on great amounts of firepower and the intervention of tanks, and when he yields, the exploitation always requires cannon. Under these conditions, every offensive still includes in some fashion a breakthrough phase in which successive objectives are imperative if one wants to ensure the precise cooperation of the different arms; and this breakthrough phase is followed by an exploitation phase, which can be successful only if one maneuvers across the successive lines or points to which enemy resistance clings.[85]

To show Foch who really commanded the French army, Pétain sent a note to his army-group commanders elaborating his operational and tactical concepts. Though Foch portrayed this later message as "conciliatory," Pétain still emphasized successive objectives.[86] And indeed, the final battles fought by the French bore a stronger resemblance to Pétain's than Foch's operational concept.

After the war British authors strongly criticized French performance in the final weeks of fighting. In the British official history, Sir James E. Edmonds highlighted what he called the "diminishing effort of the French armies" and attributed this reduction to a "policy of leaving the fighting to the British and Americans." To support this assertion he noted that the French held only sixty-five kilometers of the "active front" on November 11, 1918. Earlier in the same volume, Edmonds compared the prisoners and weapons captured by the French and British and concluded: "Which armies bore the brunt of the fighting in the last stage cannot, therefore, be doubted."[87] Although Edmonds' criticisms were colored by his desire to highlight British contributions toward winning the Great War, there is no doubt that the French army's effort and capability declined between March and September 1918 and that the French were on their last legs in the final two months of the war. After performing magnificently during the German spring offensive and allied counteroffensive, French soldiers had little left to give; heavy casualties and mental and physical exhaustion finally took their toll. A week before Foch's offensives of September 26–28, an officer in the Operations Bureau of the GQG acknowledged to an American liaison officer, "The moral[e] of French troops is very good but they are physically tired as a result of constant combat for many weeks and, in the case of many divisions, for many months."[88] Formal reports on morale highlighted the soldiers' "splendid" morale and "absolute" confidence in victory, but they also warned of increasing fatigue and more numerous complaints. A month before the armistice Colonel Auguste Laure, who later wrote a biography of Pétain and a book about the Operations Bureau in the war, told an American liaison officer, "You have many of the characteristics which we had in the early part of the war—élan, impetuosity—you are willing to assault; alas, the great losses we sustained forced us to become more conservative— probably too conservative—and your élan carries us along."[89]

Providing the Americans with massive amounts of equipment also drained the French of combat power. Of the weapons used by the Americans in combat, the French provided 3,532 of their 4,194 artillery pieces, 227 of 289 tanks, and 4,874 of 6,364 aircraft.[90] On August 19 General Buat, Pétain's chief of staff, complained in his diary about an order from Foch to provide the Americans with 24,000 horses. He wrote, "At times like this, you regret that the commander-in-chief of allied forces is French."[91] The massive transfer of weapons, equipment, and horses not only prevented Pétain from transforming his forces into what Tim Travers has called a "mechanical-warfare oriented army"[92] but also diverted artillery, tanks, and aircraft at a time when the French needed them the most. Especially during preparation of the St.-Mihiel and Meuse-Argonne offensives, the Americans required much additional support. The situation led Pétain to complain several times to Foch that the French army did not have enough equipment "to meet its own requirements."[93] In the final weeks of the war the French struggled to mount a powerful offensive on their own and required much assistance from the Americans and the British. Although they gamely organized an offensive into Lorraine, the chances of their achieving a significant victory were small.

A broader assessment of France's situation came from the former minister of war, Messimy, prior to the massive German offensive in March and the counteroffensive at Soissons on July 18. He admitted privately, "Without the American intervention, we definitely would have lost the war."[94] On the day of the armistice, General Victor Duval, the head of the Operations Bureau in Pétain's headquarters, acknowledged to a liaison officer the importance of American assistance. In his report to Pershing, the officer summarized Duval's comments:

> let me say from my heart that we French, we will feel an eternal gratitude to Americans, for without your aid we would be Boche provinces instead of a free people. You came not one hour too soon. We were nearly finished. . . . Take the all-important attack of July 18 [in which the allies gained the initiative]. Without the presence in that attack of your troops the attack would have been an utter impossibil-

ity—it would never have taken place. Your presence was absolutely essential.

A month earlier Duval had told the American liaison officer, "without you we would have been completely defeated this year."[95] Clearly, the Americans did not win the war, but without their assistance, as well as that of the British, the French probably would have collapsed amidst one of the German offensives in 1918 and certainly would not have seized the initiative from the Germans in mid-July.

The final drive on the Western Front began on October 31. By pressing forward with First Army toward Guise and Hirson and with Fourth Army toward Mézières, Pétain sought to outflank German defenses along the Aisne and thereby to open the way for Third (which had replaced Tenth) and Fifth armies. Fayolle, the Reserve Army Group commander, ordered the First Army's commander to coordinate his actions carefully with the British Fourth Army. On the first day two corps from First Army crossed a canal barring their advance, and the following day at 0630 hours they occupied Guise. Gouraud's Fourth Army also made gains during this period but only in conjunction with the U.S. First Army. On November 1 Fourth Army made small progress on the first day and more rapid progress on the second. Assisted by the Americans' energetic attacks, even larger gains on Gouraud's right came on the third day, when the French reached Le Chesne, twenty-eight kilometers east of Rethel.

On November 5 the Germans began a vast withdrawal toward the Meuse. As Pétain acknowledged in his formal postwar report, the French pursued them but "pushed forward methodically."[96] With the French Fourth Army moving north cautiously, Pershing concluded that the "honor of entering Sedan" should "fall to the American First Army."[97] His order set off an impetuous race by U.S. units across the front of Fourth Army. When the Americans rushed forward, they marched north through towns (Stonne, Chémery, Bulson, Cheveuges, and so on) through which elements of the German XIX Panzer Corps would drive south in May 1940. By the morning of November 7 the U.S. 1st and 42nd divisions were on the hills overlooking the city. To their rear, Fourth Army continued its cautious advance.

As the Americans raced and the French lumbered toward Sedan, revolution broke out in Germany. Ludendorff's replacement, General Wilhelm Gröner, gave the German War Cabinet a report that the chancellor later called "as black as could be." Gröner was particularly concerned about the American advance toward Sedan and Mézières. After a visit to Sedan, his description of the situation was even bleaker, and he told Prince Max that the Germans would have to cross the front lines with a white flag. The chancellor responded, "But not for a week at least?" "A week is too long a time," Gröner answered.[98] This grim advice came from Gröner's recognition he could not repair the disastrously unfavorable strategic and operational situations.

On November 7 at 2015 hours a German delegation, after having asked Foch by wireless the previous night for a meeting, made contact with the advance guard of First Army. The next morning, in the Compiègne forest north of Paris, Foch met the German delegates and dictated allied terms. After the departure of the Germans, Foch told allied commanders: "The enemy, disorganized by our repeated attacks, is yielding on the entire front. It is urgent to maintain and accelerate our efforts. I appeal to the energy and initiative of the commanders-in-chief and their armies to render decisive the results obtained."[99] He knew continued pressure would ensure that the Germans could not rebuild their units or rekindle their will to fight. On November 11 the German delegates returned at 0215 hours to sign the definitive text of the armistice. The allied and German representatives finished signing the formal document at 0510 hours, and at 1100 hours hostilities ceased.

The following day Pétain told French troops that they would advance into Alsace-Lorraine and Germany, and he asked them to remain disciplined and maintain respect toward their defeated enemies. He also said:

> I am touched like you by the memory of our dead, whose sacrifice has given us victory. I salute with sorrow the fathers and mothers, the widows and orphans of France, who have stopped their tears for a moment during these days of national joy to applaud the triumph of our arms.
>
> I bow before your magnificent flags.
> Vive la France![100]

Conclusion

The "Misery" of Victory

NEWS OF THE ARMISTICE unleashed a tumultuous celebration across France. In Paris crowds marched up and down the boulevards cheering wildly and singing "La Marseillaise" at the top of their voices. Thousands of people gathered in the Place de la Concorde among the captured German guns placed there for display. After ripping the crepe and mourning wreaths from the statue of Strasbourg, the rejoicing multitude covered it with garlands and the tricolor of France. A correspondent for *The Times* of London observed: "Silence has fled, perhaps to Berlin . . . but certainly far from the Paris boulevards. There is no fraction of any second that is not filled with the deep cheers of men, the shrill cheers of women, the blowing of trumpets, the singing of songs. . . . the spectacle is so extraordinary in relation to the occasion that one shrinks from the task of explaining the wild enthusiasm." The correspondent also noted, however: "Practically every woman is in deep black."[1]

France had repelled the invader and won a victory, but it had paid a terribly high price. Almost 1,400,000 men had been killed or were missing in action, and another 4,000,000 had been wounded, including some 800,000 severely wounded or permanently maimed. Much of northern and northeastern France was devastated. The fighting and deliberate German destruction had reduced many cities and villages to rubble and destroyed railways, roads, and bridges, as well as mines and water wells. Countless trenches and holes filled once-fertile fields, and stumps and splinters marked the sites of once-lush forests and orchards. Thousands of unexploded shells continued to threaten anyone traveling through the devastated countryside. The specter of severe financial difficulties also cast a long shadow. Political leaders had refused for most of the war to establish an effective income tax, and instead had financed the war through expedients, primarily by borrowing heavily and thereby putting off paying for the war until later. Long before the guns went silent, wholesale prices had quadrupled, and decades of currency stability were a thing of the past. Evidence of other significant effects appeared in the last phase of the war, when military leaders complained about the lack of discipline among new conscripts. Many of the young soldiers, the generals observed, had lost their homes and their traditional communities, had been raised in families without fathers, and seemed to lack the character and resolve of their predecessors. Much like these young recruits, France could never erase all the scars of the Great War.

Most of the losses had come from battles early in the war. By the end of the autumn offensive in 1915, after only fifteen months of conflict, France had already suffered more than 50 percent of the casualties it would experience for the entire war. In 1916 the country suffered another 20 percent of its total wartime casualties, this time primarily at Verdun and the Somme. The year 1917 yielded the lightest casualties, 10 percent of the total. Not until the Germans attacked in March 1918 did casualties rise again. In the desperate fighting from March through June 1918, the French threw everything they had into the struggle to halt the German offensive and suffered almost as many casualties as in 1917. After the counterattack on the Marne on July 18 and the resumption of the offensive, the final toll for 1918 eventually reached 20 percent of all French losses in the war.

Throughout the ordeal the French sometimes wavered, but they never quit. They had entered the war reluctantly but with grim determination to drive the Germans out of France and to recover Alsace-Lorraine. After repeated attacks failed to drive the enemy out of France, more primitive emotions of hatred and revenge, as well as a reluctance to cast aside the sacrifices already made, sustained their will to fight. Their determination was fueled by a dual conviction that France had been wronged and that Germany should be punished, and they hated the Germans for the disruption of their lives and the destruction wrought by the war. As months wore on into years, hope that the war would soon end sustained public support, but optimism waned in early 1917 amidst increased war-weariness and more numerous strikes. After wavering, public support steadied with the entry of the United States into the war. After so much effort, so much sacrifice, so many dead and wounded, French families continued to send their sons into the army. Of those conscripted, the share of young men refusing to serve declined from 2.59 percent in 1915, to 1.08 percent in 1916, to 0.88 percent in 1918.[2]

Buttressed by strong public support, every ministry from Viviani to Clemenceau remained committed to fighting the war to the finish. France entered the war because its political leaders decided to accept the risk and to support Russia in the burgeoning Balkan crisis, and it remained in the war because its political leaders refused to make peace on terms favorable to the Germans. With much of northern and northeastern France occupied by the enemy, the politicians had no bargaining chips for use in negotiations, and even those critical of the conduct of the war saw no viable alternative to continuing to fight. Only one ministry was overturned by a vote in the Chamber of Deputies—that of Painlevé in November 1917—and it fell not because of its support for the war but because of scandal and incompetence. At the lowest point of the deadly struggle, when the army was drained by casualties and weakened by mutinies, Clemenceau's rise to power and his famous words "War. Nothing but War" clearly demonstrated France's refusal to accept the disastrous effects of an unfavorable peace or of ignominious defeat.

Ordinary soldiers also refused to accept defeat. Early in the conflict the press often portrayed them as eager to fight and to die for their country. This heroic portrayal was eventually replaced by one in which they were concerned only with survival and indifferent to the outcome. More recent scholarship emphasizes a more nuanced portrait, one in which ordinary soldiers, though often weary and discouraged, remained faithful to the ideals of defending their country and doing their duty. Although many were cynical about excessively optimistic assessments and exaggerated reports of success, and sometimes angry because of a poorly organized operation or a leader's incompetence, they refused to abandon the defense of their country or to allow the sacrifices of their friends to be rendered meaningless. Toward the enemy they sometimes evinced pity for those who had experienced the same deprivation and hardships as themselves, but they hated the "Boches," who were—in the words of one soldier—"the bastards who have made me suffer so much for such a long time."[3] This anger reinforced their resolve and the resilience of the entire army. Though not eager to enter battle, the soldiers endured almost unimaginable demands in order to drive the Germans from their country.[4]

The grim quest for victory placed extraordinary requirements on France. In comparison to the other major powers, it mobilized a larger percentage of its population and suffered larger losses: while France mobilized 168 men out of every 1,000 citizens and lost 34, Germany mobilized 154 and lost 30, and Britain 125 and 16.[5] Huge demands were also placed on France's industrial base. In essence, France, which began the war with an antiquated industrial base, a backward financial system, and the loss of most of its key natural resources and factories, became the arsenal of the Entente. French soldiers began the war without much heavy artillery and without basic items such as wire cutters and trench mortars, but hastily built factories and other facilities managed almost miraculously to pour out desperately needed weapons and munitions, allowing the army to transform itself from the light, highly mobile force of August 1914 to the massively heavy one of November 1918. The sophistication and complexity of France's industrial production are illustrated by its wartime production of 52,000 aircraft, a significantly higher number than Germany's 48,000 and Britain's 43,000. At the end of the war France's air strength exceeded any other power's: 247 squadrons with 3,222 aircraft on the Western Front.[6] With production rates continuously increasing, French industry supplied weapons or munitions to all the allies at one time or another, but it provided the Americans the most—more than three-quarters of all the tanks, field artillery, and airplanes used by the Doughboys in France. Before the war no one had dreamed that France could achieve such levels of production.

Strengthened by the ordinary soldier's desire to defend his country and by the nation's outpouring of weapons and materiel, the army proved remarkably resilient. Especially noteworthy are its halting its withdrawal and going on the offensive at the decisive moment during the Marne campaign of August–September 1914. This was one of the most remarkable feats in twentieth-century warfare and amply merits the so-briquet "miracle." Similarly, its series of attacks on the Somme in late 1916 after the disastrous Artois and Champagne offensives of 1915 and the terrible losses at Verdun in 1916 demonstrated exceptional tenacity. Although these attacks proved costly, soldiers continued to endure in-credible demands until Nivelle's foolish offensive in April 1917 pushed them to mutiny. Another extraordinary performance occurred in March 1918, when Pétain threw many of them into the gap the Germans had opened along the Somme between British and French forces. By July 1918, however, the French were staggering with exhaustion, and only the support of the British and Americans kept them going.

With Germany prostrate and in chaos, the French celebrated their vic-tory; they had survived the war and had retained their independence. As they mourned their losses and erected monuments to honor the fallen, they had great hopes for the future and expected the peace treaty to dis-arm Germany, reduce the threat on their frontier, and provide reparations for damages and costs. Despite Clemenceau's best efforts, the Versailles treaty failed to alter the fundamental strategic imbalance between France and Germany. In essence France's political influence was too small to convince its allies to dismantle Germany, and its army too weak to en-force a draconian peace and destroy Germany's military power. However much the French people may have wanted revenge or security, they could not achieve them alone. Germany still had a larger population and greater industrial capacity than France, and misgivings about the future eventu-ally overshadowed the euphoria of November 1918.

With peace no longer certain, France's vision of a future war with Ger-many bore a strong resemblance to the recent conflict, for no nation can endure such an ordeal and then ignore it.[7] Gone were notions of battle as a glorious or uplifting experience. Movies, radio broadcasts, newspapers, and books frequently reminded the French of terrible battles and enor-mous losses, while battle-scarred veterans recounted grisly tales of their experiences. Reinforcing the horrific image, military journals and doctrinal publications often used terms such as "annihilating," "crushing," and "irresistible" to describe combat. Unlike Messimy in late July 1914, when he responded "bravo" to Joffre's affirmation of the army's readiness, no one expected a future war to be glorious, and no one was ready to rush to war and relive the horrific experiences of 1914–1918. Such attitudes were not necessarily defeatist or decadent and did not indicate rampant pacifism, but they ensured that caution ruled over all diplomatic and military actions and barred any possibility of an aggressive strategy in the opening days of a war. Joffre's disastrous attacks in August 1914 had demonstrated the disadvantages of an offensive strategy at the beginning of a war, and political and military leaders had no desire to incur futile losses again in a rash offensive. Especially after the unraveling in the late 1930s of the Little Entente, which was made up of countries carved out of the old Austro-Hungarian Empire, the French saw no reason to launch an impetuous attack into Germany. They preferred a more careful strategy, one that would provide time to mobilize the nation's resources and commit soldiers to prudent, thoroughly prepared operations.

The Great War had demonstrated the necessity for the entire nation to participate in a war against the Germans, and the French, though dreading the enormous destructiveness of another great war, believed they had no choice but to endure another long war should Germany attack. Numerous leaders and observers chastised the leaders of 1914 whose shortsighted efforts had cost thousands of soldiers their lives. With few voices of dissent, political and military leaders organized a military force, consisting primarily of reservists and conscripted soldiers, capable of waging a long, destructive war. They also established an elaborate system of mobilization to marshal the entire nation's resources and match or surpass the remarkable levels of industrial production achieved in the Great War. Remembering the losses of iron ore in the Briey basin and coal in the Lille region, they moved to protect the vulnerable natural resources concentrated along the northern and northeastern frontier. These efforts contributed to the building of fortifications on the northeastern frontier not only to protect valuable resources but also to provide the nation time to mobilize its entire resources for a long war. Political and military leaders thought it wise first to defend against the enemy's initial attacks and then to respond with the completely mobilized power of the entire nation.

The Great War had also demonstrated the importance of allies. At the end of the long, deadly war no one believed that France alone could defeat Germany. At the Paris peace conference France sought to ensure its future security by cementing its relationship with its allies. After the guarantees of the United States and Britain proved empty, France looked for other allies and found them in eastern Europe, but the Little Entente and other arrangements did not provide the strategic advantages that the prewar alliance with Russia or the wartime alliance with the Entente powers had conferred. As tension mounted in the late 1930s, France's leaders concluded that they had no choice but to repudiate all obligations to Czechoslovakia and follow the lead of London. In essence their desire for a powerful ally outweighed their desire for an independent policy.

Meanwhile military leaders searched for better operational methods. They knew that France had devoted considerable time and effort during the war to developing better methods, and they recalled disastrous operations early in the war in which hasty or inadequate preparation had resulted in horrendous casualties. They also remembered the failure of Nivelle's offensive and the success of Pétain's limited offensives, as well as the costly transition from the continuous to the methodical battle. Leaders in the Great War had adopted the methodical battle only after much debate and huge losses, and their successors refused to welcome new operational ideas that sounded suspiciously like the *offensive à outrance* or the continuous battle. Within the constraints of the methodical battle, rigid centralization and strict obedience—not decentralization, initiative, or flexibility—became the bywords of the officer corps. It proved easier to reject ideas from officers such as Charles de Gaulle than to replace the methodical battle with a new operational concept.

The presence of much equipment from the Great War also worked against the development of new operational methods. With some 5,412 75-mm cannon left over, for example, the trustworthy gun remained more numerous than any other artillery piece in the French army. Similarly, the French had 3,187 Renault FT-17 tanks left immediately after the war. The lightly armored two-man tank weighed 6.5 tons and had a maximum speed of 4.8 miles per hour under the most favorable conditions. Neither the 75-mm cannon nor the FT-17 tank could spark the imagination of young officers or create doubts about the combat-tested methods of the Great War. Not until the mid-1930s did new weapons begin appearing in sufficient numbers to foster new ideas about the potential of mechanized warfare.

Veterans of the war dominated the development of new ideas. The officers and soldiers of the army had greater respect for Pétain than for Foch, and Pétain, not Foch, had the largest influence upon the postwar army. His cautious methods dominated military thinking and planning. One only has to read the minutes of the Superior Council of War's meetings in the interwar years to weigh the different effects of the two men and to consider how different things could have been had Foch wielded the most influence. Another officer who played an especially important role was General Eugène Debeney, who commanded First Army in the relatively mobile battles at the end of the war. During the postwar period he served as the director of the École de Guerre and had students study every aspect of his army's mobile operations. Students at the École de Guerre often walked the ground where his army had attacked in the final months of the war, and "lessons" and insights from the study of those operations shaped multiple aspects of French doctrine. As a member of the commission that crafted the capstone doctrinal manual for the postwar army,[8] Debeney cemented the operational methods of the last months of the war into the army's thinking. As the chief of the General Staff from 1923 to 1930, he played a key role in drafting the basic laws of 1927 and 1928 that shaped the organization of the army of the 1930s and 1940s. Over the long term the methods of his army in the final months of the war provided the blueprint for the army of the future.

On the morrow of the armistice, the prestige of the Army reached its highest point. Military leaders basked in the glory of a victory that had required the best efforts from them and the entire nation. They were neither hypnotized nor blinded by their experiences in the war, and they were not bound for defeat in 1940 because they succeeded in 1918. Instead, they were confident of the methods and weapons that had given them success in the war, and they saw no reason to abandon or modify them without careful thought, thorough analysis, and challenging tests. None of them foresaw the disastrous defeat of 1940 that would inflict fewer casualties but greater damage to the ideals, institutions, and international stature of France than the Great War.

Abbreviations

AFGG	*Les armées françaises dans la grande guerre,* 11 tomes (Paris: Imprimerie nationale, 1922–1937)
AN	Archives nationales
AO	Armée d'Orient
BNF	Bibliothèque nationale de France
CA	Corps d'armée
CSDN	Conseil supérieur de la défense nationale
CSG	Conseil supérieur de la guerre
DDF	*Documents diplomatiques français*
ÉM	État-major
ÉMA	État-major de l'armée
GA	Groupe d'armées
GAC	Groupe d'armées du centre
GAE	Groupe d'armées de l'est
GAN	Groupe d'armées du nord
GAR	Groupe d'armées de réserve
GHQ	General Headquarters
GMP	Gouverneur militaire de Paris
GPE	Groupe provisoire de l'est
GPN	Groupe provisoire du nord
GQG	Grand quartier général
GQGA	Grand quartier général des armées alliées
JO	*Journal officiel de la République française*
JO, Ch. Déb.	*Journal officiel de la République française: Chambre débats*
MG	Ministère de la guerre
MMF	Mission militaire française
PRO	Public Records Office, London
PV	Procès-verbal
SHAT	Service historique de l'armée de terre, Château de Vincennes

Notes

In the notes I have adopted the convention used by other historians to identify sources in the French official history, *Les armées françaises dans la grande guerre*. For documents, *AFGG*, 612-748, p. 265, for example, designates tome 6, vol. 1, annexes, vol. 2, annex no. 748, p. 265. For the narrative in the official history, *AFGG*, 61, p. 203, for example, designates tome 6, vol. 1, p. 203. Similarly, *AFGG*, 3, p. 412, designates tome 3, p. 412.

INTRODUCTION

1. Jean-Baptiste Duroselle, *La Grande Guerre des Français: L'incompréhensible* (Paris: Perrin, 1994), p. 7.
2. The equivalent of 9,884,000 acres, or about the size of Massachusetts and Connecticut.
3. André Tardieu, "The Policy of France," *Foreign Affairs* 1 (September 15, 1922), 12–13.

1. THE TRANSFORMATION OF THE FRENCH ARMY

1. *JO* (1874), 5718.
2. *JO* (1873), 4551.
3. *JO* (1874), 5719.
4. *JO* (1872), 5165; *JO* (1888), 1964.
5. CSDN, Historique et organisation de la défense nationale de 1906 à 1939–1940, n.d., SHAT 2N1; CSDN, Décret sur l'organisation du CSDN, 28 juillet 1911, SHAT 2N1.
6. *JO., Ch. Déb.* (1888), 791, 817, 2177–78; Charles de Freycinet, *Souvenirs, 1878–1893*, 2 vols. (Paris: Delagrave, 1913), 1:405; *JO* (1890), 1869–70.
7. David B. Ralston, *The Army of the Republic: The Place of the Military in the Political Evolution of France, 1871–1914* (Cambridge, Mass.: MIT Press, 1967), pp. 190–193, 327–329, 331, 335–337; Douglas Porch, *The March to the Marne: The French Army, 1871–1914* (Cambridge: Cambridge University Press, 1981), pp. 170–176.
8. *JO, Ch. Déb.* (30 juin 1911), 2540–41.
9. Séance du vendredi 30 mai 1919, in Assemblée nationale, Chambre des députés, Onzième législature, Session de 1919, vol. 71, no. 6206 (annexe), in *Procès-verbaux de*

la commission d'enquête sur le rôle et la situation de la métallurgie en France (*Défense du bassin de Briey*, 1re partie) (Paris: Imprimerie de la Chambre des députés, 1919), p. 130.

10. Messimy à Hatto, 21/4/1899, BNF Fonds Hatto.

11. Adolphe Messimy, *Mes souvenirs* (Paris: Plon, 1937), pp. 72, 75; Séance du vendredi 30 mai 1919, in *Procès-verbaux de la commission d'enquête* (*Défense du bassin de Briey*, 1re partie), p. 132.

12. A. Marchand, *Plans de concentration de 1871 à 1914* (Paris: Berger-Levrault, 1926), pp. 4–9, 200–201.

13. *AFGG*, 11, pp. 6–7.

14. Maurice Paléologue, *Three Critical Years (1904-05-06)* (New York: Robert Speller and Sons, 1957), pp. 47–48, 173.

15. Note lue par le général de Lacroix, 15 février 1908, *AFGG*, 11-2, pp. 6–7.

16. CSG, Concentration et plan d'opérations, février 1911, *AFGG*, 11-3, pp. 7–11.

17. Note, 19 juillet 1911, *AFGG*, 11-4, pp. 12–16.

18. PV, CSG, Séance du mercredi, 19 juillet 1911, SHAT 1N10.

19. Séance du 13 mai 1919, in *Procès-verbaux de la commission d'enquête* (*Défense du bassin de Briey*, 1re partie), p. 103.

20. Joseph Caillaux, *Mes mémoires*, 3 vols. (Paris: Plon, 1943), 2:126–127.

21. Joseph Gallieni, *Mémoires du maréchal Gallieni: Défense du Paris (25 août–11 septembre 1914)* (Paris: Payot, 1928), pp. 19–21.

22. Maurice Paléologue, *Journal 1913–1914* (Paris: Plon, 1947), p. 212.

23. Ibid., p. 166.

24. David Lloyd George, *War Memoirs*, 2 vols. (London: Odhams, 1938), 1:319.

25. Jean de Pierrefeu, *G.Q.G. Secteur 1: Trois ans au grand quartier général*, 2 vols. (Paris: G. Crès, 1922), 1:96.

26. *JO* (29 juillet 1911), 6444–45; Messimy, *Mes souvenirs*, p. 82.

27. MG, ÉMA, Note indiquant les points relatifs à la situation extérieure à élucider dans la conférence du 16 octobre 1911, n.d.; ÉMA, 3e Bureau, Note pour le ministre de la guerre, 3 juillet 1911; both in SHAT 2N1.

28. CSDN, Section d'études, Note de présentation, Séance du 9 janvier 1912, p. 3, SHAT 2N1.

29. Joseph Joffre, *Mémoires du maréchal Joffre (1910–1917)*, 2 vols. (Paris: Plon, 1932), 1:22–24.

30. MG, Modifications à apporter au plan XVI, 6 septembre 1911, *AFGG*, 11-5, pp. 17–18.

31. CSDN, Séance du 11 octobre 1911, p. 5, SHAT 2N1.

32. CSDN, Séance du 9 janvier 1912, pp. 4–5, AN 509AP/5. See Guy Pédroncini, "Stratégie et relations internationales: La séance du 9 janvier 1912 au conseil supérieur de la défense nationale," *Revue d'histoire diplomatique* 91 (1977), 143–158.

33. Caillaux, *Mes mémoires*, 2:213–214.

34. CSDN, Séance du 9 janvier 1912, AN 509AP/5.

35. Joffre, *Mémoires*, 1:28; Caillaux, *Mes mémoires*, 2:209, 211–212.

36. Joffre, *Mémoires*, 1:120–121; Raymond Poincaré, *Au service de la France*, vol. 1: *Le lendemain d'Agadir* (Paris: Plon, 1926), p. 224; Conférence tenue au ministère des affaires étrangères, 21 février 1912, pp. 5–6, SHAT 2N1.

37. Joffre, *Mémoires*, 1:122-124.

38. A copy of the Military Convention of August 17, 1892, is included in Messimy, *Mes souvenirs,* pp. 407-408; Joffre, *Mémoires*, 1:128-129; Poincaré, *Au service de la France,* 1:291-292.

39. PV de l'entretien entre les chefs d'ÉM généraux des armées française et russe, 7/20 et 8/21 septembre 1910, *DDF,* 2ᵉ sér., vol. 12, no. 573, pp. 911-913.

40. Le lieutenant-colonel Pellé au général Brun, 24 mars 1910, ibid., no. 467, p. 717.

41. PV des entretiens du mois d'août 1913, 24 août 1913, *DDF,* 3ᵉ sér., vol. 8, no. 79, p. 88; M. Delcassé à M. Pichon, 21 août 1913, ibid., no. 62, p. 69.

42. PV de l'entretien du 13 juillet 1912, *DDF,* 3ᵉ sér., vol. 3, no. 200, p. 260.

43. PV des entretiens du mois d'août 1913, 24 août 1913, ibid., no. 79, pp.88, 90.

44. Ambassade de France, Attaché militaire, Le lieutenant-colonel Matton au ministre de la guerre, 21 février/6 mars 1909, SHAT 7N1535.

45. ÉMA, Communications entre la Russie & la France (traduction de la note russe), mars 1911; Communications franco-russe, juillet 1913; both in SHAT 7N1538.

46. Charles Ardant du Picq, *Études sur le combat* (Paris: R. Chapelot, 1903), p. 119.

47. Ferdinand Foch, *The Principles of War,* trans. Hilaire Belloc (New York: Henry Holt, 1920), p. 32.

48. Henri Bonnal, *La prochaine guerre* (Paris: R. Chapelot, 1906), pp. 47-48; idem, *Sadowa: Étude de stratégie et de tactique générale* (Paris: R. Chapelot, 1901), pp. 2, 181.

49. Joffre, *Mémoires*, 1:29.

50. Louis Loyseau de Grandmaison, *Deux conférences, faites aux officiers de l'état-major de l'armée (février 1911)* (Paris: Berger-Levrault, 1912), pp.22, 28.

51. France, MG, *Décret du 28 octobre 1913 portant règlement sur la conduite des grandes unités* (Paris: Berger-Levrault, 1913), pp. 48, 7.

52. France, MG, *Décret du 2 décembre 1913 portant règlement sur le service des armées en campagne* (Paris: Charles-Lavauzelle, 1913), pp. 13, 76-77.

53. France, MG, *Décret du 28 mai 1895 portant règlement sur le service des armées en campagne* (Paris: Charles-Lavauzelle, 1912), p. 178.

54. *Règlement sur le service des armées en campagne (2 décembre 1913),* p. 15.

55. Ibid., p. 78.

56. France, MG, *Règlement de manoeuvre d'infanterie du 20 avril 1914* (Paris: Chapelot, 1914), pp. 69, 139-140.

57. Joffre, *Mémoires*, 1:33.

58. Ibid., p. 40.

59. France, Ministère de la Défense, ÉMA de Terre, Service historique, *Inventaire sommaire des archives de la guerre, Série N 1872-1919,* 7 vols. (Troyes: Imprimerie la renaissance, 1968-1975), 1:153.

60. Robert M. Ripperger, "The Development of the French Artillery for the Offensive, 1890-1914," *Journal of Military History* 59 (October 1995), 605-606.

61. Frédéric Herr, *L'artillerie: Ce qu'elle a été, ce qu'elle est, ce qu'elle doit être* (Paris: Berger-Levrault, 1924), p. 4.

62. PV, CSG, Séance du mercredi, 9 juin 1909, pp. 90-93, SHAT 1N10; F. Culmann, *Tactique d'artillerie: Matériels d'aujourd'hui et de demain* (Paris: Charles-Lavauzelle, 1937), p. 21.

63. PV, CSG, Séance du mercredi, 19 juillet 1911, pp. 203, 198, SHAT 1N10; Joffre, *Mémoires,* 1:9–10.

64. Messimy, *Mes souvenirs,* p. 85; Caillaux, *Mes mémoires,* 2:208–209; Culmann, *Tactique d'artillerie,* p. 23.

65. CSDN, Séance du 9 janvier 1912, p. 6, AN 509AP/5; PV de la Séance du CSDN, 9 janvier 1912, p. 2, SHAT 2N1.

66. Quoted in Culmann, *Tactique d'artillerie,* pp. 27–28.

67. Joffre, *Mémoires,* 1:72–73.

68. CSG, PV de la séance du mercredi, 15 octobre 1913, SHAT 1N10.

69. Messimy, *Mes souvenirs,* p. 88.

70. Joffre, *Mémoires,* 1:123–124n.

71. Ibid., pp. 142–143.

72. *Règlement sur la conduite des grandes unités (28 octobre 1913),* p. 6.

73. Charles Mangin, *La force noire* (Paris: Hachette, 1911), p. 313; Adolphe Messimy, "Enquête sur le recrutement noir: Opinion de M. Messimy," *Questions diplomatiques et coloniales, revue de politique extérieure* 15 (16 février 1911), 207–210.

74. Comparison des forces qui pourraient se trouver en presence sur le théatre du nord-est, 19 octobre 1912, SHAT 2N1; CSDN, PV de la séance du CSDN, 17 mai 1913, pp. 13–16, SHAT 2N1.

75. Henri Sellier, A. Bruggeman, and Marcel Poete, *Paris pendant la guerre* (Paris: Presses universitaires de France, n.d.), p. 20; Freycinet, *Souvenirs,* 1:408.

76. Frédéric Reboul, *Mobilisation industrielle: Les fabrications de guerre en France de 1914 à 1918* (Paris: Berger-Levrault, 1925), p. 1.

77. France, Assemblée nationale, Chambre des députés, Onzième legislature, Session de 1919, vol. 71, no. 6206 (annexe), *Rapport fait au nom de la commission d'enquête (Question de Briey,* 1re partie: *Concentration de la métallurgue française sur la frontière de l'est)*(Paris: Imprimerie de la Chambre des députés, 1919), pp. 4–5.

78. Joffre, *Mémoires,* 1:93.

79. ÉMA, 3e Bureau, Plan XVII, Bases du plan, 2 mai 1913, pp. 6–7, SHAT 1N11.

80. Adolphe Messimy, "Les fêtes de Hoche à Versailles," 28 juin 1914, p. 7, typescript, AN 509AP/4.

81. Émile Fayolle, *Cahiers secrets de la grande guerre* (Paris: Plon, 1964), p. 15.

82. Joffre, *Mémoires,* 1:135–140.

83. CSG, PV de la séance du 18 Avril 1913, SHAT 1N11; Joffre, *Mémoires,* 1:169–180.

84. ÉMA, Plan XVII, Directives pour la concentration, 7 février 1914, *AFGG,* 11-8, pp. 21–22.

85. Paléologue, *Journal 1913–1914,* pp. 218–220.

86. Report by Mr. Balfour of the Conclusion arrived at on February 11, 1908, p. 3, PRO CAB 42/2/7.

87. Projet de PV, Séance du CSDN du 31 décembre 1906, p. 10, SHAT 2N1.

88. Letter from Major General N. G. Lyttelton, 26 July 1907, SHAT 7N1782.

89. CSDN, Conférence tenue au ministère des affaires étrangères, 21 février 1912, p. 2, SHAT 2N1.

90. Paléologue, *Journal 1913–1914,* p. 128.

91. Le lieutenant-colonel Huguet, Attaché militaire, Note sur la composition de l'armée anglaise, 22 janvier 1906, SHAT 7N1782.

92. Mémorandum de la conférence du 20 juillet 1911, p. 2, SHAT 7N1782.

93. 2ᵉ Bureau, Comparaison des forces qui pourraient se trouver en presence sur le théatre du nord-est, 19 octobre 1912, SHAT 2N1.

94. MG, ÉMA, 4ᵉ Bureau, Note pour l'ÉMA (3ᵉ Bureau), 4 mars 1913, SHAT 7N1782.

95. *Séance du 4 juillet 1919, Procès-verbaux de la commission d'enquête (Défense du bassin de Briey, 2ᵉ partie), p. 159.*

96. W, Prévisions de l'ÉMA (4ᵉ Bureau) relative à la durée de la concentration W, *AFGG,* 11-7, p. 20; MG, ÉMA, Instruction no. 1W, Transports de concentration de l'armée W, 31 mai 1912, SHAT 7N1783.

97. Secretary's Notes of a War Council, August 5, 1914, p. 1, PRO CAB 42/1/2.

98. See MG, Note explicative concernant les rectifications et additions apportées à l'état des approvisionnements en munitions d'Infanterie dans le Plan XVII, 4 avril 1914, SHAT 7N1778; Projet d'organisation de l'artillerie lourde dans le plan XVII, n.d., SHAT 1N11.

99. Gallieni, *Mémoires,* pp. 9–11.

100. MG, Le général Lanrezac à monsieur le général Joffre, *AFGG,* 11-19, p. 60; Charles Lanrezac, *Le plan de campagne français et le premier mois de la guerre (2 août-3 septembre 1914)* (Paris: Payot, 1921), pp. 55–56.

101. Joffre, *Mémoires,* 1:228.

102. See Kriegspiel du XVIIIᵉ corps d'armée, 17 janvier 1913, SHAT 7N436 (supplement). In addition to information about seven different war games in 1912 and 1913, this carton has information about war games in 1896, 1899, 1901, 1902, 1904, and 1911. Other assessments are in SHAT 7N1538.

103. Étude relative au théatre d'opérations russo-allemandes, mai 1914, SHAT 7N1538.

104. Commentaires du document S.R. no. 1685 du 20 Avril 1911 (Aide mémoire de l'officier d'ÉM en Allemagne), n.d., SHAT 7N436 (supplement), pp. 3, 16.

105. Joffre, *Mémoires,* 1:249.

106. Quoted in *AFGG,* 11, p. 39.

107. Joffre, *Mémoires,* 1:249.

108. Ibid., pp. 143–144.

109. Séance du 4 juillet 1919, *Procès-verbaux de la commission d'enquête (Défense du bassin de Briey,* 2ᵉ partie), p. 142; Joseph Joffre, *1914-1915: La préparation de la guerre et la conduite des opérations* (Paris: Chiron, 1920), pp. 24–25.

110. Joffre, *Mémoires,* 1:145, 190, 241.

111. Lanrezac, *Le plan de campagne français,* pp. 60–61. Dubail does not mention the incident in his memoirs; Augustin Dubail, *Quatre années de commandement, 1914-1918,* 3 vols. (Paris: L. Fournier, 1920), 1:12–13.

112. Messimy, *Mes souvenirs,* p. 78.

113. Ralston, *Army of the Republic,* p. 337.

114. Porch, *March to the Marne,* p. 237.

115. *Règlement sur la conduite des grandes unités (28 octobre 1913),* p. 4.

116. Messimy, *Mes souvenirs,* p. 232.

117. Sir A. Nicolson to Sir Edward Grey, February 24, 1913, in *British Documents on the Origins of the War 1898–1914,* ed. G. P. Gooch and Harold Temperley, vol. 9, part 2 (London: His Majesty's Stationery Office, 1934), no. 656, pp. 532–533.

2. THE WAR OF MOVEMENT, 1914

1. Jean-Jacques Becker, *1914: Comment les français sont entrés dans la guerre* (Paris: Fondation nationale des sciences politiques, 1977), p. 140; quoted in J. F. V. Keiger, *Raymond Poincaré* (Cambridge: Cambridge University Press, 1997), p. 165.

2. Raymond Poincaré, *Au service de la France,* vol. 4: *L'union sacrée* (Paris: Plon, 1927), pp. 278, 253–256.

3. Viviani à Bienvenu-Martin, St. Pétersbourg, 24 juillet 1914, *DDF,* 3ᵉ sér., vol. 11, no. 1, p. 1; Télégramme secrets du ministre des affaires étrangères à l'ambassadeur à Vienne, no. 1475, 9/22 [*sic*] juillet 1914, in René Marchand, *Un livre noir,* 2 vols. (Paris: Librairie du travail, 1922) 2:275.

4. Luigi Albertini, *The Origins of the War of 1914,* trans. Isabella M. Massey, 3 vols. (Oxford: Oxford University Press, 1952), 2:291.

5. Diary of Madame de Laguiche, vol. 2, 12 juillet/25 juillet 1914, p. 28, Laguiche family archives.

6. Lettre, Messimy à Hatto, 16/4/1915, BNF Fonds Hatto.

7. Abel Ferry, *Les carnets secrets (1914–1918) d'Abel Ferry* (Paris: Bernard Grasset, 1957), p. 21.

8. Joseph Joffre, *Mémoires du maréchal Joffre (1910–1917),* 2 vols. (Paris: Librairie Plon, 1932), 1:207–208.

9. Handwritten note on MG, ÉMA, Section d'Afrique, Note pour monsieur le ministre, 23 juillet 1914, AN 509AP/5.

10. William T. Dean III, "Mobilization of a French Colony: The Case of Morocco, August–September 1914," pp. 4–5, unpublished paper, author's possession; Albertini, *Origins of the War,* 2:597–598; Adolphe Messimy, *Mes souvenirs* (Paris: Plon, 1937), pp. 164–170; [Ministre de] Guerre à commissaire résident général Rabat, 27 juillet 1914, AN 509AP/5.

11. 162ᵉ Division, Le général commandant, Messimy à Ferry, 23 mars 1918, SHAT 3H92. Messimy insisted that the "opportune" arrival of these troops for the battle of the Marne "saved France." For an altered version of this letter with dates suggesting that the actions occurred two days later, see AN 509AP/5.

12. Raymond Recouly, *Les heures tragiques d'avant guerre* (Paris: La renaissance du livre, 1922), pp. 69–70.

13. Diary of Madame de Laguiche, vol. 2, 15/28 juillet 1914, p. 41.

14. Joffre, *Mémoires,* 1:213.

15. Note de l'ambassade de Russie, 30 juillet 1914, *DDF,* 3ᵉ sér., vol. 11, no. 301, pp. 257–258; Poincaré, *Au service de la France,* 4:383–385.

16. Viviani à Saint-Pétersbourg, Londres, 30 juillet 1914, *DDF,* 3ᵉ sér., vol. 11, no. 305, pp. 261–262.

17. Note by Abel Ferry, 30 juillet 1914, Ministère des affaires étrangères, Archives privés de Abel Ferry; quoted in Keiger, *Raymond Poincaré*, p. 175. and in Note, *DDF*, 3ᵉ sér., vol. 11, p. 262n.

18. Télégrammes secrets de l'ambassadeur à Paris, no. 210, 17/30 juillet 1914, in Marchand, *Un livre noir*, 2:290. See also *DDF*, 3ᵉ sér., vol. 11, p. 262n.

19. Albertini, *Origins of the War*, 2:608–612; Sidney B. Fay, *The Origins of the World War*, 2 vols. (New York: Macmillan, 1928), 2:486.

20. Télégramme secret de l'ambassadeur à Paris, 18/31 juillet 1914, in Marchand, *Livre noir*, 2:294; Messimy, *Mes souvenirs*, pp. 181–187.

21. Poincaré, Notes journalières, 1 août 1914, p. 138, BNF NAF 16027.

22. Georges Bonnefous, *La grande guerre (1914–1918)* (Paris: Presses universitaires de France, 1967), p. 25.

23. *JO, Ch. Déb.* (4 août 1914), 3110.

24. Quoted in Bonnefous, *La grande guerre*, p. 25.

25. Philippe Boulanger, *La France devant la conscription* (Paris: Economica, 2001), pp. 171–175.

26. Becker, *1914*, p. 489.

27. Pierre Renouvin, "Les buts de guerre du gouvernement français, 1914–1918," *Revue historique* 235 (janvier–mars 1966), 2–3; David Stevenson, *French War Aims against Germany, 1914–1919* (Oxford: Clarendon Press, 1982), pp. 9–13; Poincaré, Notes journalières, 5 août 1914, p. 147, BNF NAF 16027.

28. Handwritten memo, n.d., no. 5, SHAT 5N131.

29. Note sur la situation actuelle, 14 juillet 1915, Fonds Buat, Bibliothèque de l'Institut de France, 1/MS 5390.

30. MG, Communication téléphonique du ministre de la guerre au général Belin, 2 août 1914, *AFGG*, 11-27, p. 67.

31. MG, Instruction générale secrète pour la couverture, 2 août 1914, *AFGG*, 11-31, pp. 69–70.

32. Joffre, *Mémoires*, 1:236.

33. Ambassadeur de France en Russie, Offensive de l'armée russe, 5 août 1914, *AFGG*, 11-52, p. 85.

34. GQG, Instruction générale no. 1, 8 août 1914, *AFGG*, 11-103, pp. 124–126; GQG, Ordre particulier pour le 4ᵉ groupe de divisions de reserve, 8 août 1914, *AFGG*, 11-105, p. 127.

35. GQG, Groupement connu des forces allemandes actives, 9 août 1914, *AFGG*, 11-125, pp. 142–143.

36. GQG, Instruction particulière no. 5, 13 août 1914, *AFGG*, 11-231, pp. 239–240; Iʳᵉ armée, Instruction générale d'opérations no. 1, 13 août 1914, *AFGG*, 11-235, pp. 243–244.

37. MG, Le Ministre, 10 août 1914, SHAT 1K268; Joffre, *Mémoires*, 1:258n; Messimy, *Mes souvenirs*, p. 350. For information about the reliefs, see the four dossiers in SHAT 16N491.

38. Joffre, *Mémoires*, 1:421; Pierre Rocolle, *L'hécatombe des généraux* (Paris: Lavauzelle, 1980), p. 262.

39. GQG, Message téléphoné, Commandant en chef à commandant Iʳᵉ armée, 15 août 1914, *AFGG*, 11-301, p. 304.

40. Copie du compte rendu par la 26ème division, 14 aôut 1914, *AFGG*, 11-332, pp. 330–331.

41. IIᵉ armée, Compte rendu de la situation de la IIᵉ armée le 15 août, 15 août 1914, *AFGG*, 11-318, p. 316.

42. IIᵉ armée, Note du général commandant l'armée, 15 août 1914, *AFGG*, 11-319, p. 317.

43. GQG, Communication secrète aux commandants d'armée, 16 août 1914, *AFGG*, 11-352, pp. 343–344.

44. GQG, Instruction particulière no. 18, 21 août 1914, *AFGG*, 11-816, p. 693.

45. GQG, Instruction particulière no. 13, 18 août 1914, *AFGG*, 11-450, p. 424.

46. GQG, Commandant en chef à commandant armée Stenay, 20 août 1914, *AFGG*, 11-589, p. 530.

47. IVᵉ armée, Instruction personnelle et sécrete, 20 août 1914, *AFGG*, 11-640, pp. 559–560.

48. GQG, Général commandant en chef à ministre de la guerre, 21 août 1914, *AFGG*, 121-103, p. 93.

49. 10ᵉ Division, Ordre, 22 août 1914, *AFGG*, 11-1001, p. 807.

50. Alphonse Grasset, *Surprise d'une division: Rossignol-Saint Vincent* (Paris: Berger-Levrault, 1932), pp. 52–60, 69–70, 73–87, 108–126, 249–250; Alphonse Grasset, *Un combat de rencontre: Neufchâteau (22 août 1914)* (Paris: Berger-Levrault, 1924), p. 12.

51. IVᵉ armée, Compte rendu au GQG, 23 août 1914, *AFGG*, 11-1098, p. 871.

52. GQG, Bulletin de renseignements du 14 août, 14 août 1914, *AFGG*, 11-266, pp. 276–277.

53. Joffre, *Mémoires*, 1:268.

54. GQG, Bulletin de renseignments du 18 août, 18 août 1914, *AFGG*, 11-447, p. 422.

55. GQG, Instruction particulière no. 10, 15 août 1914, *AFGG*, 11-307, pp. 307–308.

56. GQG, Instruction particulière no. 13, 18 août 1914, *AFGG*, 11-450, pp. 424–425.

57. Vᵉ armée, Opérations du C. C. Sordet, 20 août 1914, *AFGG*, 11-648, pp. 566–567.

58. GQG, Général commandant en chef à ministre guerre, 20 août 1914, *AFGG*, 11-585, p. 528.

59. GQG, Général commandant en chef à ministre guerre, 23 août 1914, *AFGG*, 121-130, p. 112; GQG, Situation générale, 23 août 1914, *AFGG*, 11-1044, p. 842; GQG, Le général commandant en chef à ministre à guerre, 24 août 1914, *AFGG*, 121-149, p. 124.

60. Traduction d'un télégramme, Guerre à général Joffre (personnelle), 24 août 1914, SHAT 1K268.

61. IIIᵉ armée, Préparation et appui des attaques par l'artillerie, 23 août 1914, *AFGG*, 11-1088, p. 865.

62. Poincaré, Notes journalières, 24 août 1914, p. 236, BNF NAF 16027.

63. GQG, Le général commandant en chef à ministre à guerre, 24 août 1914, *AFGG*, 121-149, p. 125.

64. Traduction d'un télégramme chiffré parvenu au GQG, Section du chiffre le 8/11 1914 à 14 heures, SHAT 1K268; Ambassade imperiale de Russie à commandant en chef général Joffre, 21 août 1914, SHAT 1K268; GQG, Colonel Ignatieff, 24 août 1914, SHAT 16N491.

65. GQG, Instruction générale no. 2, 25 août 1914, *AFGG,* 121-395, pp. 278–280.

66. GQG, Note pour toutes les armées, 24 août 1914, *AFGG,* 121-158, pp. 128–129.

67. Field-Marshal Viscount French of Ypres, *1914* (London: Constable, 1919), p. 82; Joffre, *Mémoires,* 1:318–319; Charles Lanrezac, *Le plan de campagne français et le premier mois de la guerre (2 août–3 septembre 1914)* (Paris: Payot, 1921), pp. 208–211.

68. Colonel Huguet à GQG, 26 août 1914, *AFGG,* 121-634, p. 429.

69. V^e armée, Instruction personnelle et secrète, 26 août 1914, *AFGG,* 121-699, p. 466.

70. Colonel Huguet à GQG, 27 août 1914, *AFGG,* 121-829, pp. 551–552.

71. Colonel Huguet à M. le général commandant en chef, 27 août 1914, SHAT 1K268; Joffre, *Mémoires,* 1:328.

72. GQG, Général en chef à général commandant V^e armée, 28 août 1914, *AFGG,* 121-987, p. 663; Joffre, *Mémoires,* 1:332.

73. GQG, Commandant en chef à commandant armée, Laon, 29 août 1914, *AFGG,* 121-1176, p. 788.

74. Colonel Huguet à GQG, 28 août 1914, *AFGG,* 121-1000, pp. 671–672.

75. GQG anglais, 1er CA anglais aura repos le 29, 28 août 1914, *AFGG,* 121-1003, p. 672.

76. Gabriel Rouquerol, *La bataille de Guise* (Paris: Berger-Levrault, 1931), p. 40.

77. GQG, Intentions et propositions du commandement français, 30 août 1914, *AFGG,* 122-1401, p. 9.

78. GQG, Instruction générale no. 4, 1 septembre 1914, *AFGG,* 122-1792, pp. 286–287; Joffre, *Mémoires,* 1:359–360, 364.

79. GQG, VIe armée à Creil, 1 septembre 1914, *AFGG,* 122-1783, p. 281.

80. Quoted in Bonnefous, *La grande guerre,* p. 46.

81. GMP, Le général Gallieni au général Joffre, 2 septembre 1915, *AFGG,* 122-2016, p. 433; Joseph Gallieni, *Mémoires du général Gallieni: Défense de Paris, 25 août—11 septembre 1914* (Paris: Payot, 1926), pp. 60–62.

82. GQG, ÉM, 3e Bureau, Commandant Bel, 29 août 1914, SHAT 1K268; Joffre, *Mémoires,* 1:350.

83. Joffre, *Mémoires,* 1:370; Lanrezac, *Le plan de campagne français,* pp. 276–277. For additional insights, see Le général de division Lanrezac, en disponibilité, à M. le général Joffre, 29 janvier 1916, SHAT 1K268; Jules Isaac, *Joffre et Lanrezac* (Paris: Chiron, 1922), pp. 121–126.

84. Joffre, *Mémoires,* 1:370.

85. GQG, Note pour les commandants d'armées, 2 septembre 1914, *AFGG,* 122-1993, pp. 419–420; Joffre, *Mémoires,* 1:367.

86. GQG, Note personnelle pour le ministre de la guerre, 3 septembre 1914, SHAT 5N271.

87. GQG, Le général commandant en chef à M. le gouverneur militaire de Paris, 4 septembre 1915, *AFGG,* 122-2317, p. 652.

88. GQG, Général commandant en chef à commandant armée, Sézanne, 4 septembre 1914, *AFGG,* 122-2327, p. 657.

89. V^e armée, Possibilité de l'offensive, 4 septembre 1914, *AFGG,* 122-2399, p. 705.

90. Joffre, *Mémoires,* 1:388.

91. Ibid., pp. 389–390.

92. GQG, Order général no. 6, 4 septembre 1914, *AFGG,* 122-2332, pp. 660–661.

93. GQG, Note personnelle pour le ministre de la guerre, 5 septembre 1914, *AFGG,* 122-2468, pp. 768–769.

94. Colonel Huguet, Intentions du maréchal French, 5 septembre 1914, *AFGG,* 122-2480, p. 774; Colonel Huguet à ÉM Bar-sur-Aube, 5 septembre 1914, *AFGG,* 122-2482, p. 776.

95. Joffre, *Mémoires,* 1:393–394; Edward Spears, *Liaison 1914: A Narrative of the Great Retreat* (New York: Stein and Day, 1968), p. 418.

96. GQG, Proclamation aux troupes, 6 septembre 1914, *AFGG,* 122-2641, p. 889.

97. GQG, Note personnelle pour le ministre de la guerre, 5 septembre 1914, SHAT 5N131.

98. Quoted in James E. Edmonds, ed., *History of the Great War, Military Operations, France and Belgium, 1914: Mons, the Retreat to the Seine, the Marne and the Aisne, August–October 1914,* 2d ed. (London: Macmillan, 1937), p. 315.

99. GQG, Général commandant en chef à ministre guerre, 9 septembre 1914, *AFGG,* 132-2004, p. 444.

100. GQG, Instruction particulière no. 20, 9 septembre 1914, *AFGG,* 132-2008, p. 446.

101. GQG, Général commandant en chef [à] ministre guerre, 10 septembre 1914, *AFGG,* 133-2648, pp. 17–18; Joffre, *Mémoires,* 1:420.

102. GQG, Instruction particulière no. 21, 10 septembre 1914, *AFGG,* 133-2649, p. 18.

103. Joffre, *Mémoires,* 1:425.

104. GQG, Instruction particulière no. 25, 14 septembre 1914, *AFGG,* 134-4740, pp. 423–424.

105. GQG, Transports stratégiques effectués du 1er septembre au 19 septembre 1914, n.d., *AFGG,* 134-5297, p. 846.

106. GQG, Désignation du général Foch, 4 octobre 1914, *AFGG,* 142-2008, p. 674.

107. GPN, Général Foch à ÉM Romilly-sur-Seine, 9 octobre 1914, *AFGG,* 143-2487, p. 282.

108. Mission Pau près de l'armée belge, 12 octobre 1914, *AFGG,* 143-2694, p. 445.

3. SIEGE WARFARE, 1914–1915

1. Raymond Poincaré, Notes journalières, 29 septembre 1914, p. 67, BNF NAF 16028; idem, *Au service de la France,* vol. 5: *L'invasion 1914* (Paris: Plon, 1928), p. 337.

2. Joseph Joffre, *Mémoires du maréchal Joffre (1910–1917),* 2 vols. (Paris: Plon, 1932), 2:5.

3. Note sur une paix séparée de l'autriche, 8 janvier 1915, SHAT 1K268; Poincaré, *Au service de la France,* 5:5–6.

4. Joffre, *Mémoires,* 2:484–485; Raymond Poincaré, *Au service de la France,* vol. 6: *Les tranchées 1915* (Paris: Plon, 1938), p. 8; Georges Suarez, ed., *Briand, sa vie—son oeuvre, avec son journal et de nombreux documents inédits,* 4 vols. (Paris: Plon, 1938–1940), 3:91.

5. MG à M. général en chef, 15 janvier 1915, SHAT 1K268.

6. MG à M. le général commandant en chef, 14 janvier 1915; GQG, Le général commandant en chef à M. le ministre de la guerre, 15 janvier 1915; both in SHAT 1K268.

7. Commandant des divisions du 1er août 1914 au 1er novembre 1916, 25 novembre 1919, SHAT 5N269.

8. Commandant des corps d'armée du 1er août 1914 au 1er novembre 1916, 25 novembre 1916, SHAT 5N269.

9. See messages in SHAT 16N491.

10. Gaetan Gallieni, ed., *Les carnets de Gallieni* (Paris: Albin Michel, 1932), p. 117.

11. PV, 24 juin 1915, p. 2, SHAT 6N7.

12. GQG, Instruction particulière no. 29, 17 septembre 1914, *AFGG*, 141-244, pp. 234–235.

13. GQG, Note pour les armées, 17 octobre 1914, *AFGG*, 143-2958, p. 659.

14. Secretary's Notes of a Meeting of a War Council, January 13, 1915, p. 7, PRO CAB 42/1/16.

15. Télégramme, Petrograd, 3 décembre 1914, SHAT 7N1545.

16. Télégramme, Général commandant en chef à général Laguiche, 6 décembre 1914, SHAT 7N1545.

17. Télégramme, Petrograd, 19 décembre 1914, Paléologue, SHAT 7N1545.

18. *AFGG*, 2, p. 111.

19. Arthur Fontaine, *French Industry during the War* (New Haven: Yale University Press, 1926), pp. 22–54.

20. GQG, Le général commandant en chef à M. le ministre de la guerre, 20 septembre 1914, *AFGG*, 21-19, p. 13.

21. MG au général Joffre, 21 septembre 1914, *AFGG*, 21-20, pp. 13–14.

22. GQG, Le général commandant en chef à M. le général commandant l'armée . . ., 22 septembre 1914, *AFGG*, 21-26, p. 18.

23. GQG, Général commandant en chef à guerre (cabinet), 13 octobre 1914, *AFGG*, 21-65, p. 45.

24. MG à M. le général commandant en chef, 10 mars 1915, *AFGG*, 22-1136, p. 543.

25. GQG, Général commandant en chef à guerre (cabinet), 5 janvier 1915, *AFGG*, 21-551, p. 792.

26. Journal d'armements, SHAT 10N28.

27. GQG, Le général commandant en chef à guerre, 3ᵉ direction, 22 septembre 1914, *AFGG*, 21-25, p. 16.

28. Quoted in F. Gambiez and M. Suire, *Histoire de la première guerre mondiale*, 2 vols. (Paris: Fayard, 1968), 1:266.

29. Alexandre Millerand, handwritten notes, n.d., p. 6, AN 470AP/34.

30. Quoted in Pascal Lucas, *L'évolution des idées tactiques en France et en Allemagne pendant la guerre de 1914–1918* (Paris: Levrault, 1932), p. 38.

31. GQG, Note pour les armées, 2 janvier 1915, *AFGG*, 21-530, pp. 746–747.

32. Jean de Pierrefeu, *G.Q.G. Secteur 1: Trois ans au grand quartier général*, 2 vols. (Paris: Édition française illustrée, 1920), 1:106.

33. Poincaré, *Au service de la France*, 6:22–23; letter, Messimy to Poincaré, 1 August 1915, BNF NAF 16009.

34. Émile Fayolle, *Cahiers secrets de la grande guerre* (Paris: Plon, 1964), p. 67.

35. Poincaré, *Au service de la France*, 6:250–252.

36. Jean-Baptiste Duroselle, *Clemenceau* (Paris: Fayard, 1988), pp. 655–656.

37. Fayolle, *Cahiers secrets*, p. 96.

38. GQG, Instruction personnelle, 27 décembre 1914, *AFGG*, 21-478, pp. 679–680.

39. GQG, Organisations défensives de la IIIᵉ armée, 28 janvier 1915, *AFGG*, 21-747, pp. 1105–06.

40. GQG, Le général commandant en chef à M. le général commandant l'armée Châlons, 26 janvier 1915, *AFGG*, 21-734, p. 1086.

41. V^e armée, Le général Franchet d'Espèrey à M. le général commandant en chef, 1 octobre 1914, *AFGG*, 142-1782, pp. 509–510.

42. V^e armée, ÉM Romigny à ÉM Romilly-sur-Seine, 15 octobre 1914, *AFGG*, 143-2879, p. 585.

43. GQG, Note pour les armées, 12 novembre 1914, *AFGG*, 21-105, p. 114.

44. GQG, Instruction générale, Projet, 15 novembre 1914, *AFGG*, 21-121, pp. 138–139.

45. GQG, Note, 29 novembre 1914, *AFGG*, 21-227, pp. 292–296.

46. GQG, Étude, 4 décembre 1914, *AFGG*, 21-250, pp. 330–333.

47. GQG, Note, 6 décembre 1914, *AFGG*, 21-262, pp. 348–351.

48. Poincaré, *Au service de la France*, 6:500–501.

49. GQG, Note verbal pour S.A.I. le grand duc Nicolas Nicolaiewitch seul, 16 décembre 1914, no. 3954, *AFGG*, 21-365, p. 523.

50. GQG, Ordre général no. 32, 17 décembre 1914, *AFGG*, 21-378, p. 542.

51. Fayolle, *Cahiers secrets*, p. 63.

52. Général Foch, Au sujet des opérations dans le nord, 14/12/14, *AFGG*, 21-341, p. 473.

53. IVe armée, Instruction personnelle et secrète, 7 décembre 1914, *AFGG*, 21-272, p. 362.

54. 12e CA, Ordre général no. 143, 20 décembre 1914, *AFGG*, 21-420, p. 595.

55. IVe armée, Le général de Langle de Cary à M. le général commandant en chef, 13 janvier 1915, *AFGG*, 21-607, pp. 869–870.

56. GQG, Le général commandant en chef à M. le général commandant l'armée, Châlons, 15 janvier 1915, *AFGG*, 21-630, p. 910.

57. Ibid.

58. Poincaré, *Au service de la France*, 6:510.

59. IIIe armée, Note, 31 janvier 1915, *AFGG*, 21-774, p. 1143.

60. Major General G. S. Clive's Personal Diary, 23 November 1915, p. 48, PRO CAB 45/201.

61. GHQ, Memo by Major General Clive, January 10, 1915, PRO WO 158/13/1; GQG, Le général commandant en chef à son excellence M. le maréchal French, 19 janvier 1915, PRO WO 158/13/2.

62. Sir Henry Wilson, Diary, December 11, 1914, quoted in Richard Holmes, *The Little Field-Marshal, Sir John French* (London: Jonathan Cape, 1981), p. 261.

63. Le général commandant en chef à M. le ministre de la guerre, 13 mars 1915, SHAT 6N7.

64. Poincaré, *Au service de la France*, 5:411; MG, Cabinet du Ministre [Buat], Communication du commandant Herbillon, n.d., SHAT 5N271.

65. Poincaré, *Notes journalières*, 9 octobre 1914, p. 89; 23 octobre 1914, p. 126, BNF NAF 16028.

66. Joffre, *Mémoires*, 1:478–480; Roy A. Prete, "The Anglo-French Command Crisis of October–November 1914," *Research Studies* 52 (September–December 1983), 112–126.

67. GQG, Le général commandant en chef à M. le général Foch, 15 janvier 1915, *AFGG*, 21-634, p. 914.

68. GQG, Le général commandant en chef à son excellence M. le maréchal French, 19 janvier 1915, *AFGG*, 21-675, pp. 994–995.

69. GQG, Le général commandant en chef à son excellence M. le maréchal French, 16 février 1915, PRO WO 158/13/4.

70. GQG de l'armée britannique, Mémorandum du field-marshal commandant en chef l'armée britannique en campagne, à son excellence le commandant en chef de l'armée française, 23 février 1915, *AFGG*, 22-979, pp. 327–329.

71. GQG, Le général commandant en chef à M. le ministre de la guerre, 1 mars 1915, *AFGG*, 22-1041, pp. 414–415.

72. Secretary's Notes of a Meeting of a War Council, February 9, 1915, p. 3, PRO CAB 42/1/33.

73. Committee of Imperial Defence, Alexandretta and Mesopotamia, Memorandum by Lord Kitchener, March 16, 1915, p. 1, PRO CAB 42/2/10.

74. GQG, Le général commandant en chef à son excellence M. le maréchal French, 7 mars 1915, SHAT 6N7.

75. IVe armée, Instruction particulière et secrète, 28 janvier 1914, *AFGG*, 21-753, pp. 1111–12.

76. IVe armée, Le général de Langle de Cary à M. le général commandant le 17e corps, 17 février 1915, *AFGG*, 22-907, p. 222.

77. IVe armée, Compte rendu, no. 6039, *AFGG*, 22-919, p. 238.

78. GQG, Général commandant en chef à général commandant IVe armée, 20 février 1915, *AFGG*, 22-945, p. 279.

79. GQG, Note, 22 février 1915, *AFGG*, 22-967, p. 312.

80. IVe armée, Instruction particulière, 26 février 1915, *AFGG*, 22-1016, pp. 382–383.

81. Fernand de Langle de Cary, *Souvenirs de commandement, 1914–1916* (Paris: Payot, 1935), pp. 77, 187.

82. IVe armée, Note pour les corps d'armée, 7 mars 1915, *AFGG*, 22-1111, p. 511.

83. Ardant du Picq, *Études sur le combat* (Paris: Chapelot, 1903), p. 140.

84. GQG, Note pour la IVe armée, 8 mars 1915, *AFGG*, 22-1117, p. 517.

85. XVI CA, Instruction personnelle et secrète, 11 mars 1915, *AFGG*, 22-1160, p. 573.

86. XVI CA, Le général Grossetti à M. le général commandant la IVe armée, 14 mars 1915, *AFGG*, 22-1195, p. 620.

87. GQG, Le général commandant en chef à M. le général commandant l'armée, à Châlons-sur-Marne, 18 mars 1915, *AFGG*, 22-1215, p. 652.

88. De Langle de Cary, *Souvenirs de commandement*, p. 81.

89. GQG, Général commandant en chef à ÉM, rue maréchal (Bar-le-Duc), 8 avril 1915, *AFGG*, 22-1339, p. 855.

90. Détachement Gérard, Le général Gérard au général délégué du commandant en chef, 13 avril 1915, *AFGG*, 22-1382, pp. 920–923.

91. GPE, Le général Dubail au général commandant en chef, 13 avril 1915, *AFGG*, 22-1379, pp. 915–917.

92. GPE, Le général Dubail au général commandant en chef, 25 avril 1915, *AFGG*, 22-1440, p. 1004.

93. James Brown Scott, ed., *The Hague Conventions and Declarations of 1899 and 1907* (London: Oxford University Press, 1915), pp. 116, 129–130, 225, 231.

94. Olivier Lepick, *La grande guerre chimique, 1914–1918* (Paris: Presses universitaires de France, 1998), p. 65.

95. Henri Mordacq, *Le drame de l'Yser: Surprise des gaz (avril 1915)* (Paris: Des portiques, 1933), p. 94.

96. Poincaré, Notes journalières, 13 mars 1915, p. 149; 21 mars 1915, p. 173, BNF NAF 16029.

97. Mémorandum, Abel Ferry, Note du 27 avril [1915] (Conseil des ministres), AN 470 AP/14; Abel Ferry, *Les carnets secrets (1914–1918)* (Paris: Bernard Grasset, 1957), p. 69.

98. Poincaré, Notes journalières, 27 avril 1915, p. 265, BNF NAF 16029.

99. For Joffre's assessment of the war from October 1914 to March 1915, see GQG, Le général commandant en chef à M. le ministre de la guerre, 17 mars 1915, SHAT 6N7.

100. Alexandre Millerand, handwritten note, 29/3/15, AN 470AP/15.

4. AN OFFENSIVE STRATEGY, MAY–OCTOBER 1915

1. Lieutenant Colonel Clive, Conversation with Gen. Joffre, 8.30 A.M., July 30, 1915, PRO WO 158/13/24.

2. Communiqué du colonel Ignatieff, 22 février 1915, SHAT 1K268; Communiqué du colonel Ignatieff, 28 mars (10 avril) 1915, SHAT 7N1545. The earlier date is the Russian date. Russia remained on the Julian calendar during the war.

3. Télégramme chiffré, Général commandant en chef à général de Laguiche, 12 avril 1915, SHAT 7N1545.

4. GQG, Rapport du commandant Langlois sur sa seconde mission en Russie, 10 avril 1915, SHAT 7N1547.

5. Ambassade de France en Russie, Attaché militaire, 29 mai/11 juin 1915, Général Laguiche à général Joffre, SHAT 7N1545.

6. GQG, Le général commandant en chef à M. le ministre de la guerre, 17 mars 1915; GQG, Offensive en Champagne, annexe à la lettre du 17 mars N° 5668; both in SHAT 6N7.

7. Note du général Foch, fin mars 1915, *AFGG,* 31-24, pp. 40–41.

8. GPN, Le général Foch, *AFGG,* 31-20, pp. 29–30.

9. René Viktorovitch, *1915: La conquête de la méthode* (Saint-Maixent: Garnier, 1931), p. 13.

10. GQG, But et conditions d'une action offensive d'ensemble, 16 avril 1915, *AFGG,* 31-52, pp. 94–95; Joseph Joffre, *Mémoires du maréchal Joffre (1910–1917),* 2 vols. (Paris: Plon, 1932), 2:74.

11. Translation of Memo from Joffre to Sir John, 24 mars 1915, PRO WO 158/13/14.

12. GQG, Le général commandant en chef à M. le ministre de la guerre, 17 mars 1915, *AFGG,* 31-17, p. 25.

13. GQG, Prochaines attaques en Artois, 24 mars 1915, *AFGG,* 31-19, pp. 27–29.

14. Alexandre Millerand, handwritten note, Dans l'entrevenue K, 29/3/15, AN 470AP/15; GQG, Extrait du PV de la conférence du 27 mars [*sic*], 30 mars 1915, *AFGG,* 31-23, pp. 38–39; William James Philpott, *Anglo-French Relations and Strategy on the Western Front, 1914–18* (New York: St. Martin's, 1996), p. 76.

15. James E. Edmonds, ed., *History of the Great War, Military Operations, France and Belgium, 1915: Battle of Aubers Ridge, Festubert, and Loos* (London: Macmillan, 1928), p. 45.

16. Quartier général de l'armée britannique en campagne, 3 mai 1915, *AFGG*, 31-106, p. 179; GQG, Le général commandant en chef à son excellence le maréchal French, 5 mai 1915, *AFGG*, 31-121, p. 200.

17. X^e armée, Instruction personnelle et secrète, 1 mai 1915, *AFGG*, 31-95, p. 162.

18. X^e armée, Résumé des événements, 10 mai 1915, *AFGG*, 31-182, p. 268.

19. X^e armée, Aux soldats de la Xe armée, 10 mai 1915, *AFGG*, 31-188, p. 272.

20. GQG, Le général commandant en chef à M. le ministre de la guerre, 23 août 1915, *AFGG*, 32-1233, p. 671.

21. X^e armée, Ordre général d'opérations no. 223, 16 mai 1915, *AFGG*, 31-259, pp. 350–351.

22. GQG, Premiers enseignements à tirer des combats récents, 20 mai 1915, SHAT 16N1677.

23. X^e armée, Ordre général no. 253, 16 juin 1915, *AFGG*, 31-638, p. 814.

24. Raymond Poincaré, *Au service de la France*, vol. 6: *Les tranchées 1915* (Paris: Plon, 1930), pp. 271, 275.

25. Ibid., pp. 304–305.

26. Yves Gras, *Castelnau ou l'art de commander, 1851–1944* (Paris: Éditions Denoel, 1990), p. 228.

27. Poincaré, *Au service de la France*, 6:281.

28. Fernand de Langle de Cary, *Souvenirs de commandement, 1914–1916* (Paris: Payot, 1935), pp. 186–188.

29. Quoted in Émile Fayolle, *Cahiers secrets de la grande guerre* (Paris: Plon, 1964), p. 111.

30. Poincaré, *Au service de la France*, 6:311.

31. Fayolle, *Cahiers secrets*, p. 112.

32. See GQG, Le général commandant en chef à M. le ministre de la guerre, 27 mai 1915, SHAT 16N1677; Télégramme chiffré, Général commandant en chef à général Laguiche, 27 juin 1915, SHAT 7N1545.

33. GQG, ÉMA, Annexe à la note du 16 avril 1915 sur les but et conditions d'une offensive d'ensemble, 18 juin 1915, SHAT 16N1677.

34. Major-General G. S. Clive's Private Diary, 6th June 1915 to 24th March 1916, 5 July 1915, PRO CAB 45/201.

35. Conférence de Chantilly, PV, 24 juin 1915, *AFGG*, 31-736, pp. 941–943.

36. GQG, Rapport du commandant Langlois sur sa troisième mission en Russie, 20 juin 1915, SHAT 7N1547.

37. Traduction d'un télégramme chiffré, du Général Laguiche, 21 juin 1915, SHAT 7N1545.

38. Télégramme chiffré, Général commandant en chef à général Laguiche, 27 juin 1915, SHAT 7N1545.

39. Téléphoné par le capitaine Ménard du cabinet du ministre, Pétrograd, 12 août 1915, SHAT 1K268.

40. Note verbale du Général Joffre pour Lord Kitchener, 27 mai 1915, SHAT 16N1677.

41. GQG, Le général commandant en chef à M. le ministre de la guerre, 27 mai 1915, *AFGG*, 31-380, pp. 508–509.

42. Ibid., p. 508.

43. Xᵉ armée, Le général d'Urbal à M. le général Foch, 8 avril 1915, *AFGG*, 31-36, pp. 57-60.

44. GQG, Premiers engseignements à tirer des combats récents, 20 mai 1915, SHAT 16N1677; GQG, Le général commandant en chef à M. le ministre de la guerre, 30 mai 1915, SHAT 5N132.

45. GQG, Réunion des commandants de groupe d'armées du 11 juillet [*sic*], *AFGG*, 32-1150, pp. 554-558. Gamelin took notes at the meeting and mistakenly wrote July instead of August.

46. GQG, Instruction générale personnelle et secrète, 14 juin 1915, *AFGG*, 31-599, pp. 781-782.

47. GAN, Note, 1 juillet 1915, *AFGG*, 32-819, pp. 11-12; GAN, Le général Foch à M. le général commandant en chef, 1 juillet 1915, *AFGG*, 32-818, pp. 5-8.

48. GAC, Le général de Castelnau à M. le général commandant en chef, 7 juillet 1915, *AFGG*, 32-866, p. 90.

49. IIᵉ armée, Note sur les opérations, 29 juin 1915, *AFGG*, 31-792, pp. 1027-30.

50. Xᵉ armée, Instruction personnelle et secrète, 2 juillet 1915, *AFGG*, 32-835, p. 33.

51. GQG, Note sur les conditions d'une offensive d'ensemble, 8 juillet 1915, *AFGG*, 32-872, pp. 98-105.

52. Note du Général Pellé, juin 1915, SHAT 6N7; Au sujet de la note du Général Pellé, 17 juin 1915, SHAT 6N7; MG, Colonel Buat, Note pour le Ministre, 14 octobre 1915, SHAT 6N18.

53. GQG, Examen des projets d'opérations possibles de nos adversaires, 3 août 1915, AN 470AP/14.

54. GQG, Le général commandant en chef à M. le sous-secrétaire d'état de la guerre, 4 juillet 1915, *AFGG*, 32-843, p. 49.

55. GQG, No. 9861, Le général commandant en chef à M. le ministre de la guerre, 24 juin 1915, SHAT 5N132.

56. GQG, No. 9860, Le général commandant en chef à M. le ministre de la guerre, 24 juin 1915, SHAT 5N132.

57. GQG, Le général commandant en chef à M. le ministre de la guerre, 24 juin 1915, SHAT 5N132.

58. GQG, Note personnelle pour le ministre, 29 juin 1915, SHAT 16N1677.

59. Joffre, *Mémoires*, 2:126.

60. GQG, Note sur la direction de la guerre, 12 juin 1916, *AFGG*, 422-1186, p. 52.

61. PV de la conférence, 7 juillet 1915, *AFGG*, 32-860, p. 76.

62. Ibid., p. 80.

63. Conférence de Calais, 6 juillet 1915, AN 470AP/15; PV de la conférence, le 7 juillet 1915, p. 81.

64. Edmonds, *History of the Great War, France and Belgium, 1915: Battle of Aubers Ridge, Festubert, and Loos,* p. 113; Quartier général britannique, Arrêt des attaques britanniques, juin 1915, *AFGG*, 31-692, p. 893.

65. Colonel de Panousse, Idées que Lord Kitchener soutiendra à la conférence, 4 juillet 1915, SHAT 6N7.

66. Alexandre Millerand, handwritten note, 6 juillet 1915, page c, AN 470AP/15.

67. Conférence de Calais, 6 juillet 1915, AN 470AP/15; Conférence de Calais, 7 juillet [1915], AN 470AP/15.

68. Secretary's Notes of a Meeting of the Dardanelles Committee, August 20, 1915, p. 5, PRO CAB 42/3/16.

69. Report of a Meeting between Field-Marshal Sir John French and General Foch, 27 July 1915, PRO WO 158/26; GAN, Résumé de l'entretien du 27 juillet 1915, *AFGG*, 32-1026, pp. 351–352.

70. GQG, Le général commandant en chef à son excellence le maréchal French, 5 août 1915, *AFGG*, 32-1102, pp. 458–459.

71. GQG, Le général commandant en chef à son Excellence le maréchal French, 12 août 1915, *AFGG*, 32-1156, pp. 565–566.

72. GQG, Le général commandant en chef à M. le général Foch, 12 août 1915, *AFGG*, 32-1155, p. 565.

73. Edmonds, *History of the Great War, France and Belgium, 1915: Battle of Aubers Ridge, Festubert, and Loos*, p. 129.

74. GQG, Instruction pour le général Foch, 12 juillet 1915, SHAT 16N1677.

75. GAC, Projet d'opérations en Champagne, 21 juillet 1915, *AFGG*, 32-981, pp. 277–284.

76. Joffre, *Mémoires*, 2:106–107.

77. GAE, Le général de division Dubail à M. le général commandant le groupe des armées du centre, 16 juillet 1915, *AFGG*, 32-945, p. 225.

78. GAE, Le général Dubail à M. le général commandant en chef, 20 juillet 1915; GAE, Le général Dubail au général commandant, 20 juillet 1915. Both are reproduced in Joffre, *Mémoires*, 2:109–120.

79. Jan Karl Tanenbaum, *General Maurice Sarrail, 1856–1929: The French Army and Left-Wing Politics* (Chapel Hill: University of North Carolina Press, 1974), p. 54.

80. X^e armée, Le général d'Urbal à M. le général commandant le groupe d'armées du nord, 17 juillet 1915, *AFGG*, 32-957, pp. 234–238, 238n.

81. Fayolle, *Cahiers secrets*, p. 123.

82. IIe armée, Note pour les CA, 23 septembre 1915, *AFGG*, 32-1540, pp. 1134–35.

83. GQG, Note pour les généraux commandant les GA, 14 septembre 1915, *AFGG*, 32-1402, pp. 908–909.

84. GQG, Note pour les GAN et GAC, 21 septembre 1915, *AFGG*, 32-1494, p. 1064.

85. IIe armée, Le général commandant la IIe armée à M. le général commandant le groupe des armées du centre, 28 septembre 1915, *AFGG*, 33-2109, p. 404.

86. IVe armée, Compte rendu, 27 septembre 1915, *AFGG*, 33-1982, p. 288.

87. GAC, Message téléphoné, 28 septembre 1915, *AFGG*, 33-2094, p. 390.

88. *AFGG*, 3, p. 412.

89. GQG, Général commandant en chef à général de Castelnau, 2 octobre 1915, *AFGG*, 33-2518, p. 764.

90. GQG, Le général commandant en chef à M. le ministre de la guerre, 3 octobre 1915, *AFGG*, 33-2543, p. 786.

91. IVe armée, Note pour les corps d'armée, 5 octobre 1915, *AFGG*, 33-2634, p. 900.

92. See XXXV CA, 61ème Division, Le général Nivelle à M. le général commandant le XXXV corps d'armée, 17 mai 1915, *AFGG*, 31-272, pp. 364–370.

93. GQG, Lieutenant Colonel Billotte, Situation du GAC, 4 octobre 1915, *AFGG,* 33-2576, p. 833.

94. IIe armée, Situation et intentions de la IIe armée, 6 octobre 1915, *AFGG,* 33-2688, p. 954.

95. GAC, Le général de Castelnau à M. le général commandant en chef, 6 octobre 1915, *AFGG, 33*-2670, p. 940.

96. GAN, Note pour M. le général commandant la Xe armée, 26 septembre 1915, *AFGG,* 33-1796, p. 141.

97. GQG, Général commandant en chef à général Foch, 26 septembre 1915, *AFGG,* 33-1781, pp. 132–133.

98. GAN, Résumé des directives, 26 septembre 1915, *AFGG,* 33-1797, p. 142.

99. GAN, Le général Foch à M. le général commandant en chef, 27 septembre 1915, *AFGG, 33*-1953, p. 266.

100. GAN, Note pour M. le général commandant la Xe armée, 6 octobre 1915, *AFGG,* 33-2673, p. 943.

101. GAN, Extrait du journal des marches et opérations, 11 octobre 1915, *AFGG,* 33-2878, pp. 1146–47.

102. X^e armée, Ordre particulier aux CA et à l'artillerie, 11 octobre 1915, *AFGG,* 33-2887, p. 1151.

103. GAN, Opérations, 13 octobre 1915, *AFGG,* 33-2921, p. 1199.

104. GAN, Extrait du journal des marches et opérations, 15 octobre 1915, *AFGG, 33*-2961, p. 1255.

105. Edmonds, *History of the Great War, France and Belgium, 1915: Battle of Aubers Ridge, Festubert, and Loos,* p. 388.

106. GQG, Instruction générale personnelle et secrète, 22 octobre 1915, *AFGG,* 34-3000, pp. 53–55; GQG, Le général commandant en chef au général commandant le GAC, 13 octobre 1915, *AFGG,* 33-2919, pp. 1193–94.

5. THE SEARCH FOR STRATEGIC ALTERNATIVES, 1915–1916

1. Millerand to Delcassé, 5 January 1915, Archives du Ministère des affaires étrangères; quoted in Christopher M. Andrew and A. S. Kanya-Forstner, *The Climax of French Imperial Expansion* (Stanford: Stanford University Press, 1981), p. 70.

2. Secretary's Notes of a Meeting of a War Council, January 8, 1915, PRO CAB 42/1/12.

3. From the General commanding Mediterranean Expeditionary Force to M. le général de division d'Amade, 17 April 1915, *AFGG,* 811-73, p. 126.

4. D'Amade's reports of April 27, 28, 30 and May 1 are in SHAT 5N67.

5. Corps expéditionnaire d'Orient, Le général de division Gouraud à sir Ian Hamilton, 13 juin 1915, *AFGG,* 811-240, pp. 351–352.

6. Corps d'expéditionnaire d'Orient, Le général de division Bailloud à M. le ministre de la guerre, 27 juillet 1915, Rapport sur un projet d'opérations sur la côte d'Asie, AN 470AP/15.

7. PV de la conférence, 7 juillet 1915, *AFGG,* 32-860, pp. 77–78, 80.

8. GQG, Le général commandant en chef à M. le ministre de la guerre, 3 août 1915, SHAT 5N132; Raymond Poincaré, *Au service de la France,* vol. 7: *Guerre de siège* (Paris: Plon, 1931), pp. 11–13.

9. Télégramme chiffré parvenu au Ministère le 22 juillet 1915, SHAT 5N271; Foch à Joffre, handwritten note, 3 décembre 1914, SHAT 1K268; Raymond Poincaré, *Au service de la France,* vol. 6: *Les tranchées 1915* (Paris: Plon, 1930), pp. 348, 336–337; Jere C. King, *Generals and Politicians: Conflict between France's High Command, Parliament, and Government, 1914–1918* (Berkeley: University of California Press, 1951), pp. 71–74.

10. Maurice Sarrail, *Mon commandement en Orient (1916–1918)* (Paris: Flammarion, 1920), pp. 297–301; Général Sarrail, Note au sujet de la situation militaire en Orient, 11 août 1915, *AFGG,* 811-315, pp. 481–484.

11. GQG, Le général commandant en chef à M. le ministre de la guerre, 18 août 1915, *AFGG,* 811-318, pp. 486–491.

12. Poincaré, *Au service de la France,* 7:35, 37–38.

13. Ibid., pp. 64, 68–69.

14. Section d'études de la défense nationale, Note au sujet des Dardanelles, 31 août 1915, *AFGG,* 811-332, pp. 521–530.

15. GQG, Le général commandant en chef à M. le ministre de la guerre, 1 septembre 1915, *AFGG,* 811-336, pp. 539–541.

16. GQG, Le général commandant en chef à M. le ministre de la guerre, 8 septembre 1915, *AFGG,* 811-351, pp. 562–563.

17. GQG, Le général commandant en chef à M. le ministre de la guerre, 20 septembre 1915, *AFGG,* 811-365, pp. 586–588.

18. Poincaré, *Au service de la France,* 7:111.

19. Ibid., p. 102.

20. ÉMA, Le ministre de la guerre à M. le général commandant en chef, 14 août 1915, *AFGG,* 812-27, pp. 69–70.

21. Section d'études de la défense nationale, Rapport au sujet d'une intervention militaire dans la péninsule des Balkans, 4 septembre 1915, *AFGG,* 812-29, pp. 71–72; Section d'études de la défense nationale, Note au sujet des Dardanelles, 10 septembre 1915, AN 470AP/15.

22. Général Bailloud à guerre, Cabinet, no. 25, 24 septembre 1915, AN 470AP/16.

23. Général Bailloud à ministre de la guerre, 1 octobre 1915, SHAT 6N26.

24. Poincaré, Notes journalières, 23 septembre 1915, 25 septembre 1915, pp. 193–196, BNF NAF 16031; Poincaré, *Au service de la France,* 7:116, 127.

25. Secretary's Notes of a Meeting of the Dardanelles Committee, September 23, 1915, PRO CAB 42/3/28.

26. MG, Le ministre de la guerre à M. général commandant corps d'expéditionnaire Orient, 24 septembre 1915, *AFGG,* 812-41, pp. 85–86.

27. GQG, Note au sujet du télégramme en date du 23 septembre de l'attaché militaire à Londres, 24 septembre 1915, *AFGG,* 812-43, pp. 86–87.

28. AO, Note au sujet de l'intervention française dans les Balkans, 2 octobre 1915, *AFGG,* 812-96, pp. 129–134; Sarrail, *Mon commandement en Orient,* pp. 302–307.

29. GQG, Le général commandant en chef à M. le ministre de la guerre, 3 octobre 1915, *AFGG*, 812-101, pp. 137–142.

30. Ibid.

31. GQG, Note au sujet d'un télégramme de lord Kitchener, 5 octobre 1915, *AFGG*, 812-102, pp. 142–143.

32. Proceedings of a Meeting held at Calais on 11th September 1915, PRO CAB 158/13/48; Compte rendu de la conférence tenue à Calais le 5/10/15, *AFGG*, 812-108, pp. 146–150; MG, Order concernant la mission du général Sarrail, 3 octobre 1915, *AFGG*, 812-100, p. 136.

33. Alexandre Millerand, handwritten note, Calais 5/10 [1915], AN 470AP/15.

34. Cyril Falls, *History of the Great War, Military Operations, Macedonia: From the Outbreak of War to the Spring of 1917* (London: His Majesty's Stationery Office, 1933), p. 50.

35. Sir F. Elliot to Sir Edward Grey, no. 1014, October 9, 1915, in *British Documents on Foreign Affairs*, part 2, ser. H, vol. 2: *The Allied and Neutral Powers: Diplomacy and War Aims: June 1915–November 1916* (Frederick, Md.: University Publications of America, 1989), doc. 203, p. 179.

36. Poincaré, *Au service de la France*, 7:157–158, 161, 165.

37. Sarrail, *Mon commandement en Orient*, p. 19.

38. Général Bailloud, Salonique via Moudros, 12 octobre 1915, *AFGG*, 812-144, p. 180; À consul France Salonique pour gal. Sarrail, 13 octobre 1915, *AFGG*, 812-145, p. 180.

39. Le colonel Ruef au général commandant en chef, 16-10-1915, *AFGG*, 812-191, pp. 214–216.

40. Sarrail, *Mon commandement en Orient*, pp. 20, 22.

41. Ibid., p. 25.

42. Ministère des affaires étrangères, Le ministre de la guerre pour le président du conseil, 19 octobre 1915, *AFGG*, 812-206, pp. 227–228.

43. Attaché militaire, Londres, Vues de l'ÉM anglais sur la situation en Serbie, 26 octobre 1915, *AFGG*, 812-275, pp. 291–292.

44. AO, 57ᵉ division, Rapport sur l'importance de la position Vardar, Cerna, 4 novembre 1915, *AFGG*, 812-379, pp. 389–390.

45. ÉM à général cdt en chef AO, 4 novembre 1915, *AFGG*, 812-375, p. 386.

46. Le ministre guerre à général commandant AO, 13 novembre 1915, *AFGG*, 812-515, pp. 507–508.

47. Le ministre guerre à général commandant AO, 19 novembre 1915, *AFGG*, 812-579, p. 574.

48. Sarrail, *Mon commandement en Orient*, p. 42.

49. Gaëtan Gallieni, ed., *Les carnets de Gallieni* (Paris: Albin Michel, 1932), p. 221; Le ministre guerre à général commandant en chef AO, 21 novembre 1915, *AFGG*, 812-618, p. 608.

50. Quoted in Georges Bonnefous, *La grande guerre (1914–1918)* (Paris: Presses universitaires de France, 1967), p. 86.

51. Poincaré, *Au service de la France*, 7:193.

52. GQG, Le général commandant en chef à M. le ministre de la guerre, 19 [*sic;* correct date is 29] juillet 1915, *AFGG*, 811-296, p. 453.

53. Poincaré, *Au service de la France,* 7:258.

54. Joseph Joffre, *Mémoires du maréchal Joffre (1910–1917),* 2 vols. (Paris: Plon, 1932), 2:147, 151–152.

55. Poincaré, *Au service de la France,* 7:290–291.

56. Gallieni, *Carnets,* p. 211.

57. Poincaré, *Au service de la France,* 7:277–278.

58. Joffre, *Mémoires,* 2:154–155.

59. Gallieni, *Carnets,* p. 221.

60. Poincaré, *Au service de la France,* 7:296–297; Joffre, *Mémoires,* 2:157–158.

61. Gallieni, *Carnets,* p. 224.

62. Joffre, *Mémoires,* 2:156.

63. King, *Generals and Politicians,* p. 86.

64. Poincaré, *Au service de la France,* 7:12.

65. GQG, Plan d'action proposé par la France à la coalition, 2 décembre 1915, *AFGG,* 812-736, pp. 726–732.

66. Général Laguiche, Expédié de Mohileu, 26 novembre/9 décembre 1915; 29 novembre/12 décembre 1915; both in SHAT 17N571.

67. GQG, PV, 8 décembre 1915, *AFGG,* 813-820, p. 73.

68. GQG, Conclusions de la conférence, 8 décembre 1915, *AFGG,* 813-821, pp. 75–76.

69. Herbert Asquith to Sylvia Henley, 8 December 1915; quoted in David Dutton, *The Politics of Diplomacy: Britain and France in the Balkans in the First World War* (London: Tauris, 1998), p. 76.

70. Secretary's Notes of a Meeting of the War Committee, December 8, 1915, PRO CAB 42/6/6; Attaché militaire à commandant en chef, France, 8 décembre 1915, *AFGG,* 813-823, p. 77.

71. Gallieni, *Carnets,* pp. 229–230.

72. Secretary's Notes of a Meeting of the War Committee, December 13, 1915, PRO CAB 42/6/7.

73. Attaché militaire en Russie, Plan du général Alexeieff, 22 novembre 1915, *AFGG,* 812-644, pp. 639–640.

74. Cabinet du ministre, Chef d'ÉM, Situation en Russie, 8 décembre 1915, SHAT 5N139.

75. Section d'études de la défense nationale, Rapport au sujet d'une communication secrète faite par le général Alexeieff, 24 novembre 1915, *AFGG,* 812-661, pp. 653–655.

76. MMF en Russie, Le général Pau à M. le ministre de la guerre, 12 janvier 1916, SHAT 5N269.

77. Affaires étrangères, Question posées et résolues au CSDN, 8 février 1916, *AFGG,* 411-163, p. 339.

78. GQG, CSDN (séance du 10 mars 1916), *AFGG,* 412-1164, p. 300.

79. GQG, Mémorandum pour la réunion des commandants en chef des armées alliées (1 mars 1916), 15 février 1916, *AFGG,* 411-237, pp. 447–450.

80. Secretary's Notes of a Meeting of the War Committee, December 28, 1915, PRO CAB 42/16/14.

81. Conversation tenue entre le général Joffre et le général Robertson, 14 février 1916, SHAT 1K268.

82. William Robertson, *Soldiers and Statesmen, 1914-1918,* 2 vols. (New York: Charles Scribner's Sons, 1926), 2:103.

83. Ibid., p. 101.

84. Diplomatie, Paris, Pour le ministre de la guerre, 26 octobre 1915, SHAT 7N1302.

85. GQG, Le GQG à général commandant em chef l'AO, 4 mars 1916, *AFGG,* 813-1211, p. 464.

86. Chef d'ÉM impérial britannique, Au sujet des opérations à Salonique, 6 March 1916, *AFGG,* 813-1213, p. 465.

87. AO, Projet de plan d'opérations des forces alliées de Macédonie, 7 mars 1916, *AFGG,* 813-1219, pp. 470-471.

88. GQG, Le général, commandant en chef les armées françaises à M. le général commandant en chef l'AO, 10 mars 1916, *AFGG,* 813-1225, pp. 484-485.

89. GQG, Introduction à la conférence du 12 mars 1916, 10 mars 1916, *AFGG,* 412-1163, p. 298.

90. Résumé of a Discussion at the Foreign Office, Paris, March 27, 1916, PRO Cab. 28/1/ I.C.-7b; quoted in Jan Karl Tanenbaum, *General Maurice Sarrail, 1856-1929: The French Army and Left-Wing Politics* (Chapel Hill: University of North Carolina Press, 1974), p. 91.

91. GQG, PV de la conférence, 12 mars 1916, *AFGG,* 412-1212, pp. 354-357.

92. GQG, Le GQG au général commandant en chef l'AO, 20 avril 1916, *AFGG,* 813-1274, pp. 576-578.

93. GQG, Le général commandant en chef à M. le général Robertson, 25 avril 1916, *AFGG,* 813-1280, pp. 585-587.

94. Minutes of the Eighty-eighth Meeting of the War Committee, May 17, 1916, PRO CAB 42/14/1.

95. War Committee, Memorandum, 17 May 1916, *AFGG,* 813-1302, pp. 617-621.

96. GQG, Mémorandum pour la conférence de Londres, 9 juin 1916, *AFGG,* 813-1327, p. 663.

97. David Lloyd George, *War Memoirs,* 2 vols. (London: Odhams, 1938), 1:319.

98. Ibid., p. 321.

99. Foreign Office, Memorandum, 9 June 1916, *AFGG,* 813-1328, p. 664.

100. GQG, Le GQG à général commandant en chef d'AO, 20 juin 1916, *AFGG,* 813-1343, p. 686.

101. Joffre, *Mémoires,* 2:299-301; GQG, Télégramme général commandant en chef à attaché militaire, Bucarest, 26 juin 1916, *AFGG,* 813-1352, pp. 698-699.

102. Guy Rousseau, "Le Conseil des ministres en 1916, d'après les notes d'Étienne Clémentel," *Guerres mondiales et conflits contemporains* 43 (juillet 1993), 149.

103. Chef d'ÉM impérial, Au sujet de la coopération du corps expéditionnaire britannique à l'offensive dans les Balkans, 18 July 1916, *AFGG,* 813-1382, pp. 742-743.

104. Officier du GQG en mission près l'AO, Au sujet du plan d'opérations du commandement de l'AO, 17 juillet 1916, *AFGG,* 813-1381, p. 742.

105. Chef d'ÉM impérial, Au sujet des opérations à exécuter dans les Balkans, 19 July 1916, *AFGG,* 813-1384, p. 749.

106. MG, PV de la séance du 23 juillet 1916, *AFGG,* 813-1391, pp. 757-759.

107. GQG, Le GQG au général commandant en chef l'AO, 23 juillet 1916, *AFGG,* 813-1392, pp. 759-760.

108. Foreign Office, Sur le commandement à Salonika, 19 July 1916, *AFGG*, 813-1386, p. 751.

109. GQG, Le GQG au général commandant en chef l'AO, 23 juillet 1916, *AFGG*, 813-1392, pp. 759-760.

110. GQG, Mémorandum pour la réunion des commandants de groupe d'armées, 20 août 1916, *AFGG*, 511-2, pp. 9-10, 13-14, 20-21.

111. *Mémoires du général Broussilov, Guerre de 1914-1918* (Paris: Hachette, 1929), p. 224.

112. Conseil de la défense nationale, Conclusions de la déliberations, 26 octobre 1916, *AFGG*, 432-1286, p. 285.

113. GQG Russe, MMF à guerre et général commandant en chef, 13 janvier 1917, SHAT 5N140.

114. MG, Ministre de la guerre à général commandant en chef l'AO, 9 mars 1917, *AFGG*, 823-1601, p. 326.

115. Conférence du Pétrograd, février 1917, SHAT 6N68.

6. A STRATEGY OF ATTRITION, 1916

1. GQG, Le Général commandant en chef à M. le ministre de la guerre, 27 mai 1915, SHAT 16N1677.

2. Télégramme chiffré, Général commandant en chef à général Laguiche, 27 juin 1915, SHAT 7N1545.

3. Raymond Poincaré, *Au service de la France,* vol. 8: *Verdun 1916* (Paris: Plon, 1931), p. 224.

4. GQG, Note sur l'emploi des forces anglaises pendant la campagne d'hiver 1915-1916, 7 octobre 1915, *AFGG*, 33-2792, pp. 1023-24.

5. Poincaré, *Au service de la France,* 8:300; GQG, Note au sujet des conditions générales de la guerre, 7 octobre 1915, *AFGG*, 33-2793, pp. 1024-30.

6. GQG, Plan d'action, 2 décembre 1915, *AFGG*, 812-736, pp. 726-732.

7. GQG, Le général commandant en chef à M. le ministre de la guerre, 3 octobre 1915, *AFGG*, 33-2543, pp. 783-788.

8. GQG, Conclusions de la conférence, 8 décembre 1915, *AFGG*, 813-821, pp. 74-75.

9. GQG, But et conditions d'une action offensive d'ensemble, 16 avril 1915, *AFGG*, 31-52, p. 95.

10. GAN, Enseignements de tirer des dernières attaques, 6 décembre 1915, *AFGG*, 34-3122, p. 385.

11. GQG, Enseignements des batailles de septembre, 27 décembre 1915, *AFGG*, 34-3211, pp. 540-541.

12. GQG, Note sur l'emploi des forces anglaises pendant la campagne d'hiver 1915-1916, 7 octobre 1915, *AFGG*, 33-2792, p. 1023.

13. René Viktorovitch, *1915: La conquête de la méthode* (Saint-Maixent-L'École: Garnier, 1931), p. 19.

14. GQG, Instruction sur le combat offensif des grandes unités, 26 janvier 1916, *AFGG*, 34-3298, pp. 698, 701-702, 700.

15. GQG, Note annexe provisoire à l'instruction du 8 janvier 1916 sur le combat offensif des petites unités, 27 septembre 1916, p. 10, SHAT 16N1683.

16. GQG, Note pour les commandants de groupe d'armées, 5 décembre 1915, *AFGG*, 34-3117, pp. 376–377, 375.

17. Philippe Pétain, *Verdun*, trans. Margaret Mac Veagh (New York: Dial, 1930), p. 54.

18. GQG, Annexe à la note no. 14053 du 25 octobre, 13 décembre 1915, *AFGG*, 34-3153, p. 438.

19. GQG, Note pour les commandants de groupe d'armées, 11 novembre 1915, *AFGG*, 34-3065, p. 242.

20. Philippe Bernard, "À propos de la stratégie aérienne pendant la première guerre mondiale: Mythes et réalités," *Revue d'histoire moderne et contemporaine* 16 (avril–juin 1969), 360.

21. MG, Le ministre de la guerre à M. le général commandant en chef, 12 mars 1917, *AFGG*, 511-835, pp. 1536–37.

22. GQG, Le général commandant en chef aux généraux commandant les GAN, GAC, GAE, 27 octobre 1915, *AFGG*, 34-3018, pp. 91–92.

23. GQG, Le général commandant en chef à M. le général sir Douglas Haig, 26 décembre 1915, *AFGG*, 411-69, p. 162.

24. GQG, PV, 22 janvier 1916, *AFGG*, 411-116, p. 234. For an earlier discussion of attrition, see MMF, Le Colonel de Vallières à M. le général commandant en chef, 19 janvier 1916, SHAT 1K268.

25. GQG, Le général commandant en chef à M. le général sir Douglas Haig, 23 janvier 1916, *AFGG*, 411-120, pp. 239–241.

26. GHQ, From the Commander in Chief British Army in France to the Commander in Chief French Army, 1 February 1916, *AFGG*, 411-147, pp. 289–292.

27. GQG, PV, 14 février 1916, *AFGG*, 411-221, pp. 420–422; GQG, Conclusions, 14 février [1916], *AFGG*, 411-222, p. 423.

28. Robert Blake, ed., *Private Papers of Douglas Haig, 1914–1919* (London: Eyre and Spottiswoode, 1952), p. 129.

29. Émile Herbillon, *Souvenirs d'un officier de liaison pendant la guerre mondiale: Du général en chef au gouvernement,* 2 vols. (Paris: J. Tallandier, 1930), 1:227.

30. Germany, Reichsarchiv, *Der Weltkrieg, 1914 bis 1918,* vol. 10: *Die Operationen des Jahres 1916* (Berlin: E. S. Mittler & Sohn, 1936), pp. 22–41; Holger Afflerbach, *Falkenhayn: Politisches Denken und Handeln im Kaisserreich* (Munich: R. Oldenbourg, 1994), pp. 351–369; idem, "Planning Total War? Falkenhayn and the Battle of Verdun, 1916," in *Great War, Total War,* ed. Roger Chickering and Stig Förster (Cambridge: Cambridge University Press, 2000), pp. 113–124.

31. Erich von Falkenhayn, *The German General Staff and Its Decisions, 1914–1916* (New York: Dodd, Mead, 1920), pp. 239–249; Holger H. Herwig, *The First World War: Germany and Austria-Hungary, 1914–1918* (London: Arnold, 1997), pp. 179–183.

32. ÉM, Compte rendu de renseignements no. 603, 11 février 1916, *AFGG*, 411-186, p. 384.

33. Région fortifiée de Verdun, Instruction personnelle et secrète, 12 février 1916, *AFGG*, 411-211, p. 406.

34. Le général commandant en chef au général sir Douglas Haig, 22 février 1916, *AFGG*, 411-428, p. 625; GQG, Joffre to Haig, no. 15074, 22 février 1916, PRO WO 158/14/90.

35. GQG, Séance du CSDN du 10 mars 1916, *AFGG*, 412-1071, p. 176.

36. Joseph Joffre, *Mémoires du maréchal Joffre (1910–1917),* 2 vols. (Paris: Plon, 1932), 2:200–202.

37. GQG, Examen des projets d'opérations possibles de nos adversaires, 3 août 1915, SHAT 6N7.

38. GQG, Instruction générale sur le rôle des places fortes, 9 août 1915, *AFGG*, 411-4, p. 6.

39. GAE, État des organisations de la Région fortifiée de Verdun, 26 décembre 1915, *AFGG*, 411-72, p. 164.

40. Poincaré, *Au service de la France*, 8:4.

41. Fernand de Langle de Cary, *Souvenirs de commandement, 1914–1916* (Paris: Payot, 1935), pp. 225–227, 99.

42. Ibid., p. 98.

43. Quoted in *AFGG*, 41, p. 218.

44. GAC, Évacuation de Brabant, 23 février 1916, *AFGG*, 411-511, p. 674.

45. GQG, Envoyé au général de Langle, 24 février 1916, *AFGG*, 411-585, p. 723; Joffre, *Mémoires*, 2:208; Herbillon, *Souvenirs d'un officier de liaison*, 1:248.

46. GQG, Instruction pour le général commandant la IIᵉ armée, 25 février 1916, *AFGG*, 411-673, p. 775.

47. Georges Suarez, ed., *Briand, sa vie—son oeuvre, avec son journal et de nombreux documents inédits*, 4 vols. (Paris: Plon, 1938–1940), 3:249–252; Jere C. King, *Generals and Politicians: Conflict between France's High Command, Parliament, and Government, 1914–1918* (Los Angeles: University of California Press, 1951), pp. 97–100; Michel Corday, *The Paris Front: An Unpublished Diary, 1914–1918* (London: Victor Gollancz, 1933), p. 149.

48. Chef d'ÉM général, Résistance sur la rive droite, 25 février 1916, *AFGG*, 411-681, p. 781.

49. Région fortifiée de Verdun, Le général Herr à M. le général commandant le 30ᵉ CA, 25 février 1916, *AFGG*, 411-692, p. 790.

50. GQG, Le général commandant en chef à général sir W. Robertson, 26 février 1916, *AFGG*, 411-748, p. 830.

51. GQG, Général commandant en chef à général commandant en chef les forces britanniques, 26 février 1916, *AFGG*, 411-746, p. 828.

52. IIᵉ armée, Ordre général d'opérations, 26 février 1916, *AFGG*, 411-767, pp. 847–850.

53. Pétain, *Verdun*, p. 92.

54. Groupement de Bazelaire, Compte rendu, 5 mars 1916, *AFGG*, 412-1038, pp. 146–147.

55. Quoted in Jacques Péricard, *Le soldat de Verdun* (Paris: Baudinière, 1937), pp. 146–147.

56. Philippe Pétain, *La bataille de Verdun* (Paris: Payot, 1929), p. 74; Bernard Serrigny, *Trente ans avec Pétain* (Paris: Plon, 1959), p. 62.

57. GQG, Séance du CSDN du 10 mars 1916, 7 mars 1916, *AFGG*, 412-1071, p. 176.

58. GAN, Le général Foch à M. le commandant en chef, 7 mars 1916, *AFGG*, 412-1075, pp. 184–185.

59. GQG, Le général commandant en chef à M. le général sir Douglas Haig, 27 mars 1916, *AFGG*, 412-1553, pp. 775–777.

60. Blake, *Private Papers of Douglas Haig*, pp. 137, 143.

61. Minutes of the Eightieth Meeting of the War Committee, April 7, 1916, PRO CAB 42/12/5.

62. Général Haig, Le général commandant en chef l'armée britannique en France au général commandant en chef l'armée française, 8 mai 1916, *AFGG*, 421-194, pp. 295–296.

63. GQG, Résumé de l'entretien du 26 mai, 27 mai 1916, *AFGG*, 421-624, pp. 873–875.

64. Blake, *Private Papers of Douglas Haig*, pp. 144–145.

65. GQG, Mémorandum pour la réunion du 31 mai . . ., 30 mai 1916, *AFGG*, 421-704, pp. 994–997.

66. Blake, *Private Papers of Douglas Haig*, pp. 145–146.

67. GAN, Instruction personnelle et secrète, 25 mai 1916, *AFGG*, 421-581, pp. 806–807.

68. Quoted in Péricard, *Le soldat de Verdun*, p. 139.

69. Pétain, *Verdun*, p. 139.

70. GQG, Note pour la IIᵉ armée, 1 avril 1916, *AFGG*, 413-1653, pp. 4–5.

71. GQG, Général commandant en chef à ÉM Souilly, 9 avril 1916, *AFGG*, 413-1871, pp. 269–270.

72. GQG, Général commandant en chef à ÉM Souilly, 11 avril 1916, *AFGG*, 413-1962, p. 356; Serrigny, *Trente ans avec Pétain*, p. 84.

73. Poincaré, *Au service de la France*, 8:105.

74. Joffre, *Mémoires*, 2:388.

75. Poincaré, *Au service de la France*, 8:225.

76. GAC, Le général Pétain à M. le général commandant en chef, 7 mai 1916, *AFGG*, 421-129, p. 206.

77. Ibid., pp. 206–207.

78. GQG, Le général commandant en chef au général commandant le groupe d'armées du centre, 11 mai 1916, *AFGG*, 421-245, pp. 361–362.

79. IIᵉ armée, Note pour les groupements, 9 juin 1916, *AFGG*, 421-1077, pp. 1423–25.

80. André Laffargue, *Étude sur l'attaque* (Paris: Plon, 1916).

81. GQG, Général commandant en chef à ÉM, Bar, 12 juin 1916, *AFGG*, 422-1138, pp. 49–50.

82. IIᵉ armée, Aux soldats de l'armée de Verdun, 23 juin 1916, *AFGG*, 422-1472, p. 403.

83. Poincaré, *Au service de la France*, 8:251.

84. Le général de Castelnau, handwritten note, 31 juillet 1916, SHAT 16N1682.

85. GQG, Instruction personnelle et secrète, 21 juin 1916, *AFGG*, 422-1385, pp. 316–318.

86. GQG, Développement de la bataille de la Somme, 11 juin 1916, *AFGG*, 421-1151, p. 9.

87. GQG, Note sur l'offensive dans la région du nord, 17 juin 1916, *AFGG*, 422-1322, p. 214.

88. Émile Fayolle, *Cahiers secrets de la grande guerre* (Paris: Plon, 1964), pp. 161, 167.

89. Quoted in *AFGG*, 42, p. 220.

90. VIᵉ armée, Note relative à la préparation et à l'exécution des attaques, 8 juin 1916, *AFGG*, 421-1019, p. 1364.

91. GAN, Note à communiquer jusqu'aux bataillons, 20 juin 1916, *AFGG*, 422-1369, pp. 291–295.

92. Blake, *Private Papers of Douglas Haig*, p. 154; Note of Interview between Sir D. Haig and General Joffre on 3rd July 1916, PRO WO 158/15.

93. MMF, Le général des Vallières à général commandant en chef, 9 juillet 1916, *AFGG*, 422-2167, pp. 1161–64.

94. Quoted in A. H. Farrar-Hockley, *The Somme* (Philadelphia: Dufour Editions, 1964), p. 150.

95. Fayolle, *Carnets secrets,* p. 171.

96. Ibid., pp. 166, 167.

97. GAN, Le général Foch à M. le général commandant en chef, 21 juillet 1916, *AFGG,* 423-2532, pp. 162–163.

98. GQG, Extrait de bulletin de renseignements no. 695 de la VIe armée, 11 août 1916, SHAT 16N1682.

99. GQG, Instruction relative à l'utilisation des compagnies Schilt, 15 octobre 1916, SHAT 16N1683.

100. GAN, Le général Foch à M. le général commandant la VIe armée, etc., 31 juillet 1916, *AFGG,* 423-2651, pp. 321–323.

101. Pétain à général commandant en chef, 19 août 1918, *AFGG,* 423-2951, p. 717.

102. Georges Bonnefous, *La grande guerre, 1914–1918* (Paris: Presses universitaires de France, 1967), p. 122.

103. Comité Secret, Séance du 16 juin 1916, p. 4, AN 470AP/35.

104. Herbillon, *Souvenirs d'un officier de liaison,* 1:339–340.

105. Poincaré, *Au service de la France,* 8:336.

106. GQG, Conclusions de la conférence, 8 décembre 1915, *AFGG,* 813-821, pp. 74–75.

107. MMF, Le général des Vallières à général commandant en chef, 10 août 1916, *AFGG,* 423-2846, pp. 563–565.

108. GAN, Note, 11 août 1916, *AFGG,* 423-2867, pp. 595–596; Guy Pédroncini, ed., *Journal de marche de Joffre (1916–1919)* (Château de Vincennes: SHAT, 1990), p. 46.

109. GQG, Général commandant en chef à général Foch, 11 août 1916, *AFGG,* 423-2851, p. 591.

110. GQG, Le général commandant en chef à M. le général sir Douglas Haig, 25 août 1916, SHAT 16N1682.

111. ÉMA, L'usure adverse, 30 juillet 1916, *AFGG,* 423-2630, pp. 295–301.

112. Joffre, *Mémoires,* 2:251–252.

113. GQG, Mémorandum pour la réunion des commandants de groupe d'armées, 20 août 1916, *AFGG,* 511-2, pp. 9–10, 13–14, 20–21.

114. Blake, *Private Papers of Douglas Haig,* p. 162; John Davidson, *Haig: Master of the Field* (London: Peter Nevill, 1953), p. 4.

115. Major General G. W. Clive's Private Diary, 30 August 1916, PRO CAB 45/201.

116. Poincaré, *Au service de la France,* 8:313.

117. Minutes of the One Hundred and Tenth Meeting of the War Committee, August 30, 1916, PRO CAB 42/18/8.

118. Field-Marshal Sir William Robertson, *Soldiers and Statesmen, 1914–1918,* 2 vols. (New York: Charles Scribner's Sons, 1926), 1:271–272; Minutes of the One Hundred and Fifth Meeting of the War Committee, August 5, 1916, PRO CAB 42/17/3.

119. Poincaré, *Au service de la France,* 8:337.

120. Joffre, *Mémoires,* 2:263.

121. IIe armée, Groupement D.E., Ordre d'opération, 9 octobre 1916, *AFGG,* 431-924, pp. 1320–21.

122. IIe armée, Ordre particulier, 25 octobre 1916, *AFGG,* 432-1267, p. 253.

123. Winston S. Churchill, *The World Crisis,* 6 vols. (New York: Charles Scribner's Sons, 1927), 3:90, 300.

7. A STRATEGY OF DECISIVE BATTLE, EARLY 1917

1. GQG, Général commandant en chef à chefs missions militaires françaises GQG, etc., 15 octobre 1916, *AFGG,* 511-57, pp. 97–98.
2. David Lloyd George, *War Memoirs,* 2 vols. (London: Odhams, 1938), 1:541–555; Minutes of the One Hundred Twenty-eighth Meeting of the War Committee, November 8, 1916, PRO CAB 42/23/4.
3. Lloyd George, *War Memoirs,* 1:547.
4. Ibid., pp. 544–566; Maurice Hankey, *The Supreme Command, 1914–1918,* 2 vols. (London: George Allen, 1961), 2:559–561.
5. GQG, Mémorandum pour la réunion des commandants en chef, 12 novembre 1916, *AFGG,* 511-103, pp. 176, 182, 186–187.
6. Joseph Joffre, *Mémoires du maréchal Joffre (1910–1917),* 2 vols. (Paris: Plon, 1932), 2:354–358; Guy Pédroncini, ed., *Journal de Marche de Joffre (1916–1919)* (Paris: SHAT, 1990), pp. 160–161; GQG, Décisions prises, 15 et 16 novembre 1917, *AFGG,* 511-119, pp. 217–219.
7. GQG, Note annexe no. 3 au mémorandum pour la conférence du 15 novembre 1916, n.d., *AFGG,* 511-115, p. 210.
8. Lloyd George, *War Memoirs,* 1:572, 573, 574.
9. Joffre, *Mémoires,* 2:365.
10. GQG, Note relative à la préparation et à l'exploitation des attaques, 27 novembre 1916, *AFGG,* 511-183, pp. 328–331.
11. GQG, Avis du 3ᵉ Bureau, 14 novembre 1916, SHAT 16N1683.
12. GQG, ÉM, 2ᵉ Bureau, S.R. aux Armées (Contrôle Postal), Rapport sur la correspondance des troupes du 25 novembre au 10 décembre, 15 décembre 1916, SHAT 16N1485.
13. GQG, ÉM, 2ᵉ Bureau, S.R. aux armées (Contrôle Postal), Rapport sur la correspondance des troupes du 10 au 25 décembre, 1 janvier 1917, SHAT 16N1485.
14. Affaires étrangères à résident général, 14 décembre 1916, AN 475AP/194.
15. Diplomatie Paris, Pour le président du conseil, 15 décembre 1916, AN 475AP/194.
16. Note, 18 décembre 1916, AN 475AP/194. The document is a transcription of a conversation between Castelnau and François de Wendel (who lived in Paris) recorded through a wiretap.
17. Major General G. S. Clive's Private Diary, 17 December 1916, p. 123, PRO CAB 45/201.
18. Ministère de la marine, Le ministre de la marine à M. le général Joffre, 23 décembre 1916, *AFGG,* 511-337, p. 562; Joffre, *Mémoires,* 2:427.
19. Raymond Poincaré, *Au service de la France,* vol. 9: *L'année trouble 1917* (Paris: Plon, 1932), p. 22.
20. Guy Pédroncini, "La France et les négociations secrètes de paix en 1917," *Guerres mondiales et conflits contemporains* 43 (avril 1993), 131.

21. Bernard Serrigny, *Trente ans avec Pétain* (Paris: Plon, 1959), p. 82; GAC, Le général Pétain au général commandant en chef, 25 octobre 1916, SHAT 1K268.

22. Georges Suarez, ed., *Briand, sa vie—son oeuvre, avec son journal et de nombreux documents inédits,* 4 vols. (Paris: Plon, 1938–1940), 4:68.

23. Testimony of Nivelle, PV, Commission d'enquête réunie en exécution de la note ministérielle no. 18194 du 14 juillet 1917, Séance du 15 septembre 1917, p. 73, SHAT 5N255.

24. Nivelle, Note pour M. le ministre de la marine, n.d., AN 475AP/194.

25. Serrigny, *Trente ans avec Pétain,* pp. 85n, 112.

26. GQG, Ordre particulier no. 11, n.d., SHAT 16N1683; *AFGG,* 51, p. 161; Paul Painlevé, *Comment j'ai nommé Foch et Pétain* (Paris: Félix Alcan, 1924), p. 11.

27. Nivelle, Note pour M. le ministre de la marine, n.d., AN 475AP/194.

28. GQG, Le général Nivelle à M. le général sir Douglas Haig, 21 décembre 1916, *AFGG,* 511-332, pp. 554–556.

29. Robert Blake, ed., *Private Papers of Douglas Haig, 1914–1919* (London: Eyre and Spottiswoode, 1952), pp. 187–188.

30. Commission d'enquête, Réponse du général Nivelle aux questions posées spécialement par le général Brugère à la fin de la séance de la commission d'enquête du 5 septembre 1917, SHAT 5N255.

31. GQG, Instruction personnelle et secrète, 30 décembre 1916, *AFGG,* 511-365, pp. 596–603.

32. E. L. Spears, *Prelude to Victory* (London: Jonathan Cape, 1939), p. 66.

33. MMF près le GHQ, ÉM Montreuil à GQG, 23 décembre 1916, *AFGG,* 511-338, p. 563.

34. GQG, Le général Nivelle à M. le maréchal sir Douglas Haig, 2 janvier 1917, *AFGG,* 511-380, pp. 631–633.

35. Haig to Nivelle, 6 January 1917, PRO WO 158/22/114.

36. GQG, Le général Nivelle à M. le maréchal sir Douglas Haig, 11 janvier 1917, *AFGG,* 511-427, pp. 728–730.

37. Lloyd George, *War Memoirs,* 1:843.

38. Ibid., p. 865.

39. Conférence du 7 janvier 1917 (à Rome), p. 7, SHAT 7N1256.

40. Conclusions de la conférence des alliées tenue à Rome, les 5, 6, & 7 janvier 1917, SHAT 6N68; Lloyd George, *War Memoirs,* 1:857.

41. Note rédigée par le général en chef pour la conférence de Londres du 15 janvier 1917, *AFGG,* 511-446, pp. 774–776.

42. PV, Conférence du 15 janvier 1917, *AFGG,* 511-447, pp. 777–784.

43. Blake, *Private Papers of Douglas Haig,* p. 192.

44. GQG, Accord signé à Londres par le maréchal Haig et le général Nivelle, 16 janvier 1917, *AFGG,* 511-456, p. 808.

45. GQG, Général commandant en chef à ministre guerre et ÉM Beauvais, 16 février 1917, *AFGG,* 511-694, p. 1276.

46. Minutes of the Meeting of a War Cabinet, February 13, 1917, PRO CAB 23/1/64.

47. Meeting with General Nivelle on Friday, 16 February 1917, PRO WO 158/37/19.

48. Quoted in *AFGG,* 51, p. 222.

49. Proposed Organization of Unified Command on the Western Front, 26th February 1917, in *History of the Great War: Military Operations, France and Belgium, 1917, Appendices* (London: Macmillan, 1940), app. 18, pp. 62–63.

50. William Robertson, *Soldiers and Statesmen, 1914–1918*, 2 vols. (New York: Charles Scribner's Sons, 1926), 2:208.

51. Ibid., p. 209.

52. Agreement Signed at Anglo-French Conference held at Calais, 26th/27th February 1917, in *Military Operations, France and Belgium, 1917, Appendices*, app. 19, pp. 64–65; Protocole, Convention de Calais, 27 février 1917, *AFGG*, 511-739, pp. 1348–49.

53. Lloyd George, *War Memoirs*, 1:891; Hankey, *Supreme Command*, 2:619; Robertson, *Soldiers and Statesmen*, 2:216–222.

54. GQG, Le général Nivelle à M. le maréchal sir Douglas Haig, 27 février 1917, *AFGG*, 511-742, pp. 1350–52.

55. GQG, Au sujet du mémorandum du 2 mars, 6 mars 1917, *AFGG*, 511-787, p. 1448.

56. Accord entre le maréchal sir Douglas Haig et le général Nivelle pour l'application de la convention de Calais du 27 février 1917, *AFGG*, 511-847, pp. 1563–65.

57. GQG, Instructions aux GAN, GAR, GAC, 7 mars 1917, *AFGG*, 511-795, pp. 1463–64.

58. Émile Fayolle, *Cahiers secrets de la grande guerre* (Paris: Plon, 1964), p. 205.

59. Cyril Falls, *History of the Great War: Military Operations, France and Belgium, 1917: The German Retreat to the Hindenburg Line and the Battle of Arras* (London: Macmillan, 1940), p. 126.

60. Poincaré, *Au service de la France*, 9:77.

61. Painlevé, *Comment j'ai nommé Foch et Pétain*, p. 43.

62. Commandant de Civrieux, *L'offensive de 1917 et le commandement du général Nivelle* (Paris: G. van Oest, 1919), p. 66.

63. GAR, Le général Micheler à M. le général commandant en chef, 22 mars 1917, *AFGG*, 512-994, pp. 193–197; GAR, Instruction personnelle et secrète, 26 mars 1917, *AFGG*, 512-1032, pp. 259–261; Testimony of Micheler, PV, Commission d'enquête, séance du 13 septembre 1917, pp. 51–54, SHAT 5N255.

64. Fayolle, *Cahiers secrets*, p. 209.

65. Spears, *Prelude to Victory*, pp. 345–346.

66. GQG Russe, Chef MMF à guerre et général commandant en chef, nos. 1049–1050, 18 janvier 1917, SHAT 5N140.

67. MG, Télégramme parvenu au ministre le 6 février 1917, *AFGG*, 511-606, p. 1093.

68. Poincaré, *Au service de la France*, 9:68. See Conférence de Petrograd, février 1917, SHAT 6N68; MG, Rapport du général de division de Curières de Castelnau, 9 mars 1917, SHAT 6N68; Yves Gras, *Castelnau ou l'art de commander, 1851–1944* (Paris: Denoël, 1990), pp. 338–347.

69. MG, Télégramme parvenu au ministère le 27 mars 1917, *AFGG*, 512-1046, pp. 282–283.

70. Alexandre Ribot, *Journal d'Alexandre Ribot et correspondances inédites, 1914–1922* (Paris: Plon, 1936), p. 51.

71. Quoted in Jean de Pierrefeu, *L'offensive du 16 avril: La vérité sur l'affaire Nivelle* (Paris: Renaissance du Livre, 1919), pp. 61–65.

72. Testimony of Pétain, PV, Commission d'enquête, séance du 10 septembre 1917, pp. 36–37, SHAT 5N255.

73. Civrieux, *L'offensive de 1917,* p. 77.

74. Pièces remises par le Général Nivelle à la commission d'enquête, pp. 17–27, SHAT 5N255; Castelnau, PV de la réunion des commandants de groupes d'armées à Compiègne, 7 avril 1917, pp. 3–4, SHAT 5N255.

75. Pièces remises par le Général Nivelle à la commission d'enquête, pp. 17–27, SHAT 5N255; Castelnau, PV de la réunion des commandants de groupes d'armées à Compiègne, 7 avril 1917, pp. 1–10, SHAT 5N255.

76. Philippe Pétain, *Une crise morale de la nation française en guerre, 16 avril–23 octobre 1917* (Paris: Éditions latines, 1966), p. 53.

77. Émile Herbillon, *Souvenirs d'un officier de liaison pendant la guerre mondiale: Du général en chef au gouvernement,* 2 vols. (Paris: J. Tallandier, 1930), 2:56.

78. GQG, Note pour les armées, 11 avril 1917, *AFGG,* 512-1290, p. 788.

79. Lloyd George, *War Memoirs,* 1:901.

80. GQG, Situation de l'ennemi, 13 avril 1917, *AFGG,* 512-1329, pp. 826–827.

81. GQG, Le général commandant en chef au général commandant le GAR, 1 avril 1917, *AFGG,* 512-1113, pp. 422–423.

82. V^e armée, Instruction particulière concernant l'emploi des chars d'assaut, 23 mars 1917, *AFGG,* 512-1007, pp. 212–213.

83. IVe armée, Plan d'engagement, 27 mars 1917, *AFGG,* 512-1049, p. 287.

84. GQG, Général commandant en chef à ÉM Châlons, 1 avril 1917, *AFGG,* 512-1111, p. 420.

85. GQG, Directive, 4 avril 1917, *AFGG,* 512-1167, pp. 547–549.

86. GQG, Note sur l'organisation du terrain dans la bataille offensive, 12 avril 1917, SHAT 16N1686.

87. V^e armée, Le général commandant la Ve armée au général commandant le GAR, 8 mai 1917, *AFGG,* 512-1896, p. 1507.

88. Officier de liaison près le 1er CA, Situation du 1er CA, 14 avril 1917, *AFGG,* 512-1338, pp. 841–842.

89. Général Blondat, Rapport sur les opérations du 2ème corps colonial du 16 au 18 avril; quoted in Pierrefeu, *L'offensive du 16 avril,* pp. 83–84.

90. Poincaré, *Au service de la France,* 9:122; Painlevé, *Comment j'ai nommé Foch et Pétain,* p. 70.

91. Painlevé, *Comment j'ai nommé Foch et Pétain,* pp. 71, 73–74.

92. Ribot, *Journal d'Alexandre Ribot,* p. 82.

8. A STRATEGY OF "HEALING" AND DEFENSE, LATE 1917

1. John J. Pershing, *My Experiences in the World War,* 2 vols. (New York: Frederick A. Stokes, 1931), 2:142.

2. Quoted in Auguste Laure, *Pétain* (Paris: Berger-Levrault, 1941), p. 15.

3. Stephen Ryan, *Pétain the Soldier* (South Brunswick, N.J.: Barnes, 1969), p. 119.

4. C. E. Callwell, *Field-Marshal Sir Henry Wilson: His Life and Diaries,* 2 vols. (London: Cassell, 1927), 2:342.

5. David Lloyd George, *War Memoirs,* 2 vols. (London: Odhams, 1938), 1:916–919.

6. William Robertson, *Soldiers and Statesmen, 1914–1918,* 2 vols. (New York: Charles Scribner's Sons, 1926), 2:235; Déclaration faite par le général W. Robertson, 4 mai 1917, *AFGG,* 512-1816, pp. 1409–10.

7. Lloyd George, *War Memoirs,* 1:924.

8. Robert Blake, ed., *Private Papers of Douglas Haig, 1914–1919* (London: Eyre and Spottiswoode, 1952), p. 227.

9. MG, Décrète, 11 mai 1917, *AFGG,* 512-1910, p. 1520.

10. Bernard Serrigny, *Trente ans avec Pétain* (Paris: Plon, 1959), pp. 131–132.

11. Raymond Poincaré, *Au service de la France,* vol. 9: *L'année trouble 1917* (Paris: Plon, 1932), p. 131; Alexandre Ribot, *Journal d'Alexandre Ribot et correspondances inédites, 1914–1922* (Paris: Plon, 1936), p. 101. Painlevé tells a different story. See Paul Painlevé, *Comment j'ai nommé Foch et Pétain* (Paris: Félix Alcan, 1924), pp. 85, 120.

12. Émile Herbillon, *Souvenirs d'un officier de liaison pendant la guerre mondiale: Du général en chef au gouvernement,* 2 vols. (Paris: J. Tallandier, 1930), 2:84.

13. Alexandre Millerand, handwritten note, G. Nivelle, 23/5/17, AN 470AP/36.

14. Georges Clemenceau, *Grandeurs et misères d'une victoire* (Paris: Plon, 1930), p. 7.

15. Pershing, *My Experiences in the World War,* 1:141.

16. Guy Pédroncini, *Les mutineries de 1917* (Paris: Presses universitaires de France, 1967), pp. 102, 107, 132, 166–172.

17. *AFGG,* 72, pp. 192–195.

18. Raymond Poincaré, *Au service de la France,* vol. 7: *Guerre de siège* (Paris: Plon, 1931), pp. 148–149, 154–155, 156.

19. Poincaré, *Au service de la France,* 9:148; Leonard V. Smith, *Between Mutiny and Obedience: The Case of the French Fifth Infantry Division during World War I* (Princeton: Princeton University Press, 1994), pp. 184–185, 201–203.

20. GQG, Rapport, 30 mai 1917, *AFGG,* 521-372, pp. 615–624.

21. Philippe Pétain, *Une crise morale de la nation française en guerre, 16 avril–23 October 1917* (Paris: Nouvelles éditions latines, 1966), pp. 30–58.

22. Pédroncini, *Les mutineries de 1917,* pp. 309–313; Smith, *Between Mutiny and Obedience,* pp. 175–214.

23. GQG, Note pour les commandants d'armées, 8 mars 1917, *AFGG,* 521-16, pp. 31–32.

24. GQG, Contrôle postal, Rapport sur la correspondance des troupes du 10 au 25 avril 1917, 1 mai 1917, SHAT 16N1485.

25. GQG, Contrôle postal, Rapport sur la correspondance des troupes du 25 avril au 10 mai 1917, 15 mai 1917, SHAT 16N1485.

26. Pétain, *Une crise morale,* p. 97.

27. Pédroncini, *Les mutineries de 1917,* pp. 198, 307–308, 211, 185, 194–215; idem, *Pétain: Général en chef, 1917–1918* (Paris: Presses universitaires de France, 1974), p. 29. For a listing of other authors' estimates, see Pédroncini, *Les mutineries de 1917,* p. 190.

28. Nicolas Offenstadt, *Les fusillés de la grande guerre et la mémoire collective (1914–1999)* (Paris: Odile Jacob, 2002), pp. 53, 24, 252n.

29. GQG, Note relative à la discipline, 18 juin 1917, *AFGG,* 521-526, p. 870.

30. GQG, Note pour les groupes d'armées, 14 juin 1917, *AFGG,* 521-503, p. 839; GQG, Note pour les groupes d'armées, 8 juin 1917, *AFGG,* 521-460, p. 767; Télégramme pour les groupes d'armées et les armées, 8 juin 1917, SHAT 16N1686.

31. GQG, Note sur le situation actuelle, 5 juin 1917, *AFGG,* 521-426, p. 719.

32. GQG, Général commandant en chef à ÉM (Jonchery), 19 mai 1917, SHAT 16N1686; Smith, *Between Mutiny and Disobedience,* p. 192n.

33. GQG, Rapport sur la discipline, 30 mai 1917; GQG, Le général commandant en chef à M. le ministre de la guerre, 30 mai 1917; both in SHAT 16N1686.

34. Poincaré, *Au service de la France,* 9:149.

35. GQG, Résumé de l'entrevue du 2 juin à Bavincourt entre le major général et le maréchal Haig, 3 juin 1917, SHAT 16N1686; Major General G. S. Clive's Private Diary, 3 June 1917, p. 164, PRO CAB 45/201; Minutes of a Meeting of the War Cabinet, Wednesday, June 6, 1917, PRO CAB 23/3/156; Cabinet Meeting on War Policy, Minutes of the First Meeting, Monday, June 11, 1917, PRO CAB 27/6.

36. GQG, Note en réponse au télégramme no. 1932/B.S., du 27 mai, 28 mai 1917, *AFGG,* 521-349, p. 579.

37. GQG, Directive no. 1, 19 mai 1917, *AFGG,* 521-235, pp. 391–392.

38. GQG, Application de la directive no. 1, 4 juin 1917, *AFGG,* 521-418, pp. 700–701.

39. ÉMA, Note, 20 juin 1917, *AFGG,* 521-538, pp. 892–895.

40. Pétain, Directive d'études, 13 juin 1917, SHAT 16N1687.

41. GQG, Le général commandant en chef à M. le ministre de la guerre, 3 juillet 1917; GQG, Le général commandant en chef à M. le colonel chef de la MMF, 26 juillet 1917; both in SHAT 16N1687.

42. Painlevé, *Comment j'ai nommé Foch et Pétain,* p. 208.

43. GQG, Emploi des chars d'assaut à la bataille de l'Aisne, 30 juin 1917, *AFGG,* 512-1943, pp. 1587–89.

44. Pershing, *My Experiences in the World War,* 1:58–59.

45. James G. Harbord, *Leaves from a War Diary* (New York: Dodd, Mead, 1926), p. 48.

46. Ibid., pp. 47, 49–50.

47. "A Conversation with Josef-Jacques-Césaire Joffre," 2 May 1917, in *The Papers of Woodrow Wilson,* ed. Arthur S. Link, vol. 42 (Princeton: Princeton University Press, 1983), p. 189. See also Note sur l'entretien du president Wilson et du maréchal Joffre à la maison blanche le mercredi, 2 mai 1917, SHAT 14N25.

48. Entrevenue du maréchal et du général Pershing, n.d., SHAT 14N25.

49. Pershing, *My Experiences in the World War,* 1:33, 52; Robert B. Bruce, *A Fraternity of Arms: America and France in the Great War* (Lawrence: University Press of Kansas, 2003), pp. 66–67.

50. GQG, Note sur la situation actuelle, 5 juin 1917, *AFGG,* 521-426, p. 717.

51. MMF près GQG Russe, Chef mission militaire à ministre guerre et général commandant en chef, 31 mai 1917, *AFGG,* 521-379, pp. 636–637.

52. MMF près GQG Russe, Chef mission française à ministre guerre et commandant en chef, 24 juillet 1917, *AFGG,* 522-800, p. 282.

53. MMF près GQG Russe, Chef mission française à ministre guerre, 5 septembre 1917, *AFGG,* 522-1044, pp. 661–662.

54. Department of the Army, Historical Division, *United States Army in the World War, 1917–1919,* vol. 2: *Policy-Forming Documents, American Expeditionary Forces* (Washington, D.C.: U.S. Government Printing Office, 1948), p. 23.

55. GQG, Conférence entre le maréchal Haig et le général Pétain, 17 mai 1917, *AFGG,* 521-252, pp. 430–431; GHQ, Record of Conference held at Amiens on Friday, the 16th May, 1917, PRO WO 158/48/8; Blake, *Private Papers of Douglas Haig,* p. 232.

56. Callwell, *Sir Henry Wilson*, 2:354–355.

57. GQG, Le général commandant en chef au lieutenant-colonel Génie, 20 mai 1917, *AFGG,* 522-252, p. 430.

58. VIe Armée, Le général de division Maistre à M. le général commandant le GAN, 3 juin 1917, *AFGG,* 521-412, pp. 691–692.

59. Ire Armée, Le général Anthoine à M. le général commandant en chef, 15 octobre 1917, *AFGG,* 522-1216, p. 970.

60. GQG, Le général commandant en chef au général commandant l'armée, à Rexpoede, 22 octobre 1917, *AFGG,* 522-1245, p. 1013.

61. IIe Armée, Opération au nord de Verdun, 9 juillet 1917, *AFGG,* 522-675, pp. 67–71, maps 22 and 23.

62. Poincaré, *Au service de la France,* 9:254–257, 259–260.

63. IIe Armée, ÉM Souilly à ÉM Compiègne, 31 août 1917, *AFGG,* 522-1024, pp. 632–633.

64. Blake, *Private Papers of Douglas Haig,* p. 255; James E. Edmonds, *History of the Great War, Military Operations, France and Belgium, 1918: 7th June–10th November, Messines and Third Ypres (Passchendaele)* (London: His Majesty's Stationery Office, 1948), pp. 235–236.

65. Poincaré, *Au service de la France,* 9:305–306, 310; Painlevé, *Comment j'ai nommé Foch et Pétain,* p. 213.

66. *AFGG,* 52, p. 36.

67. GAN, Le général de division Franchet d'Espèrey, commandant le groupe d'armées du Nord, au général commandant en chef, 18 juillet 1917, *AFGG,* 522-751, pp. 194–197.

68. GQG, Note pour le groupe d'armées du Nord, 20 août 1917, *AFGG,* 522-939, p. 483.

69. VIe Armée, Le général de division Maistre à M. le général commandant le GAN, 9 septembre 1917, *AFGG,* 522-1064, pp. 691–693.

70. MMF, Le colonel de Bellaigue de Bughas au général commandant en chef, 30 septembre 1917, *AFGG,* 522-1140, pp. 843–844.

71. GQG, Renseignements recueillis, le 6 octobre 1917, *AFGG,* 522-1167, p. 891.

72. Minutes of a Meeting of the War Cabinet, October 15, 1917, PRO CAB 23/4/249.

73. VIe Armée, Ordre général no. 2103, 15 septembre 1917, *AFGG,* 522-1084, pp. 723–726.

74. Guy Pédroncini, *Les négociations secrètes pendant la grande guerre* (Paris: Flammarion, 1969), pp. 57–82; Fritz Fischer, *Germany's Aims in the First World War* (New York: W. W. Norton, 1967), pp. 405–450.

75. Quoted in Georges Bonnefous, *La grande guerre, 1914–1918* (Paris: Presses universitaires de France, 1967), p. 327.

76. Poincaré, *Au service de la France,* 9:291.

77. GQG, Note pour le groupe d'armées de l'Est, 9 août 1917, *AFGG,* 522–894, p. 420.

78. Pédroncini, *Pétain,* p. 111.

79. GQG, Étude sur la directive du 15 août, 17 septembre 1917, *AFGG,* 522-1093, pp. 744–754.

80. GQG, La bataille de 1918, 9 octobre 1917, *AFGG,* 611-7, pp. 11–19.

81. GQG, Avis du major général, 9 octobre 1917, *AFGG,* 611-8, p. 20; GQG, La bataille de 1918, 9 octobre 1917, *AFGG,* 611-7, pp. 12, 19.

82. GQG, Note pour le plan de campagne de 1918, 17 octobre 1917, *AFGG,* 611-13, pp. 33–34.

83. GQG, Note relative à l'opération d'Alsace, 7 octobre 1917, SHAT 16N1712.

84. GHQ, Note of General Pétain, October 19, 1917, PRO WO 158/24/286; GQG, Note pour le plan de campagne de 1918, 17 octobre 1917, *AFGG,* 611-13, p. 33.

85. GHQ, Le commandant en chef des armées britanniques en France au commandant en chef des armées françaises, 19 octobre 1917, *AFGG,* 611-16, p. 40.

86. Chief of the Imperial General Staff, Future Military Policy, November 19, 1917, PRO WO 158/24/301.

87. GQG, Le général commandant en chef à M. le maréchal Sir Douglas Haig, 23 octobre 1917, *AFGG,* 611-19, pp. 46–47.

88. Chef d'ÉM général, général Foch à général Robertson, 27 octobre 1917, *AFGG,* 522-26, p. 62.

89. MMF en Italie à ministre de la guerre, Paris, 31 octobre 1917, *AFGG,* 611-44, p. 81.

90. Lloyd George, *War Memoirs,* 2:1437; Robertson, *Soldiers and Statesmen,* 1:219–222; Painlevé, *Comment j'ai nommé Foch et Pétain,* pp. 253–255.

91. Robertson to Prime Minister, 1 February 1918, PRO 158/25/350; Robertson, *Soldiers and Statesmen,* 1:227.

92. Décisions prises à une conférence des représentants des gouvernements britanniques, français et italien, le 7 novembre 1917, *AFGG,* 611-58, pp. 109–110.

93. David Trask, *The United States in the Supreme War Council: American War Aims and Inter-Allied Strategy, 1917–1918* (Middletown, Conn.: Wesleyan University Press, 1961), p. 30.

94. Edmond Buat, Cahiers, 11 octobre 1917, Fonds Buat, 4/MS 5390, Bibliothèque de l'Institut de France.

95. Quoted in Bonnefous, *La grande guerre,* p. 346.

96. Poincaré, *Au service de la France,* 9:367.

97. MG, Le président du conseil, ministre de la guerre, à M. le général commandant en chef, 26 novembre 1917, *AFGG,* 611-114, p. 195.

98. Poincaré, *Au service de la France,* 9:402; Registre des délibérations du comité de guerre, 1917–1918 (Ministère Georges Clemenceau), $1^{\text{ère}}$ séance, 6 décembre 1917, p. 3, SHAT 3N2.

99. Poincaré, *Au service de la France,* 9:413; Comité de guerre, $3^{\text{ème}}$ séance, 12 décembre 1917, p. 8, SHAT 3N2.

100. Quoted in Jean Nicot, *Les poilus ont la parole, dans les tranchées: Lettres du front 1917, 1918* (Paris: Éditions Complexe, 1998), p. 293.

101. ÉM, Contrôle postal, Renseignements sur les corps de troupe, Deuxième quinzaine de décembre, 2 janvier 1918, SHAT 16N1485.

102. ÉM, Contrôle postal, Rapport sur le pessimisme dans le corps de troupes, 15 décembre 1917, SHAT 16N1485.

103. GQG, Note sur la situation, 12 novembre 1917, SHAT 16N1712.

104. GQG, Note pour le comité de guerre, 18 novembre 1917, *AFGG,* 611-86, p. 156.

9. RESPONDING TO A GERMAN OFFENSIVE, SPRING 1918

1. GQG, Plan d'action, 18 novembre 1917, *AFGG,* 611-86, pp. 153–158; GQG, Rapport du 2 décembre 1917, 2 décembre 1917, *AFGG,* 611-146, pp. 245–246; GQG, Plan de guerre de l'ennemi et plan de guerre de l'entente, 4 décembre 1917, SHAT 16N1712.

2. GQG, Note pour le comité de guerre, 18 novembre 1917, *AFGG,* 611-86, pp. 152–153; Comité de guerre, 1ère séance, 6 décembre 1917, pp. 2–3; 2ème séance, 10 décembre 1917, pp. 5–7; 3ème séance, 12 décembre 1917, pp. 8–9; SHAT 3N2.

3. CSG, Note collective no. 1, 13 décembre 1917, *AFGG,* 611-179, pp. 302–304.

4. Chief of the Imperial General Staff, Future Military Policy, 19 November 1917, PRO WO 158/24/301.

5. Émile Fayolle, *Cahiers secrets de la grande guerre* (Paris: Plon, 1964), pp. 245, 251, 255.

6. MG, Le chef d'ÉM général de l'armée à M. le général représentant militaire permanent français au CSG, 1 janvier 1918, *AFGG,* 611-226, pp. 410–411.

7. ÉM, Note sur la situation sur le front occidental, 6 janvier 1918, *AFGG,* 611-237, pp. 435–436.

8. Guy Pédroncini, *Pétain: Général en chef* (Paris: Presses universitaires de France, 1974), p. 247.

9. GQG, Note, 8 janvier 1918, *AFGG,* 611-242, pp. 448–450.

10. GQG, PV de la conférence tenue le 24 janvier 1918, *AFGG,* 611-287, pp. 558, 560.

11. GQG, PV de la conférence tenue le 24 janvier 1918, *AFGG,* 611-287, pp. 558–559.

12. John J. Pershing, *My Experiences in the World War,* 2 vols. (New York: Stokes, 1931), 1:303.

13. PV de la 3e séance du CSG, 30 janvier 1918; CSG Interallié, PV de la séance du 2 février 1918; both in SHAT 6N61.

14. Pershing, *My Experiences in the World War,* 1:311.

15. GQG, Le général commandant en chef au général Foch, 11 février 1917, *AFGG,* 611-355, pp. 778–779.

16. James E. Edmonds, ed., *History of the Great War, Military Operations, France and Belgium, 1918: The German March Offensive and Its Preliminaries* (London: Macmillan, 1935), p. 83; GHQ, À représentant militaire britannique, Conseil supérieur de guerre, 2 mars 1918, *AFGG,* 611-420, pp. 953–954. See Robert Blake, ed., *Private Papers of Douglas Haig, 1914–1919* (London: Eyre and Spottiswoode, 1952), p. 283.

17. Raymond Poincaré, *Au service de la France,* vol. 10: *Victoire et armistice* (Paris: Plon, 1933), p. 58.

18. Ibid., p. 62.

19. Ibid., p. 63.

20. Henri Mordacq, *Le ministère Clemenceau: Journal d'un témoin,* 4 vols. (Paris: Plon, 1930–1931), 1:186–187.

21. David Lloyd George, *War Memoirs,* 2 vols. (London: Odhams, 1938), 2:1720.

22. Ibid., p. 1714; Ferdinand Foch, *Mémoires,* 2 vols. (Paris: Plon, 1931), 2:11.

23. GQG, Note sur l'entretien des armées françaises, 14 décembre 1917, *AFGG,* 611-181, pp. 307–308.

24. GQG, Extension du front britannique, 14 décembre 1917, *AFGG,* 611-183, p. 317.

25. GQG, Le général commandant en chef à M. le ministre de la guerre, 14 janvier 1918, *AFGG,* 611-256, p. 471.

26. MG, Le président du conseil à M. le général commandant en chef, 19 janvier 1918, *AFGG,* 611-270, pp. 494–496.

27. ÉMA, Du colonel Falgalde, 13 février 1918, *AFGG,* 611-360, p. 785.

28. Pershing, *My Experiences in the World War,* 1:165.

29. Comité de guerre, 1ère séance, 6 décembre 1917, p. 2, SHAT 3N2.

30. Pershing, *My Experiences in the World War*, 1:257; Poincaré, *Au service de la France*, 10:430.

31. Le maréchal Joffre à Monsieur le président du conseil, 24 décembre 1917, *AFGG*, 611-210, pp. 372–373.

32. GQG, Résumé de l'entretien du 23 décembre 1917 (général Pétain–général Pershing), 23 décembre 1917, *AFGG*, 611-206, pp. 367–368; Poincaré, *Au service de la France*, 9:435.

33. GQG, Le général commandant en chef à M. le général commandant en chef les forces expéditionnaires américaines en France, 27 décembre 1917, *AFGG*, 611-217, pp. 393–394.

34. Forces expéditionnaires américaines à M. le général Pétain, 6 janvier 1918, *AFGG*, 611-240, p. 444.

35. GQG, Le général commandant en chef au général commandant en chef les forces expéditionnaires américaines en France, 11 janvier 1918, *AFGG*, 611-248, pp. 457–458.

36. Pershing, *My Experiences in the World War*, 1:294–295.

37. Quoted in *AFGG*, 61, p. 203.

38. Poincaré, *Au service de la France*, 10:63–64.

39. GQG, Note pour les généraux commandant les groupes d'armées et les armées, 27 novembre 1917, *AFGG*, 611-120, p. 204.

40. *AFGG*, 61, pp. 157–160; GQG, Directive no. 4 pour les groupes d'armées et les armées, 22 décembre 1917, *AFGG*, 611-202, pp. 359–362; Philippe Pétain, *Rapport du maréchal commandant en chef les armées françaises du nord et du nord-est sur les opérations en 1918, la campagne défensive (21 mars–18 juillet 1918)*, Ire partie: *La préparation de la campagne de 1918 (fin 1917–21 mars 1918)* (Paris: Imprimerie maréchal, 1921), pp. 17–18; Auguste Laure, *Pétain* (Paris: Berger-Levrault, 1941), pp. 175–177.

41. General Sir Hubert Gough, *The Fifth Army* (London: Hodder and Stoughton, 1931), pp. 222–223.

42. Minutes of the Meeting of the War Cabinet, January 7, 1918, PRO CAB 23/44B/316.

43. Tim Travers, *How the War Was Won: Command and Technology in the British Army on the Western Front* (London: Routledge, 1992), pp. 63, 65.

44. GQG, Réunion de la IIe armée, 15 janvier 1918, *AFGG*, 611-258, p. 476.

45. GQG, Réunion de la IVe armée le 16 janvier 1918, *AFGG*, 611-260, pp. 481–482.

46. GQG, Instruction pour l'application de la directive no. 4, 11 février 1918, *AFGG*, 611-351, pp. 765–766.

47. GQG, Note, 20 avril 1918, *AFGG*, 621-41, pp. 99–100.

48. GQG, Résumé du plan de guerre pour 1918, 11 février 1918, *AFGG*, 611-352, pp. 767–769.

49. GQG, Conversation téléphonique, 21 mars 1918, *AFGG*, 612-491, p. 21; GQG, Message téléphoné, 21 mars 1918, *AFGG*, 612-492, p. 22.

50. Colonel Paul H. Clark to General Pershing, Report no. 13, March 22, 1918, p. 23, USMA Library, West Point, N.Y.

51. Gough, *Fifth Army*, p. 253.

52. Clark to Pershing, Report no. 19, March 25, 1918, p. 34; Report no. 25, March 30, 1918, p. 45; Report no. 15, March 23, 1918, p. 27; Report no. 19, March 25, 1918, p. 34; all USMA Library.

53. Clark to Pershing, Report no. 16, March 24, 1918, p. 30, USMA Library.

54. Pétain, *Rapport*, IIème partie: *La bataille entre l'Oise et la Scarpe (21 mars–9 avril 1918)*, p. 15.

55. Ibid., p. 16; GHQ, Traduction, 23 mars 1918, *AFGG*, 612-587, p. 127.

56. Renseignements fournis par la 4e armée, analyse, 23 mars 1918, SHAT 16N1694.

57. Émile Herbillon, *Souvenirs d'un officier de liaison pendant la guerre mondiale*, 2 vols. (Paris: J. Tallandier, 1930), 2:228.

58. Mordacq, *Le ministère Clemenceau*, 1:227–228; idem, *La vérité sur le commandement unique* (Paris: Albert, 1934), pp. 61–62; Poincaré, *Au service de la France*, 10:86.

59. Pétain, *Rapport*, IIème partie: *La bataille entre l'Oise et la Scarpe*, p. 21; Foch, *Mémoires*, 2:14.

60. Mordacq, *Le ministère Clemenceau*, 1:232–234; idem, *La vérité*, pp. 63–64.

61. Blake, *Private Papers of Douglas Haig*, p. 297; Mordacq, *Le ministère Clemenceau*, 1:234–236; idem, *La vérité*, pp. 66–68.

62. GQG, Instruction personnelle et secrète, 24 mars 1918, *AFGG*, 612-612, pp. 149–151; Mordacq, *Le ministère Clemenceau*, 1:234–236.

63. Louis Loucheur, *Carnets secrets, 1908–1932* (Brussels: Brepols, 1962), p. 51.

64. Edmonds, *History of the Great War, France and Belgium, 1918: The German March Offensive and Its Preliminaries*, p. 427.

65. Conference at Dury, Sunday, March 24th, 1918, PRO WO 158/72/2.

66. Blake, *Private Papers of Douglas Haig*, p. 297; Major General G. S. Clive's Private Diary, 24 March 1918, p. 210, PRO CAB 45/201.

67. D. Haig, Résumé de la situation, 25 mars 1918, *AFGG*, 612-751, p. 268; Foch, *Mémoires*, 2:15; Conference at Abbeville on 25th March 1918, PRO WO 158/72/4.

68. Travers, *How the War Was Won*, pp. 66–68. See also Elizabeth Greenhalgh, "Myth and Memory: Sir Douglas Haig and the Imposition of Allied Unified Command in March 1918," *Journal of Military History* 68 (July 2004), 771–820.

69. Groupement Diébold, Instruction personnelle et secrète, 25 mars 1918, *AFGG*, 612-748, p. 265.

70. GQG, Général commandant en chef à ÉM Boulogne, 25 mars 1918, *AFGG*, 612-671:208; GAR, Ordre pour la IIIe armée et le général Debeney, 26 mars 1918, *AFGG*, 612-778, p. 293; Laure, *Pétain*, p. 191; Pédroncini, *Pétain*, pp. 311–313.

71. Three Conferences at Doullens on Tuesday, 26th March 1918, PRO 158/25/367; Georges Clemenceau, *Grandeurs et misères d'une victoire* (Paris: Plon, 1930), pp. 23–26.

72. Poincaré, *Au service de la France*, 10:88.

73. Général Foch, Le général chef d'ÉMA à M. le président du conseil, 24 mars 1918, *AFGG*, 612-603, pp. 139–140; Foch, *Mémoires*, 2:16–17.

74. MG, Accord de Doullens, 26 mars 1918, *AFGG*, 612-762, p. 279.

75. Mordacq, *Le ministère Clemenceau*, 1:245–246.

76. Gough, *Fifth Army*, p. 306.

77. Général Foch, Instruction au Général Fayolle, 26 mars 1918, *AFGG*, 612-764, p. 280.

78. Clark to Pershing, Report no. 22, March 27, 1918, p. 38; Report no. 23, March 28, 1918, p. 42; both USMA Library.

79. Pershing, *My Experiences in the World War*, 1:365.

80. Général Foch, Lettre au président du conseil, 1 avril 1918, *AFGG*, 613-1307, pp. 1–2; Le général Foch à M. le président du conseil, 1 avril 1918, *AFGG*, 613-1310, p. 5.

81. Herbillon, *Souvenirs d'un officier de liaison,* 2:241.

82. GHQ, Appui des armées britanniques par les forces françaises, 10 avril 1918, *AFGG,* 613-1598, p. 338.

83. Blake, *Private Papers of Douglas Haig,* pp. 302–303.

84. GHQ, Note remise par le maréchal Haig à la conférence d'Abbeville du 14 avril 1918, 13 avril 1918, *AFGG,* 613-1698, p. 464.

85. Clark to Pershing, Report no. 19, March 25, 1918, p. 34; Report no. 50, April 21, 1918, p. 118; Report no. 56, April 27, 1918, p. 134; all USMA Library.

86. GQG, Contrôle postal, Opinion des soldats français sur les troupes Britanniques, 13 mai 1918, SHAT 16N1485.

87. ÉM, Renseignments sur les corps de troupe d'apres le Contrôle postal, 6 avril 1918, SHAT 16N1485.

88. GQG, Le général commandant en chef à M. le général commandant en chef les armées alliées en France, 7 mai 1918, *AFGG,* 621-124, p. 256.

89. GQGA, Le général Foch à M. le général commandant en chef, 10 mai 1918, *AFGG,* 621-143, p. 296.

90. GQG, Le général commandant en chef à M. le général Foch, 24 avril 1918, *AFGG,* 613-1906, pp. 770–772.

91. GQGA, Note, 12 mai 1918, *AFGG,* 621-158, p. 319.

92. GQGA, Directive générale no. 3, 20 mai 1918, *AFGG,* 621-214, p. 401.

93. Major General G. S. Clive's Private Diary, 30 April 1918, p. 218; 19 May 1918, p. 221; PRO CAB 45/201.

94. GQG, Note sur les indices de l'offensive Allemande du 27 mai, 5 juillet 1918, p. 1, SHAT 5N256.

95. VIe armée, Le général de division Duchêne à M. le général commandant le groupe des armées du nord, 28 avril 1918, *AFGG,* 621-68, pp. 161–163.

96. Pétain, *Rapport,* IVe partie: *La bataille de l'Aisne (20 mai–5 juin 1918),* p. 8.

97. GQG, Note relative à l'attitude du commandement, 19 mai 1917, SHAT 16N1686; GQG, Note pour les généraux commandant les groupes d'armées, 1 décembre 1917, SHAT 16N1690.

98. VIe armée, Instruction personnelle et secrète, 20 mai 1918, *AFGG,* 621-218, p. 414.

99. GQG, Le général commandant en chef à M. le président du conseil, 13 juin 1918, p. 3, SHAT 5N526; GQG, Le général commandant en chef à M. le président du conseil, 13 juin 1918, *AFGG,* 622-1517, p. 721.

100. Clark to Pershing, Report no. 81, May 28, 1918, p. 208; Report no. 84, May 30, 1918, p. 216; both USMA Library.

101. GQG, Le général commandant en chef au général commandant en chef les armées alliées, 1 juin 1918, *AFGG,* 622-968, p. 111.

102. Clark to Pershing, Report no. 86, May 31, 1918, pp. 219–220; Report no. 87, June 1, 1918, pp. 221–223; both USMA Library.

103. Clark to Pershing, Report no. 87, June 1, 1918, p. 223, USMA Library.

104. Pershing, *My Experiences in the World War,* 2:71–73, 76, 82.

105. GQG, Général commandant en chef à ÉMs Sézanne, etc., 1 juin 1918, *AFGG,* 622-965, pp. 108–109.

106. Jean de Pierrefeu, *G.Q.G. secteur 1: Trois ans au grand quartier général,* 2 vols. (Paris: L'édition française illustrée, 1920), 2:189–190.

107. Clark to Pershing, Report no. 99, June 11, 1918, p. 255; Report no. 94, June 6, 1918, p. 239; Report no. 95, June 6, 1918, p. 244; Report no. 96, June 8, 1918, p. 246; all USMA Library.

108. Herbillon, *Souvenirs d'un officier de liaison,* 2:261.

109. Clemenceau, *Grandeurs et misères,* p. 40.

110. Poincaré, *Au service de la France,* 10:213.

111. GAR, Bulletin de renseignements (du 25 au 31 mai 1918), 31 mai 1918, *AFGG,* 622-895, p. 35.

112. IIIe armée, Mesures pour repousser l'attaque enemie, 6 juin 1918, *AFGG,* 622-1231, p. 403.

113. IIIe armée, Le général Humbert à M. le général commandant en chef, 16 juin 1918, *AFGG,* 623-1594, pp. 23–24.

114. Pierrefeu, *G.Q.G. secteur 1,* p. 191.

115. Pétain, Note, 16 juin 1918, SHAT 16N1697.

116. Fayolle, *Cahiers secrets,* p. 284.

117. GQGA, Note, 16 juin 1918, *AFGG,* 623-1580, pp. 4–7.

118. GQG, Le général commandant en chef à M. le général commandant en chef les armées alliées, 17 juin 1918, *AFGG,* 622-1605, p. 43.

119. GQGA, Le général Foch à M. le général commandant en chef, 27 juin 1918, *AFGG,* 623-1698, p. 158.

10. A STRATEGY OF OPPORTUNISM

1. B. H. Liddell Hart, *Foch: The Man of Orléans* (Boston: Little, Brown, 1932), p. 450.

2. Jacques Weygand, *Weygand, mon père* (Paris: Flammarion, 1970), p. 150.

3. GQG, Le général commandant en chef, à M. le général commandant en chef les armées alliées, 18 juin 1918, *AFGG,* 623-1618, p. 62; GQG, Le général commandant en chef à M. le général commandant en chef les armées alliées, 17 juin 1918, *AFGG,* 623-1604, p. 41.

4. GQGA, Le général Foch à M. le général commandant en chef, 27 juin 1918, *AFGG,* 623-1698, p. 159.

5. GQG, Directive no. 5, 12 juillet 1918, *AFGG,* 623-1928, p. 451.

6. Conversation of July 10, 1918, between General Foch and Colonels Connor & Mott, T. Bentley Mott Papers, USMA Library, West Point, N.Y.

7. GQGA, Note pour M. le président du conseil, 14 juin 1918, *AFGG,* 622-1540, p. 749.

8. David Trask, *The United States in the Supreme War Council: American War Aims and Inter-Allied Strategy, 1917–1918* (Middletown, Conn.: Wesleyan University Press, 1961), p. 95.

9. Philippe Pétain, *Rapport du maréchal commandant en chef les armées françaises du nord et du nord-est sur les opérations en 1918, la campagne défensive (21 mars–18 juillet 1918),* VIe partie: *La bataille de Champagne (30 juin–18 juillet 1918)* (Paris: Imprimerie maréchal, 1921), pp. 18–19.

10. GQG, Le général commandant en chef au général commandant le groupe d'armées de réserve, 8 juillet 1918, *AFGG,* 623-1847, p. 357.

11. Edmond Buat, Note pour le général en chef, 11 juillet 1918, SHAT 16N1697.

12. GQG, Le général commandant en chef à M. le général commandant en chef les armées alliées, 16 juillet 1918, *AFGG,* 623-2206, p. 668.

13. John J. Pershing, *My Experiences in the World War,* 2 vols. (New York: Stokes, 1931), 2:158.

14. Colonel Paul H. Clark to General Pershing, Report no. 143, July 18, 1918, p. 371; Report no. 144, July 19, 1918, p. 374; both USMA Library.

15. GQGA, Note, 18 juillet 1918, *AFGG,* 711-112, pp. 166–167.

16. Henri Mordacq, *Le ministère Clemenceau: Journal d'un témoin,* 4 vols. (Paris: Plon, 1930–1931) 2:164.

17. Quoted in Fritz Fischer, *Germany's Aims in the First World War* (New York: Norton, 1967), p. 627.

18. GQG, Le général commandant en chef à M. le général commandant en chef les armées alliées, 31 juillet 1918, *AFGG,* 711-403, pp. 423–425.

19. GQGA, Mémoire lu à la réunion des commandants en chef des armées alliées, 24 juillet 1918, *AFGG,* 711-276, p. 306; Ferdinand Foch, *Mémoires,* 2 vols. (Paris: Plon, 1931), 2:164–166.

20. GQGA, Directive générale no. 3, 20 mai 1918, *AFGG,* 621-214, pp. 401–402; Marius Daille, *La bataille de Montdidier* (Paris: Berger-Levrault, 1924), pp. 21–23.

21. GQGA, Directive particulière, 28 juillet 1918, *AFGG,* 711-355, pp. 377–378.

22. General Debeney's letter explaining his concept, reasoning, and actions are in Daille, *La bataille de Montdidier,* pp. 21–25.

23. *AFGG,* 71, p. 378; James E. Edmonds, ed., *History of the Great War, Military Operations, France and Belgium, 1918, 8th August–28th September: The Franco-British Offensive* (London: His Majesty's Stationery Office, 1947), p. 517.

24. Erich Ludendorff, *Ludendorff's Own Story, August 1914–November 1918,* 2 vols. (New York: Harper and Brothers, 1919), 2:326.

25. Fischer, *Germany's Aims in the First World War,* p. 627.

26. Ibid., p. 628; Paul von Hindenburg, *Out of My Life,* 2 vols. (New York: Harper and Brothers, 1921), 2:219–220.

27. Mordacq, *Le ministère Clemenceau,* 2:174.

28. Timothy Travers, *How the War Was Won* (London: Routledge, 1992), p. 132.

29. GQGA, Le maréchal Foch à M. le maréchal Haig, à M. le général Pétain, 12 août 1918, *AFGG,* 711-631, pp. 671–672; Foch, *Mémoires,* 2:179–182.

30. GAR, Note pour la IIIᵉ armée, 13 août 1918, *AFGG,* 711-651, pp. 690–691.

31. Ludendorff, *Ludendorff's Own Story,* 2:344.

32. GQG, Au maréchal Haig, 25 août 1918, *AFGG,* 712-835, p. 150.

33. GAR, Le général Fayolle à M. le général commandant en chef, 3 septembre 1918, *AFGG,* 712-954, p. 275.

34. GQG, Note, 6 décembre 1914, *AFGG,* 211-262, pp. 348–351.

35. GQG, Avis du major général, 9 octobre 1917, *AFGG,* 611-8, p. 20.

36. GQGA, La poursuite, 28 août 1918, *AFGG,* 712-875, pp. 185–186.

37. GQGA, Note, 30 août 1918, *AFGG,* 712-898, p. 218.

38. Auguste Laure, *Au 3ᵉᵐᵉ bureau du troisième G.Q.G. (1917–1919)* (Paris: Plon, 1922), p. 200.

39. Map réseau ferré allemand région du N.E. et Belgique, 8 mai 1918, SHAT 16N1697.

40. Pétain, *Rapport, La campagne offensive (18 juillet–11 novembre),* IVᵉ partie: *Préparation des offensives d'ensemble et opération préliminaire de Woëvre (30 août–26 septembre),* p. 24.

41. Pershing, *My Experiences in the World War,* 2:244, 246–247.

42. Quoted in Donald Smythe, *Pershing: General of the Armies* (Bloomington: Indiana University Press, 1986), p. 188.

43. Hunter Liggett, *AEF: Ten Years Ago in France* (New York: Dodd, Mead, 1928), pp. 159–160.

44. CSG, Rapport, 3 août 1918, *AFGG,* 832-583, p. 32.

45. GQG, Le général commandant en chef à M. le maréchal commandant en chef les armées alliées, 8 septembre 1918, *AFGG,* 712-1036, p. 361.

46. GQGA, Note, 23 septembre 1918, *AFGG,* 712-1257, p. 624.

47. GQGA, Note, 25 septembre 1918, *AFGG,* 712-1286, pp. 665–666.

48. Robert Blake, ed., *The Private Papers of Douglas Haig, 1914–1919* (London: Eyre and Spottiswoode), p. 329; James E. Edmonds, ed., *History of the Great War, Military Operations, France and Belgium, 1918: The Advance to Victory* (London: His Majesty's Stationery Office, 1947), p. 137.

49. GQGA, Confirmation de message téléphoné, 4 octobre 1918, *AFGG,* 721-138, p. 215.

50. GQGA, Le maréchal Foch à M. le général commandant en chef, 4 octobre 1918, *AFGG,* 721-137, p. 215.

51. Quoted in Fischer, *Germany's Aims in the First World War,* p. 634.

52. Foch, *Mémoires,* 2:218.

53. Pershing, *My Experiences in the World War,* 2:303–304.

54. Georges Clemenceau, *Grandeurs et misères d'une victoire* (Paris: Plon, 1930), p. 59.

55. GQG, Le général commandant en chef au maréchal commandant en chef les armées alliées, 30 septembre 1918, *AFGG,* 721-74, p. 125.

56. GQGA, Le maréchal Foch à M. le général Pershing, 2 octobre 1918, *AFGG,* 721-111, p. 177; Foch, *Mémoires,* 2:218.

57. Raymond Poincaré, *Au service de la France,* vol. 10: *Victoire et armistice* (Paris: Plon, 1933), pp. 368, 373–374.

58. Mordacq, *Le ministère Clemenceau,* 2:258.

59. Poincaré, *Au service de la France,* 10:368, 373–374, 377–378.

60. Clemenceau, *Grandeurs et misères d'une victoire,* pp. 64–65.

61. Frank E. Vandiver, *Black Jack: The Life and Times of John J. Pershing,* 2 vols. (College Station: Texas A & M University Press, 1977), 2:972–976.

62. Foch, *Mémoires,* 2:250.

63. Ibid., pp. 247–249.

64. Raymond Recouly, *Le mémorial de Foch* (Paris: Éditions de France, 1929), p. 43.

65. Clemenceau, *Grandeurs et misères d'une victoire,* pp. 340, 342.

66. Pershing, *My Experiences in the World War,* 2:359.

67. Clark to Pershing, Report no. 218, October 12, 1918, p. 565; Report no. 215, October 6, 1918, p. 555; both USMA Library.

68. Pershing, *My Experiences in the World War,* 2:344.

69. Clark to Pershing, Report no. 222, October 16, 1918, p. 574; Report no. 219, October 13, 1918, p. 567; both USMA Library.

70. Prince Max of Baden, *The Memoirs of Prince Max of Baden,* trans. W. M. Calder and C. W. H. Sutton, 2 vols. (London: Constable, 1928), 2:67.

71. Ludendorff, *Ludendorff's Own Story,* 2:414; Prince Max of Baden, *Memoirs,* 2:116.

72. GQGA, Directive générale, 10 octobre 1918, *AFGG,* 721-207, p. 327.

73. GQG, Le général commandant en chef au général commandant le GAC, 4 octobre 1918, *AFGG,* 721-139, pp. 216–217; GQG, Le général commandant en chef au général commandant le GAR, 4 octobre 1918, *AFGG,* 721-140, pp. 217–218.

74. GQG, Général commandant en chef à ÉMs Avize, Picardie, Souilly, Laheycourt, Bacon, 9 octobre 1918, *AFGG,* 721-197, p. 312.

75. Foch, *Mémoires,* 2:240.

76. Ludendorff, *Ludendorff's Own Story,* 2:423.

77. Prince Max of Baden, *Memoirs,* 2:206.

78. GQGA, Directive générale, 19 octobre 1918, *AFGG,* 721-307, p. 481.

79. GQGA, Le maréchal Foch à M. le général commandant en chef, 23 octobre 1918, *AFGG,* 721-349, pp. 550–551.

80. GQG, Instruction personnelle et secrète, 27 octobre 1918, *AFGG,* 721-404, pp. 638–639.

81. Mordacq, *Le ministère Clemenceau,* 2:260.

82. MG, Instruction personnelle et secrète, 7 octobre 1918, *AFGG,* 833-1378, p. 120.

83. GQGA, Le maréchal Foch à S.E.M. Orlando, président du conseil, 28 septembre 1918, *AFGG,* 721-38, p. 72.

84. GQGA, Note, 25 octobre 1918, *AFGG,* 721-380, p. 599; Foch, *Mémoires,* 2:254–256.

85. GQG à M. le maréchal commandant en chef les armées alliées, 28 octobre 1918, *AFGG,* 721-416, pp. 653–655.

86. GQG, Note pour les généraux commandant les groupes d'armées, 1 novembre 1918, *AFGG,* 721-455, pp. 707–708; Foch, *Mémoires,* 2:255.

87. Edmonds, *History of the Great War: The Advance to Victory,* pp. 584, 557.

88. Clark to Pershing, Report no. 202, September 22, 1918, p. 519, USMA Library.

89. Clark to Pershing, Report no. 213, October 4, 1918, p. 549, USMA Library.

90. Marcel Vigneras, *Rearming the French* (Washington, D.C.: U.S. Government Printing Office, 1957), p. 31; cited in Robert B. Bruce, *A Fraternity of Arms: America and France in the Great War* (Lawrence: University Press of Kansas, 2003), p. 105.

91. Edmond Buat, Cahiers, 19 août 1918, Fonds Buat, Bibliothèque de l'Institut de France, 9/MS 5391.

92. Travers, *How the War Was Won,* p. 140.

93. GQG, The General Commanding-in-Chief to Marshal Foch, 8 October 1918, in Department of the Army, Historical Division, *United States Army in the World War, 1917–1919,* vol. 2: *Policy-Forming Documents* (Washington, D.C.: U.S. Government Printing Office, 1948), p. 622.

94. Letter, A. Messimy to J. Hatto, 3 mars 1918, BNF Fonds Hatto.

95. Clark to Pershing, Report no. 243, November 11, 1918, p. 630; Report no. 212, October 3, 1918, p. 546; both USMA Library.

96. Pétain, *Rapport, La campagne offensive (18 juillet–11 novembre),* Vᵉ partie: *Offensives d'ensemble des armées alliées et poussée vers la Meuse (26 septembre–11 novembre),* p. 81.

97. G-3, First Army, Memorandum for Commanding Generals, I Corps, V Corps, November 5, 1918, in Department of the Army, Historical Division, *United States Army in the*

World War, vol. 9: *Meuse-Argonne Operation of the American Expeditionary Forces*, p. 385.

98. Prince Max of Baden, *Memoirs*, 2:292, 294n, 300; Bruce, *Fraternity of Arms*, p. 283.

99. GQGA, Maréchal Foch à général Pétain, général Pershing, général Degoutte, 9 novembre 1918, *AFGG*, 721-543, p. 837.

100. GQG, Ordre général no. 124, 12 novembre 1918, *AFGG*, 721-573, p. 882.

CONCLUSION

1. "At Last! Paris on the Great Day," *The Times*, November 12, 1918, p. 7.

2. Philippe Boulanger, *La France devant la conscription* (Paris: Economica, 2001), p. 173.

3. 1er Bureau, Service courant, Rapport sur les correspondances des troupes (10–25 avril 1916), 1er mai 1916, p. 11, SHAT 16N1485.

4. Stéphane Audoin-Rouzeau, *National Sentiment and Trench Journalism in France during the First World War*, trans. Helen McPhail (Oxford: Berg, 1992), pp. 185–188.

5. Jean-Jacques Becker, *The Great War and the French People* (Oxford: Berg, 1985), p. 6.

6. John H. Morrow Jr., *The Great War in the Air: Military Aviation from 1909 to 1921* (Washington, D.C.: Smithsonian Institution Press, 1993), pp. 295, 371, 373.

7. For a detailed analysis, see Robert A. Doughty, *The Seeds of Disaster: The Development of French Army Doctrine, 1919–1939* (Hamden, Conn.: Archon Books, 1985).

8. MG, Instruction provisoire sur l'emploi tactique des grandes unités (Paris: Charles-Lavauzelle, 1922).

Essay on Sources

An essay on sources about France in the Great War must begin with Pierre Renouvin, who served as a lieutenant in the war and was wounded two times. He played a leading role in the publication of the *Documents diplomatiques français* and served as the editor of the *Revue d'histoire de la guerre mondiale*. Many of his students and successors have used his numerous books and articles as the foundation for their research. Jean-Baptiste Duroselle, one of his students, has written a fine general history: *La grande guerre des français, 1914–1918* (Paris: Perrin, 1998). Another distinguished historian of the Great War, Jean-Jacques Becker, has written several important books that explore social dimensions of the war, including *Les français dans la grande guerre* (Paris: Laffont, 1980). Becker also wrote *1914: Comment les français sont entrés dans la guerre* (Paris: Presses de la Fondation nationale des sciences politiques, 1977). One of the rare English-language books that places France in the center of the war is Leonard V. Smith, Stéphane Audoin-Rouzeau, and Annette Becker, *France and the Great War, 1914–1918* (Cambridge: Cambridge University Press, 2003).

The best book with which to begin the study of politics in France during the war is Pierre Renouvin, *Les formes du gouvernement de guerre* (Paris: Presses universitaires de France, 1925). For a general political-military history of France in the war, see Georges Bonnefous, *La grande guerre (1914–1918)* (Paris: Presses universitaires de France, 1967). For insights into relations between the government and the military, see Jean-Marie Bourget, *Gouvernement et commandement: Les leçons de la guerre mondiale* (Paris: Payot, 1930). The best study of civil-military relations in France, however, remains Jere C. King, *Generals and Politicians: Conflict between France's High Command, Parliament, and Government, 1914–1918* (Los Angeles: University of California Press, 1951).

In recent years historians have treated France gently when examining its responsibility for the war. One of the most important works defending France is Pierre Renouvin, *Les origines immédiates de la guerre (28 juin–4 août 1914)* (Paris: Costes, 1925). Among the best recent works that defends France is John F. V. Keiger, *France and the Origins of the First World War* (New York: St. Martin's, 1983). A work more critical of France is Jules Isaac, *Un débat historique: Le problème des origines de la guerre* (Paris: Rieder, 1933). Several historians have examined France's war aims. Pierre Renouvin blazed an early trail with "Les buts de guerre du gouvernement français, 1914–1918," *Revue historique* 235 (janvier–mars 1966), 1–38. Other significant work has been done by David Stevenson in his *French War Aims against Germany, 1914–1918* (Oxford: Clarendon Press, 1982). France's diplomatic efforts are treated in Albert Pingaud, *Histoire diplomatique de la France pendant la Grande Guerre*, 2 vols. (Paris: Alsatia, 1938).

Biographies have been written on many but certainly not all of the leading political figures. Among the most important of these figures is Poincaré, and one of the most useful books, though it provides only a brief treatment of the war, is John F. V. Keiger, *Raymond Poincaré* (Cambridge: Cambridge University Press, 1997). Poincaré's multivolume memoirs and his diaries remain extremely valuable for details about political-military issues during the war. Another useful biography is Georges Suarez, ed., *Briand, sa vie—son oeuvre, avec son journal et de nombreux documents inédits,* 4 vols. (Paris: Plon, 1938–1940). Jean-Baptiste Duroselle's *Clemenceau* (Paris: Fayard, 1958) ably analyzes the most fascinating political leader of the war. Margaret Milbank Farrar examines Millerand's role as minister of war in two chapters of *Principled Pragmatist: The Political Career of Alexandre Millerand* (Oxford: Berg, 1991).

As for accounts of and by soldiers, I find Joffre's memoirs more useful than the several biographies of him. There are also several biographies of Foch, but the best general work remains B. H. Liddell Hart, *Foch: The Man of Orléans* (Boston: Little, Brown, 1932). Of the several good studies of Pétain, none matches the detail and insights of Guy Pédroncini, *Pétain: Général en chef, 1917–1918* (Paris: Presses universitaires de

France, 1974). Another impressive work is Stephen Ryan, *Pétain the Soldier* (New York: A. S. Barnes, 1969). Ryan understands aspects of the war that many English-language authors have missed. A useful biography of another important military leader is Yves Gras, *Castelnau ou l'art de commander, 1851–1944* (Paris: Denoël, 1990). Gras provides insights into Castelnau not only as a person but also as a military thinker and leader. A sympathetic and useful study of Sarrail is Jan Karl Tanenbaum, *General Maurice Sarrail, 1856–1929: The French Army and Left-Wing Politics* (Chapel Hill: University of North Carolina Press, 1974). For insights into the experiences of the French outside France, see Glenn Torrey, *Henri Mathias Berthelot: Soldier of France, Defender of Romania* (Portland, Ore.: Center for Romanian Studies, 2000).

The most valuable source on military topics pertaining to France in the Great War is the official history: *Les armées françaises dans la Grande Guerre* (Paris: Imprimerie nationale, 1922–1937). Its eleven *"tomes"* include a long, though rarely critical, narrative; more important for purposes of research, its many volumes of "annexes" present thousands of documents that are filled not only with details but also with analysis and opinion. These documents make the French official history the most useful of all the World War I official histories. Another valuable work is Pétain's postwar report, *Rapport du maréchal commandant en chef les armées françaises du nord et du nord-est sur les opérations en 1918* (Paris: Imprimerie maréchal, 1921). Like the official history, it includes volumes that tell the story of the final phase of the war and other volumes that are filled with documents.

Under the general title *Histoire de la guerre mondiale,* four authors have written books that summarize much of the information in the official history but do not always agree with its interpretation. These are Gaston Duffour, *Joffre et la guerre de mouvement, 1914* (Paris: Payot, 1937); Marius Daille, *Joffre et la guerre d'usure, 1915–1916* (Paris: Payot, 1936); Frédéric Hellot, *Le commandement des généraux Nivelle et Pétain* (Paris: Payot, 1936); and René Tournès, *Foch et la victoire des alliés, 1918* (Paris: Payot, 1936).

The best survey in French of the overall war is Fernand Gambiez and M. Suire, *Histoire de la première guerre mondiale,* 2 vols. (Paris: Fayard, 1968). The broader dimensions of the war are ably treated in John H.

Morrow, Jr., *The Great War: An Imperial History* (London: Routledge, 2004). The work of Paul de la Gorce on the army remains useful, but Anthony Clayton has provided more detailed information about the army during the war in *Paths of Glory: The French Army, 1914–1918* (London: Cassell, 2003). Numerous historical studies of World War I campaigns exist. Among the best is Henry Contamine, *La victoire de la Marne, 9 septembre 1914* (Paris: Gallimard, 1970). Another superb book on the Marne campaign is Sewell Tyng, *The Campaign of the Marne, 1914* (New York: Longmans, Green, 1935). Tyng's book is one of the best written in English on the war. Another important work is Marius Daille, *La bataille de Montdidier* (Paris: Berger-Levrault, 1924). This book was read and valued by many French officers in the interwar period. Of the many written on Verdun, I especially like Henri Colin, *Le côte 304 et le Mort-Homme, 1916–1917* (Paris: Payot, 1934).

There are many books that trace the development of ideas and weapons. One of the most useful on artillery is Frédéric Herr, *L'artillerie: Ce qu'elle a été, ce qu'elle est, ce qu'elle doit être* (Paris: Berger-Levrault, 1924). For information about tanks, see one of the numerous articles written in French military journals between the two world wars by Jean Perré. Information about tactical methods is provided in Pascal Lucas, *L'évolution des idées tactiques en France et en Allemagne pendant la guerre de 1914–1918* (Paris: Levrault, 1932). Insights into how the French developed new operational methods are provided in René Viktorovitch, *1915: La conquête de la méthode* (Saint Maixent: Garnier, 1931). Olivier Lepick has added to our understanding of chemical warfare in *La grande guerre chimique, 1914–1918* (Paris: Presses universitaires de France, 1998).

Several historians have written important works about the development of French strategy. As one would expect, Guy Pédroncini has written some of the best. His publications include "Stratégie et relations internationales: La séance du 9 janvier 1912 au conseil supérieur de la défense nationale," *Revue d'histoire diplomatique* 91 (1977), 143–158; "La stratégie du général Pétain," *Relations internationales* 35 (automne 1983), 277–289; "Trois maréchaux, trois stratégies?" *Guerres mondiales et conflits contemporains* 37 (janvier 1987), 45–62. Another useful work is David Stevenson, "French Strategy on the Western Front, 1914–1918," in *Great War, Total War,* ed. Roger Chickering and Stig Förster (Cambridge: Cambridge University Press, 2000), pp. 297–326. Finally, Douglas Porch, author of several outstanding books about the French military, also has written "The Marne and After: A Reappraisal of French Strategy in the First World War," *Journal of Miitary History* 53 (October 1989), 363–385.

Some of the best work dealing with the Great War concerns the mutinies. Once again Guy Pédroncini has written the standard work on the subject: *Les mutineries de 1917* (Paris: Presses universitaires de France, 1967). A provocative and more focused study is Leonard V. Smith, *Between Mutiny and Obedience: The Case of the French Fifth Infantry Division during World War I* (Princeton: Princeton University Press, 1994). Another interesting study, which looks not only at the mutinies but also at postwar perceptions of them, is Nicolas Offenstadt, *Les fusillés de la grande guerre et la mémoire collective (1914–1999)* (Paris: Odile Jacob, 2002).

Several books examine France's relationship with its allies. Among the best, because it rests upon extensive research in the United States and France, is Robert B. Bruce, *A Fraternity of Arms: America and France in the Great War* (Lawrence: University Press of Kansas, 2003). Another useful work despite its excessive focus on the British is William James Philpott, *Anglo-French Relations and Strategy on the Western Front, 1914–18* (New York: St. Martin's, 1996). Insights into the relationship between France and Russia can be found in Jamie H. Cockfield, *With Snow on Their Boots: The Tragic Odyssey of the Russian Expeditionary Force in France during World War I* (New York: St. Martin's, 1998). The French have been circumspect in their comments about the British, but pointed comments can be found in Charles Huguet, *Britain and the War: A French Indictment* (London: Cassell, 1928).

Numerous historical studies are available on narrow but important aspects of the war. Conscription is examined in Philippe Boulanger, *La France devant la conscription: Géographie historique d'une institution républicaine, 1914–1922* (Paris: Economica, 2001). The challenges and achievements of economic mobilization are capably examined in John F. Godfrey, *Capitalism at War: Industrial Policy and Bureaucracy in France, 1914–1918* (New York: St. Martin's, 1987). Another book that looks at conditions behind the front lines is Patrick Fridenson, ed., *The*

French Home Front, 1914–1918 (Oxford: Berg, 1992). For insights into conditions on the other side of the front line, see Helen McPhail, *The Long Silence: Civilian Life under the German Occupation of Northern France, 1914–1918* (New York: St. Martin's, 2001). The experience of prisoners during and after the war is analyzed in Odon Abbal, *Soldats oubliés: Les prisonniers de guerre français* (Paris: Études & communications, 2001). An especially interesting collection is Robert Young, ed., *Under Siege: Portraits of Civilian Life in France during World War I* (Oxford: Berghahn, 2000).

The French experience in Salonika and the Balkans is covered, often unevenly, in numerous works. One of the earliest is Albert Pingaud, "Les origines de l'expédition de Salonique," *Revue historique* 176 (1935), 448–456. A more recent work is Hervé Pierre, *L'intervention militaire française au Moyen-Orient (1916–1919)* (Paris: Éditions des écrivains, 2002). New insights into the French high command are provided in Gérard Fassy, "Le haut-commandement militaire français en Orient, octobre 1915–novembre 1918," 2 vols. (Thèse de doctorat, Université de Paris, 1998). A broader treatment of French efforts in its empire is included in Christopher M. Andrew and A. S. Kanya-Forstner, *The Climax of French Imperial Expansion, 1914–1924* (Stanford: Stanford University Press, 1981).

There are many personal accounts. The best place to begin is to review the information provided in Jean-Norton Cru, *Témoins: Essai d'analyse et de critique des souvenirs de combattants édités en français de 1915 à 1928* (Nancy: Presses universitaires de Nancy, 1993). Of the many works providing insights into the motivations and aspirations of individual soldiers, my favorite is *La dernière lettre écrite par des soldats francais tombés au champ d'honneur, 1914–1918* (Paris: L'Union des pères et mères, 1922). No other work can match the emotions communicated in those "last letters." A book that provides useful insights into the motivations of individual soldiers is Stéphane Audoin-Rouzeau, *Men at War, 1914–1918: National Sentiment and Trench Journalism in France during the First World War*, trans. Helen McPhail (Providence: Berg, 1992). Audoin-Rouzeau demonstrates that the soldiers of the Great War fought for much more than their small unit or personal friends.

An extensive, though now dated, bibliography is the New York Public Library Reference Department's *Subject Catalog of the World War I Collection,* 4 vols. (Boston: G. K. Hall, 1961). Jean Vic provides an early survey of French-language literature in *La littérature de guerre,* 4 vols. (Paris: Les presses françaises, 1923). A useful but narrow source is A. G. S. Enser, ed., *A Subject Bibliography of the First World War: Books in English, 1914–1918* (Aldershot, Hants.: Gower, 1990).

Index

Albertini, Luigi, 48, 52

Alekseev, Mikhail, 235–237, 340, 374

Allenby, Sir Edmund, 491, 502

Allies: Executive War Board, 412, 415; Supreme War Council, 400–403, 406–408, 411–412, 414–417, 419, 445, 454, 464–465, 485–486; unity of command, 103, 176, 330, 333–334, 341, 399–401, 408, 412, 414–415, 437–441, 461–462, 496

Amade, Albert d', 208–210

Amalgamation. *See* United States: amalgamation

Anglo-French relations: Balkans, 205–208, 220–221, 224–225, 233–237, 239–246; before war, 38–40; British criticisms of French, 158, 236, 240, 375, 393–394, 398, 407, 425, 436–437, 443–444, 454, 504; French concerns about Belgium, 135, 377; French criticisms of British, 79, 136, 162, 216, 281, 294, 301, 303, 334, 376, 387, 430, 432–435, 437, 445, 501–502; in 1914, 73, 77–82, 87–92, 94, 101–102; in 1915, 135–140, 156–158, 179–182, 197–199; in 1916, 258–260, 278–281, 300–304; in 1917, 311–315, 327–335, 341, 356–358, 376–378, 383, 393–394, 399, 407, 413–414, 416–418; in 1918, 433, 435–436, 443–445, 472–473

Anthoine, François, 166, 168, 348, 378–379

Artillery: as mobile reserve, 118, 370; development during war, 112, 116–118, 175–176, 255–256, 298, 317, 324, 369; prewar development of, 29–34; rolling barrage, 194, 306, 308, 323, 350, 470, 477; transition to siege warfare (1914–1915), 116–118, 120–121

Artois, battle of. *See* Operations, French: Artois

Asquith, Herbert H., 236, 242, 312, 328

Attrition, war of, 61, 167–168, 172, 250–254, 258–259, 261, 300, 308, 317, 366, 386. *See also* Operational concepts and methods: attrition

Aviation: development of, 256–257, 369, 371, 416, 511; employment of, 56, 64, 85–86, 93, 113, 193, 196, 256–257, 349, 381, 388, 433, 456, 466, 501

Bacteriological warfare, 257

Bailloud, Maurice, 210, 216, 222–223

Baker, Newton D., 371–372, 422

Baquet, Louis, 120, 175

Bazaine, Achille, 249

Becker, Jean-Jacques, 47, 54

Belgian Army: in 1914, 64–65, 70–72, 102–103; in 1918, 428, 444, 485, 489, 498; on Western Front, 108, 111, 116, 149–150, 158, 348, 379

Berthelot, Henri, 248

Bliss, Tasker H., 440–441, 445

Bolo-Pacha (Paul Bolo), 402

Bonnal, Henri, 25–26

Briand, Aristide, 238, 305, 402; as premier, 229, 336, 337, 401; changes in High Command, 319–323; concern about Verdun, 264, 266, 271–272, 285; favors operations in Balkans, 109, 204–205, 226, 232–234, 236, 242–243, 322; peace feelers, 389–391, 394; relationship with Joffre, 230–231, 234, 244, 264, 285, 300, 313, 319, 321;